Black hole tariffs and endogenous policy theory

Black hole tariffs and endogenous policy theory

Political economy in general equilibrium

STEPHEN P. MAGEE
University of Texas, Austin

WILLIAM A. BROCK
University of Wisconsin, Madison

and

LESLIE YOUNG
University of Texas, Austin

*The right of the
University of Cambridge
to print and sell
all manner of books
was granted by
Henry VIII in 1534.
The University has printed
and published continuously
since 1584.*

CAMBRIDGE UNIVERSITY PRESS

Cambridge

New York Port Chester Melbourne Sydney

Published by the Press Syndicate of the University of Cambridge
The Pitt Building, Trumpington Street, Cambridge CB2 1RP
32 East 57th Street, New York, NY 10022, USA
10 Stamford Road, Oakleigh, Melbourne 3166, Australia

First published 1989

Printed in Canada

Library of Congress Cataloging-in-Publication Data
Magee, Stephen P.
Black hole tariffs and endogenous policy theory.
Bibliography: p.
Includes index.
1. Tariff – United States – Mathematical models.
2. Protectionism – United States – Mathematical models.
3. United States – Commercial policy – Mathematical models.
4. Lobbying – Economic aspects – United States – Mathematical models.
5. Pressure groups – United States – Mathematical models.
6. Equilibrium (Economics)
I. Brock, William A.   II. Young, Leslie, 1949–   .
III. Title.
HF1757.M34   1989   382.7´0973   88-35202

British Library Cataloguing-in-Publication Data
Magee, Stephen P.
Black hole tariffs and endogenous policy theory: political economy in general
equilibrium
1. Foreign trade. Protection. Policies of governments
I. Title   II. Brock, William A.   III. Young, Leslie
382.7

ISBN 0-521-36247-4   hard covers
ISBN 0-521-37700-5   paperback

With love to our parents:

Lawrence and Edna Magee
William and Margaret Brock
Yee Fong and Lowe Soo Yee Young

Contents

vii

Contents

Preface

Warren G. Harding was President when the highly protectionist Fordney–McCumber Tariff Act was passed in 1922. He told an amazed reporter that "the United States should adopt a protective tariff of such a character as will help the struggling industries of Europe to get on their feet." (Boller 1981, p. 231)

We have tariffs and other economic policy distortions because they are efficient – that is, they are politically efficient. Because they are politically optimal, they are not aberrations, but a necessary part of any reasonable political equilibrium. We have regressive policies because income inequality is politically efficient; we have lobbies giving funds to parties because that is politically efficient; and we have politicians using these funds to educate voters who are underinformed, and this is politically efficient. For decades, economists have been stuck on the concept of economic efficiency, but this concept is too narrow to provide a proper understanding of economic policy formation. In this book we define and illustrate the concept of *political efficiency*. An action is politically efficient if it increases the chances of election of one of the political parties.

Each voter is such a tiny fraction of the electorate that he or she has no effect on the outcome. Thus, it is rational for individual voters to gather no information about candidates and issues. Thus the paradox: If individuals are rational, they will be ignorant about political issues. Even U.S. presidents (e.g., Warren G. Harding) have missed the basic economic principle that American tariffs hurt foreign industries. Information is a public good and it is underprovided.

Unfortunately, spatial voting theory, the mainstream view in contemporary political science, assumes that voters are so well informed that they are not influenced by campaign contributions. Furthermore, this theory frequently comes up with two conclusions, neither of which is very insightful:

First, that there are an infinity of possible tariff rates on auto imports; second, that politicians will choose free trade.

This book merges economics and political science to advance a new approach: *endogenous policy theory*. This replaces the spatial voting model with the probabilistic voting model of endogenous policy theory developed by Brock and Magee (1974), described in detail in Brock and Magee (1975, 1978, 1980), and expanded to general equilibrium by Young and Magee (1982, 1984, 1986).

There are many contributors to endogenous theory; a partial list appears in Chapter 2, and the theory is described in Chapter 3. All of the results presented in the book are summarized in Chapter 1.

We began working on this book in 1972. It has taken sixteen years to finish. It is true that the last 20% of any job does take 80% of the time. In the fall of 1972, I taught Monday through Wednesday at the University of Chicago and commuted to Washington to work Thursday and Friday for the Nixon White House staff. None of my Monday through Wednesday academic theories could describe the goings-on in Washington on Thursday and Friday. I felt the need for a rigorous special-interest theory that would relate these events to academics.

We develop here a Texas school of political economy approach. This is a general equilibrium version of the Stigler–Virginia public choice theory that government policies are the outgrowth of predatory and parasitic redistributive behavior. That view coincides with Justice Frankfurter's: "There are two things which you do not want to see being made: laws and sausage." This book is about the former.

In early 1973, Buz Brock and I collaborated to produce our first paper on endogenous tariff theory, which we presented to George Stigler's industrial organization workshop at the University of Chicago in January 1974 (Brock and Magee 1974). It appeared as a Chicago working paper in 1975; in May 1978 a verbal summary was published in the *American Economic Review,* and the mathematics appeared in Brock and Magee (1980). Brock and I had great fun pillorying Chicago politicians over beers in a South Side bar called Jimmy's. In the late 1970s I went to Texas and Brock went to Wisconsin, so the wisdom of Jimmy's began to fade.

At this point, we should define "endogenous policy theory." First, we did not invent this title. Others placed the label "endogenous tariff theory" on our work, so we are stuck with it. An exogenous policy is one that is unexplained. *Webster's* says that "endogenous" means "growing from the inside." For us, "endogenous policies" are those that result from all of the actors pursuing their narrow self-interest. If we followed our theory, we would have named the book "androgynous policy theory."

In 1980, Leslie Young and I began collaborating on economics and politics in general equilibrium. Our working papers started appearing in 1982, just after Leslie came to the University of Texas. He and I published our first general equilibrium version of our endogenous tariff theory in the *Review of Economic Studies* (Young and Magee, 1986, pp. 407–19). The lessons of political economy in general equilibrium are best summarized by my uncle, Stephen L. Brock, now a retired rancher in Roy, New Mexico: "When you have an economy, you have goods and services. When you have politics, you have laws and statesmen. However, when you put the two together, you ain't got nothin'." Upon this intellectual foundation is founded the model of black hole tariffs described in Part II of the book. We turn now to a non-technical overview of this special interest approach to economic policy.

Laws reflect the special interests of this generation; the bureaucracy represents the special interests of the preceding generation; and the Constitution reflects the special interests of previous generations. While this book is not about bureaucracies or constitutions, it is about how laws get passed on special-interest issues such as trade restrictions.

Politically efficient trade restrictions reduce economic efficiency. A political economy will not be in equilibrium until it reaches the production possibility curve along which political efficiency cannot increase without lowering economic efficiency. We describe in this book the politically efficient equilibrium (see Figure 3.1 for a discussion). In cooperative interactions, the welfare of both parties is improved. In selfish interactions, the welfare of the selfish party increases whereas the welfare of the other is worsened. Redistributive trade restrictions are inherently selfish, since some gain while others lose. There are parallels in nature. In nature's redistributive games, predators and parasites increase their welfares at the expense of their victims. Most interspecies relationships in nature are redistributive (e.g., carnivores eat herbivores and herbivores eat herbs). The symbiotic shark and pilot fish relationship is rare.

The pyramid of nature model dominates the Coase theorem in predator–prey relationships. (Figure 3.2 describes our construction of the Stackelberg-leadership pyramid in the endogenous policy model.) Collective welfare maximization and special interests do not fit. Special-interest behavior demonstrates the Darwinian superiority of some groups. Special interests do not lose sleep over violations of Pareto optimality and other welfare criteria. One of the superrich put it to me this way: "We don't give a *&!! about the poor."

This book is a formal analysis of economic predation as it operates through democratic political systems. The biological analogy is instructive. With predation, the prey is terminated; with parasitism, the host survives. The economic parallel is that economic predation consumes the prey's *stock* of wealth whereas economic parasitism captures part of the *flow* of the prey's income. Tariffs and trade restrictions are examples of flow redistributions. The purchasing power of many small consumers is transferred annually to more concentrated members of protectionist lobbies through the political sytem. As with biological parasitism, the parasites do not destroy the host; they simply reduce its welfare. In order to simplify the terminology, we refer in this book to both predatory and parasitic behavior as "predatory."

Pareto optimality occurs when one's welfare cannot be improved without lowering someone else's. If someone gains more than another loses, there is a potential move toward Pareto optimality, if compensation schemes were to be devised. Throughout this book we talk about potential Pareto policies of this sort; for simplicity of exposition, we refer to them as "Pareto policies."

Power is relative. There is a great joke about a lawyer and an accountant who were fishing in a stream in Alaska and saw a grizzly bear enter the water. The fishermen ran out of the stream. When they got to the bank, the lawyer stopped to take off his wading boots. The accountant said, "You can't outrun that bear, even with your boots off." The lawyer replied "No, but I can outrun you."

There is a naive view among economists that "we need to change this or that policy in order to improve economic welfare." We show here why this is impossible. The current values of policies reflect a delicate political equilibrium that balances all of society's conflicting interests. The current negative views of economists on the policy have aleady been embodied in its equilibrium value. The policy is endogenous and is outside the control of any group, including the politicians: They are merely the agents balancing all of the conflicting interests.

Part of the frustration we all experience when viewing the slow grind of government is due to insufficient political competition. A two-party country such as the United States is parallel to a duopolistic industry in economics. When there are only two firms in an industry, performance can be less than specular.

Democracy is just one party away from a dictatorship; a duopoly is just one firm away from a monopoly. There are similarities between a dictatorship and a democracy that would make the results in this book apply to a dictatorship. A dictatorship also has two major set of actors: one group in power and a revolutionary group out of power, just as U.S. Democrats wait to "overthrow" the Republicans in the next election. Special interests in both dictatorships and democracies must decide on whether to throw their funds and support to the incumbents or to the insurgents.

The commonly held view that the government is a ship of fools might be replaced with government as an island covered with pirates. The island is not economically efficient because the pirates compromise each other's objectives; but it is politically efficient because the outcomes take everything into account, particularly the underlying power structure. This is the endogenous political equilibrium.

Because most power structures are invisible, we have what an economist would call the "invisible foot" and the waste of nations described in Chapter

8. The degree of invisibility is even endogenous – witness, in Chapter 18, the optimal amount of obfuscation that parties employ. Discretionary policy and economic regulation are examples of political obfuscation.

Ideology performs many functions in endogenous policy theory. Among others, it obscures the redistributive process from voters (e.g., protection is "good" because it creates jobs, albeit lousy ones) and puts a straitjacket on politicians to keep them from deviating from the desires of their partys' underlying special interests.

The book is structured as follows: Chapters 3–8 develop endogenous policy theory in partial equilibrium. This means we describe the explicit behavior of rationally ignorant voters, two lobbies, and two political parties; however, the structure of the economy is not explained. In terms of endogenous tariff theory, this corresponds to a theory of the industry structure of tariffs: that is, why protection for steel is greater than that for shoes.

If Chapters 3–8 are a theory of why the steel industry has more political influence than the shoe industry, Chapters 9–16 explain why some countries have higher tariffs than others. There we add the maximizing behavior of the actors in two goods and two factor markets to that of the two lobbies, two political parties, and the rationally ignorant voters.

By "endogenous tariff theory" we mean protection generally, since all trade restrictions must be reduced to a tariff equivalent for meaningful measurement. We started not to include the empirical work, because much of it is preliminary; however, it emphasizes the relevance of this type of research. We encourage others to criticize and test our theory. In effect, we develop the microfoundations of national economic policies, with the tariff chosen to illustrate the theory. The results here describe any form of restriction on imports; the theory describes any government policy motivated by special interests.

This book has been fun. We particularly enjoyed devising the titles for Chapters 8 and 18. The basic distribution of labor on the book is that Magee wrote the text whereas Brock and Young wrote the Appendixes. The latter were as time consuming as the text.

We are grateful for the response of both political scientists and economists to our endogenous tariff theory. We thank the many scholars who have contributed directly or indirectly to this work (see the References for a complete list). We are especially indebted to Bob Baldwin for his kind words and encouragement, beginning in the early 1970s.

We are most grateful for the the contributions made by our parents, to whom we have dedicated this book.

January 1989 Steve Magee

Acknowledgments

We wish to thank the publishers of various papers of ours for permission to use portions of them in this book (as noted on chapter opening pages).

We are also indebted to Colin Day, Michael Gnat, Linda Hollick, and Ina Isobe of Cambridge University Press for their patience and help in bringing out this book. We are also indebted to the following individuals who have provided assistance and encouragement along the way: Peter Aranson, Robert Baldwin, David Baron, Gary Becker, Fred Bergsten, Jagdish Bhagwati, John Black, Neil Bruce, Richard Caves, Arun Chandrachud, Belinda Clark, Michael Claudon, Ken Clements, David Colander, Richard Cooper, Max Corden, Peter Coughlin, Alan Deardorff, Rudiger Dornbusch, Chrys Dougherty, Barry Eichengreen, Wilfred Ethier, Robert Feenstra, John Ferejohn, Tom Ferguson, Ronald Findlay, Mike Finger, Morris Fiorina, Jacob Frenkel, Bruno Frey, Vince Geraci, Mark Gersovitz, Herbert Giersch, Patricia Gonzales, Jack Gould, Peter Gray, Carl Hamilton, Liming Han, Xiaoyue Han, Arnold Harberger, Van Harlow, Arye Hillman, Brian Hindley, Mel Hinich, Helen Hughes, Beom-Sik Jang, Mike Jensen, Harry Johnson, Walter Johnson, Ronald Jones, Joseph Kalt, David Kendrick, Charles P. Kindleberger, Roger Kormendi, Stephen Krasner, Anne Krueger, Paul Krugman, Arthur Laffer, Leon Lasdon, Ed Leamer, Harmen Lehment, Assar Lindbeck, Melissa Marlowe, John Martin, Wolfgang Mayer, Rachel McCulloch, Jayne McCullough, Patrick Messerlin, Merton Miller, Terry Moe, Tracy Murray, Michael Mussa, Peter Neary, Dan Newlon, Tom Noe, Roger Noll, Doug Nelson, Kevin Boberts, Mancur Olson, Peter Oppenheimer, Peter Ordeshook, Melanie Payne, Sam Peltzman, Richard Posner, Ramesh Rao, Ed Ray, Michael Rebello, Bill Riker, Carlos Rodriguez, Thomas Romer, Walt and Elspeth Rostow, Carolin Schellhorn, Andy Schmitz, Thomas Schwartz, Yongjai Shin, Larry Sjaastad, Robert Stern, Laura Starks, George Stigler, Alan Stockman, Susan Strange, Lester Telser, Henri Theil, Seha Tinic, Ed Tower, Gordon Tullock, Ingo Walter, Nettie Webb, Barry Weingast, John Whalley, Martin Wolf, and Brian Wood.

List of results

This book shows how the outmoded spatial voting model can be replaced by the probabilistic voting model of endogenous policy theory.

Endogenous policy theory merges economics and politics to construct the microfoundations of economic policy in a full political–economic general equilibrium. The results from our theory are listed below by chapter.

3.   the probabilistic voting model
endogenous policies in general equilibrium
political efficiency defined
the trade-off between economic and political efficiency
policies as prices in political markets
powerless politicians

4.   the contribution specialization theorem

5.   the rationality of policies
the reverse-slope theorem
the reverse-shift theorem

6.   endogenous lobbying theory
the power function model of endogenous lobbying
the industry lobby as a noncooperative n-person game
endogenous political jurisdictions
estimating the free-rider effect

7.   a specific-factor model of short-run lobbying in the United States

8.   the invisible foot and the waste of nations
lawyers as negative externalities
evidence of slower GNP growth with more lawyers
the paradox of rising GNP with more lawyering

9.   endogenous redistribution theory
the $2 \times 2 \times 2 \times 2$ model
redistribution as a negative externality
political power as the probability of election
political parties necessarily as Stackelberg leaders

CHAPTER 1

A preview of the results

Wealth comes from two sources: *production* and *predation*. Production increases wealth whereas predation transfers wealth. Production is a cooperative effort in which direct actors may gain; predation is a noncooperative effort in which the economic prey lose. Production is cooperative; predatory behavior is selfish. Selfish individuals increase their welfare at the expense of others. This book describes how economic agents and political parties generate equilibrium levels of resources devoted to predatory redistribution. In this process, lobbying expenditures are the inputs and special-interest policies and wealth transfers are the outputs.

This book develops the microfoundations of endogenous redistribution theory. Individuals and groups will devote resources to redistribution so long as the gains exceed the costs. Self-interested actors do not care whether their income derives from cooperative or noncooperative behavior. Individuals will invest in both production and predation until the marginal returns from each are identical. At this point, a redistributive equilibrium exists.

Arbitrage between economic and political activity is the driving force behind redistributive politics. Economic wealth can create political power and political power can create wealth. It is this mutual attraction between power and money that motivates redistributive activity.

Economically efficient government policies create greater gains than losses whereas inefficient policies do the reverse. Economically efficient policies usually benefit large groups; inefficient policies usually benefit only smaller special-interest groups. Both efficient and inefficient policies have redistributive effects. It is these redistributive effects (and not the overall efficiency effects) that motivate special-interest lobbies to action.

Chapter 1 of Stephen P. Magee, William A. Brock, and Leslie Young, *Black Hole Tariffs and Endogenous Policy Theory*. New York: Cambridge University Press, 1989. Adapted from Stephen P. Magee, "Summary," mimeo, University of Texas, October 1983.

1

This book advances the notion that the unbridled pursuit of private individual gain does not maximize society's wealth because of the negative externality of redistributive activity. Adam Smith argued that the pursuit of self-interest by individuals would lead a benign invisible hand to maximize society's income. In Chapter 15, we show that the reverse is possible: We give conditions under which the pursuit of self-interest by lobbies can cause an invisible foot to minimize society's income. We call this an *economic black hole* because lobbying can drive economic income virtually to zero. The interesting feature of invisible foot behavior is that redistributors do best when their activities are invisible to the general populace. Chapter 18 shows how political parties disguise their policies in our theory of optimal obfuscation. Redistributive activity, like criminal behavior, is most successful when undetected. In Chapter 8 we present cross-national empirical evidence that redistributive lawyering does indeed lower economic performance.

The powerless politician effect suggests that there is no solution to the economic waste caused by competitive redistribution. That is, policies are determined by rational self-interested behavior of all of the players in the system. Not even the politicians are in charge because their vote-maximizing actions are determined by the technology of collecting funds from special interests and distributing those funds to garner votes from general interests. This book builds the microfoundations of party behavior, lobby behavior, and economic behavior in a self-interested world. We speculate here that successful countries such as the United States have been coincidentally blessed by a congruence of the special interests (who wrote the Constitution) and the general economic interest. One useful outgrowth of this book might be a new slant on constitution theory, particularly in how to narrow the gap between economically efficient versus politically efficient equilibria.

Part I is about how lobbies and political parties interact to redistribute income through tariffs and trade restrictions. Part II investigates the same questions in general equilibrium. Part I provides theory and evidence explaining tariff structure (tariff levels across industries) while Part II does the same for national tariff levels (a given country's tariff level through time). Chapter 2, which precedes Part I, presents a diagrammatic exposition of endogenous policy theory and endogenous lobbying theory, plus a list of some major works on the subject.

1.1   Results of Part I

Chapter 3, written largely in 1973, is the first paper publicly presented by Brock and Magee on endogenous tariffs and endogenous lobbying. The first and most important result is that *tariffs are endogenous*. To our knowledge, this was the first paper to describe tariffs as the outcome of a redistributive battle between lobbies fought through the political system, and with all of the key actors displaying maximizing behavior. Krueger's (1974) paper on rent seeking had maximizing lobby behavior, but there were no political parties and no voters present. In her model, lobbies expended efforts to obtain licenses under a fixed import quota.

In an endogenous policy model, *policies play the same role in politics as prices* play in an economy: Both are equilibrating variables that adjust until opposing forces are balanced. When the demand for wheat is high, the price of wheat is high. Similarly, powerful groups with high demands for protection will obtain higher tariffs than smaller and weaker groups. Just as prices equate demand and supply at the margin, so do redistributive policies equate, at the margin, pressures for and against a given type of redistribution. The textile lobby may obtain a 20% tariff, whereas a weaker lobby such as leather may obtain only a 5% tariff. If these are equilibrium tariffs, attempts to increase the textile tariff from 20% to 21% would encounter greater opposition than support (as would an increase from 5% to 6% for the leather tariff).

A second result is that *lobbying is endogenous.* The assumption of vigorous competition between the political parties means each lobby can only influence the electoral success of its party and not the position that the party took on tariffs. Should the lobby contribute funds to its favored party to maximize that party's probability of election? The answer is "no." The rational lobby will maximize the income of its membership, which is a weighted average of its expected income under each of the two possible political outcomes (say, Democrats vs. Republicans), less the lobbying costs. In equilibrium, the lobby's last dollar contributed to politics should generate just a dollar in additional income to the lobby membership. Anne Krueger's (1974) work on rent seeking was a pioneering paper on endogenous lobbying.

A third result is the concept of *political efficiency.* In a competitive political system, policies will proliferate so long as they increase the probability of election of the party sponsoring the policy. In an efficient political system, there is no new policy that will increase the welfare (probability of election) of one of the parties. The list will include both welfare-increasing (Pareto) and welfare-reducing (redistributive) policies.

There is a *trade-off between economic and political efficiency.* Redistributive policies that benefit one of the parties may be deleterious to the economy; similarly, the elimination of some inefficient redistributive policies may harm one or more political parties at the polls and may reduce the level of public discussion about some important political issues (because less lobbying money is available). We speculate that the most efficient economic systems will be in countries that have not achieved political efficiency (i.e., in countries where the parties have not sponsored all of the redistributive policies at their disposal). In these countries, the level of lobbying for redistributive policies will be lower; hence the level of resources to fund political campaigns will be lower. The down side to this is that all political issues will receive less public discussion. Similarly, countries with more efficient political systems will have greater lobbying, greater funds for campaigns, and more public discussion. Unfortunately, they will also have more distortionary redistributive policies, regulatory entanglements, and politically created economic inefficiency. We also define the conditions required for an *Arrow–Debreu endogenous redistributive political equilibrium*. In this model, each individual (i.e., entity) must calculate the effect of a tariff on its excess demands for each good. Each individual allocates its resources between production and predation so as to maximize its welfare.

An important result is our development of the *probabilisitic voting model,* a major theoretical alternative to the median voter model. There is a protectionist lobby that would gain from a tariff (or any form of protection), and a proexport lobby that would gain from an export subsidy (or any other form of export promotion). Each lobby contributes resources to the parties so long as the expected dollar return from the contribution exceeds its cost. Thus, the lobbies maximize their expected returns from their political investments. There are two political parties: A protectionist party sponsors a tariff, and a proexport party sponsors an export subsidy. Each party sets its policy to maximize its probability of election.

Party competition drives the *political parties to act as Stackelberg leaders.* Any party that acts as a Stackelberg follower or in Cournot–Nash fashion will have a lower probability of election than if it acts as a Stackelberg leader; consequently, it chooses the latter strategy. (A Cournot–Nash actor takes the current values of the other players' decision variables *as given* when plotting a strategy; a Stackelberg leader calculates how the other players' decision variables respond to variation *in his own* decision variable before plotting a strategy.) When a party acts as a Stackelberg leader, it anticipates how much lobbying money it will receive for all possible levels of its policy. It then picks the policy level that yields it the most votes (i.e., that maximizes its probability of election). Ironically, this means that the policy chosen by each party will be determined before any funds to be contributed by a lobby start flowing. Hence, in a sense, the level of the policy is based on anticipated rather than actual lobby contributions. We construct a *Stackelberg-leadership pyramid* to describe the game-theoretic equilibrium concept: that is, how all of the actors interact. The pyramid is realistic in that the power is greatest, the actors fewest, and the information best at the top of the pyramid.

In an endogenous political equilibrium, neither the two parties nor the two lobbies get everything that they want: Each player's optimal behavior depends on the actions of the other three players. Each player maximizes his (her/its) position, but subject to three constraints imposed by the other players. Ironically, since the parties cannot select the policies that are in the best interests of the country, we have the *powerless politician effect: Government policies are outside of policymaker control.*

The next result is the *contribution specialization theorem.* Assume that the protectionist lobby is attempting to decide on its lobbying expenditures in a two-party race. Let the protectionist party support a 20% tariff while the proexport party favors a 10% export subsidy. Because the policy positions are already set, as the parties are Stackelberg leaders, the only thing left for the two lobbies to influence are the probabilities of election of the parties. It is clear that the protectionist lobby should specialize its contributions and give only to the protectionist party. That is, the welfare of the protectionists increases with probability of election of the protectionist party, but decreases with the probability of election of the proexport party. If the protectionist lobby contributed to the proexport party, it would lower its chances of getting a 20% tariff and increase its chances of getting the unwanted 10% export subsidy. Similar arguments apply to the proexport lobby, which should give only to the proexport party. Hence, both lobbies should contribute exclusively, each to its most favored party.

There will be *nonparticipation of lobbies in Hotelling races* (in which the political parties quote identical positions). For example, if both parties quote an identical policy (e.g., both parties support a 10% tariff), neither lobby will contribute any funds because the policy chosen after the election will be the same regardless of which party is elected. A related result is the *nonexistence of a Hotelling equilibrium on special-interest issues.* Since we know that the lobbies will contribute to neither party, neither party would gain by quoting a nonzero position on the tariff – voter hostility would be encountered with no offsetting gain in contributions.

The results in Chapter 3 suggest that, as we look across countries, we should observe (1) that protariff and proexport lobbies support different parties and (2) parties will not take identical positions on the issue of protection. We do not test these implications in this book.

Chapter 4 explores the campaign contribution specialization theorem in greater detail, as well as the larger question of optimal contribution strategies of a special-interest lobby. There are three reasons why lobbies give to political parties: policies, future access, and avoidance of retribution effects. We find three exceptions to the contribution specialization theorem. The first is that a lobby *might contribute to both parties in the presence of imperfect information.* The requirement for this result is that the lobby must believe that it can influence the policy that each party will provide. Through time, however, it should learn that sophisticated parties (playing a Stackelberg-leader game) will have already anticipated their moves and set their trade policy. A second exception is that *access effects might also generate contributions to both sides.* Some donors anticipate the need for access to a party in the future (on unspecified issues) and they believe that it will be available only if they have contributed in the past. This might induce the protectionist lobby to contribute to the proexport party in the hopes that it would get some future unspecified benefits. A third exception is that a lobby may *contribute only to its nonfavored party if retribution effects are present.* Protectionist contributions to the protectionist party will be reduced to the extent that the protectionists anticipate that the proexport party (if elected) will punish them for giving to the protectionist party. If there are access effects, so that a protectionist lobby would normally give to both parties, but the proexport party is retribution prone, then a protectionist lobby might give only to the nonfavored proexport party.

There are three empirical implications of the special-interest lobbying model. The specialization effect of contributing only to the most favored party increases with the size of the contributors. Thus, *large donors are more likely to specialize their contributions* on a single party. Also, *contributions* (based on policy positions) *will be independent of the probabilities of election.* The protectionist lobby will give only to the most protectionist party (not to the party most likely to win), and the amount it will give is driven not by the probability of its election but by the *marginal probability of election.* The latter is the increase in the probability of election caused by additional lobbying funds. For example, if the protectionist party has an 80% chance of being elected, and if a large contribution will not increase that chance much (because of diminishing returns, voter satiation with advertising, etc.), then the protectionist lobby should not contribute, because of the low marginal payoff. On the other hand, if the protectionist party has a 10% chance, but a contribution will increase its chances dramatically, then a contribution by the protectionists may be rational. On the other hand, contributions for retribution and access effects do not follow this independence effect: They *will* be affected by the probabilities of election. A final empirical implication is that *polarized parties generate greater special-interest contributions.* That is, polarized elections, in which the parties are far apart on redistributive issues, generate greater lobby contributions to both parties than campaigns in which the parties are closer together.

There is a generalization of the campaign contribution specialization theorem. To how many parties should a lobby contribute when there are n parties? The *rational lobby will contribute to $n - 1$ parties,* at most. The generalized rule is never to contribute to the least preferred party.

The last result is an *empirical test of the contribution specialization theo-*

rem. The data were not taken from tariff lobbying but rather from contributions to American presidential races. This should provide a tougher test for the theorem because a presidential race is a multi-issue race and much more complicated than a tariff. In the 1964, 1968, and 1972 presidential races, 7%, 14%, and 8% of the contributors, respectively, gave to both parties. We found that the larger contributors tended to give to one side, as hypothesized, in 1968 and 1972, whereas this was not the case in 1964. Thus, the data gave modest support for the hypothesis in two out of three elections.

Chapter 5 presents the basics of *endogenous tariff theory*. Result 1 is the *reverse-slope theorem*. Imagine a two-dimensional diagram with the tariff position of the protectionist party on one axis and the export subsidy of the proexport party on the other axis. When we plot the reaction curves (the optimal strategies) of each party, we find that the slopes of the curves have opposite signs in the neighborhood of equilibrium. To label this behavior, we say that the party with the positively sloped curve "emulates" the actions of the other party (when the other party raises its policy, so does the emulator), while the party with the negatively sloped curve "counteracts" the actions of the other party.

Result 2, the *reverse-shift theorem*, suggests that certain exogenous shocks cause one of the parties to increase its policy and the other to reduce its policy. Thus, the tariff and the export subsidy will generally move in opposite directions in response to shocks. There is mild qualitative evidence for this phenomenon in the postwar period among the Western democracies: For the 1950s and 1960s, tariffs fell while export promotion grew. However, we do not examine this empirical phenomenon in this book.

The reverse-shift theorem forms the basis for results 3 and 4. Result 3 is the *policy-distance paradox*. It is possible (though not inevitable) that both the protectionist lobby and the proexport lobby become more powerful and yet the distance between the two parties falls (i.e., the sum of the equilibrium tariff and the equilibrium export subsidy falls). One possible consequence of the decline in policy distance is that contributions to both parties might fall, despite the initial increase in lobby power.

The reverse-shift theorem also generates result 4, the *distortion paradox*. Both distortions may increase, and yet the average of the two may fall. (The weights are the probabilities of election of the two parties.) This is possible when the increase in the policy of the high-distortion party causes its probability of election to fall a great deal. Next, we get a result that sounds tautological but is not: *Inconsistent parties* increase the likelihood that the endogenous policy equilibrium will be *unstable*. If each party's reaction curve is highly elastic with respect to the other party's policy, then the parties are inconsistent (i.e., they make wide swings in their positions for small changes in the position of the other party). In this case, the Cournot–Nash tariff equilibrium will not be stable. That is, if two parties are in the neighborhood of this equilibrium, they will not converge but rather diverge from it.

Next, we generalize these propositions. The *generalization of the reverse-slope theorem to many parties* suggests that if party 3 raises its tariff in response to a tariff increase by, say, party 5, then party 5 will lower its tariff in response to an increase by party 3. We suspect that the reverse-slope theorem might be quite general and applicable to most redistributive policies in a democracy. The reverse-slope theorem *generalizes to constant-sum games* between two parties (not just unity-sum games involving the probability of election). For example, it would apply to *asymmetric externality* situations in which one industry generates a negative externality (e.g., a pollutive steel plant) while another industry generates a positive one (e.g., a suburban housing development). An increase in the size of the housing development would increase the value of the steel mill, but an increase in the size of the steel mill would reduce the value of the suburb. Given certain assumptions, the reverse-slope theorem holds for constant-sum games *with many political parties*.

Chapter 6 constructs a model of the microfoundations of endogenous lobbying theory. Particularly applicable to industry lobbying, the model describes the optimal contributions by each member of a protectionist lobby, the equilibrium behavior of each member depending on the amounts given by all other members. A tariff creates a public good for all of the protectionists in a given industry, regardless of whether they contribute to the tariff effort. Thus, this chapter explores conditions required for Olson's (1965) voluntary provision of a public good. The first result in this chapter is a *model of the industry lobby as a noncooperative n-person game*. It retains the stringent assumption that each lobby member acts selfishly (i.e., only in its own interest). We do this by formalizing the importance of public-good effects relative to private-good effects for each member of the lobby. When the public-good effects dominate, free-riding is a serious problem. In this case, an individual, who is small relative to the lobby as a whole, does not perceive any effect of a contribution on group effectiveness and will not contribute. When there are firm-specific gains, however, such as the Chrysler bailout by the U.S. government, lobby contributions are greater. Almost by definition, lobby effectiveness increases with the private-good effects and decreases with the public-good effects.

Second, conditions are developed for *existence and uniqueness* of an equilibrium. Third, conditions are specified on the net marginal value products of each member, yielding *Olson's exploitation of the large by the small*. Let all of the members of the lobby be of equal size. Then increase the size of one of them. That member increases its lobby contribution while all of the smaller players decrease theirs. Total lobby contributions increase while per-member contributions decrease. In this experiment, both the total stakes increase and the shares of the gainers become more unequal. If we hold industry sales constant but increase the number of players, then total contributions decrease with the number of firms in the industry. In this case, total lobby contributions approach zero as the number of lobbying members increase. This result is consistent with the powerlessness of many consumer lobbies.

Fourth, in this same model we explore two important considerations suggested in the literature on lobbying: *perceived effectiveness and noticeability*. In addition, we develop restrictions on the contribution functions that guarantee the following three forms of Olson–Stigler lobby behavior:

1. Lobbying contributions are homogeneous of degree 1 with respect to the stakes (i.e., double the size of the industry and lobbying expenditures will double). Similarly, a doubling of the sales of each firm in an industry would double the total lobby contributions of the industry.
2. Protectionist lobbying contributions are maximized when there is only one seller, that is, a single import-competing monopolist who does not have to worry about free-riders.
3. Increases in the inequality of the benefits from a tariff increase total lobbying contributions. Conditions sufficient to give these results are the following. There is an initial phase of increasing returns of group benefits from contributing, followed by one of decreasing returns; each contributor perceives that the increase in the total group benefits from its contribution are less than its marginal cost; and the marginal private gains to each individual of contributing are identical across givers.

Fifth, we construct a *simplified model* by assuming that all of the members of the lobby are of equal size. We get four results:

1. Consider the case in which there are no private benefits to contributing to the lobby and all of the members are of equal size. In this case, there is a unique Nash equilibrium in the total level of contributions but an indeterminate composition of that total among the lobby members. Because of the latter, lobby members may contribute very unequal amounts and some may contribute nothing at all in equilibrium. Total lobbying contributions are unchanged if we add to the industry another firm that has the same level of sales as all of the other (identical) ones: A larger industry effect is just offset by a

smaller share effect. Thus, total lobbying expenditures are independent of the number of identical members. These results apply to consumer lobbies. Only if there are private benefits does the addition of another identical firm increase total lobby contributions.

2. If there are both public and private benefits present, then addition of another identical firm to the lobby will reduce per-member contributions but increase total lobby contributions. The industry is now larger and so are lobby contributions.

3. A larger number of firms in the industry but with industry sales unchanged will lead to no effect on the total lobbying effort only when the benefits of lobbying are fully private (i.e., there is no free-riding).

4. With both public and private benefits present, an increase in the number of firms in an industry of fixed size causes a decrease in total lobby contributions.

How would one use this theory to explain tariff rates across industries? The *lobbying power function* is the sixth major result. It states that industry tariffs can be explained as a simple product of a concentration measure and the value of industry sales. Given both public and private benefits from lobbying, assume that the total level of funds flowing from a protectionist lobby can be described as the product of the lobby's gain from the passage of a tariff and the Herfindahl index of the shares that each lobby member would have in that gain. If industry tariffs increase monotonically with protectionist lobbying expenditures, then the power function conforms to the usual econometric specification that industry tariffs should be positively correlated with the product of the Herfindahl index of industry structure and the total value of sales across industries. Chapter 6 highlights the number of theoretical assumptions required to obtain this specification. However, it does not solve the problem of labor and capital free-riding on each other in such a model.

Result 7 deals with the relationship between *tariffs and the size of political jurisdictions*. If aggregation of political units into larger ones increases protectionist lobbying expenditures relative to free-trade expenditures, the equilibrium tariff increases. This suggests that the senators from a U.S. state would be more protectionist than the members of Congress from the same state. It turns out that special-interest lobbying can either increase or decrease relative to general-interest lobbying as we move to larger geographical aggregations of the same individuals: The direction of the results depends on the size of the public versus private lobbying effects.

When the free-rider problem is severe, the senators will be more special-interest and favor higher tariffs than the members of Congress. Consider first the opponents of protection. For a consumer free-trade lobby, the free-rider problem is serious. From result 4 above we know that moving from a congressional district to a senatorial district might double the consumer surplus affected by a tariff but halve the share of each consumer; thus total lobby contributions by the free-trade consumer group would not change. This means that the consumer lobby contributions to all of the members of Congress from Texas might be the same as the consumer contributions to the two Texan senators. Consider now the protectionists. Large protectionist firms will have smaller free-rider problems, so total protectionist lobby contributions will rise in moving from congressional districts to senatorial districts. The increase in protectionist contributions relative to consumerist contributions suggests that the equilibrium tariff should rise in a given state as we move from Congress to the Senate (assuming for the moment that tariffs are driven exclusively by relative contribution levels).

While we do not so conclude in this book, the previous analysis suggests an eighth result, namely, the idea of *endogenous political jurisdictions*. If special-interest lobby contributions rise relative to public-interest lobby contributions as political jurisdictions get larger, then special-interest lobbies will favor centralized (i.e., national) political decision making. Centralization will continue until an equilibrium is reached where the marginal pressures for greater centralization just balance those against. Could special-interest effects such as these help explain the growth of the nation-states in the nineteenth and twentieth centuries? Or could they explain the ascendancy of Washington over state governments in the United States? Finally, Chapter 6 discusses how to estimate the free-rider effect.

Thus far in the book, the economic side of the economy has not been specified. We assumed that the model in Part I would be most applicable to industry tariff lobbies in models with immobile factors of production. However, the apparatus in Part I could be attached to a wide variety of economic models. In trade theory, two polar candidates for the economic specification are the Stolper–Samuelson model with full factor mobility and the Ricardo–Viner–Cairnes model with full factor immobility. Stolper and Samuelson assumed that both capital and labor could move to other industries in the long run; Ricardo–Viner–Cairnes assumed that it could not. If Stolper–Samuelson holds, we would expect international economic policy to be formed with the scarce factor in the economy giving lobbying resources to the protariff party and the abundant factor in the economy giving resources to the proexport party. If the Ricardo–Viner–Cairnes model holds, we would expect all of the factors in import-competing production to lobby for the protariff party and all of the factors in export production to lobby for the proexport party.

Given this, **Chapter 7** formulates *three simple tests of the Stolper–*

Samuelson theorem versus the Ricardo–Viner–Cairnes model of tariff lobby behavior in the United States. If capital and labor from a given industry are always on the opposite side of the free trade–protection issue (irrespective of their industry location), then Stolper–Samuelson would be the better model. However, the data show the reverse: Both capital and labor in import-competing industries favor protection, whereas capital and labor in the export industries favor freer trade. These results have led some to believe that fixed factor models may be the best approach to explain lobbying over tariffs. However, we have serious reservations about such a conclusion.

The most significant problem with the Chapter 7 results is that they are driven by an institutional feature of U.S. trade legislation that has been around since 1934: namely, its tendency to require renewal every four years or so. Thus, lobbying behavior tested in the three simple tests of the Stolper–Samuelson theorem apply to lobbies that are discounting future benefits for only four years into the future. Because of this short time horizon, the results are biased against the Stolper–Samuelson theorem and toward the Ricardo–Viner–Cairnes model.

For these and other reasons, we believe that the Ricardo–Viner–Cairnes model is a better description of lobbying for short-lived trade legislation and for industry-specific explanations of trade policy. However, when it comes to explaining the level of a *country's tariffs,* a politicized version of the *Heckscher–Ohlin–Samuelson (HOS)* model of international trade is *more insightful for predicting long-term behavior on trade policy.* This is true both for long periods of time and for cross-sectional studies of country tariff levels. Empirical support for this view is the alignment of blue-collar workers, a scarce factor in the United States, with the protectionist Democrats in the U.S. Congress and the alignment of many management trade associations with freer trade and with the (proexport) congressional Republicans. Similarly, tariff rates across countries are correlated with the country's endowment of capital per laborer. For this reason, our general equilibrium $2 \times 2 \times 2 \times 2$ model in Part II uses the HOS–Stolper–Samuelson model.

Chapter 8 develops a theory of the *invisible foot and the waste of nations.* It addresses the issue of protectionism at the individual level. In it we formalize Olson's (1982) hypothesis that the growth rates of economies will be inversely correlated with the time that their lobbies and political systems have had to form wasteful redistributive entanglements. We see considerable merit in the Olson hypothesis. To illustrate the difficulty of detecting the Olson phenomenon, we show theoretically how *increases in legal redistributive activity can actually increase income.* We provide a theoretical illustration of how an economy's growth rate and the level of GNP can both increase at a time of increasing redistributive activity directed at wealth. The intuition is that increasing redistribution can convert wealth into higher income and higher consumption. In the long run, however, *the negative externalities of legal activity* have adverse effects on income. Only with good measures of wealth could the Olson phenomena be detected.

We present empirical evidence in this chapter that *legal rent seeking can be detected* across countries. Data for about thirty-five countries indicate that a *relatively large proportion of lawyers in a country's white-collar labor force leads to significant declines in economic performance* (measured by GNP growth over the period 1960–80). Because of data difficulties, we used physicians as a normalizing proxy for the size of the white-collar labor force.

1.2 Results of Part II

We turn now to the chapters on endogenous tariff theory and endogenous lobbying in general equilibrium. In the late 1970s, we thought for some time about how the apparatus in Part I might be incorporated into general equilibrium. It was not immediately obvious how to proceed, due to several issues: mobile versus immobile factors, appropriate general equilibrium game-theoretic structure (who would be Stackelberg leaders and who would be followers), and so on. The problem was partially solved by a suggestion in the nice paper by Findlay and Wellisz (1982). They attached a Brock and Magee (1978, 1980) lobbying structure (just described in Part I) to a general equilibrium economy that had one mobile and two immobile factors of production. They did not have political parties but assumed that the political system would yield tariffs that increased in the protariff lobbying resources and decreased in the antitariff lobbying resources. The result was the first on endogenous lobbying in general equilibrium. The Findlay and Wellisz paper encouraged Magee and Brock to write Chapter 9, which in turn led to the work by Magee and Leslie Young in Part II of this book.

In **Chapter 9** we construct a $2 \times 2 \times 2 \times 2$ model of two goods, two factors, two lobbies, and two political parties, with all of these actors displaying maximizing behavior. When the original paper was presented at an NBER conference, Ron Findlay quipped that our model might be called the "2×4" model, partly because of its lumberyard emphasis on stark self-interest. In fact, the $2 \times 2 \times 2 \times 2$ *model* is the first major contribution in Chapter 9. In it, we attached the Brock–Magee political apparatus to a Heckscher–Ohlin–Samuelson model with full factor mobility, and assumed that the country was small so as to avoid any terms of trade motivation for tariffs. The political sector was more general than in Findlay and Wellisz: We have both political parties and voters whereas they have neither. Each of our political parties displays maximizing behavior, and our voters are rationally ignorant and choose parties probabilistically. This chapter reviews many of the issues in Part I in the context of general equilibrium.

The first problem is to describe how all of the players interact. The problem is complicated because everybody's behavior must fit with everyone else's in general equilibrium. Following Chapter 3, we used the three-tier *Stackelberg leadership pyramid* for our equilibrium concept. Each actor behaves Cournot–Nash vis-à-vis other actors on or above its tier; however, each is a Stackelberg leader vis-à-vis actors below its tier. Recall that we have political parties in the top tier, lobbies in the middle, and voters and the economy in the bottom tier. The reasons for these choices include party competition, information costs, and free-riding arguments: The higher the tier, the smaller the number of actors and the greater the power of the players. This is also reasonable because, in most countries, there are a few political parties at the top, many lobbies in the middle, and a large number of capitalists, laborers, and voters at the bottom.

How does the $2 \times 2 \times 2 \times 2$ model work? The two goods and two factor markets are perfectly competitive. The country is assumed to be an advanced one with a higher capital–labor ratio than the rest of the world. The country follows the Heckscher–Ohlin–Samuelson model in exporting the capital-intensive good and importing the labor-intensive good. We assume that each of the two factors of production organizes a lobby that engages in political activity to increase its income. To motivate the intuition behind the results and for purely expository reasons, we call the protectionist party the Congressional Democrats and the proexport party the Congressional Republicans. Following the campaign-contribution-specialization theorem, the capital lobby removes capital from production and gives it only to the Congressional Republicans; the labor lobby removes labor from the economy and gives only to the Congressional Democrats. The Democrats sponsor a tariff on imports of labor-intensive goods, which raises the domestic price of labor-intensive goods, which, by the Stolper–Samuelson theorem, then raises wages. The Republicans sponsor an export subsidy (i.e., a negative tariff), which raises the domestic price of capital-intensive goods and hence raises the returns to capital. As in Part I, the voters choose parties probabilistically, so the political parties choose their equilibrium policies by trading off the beneficial voter effects of lobby contributions against the negative voter effects of the distortionary policy. We assume, in this chapter and in all of Part II, that neither capital nor labor has a majority of the electorate. We could have added a third factor of production to the model to accomplish this, but it would have generated needless complications with only cosmetic theoretical benefits. We instead assume that part of the electorate is uninformed and that both capital and labor possess imperfect information.

What are the effects of an endogenous political system on an economy?

A priori, the political system should benefit labor relative to capital the higher the electoral success rate of the Congressional Democrats, the higher the tariff on labor-intensive imports, and the lower the export subsidy on capital-intensive exports. However, all three of these variables are endogenous and are driven by the exogenous economic and political variables in the $2 \times 2 \times 2 \times 2$ model. To understand when these a priori expectations hold, we need to understand the workings of the model.

We assume that political markets clear more rapidly than economic markets so that resources in the economy are allocated on the basis of the expected political equilibrium. Thus, the effect of the political system on relative goods prices in the economy is a weighted average of the tariff and the export subsidy, with the weights being the equilibrium probabilities of electoral success of the two parties. The expectational equilibrium is an important property of the model. It seems sensible because it fits with the long-run character of the neoclassical international trade model that we are using. It also makes this model appropriate for cross-country empirical tests, since cross-sectional data are best described by a long-run model. The only alternative to the expectational equilibrium would be to have ex post outcomes in which the economy would move to a tariff-only equilibrium when Congressional Democrats have a majority and an export subsidy-only equilibrium when Congressional Republicans have a majority. We reject this approach since it violates the stylized fact of infrequent changes in commercial policy and generates needless complexity. While we do not develop them here, models that explore ex post outcomes more fully would be welcome additions to the literature.

Is the expectational equilibrium reasonable in terms of the interaction of politics and the economy? It is especially so if we view political party competition as a continuous process, and not just confined to elections. For example, the Democrats and Republicans and their clientele lobbies compete continuously in the legislative, executive, and judicial branches in the formation and execution of protectionist policy. Even though only one of the parties controls the executive branch at a time, it takes years for a new president to change the direction of the American bureaucracy. Each party makes monthly political decisions about protectionism. Thus, if our model indicates that the Congressional Democrats have a 60% success rate in the American political system, this means that there is a 60% chance that their protection would be supported by the courts, the U.S. International Trade Commission, Congress, the voters, and so on.

An interesting feature is that the general equilibrium price distortions can be quite low from tariffs and export subsidies in our expectational equilibrium. Domestic prices in our model will be determined by the expected values of the politics and the probabilities of electoral success. Obviously, if the equilibrium tariff and export subsidy quoted by the parties are equal and the probabilities of electoral success are even, then the domestic price ratio will not differ from world prices. Even if the tariff and the export subsidy differ, the domestic and international prices can be equal. This will be true if the odds of Congressional Republican success equal the ratio of 1 plus the tariff to 1 plus the export subsidy. In this case, there would be no deadweight losses from price distortions, and the welfare losses would be confined to the lobbying costs. These results are theoretical; empirical tests would have to be performed by future researchers across economies to determine the costs of price distortions relative to lobbying. Our belief is that lobbying costs are larger than the general equilibrium price distortions. (See, e.g., Chapter 15, in which infinitesimal tariffs and export subsidies can be associated with all of the resources in the economy disappearing into lobbying.)

A second result in Chapter 9 is our first speculation about the principle of optimal obfuscation. That is, all political parties will support the same direct and efficient ("popular") redistributive policies (à la Bhagwati, 1971) if the benefiting group controls a majority of the electorate; however, each party will support a different clientele of special interests and use indirect and in-efficient ("unpopular") policies to help them when they control only a minority of the electorate. We suggest that the tariff is an inefficient and unpopular policy benefiting a minority of the electorate in most Western democracies and is better described by the obfuscation principle developed more fully in Chapter 18. Lobbies will not participate in Hotelling races (see Chapter 3). If political parties quote identical positions on popular policies, they will not raise economic resources from lobbies from their support of popular policies. If this is correct, then political parties can raise resources only from their sponsorship of unpopular policies.

One advantage of Chapter 9 is that the functional forms describing production and the probability for political success are completely general. However, this generality is a disadvantage if we want more specific results. In Chapters 10–12 we assume Leontief production functions for the two goods and a logit probability of election function for voter behavior. Chapter 13 is an empirical application of the Leontief model to U.S. tariffs over the period 1900–88. In Chapters 14 and 15, we use Cobb–Douglas functions for both production and consumer utility, coupled with the same logit probability of election function for voter behavior. Chapter 16 is a test of the endowment theory of tariffs across fifty-eight countries using 1970s data.

The first result in the Prisoner's Dilemma model of **Chapter 10** is an *explicit solution for equilibrium policies and lobbying*. The parameters in the model are a country's capital/labor endowment, the factor intensities in production of the two goods, the elasticities of political outcomes with respect to the economic resources of each party, and world product prices. The second result is that *distorted equilibria are caused by a high responsiveness of voters to the party's lobbying resources*. However, as voter responsiveness to lobbying resources decreases, a country can be transformed from a distorted equilibrium to a free-trade equilibrium.

When we investigated the equilibria in Chapter 10 generated across the entire range of possible parameter values, we came upon an interesting result. In over 40% of the equilibria, both factors were worse off by their decision to engage in lobbying. This is a puzzle. Lobbying is a voluntary act and, by definition, lobbies are special-interest organizations. How could everyone be worse off in equilibrium? The answer was a third major result in this chapter, namely, a *Prisoner's Dilemma theory of endogenous tariffs*. Out of over 70-odd possible 2 × 2 games, the Prisoner's Dilemma game yields the only pattern of payoffs in which the equilibrium is not Pareto optimal. In our Prisoner's Dilemma cases, the best strategy for each factor is to lobby for a redistributive policy, regardless of whether the other factor lobbies or not. Thus, we may have tariffs in many cases because lobby competition in a democracy leads to this degenerate equilibrium. The insight is that the lobbies are trapped by their own greed. Because of our small country assumption, the policy-induced price distortions, and the resources used in lobbying, it is impossible for both factors to be better off in our distorted equilibrium than they would be in a free-trade economy with no endogenous political sector. Thus, in all of the non–Prisoner's Dilemma economies, we found the expected "dominant player" outcome in which one of the two lobbies gained and the other lost (compared to the factor's income with free trade and no lobbying). In Chapter 11 we explore why the lobbies may not cooperate to avoid the Prisoner's Dilemma equilibrium.

Our fourth result focused on when the political outcome would be a *Prisoner's Dilemma versus a dominant player equilibrium*. We found that countries that had intermediate values of their factor endowment ratio generated Prisoner's Dilemma outcomes, whereas countries with extreme values generated dominant player outcomes. For example, if the country's capital/labor endowment was high (low), then the endogenous political equilibrium would give capital (labor) a higher income than it would have received in the nondistorted free-trade case with no special-interest politics.

The fifth result is that the equilibria display powerful constant-sum-game effects: *There are no parametric changes that make the Prisoner's Dilemma payoffs more cooperative*. Each factor must decide whether it will lobby for redistribution or not. Our simulations of parameter changes always made the payoffs more friendly for one of the players but less friendly for the other. A "friendly" payoff is one that makes the player less likely to choose the noncooperative lobbying solution.

A sixth contribution of Chapter 10 draws *insights for Prisoner's Dilemma tariffs from the experimental work on Prisoner's Dilemma games.* The likelihood of noncooperative lobbying and Prisoner's Dilemma tariffs increases (1) with economic payoffs that are unfriendly, uncertain, and unequal; (2) with tough, mean, and retribution prone lobbies; and (3) in the middle (compared with the beginning and the end) of games that are repeated many times.

A final result is that *a free-trade economy has no other equilibrium.* In addition, our simulations have revealed no cases in which an economy that had a distorted equilibrium also had free trade as one of its other equilibria. Thus, only distorted economies are prone to multiple equilibria; free-trade economies are not. The only way a country can change from a distorted equilibrium to a free-trade equilibrium is by an exogenous change in production technology, the terms of trade, the factor endowment, or the responsiveness of voters to political advertising. Perhaps this explains the worldwide absence of free trade.

Chapter 11 extends the Leontief model of the previous chapter. First, we find a phenomenon called *the compensation effect: Whenever a factor's economic fortunes decline, it turns to politics for relief.* The point can be illustrated by examining the effect of a change in the terms of trade on the level of protection. A terms of trade increase could be caused by a decrease in the price of a country's imports (e.g., the situation now facing the United States in the import surge of autos and other products from Japan and the Far East). Lower import prices place downward pressure on the prices of labor-intensive goods in the United States, and this lowers wages. Lower wages reduce the opportunity cost of lobbying for the labor lobby, so it expands its political efforts on behalf of the protectionist party (e.g., Congressional Democrats). The protectionist party increases its equilibrium tariff (or another form of protection). The higher tariff raises the domestic price of importables, and this provides an increase in wages that is a partial offset to the initial decline caused by the rise in the terms of trade (the political compensation effects cannot more than offset the wage effects of the original shock). In short, *increases in a country's terms of trade cause a rise in the country's equilibrium level of protection.* Notice that this has the same result as (but with opposite causation to) the traditional case of an increase in tariffs in a large country leading to an increase in the country's terms of trade.

Second, the compensation effect (which applies both to terms of trade and technology changes) means that *endogenous politics is progressive with respect to exogenous changes in prices and technology.* When a factor's income falls, arbitrage between economic and political activity causes the factor's lobby to get more for itself out of the political system. The injured factor lobbies harder, and the political system provides policies that generate a partial offset to the initial decline in income.

With Leontief production, we find that the *fortunes of the lobbies and the parties move together* with regard to exogenous changes in world prices. Let the price of imports decline. Labor is harmed because wages fall. Labor contributes more to the Democrats and gets a higher tariff. The Republicans counter with a lower export subsidy and receive fewer resources from the procapital lobby. We have no profound explanation for the rationale for the final result. However, when the smoke clears, the Democrats ultimately get fewer votes and the Republicans get more. In short, when world prices cause wages to fall, they also cause a decline in the fortunes of the prolabor party. We can restate the results in terms of the terms of trade, which are the ratio of the price of exports to the price of imports. An import price decrease causes a terms of trade increase, which hurts labor, the scarce factor, and thereby hurts the prolabor party. This helps capital and the procapital party.

Another result is a *pervasive tendency for multiple equilibria* to exist in our political equilibria (noted in an earlier paper by Young [1982]). The research strategy was to examine the number of equilibria that emerged as we varied the elasticity of voter responsiveness with respect to economic resources. We found that *the number of multiple equilibria in a given country increased with the responsiveness of voters to lobbying resources*. A related result is that Prisoner's Dilemma *economies are more prone to triple equilibria than are dominant player economies*.

An interesting question that was raised by Chapter 10 is the following. Why don't the lobbies simply collude in the Prisoner's Dilemma cases? That is, why don't they refuse to contribute to the political system, and drive the political system to free trade with no special-interest policies? No transfer of resources or compensation schemes between the lobbies would be necessary. Such collusion between the "prisoners" obviously avoids the noncooperative outcome in the original game. Our general equilibrium model provides insight into this question, which we call the *Prisoner's Dilemma–multiple equilibrium trap*. All of the countries we considered had two equilibria and nearly half had three. We speculate that a Prisoner's Dilemma equilibrium may be difficult to negotiate away by lobby collusion because the lobbies would fear that, instead of moving to free trade, a double cross might send the system to one of the other (even more perverse) distorted equilibria.

Compare the multiple equilibria for a given economy. There is *party–lobby schizophrenia across multiple equilibria*. We find the equilibrium with the highest wages has the lowest success rate for the protectionist party. Thus, equilibria that are good for labor are bad for the prolabor party (and similarly for capital and the procapital party).

Our simulations revealed that *70% of the countries had no equilibrium*. However, we had a loose definition of "no equilibrium" that included specialization of production (etc.) in addition to the usual absence of a core. This suggests a *passageway thesis:* Movement from a distorted equilibrium to a free-trade equilibrium by parametric changes involves *crossing a region with no equilibrium* in the sense used above. Whether this explains the difficulty that countries have in cutting their tariffs to zero is unclear.

We find that *5–15% of an economy's capital and labor is lost in predatory lobbying* in simulations across the many parameter values chosen for the model.

Chapter 12 is the only chapter that applies directly to developing countries. Here, capital is the scarce factor in the economy relative to the rest of the world. We apply the preceding model to a developing country with no barriers on international capital movements. This analysis might apply to a capital-poor country that faces capital inflows from multinational corporations or other foreign sources. We assume that tariffs and export subsidies are still the focus of policy analysis, rather than capital controls.

Historically, economists have been interested in the "tariff factory" question: that is, the role of tariffs in stimulating the creation of local factories financed through international capital inflows. In this chapter, we reverse the causation and examine the effect of capital inflows on endogenous tariffs. We assume that the developing country is a democracy. All of the results in this chapter are based on simulations using the Leontief model developed in the previous two chapters.

The most important result is that there are *increasing returns to politics: The more capital an economy has, the higher will be the returns to capital.* This runs counter to the usual story that exogenous capital inflows into a small economy would (1) decrease capital returns if the economy were closed to international trade because of diminishing returns, or (2) not affect capital returns if the economy were open to international trade, à la Rybczynski. By our assumption that the country is capital-scarce, tariffs on capital-intensive goods rise as capital flows in because the protariff capital lobby gets more powerful and gives more money to the procapital party; this, in turn, increases the success rate for the procapital party. These factors, plus Stolper–Samuelson effects, increase the returns to capital.

Second, the *equilibrium policies are fairly insensitive to changes in country factor endowments,* assuming unitary elasticities of the political outcomes with respect to campaign contributions. Increasing returns to politics suggests *geographical polarization of world capital endowments.* Countries well endowed with capital will have high capital returns and will attract even more capital, whereas labor-abundant countries should have low returns and lose capital. Could this explain the capital gap between the DCs and the LDCs? At a minimum, it reinforces the capital dominance by the developed countries.

The polarization result above suggests that *national factor endowments will be unstable* because of capital flows and endogenous political behavior. Countries that are heavily endowed with capital will provide greater political protection to capital, and this will attract even more capital. Witness the historical pattern of continued capital inflows into well endowed and politically receptive countries such as Brazil. These models generate *symmetric Marxist factor exploitation: Contrary to Marx, labor is just as likely to exploit capital* as vice versa. The results depend on whether the country has a higher factor endowment ratio than the rest of the world. Special-interest politics will lead to capital dominance in capital-abundant countries and labor dominance in labor-abundant countries.

Sixth, we find a *clout paradox*. Clout reversals are possible: That is, the pattern of a factor getting progressively stronger can be reversed. To illustrate, consider a country whose capital/labor endowment ratio is just below the world average. Since its returns to capital are below those on world markets, capital will emigrate, causing the returns to fall even further. Thus, capital has declining clout. Imagine now an exogenous change in the world price of capital-intensive goods that places the world capital return above the domestic capital return. Capital will start flowing into the country, becoming more powerful politically and increasing its clout. While this may be a bit of a curiosum, any exogenous change that causes capital's return to reverse its relationship to world capital returns can generate this result.

Seventh, because of the difference between gross and net capital returns, *capital cross flows are possible:* Capital can simultaneously flow into and out of the country. Local capital may be trapped into contributing to the local procapital party so that it earns the net return, while multinational capital may get away with not contributing to local politics and earn the gross return to capital. If the net return is below the world return while the gross return is above it, multinational capital will enter while domestic capital will leave. We speculate that countries with endowment ranges near the world average are more likely to exhibit capital cross flows than those at the extremes.

An eighth result is that *the interests of local and international capital can be synonymous:* That is, local capital may encourage rather than discourage entry of foreign capital in our model. Local capital gains from the higher tariffs generated by the contributions that new foreign capital provides to the procapital party.

Increasing returns to politics and the polarization result suggest that the world can be divided into two groups. Countries with higher capital endowments and capital returns will be blessed with the *Brazilian vitality,* whereas those with lower capital returns will be cursed with the *Indian disease.* Brazilian vitality describes a country with higher than world returns to capital: Capital enters and the returns continue to increase. The domestic capital returns may be high initially because the country has a high capital endowment or because capital is potent politically. The reverse case we characterize as the Indian disease, that is, countries with lower than world returns to capital: Capital exits and the capital returns continue to decrease. The country thus becomes increasingly labor dominant. We have no clue about how such processes end: perhaps with a bang, or a whimper, or both.

Chapter 13 is an application of endogenous policy theory to the behavior of U.S. tariffs over the period 1900–88. We use ideas generated by the Leontief endogenous policy model in Chapters 10 and 11 to select variables that might explain U.S. protection. We find empirical support for the *powerless politician effect,* that is, that trade policies are largely outside the control of the policymakers in a competitive political system. We find that protection can be explained by those exogenous variables that drive the behavior of special interests and general interests who favor and oppose protection. The *special-interest variables are factor endowments and the terms of trade; the general-interest variables are the U.S. unemployment rate and inflation.* We find that approximately two-thirds of the variability in tariffs this century are explained by these endogenous policy considerations.

There is weak empirical support for the *endowment effect* (i.e., that decreases in the ratio of labor to capital decrease protection). As labor has become a less important factor of U.S. production in this century, its political influence has waned and tariff protection has declined. The number of U.S. workers per unit of real capital today is about half what it was at the turn of the century. Following the Leontief model, the prolabor party is also suffering at the polls: Democratic presidential candidates have lost five out of the past six elections (although this correlation between the demise of the Democrats and U.S. factor endowments is probably coincidental). This follows the notion of increasing dominance by the abundant factor and increasing demise of the scarce factor.

We speculate that the public furor over protectionism in the 1970s may be an example of the *magnification paradox:* An increased magnification effect of product prices on factor prices causes both protectionist and proexport forces to devote more economic resources to politics, but to come away with a lower equilibrium level of both policies. Thus, the political noise level and the protection level can move in opposite directions. Magnification increases occur when the factor intensities of production in exportables and importables become more similar. This point is speculative, since we now have only anecdotal evidence that factor intensities have become more similar during the past forty years.

Fourth, we verify the *compensation effect.* When a special-interest group's return from economic activity declines because of any adverse shock, the group compensates by investing more resources in lobbying and politics. Its political party responds with an increase in the policy variable that benefits it. For example, increases in the unemployment rate in the past two decades have led protectionists to demand greater protection, and the U.S. political system has responded. Another example is the decline in the U.S. terms of manufacturing trade in the last decade. Advances by the Japanese and other countries in autos, steel, and textiles have reduced the world prices of U.S. importables and thus increased the U.S. terms of trade. Following the compensation principle, U.S. factors of production in importables have increased their lobbying and received more protection, particularly in these senile industries.

Republican administrations generate greater protection; Democratic administrations generate freer trade. Thus, presidential administrations in the United States generate levels of protection that apparently run counter to the desires of their special-interest clienteles. We use the macroeconomic by-product effect and the isoprotection curves to explain the paradox. The *macroeconomic by-product effect* suggests that protection is a by-product of each administration's macro policy. United States presidents do sponsor macroeconomic policies that help their interest group clienteles, and the level of protection that we observe is merely a by-product of macro policy: Republican macro policies increase protectionist pressure, whereas Democratic macro policies increase antiprotectionist pressure. Republican presidents (e.g., Reagan) generate antilabor macroeconomic policies that locate them on high isoprotection curves (high unemployment and low inflation); as a result, there are heavy protectionist pressures on Congress. This pattern has definitely held in the postwar period for Republican presidents Eisenhower and Reagan, with somewhat weaker results for Nixon and Ford. Democratic administrations favor prolabor policies such as low unemployment and high inflation. This has been true for the macroeconomic and trade policies of Democratic presidents Franklin Roosevelt, Kennedy, Johnson, and Carter.

Sixth, we estimate the slope of Magee's *isoprotection curves.* They are drawn in the Phillip's curve diagram and they show combinations of unemployment and inflation that generate equal levels of equilibrium protection. Based on 1900–80 data, we find that a one-percentage-point increase in the U.S. unemployment rate requires a two-percentage-point increase in the U.S. inflation rate to keep the equilibrium level of protection constant. *Stagflation* may not increase protectionism: Increasing unemployment raises the equilibrium level of protection, whereas increasing inflation reduces it; the net effect of stagflation on protection depends on the strengths of these two opposing forces. If the increases in unemployment and inflation move the economy along a given isoprotection curve, stagflation has no effect on the level of protection.

According to our regressions, the three presidential administrations in this century with the largest increases in protection have been those of Harding (with the Fordney–McCumber tariff, the largest increase of the century); Hoover (with Smoot–Hawley); and Reagan's first term. The actual Smoot–Hawley tariff increase was smaller than our endogenous tariff model predicted, meaning that protectionist pressure was high during the Hoover administration and that the tariff passed was less protectionist than it could have been. *Reagan's first term has the third-highest predicted increase in protection in this century* because of (1) an increase in the U.S. terms of trade index from 87 to 100; (2) a rise in the U.S. unemployment rate from 6.4% to 8.5%; and (3) a drop in the U.S. inflation rate for producer prices from 9.7% per annum to 4.2% (all compared to the Carter administration).

When compared with the rest of the century, *the 1970s were a period of low long-run protection*. We speculate that this is true even if the ad valorem equivalent of all nontariff barriers were measured along with tariff rates. The reason is that three out of four factors point to lower protection: the continued decline of labor in the U.S. factor endowment, the low level of the U.S. terms of manufacturing trade, and the high level of U.S. inflation (which mobilized consumers against protection and contributed to the weak dollar). The only protectionist pressure came from the high U.S. unemployment rate.

Increasing Republican presidential electoral success is increasing protectionism in the United States because of Republican policy preferences for high unemployment, low inflation, and a strong dollar. The Republicans have won five out of the past six presidential elections, and this has increased the level of U.S. protection.

Historically, Congress has been more protectionist than the executive branch. In the past two decades, however, *the executive branch has become increasingly protectionist* in its negotiation of voluntary export restraint agreements with the Far East and in its administrative protection (antidumping, etc.). Congress now appears to be battling the White House to regain control of protectionist policy. In addition to the current high demand for protection, Congress may wish to recapture both protectionist and pro-export lobbying resources, which have been concentrated on the White House.

The *predicted level of U.S. protection tripled during 1980–8*, increasing from the actual level of 3.1% in 1980 to a predicted level of 11.5% in 1988. What explains this increase? Roughly 40% of it was due to the decreased price of U.S. imports relative to exports (the rise in the manufacturing terms of trade); 40% was due to decreased inflation; and 20% was due to the lagged effects of the stronger dollar.

The results in Chapters 10–13 were all based on Leontief production. In Chapter 14 we use Cobb–Douglas production functions for the two goods and Cobb–Douglas utility functions for workers and capitalists; we continue, however, with our logit specification for voter behavior. A number of the results in the Leontief model carry over, although several do not.

The first major result in **Chapter 14** is *closed-form solutions* for endogenous tariffs and export subsidies, the amounts of each factor engaged in lobbying, and the equilibrium probabilities of election of the parties. Given these, all of the economic variables are also endogenous: production, consumption, prices, factor incomes, and welfare. In Chapter 10, we obtained explicit solutions for the political variables, but they had other endogenous variables on the right-hand side; here the solutions are written as functions of the exogenous variables only. These exogenous parameters are the country's capital/labor endowment ratio, the factor intensities in production, and the consumption preferences of the populace. Major results in this chapter are explicit proofs of propositions found in previous chapters by simulation.

A second result is that, with Cobb–Douglas production and consumption (and with certain symmetry assumptions about the behavior of voters with respect to resources and policy positions), *domestic politics is independent of world prices*. That is, a change in a country's terms of trade will have important distributional effects on the factor incomes, but it will have no effect on the proportion of either factor devoted to lobbying, no effect on the tariff and export subsidy, and no effect on the probability of election of either party at the polls. This contrasts with the Leontief results. Recall that with Leontief production we found, in Chapter 11, that the fortunes of the lobbies and the parties moved together with regard to exogenous changes in world prices. Let the price of imports decline: Labor is harmed because wages fall. Labor contributes more to the Democrats and gets a higher tariff. The Republicans counter with a lower export subsidy and receive fewer resources from the procapital lobby. The Democrats ultimately get fewer votes and the Republicans get more.

The third result is explicit proof of the *endowment effect*: The equilibrium tariff increases with the square root of the ratio of the country's scarce factor to its abundant factor. Similarly, equilibrium export subsidies decrease with this ratio. This generates the *policy bifurcation effect:* A change in a country's factor endowment ratio always increases one policy and decreases the other. Another implication is that the ratio of the two distortionary policies is independent of a country's factor endowment. In traditional trade theory, factor endowments played a key role in determining the pattern of trade (the Heckscher–Ohlin theorem) but did not influence factor returns (via the Rybczynski theorem and the factor price equalization theorem). With endogenous policy, relative endowments determine not only a country's trade pattern but also its structure of trade protection. An interesting implication of the Cobb–Douglas model is that *the lobbying ratio and the the election probabilities are independent of an economy's factor endowment.* The lobbying ratio is the proportion of each factor that that factor's lobby devotes to politics. The second part of the result is mildly counterintuitive, since it means that pro-capital parties will be no more successful in capital-rich countries than in capital-poor ones. Here the Leontief model was more intuitive, with pro-capital parties doing better in capital-abundant countries.

Fourth, there are *increasing returns to politics.* The factor endowment theory of protection implies that an increase in a country's endowment of a factor increases its average rate of return. Now that we have closed-form solutions to the model, we have explicit proof of the simulation result in earlier chapters that increases in factor endowments increase capital returns. The increasing-returns result causes factor returns to feed on each other so that capital will migrate to countries where it is already abundant, inducing further capital inflows. Ironically, countries with high capital/labor endowment ratios will have high returns to capital, whereas those with low capital/labor endowments will have high wages. With hindsight, the result is not paradoxical: Capital-abundant countries such as the United States provide the greatest protection to capital through both physical and intellectual property rights.

This yields a fifth result, namely, that at intermediate endowment ratios, the political clout of the two factors cancels. That is, *with countervailing power, we get Prisoner's Dilemma outcomes* in which both of the factors have lower returns than under free trade. Such a Prisoner's Dilemma outcome occurs when the opposing groups are evenly balanced in strength. This is most likely in countries with intermediate factor endowment ratios; that is, not in countries with a preponderance of capital power (such as the United States, which is long on both physical and human capital) or labor power (such as India).

The next three results examine the effects of changes in factor intensities and consumer preferences on protection. Result 6 is the *magnification paradox:* Special-interest policies can be decreasing and yet welfare can go either way. In particular, increased magnification (of factor returns with respect to product prices) can lower tariffs but can also lower welfare. The increase in magnification could have been caused by an increase in the similarity of production technologies (e.g., the capital/labor ratios in production for the two goods get closer together). Consider the following hypothetical example of this case: Japan might have a high tariff with a low fraction of lobbying by the scarce factor while the United States might have a low tariff with a high fraction of lobbying by the scarce factor. In our model, such a result could be caused by the Japanese electorate being less responsive to campaign contributions than the U.S. electorate because of the magnification effect. In short, beware of partial equilibrium reasoning. Larger welfare losses can be associated with smaller distortions. This contrasts with the usual case for lowering the level of distortions to increase welfare with exogenous policy.

The previous result dealt with a simultaneous increased sensitivity of both factor prices to product prices; consider now an increase in the responsiveness of only one factor price. Result 7 is the *factor magnification effect: An increase in a factor's price sensitivity hurts the factor's party*. Strengthen the magnification effect by increasing the responsiveness of capital returns to product prices in the economy. As expected, the capital lobby devotes an increasing proportion of its resources to lobbying because of higher expected returns from political price manipulation. We might expect that the Congressional Republicans would adopt a lower export subsidy because of the increased supply of lobbying capital (a lower subsidy is required to get the same amount of capital). We would also expect that the Republicans would have higher electoral success in the new equilibrium both because they could court voters with the more populist stance and would have more campaign funds from the lobby. The paradox is that most of these speculations are wrong: With increased magnification, the Republicans increase their export subsidy and the attendant negative voter distortion effect dominates the lobby expenditures effect so that the Republicans are worse off in the new equilibrium. Our mathematics indicates that the Democratic party lowers its equilibrium tariff so much that the probability of election of the Republicans actually declines.

The next result is a warning about *deceptively intuitive general equilibrium effects*. In deriving these results, we elicit some striking differences between the operation of political "markets" and economic markets. Increases in factor endowment and increases in the sensitivity of factor returns to commodity prices both constitute increases in the demand for protection. However, this increased demand is expressed in a way that raises the cost to the political parties of supplying the protection, so they end up supplying less for given actions of the other players. It is only because this partial equilibrium outcome is reversed by the general equilibrium interactions with the choices of the other players that we obtain the intuitive result that increased demand for protection results in an increased supply. This contrasts with the usual outcome in economic markets where partial equilibrium results are intuitive but general equilibrium effects can lead to counterintuitive results.

Finally, we *generalize* these results. The preceding results are based on voting functions in which the odds of election are unit elastic with respect to lobbying resources and (negative) unit elastic with respect to a party's policy. We find that many of them hold up with more general functional forms, whereas others do not.

In **Chapter 15** we ask the following question: Are there upper limits on the proportion of resources that can be drawn out of economic activity and consumed in lobbying and political activity? One would certainly expect so since there are diminishing returns in production, consumption, and even our voter response function (which has the marginal probability of election decreasing with successive increases in either resources or policies). First, *with risk neutrality by the factors, no more than 50% of an economy will be devoted to lobbying.* Second, with intermediate values of the degree of risk aversion, we find an *economic black hole:* Under certain circumstances, *nearly 100% of the economy can be devoted to lobbying in equilibrium.* Thus, special-interest political activity can consume the entire economy. The irony is that as the black hole is approached, the endogenous level of protection approaches zero. Both the lobbying ratios and the equilibrium policies are also driven by the magnification effect. As the magnification parameter (the elasticity of factor rewards with respect to product prices) increases, the payoff to lobbying increases, and the tariff level required to facilitate a transfer decreases.

Chapter 16 is an empirical test of the endowment theory of tariffs across fifty-eight countries, using tariff and country data from the mid-1970s. First, we find *empirical verification of the factor endowment theory of tariffs,* particularly for the developed countries. That is, tariffs decrease with increases in a country's endowment of both physical and human capital. Second, there is evidence that skilled labor in all countries gains from less protection. This suggests a competence theory of comparative advantage. The less talented factors of production in every country compete with imports while the most talented compete on world markets through exports. Third, an equation for the ratio of imports to GNP allows us to calculate *overprotection:* Deviations from the model suggest rent seeking or other factors. We estimate one equation for the degree of openness of an economy, measured by the ratio of imports to GNP. This equation indicates that there are perennially protected economies such as India, Turkey, and Japan that have excessively low import to GNP ratios. Out of the fifty-eight countries analyzed, our analysis indicates that *Japan is the third most protected country in the world.*

Chapter 17 provides justifications for *senile-industry protection.* Infant-industry protection has always been justified because the expected future benefits exceed the costs. Similar arguments apply to senile-industry protection: Industries get old just like individuals, and civilized societies protect them against market competition via social security and other conventions. Senile-industry protection may have economic benefits in the form of implicit insurance against adverse states of nature in the presence of incomplete markets. While others have developed an insurance theory of protection in some detail (Baldwin, Eaton, et al.), the discussion here is speculative and draws more on biological analogies.

A second result in Chapter 17 is that, while both are important, *economic factors explain more of the variance in tariff rates than do political factors.*

Chapter 18 investigates why we have inefficient tariffs rather than efficient factor subsidies as means of redistributing income. The first result is the *principle of optimal obfuscation.* The trade-off that parties face is that inefficient policies raise less in campaign contributions (because they benefit the lobbies less) but are less detectable by voters. If the party's vote loss from fewer resources is more than offset by the vote gains from greater voter obfuscation, then a protectionist party will choose a tariff over a factor subsidy. At the optimal level of obfuscation, these marginal effects will just balance.

The optimal level of obfuscation yields the *politically efficient policy;* but we know (from Chapter 3) that there is a trade-off between economic and political efficiency. This leads to our *theory of the second worst:* Among the choices available, parties will pick policies that are politically efficient, but these will be bad economic policies.

The *voter information paradox* suggests a final conflict between economic and political efficiency. Voters can become increasingly sophisticated in their opposition to tariffs, but the parties can respond with higher equilibrium levels of more opaque distortions, such as the voluntary export restraint agreements. This explains why protectionist parties in the Western democracies choose tariffs rather than more direct factor subsidies. We speculate that an *increase in voter sophistication can lead to reductions in welfare.* A party can resort to a more indirect policy in response to smarter voters, and these can be welfare inferior because of greater distortions than before.

CHAPTER 2

Endogenous policy theory:
a diagrammatic approach

There are at least three theories for why tariffs exist: policy theories, terms of trade theories, and political theories. In policy theories, tariffs exist to achieve policy goals: for instance, infant industry protection, industry output or employment maintenance, or government revenue. Johnson (1971) showed how to calculate the maximum revenue tariff, and the literature that followed would fit nicely into a Niskanen (1976) bureaucratic model. Policy theories fell out of favor, however, when Bhagwati (1971) and others showed that tariffs are quite inefficient at achieving most policy goals and are usually dominated by other policies (see also Bhagwati 1982). In terms of trade theories, tariffs are a tool of international redistribution: They permit a country to increase its welfare at the expense of other countries. The optimum tariff literature uses a terms of trade approach, calculating the tariff rate that would increase a country's terms of trade so as to maximize its welfare. One empirical problem with optimal tariff theory is its implication that small importers would have zero tariffs: This conflicts with our observation of especially high tariffs in many small nations.

The third class of tariff theories looks to domestic political considerations. Until about a decade ago, political explanations of tariffs were black-box theories: International economists, ourselves included, would state that tariff rates are exogenously determined by political processes beyond our understanding. While that statement is probably still true, we know a lot more today. Consider now the domestic political approach taken in this book.

Chapter 2 in Stephen P. Magee, William A. Brock, and Leslie Young, *Black Hole Tariffs and Endogenous Policy Theory*. New York: Cambridge University Press, 1989. Portions adapted from Stephen P. Magee, "Endogenous Tariff Theory: A Survey," in David C. Colander, ed., *Neoclassical Political Economy: The Economics of Rent Seeking and DUP Activities*. New York: Ballinger, 1984, pp. 41–51.

A policy such as a tariff is "endogenous" if it can be explained by rational maximizing behavior. The variables that explain the tariff are those that affect the decisions of the maximizers. *Endogenous lobbying* is the level of lobby contributions that maximizes the benefits of the lobby to the membership (see Krueger 1974). *Endogenous policy* is that level of a policy variable that maximizes the votes to the party sponsoring the policy. [See Brock and Magee (1974, 1975, 1978, 1980) for endogenous tariff theory and Pelzman (1976) on endogenous regulation.]

A *complete endogenous policy model* has both lobbying and policies endogenous, whereas a partial endogenous policy model may have only one of these two elements endogenous. Part I of this book presents a complete endogenous policy model. A *general equilibrium endogenous policy model* has both politics (the parties and the lobbies) and economics (goods markets and factor markets) based on maximization by the actors. Part II presents a general equilibrium endogenous policy model. What differs between Parts I and II is the general equilibrium specification of the economy.

What other similarities and differences exist between Parts I and II? The behavior of voters and the parties is the same in both parts. The electorate demonstrates self-interested behavior in that each individual is a rationally ignorant Downesian voter: Individuals are underinformed on the issues because each individual plays a trivial role in the electoral outcome. The political parties are also the same in both parts: A protectionist party sponsors a tariff and a proexport party sponsors an export subsidy. Throughout, there is a protectionist lobby that contributes funds to the protectionist party in exchange for a tariff. We explain in Chapters 3 and 4 why these contributions are given only to the protectionist party.

Although we use the term "tariff" throughout, the analysis would apply, with minor modification, to all forms of protection and hopefully to any government policy influenced by special interests. We assume that there is a proexport lobby that opposes the tariff and contributes funds to a proexport party that sponsors an export subsidy. The lobbies contribute to maximize the factor incomes of their membership; the parties set their policies to maximize their votes (i.e., their probabilities of election).

In Part I, we assume a partial equilibrium economic model with specific factors in which the protectionist lobby is composed of import-competing firms while the proexport lobby is composed of export firms. Because the economic side of the model is partial equilibrium, there is no limit to the number of industries and lobbies that can be considered. There is also theoretical emphasis on the Olson (1965) question of the determinants of the successful lobby. For this reason, the material in Part I can be viewed as a theory of *endogenous tariff structure:* that is, why protection for shoes, textiles, and steel might be high relative to other industries.

In Part II, we assume a long-run neoclassical (Heckscher–Ohlin–Samuelson) model in which an economy's scarce factor (e.g., labor) organizes the protectionist lobby while the economy's abundant factor (e.g., capital) organizes the proexport lobby. Following the Stolper–Samuelson (1941) theorem, the labor lobby gains from the protectionist party's tariff while the capital lobby gains from the proexport party's export subsidy. This model we call the *2 × 2 × 2 × 2 general equilibrium endogenous policy model* because it has two goods, two factors, two lobbies, and two political parties, and all actors act in their self-interest. Because the model describes both the economics and the politics of an entire country, *Part II provides a theory of endogenous national tariff levels:* that is, why the average level of protection in New Zealand is higher than in the United States. We provide both theory and empirical evidence on this question. The model can also be used to describe the movements in a country's tariff level through time. We report empirical work on this question for the U.S. tariff over the period 1900–88.

This chapter deals first with the literature on endogenous policy, then provides a diagrammatic analysis of endogenous policy theory. Finally, it examines contrasting approaches to endogenous tariff theory. An Appendix, with additional diagrams, appears toward the back of the book.

2.1   The literature

This section lists a sample of the vast literature on *endogenous policy theory.* (A literature review appears in each chapter.) Our own work on the subject is contained in Brock and Magee (1974, 1975, 1977, 1978, 1980, 1984), Magee (1980, 1982, 1984), Magee and Brock (1976, 1983), Magee and Young (1983, 1987), and Young and Magee (1982, 1984, 1986). Important empirical work on the question was also developed by Baldwin (1976a–c, 1978, 1982a,b, 1983, 1984a–c, 1985a,b, 1986a–c). Pioneering work on endogenous policy theory is provided by Lindbeck (1975a,b, 1976, 1977, 1983, 1985a,b, 1986a,b, 1987, 1988a,b). Other contributors to endogenous tariffs include Anderson (1980), Caves (1976), Hillman (1977b, 1982, 1988a–c), Lavergne (1983), Mayer (1984a), Pincus (1975), and Tharakan (1980).

The work in this book is based on the *probabilistic voting model* developed by Brock and Magee (1974, 1975, 1978, 1980). Other contributors to this literature are Coughlin (1982, 1983) and Peltzman (1976). We all build on the pioneering work by Downs (1957) on the *rationally ignorant voter.* On this question, see also Gant and Sigelman (1985), Kinder and Kiewiet (1981), MacKuen (1984), and Rose-Ackerman (1980).

The *probabilistic voting model* provides a major theoretical alternative to the traditional *spatial model,* which includes the median voter model as a subset. On the theory of spatial voting see Haefele (1971), Hinich, Ledyard, and Ordeshook (1972, 1973), Hinich and Ordeshook (1970), and Riker and Ordeshook (1973). On the *median voter model* see Bowen (1943), Downs (1957, pp. 114–25), Hotelling (1929), Inman (1978), Romer (1975), and Romer and Rosenthal (1979).

Endogenous policy theory is based on the *public choice theory* of Buchanan and Tullock (1962, 1968), Coase (1960), Hayek (1979), Tiebout (1956), and the general work of Riker and Ordeshook. Other references include Axelrod (1981), Brennan and Buchanan (1984), Johansen (1960), Moulin (1983), Mueller (1979), Ordeshook and Shepsle (1982), Plott and Levine (1978), and Sugden (1981). For related work on the theory of *public goods* see Berglas (1976), Cheung (1973), Demsetz (1970), Hamilton (1956), Hardin (1975), Oakland (1974), and Samuelson (1955). Empirical work by public choice theorists can be broken into two groups: On one side there is the microeconomic public choice work of Stigler, Peltzman, Crain, Tollison, and Wagner, which might be labeled the Chicago school; on the other side is the macroeconomic public choice analysis of Frey (1984a), Kramer (1971), MacRae (1977), and Nordhaus (1975).

On the *theory of regulation* see Cornell, Noll, and Weingast (1976), Peltzman (1976), and Stigler (1971, 1972, 1974). Alternative approaches to *special-interest modeling of policy* include Jackson (1974), Mueller (1979, chap. 6), Musgrave and Musgrave (1984), and Niskanen (1976). For a historical application of the special-interest approach to the income tax, the military–industrial complex, and the tariff see Baack and Ray (1985a,b). For generally negative results of the interest group approach applied to the administration of grants see Chubb (1984).

Serious students of endogenous policy theory should read the background works on *political institutions* by Barry (1978), Brennan and Buchanan (1985), Breton (1974), Brittan (1975), Friedman (1962), Haefele (1971), Leibenstein (1976), Lindbeck (1985a, 1987), Nordinger (1981), North (1981), Nozick (1974), Polanyi (1944), Rawls (1971), and Sen (1973, 1985). See also Brunner (1979), Goodwin (1972), Lake (1976), and Schotter (1981). For a review of the political economy and constitutional economics of rent seeking and protection see Schuknecht (1987). On the political economy of the Leviathan see Findlay and Wilson (1984). On the *theory of justice* see Frohlich and Oppenheimer (1984), Posner (1977, 1983), and Rawls (1971).

On *law and economics* see Becker (1968), Becker and Landes (1974), Becker and Stigler (1974), Coase (1960), Gould (1973), Posner (1977, 1983), Stigler (1970b), Tullock (1971b). See also Ackerman (1975), Cooter (1982), De Alessi (1980), Dewees (1983), Ehrlich (1975), Hirshleifer (1980), Landes and Posner (1975), Manne (1975), and Polinsky (1980,

1983). On the *theory of the commons* see G. Hardin (1975), R. Hardin (1971), Wallace (1983), and Wijkman (1982).

Domestic studies of political economy, redistributive activity, and rent-seeking include Borooah and van der Ploeg (1983), Inman (1978, 1981, 1982, 1985), Kau and Rubin (1982), McCormick and Tollison (1981), McKenzie (1979), Rose-Ackerman (1982), Staniland (1985), Tullock (1967a), von der Schulenberg, Graff, and Skogh (1986), and Wade (1983). For a history of the term *political economy* see Arndt (1984). He notes that contemporary political economy contains two different strands: the neo-Marxist group and the Chicago public choice school. The Stigler-type public choice theory and the present work make nearly a full circle in arriving at economic black holes and other redistributive perversities similar to the doomsday prescriptions of Marx. For an analysis of the *Marxist school* of political economy see Bowles and Edwards (1985), Foley (1975, 1978), Mandel (1978), Sherman (1979a,b, 1981), and Weisskopf (1979).

On *political efficiency* see Barro (1973), Haveman (1976), Inman (1981), Rose-Ackerman (1980), and Wildavsky (1966). For economic models of *power* see Bartlett (1978), Lindblom (1977), Rothbard (1977), and Wilson (1985). For a formal treatment of power with public goods and taxes see Aumann and Kurz (1977a,b) and Aumann, Kurz, and Neyman (1980). On the *theory of taxation* see Courant et al. (1979) and Inman (1982).

On the *theory of lobbying* see Brock and Magee (1975, 1977, 1978, 1980), Magee and Brock (1976), Moe (1980, 1981), and Olson (1965), among others. On the theory of *rent seeking* see Buchanan, Tollison, and Tullock (1980), Krueger (1974), and the survey by Tollison (1982). For a related theory of DUP activity see Bhagwati (1980, 1982a). The supply of funds to candidates comes largely from lobby contributions.

See Thurow (1980, 1985) and Thurow and Tyson (1987) for negative *welfare consequences* of redistributive activity. How candidates raise funds and use them to influence voters is described in the political science literature on *campaign contributions.* On this subject see the the review by Adamany (1977), the extensive writings of Alexander (1971, 1976), and Aranson and Hinich (1979).

A number of articles give good *historical perspectives* on the relationship among special interests, growth, and protection. In particular, see Kindleberger (1951, 1975), Kurth (1979), and Rostow (1960, 1962, 1971, 1975, 1978, 1980, 1982).

Good surveys of *international political economy* include Frey (1984a, 1984b), Kurth (1979), and Staniland (1985). On the same subject see Andrain (1980), Baldwin (1984c), Keohane (1984), Sandler (1981), and Wallerstein (1984). For works on *international relations* see Connolly (1970). Rosecrance (1981) reviews theories of international relations which stress the importance of noneconomic variables. For example, Gilpin (1975) emphasizes the importance of military and political power. On the economics of international organizations see Fratianni and Pattison (1982).

The issue of *political business cycles* is discussed in Bloom and Price (1975), Fair (1978), MacRae (1977), and Tufte (1976). For the application of control theory to macroeconomic policy see Chow (1976).

For *income distribution* generally see Bronfenbrenner (1971) and the compendium of papers in David and Smeeding (1985). For the theory of *income redistribution* see Ferejohn (1983), Gardner (1981), Hochman and Rodgers (1969), Inman (1985), Knetsch and Borcherding (1979), Peltzman (1980), Sen (1973), Thurow (1980, 1985), Tullock (1967a, 1971a,b, 1983, 1986), and Varian (1975). A related international version of redistributive activity is *imperialism:* see Cohen (1973).

Endogenous tariff theory is built on the *theory of tariffs*. For some classics see Bhagwati (1969), Corden (1966, 1971, 1974, 1975), and Johnson (1971). Alternative theoretical approaches to tariffs are provided in de Melo and Dervis (1977), Lage's (1970) linear programming approach, and Staelin's (1976) noncompetitive economy model. For empirical work see Marvel and Ray (1985, 1987), Ray (1981a,b, 1987), and Ray and Marvel (1984). For the *insurance theory of protection* see Cassing and Hillman (1981), Cassing, Hillman, and Long (1986), Corden (1974), Deardorff (1986), Eaton and Grossman (1985), Hillman (1977b, 1982, 1988a–c), and Young and Anderson (1980, 1982).

This book is not about *international theories of tariffs* and tariff negotiations: see Ahmad (1978), Brown and Whalley (1980), Cline (1982), Cline et al. (1978b), Deardorff and Stern (1979, 1981), Diebold and Stalson (1982), Fisher and Wilson (1987), Grossman and Richardson (1985), Hudec (1980), Mayer (1981), Otani (1980), and Wolff (1982). Young (1985) generalizes the *optimum tariff argument,* which we do not consider in this book.

Important work is underway on trade policy in the *new international economics framework* by Krugman (1986) and the role of policy in *computable general equilibrium models* by Whalley (1985) and others. On trade policy in the conventional international economic framework see Balassa (1967), Jungenfelt and Hague (1985), and Krueger (1978). For *customs union theory* see Balassa (1974), Collier (1979), Kemp and Wan (1976), Kreinin (1981), and Miller and Spencer (1977). On the subject of *international trade wars* see Conybeare (1984a). For studies of *trade negotiations* and proposals for specific multilateral trade policies see Bergsten and Cline (1982). For the structural effects of taxes and other distortions in factor markets see Magee (1976).

For the use of the *financial market approach* to asset valuation in the politi-

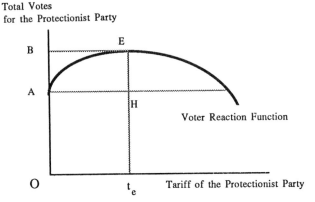

Figure 2.1. The endogenous tariff t_e maximizes the votes for the protectionist party.

cal process see Roberts (1985), who shows that politicians generate non-diversifiable risk. Magee and Brock (1986) apply the redistributive ideas in the present work to the issue of the *third world debt*.

2.2   A diagrammatic approach to endogenous policy theory

We have redistributive policies such as protection because predatory parties and lobbies gain at the expense of uninformed and unorganized prey. The gain to the protectionist party from a tariff is shown in Figure 2.1. With a zero tariff (free trade), the protectionist party would obtain OA votes. If the party acted in its own interest, however, it would set the endogenous tariff t_e, which would maximize its votes at OB and increase its votes by AB. In this framework, parties act like any other special-interest group.

To facilitate the discussion, let the protectionist party be the Democrats and the proexport party be the Republicans. Anything that causes the equilibrium point E to move to the right or left increases or decreases the endogenous tariff sponsored by the Democrats. Likewise, anything causing E to rise or fall helps or hurts the Democrats.

What happens when world prices change? (See Figure 11.2 for the effect of a decrease in import prices.) By the compensation effect, E shifts southeast so that the endogenous tariff rises to offset some of the pain imposed on members of the protectionist lobby by lowered import prices. Unfortunately for the Democrats, the number of votes for the protectionist party declines.

How did we obtain Figure 2.1? It is derived from optimal lobby and party behavior. We describe diagrammatically first the behavior of the protectionist lobby and then that of the protectionist party. We hold constant the behavior of the proexport lobby and the proexport political party (their behavior is to be modeled similarly, although not formally discussed). The diagrams in this chapter apply to all parts of the book.

The endogenous lobby contribution by the protectionist lobby to the protectionist party is described in Figure 2.2. The horizontal axis measures the dollar value of protectionist lobby contributions, and the vertical axis measures the benefits and costs of lobbying; both are in dollars. We ignore lobby organization costs, so that the total cost of a lobby's activities is equal to the campaign contributions it gives to the protectionist party: that is, the 45° line OC. The total cost line OC is independent of the tariff rate and has a slope of 1, indicating that every dollar collected from lobby members is contributed directly to the protectionist party. With lobby organizational costs, OC would be steeper than 45°.

The total benefits of the lobby's contributing to the protectionist party are shown by line OB. There is a different curve OB associated with each tariff rate. We assume that the higher the tariff supported by the protectionist party, the higher the benefit curve and the higher the value of OL_e. If the protectionist party increased the tariff rate that it supported, the OB curve would shift up. Even though the tariff set by the protectionist party is fixed for all points along the curve, the benefit curve OB is positively sloped because the lobby contributions increase the expected number of votes for the protectionist party.

At the endogenous lobbying equilibrium L_e, the vertical distance EF between the benefit curve and the cost curve is at a maximum. L_e is "endogenous" because it is the rational choice of the lobby. All other values of L are not an equilibrium and not endogenous because they do no reflect the best strategy for the lobby. The slope of the OB curve at the equilibrium point E is 1, indicating that an additional dollar contributed to the protectionist party generates a dollar worth of additional income (benefits) to the lobby. Figure 2.3 shows the marginal benefit and cost curves associated with the total benefit and cost curves in Figure 2.1. These marginal curves are the numerical values of the slopes of the total curves in Figure 2.2. At all points in the region between O and L_e in Figure 2.2, the lobby is undercontributing to the protectionist party since the marginal benefits exceed the marginal costs. The net benefit to the lobby members from engaging in political activity equals EF in Figure 2.2, which equals the shaded area between the marginal curves in Figure 2.3.

Tullock (1967a) speculated that the entire amount of producers' surplus created by a tariff might be wasted in rent seeking. In Figure 2.2 we can see

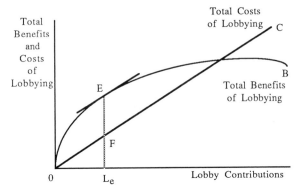

Figure 2.2. Total benefits and costs to the protectionists of lobbying generate the demand and cost curves.

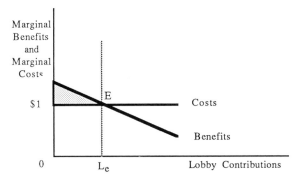

Figure 2.3. The marginal benefits and costs of lobbying.

that only FL_e is spent on rent seeking out of EL_e in total producers' surplus created by the tariff. Thus, the equilibrium proportion of total producers' surplus devoted to rent seeking is FL_e/EL_e.

Consider now the behavior of the protectionist party in Figures 2.4 and 2.5. We know that the higher the tariff it supports, the greater the level of contributions from the lobby. The greater the contributions, the greater its level of political advertising and the greater the number of votes. The votes gained from the campaign contributions funded by the lobby are shown in Figure 2.4 by curve OG, the vote gain from the tariff, which we call the "contribution effect." However, there is a trade-off: The higher the policy, the greater the voter opposition because of obvious redistribution, distorted product prices, and greater inefficiency. The votes lost from the voter dis-

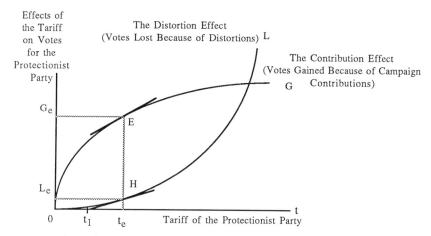

Figure 2.4. The contribution gains and distortion losses for the protectionist party.

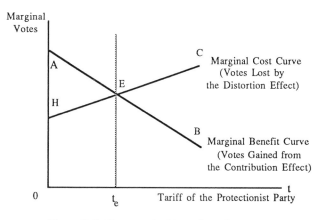

Figure 2.5. The marginal benefit and cost curves to the protectionist party generate the endogenous tariff.

affection from the distortions of the tariff are shown by the curve *OL:* This cost we call the "distortion effect" of the party's tariff. The contribution and the distortion effects are discussed at greater length in section 3.9.

The rational party will set the tariff to maximize the votes it can obtain from the policy. At t_e in Figure 2.4, the vote gain is *EH,* which, by construction, equals *EF* in Figure 2.1 and area *AEH* in Figure 2.5.

The equilibrium value of the endogenous tariff rate set by the protectionist party will be t_e because this maximizes the votes gained by the party. Figure

Table 2.1. *Contrasting approaches in early papers on endogenous tariff theory*

Paper	Modeling approach[a]	Equil.	Lobbying behavior	Party behavior	Voter behavior
Brock & Magee (1975, 1978, 1980)	$[0 \times 0 \times 2 \times 2]$	P	Endog.	Endog.	Prob.
Findlay & Wellisz (1982)	$[2 \times 3 \times 2 \times 0]$	G	Endog.	Exog.	Exog.
Feenstra & Bhagwati (1982)	$[2 \times 2 \times 1 \times 1]$	G	Endog.	Exog.	Exog.
Magee & Brock (1983)	$[2 \times 2 \times 2 \times 2]$	G	Endog.	Endog.	Prob.
Young & Magee (1982, 1984, 1986)	$[2 \times 2 \times 2 \times 2]$	G	Endog.	Endog.	Prob.
Mayer (1984a)	$[2 \times 2 \times 0 \times 2]$ & $[2 \times n \times 0 \times 2]$	G	Exog.	Exog.	Endog.

[a][Goods, factors, lobbies, parties].
Abbreviations: P, partial; G, general; Endog., endogenous; Exog., exogenous; Prob., probabilistic.

2.5 shows the marginal vote curves associated with the total vote curves. B and C are the marginal benefit and cost curves, respectively. Consider a tariff in the region of t_1. It is is not endogenous because it does not maximize the protectionist party's votes. Consider a move from $t = 5\%$ to $t_1 = 6\%$; let the additional votes obtained from the additional protectionist lobby funds equal 100,000 while the votes lost by disaffected voters equal 70,000. These are the two numbers that we would read on the vertical axis off the B and C curves in Figure 2.5. At the endogenous tariff equilibrium, the benefit to the protectionist party of raising the tariff just balances the additional vote benefits against the additional vote costs.

2.3   Contrasting approaches to endogenous tariff theory

Table 2.1 provides a brief history of recent endogenous tariff theory. Consider first some predecessors of the theory. Kindleberger (1951) had an early paper on interest groups and international trade theory. Tullock (1967b) suggested that the economic resources used to obtain the rents from tariffs and monopolies would cause their welfare effects to exceed the traditional deadweight measure. Krueger (1974) coined the term "rent seeking," which is defined as the use of economic resources to obtain politically created rents. Her contribution to endogenous tariff theory was indirect since rent-seeking resources were devoted to obtaining import licenses under an exogenously determined quota in a two-good, one-factor general equilibrium model. The term "rent" is used because the policy generating it is assumed to be fixed. Brock and Magee (1975, 1978, 1980) made both tariffs and lobbying endogenous with two lobbies and two political parties. In our game-theoretic setup, the pro- and antitariff lobbies each channeled resources to the political parties to maximize the incomes of their clienteles, and the two political parties each chose positions on the tariff to maximize their probabilities of election. We employed a partial equilibrium framework.

Findlay and Wellisz (1982) were the first to attempt a Brock and Magee-type apparatus to explain tariffs endogenously in general equilibrium. They had two fixed factors of production, one of which wanted a tariff and the other of which wanted free trade. Each employed labor optimally to lobby for their preferred policy. This paper was important but rudimentary because neither parties nor voters were introduced.

Magee and Brock (1983) followed with an analysis having two political parties explicitly maximizing their probabilities of election with one sponsoring a tariff and the other an export subsidy (i.e., a negative tariff). We also had voters who picked parties probabilistically. Our two-good, two-factor, two-lobby, two-party apparatus with all actors maximizing has been labeled the $2 \times 2 \times 2 \times 2$ model. Ronald Findlay has described our model in more colorful language, calling it the "2×4 model" because of its stark emphasis on self-interest. Feenstra and Bhagwati (1982) followed with a very different approach. They had a labor lobby pursuing a tariff, but being opposed by a beneficent government. The government would use the tariff revenue generated to reduce the demands of the tariff lobby via a subsidy and obtain an endogenous "efficient" tariff.

Because of the generality of the functional forms, both Findlay and Wellisz and Magee and Brock were able to do little more than set up the first-order conditions and provide some interesting speculations on potential applications and questions that the framework could address. Young and Magee (1982) followed with specific functional forms: Leontief production for both goods and a logit probability of election function describing voter behavior. This allowed explicit solutions for the levels of lobbying, the equilibrium policies by both parties, and even the equilibrium probabilities of electoral success by the two parties. While we obtained explicit numerical solutions for these variables, the equations were nonlinear and sufficiently complex that explicit comparative statics were not attempted. Young and Magee (1986) followed with a paper using the same logit function for voters but Cobb–Douglas functions for both production and consumption. Young devised an ingenious solution for the equilibrium levels of lobbying, the policies, and the probabilities of election of both parties, which permitted explicit comparative statics.

In Brock, Magee, and Young's work, voters were assumed to be rationally ignorant and manipulable via campaign contributions funded by special-interest lobbies. A totally different approach has been advanced by Mayer (1984a). Mayer assumes that voters are fully informed. He departs from the special-interest framework of this book in that he has no lobbies and no political parties. He follows the median voter literature and assumes that both parties will choose the tariff that is preferred by the median voter. He breaks new ground in endogenous tariff theory by showing that tariffs depend on the distribution of factor ownership among the electorate. If the median voter has a greater endowment of labor per unit of capital than the economy as a whole, then the political equilibrium will display positive tariffs if the economy imports labor-intensive goods. Second, Mayer introduces a Jones fixed-factor model in which he explains how industries with little numerical support in the electorate can receive tariffs because of voting costs. While most of the eligible electorate may lose a small amount because of a tariff, they also may not vote. While his paper cannot address some interesting questions about endogenous lobbying (since it has no lobbies, no special interests, and no parties), it merges trade theory nicely with the median voting literature.

A serious problem with Mayer's approach is that preferences are not single-peaked on redistributive issues, a requirement of the median voter approach. In contrast, we assume here that voters possess imperfect information because they rationally choose to remain uninformed, and that their choice of a party can be described by a probability of election function (e.g., logit) that is driven by campaign contributions and the policies themselves.

While he does not provide a formal model of endogenous tariffs, a provocative paper by Messerlin (1981) explains European (particularly French) tariffs in a bureaucratic context. Since the size and power of a bureau will be positively associated with the economic size of the industry it oversees (à la Niskanen 1976), import-competing bureaus sponsor tariffs whereas export bureaus sponsor export subsidies (negative tariffs). Messerlin argues that (1) if the scope of the protectionist bureau is enlarged, it will become less protectionist; and (2) politicians will be less protectionist than bureaus. This has casual empirical support in the United States where it has traditionally been true that protectionist sentiment wanes as the size of the geographical district expands as we move from the House to the Senate to the presidency. Feenstra and Bhagwati (1982) also describe this case with their assumption that lobbies will pressure the legislative branch of government for a lobbying tariff, whereas general interests will pressure the executive branch for an efficient tariff.

CHAPTER 3

The probabilistic voting model of political efficiency and powerless politicians

In this chapter we develop the following:

3.1. a review of the literature;
3.2. how endogenous policies in political markets are like prices in economic markets;
3.3. how lobbying is endogenous;
3.4. a definition of political efficiency;
3.5. the trade-off between economic and political efficiency;
3.6. endogenous redistribution in an Arrow–Debreu model;
3.7. the probabilistic voting model applied to the United States;
3.8. how competition between the political parties drives them to Stackelberg leadership and this generates non-Pareto policies;
3.9. the powerless politician effect (policies are outside of policymaker control);
3.10. the contribution specialization theorem (the protectionist lobby contributes only to the protectionist party);
3.11. lobby nonparticipation in Hotelling races;
3.12. tariffs and rents in the Corden diagram.

3.1   The literature

Our first papers on endogenous tariff theory were Brock and Magee (1974, 1975, 1978, 1980). This chapter is a revision of Brock and Magee

---

Chapter 3 in Stephen P. Magee, William A. Brock, and Leslie Young, *Black Hole Tariffs and Endogenous Policy Theory*. New York: Cambridge University Press, 1989. Adapted from William A. Brock and Stephen P. Magee, "The Economics of Politics," paper presented at the Workshop on Industrialization Organization, University of Chicago, January 1974.

(1974) and contains the outline and the simple mathematics describing a formal theory of endogenous policy. This work builds on Stigler's (1971) microeconomic views of political economy; the Lindbeck (1975a,b, 1976, 1977, 1985a) macroeconomic school of endogenous policy; the Buchanan and Tullock (1962, 1968) approach to public choice theory; and the Olson (1965) notion of collective action. The basic idea is that political behavior and economic behavior are identical in that both are driven by self-interest. Many limbs have branched from this tree, but two are worth mentioning here: Peltzman's (1976) theory of regulation, which paralleled our own, and Baldwin's (1976a–c, 1983, 1984a, 1985b, 1986c) work on the political economy of U.S. tariffs. These are summarized in more detail in Chapter 6, along with a sample of the following works related to tariff structure: Caves (1976), Helleiner (1977), Marvel and Ray (1985), and Takacs (1981).

Lindbeck (1985a) has organized redistributive policies into four groups:

1. *broad horizontal redistributions,* that is, those among classes (e.g, between labor and capitalists or between debtors and creditors via inflation);
2. *life cycle and insurance-type redistributions,* such as social security;
3. *vertical redistributions* (e.g., from the rich to the poor or vice versa);
4. *fragmented horizontal redistributions,* such as those occurring via lobbying groups for large numbers of minority special-interest groups.

Several authors note that horizontal redistribution, the type considered in this book, is not as likely with direct voter referenda (compared to representative democracy, in which intermediaries determine policies). Lindbeck notes that agricultural protection is an example of the first type of redistribution and is broadly based (farmers in Europe in the past century constituted more than half of the population). He shows that while life cycle and insurance forms of redistribution are the most important in the first six decades or so of this century, fragmented horizontal redistributions of the lobbying type have been more important in recent decades. One reason for this is the increasing socioeconomic diversification of modern industrial societies. He also argues that special interests that benefit from subsidies get the entire marginal benefit while paying only the average tax increase for all groups in society.

We might expect the future demand for protection to increase for the following reasons. Because of the increasingly crowded agendas for subsidy transfers, and growing public deficits (which are inherently a transfer of the wealth of future generations to the present generation), politicians would prefer indirect and less obvious forms of redistribution such as protectionism. Hence, as Lindbeck (1985a) points out, protection provides nonbudget methods of redistribution; this helps explain why tariffs are politically superior to production subsidies and consumption taxes.

Baldwin (1986b) provides a survey of alternative approaches to tariff modeling in his review of trade policies in developed countries. While the special-interest model is in vogue, he also cites Caves's (1976) adding machine model, based on the voting strength of an industry; Cheh's (1974) adjustment assistance model, in which governments minimize short-run adjustment costs; the equity-concern model of Baldwin (1982b), Ball (1967), Constantopolous (1974), and Fieleke (1976), which fosters government concern for low-income workers; Lavergne's (1981) and Ray's (1981a,b) comparative cost model, which shows that tariffs can be explained by simple comparative disadvantage; Helleiner's (1977) international bargaining model, which suggests that developed country protection will be higher on imports from developing countries because the latter have high levels of protection; and Lavergne's (1983) status-quo model, which argues that protection today is correlated with the protection of yesterday. This last has theoretical underpinnings in the conservative social welfare function of Corden (1974, pp. 107–11; 1984b).

For classic international political economy background works see Bowls and Whynes (1981), Frey (1978, 1984a), Hirschman (1945), Katzenstein (1978), Kegley and McGowan (1981), Keohane and Nye (1977), Kindleberger (1951, 1970b), Knorr (1973), Krasner (1978), Lindbeck (1985a), and Walter and Areskoug (1981). For surveys of theories of the domestic theory of taxation and public goods see Atkinson and Stiglitz (1980) and Mueller (1979).

The model used throughout this book is based on probabilistic voting, derived from Brock and Magee (1974), also used by Coughlin (1982, 1983), and Peltzman (1976). For probabilistic models applied more generally to group decision making see Niemi and Weisberg (1972). These models are based on the work of Downs (1957) showing that voters are rationally ignorant. Riker and Ordeshook (1973) extend this work noting that, since voters have little likelihood of influencing the outcome of an election, they will gather insufficient information. That voters are underinformed makes advertising (funded by campaign contributions) valuable.

Sen (1970) and subsequent researchers have found that, even when voters are fully informed, majority rule may not produce a single determinate winning outcome. Alternative approaches are provided by Hinich (1981), who argues that voting is like a campaign contribution, whereas Banzhaf (1965) argues against weighted voting. A survey of various probability models applied to voting is provided by Paldam (1981). Kramer (1966) emphasizes the complexity of voting. Bernholz (1966, 1974, 1977) shows, among other things, that instability in some spatial voting models can be stabilized by the formation of interest groups.

On the issue of efficient versus inefficient political outcomes, see Rose-Ackerman (1980). She discusses the phenomenon of inefficient outcomes produced by myopia (excessive preoccupation with the short run) caused by migration of voters. On the issue of economic versus political competition see Stigler (1972). For an interesting paper on competition and stability in political markets see Crain (1977). While many assumptions are possible about the maximizing behavior by politicians, see Frohlich and Oppenheimer (1974) for one model of leadership.

Glazer, McMillan, and Robbins (1985) point out that, in politics, the all-or-nothing nature of contests emphasizes comparative advantage: Only relative power matters. They note the Darwinian effect that survival of a species depends less on the food supply or on climate than on the quality of the other species sharing the niche. For example, sequoia trees are more resistant to fires than are Douglas firs. Thus, though a fire hurts both types of tree, it hurts sequoias less; thus fires actually promote the spread of sequoias. The political parallel is that restrictions on a campaign contribution reduce a politician's ability to communicate with the public. One might think that such restrictions would hurt incumbents, but this is not so: Restrictions hurt challengers relatively more than they hurt incumbents, thereby working to the benefit of incumbents.

For a formal definition of power using some clever arbitrage arguments see H. P. Young (1978b), who addresses the question of the power of representatives versus senators versus the president. (The vice president is ignored, assuming that he is simply another senator.) How much power is required to get a bill passed? The minimum winning coalition is either a majority of both houses of Congress plus approval by the president, or a two-thirds override by both houses of Congress when the president disapproves. Thus, when the president approves a measure, the minimal winning coalition comprises 218 representatives, 51 senators, and the president. When the president opposes, however, the minimum winning coalition comprises 290 representatives and 67 senators. The president is therefore as powerful as a combination of 72 representatives and 16 senators (the number required to override a veto). Young argues that it should not require more money to obtain the vote of a senator than a representative (since there are 33 senators excluded from the winning coalition who would compete to vote for most proposals at a low price). If representatives and senators are equally powerful, then Young argues that the president's power is 88 times as great as that of an individual representative or senator. The arbitrage argument is that the rational lobby would be indifferent between paying $88 million to the president for a measure versus paying $1 million to each of 88 representatives and senators to vote for the override of a veto. For a formal treatment of power and taxation see Aumann and Kurz (1977a). Gardner (1981) provides an examination of power in a different voting system. The power of various groups within a society need not come only from lobbying and group organization: Politicians can also identify and coalesce unorganized groups into voting coalitions.

Shubik and Van der Heyden (1978) examine the following question: If there is logrolling and vote trading present in a legislature, does this imply that a market price for votes will emerge so that the political process resembles a market economy? They find that this will occur only in the trivial circumstance in which all voters most favor the same project. This is equivalent to assuming that all voters are identical in terms of their preferences. Thus, it appears that vote trading cannot replicate a market outcome on redistributional issues, because voters have conflicting preferences.

Enelow and Hinich (1982a) find that minority interests (and presumably special-interest lobbies) are better served in representative democracies than they would be under referenda (in which policy making is handled directly by voters). A contrasting point is that representative democracies prevent exploitation of minorities and reduce revolutionary activity by frustrated and radical groups.

3.2   Endogenous policies as prices in political markets

There is a connection between economic and political markets, both in their operation and in the analytical tools used to describe them. Consider the following parallels.

First, in both economic and political markets, there is a process for resolving conflicting goals: In economic markets the desired quantities traded by buyers and sellers are equilibrated by the price mechanism; in political markets, the levels of power exercised by conflicting groups are balanced by the policies that are enacted. Policies in political markets are like prices in economic markets: They are equilibrating mechanisms that adjust to balance opposing forces. In Figure 2.5, the endogenous tariff serves to equate the benefits and costs of protection to the protectionist through the medium of votes. The marginal benefit and cost curves are a direct parallel with the demand and supply curves of traditional economic analysis.

Second, a successful conclusion to conflict resolution in each market is described analytically as an "equilibrium." Economic markets reach their equilibrium level whenever prices are such that the quantities offered by suppliers equal that demanded by buyers. Political markets are in equilibrium whenever the policies (tariffs, bureaucratic practices, judicial processes, regulatory laws, etc.) adjust to the point where the political value of additional (marginal) resources deployed by opposing forces is equal. In equilibrium, neither the protectionist nor the antiprotectionist party is willing to devote more effort to the battle.

Third, students of both markets postulate that agents in the markets maximize some objective function. In both cases, the variable maximized is a nonobservable construct: In economics it is welfare, whereas in politics it is power. In the first part of this book, we make the nonobservables more concrete by assuming that lobbies maximize the expected dollar returns on their political investments for their economic interest group. Throughout, we assume that parties maximize their expected votes or their probabilities of election. Lobbies seek wealth for their economic clientele; parties seek electoral success. The probability of electoral success is an ex ante measure of a party's political power.

Fourth, politics and economics interact because politics can redistribute wealth and economic resources can enhance political power (electoral success). Special-interest lobbies and political parties form coalitions to exploit the mutual gains created by this interdependence.

In this chapter, we provide explicit calculations of economic lobbies' investments in and returns from political activity and of the response of parties in creating special-interest legislation. While the theory is general, we apply it to the formation of a country's international economic policy. Assume that the textile lobby requests that Congress raise the tariff on U.S. imports of textiles. In order for the analysis to apply to special-interest policies generally, assume that the optimum tariff is zero for the United States vis-à-vis foreigners. This is the case for either a small country or a large country facing retaliation by foreigners against its exports. The individual member of Congress faces a trade-off between the social cost that the tariff will impose on unorganized voters and the benefits of the campaign contributions that the textile lobby will provide (the latter is an increasing function of the tariff level he or she supports). We assume that each congressperson supports policies that maximize his or her probability of election. After the tariff is passed, the lobby's investment yields redistributive returns to fixed factors in economic markets in the short run, because of the higher price of textiles, and permanent redistributions of income toward the intensive factor in the textile industry in the long run. The appropriateness of the redistributive approach to politics is documented by Hughes (1979) who notes that purely economic analysis is rarely used or seriously sought in congressional decision making.

3.3   Endogenous lobbying

Consider the public-goods aspect of political behavior discussed by Olson (1965), Stigler (1974), and others. In general, a group will underachieve a common goal to the extent that some part of the group "free-rides" on the efforts of the rest of the group. Group effectiveness depends on many factors: size, costs of organization, and so on. However, an important determinant of group power is the mechanism by which the costs are shared by the members of the group. Technical, legal, social, economic, and geographic factors that induce group members to contribute more to the group effort (or that reduce the group's relative costs of policing free riders) give that group an advantage over other groups.

The goal of every group is to obtain legal sanctions, through political investments, that reduce the costs of policing free riders. A priori, the policing costs are lower for highly concentrated groups. In the limit, an industry consisting of a single firm (i.e., a monopolist) would not face the free-rider problem for industry lobbying because it would not have to share the benefits with other firms. When there are large numbers in a group, the problem is more complicated. In the case of lobbies, one way to reduce policing costs is to raise the expected cost to noncontributors by threatening to exclude them from the industry. The degree of exclusivity that a group can exercise is partially explained by all of their past investments in political activities (including the receipt of a legal sanction for enforcing exclusion). However, there are other techniques. The nation-state has partially solved the free-rider problem in taxation through legal compulsion; firms have solved the problem by a long history of practice and common-law development permitting free riders to be fired or discharged from the firm; and labor unions have obtained exclusionary privileges for closed shops. Notice that even the federal government, which produces a number of public goods, does not enjoy completely monopolistic power in collecting taxes, despite the power of the U.S. Bureau of Internal Revenue. The point is that it is not economically feasible to force all members to contribute to group goals. From the group's point of view, the optimal percentage of group participation occurs where the marginal contribution to the group effort just equals the marginal policing cost. For some groups, participation rates are low (American Association of University Professors, National Association of Manufacturers, etc.) while for others it is high (closed-shop unions). Because participation rates decrease with size, we observe disproportionate power by numerically small voter groups (doctors) and underrepresentation of some larger groups (consumers). A formal model of the microeconomics of free riding within the lobby and related problems are handled in subsequent chapters.

Consider the groupings for and against the tariff, a policy (price) that clears the political market between groups for and against higher-priced importable goods. If those favoring higher prices for importables dominate, the tariff will be positive; if those favoring higher prices for exportables are more powerful, the tariff will be negative (there will be a subsidy on exports). What economic forces will join the pro- and antitariff groups? The economic literature on this suggests that the answer depends on the time horizon of the analysis.

In short-run economic models, groupings will occur along industry lines:

Those favoring a tariff would be import-competing firms (both capital and labor) and those opposing tariffs would be exporters, consumers, and firms using imports as inputs. In intermediate-time-horizon models, an early paper by Mayer (1974) showed that both factors in an industry can gain from a tariff in the short run if one factor is perfectly mobile and the other adjusts slowly to price changes. If the discount rate is high enough, if adjustment to a new equilibrium is very slow, or if the factors of production look only at short-run effects, then protariff lobbies will form on an industry basis, ceteris paribus. In long-run models, pro- and antiprotectionist groups will organize along scarce-factor/abundant-factor lines. Stolper and Samuelson (1941) showed that if the Heckscher–Ohlin theorem holds, the country's scarce factor would favor a positive tariff while the abundant factor would favor a negative one. In general, the intensive factor in an industry that is given favorable treatment will benefit relative to the other factor. The analysis in Part I of this book emphasizes short-run, industry-specific protection and lobbying, whereas Part II emphasizes the long run.

3.4   Political efficiency

In a competitive political system, policies proliferate if they increase the probability of election of one of the parties. In a competitive political equilibrium, all of the policies that will enhance each party's electoral chances will be introduced. In an *efficient political system* there is no new policy that will increase the probability of election of one of the parties. By policies, we mean both those that increase general welfare (Pareto policies) and special-interest welfare (redistributive policies). A policy is potentially *Pareto optimal* if the benefits to the gainers exceed the losses to the losers. Since redistributive policies usually hurt large groups more than they help smaller groups, why do they persist? One theory is voter ignorance.

Downs (1957) showed that the rational voter will be imperfectly informed. If voters are imperfectly informed, then they can be swayed by advertising. If political parties that have more resources can advertise and defeat parties with fewer resources, then parties will attempt to raise campaign funds. Political parties sell redistributive policies that transfer wealth from poorly organized groups to well-organized ones in exchange for campaign funds. This redistributive process is self-limiting, the limits being the strength of organized opposition, a general voter awareness of the social costs of policy distortions, and the extent to which the acceptance of campaign contributions from special interests are exploited by political opponents. In the case of redistributive policies, a party purchases a private good (campaign contributions) by selling a negative externality (the distortionary policy). Economists mistakenly argue that competition between the political parties will yield

Pareto optimality. This argument is usually based on a strong but hidden assumption that voters are fully informed. In this book, we find that uninformed voters plus party competition drives parties to Stackelberg leadership (see section 3.8) and non-Pareto redistributive policies because voters are uninformed.

The creation of non-Pareto redistributive policies by democratic political systems follows directly from three propositions:

1. Organizational costs for coalitions for and against special-interest legislation are unequal.
2. It is rational of voters to remain uninformed on public issues, including redistributive questions.
3. Political markets are efficient, with the political benefits of redistributive political activities being competed away by the parties.

If government turnover is a criterion, the developing countries are more politically efficient than the developed countries. For example, Bolivia has had more than 185 governments in the past 185 years. That is a competitive political system. Developed countries have constitutions that limit predatory redistributive activity, thereby reducing political efficiency but promoting economic efficiency. (For a graph that shows high tariff rates in developing countries relative to advanced countries, see Figure 16.1.)

3.5   The trade-off between economic and political efficiency

Ironically, the more efficient the political system, the more likely are economically inefficient redistributive policies. Thus, there is a trade-off between *political efficiency* and *economic efficiency*. Economic agents take all actions that increase their welfare; political parties take all actions that increase their electoral welfare. It is obvious that a movement toward political efficiency involving an increase in redistributional policies usually lowers economic welfare. At the same time, a movement toward economic efficiency that dismantles economically inefficient redistributive policies would lower political efficiency (because their reinstitution would enhance the electoral success of one or more parties).

Consider the behavior of the protectionist party. In the context of the model in this book, economic efficiency is a zero tariff and political efficiency is the endogenous tariff. In Figure 3.1, E denotes economic efficiency and P denotes political efficiency. A small open economy cannot have its GNP exceed the level at point E, which corresponds to that at free trade. Similarly, the votes obtained by the protectionist party cannot exceed those at P, obtainable at the endogenous tariff t_e, shown in Figure 2.1. At any tariff be-

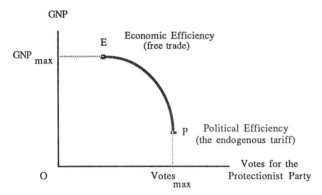

Figure 3.1. The production possibility curve *EP* between economic and political efficiency.

tween zero and the endogenous tariff, the votes obtained by the protectionist party will fall somewhere on the locus *EP*.

EP is the maximum level of GNP that the economy will produce, for any given level of distortions imposed by the protectionist party. In another context, *EP* can be viewed as a production possibilities curve between efficiency and redistribution (equity).

Both economic and political efficiency are impossible: Redistributive political policies prevent the former, and constitutional restrictions on egregious forms of redistribution prevent the latter. Economic efficiency must be defined holding political variables constant, and vice versa. For a discussion of which policy will be chosen see section 18.2.

3.6   Endogenous redistribution in an Arrow–Debreu model

A full political–economic general equilibrium occurs when both the political parties and the economic individuals achieve their objectives, given the behavior of all of the other players. This book shows how the political–economic equilibrium is achieved for a single policy, namely protection. There are obviously more efficient ways of performing the redistribution that is provided by protection. In Chapter 18 we analyze why protection is chosen over other redistributive mechanisms (e.g., production subsidies, factor subsidies). Because political parties generate misinformation, we formulate a theory of optimal obfuscation based on political efficiency.

A formal definition of an Arrow–Debreu political–economic equilibrium with *P* parties and *A* economic individuals is provided in the Appendix. It states that each individual allocates its resources between production and predation so as to maximize its welfare (given the behavior of the political parties). Each political party will set its policies to maximize its welfare (given the behavior of the individuals). The decision variables for the economic individuals are their predatory lobbying expenditures; those for the parties are their policy positions on protection. In a full political–economic equilibrium, no individual or party can improve its position by altering its decision variable.

Consider first the welfare of each of the individuals that contribute to the parties. The goal of each individual is to maximize its welfare. Individual welfare is determined by the tariff, by one's own contribution, and by the contributions of others. The solution for all of the individuals can be written as $C(t)$; that is, the total contributions by all individuals depend on the vector of the tariff levels chosen (by the parties). The logic of the equilibrium is as follows. Individual a forms expectations on the positions of the parties and on the level of contributions by all of the other individuals. It then calculates its best response by maximizing its welfare, using its political contribution. Equilibrium holds when each individual's expectations are realized with respect to all of the variables. There will be different contribution equilibria for different values of the tariff vector t.

We assume that the political parties are Stackelberg leaders (the reason for this will be demonstrated shortly). This means that the parties incorporate the optimal lobbying solution by the individuals into their own calculations of their optimal tariff. Each party forms expectations on tariff stands taken by all of the other parties, calculates the expected contribution equilibrium of the individuals' game, and then selects the tariff that maximizes the party's welfare. Parties are in equilibrium when their expectations are fulfilled. No party has an incentive to deviate from its equilibrium play, provided the others play their equilibrium strategy.

3.7 The probabilistic voting model: application to the United States

Let us simplify the Arrow–Debreu model by considering only two parties and two lobbies. Assume that the bulk of the voters favor free trade but are imperfectly informed, and that each party maximizes its probability of election. The four players are (a) a protectionist lobby, which gains from a tariff; (b) a proexport lobby, which favors a negative tariff (i.e., an export subsidy); (c) proexport party 1; and (d) protectionist party 2. The voters are rationally ignorant Downesians who collect little information and behave in a nonstrategic manner. There is no loss of generality from our numbering of the parties; further, p is the probability of election of protectionist party 2 and

q is the probability of election of proexport party 1. The strategies of the players are for the lobbies to maximize the expected incomes of their membership and for the parties to maximize their probabilities of election. [See equations (3.3)–(3.6) in the Appendix.]

A political equilibrium exists in the redistributive policy model when the optimal choices of each of the four players are consistent with the choices made by the other three. The model is best motivated by applying it to the United States. Baldwin (1986c) has shown that, in recent years, the Democrats in the U.S. Congress are more protectionist than are the Republicans. Therefore, think of party 2 as the more protectionist congressional Democrats and party 1 as the proexport congressional Republicans. Since the Democrats offer a positive tariff, the protectionist lobby will have a higher income under protectionist party 2 than under party 1 ($r^2 > r^1$). We summarize the model by discussing the objective function of the protectionist lobby [equation (3.4)] and the objective function of the protectionist party [equation (3.6)] shown in the Appendix.

The strategy of protectionist lobby 2 is

$$\max_{C^1, C^2} R = (1-p)r^1 + pr^2 - C^1 - C^2 \tag{3.4}$$

The strategy of protectionist party 2 is

$$\max_{t} p = p(\underset{-}{C^1}, \underset{+}{C^2}, \underset{+}{s}, \underset{-}{t}) \tag{3.6}$$

where

R	=	expected total income of the protectionist lobby
p	=	probability of election of the protectionist party
$(1-p)r^1, pr^2$	=	expected income of protectionist lobby when party 1 or 2 is in office
C^1, C^2	=	lobby contributions to party 1 and 2
s	=	export subsidy favored by party 1
t	=	tariff favored by party 2

The strategy of the protectionist lobby in (3.4) is to maximize R, the expected income of lobby members, net of all political costs, by its choice of C^1 and C^2. We ignore the lobby's organizational and policing costs and assume that the only political costs incurred by the lobby are their campaign contributions, $C^1 + C^2$. The income of the lobby members is r^1 if party 1 is elected and r^2 if party 2 is elected. The expected revenue to lobby members equals r^1 and r^2 weighted by the probabilities of election of the two parties: that is, $(1-p)r^1 + pr^2$ (expectational notation has been dropped for simplicity). When we subtract lobby contributions (C^1 and C^2) from this expected revenue, we have the expected income of the lobby membership, taking expected future political events into account. The proexport lobby behaves similarly in its choices of $C^{1\prime}$ and $C^{2\prime}$. Notice the generality of the analysis: The incomes variable R captures both expected economic and political events.

The strategy of the protectionist party is to choose its tariff t so as to maximize its probability of election in (3.6). The strategy of the proexport party is to choose its export subsidy to maximize its probability of election. Since the probabilities of election sum to 1, each party's strategy is equivalent to minimizing the probability of election of the other party. For expositional purposes only, let us assume that maximizing the probability that one's party wins is equivalent to maximizing the party's votes.

The decision to contribute to the political process and the announcement of policy positions are assumed to occur before elections. Thus, the lobbies maximize their expected returns from contributing while the parties maximize their expected probabilities of election. The equilibrium concept here is an ex ante one. It describes actual short-run behavior if political markets clear more frequently than economic ones. This may be realistic given the long lives of many capital projects relative to the shorter terms of most elected officials. Another parallel is that the R shown in equation (3.4) corresponds to the long-run factor incomes of the protectionist lobby, and the probability of election in (3.6) corresponds to the long-run success rates of the protectionist parties. For example, $p = .6$ implies that the protectionist party would be in control 60% of the time.

3.8 Competition between the political parties drives them to Stackelberg leadership and non-Pareto policies

Thus far, the game-theoretic equilibrium concept has not been discussed explicitly. We consider three: Cournot–Nash, Stackelberg leadership by the lobbies, and Stackelberg leadership by the parties [see Intriligator (1971) for an exposition of these concepts].

The Stackelberg concept has one of the players (the "Stackelberg leader") dominating the other (the "Stackelberg follower"). In this equilibrium, the Stackelberg leader improves its welfare while the Stackelberg follower's welfare declines (both compared to their Cournot–Nash welfare level). The Cournot–Nash and the Stackelberg-follower situation both assume that the players take as given the value of the other players' strategic variables. The Stackelberg concept requires that the leader (the more sophisticated player) have superior knowledge compared to the follower. However, this information comes at a cost: The leader must calculate the effect of its actions on the behavior of the follower and then incorporate this reaction of the follower into its own decision-making process. Ignoring information costs, the Stackelberg leader does better in this situation than when playing a Cournot–Nash strategy and not making such calculations.

Rationally ignorant Downsian voters are not sufficient to yield non-Pareto redistributive policies. If the parties behave in either Cournot–Nash or Stackelberg-follower fashion (in the latter case the lobbies would be the Stackelberg leaders), the parties will still enact Pareto policies. When the protectionist party is too lazy or uninformed to calculate how contributions will flow to it from the protectionist lobby, then it takes C^2 as given in (3.6). Thus, when the protectionist party raises the tariff t, it generates only voter hostility (notice the minus sign below the t in the voter's probability of election function p). Thus, the protectionist party leaves t at zero and selects free trade as its vote-maximizing policy. Similar reasoning would apply for the export subsidy chosen by the proexport party. The result: Only naïve Cournot–Nash parties will quote Pareto free-trade policies. The parties reason correctly that any positive redistributive policy will just lose votes, but they are naïve in not calculating that their policy will raise sufficient funds to purchase even more votes with advertising. We shall see shortly that if resources matter sufficiently in getting people elected, then naïve parties that vote for Pareto optimality will have less electoral success and will be replaced by more sophisticated parties employing Stackelberg strategies.

Thus if a protectionist party either adopts a Cournot–Nash strategy or is a Stackelberg follower vis-à-vis its lobby, then it will not deviate from Pareto optimality and set positive special-interest policies. Since this case appears to be irrelevant empirically, consider next the behavior of a political party that adopts the more sophisticated Stackelberg strategy vis-à-vis the lobby that channels funds to it. Let the protectionist party play a Stackelberg leadership game vis-à-vis the protectionist lobby, so that it incorporates the lobby's optimal reaction to its tariff rates into its own tariff decision.

The optimal value of a variable for any player, given the choices by the other players, is called the player's *reaction function*. When the protectionist party acts as a Stackelberg leader, it calculates the reaction function of the lobby with respect to the protectionist party's tariff rate. This reflects the protectionist lobby's contribution level that maximizes the income of lobby members, given the tariff level t and the export subsidy s quoted by the two parties. In the Appendix, equation (3.8) shows how the optimal lobby contributions to the protectionist party change with the party's tariff. When the protectionist party acts as a Stackelberg leader, it uses this information [see equation (3.12)]. We assume at this stage (for reasons to be explained shortly) that all of the protectionist lobby contributions go to the protectionist party, and that all of the proexport lobby's contributions go to the proexport party.

The important result here is that parties get ahead by employing the more sophisticated Stackelberg strategy. Thus, we hypothesize throughout this book that party competition drives parties to employ Stackelberg strategies vis-à-vis their clientele lobbies. More enterprising parties will actually recruit and organize lobby efforts in their behalf, in exchange for redistributive policies. In Chapter 5, we discuss how the redistributive policies themselves are selected, which turns out to be for their political efficiency, not their economic efficiency. One possible implication of this observation is that political régimes in less developed countries may be more politically efficient than those in advanced countries. That is, greater party competition drives lower-income countries toward more redistributive policies. There is a clear trade-off between economic and political efficiency.

The assumption that the parties Stackelberg-lead is a reasonable one from another perspective. In most electoral systems there are few political parties but many special-interest groups. This gives the parties power over the lobbies because there are so few parties; the lobbies must work much harder to get the attention of a party because of their own large numbers. Thus, it is reasonable to assume that the parties get relatively more of the benefits from special-interest activity than the lobbies. The plausibility of the parties acting as Stackelberg leaders is tested indirectly in the next chapter.

The equilibrium concept can be demonstrated by the following tale: The parties will establish their optimal positions on trade policy before the lobbying contributions start to flow. The protectionist lobby can increase its redistributive returns only by helping the protectionist party get elected: that is, by increasing p, the probability of protectionist party electoral success. The redistributive income levels (the r's) are determined after the parties have set their trade policies. The effect of the lobby funds on the Democrats' tariff level itself occurred to the protectionist party leaders in equation (3.6), so it cannot be measured a second time in the protectionist lobby calculations of equation (3.4).

We can visualize our game-theoretic equilibrium structure as a pyramid: There are three tiers in the game. Those on higher tiers are Stackelberg leaders vis-à-vis the actors directly below them; all players on the same tier display Cournot–Nash behavior toward each other; and all players display Cournot–Nash behavior toward players on higher tiers. Thus, the two parties are Stackelberg leaders vis-à-vis their own lobbies and the voters; the two lobbies are Stackelberg leaders vis-à-vis the voters. This structure is shown graphically in the pyramid in Figure 3.2. Stackelberg leadership describes all vertical relationships in the diagram.

There is a gap down the middle of the top two tiers, which Stackelberg leadership does not cross. The protectionist party does not incorporate the reaction function of the proexport lobby in its calculations: only that of voters and its own lobby. There are two justifications for this: One is that the in-

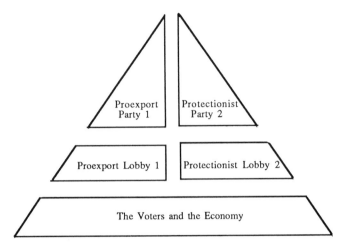

Figure 3.2. The Stackelberg-leadership pyramid of the endogenous policy model.

formational complexities of anticipating the behavior of all other lobbies in a complex democracy would be staggering. A second is that if party 2 were to anticipate the behavior of lobby 1, it would no longer be playing a Cournot–Nash game with party 1 (since lobby 1's decisions are influenced by party 1's choice of policy). In this case, Stackelberg indeterminacy (no equilibrium) would occur.

The three-tier "pyramid" Stackelberg equilibrium is also reasonable based on the number of players in the game: There are fewer players and greater power the higher one is on the pyramid. As an empirical matter, there are usually only two effective political parties, each of which is powerful; there are many lobbies, all of whom have to compete to get the attention of the parties; and there are millions of voters, capitalists and laborers, all of whom have little personal incentive to collect political information and very little political power. Power increases and free riding decreases as one ascends the pyramid. Our Stackelberg-leadership structure assumes this pyramid of power and holds for the entire book.

3.9   The powerless politician effect: endogenous policies are outside of policymaker control

We have determined that, in the long run, rational parties will be driven by electoral competition to act in a sophisticated way toward the lobbies: that is, to act as Stackelberg leaders vis-à-vis the lobbies and the voters. The lobbies will Stackelberg-lead only vis-à-vis the voters, meaning that they will incorporate the voters' reaction function. We discuss next the optimal behavior of the protectionist lobby, and then that of the protectionist party.

A striking implication of the assumption that parties maximize votes is that *they exert no independent influence over policy*. To do so would lower their probability of election. Thus the powerless politician effect: *Endogenous policies are outside of policymaker control*. This contrasts with the views of Nordlinger (1981), for example, who argues that the autonomous state can circumvent societal constraints.

The assertion that politicians are powerless is supported by the observation that barriers to entry by challengers are low. There is a highly elastic supply of politicians at low prices. Such potential entry by challengers in both parties forces incumbents to support policies that maximize their votes. In this sense, politicians are like business managers: Those with more talent replace those with less. Politicians with greater talent can obtain more votes with the same level of economic resources. The notion that politicians are powerful suggests that they are free to pursue strategies that do not maximize votes. This is incorrect. Only an incumbent who is more talented than the best potential entrant can deviate from vote maximization, and then only by the difference between the incumbent's power and that of the best challenger.

How do we measure power?: by a politician's expected performance at the polls relative to the most serious challenger. If an incumbent expects to receive 53% of the vote and the challenger 47%, the incumbent is free to exercise discretionary power only up to losing 3% of the votes. Politicians are powerless if they can command no more votes than their best potential opponent. To survive, they will be powerless to prevent distortionary special-interest policies that hurt the many in exchange for funds from the few.

There are flaws in the view that the power of incumbents makes them oblivious to oblations. Incumbents are the prime targets of the special interests. Consider the optimal contribution level of the protectionist lobby to the protectionist party in equation (3.14), where C^2 represents the contributions by the protectionist lobby to the protectionist party:

$$dR/dC^2 = \underset{+}{dp/dC^2} \underset{+}{(r^2 - r^1)} - 1 = 0 \quad \text{yielding } C^2 > 0 \quad (3.14)$$

[marginal political   [marginal
revenue]   cost]

We will use a discrete example to illustrate the continuous calculus in (3.14). Consider a \$1 million contribution by the protectionist lobby to the House Democrats and assume that the income of the membership of the protectionist lobby would equal $r^2 = \$20$ million under the protectionist House Democrats but would be $r^1 = \$15$ million under the proexport House Republicans. The protectionist lobby should contribute to the Democrats so long as the expected marginal political revenues exceed the expected marginal political costs. Equation (3.14) states that the change in the probability of election caused by the contribution, multiplied by $5 million, must exceed or equal the $1 million cost of the contribution. In this case, the contribution must change the probability of election by at least .2 in order for it to be worthwhile. Thus, if the chances of the Democrats increase by more than 20%, then the protectionist lobby is behaving rationally. The lobby will continue giving until diminishing returns drive the expected marginal political revenue to just equal the marginal cost: that is, the condition in (3.14). The proexport lobby contributes to its party similarly (see the Appendix).

Consider now the protectionist party's vote-maximizing tariff:

$$dp/dC^2(dC^2/dt) \quad + dp/dt \quad = 0 \qquad \text{yielding } t > 0 \qquad (3.16)$$

$$\underset{\substack{+ \\ \text{[positive contribution} \\ \text{effect]}}}{} \quad \underset{\substack{- \\ \text{[negative} \\ \text{distortion} \\ \text{effect]}}}{}$$

The first large term on the left of (3.16) is positive: An increase in the tariff will increase the protectionist contributions, and the increased contributions will help the protectionist party get elected. The second term is negative: Voters oppose distortionary and redistributive policies. The first term we call the positive *contribution effect*; the second is the negative *distortion effect*. If the marginal contribution effect on votes exceeds the marginal distortion effect on votes starting from $t = 0$, then the protectionist party will quote a positive tariff ($t > 0$). Equation (3.16) provides the vote-maximizing tariff for the protectionist party, that is, the equilibrium value of the endogenous policy.

3.10   The contribution specialization theorem: the protectionist lobby contributes only to the protectionist party

An interesting consequence of the endogenous policy model is that contributors in a two-party race should give to only one side. This result we call the *contribution specialization theorem*. The rational lobby should contribute only to the party that offers it the highest return. A contribution to the other party hurts the lobby by reducing the probability of election of its most favored party. This result is generated in the endogenous policy model because the lobbies can affect only electoral outcomes. To illustrate: A protectionist lobby might give $1 million to the House Democrats and increase their electoral chances by .05. If it also gives $1 million to the House Republicans, this might lower the electoral chances of the House Democrats by, say, .05. It is clear that a lobby's contribution to its nonfavored party is self-defeating, since it cancels out the value of its contribution to its favored party. This result exposes a fallacy in the folk wisdom surrounding con-

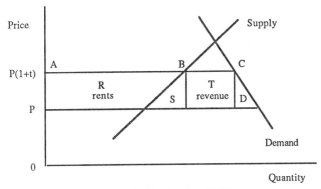

Figure 3.3. Rents in the Corden (1957) diagram.

tributing to both sides. Exceptions to the rule are considered in the next chapter.

3.11 Lobby nonparticipation in Hotelling races

One property of the endogenous policy equilibrium is that there will be no special-interest campaign contributions when the two parties play a median voter (i.e., a Hotelling) strategy and both choose the same level of protection: $t^1 = t^2 = t$. Notice that for equations (3.13) and (3.14) the left-hand sides are both negative, since the first term equals zero because $(r^2 - r^1) = 0$. The logic is as follows: If both parties set a tariff of 20%, the protectionist lobby will contribute to neither party because it gets a 20% tariff no matter who is elected. Rational lobbies will sit out races in which all of the candidates are identical. The Hotelling outcome cannot be an endogenous policy equilibrium.

3.12 Tariffs and rents in the Corden diagram

Figure 3.3 shows the rents for import-competing producers created by a tariff. An ad valorem tariff of t on imports of a good raises the domestic price from $0P$ (the world price) to $0P(1 + t)$. Consumer welfare falls by $(R + S + T + D)$. The tariff transfers the rents R to import-competing protectionists and tariff revenue T to the government. S and D are welfare-loss triangles. This book explains how the protectionist party will set the tariff t and how much the protectionist lobby will pay to obtain the rents R. Chapters 4 and 6 explain how only a fraction of the rents R will be spent in lobbying.

CHAPTER 4

Endogenous lobbying theory and the contribution specialization theorem

There are three motivations driving lobby behavior: policy effects, access effects, and retribution effects. The *policy effect,* discussed in Chapter 3, captures the economic benefit to the lobby of the policy of its favored party. For the protectionist lobby, the policy effect is the value or the tariff received from the protectionist party. The policy effect is the focus of this book; in this chapter only, we consider the two others. The *access effect* is the expected economic value to the lobby of having greater input into party decisions in the future. The *retribution effect* is the expected cost imposed on the lobby by the winning party of lobby contributions to the other party. The chapter is organized as follows:

4.1. the literature;
4.2. three exceptions to the specialization theorem, due to imperfect information, access, and retribution effects;
4.3. three empirical implications:
the largest donors are least likely to give to both sides;
policy contributions will be independent of a party's chances;
polarized candidates will generate more contributions;
4.4. contribution to (at most) $n - 1$ parties, given n parties; and
4.5. mild empirical support for the specialization theorem, based on contribution data for the 1964, 1968, and 1972 U.S. presidential campaigns.

Chapter 4 in Stephen P. Magee, William A. Brock, and Leslie Young, *Black Hole Tariffs and Endogenous Policy Theory.* New York: Cambridge University Press, 1989. Adapted from Stephen P. Magee and William A. Brock, "The Campaign Contribution Specialization Theorem," mimeo, University of Chicago, February 1976.

4.1 The literature

A classic in the modern theory of lobbying is Tullock (1967), who speculated that possibly the entire area of producers' surplus created by a tariff might be wasted by lobby expenditures. Krueger (1974) followed with the first paper that explicitly solved for the optimal level of lobbying expenditures to acquire a fixed sized import quota; she also coined the term "rent seeking." For a survey of rent seeking see Tollison (1982). For a study in which expenditures are made to acquire the revenue generated by a tariff see Bhagwati (1980). Do resources matter in getting parties elected? Do they matter in voting on trade bills? Baldwin (1976a) showed that the probability of a member of Congress voting as a protectionist on the 1973 trade bill was a significant increasing function of the campaign contributions received from trade unions.

H. P. Young (1978b) models how lobbyists should rationally allocate their funds most effectively among voters in a legislature. He notes that Republicans outspent Democrats by a ratio of approximately 2 to 1 in 1952, 1956, and 1968, all years in which they won the White House.

Berg, Eastland, and Jeffe (1981) look at the demographic and social characteristics of large campaign contributors. They examine a sample of 800 large contributors who gave $500 or more to political campaigns (ranging from state legislative races to the presidency) during the period 1968–72. They find that 90% of the large contributors are male; 60% have gross personal incomes in excess of $80,000 per year; 75% are registered Republicans; and 83% consider themselves "moderate." Of the donors who earn $150,000 or more 63% talk to public officials frequently about political matters, giving indirect support to the notion of access effects.

Brown, Hedges, and Powell (1980) investigate contributions to the 1972 presidential race. They show that 27% of campaign contributors have incomes in excess of $100,000 and 76% completed college. Furthermore, their dollar contributions are a small part of their participation in the political process: About half actively work in multiple campaigns (state, congressional, and presidential); one-third have held appointive office; two-thirds have been asked to help with state, local, or national government; and over 95% of them are active voters. In short, campaign contributors are members of the socioeconomic élite. This suggests that an individual's influence in the electoral process may be approximated by his or her net worth. So much for the view of one man, one vote.

Aranson and Hinich (1979) find that federal restrictions on campaign contributions help those with high initial probabilities of election, namely incumbents. Malbin (1979) discusses campaign financing. Gary Jacobson (1978) examines the effects of lobby expenditures on congressional elections.

For a good theoretical treatise on the internal dynamics of lobbies see Moe (1981). On this subject, see the extensive writings of Alexander (1971, 1976) and the review by Adamany (1977). Ferguson (1984) develops an investment theory of political parties. Moe (1980) contrasts the pluralist model of interest groups with that of Olson (1965), whereas Hartle (1983) reflects on the theory of rent seeking. For an early theoretical paper on the economics of campaign finance see Welch (1974). For another theoretical paper on the optimal allocation of campaign contributions over n constituencies during an election see Cook, Kirby, and Mehndiratta (1974). For two recent papers on campaign finance see Conlon (1987) and Sabato (1987).

Gary Jacobson (1978) finds a puzzle in campaign contribution data across congressional elections: when incumbents spend a lot, they do poorly. The explanation is that incumbents spend money only in response to challengers, so the more spent, the more serious the threat. This suggests theoretical modeling in which the incumbent is a Stackelberg leader vis-à-vis his or her opponents, rather than Cournot–Nash specification between parties. For challengers, Jacobson asserts that the amounts of campaign contributions received will be directly proportional to the probability of election. Both of these predictions are at variance with the specifications derived in this chapter, where optimal contributions are related to the marginal probabilities of election. He finds that, in the early 1970s, successful challengers in congressional elections spent about $21,000 more than unsuccessful ones. He also finds that, for both challengers and incumbents, each one-percentage-point increase in the vote won by the challenger's party in the previous election increases contributions in the current period by approximately $1,000.

On the issue of policy distance see Poole (1986), who finds that policy distance is greatest between interest groups, next largest among legislators, and smallest among elected presidents.

Hardin (1979) notes that in the 1970s there were approximately one million environmentalists in the United States, with an average expenditure per environmentalist of only ten dollars. Nevertheless, this $10 million in expenditures, combined with their votes, has an enormous political impact: Upwards of $15 billion is spent every year on pollution abatement.

Several writers show that the campaign financing reform movement of the 1970s, which reduced spending by candidates, inherently favored incumbents. When the government share of GNP is nearly one-third, it is clear that the amounts to be spent on political campaigns should be correspondingly large. In this context, the amount spent on political campaigns is small.

Kau and Rubin (1982, pp. 116–19) found the following results in their examination of contributions to members of the House of Representatives in 1978. Contributions from labor unions were associated with liberal recipients; those from the medical lobby were associated with conservative recipients; and those from business were neutral. Their data revealed the enormous power of the American medical lobby. Contributions to winning candidates by organized groups were (in millions): medical, $6.3; business, $5.4; and labor, $4.8.

Glazer, McMillan, and Robbins (1985) find little evidence for the effect of politics on corporate profits. They speculate that one possible explanation for their results is that in politics an issue is rarely closed: There is continual legislative review, Supreme Court decisions can be appealed, and so on.

4.2   Three exceptions to the specialization theorem: imperfect information, access, and retribution effects

In Chapter 3, we examined policy effects only and discovered the following. Rational parties will act as Stackelberg leaders and set their policies independently of the amounts they actually receive: Their policies will be based on expected optimal contributions, not actual receipts. However, the lobbies may not understand this if information about election probabilities is poor, the positions of the parties are ambiguous, or if the parties cloud the information process in order to solicit funds. How will lobbies contribute in these situations?

Assume that, before the election, proexport party 1 will announce its vote-maximizing export subsidy s while the protectionist party 2 will announce its vote-maximizing tariff rate t. If the lobbies believe that they cannot control the policy levels, the protectionists will contribute only to the protectionist party and the proexport lobby will contribute only to the proexport party, following the specialization theorem.

Assume now that the lobbies believe that they will receive *access* and other nonpolicy benefits from contributing to each party. The analysis here would apply equally to situations in which a lobby is imperfectly informed or irrational. We ignore the joint-product problem of the lobby's simultaneously purchasing both a policy and an access effect and the inconsistency involved in both the lobby and the party attempting to play a Stackelberg-leadership role. We perform the analysis for the protectionist lobby only, although the results apply equally to both lobbies.

Should the protectionist lobby give to the proexport party? If it does so, conflicting effects are generated: There is the positive effect of gaining greater access to the proexport party after the election, but the negative effect of increasing the electoral chances of the antiprotectionist party. If the access effect is larger, the protectionist lobby will contribute to the nonfavored proexport party. Two considerations favor this result. First, this is more likely the smaller the negative policy effect: that is, the lower the protectionist party's tariff and the lower the opposing party's export subsidy. Second, it is also more likely the higher the probability of election of the proexport party (this increases the value of access).

Another consequence of the access effect is that the two parties can choose identical (Hotelling) positions on the issues (i.e., both could be equally protectionist so that $r^1 = r^2$) and yet the lobby might contribute to both parties. We found at the end of Chapter 3 that, with only policy effects present, a lobby will contribute to neither party.

Consider now *retribution:* situations in which parties punish lobbies that contribute to the opposition. Vindictiveness is not uncommon politics: Richard Nixon, Richard J. Daley of Chicago, and Lyndon B. Johnson used retribution schemes that reduced resource flows to existing or potential political opponents. Assume that both parties punish contributors to the other party.

Three results follow from retribution behavior. First, the protectionist lobby may not contribute to its preferred protectionist party 2 if the expected punishment by the proexport party is sufficiently large. Second, the retribution effect diminishes total contributions to the campaign, since it introduces added costs to political participation. Third, retribution behavior is most effective for front-runners because the probability of punishment is greater (by definition, front-runners are the most likely to be elected).

The three effects of contributing can be seen mathematically by examining the first-order condition for the protectionist lobby's contribution to its favored protectionist party 2 (see the Appendix):

$$dR/dC^2 = dp/dC^2 \ (r^2 - r^1) + p(dr^2/dC^2) + (1-p)(dr^1/dC^2) - 1 = 0 \qquad (4.7)$$
$$\underset{[\quad \text{policy effect} \quad]}{\overset{+}{}\overset{+}{} \overset{+}{}} \quad \underset{[\text{access effect}]}{\overset{+}{}} \quad \underset{[\quad \text{retribution effect} \quad]}{\overset{-}{}}$$

Recall the numerical example in Chapter 3: Assume that the -1 in (4.7) represents the $1 million cost of a contribution by the protectionists to the protariff party; that $(r^2 - r^1)$ equals $5 million; and that the contribution increases the probability of election by .2. If the access effects and the retribution effects were zero, the lobby would have been indifferent between making the contribution or not. Assume now that the $1 million contribution increases the expected income of the protectionists by $2 million ($= dr^2/dC^2$) because of the lobby's greater access to the protariff party on all future matters. Assume also that the $1 million contribution lowers the expected future income of the protectionists by $3 million ($= dr^1/dC^2$) because the protariff party 1, if elected, will inflict retribution on them by denying them political privileges and so on – in addition to the harm that the export subsidy inflicts on the protectionists. The decision of whether the protectionist lobby should contribute at all to the protectionist party hinges on the value of the following: $p(\$2 \text{ million}) + (1-p)(-\$3 \text{ million})$. If p, the expectation of electoral success by the protectionist party, exceeds .6, then the positive access effect will outweigh the negative retribution effect and the protectionist lobby will contribute to the protectionist party; if p is less than .6, the protectionist lobby will not contribute.

4.3 Three empirical implications

1. Specialization is more likely for large contributors.
2. Policy contributions are independent of the party's electoral chances while access and retribution contributions are not.
3. Polarized policies generate greater contributions.

The endogenous policy model suggests several results that might appear in the data. First, large contributors are more likely to specialize their contributions on their most favored party. We define a large contributor to be one whose contribution is large enough to change the probability of election. Notice in equation (4.7) that if the lobby is too small to change the probability of election, the policy effect (the first term) will be zero and the protectionist lobby might not even contribute to the favored protectionist party. A medium-sized lobby, by definition, cannot affect the probability of election, so its only rationale to contribute is the access effect. With both policy and access effects present, a priori, a large lobby is more likely to specialize its contributions: A contribution to its nonfavored party has a negative effect on the policy value of its favored party.

Second, how important will the policy effect be compared to the access and the retribution effects? The policy effect predicts that campaign contributions will be independent of the probabilities of election since it is based on the marginal probability of election. Paradoxically, *front-runners will have no edge in obtaining lobby contributions for policy purposes.* The access and retribution effects will be an increasing function of the recipient party's electoral chances.

Third, the more polarized the party positions on policies, the greater will be the contributions by each lobby to its favored party. The farther apart the parties on the issue of protection, the larger will be $(r^2 - r^1)$; hence the greater the amount contributed by the protectionist lobby to the protectionist party. (By the same logic, the proexport lobby will contribute more to the proexport party.) The larger is $(r^2 - r^1)$, the greater the marginal revenue from contributing to one's favored party.

4.4 The specialization theorem with n parties: contribution to n − 1 parties, at most

Consider the standard endogenous policy model in which there are no access or retribution effects (only a party's position on the issues matters in generating income for the lobbies). We illustrate the general case by considering three parties (or equivalently, three candidates). Let t^i be party i's position on the tariff. Should the protectionist lobby give to more than one party? Let party 3 be the most protectionist and party 1 be the most free-trade party. It turns out that the protectionist lobby may contribute to both parties 2 and 3. The reason for giving to party 3 is obvious. The chances of giving to party 2 are greater:

1. the more party 2 takes votes away from (the least favored) party 1 rather than (the most favored) party 3 when it receives funds; and
2. the farther party 2's tariff is from party 1's.

The generalized specialization theorem states that a lobby will contribute to, at most, $n - 1$ parties in an n-party race. Lobbies in France have more tedious calculations to make than their American counterparts.

4.5   An empirical test of the contribution specialization theorem

The data used to test the specialization theorem are taken from the contributions to the parties in the presidential election years 1964, 1968, and 1972. These data were used primarily because of availability: Alexander (1971, 1976) compiled lists of split contributors for each of these races. His data are better for 1972 than for the other two races.

Using presidential election data to test the specialization hypothesis raises some questions. In one sense, it provides a strong test of the theory since it assumes that contributors can reduce the entire vector of a party's positions on the issues (instead of just the tariff) to a single value. On the other hand, Alexander's data for 1964 and 1968 are a problem because contributors may give to both parties in a given year, even though they are specializing their contribution at different points in time. For example, a firm with Defense Department contracts might have given to George Wallace before the 1968 Democratic national convention and to Richard Nixon after the convention. This would appear in the 1964 and 1968 data as a split contribution even though the contributor had actually specialized in the candidate who was most hawkish at the time. The 1972 data are better, showing amounts actually given to Nixon and McGovern.

Consider the evidence on the specialization theorem. We assume a cutoff between split and specialized contributions. We consider a contributor's funds to be specialized (nonsplit) if 92% or more of his (her, its) total contributions go to one candidate. Given this definition, Table 4.1 presents the dollar value of contributions in each category. The split contributions increased from 7% to 14% between 1964 and 1968. One explanation of this increase is the large number of contributors in 1968 who gave to antiwar

Table 4.1. *Contributions to parties (1964 and 1968)[a] and candidates (1972, Nixon and McGovern) in millions of dollars (and percentages)*

Year	Specialized contributors[b]	Split contributors	Total
1964	2.05	0.15	2.20
	(93)	(7)	(100)
1968	10.51	1.69	12.2
	(86)	(14)	(100)
1972			
(PACs)[c]	1.32	.11	1.43
	(92)	(8)	(100)
Individuals[d]	31.78	.26	32.04
	(99)	(1)	(100)

[a]All data, except those for 1972, are for contributions over $10,000 per donor.

[b]Specialized contributors are those who contribute 92% or more of their funds to one candidate; all others are split contributors.

[c]PAC contributions for business, agriculture, health, and labor were reported by Common Cause.

[d]Estimates from the Citizens' Research Foundation Listing of Political Contributors and Lenders of $10,000 or more in 1972.

candidates of both parties before the conventions. The 1972 data are divided into Political Action Committee (PAC) contributions and individual contributions. Of the PAC contributions, 8% were split between Nixon and McGovern, whereas only 1% of the individual contributions were split.

Consider the 1968 data. Is there any evidence that the largest contributors specialized their contributions in a single party, as endogenous policy theory suggests? We examine a sample of contributors who gave more than $10,000. For eight of the nine individuals contributing over $35,000, at least 94% of their money went to a single candidate. The one exception is the antiwar contributor Stewart R. Mott, heir to the GM fortune, who contributed $210,000 to Eugene McCarthy, $100,000 to Nelson Rockefeller, and another $55,000 to antiwar candidates in Congress. We eliminate him from the calculations that follow because he was contributing to different candidates and at different points during the campaign. He was, however, consistently specialized in the most antiwar candidate.

Table 4.2. *Summary of contribution data and test statistics*

Year	N	Contributions ($) standard Mean	Deviation	Test of equivalence of means[a] Statistic[b]	Signif.
1964					
Split $(H < 1)$[c]	27	18,500	9,200	(W) −1.38	(0.08)[d]
Nonsplit $(H = 1)$	103	16,100	9,200		
1968					
Split $(H < 1)$	35	18,700	8,900	(W) 2.75	0.004
Nonsplit $(0.85 < H < 1)$	23	45,266	45,000		
1972					
Individuals					
Split $(H < 0.85)$	11	23,200	28,600	(t) 0.85	0.20
Nonsplit $(H > 0.85)$	111	50,400	104,800	(BF) 2.07	0.02
				(W) 1.32	0.10
PACs					
Split $(H < 1)$	13	9,000	8,700	(t) 0.63	0.30
Nonsplit $(H = 1)$	91	14,500	30,800	(BF) 1.36	0.07
				(W) −1.63	(0.05)[d]

[a] H_0 is the hypothesis that there is no difference in the ranks of the split and the nonsplit contributors.
[b] The test statistics are as follows: t is the student t, BF is the Behrens–Fisher t-statistic (for which the variances of distributions are unknown and unequal), and W is the Wilcoxon rank sums test. A positive Wilcoxon indicates the nonsplit contributors gave more than the split contributors.
[c] H is the Herfindahl index.
[d] For these two cases, the split contributions were significantly greater than the specialized contributions at the significance levels shown.

In Table 4.2 we test whether the means of the specialized contributors are significantly greater than the means of the split contributors. The evidence in Table 4.2 refutes the specialization theorem in 1964 (at the 8% level). However, the specialization theorem is partially confirmed in the 1968 data and in the individual data for 1972, using the Behrens–Fisher and the Wilcoxon tests of differences in means of two distributions. A useful piece of future research would be an empirical test of the specialization theorem using contributions by protectionist and proexport lobbies.

While we do not show such a graph here, the contribution specialization theorem could be illustrated by plotting the total amounts contributed by each donor on the y axis (to both candidates) and the percentage of each donor's total contribution given to his preferred candidate on the x axis. The theorem implies that larger contributors should be more specialized, so the scatter diagram should show a positive correlation between the variables on the axes: The larger the contribution, the larger the percentage given to the preferred candidate.

CHAPTER 5

Endogenous tariff theory

After an examination of the literature (section 5.1), this chapter develops seven results describing the equilibrium positions that two parties will take on the issue of protection before an election:

5.2. the reverse-slope theorem;
5.3. the reverse-shift theorem;
5.4. the policy distance paradox;
5.5. the distortion paradox;
5.6. inconsistent parties and unstable tariff equilibria;
5.7. three generalizations of the reverse-slope theorem; and
5.8. rational policies.

Since all of the actors act in their self-interests, the preelection tariff and the export subsidy are endogenous. We do not explore the extent to which parties adhere to their ex ante positions after an election. In this and all subsequent chapters, we ignore the access and retribution lobbying effects discussed in Chapter 4 and analyze only the basic endogenous policy model described in Chapter 3.

The basic idea is that politicians in democracies are intermediaries between large uninformed groups of voters and small informed groups called lobbies.

Chapter 5 in Stephen P. Magee, William A. Brock, and Leslie Young, *Black Hole Tariffs and Endogenous Policy Theory*. New York: Cambridge University Press, 1989. Adapted from William A. Brock and Stephen P. Magee, "The Economics of Pork-Barrel Politics," Report 7511, Center for Mathematical Studies in Business and Economics, University of Chicago, February 1975; William A. Brock and Stephen P. Magee, "The Economics of Special-Interest Politics: The Case of the Tariff," *American Economic Review* 68 (May 1978), 246–50; William A. Brock and Stephen P. Magee, "Tariff Formation in a Democracy," in John Black and Brian Hindley, eds., *Current Issues in Commercial Policy and Diplomacy*. New York: St. Martin's Press, 1980, pp. 1–9; and William A. Brock and Stephen P. Magee, "Reverse-Sloped Reaction Functions in Constant Sum Noncooperative Games," mimeo, University of Chicago, January 1976.

The information asymmetry grows as societies become more specialized and complex. The political parties, facing increased difficulty in processing information, become more dependent on the lobbies. The parties need more funds for campaigns to inform voters; lobbies are the only easy source of such funds. We can thus expect protection and other special-interest policies to increase over time. This result is consistent with Olson's (1982) economic sclerosis and Lindbeck's (1985a) growth of the public sector thesis.

5.1   The literature

The rationally ignorant probabilistic voter model developed in this book is based on the work of Brock and Magee (1974, 1975, 1978, 1980). See also Coughlin (1982, 1983), Downs (1957), and Peltzman (1976). This chapter is about endogenous policy. An important early contributor to endogenous macroeconomic policy theory is Lindbeck (1975a,b, 1976, 1977, 1983, 1985a,b, 1986a,b, 1987, 1988a,b).

There is anecdotal evidence for the rationally ignorant voter. Tullock (1983) points out that the average U.S. citizen does not even know which party controls Congress. McKenzie (1979) notes that philosophy majors are slightly better than economics majors in assessing the effects of government economic policy. Will two candidates take identical positions empirically? Empirically, they appear to be closest together in fairly open contests (e.g., every eight years with two new presidential candidates). Ingberman (1985) shows that challengers will take more extreme positions the more senior the incumbent.

An alternative is the median voter model used by Mayer (1984a) to describe tariffs. While political scientists speak with less than unanimity, Aranson and Ordeshook (1981, p. 77) argue that "the median voter hypothesis cannot be applied, and indeed makes little sense, in the context of elections entailing redistributive issues" because of the absence of single-peaked preferences. Thus, the Mayer approach has a conceptual flaw.

Magee and Noe (1989) illustrate that, with endogenous voter preferences, voting cycles and Arrow paradoxes will always emerge on redistributive issues. This can be illustrated with the following example. Let there be three individuals voting on the level of protection that each will receive for their products. Assume that each produces only its own product and consumes the other two products. Thus, each individual prefers high protection for its own good and low protection on the other two goods. Let A represent protection for voter A; B represent protection for voter B; and C represent protection for voter C.

Consider simple majority voting by these three voters on which of them will be granted protection. Each will always prefer protection for itself over protection for the other two. Whether an unambiguous noncyclical outcome emerges depends on the second and third preferences of each voter. Magee and Noe (1989) illlustrate that rational second and third choices by the voters will always prevent a noncyclical win by anyone. This generates cyclical voter preferences on protection of the following sort:

Voter A	Voter B	Voter C
A	B	C
B	C	A
C	A	B

Notice that two out of three voters prefer more protection for A than for B, and two prefer more for B than for C. Thus, transitivity would dictate that A receive more protection than either B or C. However, the preferences violate transitivity because any vote comparing A and C will result in two votes for C receiving more protection than A. Thus, the outcome is politically indeterminant and depends on the arbitrary order in which votes are taken.

The basic idea illustrated by Magee and Noe (1989) is that, on matters of redistribution, self-interested individuals will care little about their second and third choices and will alter those choices to block someone else from winning. If anyone unambiguously wins, the other two lose. Thus, second and third choices will be altered to guarantee the cyclical outcome, as in the case illustrated above.

Condorcet (1785) offered the following simple solution to a voting cycle with many voters in which A defeats B, B defeats C, and C defeats A. H. P. Young (1977a) illustrates Condorcet's solution as follows: If A defeats B by a votes, B defeats C by b votes, and C defeats A by c votes, where $a > b > c$, then break the cycle by eliminating the weakest link (C), thereby declaring A the winner. This technique will work on some issues but, because it assumes preferences are exogenous, it cannot solve the redistributive voting problem. In a sense, the campaign contribution approach in this book resolves the problem of voting cycles because it reveals the relative strength of the players' preferences: Players in lobbies have stronger preferences than those not in a lobby, and preference strength is revealed by amounts contributed.

Brennan and Buchanan (1984) make the point that neither contributors nor voters get to vote on the policies they want. Rather, they contribute to or vote for intermediaries (politicians), each of whom has a small role in delivering the desired policy. There is an obvious logic to this – the intermediaries will gather more information than do the voters, and hence provide a partial solution to the rationally ignorant Downsian (1957) voter.

Why are tariffs used rather than more efficient forms of redistribution? For interesting work on this, see Mayer and Riezman (1987). They note that political economy models cannot explain why tariffs are preferred as redistributive mechanisms over factor or production subsidies. They also argue that high-income groups may favor tariffs because this reduces their tax burden in a progressive tax system. Their empirical implication is that tariff rates should increase with the progressivity of a country's tax system – a testable proposition.

We pose one solution to Mayer and Riezman's interesting question in our Chapter 18 by arguing that politicians prefer indirect and opaque redistributive mechanisms. Hence, they will choose tariffs over consumption taxes and production subsidies because tariffs satisfy the principle of optimal obfuscation.

Another solution has been advanced by Lindbeck (1985a). He observes that tariffs provide nonbudget methods of redistribution, which are politically superior to production subsidies and consumption taxes. Tariffs are preferred to taxes and subsidies in developing countries because of the bureaucratic costs of administering the more complicated production subsidies and consumption taxes. There is less political opposition to hidden taxes in the form of price increases via tariffs than in more visible ones such as direct taxes and subsidies.

An alternative to the special-interest group model here is provided by Caves's (1976) adding machine model, which states that industries with high labor-output coefficients will have higher protection simply because they have more voters. Anderson (1980) suggests that the interest-group model can be thought of in a supply and demand context. Interest groups generate the demand for protection; supply of protection is provided by the political system. He applies the model to Australian protection in the 1970s. For an artful application of the demand and supply approach applied to legislators, see Denzau and Munger (1984).

Schattschneider's (1935) analysis of the Smoot–Hawley tariff bill led him to the following conclusion: "Some businessmen are occupied with politics so continuously that they are substantially politicians." Thus, the line that we draw in this chapter between lobbies and political parties may be a gray one.

For evidence on self-interested behavior on the part of members of Congress, see Niskanen (1976), who noted that the rational congressperson will spend most of his or her time invested in constituent work to obtain votes, rather than in supervising the functions of government.

H. P. Young (1978) contrasts minimum winning coalition versus vote maximization models. Consider three states, two with ten electoral votes and one with one electoral vote, with a majority of eleven electoral votes needed to win. The strategy of vote maximization would imply that a candidate should concentrate on the first two states; the minimum winning coalition strategy would include the third state along with one of the other two.

For an ambitious attempt at empirical estimation of a spatial model see

Poole (1986). In contrast to this work, Lindbeck and Weibull (1987b) find conditions under which parties will converge on identical positions on redistributive issues, as predicted by Hotelling (1929). They also derive conditions under which Director's Law is not generally valid. Director's Law of income distribution states that public expenditures are made primarily for the benefit of the middle class but are funded in considerable part by taxes levied against the rich and the poor (see Stigler 1970a). Lindbeck and Weibull state rather that both parties will favor voters who are marginal in that they are indifferent between voting and not voting.

What is the role of ideology? Lindbeck (1985a) and Hochman and Rogers (1969) discuss the role of ideology and entitlement principles in determining redistribution. According to their view, ideology provides intellectual and emotional justification for certain patterns of distribution and redistribution. For example, it provides individuals with the view that they are "entitled" to their factor return. In the context of protection, the parallel is the justification of protection for certain groups based on the importance of preserving jobs, employment, and other virtues. On the issue of ideology see Kalt and Zupan (1983, 1984). For a paper indicating that ideology is important in determining congressional voting power see Kau and Rubin (1979).

Hinich (1981) rationalizes voting in a marginal cost and marginal benefit model. Hinich (1978) argues that the indeterminacy of spatial voting models can be overcome when there is a sufficient divergence of beliefs and preferences about the ability of candidates.

5.2   The reverse-slope theorem

Consider the behavior of the two political parties. The endogenous policy model suggests that the most important considerations for the parties are resources and issues. We demonstrated in Chapter 3 that party competition will drive the parties to act in a sophisticated Stackelberg manner toward the lobbies. Hence, the objectives of the two parties can be written solely in terms of the policy variables. Recall that p is the probability of election of the protectionist party, t is the tariff rate that it sets, and s is the export subsidy set by the proexport party. The party strategies are as follows:

$$\text{the proexport party 1} \qquad \min_{s} p(s,t) \tag{5.1}$$

$$\text{the protectionist party 2} \qquad \max_{t} p(s,t) \tag{5.2}$$

These are reduced-form versions of equations (3.11) and (3.12) (see Appendix). With two parties, party 1's choosing s to minimize p is equivalent to choosing s to maximize q.

We show in the Appendix how the phenomenon of one party maximizing p and the other party minimizing p causes the slopes of the party reaction functions to have opposite signs near any equilibrium. This reverse-slope

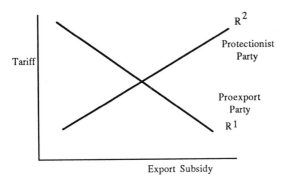

Figure 5.1. Democrats emulate, Republicans counteract.

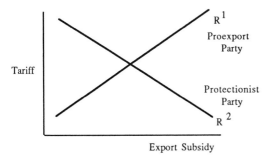

Figure 5.2. Republicans emulate, Democrats counteract.

theorem means that all political equilibria can be described geometrically by one of the two cases described in Figures 5.1 and 5.2. To facilitate the exposition, assume that the House Democrats sponsor a tariff and the House Republicans sponsor an export subsidy. The party whose slope is positive is an "emulator" in that its special-interest policy always moves in the same direction as that of the opposing party. Consider Figure 5.1.

The protectionist Democrats emulate the policy behavior of the Republicans: That is, an increase in the export subsidy of the Republicans in the neighborhood of equilibrium causes the Democrats to increase their tariff. The party whose slope is negative is a "counteractor": If the other party increases its policy, the counteractor reduces its policy. In Figure 5.1, the Republicans counteract the moves of the Democrats: Higher tariffs by the Democrats elicit lower export subsidies from the Republicans. The reasons for both types of behavior are embedded in the voting function p and the assumption of party competition. We generalize the theorem later in this chapter. The theorem may also be extended to Barro-type (1973) cases in which parties garner economic income in their payoff functions. In the specialized political game analyzed here, the parties obtain no economic income, so party welfare is described simply as the probability of electoral success.

While the emulator–counteractor strategies are driven by the mathematics of strategic maximization, there are behavioral parallels. Emulative politicians carry a pejorative label of following "me too" strategies. The contempt voters have for emulative politicians may be deserved ("They aren't bright enough to formulate their own program"). However, another possibility is that the emulator is simply following a vote-maximizing strategy.

Think of higher values of either policy as being increasingly "special-interest," and lower values as being increasingly "populist" or "proconsumer." We speculate that the emulator will be the party whose lobby contributions are most responsive to its policy. Thus, if the emulator increases its policy and the other party increases its policy, the emulator has gained relatively more in funds. The counteractor party becomes increasingly populist when the other party raises its policy and increasingly special-interest when the other party lowers its policy.

5.3   The reverse-shift theorem

This is a curious result. Both parties can become increasingly special-interest, but one of the equilibrium policies can fall. The reverse-shift theorem shows that it is possible (though not necessary) for one redistributive policy to fall even though both parties increase their desire for redistribution. Assume that the political equilibrium is stable and that both the protectionist and the proexport parties increase their desire for greater redistribution. Mathematically, this means that each party will prefer a higher level of its redistributive policy than before, for each and every fixed value of the opponent's policy. In terms of Figure 5.3 (using the proexport-emulator case in Figure 5.2), the reaction curve of the protectionist Democrats shifts upward (to higher tariff levels) and the reaction curve of the proexport Republicans shifts to the right (to higher export subsidy levels). The reverse-shift theorem specifies the conditions under which the equilibrium policy of one of the two parties will actually fall. In Figure 5.3, the equilibrium tariff falls because the shift to the right in the Republican reaction curve was larger than the upward shift in the Democratic reaction curve.

When reverse shifts occur, it is always the counteractor's policy that falls. Notice in Figure 5.3 that the protectionist Democrats are the counteractor and that the tariff is the policy that declines. Had the Republicans been the counteractor, the export subsidy would have been the only policy that could have declined following the increased desire for redistribution by the two parties.

The likelihood of a reverse shift is greater (1) the more negative the slope of the counteractor's reaction curve and (2) the greater the outward shift

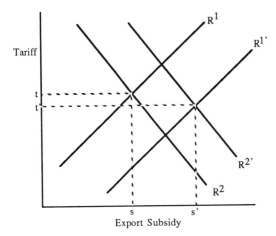

Figure 5.3. The reverse-shift paradox: Both parties become more special-interest but the equilibrium tariff falls.

in the emulator's reaction curve. Note in Figure 5.3 that condition 1 means that the R^2 curve is more vertical (more perpendicular to the s axis), and condition 2 means that the proexport Republican curve R^1 shifts to the right a great deal relative to the upward shift in the protectionist Democrat's curve R^2.

We have not investigated the cause of the increased preference by the parties for greater redistribution. If it were caused by increased contributions from the lobbies, there would appear to be a contradiction involved. Why would a protectionist lobby increase its contributions just to receive a lower tariff? Is this behavior irrational? The answer is "not necessarily," since net political returns to the lobby could increase, even with a lower tariff. The increased contributions may be due to a fall in the cost of policing free-riders: Net returns to lobby members can increase if lobby costs fall more than lobby revenues. We speculate that an economic parallel is the increase in a firm's output following a technological change that increases production efficiency. Higher output lowers product prices (the lower tariff), but firm profitability (protectionist lobby net revenue) can still increase if the firm's (lobby's) costs fall.

What are the empirical implications of the reverse-shift theorem? Technological innovations such as television have increased the importance of economic resources for party electoral success in the past few decades. This would lead us to expect both parties to prefer higher special-interest policies than before in order to raise campaign funds.

Casual empiricism suggests that protection declined in most Western democracies during the 1950s and 1960s at the same time that proexport (promultinational) policies were proliferating. If it were true that both the Democrats and Republicans in Congress preferred higher redistributive policies because of the campaign funds effect but t fell while s rose, this could be a reverse-shift effect. If there is any empirical content to this speculation, the congressional Republicans are the emulator party and the Democrats are the counteractor. This would make Figure 5.2 more relevant empirically. It also fits with the earlier speculation that the emulator Republicans face a supply of campaign funds that is more responsive to an increase in their export subsidy than is the case for funds going to the protectionist Democrats.

A second empirical insight applies to testing protectionist models across congressional districts. Consider a cross-sectional study that attempts to relate the preferences of Democratic members of Congress to import-competing employment in their districts. In the usual case, congresspeople would prefer greater protection the higher the level of import-competing employment; however, the reverse-shift result suggests that this is not inevitable. The vote-maximizing level of protection preferred by Democratic members of Congress can be lower in some heavily import-competing districts. This would reduce the statistical fit and hence the R^2 in a cross-sectional regression.

5.4   The policy-distance paradox

The policy-distance paradox suggests that both parties could prefer increased redistribution, and yet the equilibrium redistributive policies might fall. Since one policy might rise and the other fall, the result is best stated in terms of the distance between the policies (since the export subsidy is simply a negative tariff). The tariff raises the ratio of the price of importables to exportables; the export subsidy lowers the ratio. The difference in this price ratio under the protectionist party relative to the proexport party is approximately equal to the sum of the equilibrium policies, $s + t$. We call this sum the "policy distance" between the parties because it measures the postelection difference in the political impact on relative prices in the economy. Policy distance is the decline in the price of importables relative to exportables that occurs in any change from a Democratic to a Republican national political régime in the United States.

We continue to analyze the case in which there is an increase in the redistributive desires of both parties (i.e., an outward shift in both reaction curves). What happens to the policy distance between the parties following such a change? Normally, this would cause both special-interest policies to increase. For example, the Democrat's tariff might go up from, say, 10% to 15% and the Republican's export subsidy would go up from 7% to 13%. The initial policy distance is 17 percentage points; after the change, it increases to 28 points.

The policy distance between two parties is important because it determines campaign contributions from the lobbies. From the lobby's viewpoint, the greater the policy distance between the parties, the more each lobby will contribute to its favored political party. This is true because, in equation (3.14), the higher the tariff, the larger is r^2 (the returns to the protectionists under the congressional Democrats) and the higher the export subsidy, the lower is r^1 (the returns to the protectionists under the Republicans). Thus, marginal political revenue from protectionist lobbying rises because $(r^2 - r^1)$ increases with policy distance; hence protectionist lobby expenditures increase with policy distance.

Under what conditions will the equilibrium policy distance decrease in the face of an increased preference for redistribution by both parties? As shown in equation (5.22), the likelihood of the paradoxical outcome is greater the more negative the slope of the counteractor's reaction curve and the greater the shift in the emulator's reaction curve. These were the same conditions that increased the likelihood of the reverse-shift paradox in section 5.3.

One empirical implication of the policy-distance paradox is that both lobbies might become increasingly vocal for their constituencies and hence both parties might favor, ex ante, increasing redistributive distortions; yet the equilibrium level of resources contributed to the parties could fall (because of the decline in the policy distance). Because declining policy distance is counterintuitive, it may be the empirical exception rather than the rule.

5.5   The distortion paradox

In the long run, the economic distortions imposed on an economy by the tariff and the export subsidy can be approximated by the mean distortion D, that is, the average value of s and t, where the weights are the probabilities of election of the parties:

$$D = [1 - p]s + pt \qquad\qquad (5.21)$$

What happens to the mean distortion when both parties prefer increased redistribution? Most of the time, D will increase; however, there are times when it will not. This case generates the distortion paradox: Both parties want greater redistribution but the average level of the two distortions falls.

What conditions generate distortion paradoxes? Consider first the case in which the reverse-shift theorem does not hold, so that the equilibrium values of both s and t increase following the increased desire of both parties for greater redistribution. It might not seem possible that the average distortion could fall in this case; however, the average distortion can fall if the increase in the policy of the high-distortion party is accompanied by a sufficiently large decline in its probability of election. For example, let the initial probability of election be .5 for both parties; let $s = 10\%$ and $t = 30\%$ so that the mean distortion is 20%. Now let both parties increase their redistributive policies, so that s increases to 15% and t increases to 35%. Had the probabilities remained at .5, the mean distortion would have increased to 25%. However, assume that the increased tariff position of the Democrats hurts it dramatically with the voters relative to the increased export subsidy for the Republicans. Let the Democrats' equilibrium probability of election p drop to .2. In this case, the new level of the mean distortion declines to 19% (= .2[35%] + .8[15%]).

Consider second the case in which the reverse-shift paradox holds. The distortion paradox can occur in this case if the party with a high probability of election reduces its policy sufficiently. To see this, let the initial probability of election be $p = .8$ for the Democrats; let $s = 10\%$ and $t = 30\%$. Following the increased preference for redistribution by both parties, let p remain at .8 but let the tariff fall to 20% and the export subsidy rise to 15%. The initial average distortion is 26% (= .8[30] + .2[10]) whereas the final average distortion is 19% (= .8[20] + .2[15]).

The empirical implications of the distortion paradox are clear. Both parties in a country can experience an increased preference for redistribution and yet the long-run average level of policy distortions in the country can fall (and vice versa). Again, political hoopla for change may not be accompanied by the expected results.

5.6   Inconsistent parties and unstable tariff equilibria

An inconsistent party is one that varies its program widely in response to policy changes by its opponent. Inconsistency, in turn, leads to an unstable political equilibrium. The slope of each party's reaction function with respect to its own policy axis has an interesting interpretation. When it is nearly perpendicular, the party is "consistent": Large changes in its opponent's positions generate small changes in its own. When it is nearly parallel, the party is "inconsistent": Small changes by the opponent generate large changes in its position. This point is illustrated in Figure 5.4. Given these reaction functions, the equilibrium is unstable and the adjustment process explodes. Start at point J, with the export subsidy equal to s^0. The Democrats respond with tariff t^1; the Republicans counter with export subsidy s^2; the Democrats go to t^3; and so on. There are problems with the interpretations of instability of simple Cournot–Nash equilibria. These notwithstanding, it is clear that if one or more of the parties are sufficiently inconsistent, the political equilibrium will be unstable on almost any specification of the dynamic adjustment process. In many situations institutional checks limit political inconsistency. Both the press and rival candidates make it costly for parties to make significant changes in previously announced positions.

The behavior of the inconsistent party described here might be compared to

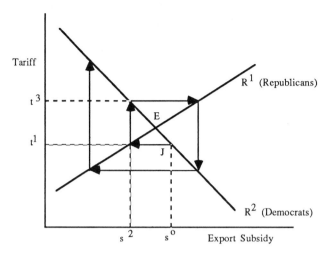

Figure 5.4. An unstable policy equilibrium caused by inconsistent party behavior.

the party that always attempts to outdo the moves of its opponent in one direction or the other. On the surface, it might appear that populists, such as Huey Long, would contribute to instability: In the absence of large campaign chests, they might vary their policy positions widely (outdo the moves of their opponents) in order to remain competitive. Long once ran against a candidate who was even more populist than he. The opponent had been poor as a child and had walked long distances to school barefooted. Long's response on the campaign trail: "I was so poor as a child that I was born barefooted."

We do not prove, but offer as a speculation, that parties have consistent reaction curves if the contribution functions from their lobbies are either very responsive or very unresponsive to the party tariff positions. We leave to interested readers the development and implications of this point. Populists, who usually cannot attract special-interest funds, may have low levels of funding and may favor low tariffs. Special-interest parties may have wide ranges over which they can vary their policies in order to attract funds.

5.7   Three generalizations of the reverse-slope theorem

5.7.1   A unity-sum policy game with many political parties

With many political parties the generalized reverse-slope theorem states that if party i's reaction function is positively sloped in $t_i t_j$ space, then party j's reaction function must be negatively sloped in the same space. We show [in Appendix section A.5.4(1)] that the slope of the reaction function for any party i has the same sign as the change in its own marginal probability of election (dp^i/dt_i) with respect to t_j. If an increase in t_j increases (decreases) this marginal probability of election, then the party is an emulator (counteractor). These results assume that each party takes different tariff positions with many parties present.

5.7.2   A constant-sum policy game with two political parties

Thus far in this book, the probabilities of election of the political parties have summed to unity. We now generalize the two-party policy game to a constant-sum game. This allows the sum of the two values being maximized by the parties (when they choose their policy position) to equal any value. We find that the reverse-slope theorem still holds in this case and is similar to a two-player market game with asymmetric externalities. The reverse-slope theorem can explain pollution games. An example of the latter is a real estate development whose expansion benefits a local steel mill (since the supply of labor increases) although steel mill expansion harms the development (assuming the dominance of the negative pollution effects). In the case of the parties, each might maximize the present value of its policy strategy and these values need not sum to 1. An example might be parties that maximize the present values of their probabilities of future election, or this plus some measure of wealth. A party that merely maximizes its probability of election in the next election might choose a tariff higher than one that maximizes the present value of its future political power. The Appendix indicates that the reverse-slope theorem applies to this more general game.

One economic example of two-player games with asymmetric externalities is two-player market share games. Consider the economic market share game in which each player i charges a price (e.g., t_i), so as to maximize its market share (measured in percentage terms), $p_i(t_i, t_j)$. In this game, the reverse-slope theorem holds, notwithstanding the observation that market share games do not satisfy the survival principle (which states that firms that do not maximize profits will be replaced in the long run by firms that do).

When there are many issues, we speculate that the reverse-slope theorem still holds, assuming the matrix p_{11} is negative definite and p_{22} is positive definite. The reverse-shift theorem may not hold without stronger assumptions about the p_{ij} matrices. We ignore problems of Arrow cycling and the other issues.

5.7.3   A constant-sum policy game with many political parties

When there are many parties, the reverse-slope theorem holds for a constant-sum game if assumptions are made about the relative strengths of policy-change effects across parties. For example, if two parties' policies have greater impacts on each other than they have on every other party combined, then the reverse-slope theorem holds for this pair of parties. The assumptions required for reverse-shift result are left as an exercise for the interested reader.

5.8   Rational policies

A frequently heard statement is that some government policy "makes no sense." This is only partially correct.

All government policies are rational to some group. To the gainers they make sense; to losers, they do not. The statement was made by a loser. To understand the policy, look for the gainers.

CHAPTER 6

The power function model of endogenous industry lobbying

This chapter explains how the level of political contributions by an industry lobby is explained by the size and number of the members. The topics examined are as follows:

6.1. a review of the literature;
6.2. the industry lobby as a noncooperative n-person game;
6.3. the existence and uniqueness of an equilibrium;
6.4. the exploitation of the large by the small;
6.5. the effect of industry concentration versus homogeneity;
6.6. lobbying contributions when the firms are of equal size;
6.7. the lobbying power function – industry lobbying power equals the product of the Herfindahl times industry sales;
6.8. how industry lobbying expenditures vary with the size of political jurisdictions (including why protectionist sentiment falls from the House to the Senate to the White House, and the optimal size of political jurisdictions); and
6.9. how to estimate the free-rider effect.

Chapter 6 in Stephen P. Magee, William A. Brock, and Leslie Young, *Black Hole Tariffs and Endogenous Policy Theory*. New York: Cambridge University Press, 1989. Adapted from William A. Brock and Stephen P. Magee, "An Economic Theory of Politics: The Case of the Tariff," mimeo, University of Chicago, May 1974; William A. Brock and Stephen P. Magee, "Understanding Collective Action: A Formal Analysis of the Voluntary Provision of Public Goods," mimeo, University of Chicago, December 1977; and William A. Brock and Stephen P. Magee, "The Economics of Special-Interest Politics: The Case of the Tariff," *American Economic Review* 68 (May 1978), 246–50.

6.1   The literature

Significant portions of this chapter formalize the work of Olson (1965) and Stigler (1971, 1974). Olson (1965) examines *lobbying*. He argues that organization is easier: with fewer numbers; in more concentrated industries; with more similar members; and with greater external threats. Stigler (1971) advances the microfoundations of the self-interest model and provided evidence across U.S. industries for its value in explaining regulation. Becker (1983) also argues that small groups will be successful in taxing larger groups for their subsidies. Taussig (1931) suggests that special interests caused the proliferation of protection across industries and over time in the United States.

One of the issues in the theory of lobby success is the *free-rider problem,* on which see Baldwin (1986a), Kim and Walker (1984), Marwell and Ames (1979), and Stigler (1974). For middle-of-the-road candidates see Rosen and Einhorn (1972). Lindbeck and Weibull (1987b) found that free-riding will be an inevitable consequence of social interaction with altruistic agents.

Some experimental results testing Olson's (1965) hypotheses are provided by Chamberlin (1978), who confirms the following two Olson predictions: The larger the group, the larger the amount of the collective good provided; and the larger the group, the farther it will fall short of providing the optimal amount of the collective good. However, Chamberlin was unable to find support for a Olson's "exploitation of the large by the small." For discussion of pressure groups in the United States see Gates (1981) and Walker (1983).

For theoretical papers on the issue of free-riding and voluntary provision of public goods see Austen-Smith (1981), Bliss and Nalebuff (1984), Darley and Latane (1968), Dawes (1980), Dawes, Orbell, and van de Kragt (1985), Grossman and Hart (1980), Hansen, Palfrey, and Rosenthal (1987), Harsanyi (1967–8), Isaac, McCue, and Plott (1985), Isaac, Walker, and Thomas (1984), Kim and Walker (1984), Marwell and Ames (1979), Palfrey and Rosenthal (1984, 1985), Rappaport (1985), and R. D. Roberts (1984). For a formal analysis of the tactical lobbying game between two lobbyists on opposite sides of an issue see H. P. Young (1978a).

Becker (1983) offers the insight that, in a world of free-riding across lobbies, the relevant consideration is free-riding for each lobby *relative* to free-riding by other lobbies. Thus, a lobby might have a lot of free-riding among its membership but be powerful because its free-riding is low relative to all other lobbies. Power is relative. Marwell and Ames (1979) found that, in experiments on graduate students, those majoring in economics were much more likely to free-ride in games than were those in any other subject area. Pugel and Walter (1985) attempted to test the free-rider phenomenon and the preferences of corporations on protection, but obtained poor results. The sample of 68 companies out of the U.S. *Fortune* 1,000 industrial corporations in 1980 revealed that companies favoring free trade tended to have higher ratios of R&D per sales, higher advertising to sales ratios, and more diversified product structures. Their explanation is that each of these variables is positively correlated with the degree of multinationality of the firm.

Campaign contributions solve several *shirking* problems in politics. For an important model describing these results see Baron (1986). A candidate can promise policies to groups of voters but, because of the secret ballot, voters can shirk on their provision of votes to that candidate. The provision of campaign funds is a way that high-income voters ensure their commitment to a candidate. Second, candidates, once elected, can shirk on their delivery of policies to a lobby. For challengers, this is reduced by publicly stating their positions before the election, adopting ideologies that guarantee predictable positions on certain issues, accepting "pledges" for funds that are received after the election when policies are delivered, and realizing that shirking will cost them future campaign contributions from all potential contributors. Incumbents have an advantage over challengers in reducing risks for their contributors: Since they campaign continuously, they can provide current policies in exchange for campaign funds. Third, lobbies would prefer to contribute only to winning candidates; however, the requirement of funds before elections forces lobbies to commit to candidates and vice versa. Gary Jacobson (1978) finds that campaign expenditures by challengers increased their votes, whereas those by incumbents did not .

Conybeare (1983a) discovered an interesting solution to Baron's (1986) voter-shirking problem in Australia. There, after an election, the elected government provides greater protection to industries concentrated in those geographic regions that supported them in the election. In this case, protection is an ex post payoff directly to voters. Another shirking issue is the theft of technology. There is an appropriability argument for U.S. protection against goods produced abroad using U.S. technology that was not paid for. This was one of many issues in the semiconductor protection directed at the Japanese recently. On the appropriability question, though not in a political context, see Magee (1977a,b,c).

Lindbeck (1985a) argues that agricultural protection, rent control, and tax concessions to home-owners in Western democracies all indicate redistributional benefits that favor large, diverse, and unorganized interests. We argue in Chapter 11 that both agricultural protection and rent control emerge because of compensation effects: Sudden drops in income motivate these actors to obtain political protection.

There is no paradox in both large and small groups obtaining redistributional benefits. Small groups are effective because of homogeneity and low organization costs; large groups may be effective because of their voting power. This suggests that there might be an inverted-U relationship between the tariff rate and the power function introduced in this chapter. The power of highly concentrated groups will be determined by the Herfindahl index; the power of unconcentrated groups will be determined exclusively by size. This suggests a separation of the Herfindahl index and the size variable. On the nonlinearity of the size variable in determining power see Pincus (1975).

Several *historical* works are insightful, particularly Rostow (1960, 1971, 1975). Kurth (1979) argues that the power of various industries politically has a long historical tradition. For example, he shows that each major industrial country has followed the same sequence of industrialization: first textiles, then steel, then steel derivatives such as shipbuilding, rails, and autos. Gourevitch (1977) provides a historical comparison of tariffs in the late nineteenth century for the United States, Germany, France, and Great Britain. He finds the following pattern of winners over losers across all the countries: producers over consumers; heavy industrialists over finished manufacturers; big farmers over small farmers; and property owners over laborers. Substantial landowners and large-scale basic industry were consistent winners. Bauer, de Sola Pool, and Dexter (1963) conducted a survey in the 1950s that throws light on individuals in free trade and protectionist lobbies. They found that free traders are better educated, wealthier, more politically active, and in the Republican party, whereas ultraprotectionists are more likely to be found in the Democratic party. Nelson (1987) found that the protectionist bias of lobbying organizations finds its way into institutions as well.

On the *law of the excluded middle,* Guttman (1977) argues there will be a Pareto-optimal provision of a nonexcludable public good with any number of actors and perfect information because the actors will voluntarily match each other's contributions dollar for dollar. He argues that the free-rider problem in lobbies emerges because of imperfect information. For the political science view see Gowa (1986), who argues that potential group members weigh the participation benefits of joining against the free-rider benefits of not joining. On the issue of the excluded middle see the paper by Rosen and Einhorn (1972) on the attractiveness of "middle-of-the-road political candidates."

For evidence of the *compensation effect,* which we discuss in Chapter 11, see Glazer, McMillan, and Robbins (1985). The compensation effect states that recently disadvantaged economic actors will lobby harder than others. Glazer, McMillan and Robbins note that undue political influence is much more prevalent in competitive industries than in oligopolistic or monopolistic ones.They point in particular to used-car dealers, realtors, truckers, doctors, dentists, trial lawyers, and funeral directors. This provides a potential explanation for the failure of concentration ratios to work well in explaining industry tariff rates.

Consider the *political impotence* view. There is evidence, for example, that firms in concentrated industries are not particularly successful in obtaining political benefits: See, among others, the work of Caves (1976). Stigler (1971) found that regulation of electric utilities had little effect on electricity prices and that securities laws did not cause the price of securities to decline. In related work, Kalt and Zupan (1984) found that the economic interests of a state is less important than its senator's ideology in explaining how he or she will vote on issues. Some of these results fail the rationality test: In the long run, industries should not spend large sums on unsuccessful ventures.

Industry tariff studies include Marvel and Ray (1985), who examined both tariffs and nontariff barriers in the United States. They found that tariffs were higher in U.S. industries with higher concentration (the share of the four largest firms in the industry); weaker opposition (measured by the consumer goods ratio); weaker international competitiveness; and slower U.S. growth. Caves (1976) reports one of the first efforts to test alternative theories of endogenous tariff structures. He examined 1963 Canadian data that marginally favored the interest group model over the vote maximization and the national policy models. An alternative approach to Canada's tariff structure was suggested by Helleiner (1977), who used time series data for 1961–70 to establish that labor favored protection whereas multinationals favored free trade. By contrast, Lavergne's (1983) test of tariff structure for 300 U.S. manufacturing industries is pessimistic regarding the role of pressure groups. These models are discussed in Frey (1984a, chap. 3). Cable and Rebelo (1980) estimate cross-industry import penetration in the United Kingdom and find protection to be significant and with the expected sign.

For other industry tariff studies see Balassa (1965), Baldwin and Lewis (1978), Basevi (1966), Cook (1981), Fieleke (1976), Jenkins (1981), Lundberg (1981), Pelzman and Rousslang (1982), Riedel (1977), and Saunders (1980). For the theory of tariff structure see Corden (1966) and Falvey (1979). For empirical studies of trade protection in the United States by industry see Marvel and Ray (1987), Ray (1981a,b, 1987), and Ray and Marvel (1984). Ray and Marvel have been particularly effective at finding results in the data that have eluded others: for example, the expected positive sign on concentration. See Fieleke (1976) and Saunders (1980) for a model of effective protection in Canada. For studies on the effects of Japanese trade on American protection and employment see Staiger, Deardorff, and Stern (1985a–c). Fieleke (1976) argues that industry tariffs cannot be explained by the degree of import competition, the general health of the industry, or the industry's involvement with the national defense. The only variable he finds that works across industries is the wage rate, and that explains only a fraction of the total variation in interindustry tariffs. Dougan (1984) emphasizes that, irrespective of an industry's political power and organizational efficiency, the industry will not find it either easier or profitable to obtain high price supports if it faces an elastic demand for its product. He shows how tariff rates are influenced by domestic demand and supply elasticities.

Marvel and Ray (1987) argue that growing *intra-industry trade* reduces protection. This occurs for two reasons: there will be export opposition to the protection within an industry because of the likelihood of foreign retaliation and import computing firms will be importing components and perhaps re-exporting them. Marvel and Ray (1985) argue that there is less trade liberalization in concentrated U.S. industries than in other ones. While it has been difficult to show relationships between concentration and tariff levels, Marvel and Ray do find the expected effect of concentration on tariff reductions.

6.2 The industry lobby as a noncooperative n-person game

Consider n individuals who stand to obtain supplier surplus gains and m individuals who stand to lose consumer surplus amounts if an industry's tariff is changed from 0 to t. We postulate that the perceived net gain G_i to individual i of using his (her, its) wealth to back the tariff is a function of the total perceived backing for it X, total lobbying against the tariff Y, i's own lobby expenditures x_i (which is above and beyond his contribution to the perceived total X), and his supplier surplus gain $S(t)$ if the tariff passes.

The variable t itself is not a function of X,Y because it is already reflected in $G_i(X,Y,x_i,S_i(t))$, following the Stackelberg formulation of the endogenous policy model. Two definitions are advanced in the mathematical Appendix. According to definition 1, a noncooperative equilibrium exists when each player prefers not to alter his (her, its) contributions, given the contribution levels of all of the other players. We choose this notion of equilibrium because of our assumed inability of the players to write enforceable legal contracts. By definition 2, if a noncooperative equilibrium exists, then we can write lobbying functions for the total amounts contributed to the political process as a function of the policy variable t.

What is the shape of an individual's gain function G_i? Since G_i measures the net benefit to individual i ($G_i = B_i - x_i$, where B_i equals the gross benefit and x_i equals the amount contributed to the campaign), it is reasonable to postulate that G_i increases for small values of x_i and then decreases for large values. We would expect B_i to increase for low values of x_i because individual i: (1) may feel that he has an impact on the chances of passage of the legislation above and beyond the total contribution X; (2) derives personal satisfaction from defending his group's interest; and (3) feels negatively about his noticeability and group sanctions that might be levied against him if he does not contribute. It is plausible to suppose that G_i is decreasing in Y, the contributions by the opponents of protection. The arguments X and x_i in G_i are an attempt to capture precisely Olson's (1965) notions of perceived effectiveness and noticeability, respectively. Also it seems reasonable to postulate diminishing returns to (X,x_i) at least for large values of X and x_i. These conditions are described in assumption 1 in the Appendix.

It is worth mentioning that insertion of X and x_i into G_i capture spillover effects and appropriability effects analogous to those attending the free-rider problem in the pure theory of public goods. The reader may ask why we don't use the Groves and Ledyard (1977) solution to the free-rider problem. The answer is that their solution requires the existence of a government that has the power to collect the taxes. The Groves and Ledyard problem is to construct demand-revealing processes that prevent underrevelation of preferences in such a way as to guarantee a Pareto optimum, given that there is a government to enforce the rules. Political lobbying involves the voluntary provision of public goods in which there is no government to force payment of tax-type contributions. The Olson (1965) problem of the voluntary provision of public goods differs from the problem of constructing a demand-revealing process. For a discussion of contingent contracts such that Groves and Ledyard might be applied to the lobbying problem see Brock (1980).

The reader might also ask why we don't make use of Olson's (1965) by-product argument that lobbies such as the AMA finance their lobbying expenses via the sale of private services such as journals and conferences. The reason is that this requires a much more elaborate model of the microeconomics of the lobby and the demand for such tied services than we provide here. As an aside, one criticism of Olson's by-product argument is that competing organizations could offer journals and conferences cheaper than the AMA, and hence doctors belonging to these competing organizations could get the private goods cheaper and free-ride on the public good. A way around this criticism is a von Neumann-type model, say, of private medical practice in which organizational output emerges as a joint product of private optimizational activity. If a profit-maximizing AMA did not try to capitalize on this organizational output, it would be run out of business by an organization that did. Two problems are that (1) organizational output is hard to define, and (2) it is difficult to determine what it is in the von Neumann activity analysis of a particular professional or special-interest group that leads to the joint product of organizational structure in the pursuit of private profits. Thus, while Olson's by-product argument is hard to model precisely, it has merit. Ignoring these complexities, let us return to the gain function G_i and the function describing the losers from tariffs, L_j.

Under what condition will the gains and losses from tariff-induced price changes be large? When the factors of production in an industry are inelastically supplied and immobile, the present values of the producer and consumer quasi-rents will be large relative to industries with more elastic and mobile factor supplies. Since lobbying expenditures increase with immobility, we expect immobile factors to be more active in politics than mobile factors. If factors become more immobile the longer they are in an industry, then lobbying should increase with industry age.

6.3   Existence and uniqueness

If the perceived net marginal value product of x_i is well behaved (see 6.17), then the lobbying equilibria exist and are unique, holding constant the contributions of the proexport lobby. The net marginal value product of x_i is the net gain to protectionist contributor i of an additional dollar donation to politics. Sufficient conditions yielding existence and uniqueness are that the net marginal value product of x_i be continuous, decreasing in x_i and X_i, and increasing in the stake S_i.

6.4   Exploitation of the large by the small

Assume that the perceived net marginal value product of x_i for the protectionists is independent of the amounts contributed by the proexport lobby. Then an increase in the stake of one of the protectionists makes him (her, it) contribute more while each of the other protectionists contributes less. The total contributions of all of the protectionists increases, however. If all of the protectionists were of equal size initially, then we would have free-riding by the small protectionists at the expense of the larger protectionist. This is Olson's exploitation of the large by the small.

The existence and uniqueness results for the protectionists in section 6.3 assumed that the level of contributions of the proexport lobby is held constant. When both of the lobbies behave optimally, it is possible that there is no equilibrium or that there are multiple equilibria (see Appendix Figures A.6.5 and A.6.6).

The comparative statics from this generalized model are reasonable. If the stake of one of the protectionists increases, the equilibrium level of total protectionist lobby contributions increases while the total level of all proexport lobby contributions decreases. The interesting feature of this result is that the rational level of expenditure by any lobby is a function not just of its own structure, but also of the level of expenditures by opposing lobbies.

6.5   Perceived effectiveness and noticeability: concentration and homogeneity

In order to obtain empirical implications, we shall work from this point with simplified and specific lobbying functions to illustrate spillover and free-rider effects. These functions capture Olson's perceived effectiveness and ("free-riding") noticeability coefficients. These ideas apply to both the protectionist and the proexport lobbies.

There are two important coefficients in our formalization of Olson. Coefficient a captures the noticeability effect and provides a measure of the free-rider problem. The larger is a, the greater the free-riding problem (the greater the benefits accruing to i of contributions by others). If a is large, then the contributor in question is not noticeable and can free-ride. Coefficient b captures perceived effectiveness, that is, the effect of individual j's own contribution on his own gain, apart from his contribution to the total. It may be helpful to view b as political access or future unspecified benefits. For reasons discussed in the Appendix, the sum $(a + b)$ must be less than or equal to unity. The case of no free-riding would be $b = 1$; that of complete free-riding would be $a = 1$. All other combinations fall in between.

Appendix equations (6.33)–(6.40) derive the implications of this Olson-type (1965) model of the voluntary provision of public goods. The least surprising result is (6.33) and (6.34), in which no actor contributes more than his stake (i.e., what he will get back from the political system). For example, if a proposed tariff change would cause an import-competing producer to gain $50,000, he will not contribute more than this amount to a lobby to obtain the change.

The superiority of the monopolist lobby is reflected in (6.35) and (6.36). Total lobby contributions are maximum for a single-member lobby, holding the total stake constant. This is reasonable in light of free-riding and is anecdotally supported by the observation that one-firm lobbies in developing countries (frequently large multinational corporations) wield considerable influence over the local government.

A related result is Olson's "enhancement of concentration" result, shown in (6.37) and (6.38). Any increase in the inequality of the stakes increases the level of total lobby contributions. This economic result runs counter to the sociological result that group effectiveness decreases with the homogeneity of the membership. If this sociological view were correct, lobbying effectiveness should fall with greater concentration. However, a lot of sociologists agree that dominant figures contribute more than their pro-rata share of the effort in group activity.

Lobby contributions are homogeneous of degree 1 with respect to the stakes. That is, if the industry's size is doubled, its equilibrium lobbying effort should double as well (ceteris paribus). In (6.35) and (6.36), if each lobby member's stake increases by a factor of q, then the entire lobby's effort rises by q.

Tariff cascading or tariff escalation is one implication of the Olson–Stigler concentration results. Lobbying theory would predict that tariff rates should

Table 6.1. *Tariff escalation: post-Tokyo Round tariff rates*

Product	Primary goods	Semifinished goods	Final goods
Sugar (Japan)	35	40	32
Cocoa (Japan)	0	2	25
Leather (U.S.)	0	3	14
Wood (EEC)	0	2	4
Pulp and paper (EEC)	0	0	4
Wool (U.S.)	4	9	41
Cotton (U.S.)	2	7	7
Jute (Japan)	0	8	20
Iron (U.S.)	0	1	4
Copper (U.S.)	0	1	2
Aluminum (Japan)	0	9	12
Lead (U.S.)	0	4	8
Zinc (EEC)	0	2	7
Tin (U.S.)	0	0	2
Simple average:	3	6	13

be low on goods that have large domestic purchasers, and high on goods with small atomistic purchasers. Since raw materials have the largest purchasers in most economies, they tend to have low tariff rates; tariffs on semimanufactured goods are somewhat higher, whereas those on final goods tend to be highest because they have the most atomistic consumers. For interesting discussions of tariff escalation see McKinnon (1973, p. 135) and Yeats (1984). Yeats (1984) provides the data shown in Table 6.1 on post-Tokyo Round tariff rates by processing stage. Typically, there are a few large importers of primary products, so their political influence would be for free trade and with considerable lobbying clout. However, in the face of final goods, there will be many fragmented consumers of the product, so their opposition to protection would be much less effective. Thus, tariff rates on these products are typically higher.

6.6 A simplified model: firms of equal size

We simplify the model further by assuming that each of the protectionist firms is the same size and that each of the proexport lobby firms is the same size. In this case, the per-member contributions by the protectionists x

can be written

$$x = S(a/n + b) \qquad (6.41)$$

and the total contributions by the protectionists X can be written

$$X = S(a + nb) \qquad (6.42)$$

where S is the gain of each individual protectionist if the tariff changes from 0 to t (we repeat the equation numbers used in the Appendix). A similar formulation applies to the proexport lobby. Recall that complete free-riding corresponds to $a = 1$, whereas no free-riding implies $b = 1$. Three results follow immediately.

1. Addition of another member with an identical stake leads to a fall in x (per-member contributions) but a rise in X (total contributions). This corresponds to a rise in n in the two equations above. The empirical implication is that per-member contributions should fall with group membership, while total contributions should increase.
2. In the same case, the addition of another member with an identical stake has no effect on the total lobbying effort only if there is complete free-riding: that is, if $a = 1$. This is the case if each lobby member feels that his (her, its) contribution has no effect on total contributions by the lobby.
3. What happens to total lobby contributions if the number of protectionists is increased but the total dollar value of the protectionist stake remains unchanged? From (6.41), the effect on total lobby contributions appears to be ambiguous since the number of protectionists n increases but the per-protectionist stake S decreases. As shown in the Appendix, however, the total level of contributions X unambiguously falls as the number of players increases. Thus, a regression attempting to explain total lobby contributions should be decreasing in the number of members in the lobby (holding stakes constant).

6.7   The lobbying power function

If we multiply the Herfindahl concentration index by the value of the total stakes in an industry, we have a "power function" measure of the dollar amount that a protectionist lobby would contribute for tariffs:

$$P = P(S_1, \ldots, S_n) = H\left(\sum S_i\right) \qquad (6.49)$$

Recall that the Herfindahl ranges from 0 to 1, with a single firm in the industry corresponding to $H = 1$ and many small firms in the industry corresponding to H approaching 0. If there are five equal-sized firms in an industry, $H = .2$ (or, with n firms, $H = 1/n$). Given certain simplifying assumptions, the optimal contributions by the protectionist lobby (derived earlier) will equal those predicted by the power function in equation (6.49). As predicted earlier, an empirical implication of the power function model is that total contributions should fall with the number of firms in the lobby group, and total contributions should increase with the size of the industry.

6.8   Endogenous lobbying and the size of political jurisdictions

How are the levels of lobbying expenditures by well-organized protectionists (or by relatively less organized consumer groups) affected by the size of the political jurisdiction? The answer to this question would provide theoretical insight into whether members of the U.S. House of Representatives would be more or less protectionist than the senators from the same state. We examine here the net contributions for protection, which equal the total protectionist contributions minus the proexport (or proconsumer) lobby contributions.

Suppose that all political jurisdictions (districts) are of equal size and that there are n identical gainers and m identical losers in each of the D districts ($d = 1, \ldots, D$). We shall examine the net protectionist contributions over the union of the districts. Now suppose the D districts are consolidated into one large district with one representative to represent it. The equilibrium in the larger geographical district (i.e., after consolidation) is indicated by a prime ($'$). Appendix Figure A.6.8 shows these functions, assuming that both protectionist and proexport lobbying funds are an increasing function of the tariff rate. We assume for the purposes of this section that the equilibrium tariff is determined simply by the intersection of the protectionist and the proexport lobbying curves.

Before considering consolidation, notice that if either C' (the per-member stake by the antiprotectionist lobby after consolidation) or m (the number of antiprotectionists) increases, then expenditures against the tariff increase and net protectionist lobbying expenditures will fall. If the equilibrium tariff is determined by the equality of the funds contributed by protectionists and antiprotectionists, the equilibrium tariff will fall. Conversely, if S' (the per-member stake by the protectionist lobby after consolidation) or n (the number of protectionists) increases, protectionist lobbying expenditures rise and the equilibrium tariff rises, ceteris paribus.

With geographical consolidation, the net pressure for a tariff can go either way: Figure A.6.8 indicates that if $a = 1$ (i.e., $b = 0$, meaning complete free-riding by the protectionists), and $B > 0$, then net protectionist pressure (and hence the tariff) falls with geographical consolidation because the Y curve shifts up but the X curve stays put. When there is complete free-riding, protectionist i feels that increasing his contribution x_i by one dollar reduces the expected contribution by the rest of the protectionists by one dollar. If $b > 0$, there is not complete free-riding, so there is a positive expected gain to i when he contributes. If $B = 0$ (complete free-riding by the antiprotectionist lobby), then net pressure and the equilibrium tariff rise (assuming that $a > 0$) because the X curve shifts up but the Y curve stays put. The situation of $B = 0$ is similar to that of the average writer of a letter to the President of the United States. Since only the total number of letters matters, another individual letter has no impact.

6.8.1   Why protectionist sentiment falls from the House to the Senate to the White House

Geographical consolidation will increase net protectionist lobbying and increase the tariff when $B = 0$. That is, when consumers – the losers – feel anonymous, then consolidation generates more special-interest behavior and hence a higher tariff. The logic goes as follows. Consolidate two equal-sized congressional districts into a state: There are now twice as many gainers and losers. Contribution per person of the losers falls but, if $B = 0$, total contributions of the losers remain the same. That is, contribution per person falls so much that, even though there are twice as many contributors, total lobbying in the state is the same as the lobbying directed to each of the two representatives in the congressional districts. Things are different with the firms, however. Since firms are larger, they feel less anonymous (i.e., $b > 0$). Thus, even though lobbying per firm falls due to free-riding ($a > 0$), total protectionist lobbying expenditures rise. Thus, special-interest contributions can increase relative to general-interest contributions as we move to larger political jurisdictions.

What are the empirical implications? If the forces for free trade are largely disorganized consumers, then the theoretical arguments just presented imply that protectionist forces should get more powerful as we move from the House to the Senate to the President of the United States. Since the reverse appears to be true, the following approach is more plausible. Major opponents of protection in the United States for the past half-century have been U.S. multinational corporations. As they appear to be more concentrated in their industries than are the protectionist firms in theirs, our model predicts that multinationals will become increasingly influential relative to protectionist firms as we move to larger geographical areas (i.e., from the House to the Senate to the White House). Supporting this view is Ferguson's evidence that U.S. multinationals provided political backing and campaign contributions to Roosevelt in 1932 that resulted in Roosevelt's free-trade Reciprocal Trade Agreements Act of 1934.

6.8.2 The optimal size of political jurisdictions

The analysis above suggests that there are optimal geographical jurisdictions. The system that most favors relatively concentrated interests is at the national level; the one that favors less concentrated interests is at the local level. Perhaps this explains why very large money-center banks and large U.S. multinationals are most effective at the White House level, whereas unconcentrated industries (such as textiles) have so much political support for protection in the House of Representatives. A welfare implication is that geographical consolidation will lessen the deadweight losses for some special-interest policies but increase it for others. The methodology also has implications for political reform. Generalists' interests would be best served by having special-interest decisions made at the level that moves the system closest to Pareto optimality. There are two reasons why this is unlikely to occur. First, the optimal geographical level at which to make special-interest policy decisions differs from policy to policy: What is best for protection may not be best for bank regulation. Second, following the powerless politician effect, adoption of such a system is outside of the control of policymakers because of the lobbies. If the lobbies are sufficiently powerful at the time the constitution is established, we can almost be certain that the geographical level at which decisions are made would be influenced by the lobbies.

6.9 How to estimate the free-rider effect

The lobbying power function discussed above could be estimated for protectionists as follows. First, estimate the value of the total protectionist stake for the industry V as the product of industry sales and the tariff rate ($t \times$ sales). Then, estimate the following power function:

$$\log X = a_0 + a_1 \log H + a_2 \log V \tag{6.52}$$

Unfortunately, the coefficients are not precise estimates of the perceived effectiveness and noticeability coefficients. The coefficients a and b can be estimated as follows:

$$r = X/V = aH + b \tag{6.54}$$

where

r = the lobbying ratio (ratio of lobbying expenditures to the value of the stakes)

X = total lobbying expenditures by the industry for protection

V = value of the industry stake (= tariff rate times industry sales)

H = Herfindahl index of concentration for the industry ($0 \leq H \leq 1$)

This regression provides an explicit test of our assumption that $a \geq 0$, $b \geq 0$, $a + b \leq 1$, and so on. A diagram of interest would be the plot of r on H or n. Positive residuals (actual values exceeding predicted ones) would indicate above-average lobbying success by an industry. The coefficient a measures an external effect and b measures an internal effect: If $a = 0$, there are no externality effects; if $b = 0$, individual effort has no effect. This provides an explicit method of testing for the relative importance of the free-rider effect across industries. We leave empirical tests of this model to interested readers.

CHAPTER 7

Three simple tests of the Stolper–Samuelson theorem

Second only in political appeal to the argument that tariffs increase employment is the popular notion that the standard of living of the American
worker must be protected against the ruinous competition of cheap foreign
labor. (Stolper and Samuelson 1941, p. 333)

This chapter examines how alternative models predict lobbying positions on
the issue of freer trade versus protection. The following topics are addressed:

7.1. a review of the literature;
7.2. Stolper–Samuelson versus Ricardo–Viner–Cairnes;
7.3. the three tests that would confirm a Stolper–Samuelson explanation
of lobbying: (1) capital favoring free trade and labor preferring protection; (2) each factor being unanimous in its choice of free trade
or protection; (3) each factor's policy choice being independent of
whether it was producing export- or import-competing goods; and
7.4. caveats and conclusions.

7.1   The literature

Harry Johnson made important contributions to many fields, including the pure theory of international trade. His influence was especially
significant in the theory of tariffs: Witness the collection of classic papers in

Chapter 7 in Stephen P. Magee, William A. Brock, and Leslie Young, *Black Hole
Tariffs and Endogenous Policy Theory*. New York: Cambridge University Press,
1989. Adapted from Stephen P. Magee, "Three Simple Tests of the Stolper–
Samuelson Theorem," in Peter Oppenheimer, ed., *Issues in International Eco-
nomics*. Proceedings of the Oxford International Symposium in Honor of Harry G.
Johnson. London: Oriel Press, 1980, 138–53.

his *Aspects of the Theory of Tariffs* (1971). An important question in tariff theory is the effect of a tariff on the distribution of income. The Stolper and Samuelson (1941) theorem asserts that, in a two-factor world with complete mobility of factors within a country, liberalization of international trade will lower the real income of one factor of production and increase the real income of the other. It is one of the four central propositions in the 2×2 theory of international trade, along with the factor price equalization, Heckscher–Ohlin, and Rybczynski theorems. For an extension of the theorem see Bhagwati (1969, chap. 7).

The most extreme theoretical alternative to the Stolper–Samuelson theorem is the theory of noncompeting groups advanced by Cairnes (1884). The same approach is contained in the Ricardo–Viner model. For a discussion of these models see Jones (1971), Mayer (1974), Mussa (1974), and Neary (1978). They suggest that factors of production are industry-specific even in the long run, so that trade liberalization would benefit all factors in the export industry but hurt all factors in the import-competing industry. Studies by Mayer (1974) and Mussa (1974) combine short-run immobility with long-run factor mobility to yield intermediate results: One factor will, say, unambiguously gain both in the short and the long run; the other will gain in the short run but lose in the long run from trade liberalization. This intertemporal conflict could be resolved by present-value calculations, if the factors have sufficient information about the adjustment path. Although these present-value calculations would be tedious, they could be done.

7.2   Stolper–Samuelson factor mobility versus Ricardo–Viner–Cairnes factor immobility

The intertemporal consideration highlights the difficulty of constructing direct statistical tests that would establish the empirical relevance of the Stolper–Samuelson versus the Ricardo–Viner–Cairnes model. The researcher would have to determine factor intensities, factor elasticities of substitution, all variables affecting interindustry movements in the factors of production (moving costs and geographical dispersion of plants), discount rates, expectations of the likelihood of government adjustment assistance, and so on. The enormity of this task explains the shortage of direct empirical tests of the two models.

The original Stolper–Samuelson article itself suggests an indirect approach. Tariffs are set by politicians. This book suggests that tariffs can be thought of as prices that clear political markets. An important question, using this approach, is the manner in which coalitions form. Any theorem regarding the redistributional effect of a tariff also implies the way in which coalitions are likely to form for and against tariffs: Stolper–Samuelson suggests that lobbying activity will occur along factor lines (capital vs. labor), whereas Ricardo–Viner–Cairnes suggests that they will occur along industry lines (import-competing vs. export). This chapter provides three tests of these contrasting forms of lobbying behavior. We assume that the factors of production base their lobbying on rational present-value calculations based on their self-interests. If the present value of income streams (inclusive of non-pecuniary considerations and taking lobbying costs into account) would be increased by free trade, we can expect them to lobby for freer trade (and vice versa). This "revealed-preference" approach to testing for the redistributive effects of tariffs shifts the voluminous amount of information required for an empirical test from the researcher to the lobby representatives of the factors of production.

Three revealed-preference tests of the competing theorems are performed on 1973 U.S. data in section 7.3. Section 7.4 discusses limitations, alternative interpretations, and some implications of the tests. The results generally reject Stolper–Samuelson and accept the Ricardo–Viner–Cairnes approach. This is consistent with the view that factors are less mobile between industries in advanced industrial societies because of sector-specific human capital and high-technology physical capital (a point suggested to us by Franz Gehrels). Another interpretation is that lobbying costs and free-rider problems are lower for industry lobbies than for factor lobbies. The most important explanation of these results, however, is probably the institutional fact that, since 1934, U.S. trade legislation must be renewed approximately every four years. This causes U.S. trade lobbying to display a short time horizon.

7.3   The three empirical tests

> In other words, whatever will happen to wages in the wage good (labor intensive) industry will happen to labor as a whole. And this answer is independent of whether the wage good will be imported or exported. (Stolper and Samuelson 1941, p. 344)

Simplicity, statistical methodology and data availability dictated that the tests be limited to two factors of production, capital and labor. The cost of this limitation is that we may be testing other relationships (e.g., substitutability or complementarity between two out of many factors) rather than the two competing theories.

Capital and production labor in the United States were chosen to illustrate the tests. The American labor movement has been actively engaged in lobbying on trade policy during the past decade. Most of the headlines have placed labor on the side of greater protection, although we shall see shortly that this position is far from unanimous. Similarly, management in many industries has lobbied actively. Since management is chosen by stockholders, we assume that management's interests coincide with the owners of the firm's physical capital. Regardless of the positions of the factors not considered here (land, skilled labor, etc.), it is of some interest whether production labor and capital are protagonists or antagonists on the question of freer U.S. trade.

The empirical evidence used in this paper is taken from the Summary of Testimony for the Hearings before the Committee on Ways and Means in the U.S. House of Representatives on the Trade Reform Act of 1973, May–June 1973. These summaries revealed the preferences of twenty-nine trade associations (representing management) and twenty-three unions for either freer trade or greater protection. A summary of the results and the related Standard Industrial Classification (SIC) codes are shown in Table 7.1. In cases where the information was ambiguous or where no information was given, the staff of the Ways and Means Committee and other experts in Washington were consulted. Table 7.1 should not be read in terms of each group's position on specific items in the 1973 trade bill, but rather its general position on freer versus more restricted trade. This position is presumed to reflect its preference both for itself and other industries since trade bills are seldom industry-specific. "P" stands for a protectionist position, "F" for freer trade, and "M" for mixed positions (i.e., powerful subgroups within the organization on both sides). The quotation from Stolper and Samuelson (1941) at the beginning of this section suggests three empirical implications of their theorem in a simple two-factor world.

1. Capital and labor in a given industry will oppose each other on the issue of protection (or free trade) for that industry.
2. For the country as a whole, each factor will favor either free trade or protection but not both.
3. The position taken by capital or labor in an industry on the issue of protection will be independent of whether the industry is export- or import-competing.

These implications form the basis of our three tests.

7.3.1   Test 1: capital versus labor opposition on protection

The first implication suggests that we could test the competing hypotheses for two factors of production with a 2×2 contingency table, as shown in Figure 7.1. Each industry can be placed in one of the four mutually exclusive and exhaustive cells, depending on the position of its capital and labor on trade policy.

Position of Industry Labor

	1 Protectionist	2 Free Trade
1 **Protectionist**	11 Ricardo- Viner- Cairnes (import- competing)	12
2 **Free Trade**	21 Stolper- Samuelson (all industries)	22 Ricardo- Viner- Cairnes (exports)

Position of Industry Capital (row label at left)

Figure 7.1. Implications of traditional international economic theories for U.S. lobbying.

The Stolper–Samuelson theorem asserts that capital and labor will oppose each other on trade policy; thus the diagonal elements should equal zero. Furthermore, all labor will support one policy while capital will do the reverse. Since the United States is capital abundant and labor scarce, capital should favor free trade or even export expansion, and labor should favor protection. Thus, Stolper–Samuelson asserts that the lower left quadrant in Figure 7.1 will have all n industries while the other will contain none.

The Ricardo–Viner–Cairnes factor-specific model predicts sharply contrasting results. With immobility of both factors, the prices of capital and labor move with the price of industry output. Thus, capital and labor in an industry will work together on trade policy, implying that the only nonzero elements in the matrix will be in one of the two diagonal boxes: Import-competing industries will be in box 11, and the export industries will be in box 22.

The results of this test for twenty-one of the U.S. industries in Table 7.1

Table 7.1. Positions of lobbying groups on U.S. trade policy by industry

SIC	Industry	Trade balance[a]	Trade association	Position[b] Capital	Labor	Labor union
2015	Poultry	41	Poul. and Egg Instit. of Am.	F		
2026	Dairy	–1	Nat'l. Milk Prod. Fed.	P		
2085	Distilling	–416	Dist. Spirits Council	P	P	Dist., Rect., Wine and Allied Wkrs.
2092	Soybeans	320	Nat'l. Soybean Processors	F	F	
21	Tobacco	130	Tobacco Institute	P	F	Tab. Int'l. Workers Union
22	Textiles	–418	Am. Txt. Manuf. Inst.	P	P	Text. Wkrs. Union of America
23	Apparel	–486	—c	P	P	Amalg. Clothing Wkrs.
26	Paper	–632	Am. Paper Inst.	F	F	United Papers Wkrs. Int'l.
2815	Chemicals	81	Synth. Org. Chem. Manuf.	P	P–M	Int'l. Chem. Wkrs. Union
2821	Plastics	527	Society of the Plast.	P	P	United R.C.L. & Plast. Wkrs.
2911	Petroleum	–505	Am. Petrol. Inst.	F	P	Petroleum Wkrs. Union
30	Rubber	92	Rubber Manuf. Assn.	M	P–M	United Rubber Wkrs.
3021	Rubber shoes	–82	Rub. Manuf. Assn. – Footwear	P	P	United Rubber, C, L and P
31	Leather	–364	Tanners Council of Am.	P	P	Int'l. Leath. Goods Wkrs.
3141	Shoes	–471	Am. Footwear Assn.	P	P	United Shoewkrs. of America
32	Stone, etc.	12	Stone, Glass & Clay C. Comm.	P	P	United Glass & Ceramic Wkrs.
331–2	Iron/steel	–1,923	Am. Iron and Steel Inst.	P	P	IAIW and United Steelwkrs. of America
3732–3	Lead/zinc	–137	Lead/Zinc Prod. Comm.	M		
3334	Aluminum	–95	Alum Assn.	F	M	Alum. Wkrs. Int'l. Union
3421	Cutlery	–16	Nat'l. Assn. of Scissors M.	P	P?	—c
3423	Hardware	38	Bldrs. Hardw. Manuf.	P	P	Int'l. Assn. of Tool Craftsmen

35	Machinery	4,029	Mach. and Allied Prod. Inst.	F	F	Int'l. Assn. of Machinists
3522	Tractors	146	Caterpillar Tractor	F	F?	—[c]
3541	Mach. Tools	25	Nat'l. Mach. Tool Bldrs.	M	P	Int'l. Assn. of Tool Craftsmen
3562	Bearings	23	Anti Fr. Bearing Manuf.	P	P?	—[c]
3572	Bus. Eq.	-21	Comp. and BE Manuf. Assn.	P	M?	—[c]
36	Electrical	701	Nat'l. Electr. Manuf. Assn.	M	P	Int'l. Broth. of Elect. Wkrs.
3711	Cars	-1,730		F	P	United Auto Wkrs.
3713	Trucks	1,203	Hvy. Duty Truck Manuf.	F	F	Transport Wkrs U. of America
3720	Aviation	1,695	Gen. Aero Manuf. Assn.	F	F	Int'l. Assn. of Mach. and Aerospace
3751	Bicycles	-296	Cycle Parts and Acc. Assn.	P	P	
3871	Watches	-126	Am. Watch Assn.	P	P	Am. Watch Wkrs. Union
3941	Toys	-51			P	Int'l. U. of Dolls, Toys

[a]Trade balances are given in millions of dollars (1967).

[b]Positions: P = protectionist; F = free trade; M = intermediate (ambiguous).

[c]Position determined from other sources.

Source: United States Congress (1973).

Position of the Industry's Labor

	1 Protectionist	2 Free Trade
1 **Protectionist**	**1 1** distilling textiles apparel chemicals plastics rubber shoes leather shoes stone products iron & steel cutlery hardware bearings watches	**1 2** tobacco
2 **Free Trade**	**2 1** petroleum	**2 2** paper machinery tractors trucks aviation

Position
of Industry
Capital

Figure 7.2. Empirical results for lobbying on the Trade Reform Act (United States Congress 1973).

are shown in Figure 7.2. It is apparent that the data are dominant diagonal and strongly supportive of the Ricardo–Viner–Cairnes factor-specific model and reject the Stolper–Samuelson hypothesis. In only two industries do labor and management oppose each other: Management is for free trade in petroleum and protectionist in tobacco, with labor being the reverse. The petroleum industry is complicated by the split between the major oil companies and the independents, with the latter opposed to free trade. In nineteen out of twenty-one industries, labor and management work together on the question of protection. To perform a test of statistical significance would belabor the obvious.

7.3.2   Test 2: factor unanimity on policy preference

The second implication of the Stolper–Samuelson theorem is that all of labor will favor either free trade or protection (similarly for capital). We find that only 63% of the industries selected show capital supporting their preferred alternative (protectionism). Stolper–Samuelson predicts that all capital would choose one alternative or the other (100% vs. 0%) and should not split this way (63% vs. 37 %).

Consider capital: In the Appendix to this chapter, we test for statistical significance and find that, for capital, the results reject the factor-mobility hypothesis implicit in Stolper–Samuelson but cannot reject the factor-specific Ricardo–Viner–Cairnes hypothesis. The sample proportion of labor favoring protection is 0.76: Both Stolper–Samuelson and Ricardo–Viner–Cairnes are rejected, with the latter rejected more decisively. The results for labor are thus inconclusive.

7.3.3   Test 3: independence of industry location and policy preference

Test 2 indicated the degree of unanimity (or lack thereof) that a factor has for a specific trade policy. Test 3 indicates whether or not a factor prefers a policy that is beneficial to the industry in which it is currently employed. If it does, factor specificity is implied; if not, factor mobility (among other things) is more likely. Two versions of this test are conducted: The first is a proportions test; the second allows continuous variation in the industry's trade balance.

The results in the Appendix indicate that both capital and labor differ significantly from the hypothesized Stolper–Samuelson independence of lobbying positions and sectoral location. The Stolper–Samuelson theorem is refuted for capital at the 5% and labor at the 10% significance level.

A limitation of this quantitative test is that it does not consider the association between a factor's position on trade policy and the extent to which each industry is export- or import-competing. We could have remedied this problem partially by testing, for each factor, whether there are significant differences between the trade balances in industries containing free traders versus industries containing protectionists. If more positive trade balances are associated with the free trade position, we can reject the Stolper–Samuelson theorem. If there is no significant difference in the trade balances, then the positions are independent of sectoral location and we can reject Ricardo–Viner–Cairnes. We do not report the specifics of that test here. We did find that the average trade balance in industries in which capital supported free trade was $689 million; it was –$254 million if capital was protectionist. The difference was statistically significant using three different tests for equality of the trade balances of the two groups. The average trade balance in industries in which labor supported free trade was $1,985 million, whereas it was –$321 million in labor-protectionist industries. These differences were significant for two out of three of the tests. We conclude from both versions of test 3 that both capital and labor lobby for protection in ways more consistent with the Ricardo–Viner–Cairnes model.

7.4   Caveats and conclusions

Tests 1 and 3 provide refutation of Stolper–Samuelson relative to Ricardo–Viner–Cairnes. In test 2, Stolper–Samuelson was rejected for capital while labor was impossible to classify as mobile or specific; this is not inconsistent with the a priori assumptions made in early theoretical discussions by Mayer (1974) and Mussa (1974) that capital is *quasi*-fixed in the short run relative to labor. What conclusions are we to derive from these results?

Although this chapter provides a fascinating exercise, we do not reject the Stolper–Samuelson theorem based on these results. The Stolper–Samuelson theorem is a long-run proposition; trade policy lobbying in the United States is a short-term phenomenon. Since 1934, U.S. trade bills have been subject to congressional renewal every three to five years. These short time horizons clearly bias the tests toward spurious rejection of the Stolper–Samuelson theorem. As we watch the free-trade behavior of the U.S. multinational corporations and the protectionist (and immigration-restrictionist) moves of American labor since World War II, it is clear that the Stolper–Samuelson theorem is a useful guide to the long-run political interests of American capital and labor.

As American industries age, the comparative advantage of the United States in heavily capital-intensive industries has been diminished by the Far Eastern countries, but not reversed. Vis-à-vis most countries of the world, it is still true that America's most abundant factors are physical and human capital. Our work in Part II of this book builds on this fact.

CHAPTER 8

The invisible foot and the waste of nations: lawyers as negative externalities

Adam Smith's invisible hand symbolizes the unseen benefits that economic competition confers on the coordination of economic activity. The "invisible foot" developed here symbolizes the unseen costs that redistributive activity imposes on an economy. It captures the negative welfare effects of competition over distributive shares. The adjective in the label emphasizes the difficulties of observation, quantification, and measurement. This chapter is an extension of the ideas in Mancur Olson's *The Rise and Decline of Nations* (1982). In general, we agree with Olson's view that redistributive lobbying leads to institutional sclerosis and economic waste. However, the economic effects of redistributive activity are more complicated than he envisioned.

The following topics are covered in this chapter:

8.1.   a review of the literature;
8.2.   legal activity redistributing wealth;
8.3.   legal activity redistributing income in a static model;
8.4.   legal activity redistributing income in a dynamic model; and
8.5.   evidence on the negative effect of lawyers on economic growth.

We investigate the effects of redistributive activity at the individual level. We assume that there are two classes of labor in an economy: One is productive, the other redistributive. Think of the former as engineers and the latter as redistributive lawyers. What are the economic effects of increases in the number of lawyers relative to engineers? Our intuition tells us that economic

Chapter 8 in Stephen P. Magee, William A. Brock, and Leslie Young, *Black Hole Tariffs and Endogenous Policy Theory*. New York: Cambridge University Press, 1989. Adapted from William A. Brock and Stephen P. Magee, "The Invisible Foot and the Waste of Nations," in David C. Colander, ed., *Neoclassical Political Economy*. Cambridge, Mass.: Ballinger, 1984, pp. 177–85.

performance should decline. This is true in the long run; however, this need not occur in the short run. This chapter develops the counterintuitive result that economic performance can improve temporarily as a result of increased legal activity. The effects depend, in part, on whether redistributive activity is directed toward income or wealth. To illustrate this we develop here three models of redistributive lawyering: Model 1 investigates wealth redistribution, and models 2 and 3 develop income redistribution. This chapter extends earlier theoretical work on the Olson hypothesis by Hicks (1983) and Mueller (1983). See also Wellisz and Findlay (1988).

We demonstrate the difficulty of observing invisible foot behavior by providing examples of economies with an Olson scenario but with opposite effects; for instance, in model 1 we find that increases in labor devoted to wealth redistribution can increase (rather than decrease) GNP and GNP growth. An example of this phenomenon is an attorney who is paid a contingency fee of, say, one-third of the wealth that he or she successfully transfers from one individual to another. The attorney's fee is a transformation of wealth into income, and if this fee exceeds what the attorney would have earned in nonredistributive activities (which it will), such predatory behavior increases measured GNP in the short run. Successful quantification of this effect would require better measurements of wealth than we now have.

Model 2 analyzes income redistribution in a static world, and model 3 analyzes dynamic income redistribution. Both models are formalizations of an Olson approach. In some cases they reinforce his points; in others, they conflict with his views. There are four major results in model 2. First, as in model 1, large and positive growth rates of GNP are compatible with growth of redistributive activity. Second, the growth rates of productive and redistributive activity converge in the long run. Third, a negative association between growth rates of GNP and growth in redistributive activity is most likely early in the redistributive process rather than later. This conflicts both with Olson's view that negative correlation occurs in older economies, and with model 1, in which negative correlation occurs in "middle-aged" economies. Fourth, model 2 is consistent with redistributive activity being countercyclical over the business cycle.

Model 3 explores income redistribution in an intertemporal model. First, we find that the more wealthy an economy, the more resources will be devoted to redistribution. Our result may be difficult to separate empirically from Olson's thesis that redistributive battles increase with the age of the economy. In our model, the result comes from the first-order condition showing that more labor will be devoted to redistribution the higher the capital stock. In other words, redistributive conflict over shares increases with the size of the pie. This emerges despite our behavioral specification that redistributive activity is directed at income rather than capital. We speculate that care must be exercised in empirical work to disentangle Olson effects (old economies growing slower because of redistributive entanglements) from normal diminishing returns to capital (old economies having slower growth of the capital stock and hence slower GNP growth).

Second, the intertemporal equilibrium demonstrates clearly our assumption of arbitrage between productive and redistributive activity. In equilibrium, identical workers will be indifferent between devoting their efforts to productive versus redistributive activities. This causes the equilibrium proportion of the labor force devoted to redistribution to be inversely related to the wage rate.

A third and unexpected result of dynamic income redistribution is that the equilibrium capital–labor ratio is independent of the level of redistributive activity. This occurs because redistribution reduces GNP, the capital stock, and the labor force by the same proportion in the long run in model 3; thus, the ratios of any two of the three variables are unaffected. The result implies that if we attempted to correlate some independent measure of redistribution with capital–labor ratios across economies, we should find no relationship. Fourth, as in the previous models, there is no association between growth rates of economic variables and redistributive waste in the long run.

The three models suggest that the relationship between GNP growth rates and redistributive activity is subtle and not easily predicted by ad hoc intuition. We are not surprised at Pryor's (1983, 1984) empirical rejections of the Olson growth rate hypothesis.

These theoretical results notwithstanding, the final section of the chapter reports some empirical results showing that GNP growth across thirty-four countries in the period 1960–80 is negatively correlated with the ratio of lawyers to physicians.

8.1   The literature

The idea that redistributive activity can lead to the maximum level of waste is pursued formally in Chapter 15 (on black hole tariffs). Here we address the measurement problem. Becker and Stigler (1974) argue correctly that the cost of litigation is simply a transaction cost that an orderly society must bear to ascertain facts, reduce doubts, and resolve conflicts. However, they go too far in stating that "the view of enforcement and litigation as wasteful in whole or in part is simply mistaken" (p. 16). Our view is that rules are a public good whereas redistributive activities confer private benefits: The usual underprovision of public goods dictates that conformity to rules will be underprovided and redistributive activity will be overprovided. In fact, lobbying and rent seeking are ways that groups attempt to convert rules into private goods. The conflict between private rationality (redistribution) and collective goods is resolved in the Prisoner's Dilemma case (see Chapter 10) by the Pareto-inferior outcome of excessive redistributive competition.

On the growth of government see Foley (1978), Lindbeck (1985a, 1987), Meltzer and Richard (1981), Peltzman (1980), Spann (1977), and Worth (1984). For articles on growth theory see Barry (1986), Johansen (1960), and Kormendi and Meguire (1984a). On economic growth see Barry (1986) and Rostow (1960, 1962, 1971, 1975, 1978, 1980, 1982). This chapter measures the effects of redistributive activity on the growth of economic productivity. On the subject of productivity measurement see Rees (1980). The measures of the number of lawyers per economy were derived from studies by Dunn (1983) and Neville (1986). For an extension of Olson's work on the effects of redistributive activity on economic growth see Olson and Landsberg (1973). For a discussion of slow growth in the United States see Dunn (1980). Persson and Wissen (1984) studied tax evasion and argue that the distribution of total income (taking all redistributed activity into account) is more unevenly distributed than is measured income. Lasswell (1974) notes that legal activity is essentially a private good. The contribution of our adversarial legal system to economic efficiency is declining because of the free-rider problem.

8.2   Model 1: wealth redistribution

Olson (1982) argues that over time GNP growth will fall for two reasons in invisible foot economies: because resources are being removed from productive activity and because perverse policies lead to economic sclerosis and inefficiency. This chapter deals with the first of these two. The perverse economic effects of redistribution can be harder to detect than Olson imagined. In some cases, increased redistributive action can actually lead to an increase in the level of GNP and in a country's growth rate.

To see this, let us first assume that redistributive activity is directed at wealth rather than income. Assume that the total labor supply T follows one of two activities: L is engaged in productive activity while R pursues redistributive activity.

$$T = L + R \tag{8.1}$$

Productive labor helps produce economic income, whereas redistributive labor transfers it from one member of society to another. This process is determined by an exogenous social technology of law, accounting, economics, and tradition. We also assume that all redistributed wealth is converted to income. Total income Y in the invisible foot economy then comes from two sources – economic income F and redistributive income Kr:

$$Y = F(K,L) + Kr(R) \qquad (8.2)$$

where

K,L = capital and labor in production;
r = fraction of capital that is redistributed each period and converted to income; and
R = labor engaged in redistributing capital.

In contrast, total income in the invisible hand economy can be written

$$Y = F(K,T) \qquad (8.3)$$

Assume that the two economies have identical labor forces and identical capital stocks. From Eqs. (8.2) and (8.3) it is clear that the hand economy will have more economic income because $T > L$, but the foot economy will have positive redistributive income (if $r > 0$) because redistribution converts parts of the capital stock back into income each period. *GNP and GNP per capita can be higher* in the invisible foot economy. This should be true if r is sufficiently high and early in the redistribution phase. Consider the transfer of one unit of labor from economic activity to redistributive activity in equation (8.2), starting at a low R. The labor would not have made the transition voluntarily unless the income it received from redistribution exceeded the foregone wage. But this is the very condition that guarantees that the transfer to redistribution increases GNP. This result ignores defensive actions by the redistributees to prevent the transfer: These may or may not provide an offset to the income-increasing effect. If people finance their redistribution defenses out of wealth rather than income, this too increases measured GNP, at the expense of wealth (e.g., the income of locksmiths and defense attorneys appears in national income).

Another result that emerges from this simple framework is that, early in the redistribution period, *wages are higher and returns to capital are lower* in the invisible foot economy (when compared to an invisible hand economy with an identical capital stock and total labor force). Since there is less labor in economic production, the capital–labor ratio is higher, the marginal product of capital is lower, and the marginal product of labor is higher in the foot economy. Thus, any economy with increasing redistributive activity should show a rise in wages relative to rentals and *factors market pressures for labor immigration and capital emigration.*

What are the effects of redistribution on growth? Consider the growth rates of income in two economies, each starting with identical stocks of capital and labor with identical production and redistribution technologies. Invisible foot economies entering periods of wasteful redistribution will have *unambigu-*

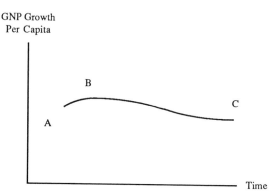

Figure 8.1. Effects of legal redistributive activity on per capita GNP growth over time.

ously higher growth rates of GNP than invisible hand economies. The reason is simple: Collectors of GNP statistics value all services at the amount the wage earner receives. They do not ask whether redistributive services were socially productive, nor do they inquire whether wealth was extinguished to pay them. In the United States, it is illegal for lawyers and criminals not to report their successful redistributive ventures as taxable income. We do not know the extent to which transfers of wealth into criminal income are counted in U.S. GNP.

Early in invisible foot economies, we find that *GNP growth rates will be higher the more rapid the growth of labor in the redistributive sector*; that is, so long as the economy's redistribution equilibrium in labor markets has not yet been reached. Early in the redistributive process, the marginal payoff to entering redistribution will also increase with the capital stock. In many cases, *capital-abundant economies will demonstrate more rapid growth with increasing redistribution than labor-abundant economies.*

Once the proportion of the labor force devoted to redistribution has grown sufficiently in the invisible foot economy, diminishing returns to redistribution will lead to an equilibrium in labor markets. The marginal returns from redistributive activity will equal those in economic activity; that is, the salaries of marginal lawyers will equal those of marginal engineers. Late in the short run of the redistributive process, the growth rate of GNP in the invisible hand economies may be above or below that in invisible foot economies. The invisible foot economies are aided by the growth of income due to the consumption of the capital stock, but the GNP growth rate is reduced because the capital stock growth is retarded by redistributive activity. Of course, the capital stock declines every period by the amount of redistribution.

These theoretical effects of legal redistributive activity on GNP growth are shown in Figure 8.1. In the short run, redistributive activity increases GNP growth (region AB). When the medium run arrives, there should be a negative effect of legal activity on GNP growth (region BC). In section 8.4 we shall see that legal activity should have no discernible effect in the long run (to the right of C).

8.3   Model 2: static income redistribution

In this model, we assume that each individual must allocate some fraction of his (or her) effort between economic and redistributive activity. However, the returns to his own redistributive activity are a decreasing function of the amount of redistributive activity being done by others (reflecting diminishing returns and the negative-sum nature of the game). The situation is analogous to an arms race or a Prisoner's Dilemma (see Chapter 10 for Prisoner's Dilemma outcomes in lobbying equilibria over tariff setting).

By definition, observable GNP is equal to all earnings of labor, both productive and redistributive. The mathematical analysis of this model in the Appendix yields four conclusions. First, in the short run, just about any patterns of rates of growth of real output are possible. As in the first model, large positive rates of growth of GNP are compatible with large positive rates of growth of both productive activity and redistributive activity.

Second, consider the class of cases in which the share of labor devoted to redistribution stabilizes through time. Here, too, the share of GNP going to redistribution settles down in the long run. Then, the growth of productive and redistributive labor will be the same, as will, therefore, the growth of economic activity and redistributive activity in the long run.

Third, any negative association between rates of growth of redistribution and rates of growth of economic activity is more likely to show up in young countries. This is the reverse of the results of both our model 1 and Olson (the latter's result being that older countries display slower growth because of redistribution).

Fourth, this model is consistent with the stylized fact of the redistributive activity being countercyclical. As an economy goes into recession, there is a decline in the rewards of production relative to redistributive activity (see the compensation effect in Chapter 11). Hence, the proportion of labor devoted to redistribution rises in troughs and falls in peaks of business activity.

8.4   Model 3: dynamic income redistribution

We explore next the economic impact of income redistribution in an intertemporal model. We assume that N homogeneous individual households maximize their life-cycle utility. Assume that the households are homogeneous and have time-stationary preferences. Production is assumed to occur under constant returns, there is no technical progress, and there is no population growth.

A first result is that *the long-run capital labor ratio is independent of redistributive activity*. In other words, the steady-state capital–labor ratios of redistribution-prone economies, such as the United Kingdom, should equal those of presumably more efficient economies, such as Japan (holding other factors, such as country age, constant). Although the national capital stock and national output are smaller in invisible foot economies, so is the amount of labor devoted to productive activity. *In equilibrium, the fraction of redistributive waste is the same for labor, capital, and national income.*

Second, *economies with higher ratios of capital incomes rK to labor income in the productive sector wL have higher propensities to redistribute.* Thus, a high-capital-income economy has to invest more to protect its capital. Therefore, waste and wealth should be positively correlated, giving an alternative explanation to Olson's for greater redistribution in wealthier economies. *The larger the pie, the larger the fraction of labor devoted to fighting over shares of the pie.* The more wealth in an economy, the more resources are used in protecting wealth from redistribution. Both offensive and defensive activity increase with the amount of wealth at stake. Thus, *increasing criminal and predatory redistributive legal activity may be a necessary evil in advanced capitalistic societies.*

Third, in the steady state all growth rates will be the same. Hence, *there is no association between growth rates of economic variables and redistributive waste in the long run.*

8.5   Empirical evidence: the negative effect of lawyers on country economic growth

Is there any evidence that redistributive lawyering reduces GNP growth rates? We examine the data on this question as well as correlations between lawyers per capita and the level of protection for thirty-four countries. Figure 8.2 shows a plot of lawyers per physician versus the

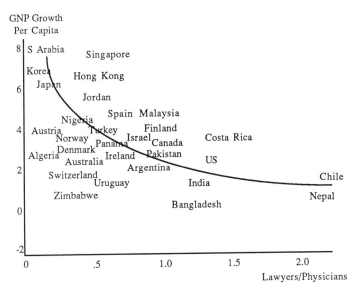

Figure 8.2. GNP growth per capita during 1960–80 versus the ratio of lawyers to physicians.

growth of GNP per capita over the period 1960–80. We had to normalize by physicians because lawyers and other white collar workers are stage-of-development dependent: The higher the GNP per capita of the country, the larger the proportion of both of these groups in the labor force. Apparently, the normalization succeeded: Our ratio of lawyers per physician is uncorrelated with GNP per capita across countries. We would have preferred to normalize by engineers, but the engineer data have been harder to obtain. The data on lawyers come from studies by Dunn (1983) and Neville (1986), who obtained it from the International Bar Directory (1985); see Table 8.1.

Notice the negative correlation: The more lawyers per doctor, the lower the country's per capita growth rate. There are only six countries in the figure with more lawyers than doctors: The United States and India are included in this group. Appendix Figure A.8.3 shows that individual rent seeking appears to be correlated with protection: High-tariff countries also have more lawyers. An important area for future research is quantification of the negative externality imposed by legal redistributive activity.

Table 8.1. *Lawyers and physicians*

Country	Growth in GNP	Population (1980) (millions)	Ratio of population to physicians	No. of physicians (1980)	Ratio of lawyers (1983) to doctors (1980)	No. of lawyers (1965)	No. of lawyers (1983)	GDP (1985)
Algeria	3.2	18.9	2,630	7,186	0.11	80	800	58,180
Argentina	2.2	27.7	430	64,419	0.78	12,000	50,000	65,920
Australia	2.7	14.5	560	25,893	0.27		7,068	162,490
Austria	4.1	7.5	400	18,750	0.12	200	2,200	66,050
Bangladesh	0.0	88.5	10,940	8,090	1.11	8,000	9,000	16,110
Belgium	3.8	9.8	400	24,500	0.5	5,600	12,300	79,080
Canada	3.3	23.9	550	43,455	0.92	14,100	40,000	346,030
Chile	1.6	11.1	1,930	5,751	2.14	5,000	12,300	16,000
Costa Rica	3.2	2.2	1,460	1,507	1.3	723	1,959	3,810
Denmark	3.3	5.1	480	10,625	0.28	2,250	3,000	57,840
Finland	4.0	4.9	530	9,245	0.97	4,475	9,000	54,030
France	3.9	53.5	580	92,241	0.3	14,900	27,215	510,320
Germany	3.3	60.9	450	135,333	0.32	24,300	43,100	624,970
Hong Kong	6.8	5.1	1,210	4,215	0.32	346	1,332	30,730
India	1.4	673.2	3,690	182,439	1.23	70,000	225,000	175,710
Ireland	3.1	3.3	780	4,231	0.59	1,300	2,500	18,430
Israel	3.8	3.9	370	10,541	0.71	3,500	7,500	20,270
Italy	3.6	56.9	340	167,353	0.28	39,400	46,600	358,670
Japan	7.1	116.8	780	149,744	0.09	8,800	14,000	1,327,900
Jordan	5.7	3.2	1,700	1,882	0.37	400	700	3,450
Malaysia	4.3	13.9	7,910	1,757	0.74	750	1,300	31,270

Country								
Nepal	0.2	14.5	30,060	482	2.07		1,000	2,340
Netherlands	3.2	14.1	540	26,111	0.15	2,270	4,000	124,970
Nigeria	4.1	84.7	12,500	6,776	0.3		2,000	75,300
Norway	3.5	4.1	520	7,885	0.27	1,650	2,100	57,910
Pakistan	2.8	82.2	3,480	23,621	0.93	11,000	22,000	28,240
Panama	3.3	1.8	980	1,837	0.49		900	4,880
Singapore	7.5	2.4	1,150	2,087	0.47	300	990	17,470
Spain	4.5	37.4	460	81,304	0.68	30,000	55,000	164,250
Switzerland	1.9	6.5	410	15,854	0.21	2,100	3,300	92,690
Turkey	3.6	44.9	1,630	27,546	0.65	10,000	18,000	48,820
U.K.	2.2	55.9	650	86,000	0.62	29,500	53,000	454,300
U.S.	2.3	227.7	520	437,885	1.29	355,000	565,000	3,946,600
Uruguay	0.7	7.4	6,580	1,125	0.27	200	300	4,530

Sources: For the lawyer data see Dunn (1983), International Bar Directory (1985), and Neville (1986). The remaining data come from the World Bank (1982 and subsequent annual reports).

CHAPTER 9

The $2 \times 2 \times 2 \times 2$ model of endogenous redistribution theory

Part I of this book was about endogenous lobbying and endogenous politics in partial equilibrium. There two lobbies channeled resources in a self-interested way to a protectionist and a proexport political party. The parties exploited voter ignorance by using resources from the lobbies to advertise and get elected. In Part I, the structure of the economy was unspecified. In Part II, we attach a general equilibrium trading economy to the political apparatus developed in Part I.

The $2 \times 2 \times 2 \times 2$ model is a general equilibrium endogenous policy model of redistribution with two goods, two factors, two lobbies, and two political parties, with all actors pursuing their own interests. We have a choice of whether to use a short-run or a long-run model to describe the economy. Following the arguments in Chapter 7, it appears that a short-run model would be best for describing lobbying behavior. However, there are two reasons for not taking a short-term approach. First, our interest is in long-run policy behavior within an economy and in the levels of protection across economies. The levels of total protection change slowly over time. Second, we noted in Chapter 7 that those tests of the Stolper–Samuelson theorem were biased toward short-run results because of the short time horizons and periodic renewal of U.S. trade legislation. For these and other reasons, we take a long-run approach to the specification of the economic side of the country in Part II of the book.

Chapter 9 in Stephen P. Magee, William A. Brock, and Leslie Young, *Black Hole Tariffs and Endogenous Policy Theory*. New York: Cambridge University Press, 1989. Adapted from Stephen P. Magee and William A. Brock, "A Model of Politics, Tariffs and Rent Seeking in General Equilibrium," in Burton Weisbrod and Helen Hughes, eds., *Human Resources, Employment and Development. Vol. 3: The Problems of Developed Countries and the International Economy*. Proceedings of the Sixth World Congress of the International Economic Association held in Mexico City, 1980. London: Macmillan, 1983, pp. 497–523.

We describe the economic behavior of a country by the standard neoclassical Heckscher–Ohlin–Samuelson two-factor, two-commodity model. All of the actors in our model maximize their welfare. Each factor of production receives its marginal product in competitive factor markets; each lobby maximizes the returns to the factor of production it represents; each party maximizes its probability of election by its optimal choice of a redistributive policy variable; and voters are rationally ignorant in that they underinvest in information. Our probabilistic voting function assumes that voters pick the party that provides them with the most favorable information–policy trade-off.

Given this framework, we derive the equilibrium values of both commercial policies (a tariff and an export subsidy), the equilibrium amounts of capital and labor removed from the private economy to engage in lobbying, and the equilibrium probability of election of both parties. The equilibrium distribution of income between capital and labor is also determined. In deriving these results, we assume that no single factor of production has a majority of voters. Thus, each redistributive policy redistributes income to a minority of voters (i.e., all of those individuals constituting the factor of production that lobbies for this policy). With only two factors, one of the two should always have a majority of the electorate and dominate the political contest. However, special-interest politics, by definition, involves minorities of the electorate exploiting large disorganized groups. Our assumption would be more realistic in a three-or-more-factor model. It was made with the feeling that the increased voter realism of a three-factor model is not worth the additional computational complexity.

Each factor of production is represented by a lobby that contributes economic resources to a political party. This party supports an economic policy that alters relative product prices in a manner benefiting the real income of the sponsoring factor. As before, we assume that American labor would support the House Democrats, who sponsor a tariff on imports of labor-intensive goods, whereas capital would support the House Republicans, who sponsor a subsidy on exports of capital-intensive goods. Republicans also support policies that increase the profits of U.S. multinational corporations, the latter representing the highest expression of the U.S. comparative advantage in skilled labor. Each policy benefits its respective factor of production more (1) the more efficacious its lobby at channeling economic resources to the party sponsoring the policy and (2) the lower the voter's perceived economic cost of the policy.

In what follows we consider almost exclusively "unpopular redistributive policies" (ones benefiting only a minority of the electorate). Voters are assumed to act rationally. Unpopular policies exist because they are necessary for the provision of a quid pro quo (such as information) and because voters are rationally uninformed. Because public funds underprovide voters with information, each party will seek its own clientele of organized supporters. How and why certain historical patterns of lobby–party specialization develop is beyond the scope of this book. Although the information-redistributive policy quid pro quo is admittedly a second-best situation, voters actually gain from increases in redistributive policies so long as the marginal benefit of the information they receive exceeds the marginal economic cost of the distortion. If the resources provided by lobbies are used for bribes and chicanery rather than to provide information to voters, then the voter gains from lobbying are exaggerated.

For general equilibrium, as in partial equilibrium, each lobby follows the "contribution specialization" theorem, specializing its economic resource contributions on the party providing it the highest real income. Because the economy under consideration is like the United States and is capital-abundant (including human capital), it conforms to the Heckscher–Ohlin theorem and exports the capital-intensive good. The specialization theorem implies that the capital lobby contributes only to Republicans and the labor lobby contributes only to Democrats. Since this is not a monetary model (as was the case in Part I), we simplify it by assuming that the capital lobby gives only physical capital to Republicans and the labor lobby gives only labor to Democrats.

Because of the voter information–social cost trade-off, the two parties do not adopt identical policies à la Hotelling. Because it is difficult for voters to understand (and for economists to measure) the economic costs of distortionary policies, we assume that voters are not sophisticated enough to make second-best policy judgments. We assume that voters oppose increases in any redistributive policy, based in first-best reasoning.

Why do parties pick tariffs and indirect means to redistribute income rather than direct factor subsidies? Because each party will pick the redistributive policy whose optimum value maximizes the party's probability of election, vis-à-vis a given lobby. But what are the calculations underlying *which* policy is chosen? Assume that, because of information costs, the *perceived* distortionary costs to voters of redistributive policies are lower the more indirect the policy. Now, arrange the redistributive policies that benefit a lobby from the most direct policy to the most indirect, with each policy set at the value that maximizes the probability of election of the sponsoring party. Each party will follow a "principle of optimal obfuscation" in choosing its policy; it will move toward a more indirect policy so long as the increased probability of election from increased voter obfuscation exceeds the decreased probability of election emanating from lesser lobbying resources (caused by the adoption of a more indirect policy). This principle explains the apparent preference of Western democracies for indirect redistributive policies. We argue that Bhagwati's efficiency rankings of policies from most direct to most indirect would be the politically preferred ranking only in countries where a single factor of production had a majority of the votes. For special-interest policies, the principle of optimal obfuscation suggests the reversal of Bhagwati's rankings.

Assume that Democrats have settled on a tariff as their preferred policy and that Republicans have picked an export subsidy. The equilibrium probability-of-election-maximizing tariff rate for the Democrats is one that balances at the margin the favorable voter effect of resource flows against the negative voter reaction to the distortionary policy. We assume, as in Part I, that political markets clear more rapidly than economic markets; hence economic resources are allocated at the *expected value* of domestic relative product prices (which incorporate election probabilities and equilibrium party positions on tariffs and export subsidies). This assumption is justified if elections occur frequently and the economic adjustment process is slow, or if we interpret the probability of electoral success more broadly to include not just elections but all legislative votes, judicial decisions, and bureaucratic acts that affect the two policies. The assumption also simplifies the model by avoiding distinctions between *ex ante* and *ex post* (pre- and postelection) equilibria. Another important point is that our ex ante equilibrium is the proper long-run view of protection, since we have a long-run economic model.

Once a party has chosen its redistributive policy, the party's optimal (probability-of-election-maximizing) value of that policy is that which maximizes the expected difference between the value of the information to voters and its perceived cost to them. Notice that voter welfare could actually increase above the free trade (no distortion) level if the value to voters of the information that political advertising provides were large enough to offset the policy distortion costs and the lobbying costs.

Political advertising is like product market advertising: Some is redistributive and wasteful, and some is beneficial. It is difficult to separate welfare-increasing political advertising from the rest. For this reason, we do not attempt such a separation in this book.

The results above are built upon our equilibrium concept that political parties are Stackelberg leaders vis-à-vis the other actors. If neither the political parties nor the lobbies attempt to "game" the other group's behavior, then free trade will be the outcome: The parties will choose equilibrium tariffs and export subsidies equal to zero. In Part II we continue the assumption that party competition will drive the parties to Stackelberg leadership. Given this assumption, we find in Chapter 10 precise conditions under which redistributive policies and lobbying will and will not emerge.

The model determines the equilibrium level of lobbying, the probabilities of party success, the equilibrium distribution of factor incomes, and so on. The last is determined simultaneously with all of the others. In contrast to Marx, this model provides "symmetric exploitation." There appears to be no a priori reason why one factor's political exploitation via lobbying will succeed any more than the other in general equilibrium. Capital and labor engage in economic conflict, but in democracies the battles are carried out via the lobbies. In general, capital has an advantage in raising funds, whereas labor has the advantage of superior numbers at the polls. Capital is not alone in its political exploitation of labor: Both capital and labor will exploit one another through the political system until a redistributive equilibrium is reached. In such an equilibrium, neither factor is willing to devote additional energy to exploitation because the expected benefits are lower than the costs.

Our intuition tells us that lobbying has negative effects on overall welfare. The primary cause of tariffs and other special-interest policies is lobbying to achieve domestic redistribution. In a two-factor model, if neither capital nor labor lobbies, both would usually be better off than if both lobby. However, if either lobbies while the other does not, the lobbyer gains the most. Like arms races, lobbying and competition over shares of the pie are ultimately a negative-sum game. This Prisoner's Dilemma view of protection is modeled explicitly in Chapter 10.

Before proceeding, consider the three major sets of actors. The simplest equilibrium concept linking the economy, voters, lobbies, and political parties would be Cournot–Nash; that is, the actor in each subsystem would take as fixed the policies of the other actors. This is reasonable for the private economy because production is atomistic; hence producers can be assumed to take domestic product prices as given. Similarly, voters are atomistic and face high information costs vis-à-vis both lobbies and political parties. However, the two large lobbies and the two political parties possess discretionary power: The lobbies can affect political outcomes by their allocations of resources, and the parties can affect the distribution of income by their choices of policies. For this reason, we assume that both the lobbies and the parties act as Stackelberg leaders vis-à-vis the economy and voters.

Our decision to continue the assumption in Part II that the political parties Stackelberg-lead vis-à-vis the lobbies (rather than vice versa) is supported in general equilibrium by several considerations. There are higher barriers to entry for parties than for lobbies; the goals of lobbies are more transparent than those of parties; there is a broader range of policy tools available to political parties to affect redistribution (limited, in fact, only by the human imagination) compared to the tools available to lobbies to affect political outcomes; and, significantly, the political system sets, enforces, and adjudicates the rules under which the lobbies operate.

Finally, recall that the model can be summarized by enumerating three layers of actors – (1) the parties, (2) the lobbies, and (3) the economy and voters – and notice that, as in Part I, each layer internalizes the optimal behavior of layers below it. For a summary of this logic see the discussion of Figure 3.2 in Chapter 3.

9.1   The literature

One difference between an export subsidy and a tariff is that the former is an explicit form of public redistribution whereas the latter is implicit. Since explicit redistributions are easier to detect by voters, export subsidies are less common than import protection.

In a frictionless economy, the determinants of the distribution of income are (1) the ownership of the factors of production and (2) the prices of final products (see Dantzig 1975). Factor prices and factor incomes will be determined by competition and the technology of production. In our model, each factor uses part of its resources to alter product prices through political lobbying for protection, export subsidies, and so on.

An important inspiration for our general equilibrium $2 \times 2 \times 2 \times 2$ model is the work of Findlay and Wellisz (1982, 1983). However, since protection is very much a long-term phenomenon, we choose not to use their short-run model. The approach in Part II of this book is to build a political economy model based on long-run economic behavior. For the development of the Heckscher–Ohlin theory with market power see Staiger (1985). The emphasis in general equilibrium is on commodity prices and factor prices [see, for example, Cassing (1981)]. For a model developing the relationship between fiscal policy and the Heckscher–Ohlin model see Barry (1987). Hamilton and Svensson (1984) find that a Jones–Krueger many-commodity, many-country formulation of the Heckscher–Ohlin–Samuelson model received considerable empirical support, except in the case of Australia.

By focusing on tariffs and export subsidies, we are really analyzing changes in a single relative price. The idea that protection implicitly taxes exporters whereas export subsidies implicitly tax import-competing firms has been around since Lerner (1936). For a recent study see Clements and Sjaastad (1984). For the rather complicated relationship between product prices and factor prices with many goods and factors see Cassing (1981), Jones (1979), and Jones and Scheinkman (1977).

Helleiner (1977) studied Canada's tariff structure using time series data for 1961–70. He found that labor favored protection whereas multinationals favored free trade. This supports the assumption underlying Part II of this book; namely, that capital will favor export subsidies and labor will favor protection. Casual observation in the United States yields a similar view: U.S. multinationals and human capital gain from freer trade and even greater exports whereas unskilled labor benefits from protection. A broad view of trade policy is advanced by Cooper (1987), who argues that U.S. tariff policy was driven by redistributive considerations primarily in the period 1920–34. Since then, trade policy became increasingly general-interest in scope (similar to macroeconomic policy) or an extension of other foreign policy.

For studies of the relationship between tariffs and labor see Ball (1967) and Constantopolous (1974). For a study of how protection helps labor in eight advanced countries see Anderson and Baldwin (1981). Conybeare (1984b) shows that protection favors labor in Australia. On general equilibrium models of tariffs, though generally not in a political economy framework, see Boadway and Treddenick (1978), Deardorff and Stern (1978, 1979, 1981, 1983, 1984a,b), and Evans (1971). On export subsidies see Fleisig and Hill (1982) and Mutti (1982).

For a study of subsidies in international trade see Hufbauer and Erb (1984). For a good analysis of the export–import bank in the United States see Baron (1983). For an interesting discussion of trade theories see Johns (1985). Grilli (1980) found that Italian industries were subsidized by the government to keep them from pushing for protection.

Recall from Chapter 5 that Director's Law states that public expenditures are for the benefit of the middle class but funded by taxes levied on the rich and the poor (see Stigler 1970a). For discussions of income distribution see Goldberg (1977), Lindbeck (1985a), and Sen (1973, 1981). Goldstein (1986) states that escape clause recipients in the United States tend to be relatively well off – a comment made about the U.S. farm program.

Bauer, de Sola Pool, and Dexter (1963) found that the United States generated an asymmetry favoring tariffs rather than export subsidies. Mainly, the prospect of a loss created by foreign imports stimulates more political action than the prospect of gain through expanded exports. As an aside, this result would be predicted by declining marginal utility and initially identical incomes. When Bauer et al. surveyed business executives, they found sentiment favoring expanded trade 3 to 1; however, they discovered that letters to members of Congress ran 2 to 1 against freer trade.

Rosen (1980) examines the effect of price incentives on factor supplies. He finds that the effect of the net wage upon the hours of work is significant for married women but insignificant for prime-age males.

9.2   The economy

The mathematics of the model are outlined in the Appendix. We use a standard "two-by-two" pure trade model producing two goods by two factors of production. To simplify, we assume that this economy is small, so that world prices are unaffected by its behavior. A useful extension of this work would be to analyze this model in a large economy. Production of the two goods, X and Y, is linearly homogeneous in the two inputs, capital and labor. Profit maximization and competition dictate that each industry earns competitive returns.

We deviate from the standard economic treatment by suggesting that factors of production will be devoted both to economic activities (producing goods X and Y) and to political activities (devoting capital and labor to politics). Since we take a long-run view, full employment holds. Real income available to consumers, evaluated at world prices, equals the value of their production plus their receipts of tariff revenue on imports, expressed in terms of good X. Consumption of the two goods (X^c and Y^c) plus resources transferred to the government (lump sum) to fund the export subsidy is assumed to satisfy the budget constraint. The utility of identical and homothetic consumers is maximized, yielding the usual competitive product market equilibria. When goods markets clear, exports of X (E) and imports of Y (M) equal the difference between domestic demand and supply for each of the products. When all markets clear, both trade and the government budget are balanced.

We assume that the country is capital-abundant and conforms to the Heckscher–Ohlin theorem; thus, the country has a comparative advantage in the export of good X, the capital-intensive good. It also conforms to the Stolper–Samuelson theorem in that increases in P^d lead to rises in the price of good Y domestically, and this raises the real wage, since good Y is labor-intensive.

Finally, we define the link between the domestic relative price of Y and the international price. This link is determined by the equilibrium values of the commercial policy variables (the export subsidy on good X and the import tariff on good Y) and the probabilities of election of the two parties. The higher the equilibrium tariff, the higher the domestic price ratio P^d of the labor-intensive good; the higher the equilibrium export subsidy, the lower the domestic price ratio.

An important economic consideration underlies the model. If the economy adjusted rapidly to elections, the economy would face a high relative price of labor-intensive goods when the prolabor protectionist party was in office and a low price when the procapital party was in office. This is unsatisfactory for a model describing long-run political equilibria; thus we assume that the political market clears more frequently than the economic market, so that the economy stays at the long-run "expected value" of the relative goods prices. If one thinks of the probability of success of the protectionist party in the broader context of all bureaucratic decisions, court decisions, and legislative decisions on protection, then the ex ante approach is reasonable. Also, if political decisions occur frequently, then this formalization is appropriate.

9.3   The voters

We assume that each voter acts rationally (in his or her own self-interest) in not investing in information about political issues. We describe voter behavior using the probabilistic voting function developed in Part I.

Recall that, in that formulation, voters know that special-interest policies are bad and their opposition increases continuously with the level of the policy. For example, voters will oppose a 20% tariff with approximately twice the vehemence of a 10% tariff. Similarly, voters are twice as likely to vote for a party with a $100 million advertising budget versus one with a $50 million budget. There are four issues with respect to voter behavior: probabilistic voting, trade policies as unpopular issues, the information–social cost trade-off, and single-peaked preferences.

9.3.1   The probabilistic voting model

Voter information costs and free-rider problems explain why voters leave information-gathering and policy-making processes to intermediaries such as political parties. The amount of information increases with the resources provided to the party by the lobby, and the social costs of each policy increase with the level of the distortion. Thus, each party provides one distortionary policy and collects resources from one factor of production's lobby; these are used to gather and disseminate favorable information about the sponsoring party and unfavorable information about the other party and lobby.

We could generalize the process to many factors, many parties, and many lobbies. In our framework, modeling would require as many parties and policies as there are lobbies. However, in Part II we deal with only two parties and two policies. Since the export subsidy is a negative tariff, the analytical problem is really one-dimensional. The game is played over a single relative price: the price of importables relative to exportables. By the contribution specialization theorem, each lobby contributes to only one political party. To simplify the exposition, we will label the probability of election of the procapital party π and the probability of election of the prolabor party $1 - \pi$. The procapital party supports an export subsidy that raises the price of good X, the capital-intensive good. Via the Stolper–Samuelson theorem, this will increase the real income of capital. This leads to the following function defining the probability of election of the procapital party.

If procapital party 1 raises the level of export subsidy it supports, this hurts it with voters, but it has more capital resources at its disposal. If it is still below the vote-maximizing export subsidy, the increased export subsidy raises the probability of election for the procapital party. Similar arguments hold for contributions of labor to protectionist party 2 and a higher tariff supported by it. To simplify, we assume that the capital lobby contributes only capital to the political process, and the labor lobby contributes only labor. The value of this simplification is felt to exceed the cost of more tedious calculations involved in supposing that each lobby contributes both capital and labor to its favored party. A more general model of that kind is an important extension but is left to interested readers. Another simplification is that the capital lobby does not attempt to bribe the protectionist party into reducing the tariff it supports. This, again, would be an interesting extension.

To summarize, each party is provided resources by one lobby and, in turn, sponsors one policy that benefits that lobby. Voters respond positively to the resources that a party possesses but negatively to the welfare-distorting policies. The rational party will set its policy to maximize its votes.

9.3.2   Trade policies as unpopular issues

In analyzing the behavior of voters in the face of redistributive policies, it is important to determine the degree of voter opposition to the policy and whether an economic lobby exists to channel resources to the sponsoring party. A given redistributive policy is said to be "popular" if it benefits a majority of voters. Consider first a popular redistributive policy.

If either capital or labor is a majority of the electorate, both parties will support a policy that would maximize the income of that factor. For example, if labor has 70% of the votes, both parties will move toward a Hotelling outcome, supporting identical positions on the most efficient policy to maximize the real income of labor. Such a policy would be a wage subsidy that would force specialization of the economy in the labor-intensive good and eliminate both production and exports of the capital-intensive good. If, for some reason, the parties were constrained to use a less efficient policy such as the tariff, both parties would support a prohibitive tariff; this would eliminate international trade and set wages at their autarkic levels (in autarky, imports cease). The only pitfall to this observation is the empirically unsupported prediction that international trade would be driven to zero in all economies where trade restrictions benefit a factor of production with more than 50% of the votes. A more difficult theoretical task is explaining unpopular special-interest policies benefiting a factor of production that is a minority of the electorate.

We assume in what follows that neither capital nor labor holds a majority of the votes. This is an admittedly artificial assumption in a two-factor model; however, the disadvantage of the additional economic complexity of moving to a three-or-more-factor model outweighs the advantages.

9.3.3   The information–social cost trade-off

We assume that many other issues beside redistributive policies lurk in the background and are of concern to voters. Also, since neither capital nor labor has a majority of votes, each party must appeal to uncommitted voters.

On unpopular redistributive issues such as tariffs, uncommitted voters are worse off the higher the tariff because of the redistributive effect and the economic deadweight loss. It is in the voters' interests to tolerate positive tariffs only if the social costs are necessary for the provision of some social gain. We speculate that one such gain is the information value to the voters of the resources provided by the protariff lobby. A mistake in the choice of candidates sometimes has high social costs. Thus assume that the labor lobby asks society through the Democratic party for a 10% tariff on imports of labor-intensive goods; that the distortionary tariff would cause a 1% reduction in the income of uncommitted voters; that the labor lobby provides the Democratic party with resources that the latter can use to unearth unfavorable (though socially valuable) information about the Republican party; and that the total value of this information to uncommitted voters is equal to 3% of their income. Even an anarchist can see some virtue in this trade-off: The information gain exceeds the distortion loss. Symmetric arguments hold for Republican party sponsorship of an export subsidy that benefits capital. The most favorable view of this admittedly sleazy process is that redistributive policies are a quid pro quo that funds party competition through second-best lobby competition.

9.4   The lobbies

Because of party competition, the parties internalize the optimal behavior of the lobbies before setting their policies. Thus, the policies chosen are outside the control of the lobbies, who must take the announced policy positions as given at the time they contribute. From the contribution specialization theorem, a lobby should give to no more than one party in a two-party race. Recall the logic behind the theorem: Let the capital lobby contribute $1 million to the first party, thereby raising its probability of election from .55 to .60. If the capital lobby then contributes $1 million to the second party and lowers the first party's chances of election by .05, then the lobby would be back where it started, except for having wasted $2 million. This illustrates the illogic of contributing to both parties. We employ this theorem in Part II.

An important problem plaguing all lobbies is free-riding. If three-fourths of labor in an economy contribute to the lobby's success, the remaining one-fourth of labor obtains benefits at no cost. This tendency reduces the effectiveness of lobbies in most democratic societies. We model the phenomenon, albeit ad hoc, by adding an appropriability parameter to the lobbying functions. The parameter has a value of 0 if there is complete free-riding and 1 if there is none. In all subsequent chapters, we set the appropriability parameter equal to 1. A useful extension would be relaxation of this assumption.

What are the general equilibrium economic effects of the labor lobby giving another million dollars worth of labor time to the House Democrats? The benefit to the labor lobby is that the electoral success of these Democrats increases. Since the Democrats sponsor the tariff, the long-run relative price of labor-intensive goods will be higher: With a higher U.S. price of textiles, for example, the textile industry expands, hiring relatively more labor than capital; these pressures on factor markets cause wages to rise and capital returns to fall. So long as the marginal benefits to the labor lobby of the higher total wages exceed the marginal lobby costs of the additional labor in lobbying, the lobby should increase its level of its activity. Because of diminishing returns, lobbying will have greater marginal benefits the larger the initial proportion of the factor in productive activities.

9.5 The political parties

There are two questions facing each party:

1. Which special-interest policy should be chosen to enrich its clientele lobby?
2. What should be the level of that policy?

For example, on question 1 the Democrats must decide whether to sponsor a factor subsidy for labor, a production subsidy on labor-intensive production, a tariff, a quota, a voluntary export restraint agreement by foreign exports of labor-intensive goods, or some other policy. Once the Democrats decide on a tariff, they must then determine its vote-maximizing level. In general, each party should solve problem 2 for each policy, then pick the policy whose optimum value yields the greatest number of votes.

9.5.1 The principle of indirection: optimal obfuscation

How do the parties decide which policy to adopt? International economists have difficulty understanding the use of tariffs and other inefficient redistributive devices by Western democracies. Bhagwati, among others, has shown that the economically efficient way to introduce distortions into an economy is "to choose that policy intervention that creates the distortion affecting directly the constrained variable" (1971, p. 77). He shows that if factor employment in a sector is a constraint, then the ranking of policies would be as follows: first-best, factor subsidy; second-best, production subsidy; third-best, a tariff; and so on. Economic efficiency would dictate that redistribution be undertaken by the most efficient policies possible: that is, by the principle of "economic direction."

It is our view that Bhagwati's principle applies only to popular issues. That is, it is likely that a democratic society would adopt a factor tax or subsidy as a redistributive policy, but only in countries where a single lobby possesses a majority of the voters. Consider a country in which 70% of the voters are laborers. In this case, the labor lobby, both parties, and the median voter (who is a laborer) all prefer that the most efficient policy tool be undertaken to increase the real wage. Because the median voters are members of the lobby itself, it is in their interest that the political system benefit them with a minimum of economic deadweight loss. However, we noted earlier in the discussion of the lobbies that, when both parties adopt identical policies, they cannot use their positions on these issues to accumulate economic resources (because of zero contributions for popular policies). Thus, we speculate that political parties will not accumulate resources from dominant-factor lobbies. In the cases considered in this book, protection benefits only a minority of the populace.

We hypothesize that the parties follow a "principle of optimal obfuscation" when they choose protection as a redistributive mechanism. We analyze this concept at greater length in Chapter 18. Parties choose indirect means of redistributing income to disguise the process. This has the effect of making it more difficult for voters (as well as economists) to measure their costs. Since it is easier to detect and measure the costs of direct redistribution policies, parties cannot use them to enrich voter minorities. To illustrate our principle of optimal obfuscation, arrange all of the policies from which a protectionist party might choose from the most direct to the most indirect; then set the optimum value of each policy. The principle of optimal obfuscation suggests that a party will shift to more indirect policies for redistributing income so long as the electoral gains in voter obfuscation exceed the electoral cost of receiving fewer resources from the clientele lobby. With weak restrictions on the probabilistic voting function, one policy will dominate the rest. Judging from what we observe empirically, it will seldom be the most direct.

The principle explains the reverse-efficiency ordering of trade policies chosen by many Western democracies. The evidence is the scarcity of direct factor subsidies and production subsidies to labor-intensive industries by parties that are supported by well-organized labor lobbies. Unpopular policies such as tariffs are disguised by protectionist lobbies with arguments to camouflage their redistributive intent. The domestic employment argument is one such disguise. Economists have difficulty understanding the logic of preserving employment in low-wage industries in which the economy is most inefficient (import-competing industries are those in which an economy has the greatest comparative disadvantage). Paradoxically, during the past twenty years in the United States, continuing pressure for freer trade by economists and consumer lobbies may have had a perverse effect. Increased voter sophistication about the welfare costs of tariffs increased the obfuscation needs by the protectionists. This pushed the system toward quotas, voluntary export restraints, and more inefficient forms of protection. Thus, we have the paradox of consumerist pressure for free trade eliciting increasing levels of protection.

In the rest of the book, we assume that the prolabor party has picked the tariff and the procapital party has picked the export subsidy as the most favorable policy. While we use the term "tariff" throughout, the analysis here could be extended to include most forms of protection. At what level, then, will the tariff and the export subsidy be set?

9.5.2   Equilibrium tariffs and export subsidies

The equilibrium tariff maximizes the votes of the prolabor party whereas the equilibrium export subsidy maximizes the votes of the procapital party (balancing the electoral benefits of the lobbying resources against the electoral costs of the distortionary policy).

We must choose between one of two types of Stackelberg leadership by the parties. The first is a "limited-information Stackelberg equilibrium," in which the political parties have knowledge of and take into account the effect of their policy only on the lobbying resources that flow from their lobby to them. If it is difficult for parties to calculate the effect of their own policies on resource flows to the other party, this is a reasonable assumption. The other equilibrium concept is that of a "full-information Stackelberg equilibrium," in which each party must calculate all resource flows to all parties as a result of the party's policy choice. For both logical and pragmatic reasons, we choose the limited-information approach.

Given the model, the following variables are simultaneously determined by all of the other variables: The *political variables* are the policies (export subsidy and tariff) and the probabilities of election of the two parties; *lobbying variables* are the amounts of capital and labor contributed by the respective lobbies to their associated parties; and the *economic variables* are the politically determined domestic price of importables relative to exportables, the levels of production, consumption, and international trade of the two goods and, most important, the factor rewards to capital and labor.

9.6   Endogenous redistribution theory

There are important distributional implications of the approach taken here. The first is cynicism about the ability of democratic governments to generate altruistic income redistributions. Political parties seek out economic lobbies that will fund their economic requirements in exchange for distortionary policies. This leads to an actual distribution of income that is determined by the microeconomics of policing free-riders, the marginal productivity of economic resources used to influence voters, and other variables. In societies where capital is well organized relative to labor, the distribution of income will be skewed toward capital; the reverse will be the case in societies with effective labor lobbies.

It is well known that the distortionary effects of any one policy should not be measured in isolation. This model provides a framework in which the negative welfare effects of relative price distortion can be compared with the welfare loss generated by the two lobbies in rent seeking. Extensive work has been done on the welfare cost of price-distorting policy. In contrast, Tullock (1967b) speculates that the resources expended by rent seekers attempting to obtain politically determined scarcity rents might be quite large relative to the deadweight loss effects. Obviously, resolution of this question is empirical, depending on the parameters and structure of the economy, the lobbies, and the political system.

We note in passing that if the equilibrium value of the equilibrium probability of election of party 1 is .5 and the two parties support commercial policies at identical rates (that is, an export subsidy and tariff of 20%), then the deadweight loss triangles would be irrelevant and all the social costs of tariff formation in a democracy would be the lobbying component. This result grows out of our assumption that political markets clear much more rapidly than economic markets. Bhagwati and Srinivasan (1980) present an interesting exception in which lobbying can lead to a welfare improvement rather than a welfare decline. They show that if increased rent seeking results in a sufficiently large improvement in a country's terms of trade, then the welfare cost of that rent seeking would be negative (that is, a gain for the economy). We show in Chapter 15 theoretical conditions under which large portions of an economy can disappear into lobbying. Krueger (1974) presents empirical estimates of rather large amounts of resources expended on rent seeking in Turkey and India. Altruism may affect voters, but equilibrium income distributions are also driven by self-interested lobbies.

A second implication is the alternative scenario that the model provides for the Marxian conflict between capital and labor. With political competition, the economic interests of capital and labor are at variance in both advanced and developing economies. Marx suggested that the class structures of societies and their political systems would be influenced by the way in which the societies produced goods and services. In the model presented here, capital and labor engage in a conflict no different from that suggested by Marx; however, this framework provides an explicit distributional outcome. Both factors of production are limited in their ability to exploit the other by lobby budget constraints, free-rider problems within the lobby, the microeconomics of campaign contribution effectiveness, and all of the other variables affecting rent-seeking. This theory of the "exploitation hypothesis" is that either factor of production can exploit the other if it accumulates sufficient economic lobbying power. Our view is that Marx's predictions failed because of organized labor's political and organizational success.

Marx suggested that capital–labor conflict would lead to increasing class warfare until capitalism was finally overthrown. We, too, can visualize potentially degenerate outcomes, but these grow out of the lobbying process. The increased compactness of Western economies, improved effectiveness of the appropriation mechanisms of large portions of the industrial sector, and learning behavior by lobbies [à la Olson (1982)] all suggest increased lobbying over time. In this case, the vision is not Marx's big bang but a slow economic decline from political sclerosis. The closest we can come to Marx's pessimism is an economic black hole in which all of an economy's resources are consumed in redistributive lobbying.

CHAPTER 10

A Prisoner's Dilemma theory of endogenous protection: the Leontief model

Competition among lobbies over the issue of protection can lead all of them to be worse off than under free trade. Furthermore, this perverse outcome can persist, meaning that it can be a stable equilibrium. This result, known as the Prisoner's Dilemma, was first suggested as a theory of tariffs by Messerlin (1981). This chapter introduces explicit functional forms in order to derive specific results. We assume risk neutrality, Leontief production, and a logit probability of election function. This special case allows us to derive explicit reaction functions of the four major actors: the protectionist and proexport lobbies and the protectionist and proexport political parties. In addition, we have a complete general equilibrium model operating that computes values for all production, consumption, factor incomes, and so on.

This chapter covers the following:

10.1.   a review of the literature;
10.2.   explicit solutions to the Leontief model with logit voting;
10.3.   distortionary policies such as protection being due to high voter responsiveness to campaign contributions by the parties;
10.4.   the frequency of Prisoner's Dilemma outcomes across countries;
10.5.   Prisoner's Dilemma economies having intermediate capital–labor factor endowment ratios; and
10.6.   the nonexistence of parametric changes that make the game more cooperative for both lobbies.

Chapter 10 in Stephen P. Magee, William A. Brock, and Leslie Young, *Black Hole Tariffs and Endogenous Policy Theory.* New York: Cambridge University Press, 1989. Adapted from Leslie Young and Stephen P. Magee, "A Prisoner's Dilemma Theory of Endogenous Tariffs," a paper presented at the Econometric Society Meetings, December 1982, and at the Conference on Rational Actor Models in Political Economy, Stanford University, April 1984.

The Prisoner's Dilemma entailed by this political structure is examined at three levels. First, we show that free trade will be an equilibrium of the above tariff-setting game if voters are unresponsive to campaign expenditures, but will never be an equilibrium of the game if voters are responsive to them. By "free trade" we mean zero lobbying by both factors and zero tariffs and export subsidies. Second, simulations of the equilibria of the tariff-setting game reveal that, in many cases, both lobbies end up worse off than under free trade. Although political activity is readily understandable when one lobby gains, why does it occur when no one gains? This question is considered in a second-level "metagame" in which the two lobbies decide unilaterally whether or not to contribute to politics. We find that the payoff matrix for the metagame conforms to that of the classic Prisoner's Dilemma about 40% of the time. Thus, the mutually harmful decisions of the lobbies to contribute to politics are the outcomes of dominant strategies in the metagame. Third, lobbies might fail to obtain the benefits of not lobbying, even if the metagame is repeated. The presence of multiple equilibria in the tariff-setting game can undermine the usual arguments for cooperation with repetitions of the Prisoner's Dilemma game. This theme is developed in detail in Chapter 11.

Recall from Chapter 9 that, by contributing capital to the procapital party, the capital lobby can increase the probability of a high domestic relative price for the exportable good 1 (X). This increases capital rental rates via the Stolper–Samuelson effect. However, increased capital contributions mean that the higher rental rate is earned by fewer units of productive capital. Similarly, the labor lobby must trade off the higher expected wage rate from political contributions to the prolabor party against the reduction in the units of productive labor earning the higher rate. The procapital party can enter the redistributive policy game by announcing a policy of subsidizing exports of good 1. They calculate, in a Stackelberg fashion, that an increased subsidy rate will "purchase" more political contributions from the capital lobby, which will increase their probability of election. A partially offsetting cost is the increased voter hostility excited by their intervention. Similar remarks apply mutatis mutandis to the prolabor party.

Consider the Prisoner's Dilemma economy in Figure 10.1, which was generated by simulations of our model described later in this chapter. The incomes described equal actual factor incomes divided by their free trade (no lobbying) values. For example, if both capital and labor lobby, capital's income falls to 93% and labor's income falls to 95% of its free trade value. The best situation for a factor is to lobby while the other factor does not; the next best is free trade; the third best is when both lobby; the worst is to be the only factor that does not lobby. If either factor does not lobby, the associated party does not deviate from its free trade value of a zero distortion policy. For

Labor

	1 No Lobbying	2 Lobbying
1 No Lobbying	Outcome 11 1.0	Outcome 12 0.26
2 Lobbying	Outcome 21 1.21	Outcome 22 0.93

Capital (left label)

(a)

Labor

	1 No Lobbying	2 Lobbying
1 No Lobbying	Outcome 11 1.0	Outcome 12 1.79
2 Lobbying	Outcome 21 0.67	Outcome 22 0.95

Capital (left label)

(b)

Figure 10.1. A Prisoner's Dilemma economy: (a) capital income, (b) labor income.

example, if capital does not lobby and labor does, the export subsidy chosen by the Republicans equals zero while the Democrats sponsor a tariff. As a result, capital's income falls to 26% of its free trade value while labor's income rises 79% above its free trade value. This illustrates the devastating consequences of not lobbying when the other factor lobbies.

In Figure 10.1(a), capital's income is highest in row 2, irrespective of labor's decision of whether to lobby. Similarly, in Figure 10.1(b), notice that labor's income is highest in column 2, irrespective of capital's decision.

Thus, in the absence of communication between the two lobbies, capital will choose row 2 and labor will choose column 2, yielding outcome 22 as the equilibrium of the game. Each factor's dominant strategy is to lobby, no matter what the other factor does.

This is called the "Prisoner's Dilemma" game because individual rationality yields an equilibrium that is not in the best interest of the two players. It is best illustrated by two prisoners who are interrogated separately about a crime that they have committed jointly. Good interrogators set up the perceived payoffs so that each has an incentive not to cooperate with, but to tell on, the other (outcome 22). Of all possible 2 × 2 games of this sort, the Prisoner's Dilemma shown in Figure 10.1 is the only one in which the non-cooperative equilibrium (outcome 22) differs from Pareto optimality (outcome 11). Full knowledge by a lobby of what the other lobby plans to do does not avert this outcome. In our grid search through all possible general political equilibria, we were surprised to find that the Prisoner's Dilemma outcome occurred as much as 40% of the time.

10.1   The literature

For a historical discussion of the Prisoner's Dilemma in game theory see Luce and Raiffa (1957). Rappaport and Chammah (1965) report experimental evidence on the tendency for cooperation to emerge in repetitions of the Prisoner's Dilemma game. The possibility that political competition through trade instruments can lead to a Prisoner's Dilemma is ironic in view of Luce and Raiffa's (1957, p. 97) suggestion that the role of government is to resolve Prisoner's Dilemmas amongst its citizens. In our model of political competition, the Prisoner's Dilemma is caused by the government interacting with self-interested lobbies.

As noted earlier, Messerlin (1981) applied the Prisoner's Dilemma to tariffs in a bureaucratic model, building on Niskanen's (1976) theory of bureaucracy. See also Pommerehne and Frey (1978). For an application of the Prisoner's Dilemma to international political economy see Conybeare (1984c). For the growth of bureaus in the United States see Casstevens (1984). For the relationship between the Prisoner's Dilemma and Olson's analysis of collective action see Hardin (1971). For an early paper on supergames in the modeling of Prisoner's Dilemma equilibria see Friedman (1974); for a recent paper see Rubinstein (1986). For an application of reputation effects and political leadership in Prisoner's Dilemma situations see Calvert (1986). Palfrey and Rosenthal (1985) provide a description of the many forms of 2 × 2 games involving social dilemmas (e.g., Chicken, No fear, Control, Poison). All of the aforementioned deal with Prisoner's Dilemmas applied to protection or related matters.

We turn now to insights for endogenous policy theory from the literature on experimental Prisoner's Dilemma games. We want to know conditions under which the noncooperative Prisoner's Dilemma outcome with tariffs is more likely to happen than the cooperative free trade outcome with no lobbying.

There are three broad classes of result from the experimental Prisoner's Dilemma literature that have implications for endogenous tariff theory. The first deals with characteristics of the payoffs themselves; the second describes characteristics of the players; and the third pertains to the length of the game. For a good characterization of the issues in the Prisoner's Dilemma game see Axelrod (1980a,b).

10.1.1 The payoffs

Prisoner's Dilemma payoffs vary in terms of friendliness, noisiness, certainty, and equality. We examine each in turn, starting with friendliness [see Goehring and Kaham (1976) and Rappaport and Chammah (1965, p. 48)]. Consider the payoffs to capital in Figure 10.1(a) (the arguments for labor are symmetric). The game is more "friendly" if the payoffs in row 2 decline because this reduces the likelihood that capital will choose the non-cooperative lobbying strategy. Anything that increases the friendliness of the payoffs to the lobbies should decrease the likelihood of Prisoner's Dilemma tariffs. We noted above that all economic parameter changes in our model that increase the friendliness of the Figure 10.1 payoffs for one of the factors always decrease the friendliness of the game to the other factor. The road to voluntary cooperation is a rocky one.

Rappaport and Chammah (1965, p. 54) find that increased noise introduced by frequent changes in the payoff matrices reduces the incentive effects of friendly versus unfriendly payoffs. Increased noise thus has a two-edged effect: Cooperation is reduced by increased noise when the payoffs are friendly, and is increased when the payoffs are unfriendly. The implication is that rapidly changing environments will (1) weaken tendencies toward free trade if the payoffs are friendly and (2) weaken tendencies toward distortions if the payoffs are unfriendly. In another experiment, Rappaport and Chammah (1965, p. 54) find that incomplete knowledge about the payoffs to the other player decreases the likelihood of cooperative behavior. Thus, the less each lobby knows in a tariff game about what the other is getting out of the political system, the less likely is free trade. Finally, Pruitt and Kimmel (1977) report that the more equal the payoffs to players, the greater the likelihood of a cooperative outcome. Whether this result carries over to endogenous tariffs is unclear. To test this, the interested reader might examine whether lobbying activity and income inequality were correlated across countries.

10.1.2   The players

Consider next four characteristics of the players in the repeated Prisoner's Dilemma games: niceness, toughness, predictability, and responsiveness. Several studies report that consistently nice players are exploited by tougher players (Pruitt and Kimmell 1977, p. 380). A consistently nice player is equivalent to an absence of lobbying by one of the two factors in our game. Excessive cooperativeness thus suggests a single distortion economy in our framework (although this should not hold in the long run since the dormant factor would organize): Depending on which lobby is nice, we get either a tariff-only outcome in Figure 10.1 (case 12) or an export-subsidy-only outcome (case 21). Ironically, this suggests that free trade might be facilitated in the long run by helping the dormant factor organize. The idea is a second cousin of Bhagwati's (1982) notion that a lobby might be directly unproductive but, in a second-best world, evil begets good.

Several studies (see especially Axelrod 1980a,b) find that tough, mean, and retribution-prone players drive the system to mutual noncooperation. This has obvious implications for tariffs if spiteful lobbies are present. Axelrod (1980a,b) and others find that predictability leads to greater cooperation whereas random play leads to the reverse. Thus, random lobbying effectiveness by consumerist lobbies might encourage protection. Olson (1965) certainly documents the random effectiveness of consumer lobbies. An example of retribution is tariff retaliation of the sort that occurred in 1930 during the Smoot–Hawley period. Most of the major industrial economies resorted to selfish nationalistic strategies in an effort to protect their domestic economies from the onset of the Great Depression.

We can combine the previous three results in discussing the effects of player responsiveness. Predictably nice (but not tough) players get exploited; predictably tough (but not nice) players elicit retribution; ironically, predictably nice but tough players do very well in repeated Prisoner's Dilemma games. The latter point is combined in the quite successful dynamic strategy, tit for tat [see Axelrod (1980a,b), Pruitt and Kimmel (1977), and Wilson (1971)]. The tit for tat strategy is to cooperate on the first round. Thereafter, it is nice in that it is never the first to defect (to noncooperation) but rewards every cooperative move by an opponent with cooperation on the next round; it is tough in that every defection by an opponent results in its defection on the next round; it is totally predictable; and it is responsive in that it allows the other player to dictate the outcome.

The two tournaments held by Axelrod (1980a,b) among game theorists and other experts was interesting in that tit for tat beat all of the experts, even though all players knew in advance that the tit for tat strategy was entered. Most of the other strategies could beat tit for tat head to head, but they compiled poorer scores against each other. The tournament championship was determined not by head to head scores, but by each entrant's score against everyone entered. Tit for tat won because the others frequently generated noncooperative outcomes when playing each other.

10.1.3   The length of the game

Finally, time and length of play of games generate three effects on the outcomes: polarization, U-shaped cooperation, and experience. With regard to polarization, the longer the game is played, the more results gravitate toward either mutual cooperation or mutual defection by both players. This makes the payoffs in Figure 10.1 evolve toward dominant diagonality. Rappaport and Chammah (1965, p. 99) report that the proportion of case 11 plus case 22 outcomes rose from .60 early in games to .90 in the end. Thus, with time, the players tend to become more and more alike as they emulate one another's behavior. The implication is that economies will polarize toward patterns of either free trade with little lobbying or complete distortions with everyone lobbying. This observation is consistent with the pattern between World War II and the 1970s of increased free trade among advanced economies and increased trade intervention in developing countries.

Goehring and Kahan (1976), Pruitt and Kimmel (1977), Rappaport and Chammah (1965), and Wilson (1971) all find evidence that the pattern of cooperation through time is U-shaped. That is, mutual cooperation drops early in the game but then rises until the end of the game. The implications for tariff analysis are that economies will display decreasing and then increasing lobby cooperation for free trade over certain time intervals. If lobby cooperation is U-shaped, then the pattern of tariffs over the past 100 years displays a pattern of occasional increases followed by continuous decreases. This evidence, unfortunately, is consistent with U's, inverted U's, and other letters of the alphabet.

What are the effects of the experience of the players as they play longer and longer? The evidence from many of the studies indicates that, after the initial period of noncooperation, cooperation steadily rises until the end of the experiments, provided that the payoffs are not too unfriendly [Komorita and Lapworth (1982), Pruitt and Kimmel (1977), Rappaport and Chammah (1965), and Wilson (1971)]. Further, cooperation is higher at the end of the game than at the beginning: Rappaport and Chammah found that the proportion of mutual cooperation (outcome 11) increased from .24 early in the games to .68 at the end of 300 plays.

This contrasts with the Olson (1982) hypothesis that lobbies will become more efficient as they learn to overcome the free-rider problem. Olson's theory deals with internal lobby effectiveness whereas the experimental results being reviewed here apply to relationships between lobbies. Quite apart from this, the theories have contrasting implications. Until about 1980, protection had declined over the past half-century in the advanced countries, providing modest support for the experimental results.

10.2 Explicit solutions for the endogenous policy model: Leontief production and logit probabilistic voting

This chapter develops the endogenous policy model when economic goods are produced with Leontief production functions. This means that the capital–labor ratios in production are fixed in each industry by engineering or other constraints. Good 2 is labor intensive while good 1 is capital intensive. By choice of units, the capital–labor ratio for good 1 equals 1, and the capital–labor ratio for good 2 is $A < 1$. Increases in A bring the factor intensities of production for the two goods closer together, which increases the magnification effect (the responsiveness of factor prices to relative product prices). The magnification effect is important in endogenous tariff theory because it accentuates the payoff of manipulating factor rewards through changes in relative product prices. The second economic parameter is P, the relative price of labor-intensive good 2 on the world market. When P rises, the price of textiles, for example, is higher, and this raises domestic wages because textiles are labor intensive in production. When P falls, returns to capital rise via similar reasoning. The third economic parameter is the capital–labor endowment of the economy.

To describe voters, we use a logit probability of election function. We are not introducing this to capture the effects of risk aversion since the economic actors and voters are risk neutral. The probabilistic voting function best captures the behavior of rationally uninformed voters. With the logit function, the logarithm of the odds of election of a party is a linear function of the logarithms of the variables that describe voter behavior. In this function, the odds that the procapital party is elected:

> increase with the capital it receives from the capital lobby;
> decrease with the export subsidy it sponsors;
> increase with the tariff sponsored by the prolabor party; and
> decrease with the labor contributions to the other party.

Each of these variables affects the odds of election with elasticities that range from 0 to 1. For example, if the elasticity of the odds with respect to capital lobby contributions is 1, then a 10% increase in capital lobby contributions increases the odds of the procapital party's victory by 10% (e.g., from 2/1 to 2.2/1).

10.3   Redistributive policies due to high voter responsiveness to campaign contributions

The equilibrium values for the amounts of capital and labor devoted to lobbying are described in Theorems 1 and 2; the levels of the equilibrium export subsidy s and the equilibrium tariff t are described in Theorems 3 and 4 (see the Appendix). To simplify the notation in those theorems, we use the terms T ($= 1 + t$) and S ($= 1 - s$). Under free trade, $S = T = 1$, whereas under redistributive policy intervention by both parties, $S < 1 < T$.

When will the lobbies contribute and the parties intervene with redistributive policies? When the elasticities of electoral outcomes with respect to resources are low, the lobbies desist from contributing and the parties do not introduce redistributive policies. Theorem 5 indicates precise conditions that yield free trade as an equilibrium outcome. Theorem 6 indicates that, when the elasticities of electoral outcomes with respect to money are high, at least one lobby will contribute and at least one party will intervene with a redistributive policy. In general, it appears that redistributive party intervention occurs when the positive elasticity of the party's electoral chances with respect to lobby contributions is large relative to the negative elasticity of the party's electoral chances with respect to the policy it sponsors. Theorem 7 advances the following result: For some equilibria, one party will introduce a special-interest policy while the other will not. In all such equilibria, the lobby associated with the special-interest party is better off than under free trade; the other party is worse off.

10.4   A Prisoner's Dilemma theory of endogenous policy

We turn now to simulations of the model to investigate conditions under which both factors can end up worse off with lobbying and special-interest policies. We do this by varying the exogenous parameters that the economy faces over wide ranges. These parameters are the economy's capital endowment, the relative price P of the labor-intensive good on world markets, the capital–labor ratio A of good 2 relative to good 1, and the proxies for effectiveness of capital and labor lobbying resources in influencing voters. We are interested in discovering how many of the distorted economies are characterized by Prisoner's Dilemma outcomes. Theorem 7 tells us that both factors can be worse off only if both parties espouse intervention. Theorem 6 indicated that this would occur if capital and labor lobbying resources are effective in influencing voters.

We construct a grid covering the entire range of values for three of the parameters (prices, factor intensities, and country factor endowments). These parameters are constrained so that, under free trade, both goods were pro-

Table 10.1. *Actively redistributive economies*

Economies	No.	%
1. Prisoner's Dilemma economies (both factors worse off than under free trade)	24	40
2. Capital-dominant economies (capital better off and labor worse off than under free trade)	10	16
3. Labor-dominant economies (labor better off and capital worse off than under free trade)	27	44
Total distorted economies	61	

duced and both factors are fully employed. Given our assumptions and the mesh of the grid, we generate 204 different logical possibilities, each described as a "different economy," even though two "economies" may differ only in the international price they face. Of the 204 economies, 61 had equilibria in which both parties proposed intervention; that is, where the protectionist party proposed a positive tariff ($t > 0$) and the proexport party proposed a positive export subsidy ($s > 0$) and where both goods were produced and both factors were fully employed. We investigate these cases in detail.

The sixty-one economies with active redistributive activity by both parties fell into three groups, as shown in Table 10.1. It is impossible for there to be a fourth category in which both factors are better off than under free trade because GNP (and hence total factor income) is maximized under free trade for a small open economy. The redistributive battle over relative prices alters the shares of a smaller pie (since lobbying reduces the factors devoted to producing the pie); thus, the absolute amount of pie going to each factor cannot increase for both. In the Prisoner's Dilemma economies, the changes in the factor shares are small, so the decline in the size of the pie causes both factors to be worse off. In the capital-dominant economies, capital's share increases sufficiently to offset the declining pie effect; the reverse is true for the labor-dominant economies.

The Prisoner's Dilemma economy was shown in Figure 10.1; the capital-dominant economy is given in Figure 10.2, and the labor-dominant economy in Figure 10.3. As before, row 2 is the dominant strategy for capital in 10.2(a), whereas column 2 is the dominant strategy for labor in 10.2(b). Thus, the equilibrium is outcome 22. Note, however, that capital is better off in the special-interest equilibrium (hence the term "capital-dominant") while labor is worse off, both compared to free trade. The reverse is true in Figure 10.3: Labor gains relative to free trade while capital loses.

	Labor	
	No Lobbying	Lobbying
No Lobbying	Outcome 11 1.0	Outcome 12 0.8
Capital		
Lobbying	Outcome 21 1.9	Outcome 22 1.2

(a)

	Labor	
	No Lobbying	Lobbying
No Lobbying	Outcome 11 1.0	Outcome 12 1.3
Capital		
Lobbying	Outcome 21 0.4	Outcome 22 0.6

(b)

Figure 10.2. A capital-dominant economy: (a) capital income, (b) labor income.

	Labor	
	No Lobbying	Lobbying
No Lobbying	Outcome 11 1.0	Outcome 12 0.5
Capital		
Lobbying	Outcome 21 1.3	Outcome 22 0.6

(a)

	Labor	
	No Lobbying	Lobbying
No Lobbying	Outcome 11 1.0	Outcome 12 1.8
Capital		
Lobbying	Outcome 21 0.9	Outcome 22 1.3

(b)

Figure 10.3. A labor-dominant economy: (a) capital income, (b) labor income.

An important point for all of the figures in this chapter is that the free trade outcome 11 is never an equilibrium of the game. A necessary condition for a free trade equilibrium would be for the lobbies to collude and jointly refuse to contribute to politics. Even is this were an equilibrium for the lobbies, it could not be an overall equilibrium because it ignores party behavior.

The original Prisoner's Dilemma game involved no communication between the players, and this is cited as one reason for the perverse outcome. Assume for the moment that only one equilibrium exists and that the lobbies are free to communicate: It would be rational for the capital and labor lobbies to agree to contribute nothing to either party. In this situation, neither party would advocate a distortionary policy since it would encounter voter hostility with no redeeming economic resources. The result would be a move to free trade with both factors of production being better off. If either lobby–party coalition chiseled on the agreement, the other could follow suit: The worst that could happen to either lobby is that it return to the original Prisoner's Dilemma equilibrium. In other words, there is no long-run downside risk to a move to free trade when there is only one equilibrium. We would expect free trade to emerge in most of these situations. In Chapter 11 we show why multiple equilibria and the possibility of double crosses might cause the Prisoner's Dilemma equilibrium to persist even with communication between the players.

10.5 Why Prisoner's Dilemma versus dominant-player economies?

What economic characteristics do labor-dominant economies have vis-à-vis capital-dominant and Prisoner's Dilemma economies? Since the elasticities of the electoral outcomes with respect to both capital and labor were both set near 1 in the 204 economies for which we examined the Prisoner's Dilemma versus dominant-player question, the only exogenous parameters that can explain the phenomenon are the country's capital–labor ratio, the relative factor intensities of production for the two goods, and the terms of trade that the economy faces on world markets. Our simulations reveal that the endogenous political systems of *labor-dominant countries* display

> higher tariffs,
> higher probabilities of election of the prolabor party, and hence
> higher wages

compared to the values of these variables in the same economies without redistributive conflict (i.e., under free trade). Symmetrically, the *capital-*

dominant countries display

> higher export subsidies,
> higher success rates for procapital parties, and hence
> higher returns to capital,

again, compared to free trade without lobbying. Since Prisoner's Dilemma countries will be intermediate between these two extremes, they will have intermediate values of these variables.

What are the effects of *factor endowments* on capital versus labor dominance? Labor-dominated economies have low capital–labor endowments, capital-dominated economies have high capital–labor endowments, and Prisoner's Dilemma economies have intermediate capital–labor endowments. This analysis ignores differences in national political institutions.

Consider now *world product prices* and the *factor intensities* of production. In the long run, these variables would be identical for all economies since every country can presumably trade in the world market and each has access to the same world production technology. Thus, these two parameters alone should not explain why one country might display a Prisoner's Dilemma equilibrium and another a dominant-player equilibrium, except in the short to medium run: Only the country factor endowment ratios should have any explanatory power in the long run.

Exogenous changes in world prices and technology have the long-run effect of pushing all countries either in the direction of labor dominance or capital dominance. Consider now the effect of an increase in the world price of labor-intensive goods. Since these goods are imported, the world price change is equivalent to a decline in the country's terms of trade. By the Stolper–Samuelson effect, wages rise worldwide and returns to capital fall. In this situation, all of the labor lobbies of the world face higher costs of lobbying while the capital lobbies face lower costs; thus, labor lobbying declines. In general, the labor lobbies will work less hard at politics while the capital lobbies will work harder. Ironically, the higher wages (caused by the declining terms of trade) reduce the political influence of labor, and this causes the equilibrium tariff to fall and the export subsidy to rise. All of these effects generate moves in the economies toward capital dominance. The endogenous political effects just described provide a partial offset to the initial economic gain of labor that was caused by the decline in the country's terms of trade. Similar results to those just outlined occur when production technologies change so that the labor-intensive good becomes even more so in production: Wages rise, labor lobbies less, the equilibrium tariff falls, and so on. The economic change favoring labor reduces its political activity. The point just made illustrates a pattern that we observe empirically: Political involvement increases when market returns fall, and decreases when economic rewards rise. In Chapter 11 we call this the *compensation effect*.

	Labor	
	No Lobbying	Lobbying
No Lobbying Capital	cap income = 1.0 labor income = 1.0 s = 0 t = 0 p = .5	cap income = .26 labor income = 1.79 s = 0 t = .91 p = .19
Lobbying	cap income = 1.21 labor income = .67 s = .42 t = .00 p = .63	cap income = .93 labor income = .95 s = .39 t = .12 p = .19

Figure 10.4. The Prisoner's Dilemma economy of Figure 10.1.

As in politics, the language of our model is deceptive: Capital is politically dominant when it is economically weak; that is, capital gets the most out of politics when it is forced to by economic markets. Recall that capital dominance means that capital's returns are higher in the endogenous political equilibrium than they would have been with free trade and no lobbying. But capital gets these higher returns only when the returns to capital are so low under free trade that it must devote a lot of its resources to lobbying. Prisoner's Dilemmas characterize intermediate ranges of the possible values of a country's terms of trade.

10.6 The constant-sum-game effect: no parametric changes that make the game more cooperative

Consider the Prisoner's Dilemma country in Figure 10.4 (the case in Figure 10.1). Are there any changes in the three exogenous economic variables that might make the payoff matrix more conducive to cooperation for both players? Such changes would lower the payoffs to noncooperative activity, that is, lower the row 2 payoffs for capital and the column 2 payoffs for labor.

Surprisingly, the answer is no. Our simulations reveal that a change in each of the three key economic parameters always changes these payoffs so that one of the players faces more cooperative payoffs while the other faces less cooperative payoffs. For example, an increase in a country's capital endowment gives capital more clout in the political system and increases its returns in row 2 compared to row 1. Labor, meanwhile, loses politically and experiences a decrease in column 2 payoffs relative to column 1. Capital becomes less prone to cooperate while labor becomes more so. This is not surprising in a constant-sum political game.

CHAPTER 11

The compensation effect and the multiple equilibrium trap

This chapter contains simulation results from the Leontief general political equilibrium model of Chapter 10, and covers the following:

11.1. a review of the literature;

11.2. the compensation effect – endogenous policies compensate for price and technology shocks (e.g., a decline in import prices causes the endogenous tariff to rise);

11.3. endogenous politics are progressive with respect to price and technology shocks;

11.4. there is a pervasive tendency for multiple equilibria;

11.5. multiple equilibria generate political schizophrenia (i.e., the lobbies and parties prefer different equilibria);

11.6. the multiple equilibrium trap prevents escape from the Prisoner's Dilemma of protectionism;

11.7. no equilibrium occurs 70% of the time;

11.8. the passageway thesis – that there is a region of no equilibrium between protectionist and all free trade equilibria; and

11.9. predatory lobbying costs in our simulations range from 5% to 15% of GNP.

We summarize the model as follows: A small open economy follows the Heckscher–Ohlin theorem in exporting the capital-intensive good and importing the labor-intensive good. The prolabor party sponsors a tariff that

Chapter 11 in Stephen P. Magee, William A. Brock, and Leslie Young, *Black Hole Tariffs and Endogenous Policy Theory*. New York: Cambridge University Press, 1989. Adapted in part from Stephen P. Magee, Leslie Young, and William A. Brock, "The Compensation Effect of Endogenous Tariffs in General Equilibrium," paper presented at the Conference on International Political Economy, Department of Finance, University of Southern California, March 1984.

raises wages while the procapital party sponsors an export subsidy (economically equivalent to a negative tariff) that raises the returns to capital. The model parallels the U.S. economy in that:

> the United States is (both physical and human) capital abundant;
>
> it imports labor-intensive products and exports capital-intensive products;
>
> the Congressional Democrats receive support from the labor lobby and sponsor tariffs that raise labor incomes; and
>
> the Congressional Republicans receive support from capital and the multinationals and encourage free trade and export incentives.

The behavior of the rationally ignorant voters is probabilistic. Our logit probability function for voters assumes that they are more likely to vote for a party the more resources it has (since this will be directly related to the amount of information it can convey to them), but less likely to vote for a party the larger the value of its distortionary policy. The rational party will increase its redistributive policy so long as the vote gains from the increased campaign contributions outweigh the vote losses from the policy distortion and resentment over the redistribution. The economic model in Chapters 10–12 assumes Leontief production.

11.1   The literature

The compensation effect is an important result in this chapter. Glismann and Weiss (1980) provide direct evidence on a compensation effect with respect to income using German data between 1880 and 1978. After normalizing for trend, they find that increases in income reduce the level of German protection. For contrasting results see Cassing and Hillman (1986), who suggest that, as dying industries become smaller, their political support fades, so that politics may reinforce the death of an industry. On the latter, we find the reverse: There is less variance in factor rewards caused by terms of trade or technical change because of the political system. For example, when wages decline, labor lobbies more and gets a larger endogenous level of protection, which partially offsets the higher lobbying costs and part of the initial wage decline. Corroborating evidence is provided by Gallarotti (1985), who finds that tariff changes in the United States and Germany in the nineteenth and twentieth centuries increased during troughs of business cycles.

Hillman (1982) finds that a decline in the world price of a product has two consequences for the domestic political equilibrium. First, the political authorities may partially offset the decline by increased protection for the affected industry. This is consistent with our compensation effect. However, the decline in the world price may cause the domestic industry to become so politically weak that the domestic political authorities actually reduce the level of domestic production and hence accelerate the decline in the industry.

Some excellent evidence for the compensation effect is provided by McKeown (1983), who found that, in the nineteenth and twentieth centuries, the major motivation for reductions in national tariffs was world prosperity. In contrast, increases in protection generally occurred during periods of worldwide depression. For an application of the relationship between terms of trade changes and rent seeking see Hamilton, Mohammad, and Whalley (1984). For early discovery that multiple equilibria occur in political economy models of this sort see Young (1982). On the compensation effect, Johnson (1965) argues that countries whose competitiveness in world markets is improving tend to favor free trade, whereas countries whose competitiveness is deteriorating favor protection.

The compensation effect in this chapter is a long-run general equilibrium effect and provides an offset to economic shocks. This is the reverse of short-run lobbying effects, which can add volatility to income. For example, let there be a shock that reduces world income. An increase in protectionist lobbying will lead to a further reduction in productive output because of its wasted resources. Successful protectionism will reduce imports, and this will stimulate import-competing production, although it acts as a tax on all other production in the economy, including exportables. Corden (1974) discusses the medium- to long-term cost to the economy of the inefficiency (deadweight) losses that protection brings. For evidence of the compensation effect see Glazer, McMillan, and Robbins (1985), who note that political influence is much more prevalent in competitive industries than in oligopolistic or monopolistic ones.

Some authors argue that it is impossible to justify on efficiency grounds any deviations from the status quo for metropolitan political organizations. This summarizes well a reconciliation between the conservative social-welfare-function tariff theorists and the special-interest theorists. Any shock to an economic system necessarily alters the political equilibrium. Both the insurance theory and the special-interest theory predict that disadvantaged groups will intensify their pressure for government assistance. Both approaches have the same predictions.

The insurance argument for protection can thus be explained by the compensation effect. Lindbeck (1985a) argues that agricultural protection and rent controls have emerged from sudden drops in the income of certain groups. Rent controls are an interesting counterfactual in that they benefit large and disorganized renters relative to the wealthy and more concentrated homeowners.

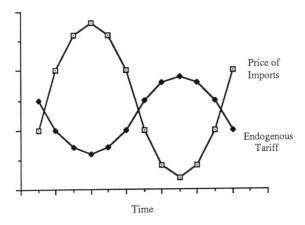

Figure 11.1. The compensation effect of endogenous tariffs.

11.2   The compensation effect: endogenous policies compensate for price and technology shocks

In the Leontief model, a decrease in import prices generates political forces that increase tariffs. While labor is hurt by decreased import prices, it is partially cushioned from the full effect by a higher tariff. Thus, endogenous policies provide a compensation effect against product price movements. This effect is illustrated in Figure 11.1. Whenever the price of a country's imports falls, the endogenous tariff rises, and vice versa.

The lowered price of imports puts downward pressure on wages because the import-competing industries are labor intensive. Lower wages stimulate labor to substitute out of economic activity and into political activity. The labor lobby expands its contributions to the Democrats because lower wages reduce labor lobby costs. The Democrats then offer a higher tariff.

To illustrate, consider the importation of automobiles into the United States from Japan. The entry of Japan into the world auto market lowered the world price of autos; this lowered the price of imports into the United States; and this stimulated pressures by labor and protectionists to keep the autos out. The result was the voluntary export restraint agreement between the United States and Japan, which was, in some ways, like a higher tariff. Thus, the rise in the terms of trade caused by the decline in U.S. import prices caused the U.S. endogenous political equilibrium to shift to greater protection.

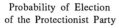

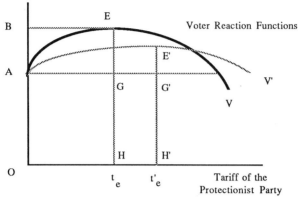

Figure 11.2. A fall in import prices raises the endogenous tariff (generating a compensation effect for labor) and reduces the probability of election for the protectionist party.

The political effects of the fall in import prices are shown in Figure 11.2, which is adapted from Figure 2.1. The endogenous tariff rises from OH to OH', but the probability of election of the Democrats falls from EH to $E'H'$. The only explanation we have for the voter reaction curve shifting down is the following: although the Democrats are helped with voters because they have more campaign funds, apparently they are hurt more by the decreased export subsidy quoted by the Republicans.

We can also illustrate the effect of a drop in U.S. import prices on the tariff equilibrium in Appendix Figures A.2.1–A.2.3. Increased market pressure on U.S. importable industries causes their wages to fall. The labor lobby has lower total costs and thus expands its operations and greater labor contributions to flow to the protectionist party. This can be shown in Figure A.2.1 as a rotation to the right in the protectionist lobby cost curve OC. This rotates the protectionist party's supply curve of funds, OS in Figure A.2.2, to the right. The curve OS also rotates to the right in Figure A.2.3, forming a new tangency with the isovote loci at a higher tariff and a higher level of protectionist lobbying expenditures. There are other general effects at work. After all of the general equilibrium adjustments, the proexport party reduces its export subsidy. This increases the electoral cost to the protectionist party of its tariff. We know from the mathematics that this effect causes the isovote loci to change in such a way that the probability of election of the protectionist party falls. Thus, the new point E in Figure A.2.3 involves fewer votes than before for the protectionist party.

In general, an increase in a country's terms of trade causes the equilibrium level of protection to rise and the export subsidy to fall. The terms of trade are the ratio of the price of a country's exports over that of its imports.

Similar results to those just outlined occur when production technologies change so that the labor-intensive good becomes more capital intensive in production (i.e., wages fall, labor lobbies more, the equilibrium tariff rises). The economic change hurting labor increases its political activity.

11.3 The progressivity of endogenous politics with respect to price and technology shocks

Do endogenous political forces reinforce or offset natural economic advantage? We shall find in Chapter 12 that international capital movements are regressive in that they reinforce economic advantages: The larger the capital endowment of a country, the more the political system increases the returns to capital and lowers the returns to labor. However, we have just shown that the reverse is true of international changes in product prices and production technologies. Product price changes that raise world wages cause labor lobbies in all countries to substitute away from politics, and this reduces part of the previous political support of the wage rate. Thus, economic increases in wages generate offsetting political offsets that partially reduce wages. The increase in domestic wages caused by a rise in world wages is lower with endogenous domestic politics than without.

The incomes of both capital and labor are much more stable with endogenous politics than with free trade. Thus, endogenous politics is progressive with respect to price and technology shocks. This is a potential explanation of why we have protection: an implicit insurance motive.

The progressivity result also holds for exogenous changes in production technology. The variable A is the capital intensity of the labor-intensive good. When this capital intensity rises, returns to capital rise and wages fall. With endogenous politics, capital income can actually fall and wages continue to fall, although by a lesser amount than before.

11.4 Multiple equilibria

This endogenous policy model displays a pervasive tendency for multiple equilibria. We looked for multiple equilibria following earlier work on political economy by Young (1982). Table 11.1 summarizes the number of multiple equilibria out of the sixty-one economies with a normal (type A) redistributive policy equilibrium (both parties sponsoring nonzero redistributive policies, both lobbies contributing, both goods being produced, and both factors fully employed). Significantly, all of these sixty-one economies had multiple equilibria. In no case was one of the multiple equilibria a free trade

Table 11.1. *Simulation results for all economies with at least one equilibrium with positive tariffs and export subsidies*

Type of economy	Total number of economies	Number of equilibria		
		3	2	1
1. *Prisoner's Dilemma*	24	16	8	0
2. *Dominant-factor*				
a. Capital-dominant	10	5	5	0
b. Labor-dominant	27	4	23	0
Total	61	25	36	0

Note: These data are from the simulations using the Leontief model in Chapter 10.

equilibrium. In addition, the Prisoner's Dilemma economies were more prone to triple equilibria than were the dominant factor economies: About 67% of the Prisoner's Dilemma economies had three equilibria, as compared to roughly 24% of the dominant-factor economies. As expected from Theorem 6 (Chapter 10), the assumption that voters had a unitary elasticity of electoral outcomes with respect to lobbying contributions was sufficient to ensure that none of the sixty-one economies had free trade as an equilibrium.

In our Leontief model of the tariff-setting game, four types of equilibrium are possible:

A. both a tariff and an export subsidy;
B. a tariff only;
C. an export subsidy only;
D. free trade.

In the type B equilibrium, the optimal strategy for the procapital party is to set its export subsidy equal to zero; the same holds for the prolabor party and the tariff in the type C equilibrium. In the type D equilibrium, the optimal strategy for both parties is to quote zero values for their redistributive policies. The type B(C) equilibrium should not be confused with an "outcome 12(21)" in the sense of Figures 10.1–10.3. The former is an equilibrium of maximizing choices by all the players; the latter involves one lobby behaving suboptimally and voluntarily desisting from lobbying. In our simulations to date, we have not found an economy with a distorted equilibrium (A, B, or C) that also had free trade as an equilibrium (and vice versa).

Some economies display all three of the distorted equilibria. Table 11.2 illustrates one of the twenty-five economies that had three equilibria. Notice

Table 11.2. *An economy[a] with three equilibria*

	Type of equilibrium		
	C	A	B
	(export	(both	(tariff
Variable	subsidy only)	distortions)	only)
Percent of capital lobbying	6%	11%	26%
K^*	4.806	9.081	20.813
Percent of labor lobbying	12%	15%	20%
L^*	11.793	15.262	19.893
Export subsidy (%)	47%	27%	0%
S^* (S')	0.535	0.726	1.0 (2.0)
Tariff (%)	0%	25%	106%
T^* (T')	1.0 (0.808)	1.246	2.061
Probability of election of			
the procapital party	18%	35%	68%
π	.179	.350	.683

[a]This economy was one of the twenty-five economies with triple equilibria, based on the Leontief model in Chapter 10. The type A distortion above includes both Prisoner's Dilemma and dominant-factor cases.
Parameters: $A = .20, P = .50, K = 81, L = 101, K_1 = 1, L_1 = 1$ (free trade $\pi = .5$).

that, depending on the equilibrium, tariffs could be 0%, 25%, or 106%, and the equilibrium export subsidies could be 47%, 27%, or 0%, respectively. Thus, these three economies could be identical along every economic and political dimension yet display tariffs as far apart as 0% and 106% and long-run success ratios of the procapital party ranging from 18% to 68%. Alternatively, the same economy could move from one equilibrium to one of the others with no change in any of the variables that a political economist might deem important. *Multiple equilibria may explain poor fits in econometric models of tariff setting.* For empirical estimates of tariff models see Caves (1976) and Pincus (1975).

What causes multiple equilibria? We find that they are more likely when the electoral outcomes are more responsive to funds from the lobbies. Figure 11.3 shows an economy that displays this behavior. In that economy, we held the elasticities of the electoral odds with respect to both policies constant at −1 (meaning that a 10% increase in a party's policy reduces its odds of election by 10%, ceteris paribus). We then held the elasticity of the electoral odds near 1 for capital contributions to the procapital party and increased the elasticity of the odds for the effectiveness of labor contributions from 0 to 1. This is equivalent to movement down the vertical axis in the figure, and corresponds to the movement from both parties supporting free trade to no equilibrium, to a single equilibrium, to two equilibria, and finally to three equilibria as labor contributions influence voters more (as the horizontal axis is approached).

To summarize: *The more important is money in politics, the greater the number of multiple equilibria in a country.* Thus, increases in the effect of a lobby's contributions on its party's election increases the number of equilibria in a progression from free trade to no equilibrium, to one equilibrium, to two equilibria, to three.

11.5 Political schizophrenia: party–lobby conflict with multiple equilibria

For all twenty-five economies with three equilibria (A, B, C), the following pattern emerged:

> the procapital party does best with B, intermediate with A, and worst with C;
> capital does worst with B, intermediate with A, and best with C;
> labor does best with B, intermediate with A, and worst with C.

For economies with only two equilibria, the above rankings held whenever applicable. Thus, a type B (zero-subsidy) equilibrium always involved the highest probability of victory for the procapital party, the lowest expected income for the capital lobby, and the highest expected income for the labor lobby.

Similar results hold when type B and C outcomes were compared with those under free trade FT (recall that free trade is not an equilibrium, just a reference point):

> the procapital party does best with B, intermediate with FT, and worst in C;
> capital does worst with B, intermediate with FT, and worst with C;
> labor does best with B, intermediate with FT, and worst with C.

In fact, the second and the third of these results follow directly from Theorem 7 in the Appendix to Chapter 10.

The schizophrenia result asserts that *with multiple equilibria, an equilibrium that is bad for a lobby is good for its party and vice versa.* Notice in the type B equilibrium that the procapital party sponsors a zero subsidy but has a 68% probability of election. Even though it sponsored a zero export subsidy in that case, it still received contributions from the proexport capital lobby. In fact, it received the largest percentage of capital devoted to lobbying (26%)

of all of the equilibria. This caused the type B equilibrium to yield the lowest expected income for capital. Another interesting feature of the schizophrenia case is that *each party does best in that equilibrium in which it is the least interventionist politically*. We do not have good intuitive explanations for these results.

11.6   The multiple equilibrium trap: why negotiation may provide no escape from the Prisoner's Dilemma

While the Prisoner's Dilemma model provides an explanation for tariffs, it also raises questions. The traditional query by economists was this: Why don't the losers from tariffs bribe the gainers into not seeking tariffs? In a small economy, the losers will always have money left over after they pay the bribe. Previously, the best answer has been information costs, unorganized general interests, and the absence of institutional arrangements facilitating payoffs among the lobbies (although the parties could provide this). However, it would appear that Prisoner's Dilemma tariffs could easily be avoided by simple negotiation since the factors could simply agree not to lobby. Our model generates multiple equilibria, and this, as we shall see, provides a reason why negotiation between the lobbies may not be enough to avoid the noncooperative tariff equilibrium.

The point that cooperation and Pareto optimality should emerge has also been made in many versions of the repeated Prisoner's Dilemma game. See, for example, the Axelrod (1980a,b) tournament and the empirical literature reviewed in Chapter 10. The argument is that, although each player then has an incentive to double-cross the other to obtain the still more favorable off-diagonal payoff, he (or she) is restrained from acting noncooperatively because, in the following period, his opponent can play noncooperatively. Hence, the double crosser stands to make only a one-period gain and then suffer future losses. Meanwhile, the potential victim of a double cross stands to make only a one-period loss, after which he could attain at least his original payoff under the noncooperative solution. Thus, there are incentives to enter into cooperative agreements. Why does cooperation not emerge among domestic lobbies so that Pareto (zero-tariff) policies emerge?

The multiple equilibrium trap suggests that *multiple equilibria may prevent a move to free trade because they provide worse alternatives to the Prisoner's Dilemma outcome*. When multiple equilibria are present, the lobbies will be reluctant to leave the Prisoner's Dilemma equilibrium for free trade because a double cross could take them to another equilibrium even worse than that of the Prisoner's Dilemma. Suppose that the lobbies initially both choose noncooperation; that both parties choose positive policies; and that the equilibrium involves both factors being worse off with lobbying than they would have been with free trade. The type A equilibrium shown in Table 11.2 has a

Prisoner's Dilemma metagame of this sort. Consider negotiations between the lobbies to move away from this type A equilibrium to free trade. Notice that both capital's and labor's income would rise by approximately 10%. In evaluating the costs and benefits of this cooperative move to free trade, each lobby must reflect that, if it is double-crossed, there is no guarantee that it can return to the original type A equilibrium: It might end up in a type B or C equilibrium, in which case its payoff could be worse than in the original Prisoner's Dilemma case. Note that, compared to the type A equilibrium, capital would be worse off under a tariff-only equilibrium (type B) and labor would be worse off under an export-subsidy-only (type C) equilibrium. With sufficient risk aversion, it would be rational for both lobbies to stay at a type A noncooperative equilibrium, even when the metagame is repeated.

There are, of course, other reasons for the absence of free trade. An interesting one seldom mentioned in the economics literature is the difficulty of compensating the losing actors in a negotiated movement to free trade. Both economic agents and political parties would be injured. In our model, the movement to free trade would almost always leave one of the political parties with a lower probability of election. Hence, *free trade may not emerge because of institutional difficulties in compensating the losing political party.* In a more complicated model with both special interests and general (unrepresented) interests, it would be reasonable for special-interest lobbies to prevent the evolution of institutional mechanisms for party compensation that would lead to free trade. Such mechanisms would reduce the power of special-interest lobbies relative to that of general interests. This can cause redistributive perversities to emerge in the formation of constitutions.

Intercountry agreements such as GATT avoid Prisoner's Dilemmas at the country level. However, voluntary export restraint agreements are obvious deviations from GATT-type agreements. VERs are parallel to price chiseling by firms in a price-setting cartel. With large numbers of lobbies pressing for redistributive policies of all types, multilateral agreements to refrain from protectionist activity are difficult to police. In every country, at least one political party has an incentive to cheat secretly on the free trade cartel and receive funds in exchange for invisible forms of protection, such as VERs. International trade agreements cannot be understood without knowing the domestic gainers and losers, both economic and political. Anything that improves one domestic group's economic welfare usually harms one of the political parties.

11.7   No equilibrium

The nonexistence of an equilibrium may be of some interest for future research because it is so common in this model. Even when the elasticities of the electoral outcomes were high with respect to economic resources, we were able to find a type A political equilibrium (i.e., two interventionist policies, nonspecialized production, and full employment) in only 61 out of 204 countries examined (i.e., only 30% of the time). What does it mean if we cannot find a political-economic equilibrium 70% of the time?

"No equilibrium" cases include all economies in which the political system drove one of the two industries out of business and/or caused unemployment of one of the factors. Since we are interested in long-run effects, it is not reasonable to include unemployment cases as an equilibrium. Another interpretation of "no equilibrium" is that production may be nonspecialized and full employment may hold, but nonlinearity of the equilibrium conditions may simply mean that not everybody can be happy and get what they want in a general political-economic equilibrium. In this case, there are no values of the policies and of the lobbying expenditures that can simultaneously make the two lobbies and the two political parties happy: Given two lobbies and two parties, there is always at least one of the four actors who will be dissatisfied. The parallel in traditional supply and demand analysis is nonintersection of the supply and demand curves. *An empirical prediction might be political turbulence.* The latter has implications for politics in the developing countries and is a useful area for future research. Unfortunately, time did not permit us to determine which of these two interpretations explains some or all of the "no equilibrium" cases: We leave this question to other scholars.

The absence of an equilibrium in an economy is related to the effectiveness of lobbying resources in helping political parties get elected. Figure 11.3 shows how the number of equilibria in an economy depends on the effectiveness of capital and labor lobbying in influencing voters. Low values of K_1 and L_1 imply that capital and labor are effective in obtaining votes; high values imply the reverse. Notice that intermediate values of K_1 and L_1 are associated with no equilibrium.

11.8   The passageway thesis: the no-equilibrium region between protection and free trade

There is another result suggested by Figure 11.3. As the underlying parameters change so that a country moves from a distorted equilibrium (with positive tariffs and export subsidies) to free trade it crosses a "no-equilibrium region." We have not explored the passageway thesis extensively to see whether the no-equilibrium region must *always* be crossed in moving from distorted equilibria to free trade economies. That is, we did not investigate the passageway thesis for many values of the terms of trade P and the factor intensity parameter A. Such research would be useful.

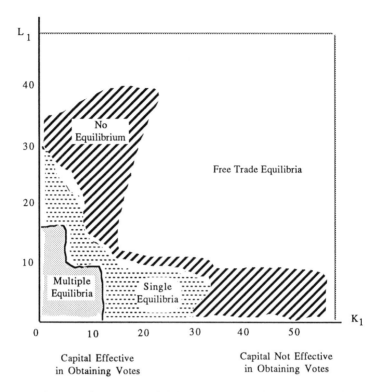

Figure 11.3. The no-equilibrium passageway between protection and free trade (simulation based on $A = .3$, $P = .6$, $K_0 = 90 + K_1$, $L_0 = 100 + L_1$).

If the no-equilibrium region is empirically meaningful, it suggests two insights. First, it might be a theoretical explanation of political turbulence in many developing countries. According to the model, such countries will have low to intermediate values of the elasticity of electoral outcomes with respect to economic resources. Second, equilibrium movements to free trade may require drastic rather than small changes (in order to cross the no-equilibrium region) in the responsiveness of electoral outcomes to economic resources (e.g., the drastic trade liberalization experiment in Chile in the 1970s). Note in Figure 11.3 that *in order for the political equilibrium to move from multiple distortions to free trade, there must be a decline in the effectiveness of money in political campaigns* (e.g., caused by an increase in voter sophistication). Theorems 5 and 6 in the Appendix to Chapter 10 give explicit conditions relating K_1 and L_1 to presence of tariffs versus free trade.

11.9   Predatory lobbying costs: rent seeking

How much of the national economy gets burned up in resources devoted to lobbying? The three equilibria for the economy described in Table 11.2 have proportions of capital devoted to lobbying ranging from 5% to 21% and proportions of labor in lobbying ranging from 12% to 20%.

These rent seeking proportions are typical of those in the sixty-one economies with positive tariff and export subsidy rates in Table 11.1. In the vast majority of those cases, the proportions of capital and labor devoted to lobbying fell between 5% and 15%. If these are empirically representative, rent seeking is a much larger loss than the typical 1–2% inefficiency (deadweight) losses.

CHAPTER 12

Increasing returns to politics and factor endowments: economic development and Brazilian vitality versus the Indian disease

This chapter analyzes a small developing economy that is capital scarce but labor abundant. It differs from the rest of the book, which describes an advanced economy, such as the United States, in which capital is abundant but labor is scarce. In this chapter, the procapital party favors protection since imports are capital intensive, and the prolabor party favors export promotion because exports are labor intensive. Mathematically, the formulas developed in the previous chapters can be used here simply by reversing the symbols.

One of the most interesting implications of this chapter is that *with endogenous politics, there are increasing returns to an economy's factor endowment. That is, the more capital an economy has, the higher will be the returns to capital.* This contrasts with the Rybczynski result that capital returns will be independent of factor endowments for an open trading economy, and with the diminishing returns result that capital returns will decline with more capital in a closed economy. We speculate that our result explains both Brazilian vitality and the Indian disease.

The pure theory of international trade is long on demonstrations that tariffs can induce capital accumulation in capital-scarce economies. The same idea appears in the literature on tariff factories (see Kindleberger 1963, chap. 12) and earlier in discussions of tariffs as engines of capital formation through redistribution effects toward savers (Johnson 1908). The traditional literature

Chapter 12 in Stephen P. Magee, William A. Brock, and Leslie Young, *Black Hole Tariffs and Endogenous Policy Theory.* New York: Cambridge University Press, 1989. Adapted from Stephen P. Magee and Leslie Young, "Multinationals, Tariffs and Capital Flows with Endogenous Politicians" in Charles P. Kindleberger and David Audretsch, eds., *The Multinational Corporation in the 1980s.* Cambridge: MIT Press, 1983, pp. 21–37.

examines *the effects of tariffs on international capital movements.* In this chapter *we reverse the causation and examine the effects of international capital flows on tariffs.* We explore how politics and the economy interact in situations analyzed by Hymer (1970) and Barnet and Mueller (1974). A useful extension of this work would examine the effects of capital flows on endogenous capital restrictions. Findlay and Wellisz (1982) examine the optimal inflow of foreign capital and the domestic conflict between opposing interests with and without tariffs. A good survey of the political determinants of economic policy decisions in trade and direct investment models is provided in McCulloch (1979).

Why are there extensive restrictions on multinationals in tariff-protected markets in developing countries? Consider a small developing economy in which capital and labor are engaged in the distributional squabble outlined in earlier chapters. Assume that the trade policies emerging from the political equilibrium result in a higher domestic price of the capital-intensive good than would be true with free trade. If foreign capital cannot be induced to contribute to the capital lobby, it will enter, since the domestic return exceeds the world return (we ignore risk here). If it must join local capital in contributing to the procapital party, it will enter only if the returns net of lobbying costs exceed the world return. We speculate that local capital in these situations prefers licensing over subsidiaries, local equity participation over full foreign ownership, and controlled versus uncontrolled multinational subsidiaries, once these political considerations are taken into account. Controls over foreign capital, even if implemented initially by the prolabor party, can be co-opted by the procapital party and used to force foreign capital to help generate political returns to capital.

Local capital will pressure for restrictions to force multinationals to contribute to the political effort. Thus, restrictions on foreign capital provide Olson (1965) appropriation mechanisms for local capital. If the restrictions did not exist, multinationals would quickly erode the politically created capital scarcity caused by high tariffs. In what follows, we do not examine how these ancillary mechanisms develop; we merely assume that they exist and are effective. We assume that the appropriation mechanisms work so that multinationals contribute the same proportion of their capital to the local procapital party as do local capital owners. The framework here is symmetric in that each factor attempts to exploit the other through the political process.

The results are based on simulations generated by the model in Chapter 10 of Leontief production with logit probability of election functions. This chapter covers the following:

12.1.   a review of the literature;
12.2.   the endowment effect – there are increasing returns to politics;

12.3.   policy insensitivity – the tariff rate does not rise dramatically with increases in a country's capital–labor endowment ratio;

12.4.   world polarization into capital- versus labor-abundant economies;

12.5.   the instability of country capital endowments – countries with a lot of capital gain more and vice versa;

12.6.   symmetric Marxist factor exploitation – each factor attempts to exploit the other through politics;

12.7.   clout reversals – the ability of international price changes to cause the pattern of domestic factor exploitation to reverse;

12.8.   the possibility of capital cross flows – international capital enters without paying lobbying costs while domestic capital leaves to avoid the high lobbying costs;

12.9.   local capital benefits from capital inflows if international capital contributes to the lobbying effort; and

12.10.   Brazilian vitality versus the Indian disease – international capital expands rapidly in Brazil where it is abundant (because politically protected) while capital leaves prolabor environments such as India.

In our model, a small developing economy produces two goods using two factors of production, capital and labor. The two factors of production are devoted either to producing goods or to political lobbying. We take a long-term view so that full employment holds. There is an export subsidy s on good Y, the import tariff t on good X, and a probability of election π of the procapital party. The political market clears more frequently than the economic market, so that the economy stays at the "expected value" of the relative goods price ratio rather than moving to either of the two extreme realizations following each election.

We are interested in examining effects of international capital investments in which a multinational corporation (abbreviated MNC) enters and joins the local capitalists in contributing to the procapital party. What happens to the equilibrium tariff rates, returns to capital, and electoral outcomes with endogenous politics? We answer this question using simulations. Good X is relatively capital intensive and is imported in the absence of distortions. The capital lobby contributes capital to party 1, which sponsors a tariff t on imports of good X. The labor lobby contributes labor to party 2 in exchange for an export subsidy on the labor-intensive good. We choose values of the parameters so that production is not specialized (i.e., so that both goods are produced): The international price of good Y is set at 0.64 while the capital–output ratio for good X is 1.0 and the ratio for good Y is $A = 0.20$. The labor–output ratios for both goods equal 1.0. The economy's labor endowment is fixed at 100, and the capital endowment is varied from 28 to 84. Both goods are produced and full employment holds. As in previous chapters, we

Table 12.1. *Simulation results for an economy with four different capital–labor ratios*

	Case			
	A	B	C*	D
Capital–labor ratio	0.280	0.319	0.597	0.840
Equilibrium policies are insensitive to an economy's capital–labor ratio	Equilibrium policies (%)			
Tariff on X	35.9	36.5	39.5	41.2
Export subsidy on Y	10.9	9.7	4.1	1.1
Increasing returns to capital: Capital returns are positively related to the economy's capital–labor ratio				
Success of the procapitalist party	0.199	0.210	0.266	0.301
Domestic price of good Y	0.650	0.640	0.592	0.566
Return to capital				
Gross	0.438	0.450	0.510	0.543
Net of lobbying costs	0.385	0.396	0.450	0.480
(International return to capital = 0.450)				
Polarization of capital: Capital exits from the economy for K/L values below the watershed value of $(K/L)^* = 0.60$ in case C; capital enters for $K/L > 0.60$				
The wage rate drops as the capital–labor ratio rises				
Gross wages	0.562	0.550	0.490	0.457

Note: International parameters for good Y: relative price $P = 0.64$; capital–output ratio $A = 0.20$.

assume a logit probability of election function for party 1 in which the elasticities of the odds that a voter will vote for the procapital party are unit elastic with respect to capital lobbying and the tariff, and (minus) unit elastic with respect to labor lobbying resources and the export subsidy. The generality of the results (or the lack thereof) could be established by empirical testing. Our results for this chapter are summarized in Table 12.1.

12.1   The literature

Mundell (1957) found that, in the presence of a tariff, capital mobility could lead to the same distribution of income in an economy as would be the case without the trade. The results in this chapter provide an important exception to that rule. We find that, since the domestic political equilibrium is affected by a country's factor endowment, the distribution of income is also affected by factor endowments.

Findlay and Wellisz (1983) examine a Ricardo–Viner model of a developing country in which there is one mobile factor of production (labor) and two immobile factors (capital and land). Capital is employed in producing manufactured goods, the importable, while land is used in the production of the exportable good, agricultural products. Findlay and Wilson (1984) show that the optimal tax on foreign inflows of capital is positive when there is a positive tariff rate. However, they note that, in the presence of a tariff, inflows of foreign capital will reduce the return of both capital and land while improving the wage of labor. Thus, they get the result that if capitalists and landowners lobby together against foreign capital inflows and attain a tax against the inflows, then national welfare will rise. Ethier (1986) develops a formal model in which technology transfers involving simple technologies can occur through the market; those that are more complicated must be undertaken through multinational firms.

For the interaction of capital mobility and commercial policy see Miyagiwa and Young (1986). For a model in which rigidities lead to greater factor price equalization across countries with factor mobility see Neary (1985). For stylized facts on U.S. foreign investment see Lipsey (1982). For economic growth see Rostow (1960, 1962, 1971, 1975, 1978, 1980, 1982).

There is a large literature on multinational corporations, which will not be reviewed here. We mention in passing the work of Caves (1971), Kindleberger (1969, 1970a), Kindleberger and Audretsch (1983), and Vernon (1966); the internalization theories of Buckley and Casson (1976) and Dunning (1973); the appropriability theory of Magee (1977a–c); the scale economies theories of Ethier (1979, 1986), Helpman (1984), Helpman and Krugman (1985), and Krugman (1979, 1981); and the hierarchy theory of Williamson (1975). For surveys see McCulloch (1985) and Rugman (1980).

For an application of the special-interest ideas in this book to the third world debt problem see Magee and Brock (1986). For an analysis of public finance in developing countries see Lindbeck (1986b). On the issue of international factor mobility see Neary (1985). On political groups and the development process see Leff (1979). Bhagwati (1987) has suggested quid pro quo direct foreign investment: A country will invest in a host country at a loss, but this will reduce host-country protection against it in subsequent periods. Dinopoulos (1987) finds evidence for this phenomenon: Although rates of return in the Japanese automobile industry were eight times those in the United States, the Japanese industry undertook investments in the States, apparently to reduce the effects of possible U.S. restrictions against their cars.

For the effects of protection on developing country exports to advanced countries see Hughes and Krueger (1982) and Michaely (1985). For studies on preferential treatment of developing country exports to advanced countries see Brown (1985a,b), Ray (1985), and Sapir and Lundberg (1982). Brown (1985a) found that the U.S. generalized scheme of preferences favored the high-income developing countries and hurt agriculturally based economies.

On the issue of rent seeking in developing countries see the discussion of Whalley's work our Chapter 15 and the case study by Ross (1984). Bornschier (1980) finds that direct investment by multinational corporations increases the growth rate in developing host countries in the short run but lowers growth subsequently.

For an examination of the "Dutch disease" (price increases in one sector causing contractions in other sectors) see Corden (1984a) and Dornbusch and Frankel (1987). Brittan (1975) discusses the "British disease" (slow growth and high inflation), caused by the government preventing real wage adjustment through unemployment benefits and social programs. A closely related disease is stagflation (rising unemployment and inflation). Davis and Minford (1986) analyze the "European disease," which is permanently high unemployment and low output growth. Neary and O'Grada (1986) report the inconsistent behavior of the Irish government in the early 1930s: introducing high tariffs and, simultaneously, preventing foreigners from setting up factories made profitable by the tariffs.

12.2 Increasing returns to politics: the endowment effect

We observe increasing returns: The more capital an economy has, the greater its political clout and the higher the returns to capital. In our model, the returns to capital are positively (rather than negatively) related to the economy's endowment of capital because as capital accumulates, the procapital party's equilibrium tariff increases and its electoral success increases. Both considerations increase the domestic price of the capital-intensive good, increase the return to capital, and lower wages. Table 12.1 shows that the success ratio of the procapitalist party increases from 19.9% in case A to 30.1% in case D. These results are diametrically opposed to the more traditional outcome in a closed economy, in which an increase in an economy's capital stock drives down the return to capital (i.e., until the domestic returns equal international returns).

The increasing returns to factor endowments caused by endogenous politics are illustrated in Figure 12.1. The more capital the economy has, the higher the electoral success rate of the procapital party and the higher the policy favored by the procapital party (i.e., in this chapter only, the tariff). Our

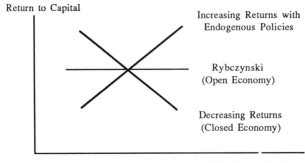

Figure 12.1. Increasing returns to factor endowments with endogenous politics contrasted with two traditional cases.

results (the positively sloped line in Fig. 12.1) are in direct conflict with the traditional theory of diminishing returns to a factor in a closed economy (the negatively sloped line) and the independence of factor returns and factor endowments predicted by Rybczynski for a small open economy (the horizontal line).

The same point can be made in Table 12.1. The increased success of the procapitalist party causes the expected domestic price of the labor-intensive good to fall from 0.650 to 0.566 (in moving from case A to case D). Because of the magnification effect, the gross return to capital rises from 0.438 to 0.543. The return to capital net of lobbying costs also increases. Thus, because of the higher success rate of the procapital party with a larger endowment of capital in the economy, there is a positive relationship between capital returns and the capital stock.

Similar arguments explain why this model predicts that wage rates fall as foreign capital enters the economy. Wage rates drop from 0.562 to 0.457 as capital increases. Similar results are discussed in the popular press (see Barnet and Mueller 1974). These political considerations help explain labor and Marxist opposition to multinationals in developing countries.

12.3   Policy insensitivity

In the simulations done here, the equilibrium policies are generally insensitive to changes in an economy's endowment of capital. They show that if the capital–labor endowment ratio for a country triples (from 0.28 to 0.84), the equilibrium tariff rate only increases from 35.9% to 41.2%. This suggests that, when a multinational corporation brings capital into a small economy, the procapital policy changes may be hard to detect.

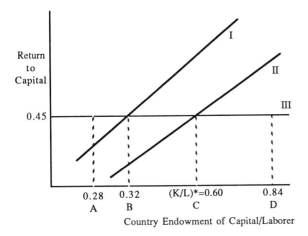

Figure 12.2. Returns to capital with endogenous policies: I, gross domestic returns to capital (free-riders earn this); II, returns net of lobbying costs (lobby contributors earn this); III, international returns to capital.

12.4   World polarization into capital- versus labor-abundant economies

Increasing returns to factor endowments generate a polarization effect. Given the other economic parameters, there is a "watershed" value of an economy's capital stock at which the domestic capital returns equal the returns on world markets. If a country's capital endowment is below this value, domestic returns are lower than international returns and capital leaves the economy, causing its capital stock to decline to zero. If the capital endowment is above the watershed value, the capital stock expands indefinitely until revolution or factors outside our analysis intrude. The capital stock watershed value is an unstable equilibrium: At all other endowments, the capital stock expands or contracts because of domestic special-interest behavior.

These results are illustrated in Table 12.1 and in Figure 12.2. Note that the net return to capital increases from 0.385 in case A to 0.480 in case D. By assumption, capital on the world market earns a rental equal to 0.450. Thus, both local and international capital tend to leave this economy if its endowment is below 0.597 units per person, and international capital will join local capital in entering the economy if the endowment exceeds 0.597. Case C represents this "watershed" value of the economy's factor endowment. For capital–labor ratios below C, the capital stock implodes; above C, it explodes. Point C corresponds to Rostow's (1960) takeoff.

12.5   Unstable capital endowments

An empirical implication is that developing economies will segment into two groups. Those with low capital endowments would have slow or negative growth of their capital stocks, whereas those with high endowments of capital would show increasing capital and positive growth. This contrasts with the usual economic prediction that undercapitalized economies would engage in capital deepening, whereas overcapitalized economies would show slow or even negative growth of their capital stocks. This is a useful area for future empirical work.

12.6   Symmetric Marxist factor exploitation

For decades economists have taught their students that only relative prices matter. A similar proposition holds in special-interest politics: Only relative power matters. In Figure 12.2, capital and the procapital protectionist party become increasingly powerful if the economy is initially endowed with more than 0.60 units of capital per person; labor and the proexport labor party, on the other hand, become increasingly powerful when the economy is initially endowed with less than 0.60 units.

There have been forests of material written by Marxists and anti-Marxists on this question. There is no a priori reason to believe that capital will be more or less politically successful than labor in Western democracies. Capital has concentrated wealth, which can buy votes, but labor has greater numbers and more votes. Since power is relative, what matters for local political success is determined by a country's factor returns *relative* to those on the world market. Changes in wages and capital returns on world markets can alter the balance of power in domestic markets, particularly for countries whose endowments are near the watershed endowment ratio. Presumably, these would be countries near the world average endowment ratio.

12.7   Clout reversals

Political power is determined by economic clout. We have just seen that if a country has relatively more capital per person than does the world economy, that it will have higher capital returns. This generates an interesting paradox: Local capital's welfare can rise in response to a decrease in world capital returns.

To see this result, assume that labor has more clout in an economy than capital, so that the domestic capital–labor ratio is below the world average – say, at B in Figure 12.2 (= 0.32). In this case, capital is emigrating, labor is becoming increasingly powerful politically, and the tariffs that protect domestic capital are falling. Now let the world returns to capital fall substantially below 0.45. If the domestic return to capital (measured along II) at endowment point B is now higher than the return on world markets, labor's exploitation of capital will reverse. Capital will start to enter the country, the procapital protectionist party will become more successful, and labor will be exploited. In short, *changes in world factor returns can reverse patterns of factor exploitation in countries near the world average endowment ratio.*

12.8   Capital cross flows

If international capital fails to contribute to the procapital party, capital cross flows are possible at endowment levels just below the watershed capital stock. There, international capital that entered would earn the gross return to capital , whereas local capital would earn less because of the cost of contributions to the procapital party (local capital earns the net return). Since the international return is between these two values, local capital leaves and international capital enters. This phenomenon is called a *capital cross flow.*

We speculate that local capital in many economies will use enforced licensing regulations, required sharing of equity with local capital holders, and other schemes to induce international owners of capital to share the politically created scarcity rents with them, contribute to their creation, and prevent their erosion via entry. Obviously, both domestic and international investors will attempt to free-ride on the political investments already made to the domestic procapital party.

12.9   Local capital benefits from capital inflows

Local capital will favor rather than oppose entry of foreign capital at all possible endowment levels so long as the international capital contributes to the lobbying effort. The net returns to local capital (i.e., returns minus all lobbying costs) appear to increase with entry of foreign capital. This result assumes, however, that the new foreign capital allocates the same proportion of itself to lobbying as does domestic capital. Let the gross rental rate be 1.0 and let the local capital lobby allocate 80% of each machine to economic production. The rental rate net of lobbying costs is then 0.80. Assume that a multinational entered, contributed to the lobby, and that the increased success of the procapital party caused gross returns to capital to rise to 1.1. Our simulations reveal that the fraction of the capital devoted to economic production increases slightly with larger capital endowments; thus, let this fraction rise to 0.82. As a result, the net return to local capital rises to 0.90 (= 1.1×0.82).

12.10   Brazilian vitality versus the Indian disease

Increasing returns to politics might help explain certain empirical phenomena. Over the period 1960–80, the World Bank reports that the average annual growth rate of GNP per capita was 5.1% in Brazil and only 1.4%

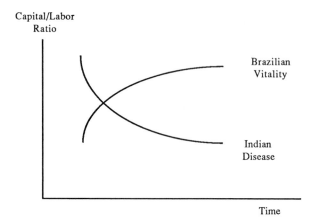

Figure 12.3. The evolution of an economy's capital–labor ratio over time.

in India. This occurred despite the fact that population grew more rapidly in Brazil. We divide the world's countries into two groups. Those with higher capital endowments and capital returns will be blessed with Brazilian vitality; those with lower capital returns will be cursed with the Indian disease. We lump the advanced countries into the Brazil group.

Brazilian vitality describes a country with higher than world returns to capital so that capital enters and the returns continue to increase. The domestic capital returns may be high initially because the country has a high capital endowment or because capital is potent politically. The reverse case we characterize as the *Indian disease;* i.e., countries with lower than world returns to capital so that capital exits and the returns continue to decrease. The country becomes increasingly labor dominant. The process is not self-correcting because of increasing returns to politics: The dominant factor gets stronger over time. This process will end with a bang, a whimper, or both.

Figure 12.3 illustrates the proposition. Over time, capital-rich countries continue to prosper because of favorable policy changes and increased growth in property rights both for physical and human capital. These are called advanced countries and are characterized by the Brazilian vitality curve. In contrast, countries dominated by labor experience decreasing protection for capital and the reverse. They are described by the Indian disease curve.

Our polarization result in this chapter suggests a formal theory for the absence of countries with intermediate factor endowments and hence intermediate values of GNP per capita. As Figure 17.1 will show, there were few countries in 1980 with GNP per capita in the midrange of $4,000–$8,000.

CHAPTER 13

Endogenous protection in the United States, 1900–1988

This chapter applies endogenous policy theory to U.S. protection since 1900. The work is preliminary since we do not test rival models. However, endogenous policy theory points to several variables that work moderately well in explaining tariff protection during this century. Empirically, long-run protection is explained by those exogenous variables that drive the behavior of groups (both broad and narrow) that favor or oppose protection (just as prices can be explained by the exogenous determinants of supply and demand). The U.S. variables explaining U.S. tariffs since 1900 are the labor–capital ratio, the terms of trade, the real foreign exchange rate, the unemployment rate, and the inflation rate. Since 75% of the variance in U.S. tariffs can be explained by these economic variables, we have indirect evidence for the powerless politician effect (that policies are outside of policymaker control).

We cover the following in this chapter:

13.1. a review of the literature;
13.2. the politics of U.S. protection (summary);
13.3. endogenous tariff theory and U.S. protection since 1900;
13.4. the empirical results;
13.5. the isoprotection curve and the macroeconomic theory of Republican protectionism; and
13.6. the Republican protectionism of the 1980s.

Chapter 13 in Stephen P. Magee, William A. Brock, and Leslie Young, *Black Hole Tariffs and Endogenous Policy Theory*. New York: Cambridge University Press, 1989. Adapted from Stephen P. Magee and Leslie Young, "Endogenous Protection in the United States, 1900–1984," in Robert M. Stern, ed., *U.S. Trade Policies in a Changing World Economy*. Cambridge: MIT Press, 1987, pp. 145–95.

The empirical results strongly support the compensation effect at work in the United States, both through the terms of trade effect and the unemployment rate. Among other things, we find that:

stagflation can have neutral effects on protection;
the three most protectionist administrations of the century were Republican – Harding, Hoover, and Reagan;
Republican electoral success is increasing protectionism;
the president is replacing Congress as the primary source of protection in the United States; and
protectionist pressure was low in the 1970s and high in the 1980s.

13.1   The literature

The history of U.S. tariff legislation for most of this century is well summarized by Baldwin (1983, 1984a, 1985b, 1986c) and Ratner (1972); for earlier periods see Taussig (1931) and Lake (in Frieden and Lake 1987, chap. 9); for a discussion of recent protectionism see Salvatore (1985). Several generalizations emerge from these studies. First, early in this century, Democratic presidents favored freer trade, whereas Republicans favored greater protection. We confirm Ferguson's observation that even recent Republican presidents (Eisenhower, Nixon, Reagan) are more protectionist than recent Democratic ones (Kennedy, Johnson, Carter), as was the case early in the century. Second, the House of Representatives is generally more protectionist than the Senate or the president. Third, a major set of changes occurred in the 1930s. Prior to 1934, Congress largely controlled tariff levels; thereafter, the Executive Branch was the dominant force.

The locus of protectionist pressure in the House of Representatives has switched from the Republican party in 1900 to the Democratic party today. Baldwin (1976a, 1986c) has examined this switch by House Democrats from free trade to protectionism. In the 1970 discussions of the protectionist Burke–Hartke proposal, Democrat Wilbur Mills deviated from his long-standing support of liberal trade policies and sponsored a bill establishing import quotas on textiles and footwear. The House Democrats voted for the protectionist Ways and Means Committee bill (137 for and 83 against) while the Republicans were slightly opposed (78 for and 82 against). These results were reinforced in Baldwin's analysis of the vote on the 1973 Trade Bill: Democrats in both the House and the Senate were significantly more protectionist than were Republicans, and protectionist labor union contributions were given primarily to those representatives who voted against the act. Baldwin (1986c) finds that both the president and Congress are more likely to adopt protectionist legislation just prior to an election. Baldwin (1985b) has a good discussion of the trade policies of the Reagan administration's first term.

Ferguson (1984) argues that a major realignment occurred in the United States under the New Deal whereby labor-intensive industries became nationalists, whereas capital-intensive industries became internationalists. The internationalists associated themselves with the Democrats, and the nationalists were associated with the Republicans. For a historical description of U.S. tariff policies see Pincus (1984).

Lindbeck (1975a, 1976, 1983) has developed the notion of endogenous politicians within the political business cycle. The result can best be described in the Phillips curve diagram with unemployment on the horizontal axis and the rate of inflation on the vertical axis. Presume that international markets or other outside forces generate a level of inflation consistent with external balance for the country. So long as the country is below this level of inflation, there will be external surplus in a fixed-exchange-rate period; the converse will be true above this rate of inflation. Because of domestic political pressures for external balance, Lindbeck shows that the equilibrium will cycle in clockwise loops generated by domestic policy and international market forces. In Lindbeck (1975a) the loops are shown for the period 1948–74. Domestic politicians are endogenous in this model because of the constraints put upon them by the lack of internal or external balance. The model is also useful in predicting where monetary and fiscal policy must take the economy within the Phillips curve diagram. In a slightly different context, Lindbeck (1983) describes the vicious circle of budget expansion. In it, political competition generates demands for budget expansion, which lead to higher taxes, which increase inflation, which reduces international competitiveness, which increases the rate of unemployment, which then reduces the tax base, leading to higher budget deficits. Continual pressure from the political side to increase spending leads to a repeat of the cycle. Lindbeck and Snower (1987b) explain that Europe's lack of success in reducing its unemployment after the recession in the early 1980s is explained by the more widespread influence of unions in Europe.

Paldam's (1981) survey indicates that about one-third of the variations in party popularities across countries are explained by macroeconomic variables. Sachs and Alesina (1986) find that, since World War II, Democratic administrations expand the economy during the first two years of their terms, whereas Republican administrations contract the economy. For an analysis of the relationship between interest groups and macroeconomic policy see Hibbs (1977, 1987). In examining twelve Western European and Northern American nations, he finds that countries with predominantly leftist governments are characterized by lower unemployment and high inflation while the reverse pattern is true in countries dominated by centrist or rightist parties.

Kurth (1979) develops some interesting special-interest origins of macroeconomic stabilization policy in Germany. He notes that the German steel industry was particularly active in pressuring and obtaining government support for expansion of the German naval budgets following depressions. For example, Germany experienced a depression in 1883, and Bismarck initiated a 20% increase in the German naval budget in 1884. The depression of 1890 was followed by a 60% increase in the German naval budget of 1891. Similar increases in the budget followed the depressions of 1901 and 1908. Early in the twentieth century, the steel industries of Britain and Germany competed directly with each other through the building of warships so that an Anglo–German naval race ensued. Although Kurth does not attribute World War I to this race, he shows that it did place significant barriers to detente between Britain and Germany.

Dornbusch and Frankel (1987) list four structural reasons for protection: shifts in productivity, the Dutch disease (price increases in one sector putting pressure on other sectors), wage misalignments, and import pressure from developing-country needs to pay debts. On international relationships between trade and unemployment see Cohen (1983). For an attempt to measure the procyclicality of protection see Cassing, McKeown, and Ochs (1986). Curzon and Price (1984) raise the question of whether the current rise in protection is a secular or cyclical phenomenon. Rogoff and Sibert (1985) model macroeconomic effects on elections as an equilibrium-signaling process, using taxes, government spending, and money growth as policy variables. For studies of macroeconomic and/or tariff policies see Chow (1976), Curzon and Price (1984), Dornbusch (1987), Gupta and Venieris (1981), Hall (1980), Henderson (1979), Hibbs (1977, 1987), Kormendi (1983), Kormendi and Meguire (1984b), Lindbeck (1976), and Spinelli (1985).

For evidence on the political business cycle in the United States see Frey and Ramser (1976), Nordhaus (1975), and Tufte (1976). On macroeconomics and protectionism generally see Magee (1982), and on macroeconomic interdependence among countries see Ishii, McKibbin, and Sachs (1985). For an analysis of the effects of terms of trade changes on an economy see Stulz (1984). In addition to Baldwin's (1983, 1984a, 1985b, 1986c) studies of trade policies in the United States see Baack and Ray (1983), Ferguson (1984), Frey and Schneider (1978), Krasner (1977, 1978, 1985), and Takacs (1981). For an analysis of macroeconomic policy in an open economy see Henderson (1979). Klein (1985) calculates the economic benefits of worldwide tariff reductions of 5%: He finds that domestic inflation is reduced for two years on the OECD countries and then rises for the next four years, although not significantly.

We generally think of governments as providing macroeconomic stabilization. However, Frey and Lau (1968) suggest that the reverse may be true:

The political system may increase rather than decrease variance in economic activity. Frey and Schneider (1978) find that increased inflation and unemployment hurt presidential popularity in the United States, whereas the growth in nominal consumption improves presidential popularity. Interestingly, they find that nondefense government expenditures and the number of civilian government jobs both increase significantly as elections approach, whereas government transfers are not significantly related to the time before the election. One other insight from this work is that, when presidents are confident at winning elections, they allow their ideological views greater freedom. Frey (1979) finds that, in certain countries (the United States, Germany, Sweden, and the United Kingdom), government popularity is negatively affected by inflation and unemployment, but positively affected by the growth in real income.

There are at least two scholars who believe that politics has little or no effect on the macroeconomy. Stigler (1972) believes that the political business cycle literature is without foundation and that rational voters will prevent politicians from successfully manipulating electoral outcomes through inflation or unemployment policies. In Tullock's (1979) view, the empirical effects of the political business cycles are statistically significant but small.

Baack and Ray (1985a) argue that U.S. tariffs declined and the income tax was instituted early in this century because big business wanted trade liberalization while the populists wanted more equitable taxation.

Ahmad (1983) generates macroeconomic evidence for the compensation effect. Using time series data he finds that, in the United States, federal expenditures on goods and services as a percentage of GNP increase with the rate of inflation and with the unemployment rate, but decrease with the growth of income.

McKeown (1983) documents a business cycle compensation effect. He notes that, in both the nineteenth and the twentieth centuries, more open world trade has occurred during periods of world prosperity, whereas closure of the system and greater protectionism occurred during periods of world depression. He cites slightly different motivation for tariff increases during depressions. Since the principal source of government revenues is custom duties, and these decline in depressions, the government officials themselves favor increasing tariffs to make up for the revenue shortfalls. Government officials are also motivated to vary tariffs in countercyclical ways for the following reason: At peaks of business cycles, governments enjoy high popularity because of the prosperity, and hence can afford to implement tariff reductions. Conversely, governments are unpopular during depressions and attempt to recoup popularity through tariff increases. This generates an "unpopular government" theory of protection.

In the future, U.S. protectionism will escalate as high-tech industries such

Table 13.1. *Major U.S. trade legislation*

Act	Year	Trade effects	Party/president	
Dingley	1897	protectionist	R	McKinley
Payne–Aldrich	1909	marginally freer trade	R	Taft
Underwood–Simmons	1913	freer trade	D	Wilson
Fordney–McCumber	1922	very protectionist	R	Harding
Smoot–Hawley	1930	very protectionist	R	Hoover
Reciprocal Trade Agreements Act	1934[a]	freer trade	D	Roosevelt
International Trade Negotiations:				
Geneva	1947			
Annecy	1949			
Torquay	1950–1			
Dillon Round	1956–61			
Trade Expansion Act	1962	freer trade	D	Kennedy
Kennedy Round Trade Negotiations	1964–7			
Burke–Hartke Bill[b]	1970	very protectionist	R	Nixon
Trade Act of 1974		freer trade	R	Nixon/Ford
Tokyo Round Trade Negotiations	1974–9			
Trade Act of 1979		freer trade	D	Carter
Trade Act of 1988		somewhat protectionist	R	Reagan

[a]Renewed by Congress eleven times, 1934–62.
[b]Did not pass.
Sources: Baldwin (1983), Pugel and Walter (1984), and Ratner (1972).

as electronics become import competing because of their accumulated political experience as defense contractors. Gates (1981) analyzes pressure-group politics and land policies in the United States. For an important study of nontariff protection in the United States in thirty-one industries see Hufbauer, Berliner, and Elliott (1986) and the data from this study discussed in Chapter 18.

13.2   The politics of U.S. protection

The chronology of U.S. tariff legislation in this century appears in Table 13.1. With a few exceptions, the major early protectionist tariff acts were passed during Republican administrations (McKinley, Taft, Harding, and Hoover); similarly, major nontariff barriers, such as the oil import quota (Eisenhower) and voluntary export restraint agreements (Nixon and Reagan), have been imposed or negotiated primarily by Republican presidents. Trade liberalizing acts have been the rule under Democratic presidents: Wilson,

Franklin Roosevelt, Kennedy, and Carter. This behavior can be described as Republican protectionism: Procapital Republican presidents support protection, whereas Democratic presidents support freer trade. The other surprise is how the American presidency, beginning with the late Nixon administration, has become more protectionist than Congress and a source of inefficient voluntary export restraint agreements, administrative protection, and so on.

13.3 Endogenous policy theory and U.S. protection

In general, we find empirical support in this chapter for the *powerless politican effect;* that is, that trade policies are largely outside the control of the policymakers in a competitive political system. We find that protection can be explained by those exogenous variables that drive the behavior of special interests and general interests who favor or oppose protection. Approximately 75% of the variability in tariffs during this century is explained by endogenous policy considerations (factor endowments, the terms of trade, unemployment, and inflation).

This chapter examines the level of protection for the United States as a whole. The variable to be explained is the average U.S. ad valorem tariff rate *t*, calculated as total U.S. tariff revenue divided by the value of U.S. total imports. In the U.S. context, we suppose that labor is used more intensively in import-competing industries and benefits in the long run from tariffs, whereas capital (both physical and human) is used more intensively in export industries and benefits from negative tariffs (i.e., export subsidies). On this point see, inter alia, Baldwin and Hilton (1983) and Stern and Maskus (1981). Evidence from Baldwin (1976a, 1986c) indicates that the House Democrats favor protection, whereas House Republicans favor freer trade. In our modeling, we assume that the Democratic party supports a tariff and the Republicans support a negative tariff (export subsidy). Given the lobbying resource flows, each sets its policy to maximize its probability of election. Since tariff levels are determined as the equilibrium of the political game, tariffs can be explained by variables that affect the protectionist lobby, the proexport lobby, and voters. Another point to stress is that protectionism is not a two-player game between protectionists and voters; rather, it is a three-player game among protectionists, proexport interests, and voters (with the parties acting as intermediaries). For this reason, we model both protectionist and proexport special interests. Consider first variables that measure *special-interest pressures for protection: the country factor endowment, magnification effects, and two compensation measures* (the terms of trade and the unemployment rate).

There is weak empirical support for the *endowment effect* (that changes in U.S. factor endowments alter the political power of special-interest lobbies

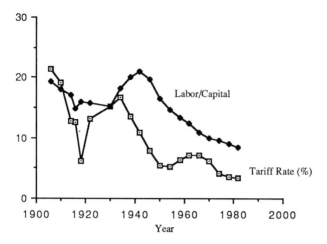

Figure 13.1. U.S. tariffs and the number of U.S. laborers per $100,000 in real capital.

representing the factors of production). As labor has become a less important factor of production in the United States during this century, its political influence has waned and tariff protection has declined. Following the Leontief model, the prolabor party should suffer at the polls as the relative importance of labor falls. Although this may be coincidental, Democratic candidates have lost five out of the past six presidential elections.

In earlier chapters, tariffs were related to country capital–labor ratios; for expositional convenience, and with no loss of generality, we invert the endowment ratio in this chapter. Since labor has become less important in the U.S. factor endowment, the theory predicts that tariff levels should decline. The readiest measure of the relative strength of labor is the ratio of labor to capital for the United States as a whole. *The number of U.S. workers per unit of real capital today is about half what it was at the turn of the century.* Figure 13.1 is a plot of U.S. tariff rates and the U.S. endowment of the number of workers per $100,000 of real U.S. capital (in 1972 dollars) since 1900. The only rise in the U.S. labor–capital endowment ratio came in the 1930s–1940s, because of the Great Depression.

The capital deepening that occurred in the advanced countries from World War II to the early 1970s was accompanied by decreases in tariffs on labor-intensive imports and increases in export subsidies, as endogenous policy theory suggests. Capital accumulation slowed in the 1970s and protectionism increased. The Leontief paradox notwithstanding, the endowment effect is supported by Ray's (1981a) cross-sectional evidence that U.S. tariffs are significantly lower in industries with higher capital–labor ratios and Finger, Hall, and Nelson's (1982, p. 460) result that nontariff protection is significantly lower in industries with high capital–labor ratios. The survey evidence by Pugel and Walter (1985) indicates that U.S. firms favoring free trade tend to be large, a result consistent with Ferguson's (1984) thesis that capital-intensive U.S. multinationals have been a powerful political force for free trade in the United States over the past fifty years.

The public furor over protectionism in the 1970s might be an example of the *magnification paradox*. Our Cobb–Douglas model predicts that increased magnification effects of product price on factor prices causes both protectionist and proexport forces to devote more economic resources to politics but to come away with a lower equilibrium level of protection. Thus the political noise level and the level of protection can move in opposite directions. In more detail, consider an increase in magnification caused by a decrease in the share of capital income in the production of U.S. exportables. This increases the elasticity of wages with respect to product prices. With increased magnification, labor becomes more interested in manipulating its wages through the political system. Consequently, it increases the proportion of its resources that are channeled to the Democratic party. For similar reasons, capital increases its political contributions to the Republicans.

With increased magnification, both parties find it optimal to offer less extreme policies in order to attract resources from their lobbies. Thus, both tariffs and export subsidies should decrease. In effect, the party gets the luxury of more resources from the protectionist lobby as well as lower voter hostility from its lower tariff. The magnification paradox suggests that *observers of protectionism must be careful not to confuse increased demands for protection with the actual supply of protection.* For example, the demand for protection appeared to increase in the 1970s while the supply apparently dropped (witness the Trade Bill of 1979). The magnification effect predicts that the tariff should move directly (while the level of protectionist lobbying should move inversely) with the share of capital income in U.S. production.

We were unable to devise a long series for the shares of capital and labor in exportable and importable production (which would be proxies for factor intensities, assuming a Cobb–Douglas production function). This would be an important exercise for future research. As a crude proxy, we calculated the capital share of all of U.S. national income since 1900. There was a secular decline during this century, and a generally procyclical movement of the series. Oddly enough, the coefficient on this variable often had the wrong sign, and was occasionally significantly wrong-signed. These experiments are not reported in the empirical work below. However, the significantly wrong signs might be a useful area for future research.

When any factor's economic fortunes decline, it transfers effort out of economic activity and into lobbying and political activity. This is called the *compensation effect*. When applied to tariffs, this effect applies to all variables affecting the economic fortunes of protectionists. The protectionist political party responds with a higher tariff. For example, increased unemployment, a rise in the terms of trade, and a strengthening of the real dollar exchange rate all reduce economic returns and cause protectionist forces to devote more resources to lobbying for protection. The result is an increase in the equilibrium tariff level. The votes of the Democrats decline during this process (see Chapter 11).

We apply the compensation effect to an increase in the U.S. *terms of trade* caused by the relative decline abroad in the price of U.S. importables (e.g., the Japanese automobile phenomenon). The results described here follow the Leontief model. (In Chapter 14, with the Cobb–Douglas model, the equilibrium lobbying ratios, tariffs, and probabilities of electoral outcomes are all independent of a country's terms of trade.) Since importables are labor intensive, the initial effect of the terms of trade increase is for U.S. blue-collar wages to fall. This, in turn, lowers the opportunity cost of lobbying for labor. Labor substitutes out of economic activity and into political activity (i.e., increases its protectionist lobbying pressure and its campaign contributions to the Democrats), with the result that U.S. tariffs increase. Recall that even with the higher tariff, wages of labor still fall; that is, the tariff provides only a partial offset to the increase in the terms of trade.

What happens to the export subsidy and electoral outcomes when the terms of trade increase? Recall that, in the Leontief model, the congressional Republicans should offer a smaller export subsidy than before to obtain general-interest votes; however, they will also receive fewer contributions from capital. The net effect of both of these changes is to raise the electoral cost to the Democrats of their higher special-interest tariff. It turns out that this increased cost to the Democrats dominates the benefits of greater contributions from labor, so the Democratic party is worse off (its electoral chances fall). In sum, the welfare of labor and the Democrats' electoral fortunes move together in response to an increase in the terms of trade: Labor's income falls and the Democrats lose votes.

A final point relating to estimation: The terms of trade effect on tariffs is in the same direction as the traditional tariff effect on a large country's terms of trade. We find that terms of trade increases raise the equilibrium tariff level, in contrast to the traditional result that increases in tariffs improve a large country's terms of trade. If the latter effect is at work, simultaneous equation bias may cause the significance of the terms of trade effect on tariffs to be overstated.

Figure 13.2 plots U.S. tariffs against the U.S. terms of trade for manufactured goods during this century. The improvement in the terms of trade in

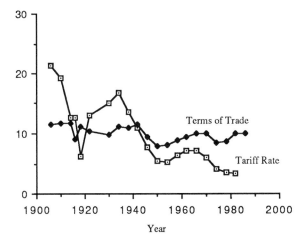

Figure 13.2. U.S. tariffs and the U.S. terms of manufacturing trade (price of exports/price of imports).

the 1930s may have been assisted by our Smoot–Hawley tariff being more beggar-thy-neighbor than those of our trading partners. However, note that the U.S. terms of trade increased from 1926 to 1930, well before Smoot–Hawley. Note also the steady rise from 1950 until 1970, which may have contributed to the Burke–Hartke protectionism of 1970. Note too the rise from Ford through Reagan, which contributes to current protectionist pressure.

Given the industrialization of the third world over the next few decades, *we can expect further relative declines in the prices of labor-intensive goods on world markets, continued increases in the U.S. terms of trade for manufactures, and greater protection.* This occurs because the downward pressure on wages will cause low-wage labor to substitute toward more protectionist lobbying. It also suggests a lowered electoral success rate for the prolabor Democrats, although the empirical importance of this effect is undetermined.

The other compensation variable is the *unemployment rate,* shown in Figure 13.3. Increased unemployment should render voters less hostile to the protection of jobs, and hence should increase the supply of protection even while it increases the demand for protection (via compensation behavior by labor). Higher unemployment also causes greater protection through compensation behavior by labor: They demand higher protection and devote more lobbying resources to protectionist lobbying during periods of high unemployment.

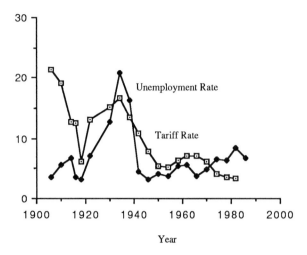

Figure 13.3. U.S. tariffs and unemployment.

Consider now a variable that proxies the behavior of *general interests,* namely *voters.* We assume that individual voters remain rationally ignorant about many economic issues, including protection. A single voter has a negligible probability of affecting the outcome of most elections; thus, the expected gain from collecting information about tariffs and other issues is minimal. We assume that the median voter generally opposes protection, but is insufficiently informed for it to go away. Hence, he or she is malleable via advertising financed by lobby contributions.

Apparently, one situation that rouses voters out of their normal stupor is a period of high *inflation.* Older macroeconomic arguments about the effect of inflation on protection asserted that higher U.S. inflation would increase U.S. imports; this pressure on the import-competing sector would cause it to lobby for greater protection. However, here arguments similar to the compensation effect dictate the reverse: When consumers experience unanticipated losses caused by inflation, they too substitute into political activity. During high inflation, voters and consumers become more politically vocal: Protectionism is one of their many targets. This lowers the equilibrium level of protection. Accordingly, the high inflation period of the 1970s generated pressure for import liberalization, whereas the low inflation period of the 1980s encourages greater protection. The inflation rate for U.S. producer prices plotted against U.S. tariffs is shown in Figure 13.4. Note the negative correlation between these variables, both in levels and in changes: the deflation under Harding and the rise in tariffs under Fordney–McCumber; the

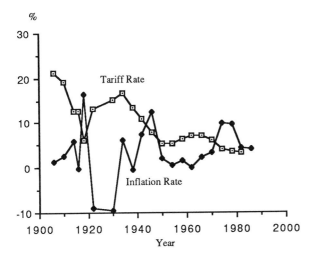

Figure 13.4. U.S. tariffs and the U.S. inflation rate (producer prices).

deflation of the 1950s and the rise in protection under Eisenhower and
Kennedy; and the inflation of the late 1970s associated with the drop in tariffs
then. Inflation has a significantly negative effect on U.S. tariffs in our regressions.

There is a second mechanism by which higher inflation reduces protectionist pressures. Periods of high inflation are correlated with declines in the
real exchange rate during floating rate periods. The rise in the dollar prices of
U.S. importables reduces compensation pressures for protection through
lobbying. We found negative correlation between U.S. inflation and the real
value of the dollar during this century: The simple correlation between the
two is –.38, which is significant at the .10 level. Thus, periods of low U.S.
inflation are associated with a strong real dollar (high U.S. price levels relative to foreign prices) and hence compensating behavior by U.S. special interests toward greater protectionist pressure. Thus, not all of the inflation
effect can be traced to the behavior of general (voter) interests.

13.4   The empirical results

When economic and political agents act rationally in the setting
of redistributive policies, they do so indirectly through lobbying, campaign
contributions, and logrolling, and they must operate through multiple
branches of government. Here, we abstract from these complications and
simply estimate a reduced-form equation for tariffs. Second, a long time

series is required to capture the political consequences of the long-run neo-classical determinants of protection such as factor endowments, factor in-tensities, and terms of trade effects. The information in Table 13.1 suggests a way to organize the data for an empirical estimation of the determinants of U.S. tariff levels in this century. Only four observations were taken on tariffs before Franklin Roosevelt, corresponding to the presidential administrations of the major tariff acts: Payne–Aldrich, Underwood–Simmons, Fordney–McCumber, and Smoot–Hawley (the results are not much different if all eight terms before 1932 are included). After 1934 (inclusive), the tariff level of each of the twelve administrations from Franklin Roosevelt through Carter is included, because of the continuous renewal of the trade acts and their non-specific nature. For our sixteen administrations, we regressed the average tariff level in the presidential administration of the act to exogenous variables in that or the previous administration (depending on whether or not the exog-enous variable is lagged). Our statistical modeling was constrained by the following consideration: We wanted observations longer than one year be-cause of the long-run nature of the political process that determines tariffs. Four years seemed appropriate for observation length because it coincides with the length of presidential administrations, and there has typically been about a four-year lag between renewals of trade acts since 1932; but four-year observation intervals generate only sixteen observations. This limited the number of exogenous variables that could be successfully included in a given regression equation. Fortunately, there is considerable variation in most of the series over this period, as can be seen in Table 13.2. (Our data are pre-sented by year in Appendix Table 13.1.)

Table 13.3 reports the tariff regressions using ordinary least squares over the sixteen administrations in the period 1905–80. (Appendix Table A.13.2 lists the variables used in the regressions and their sources.) In each equation the log of $(1 + t)$ is regressed on the exogenous variables, where t is equal to tariff duty revenue collected by the U.S. divided by the value of all U.S. imports for each observation (it does not include nontariff barriers). In effect, the dependent variable can be approximated by the value of t (since the log of 1 is zero). Equation 1 thus reports the regression of t on a set of macro variables that our intuition initially suggested might be important in explain-ing protection: the unemployment rate, the value of the real U.S. trade bal-ance, and the inflation rate. No lags are present, meaning that the average tariff rate for a given four-year period is being explained by the macro vari-ables for the same period. The fit is not good, with an adjusted R^2 of only .35; there was serious positive serial correlation in the residuals; and only unemployment was significant. When the same variables were lagged one administration, the fit was much worse, with an adjusted R^2 that was actually negative.

Table 13.2. *The data by administration*

	Mid-year	Tariff rate	Unem-ploy-ment	Inflation PPI	Terms of trade	Labor per $100,000 K	Capital per laborer
T. Roosevelt	1902	27.8	3.1	1.6	119.7	20.50	4,875
T. Roosevelt	1906	21.3	3.6	1.4	115.5	19.32	5,175
Taft	1910	19.2	5.6	2.5	117.9	17.98	5,561
Wilson	1914	12.7	6.7	5.9	117.0	17.11	5,845
Wilson	1918	6.2	3.1	16.5	111.0	15.98	6,258
Harding	1922	13.1	7.1	-9.1	103.4	15.70	6,371
Coolidge	1926	12.6	3.6	-0.3	91.2	14.75	6,778
Hoover	1930	15.1	12.8	-9.4	97.8	15.15	6,600
F. Roosevelt	1934	16.7	20.8	6.0	111.2	18.25	5,479
F. Roosevelt	1938	13.5	16.3	-0.5	109.6	19.97	5,007
F. Roosevelt	1942	10.9	4.4	7.4	114.9	20.91	4,781
Truman	1946	7.8	3.1	12.4	93.6	19.61	5,100
Truman	1950	5.4	4.1	2.0	78.5	16.46	6,074
Eisenhower	1954	5.3	3.8	0.6	80.4	14.56	6,868
Eisenhower	1958	6.4	5.4	1.6	89.4	13.23	7,557
Kennedy	1962	7.1	5.6	0.1	93.8	12.41	8,061
Johnson	1966	7.2	3.8	2.2	100.1	10.86	9,211
Nixon	1970	6.1	4.9	3.3	100.0	9.90	10,104
Ford	1974	4.1	6.6	9.9	84.7	9.58	10,435
Carter	1978	3.6	6.4	9.7	87.0	8.92	11,215
Reagan	1982	3.4	8.5	4.2	99.7	8.43	11,864
Reagan	1986	3.6	6.7	4.1	99.7	8.04	12,442

Sources: See Appendix Table A.13.2.

We next added two variables suggested by the discussion above on endogenous tariffs: the U.S. labor–capital factor ratio to capture the endowment effect, and the U.S. terms of manufacturing trade to pick up other compensation effects. Both variables were lagged one administration because they were expected to have longer-run effects. The terms of trade effect was positive and significant, whereas the endowment effect had the right sign but was not significant at the .10 level. These results are shown as equation 2. The equation appears to be a significant improvement over equation 1. It indicates that U.S. tariffs fall with decreased importance of labor in the U.S. factor

Table 13.3. *The U.S. tariff regressions*

	Equation number and dependent variable						
	1	2	3	4	5	6	7
	LTAR	LTAR	DTAR	DUNEMP	DINFLATE	LTAR	LTAR
CONSTANT	.05	−.80	−.003	−1.04	−1.08	−1.02	−1.23
	(2.5)	(−3.1)	(−.7)	(−.7)	(−.5)	(−3.8)	(−3.2)
LAGLPERK		.05				.069	.053
		(1.5)				(1.9)	(1.4)
LAGTMT		.16				.20	.256
		(2.5)				(3.0)	(2.7)
INFLATE	−.0019	−.0024				−.0037	−.0036
	(−1.1)	(−1.9)				(−2.9)	(−2.7)
UNEMP	.0057	.0045					.0031
	(2.7)	(3.1)					(1.8)
DTMT			.115				
			(2.4)				
DUNEMP			.0024				
			(2.4)				
DINFLATE			−.0016				
			(−3.1)				
REPUB				3.80			
				(1.7)			
DREPUB					−6.26		
					(−2.0)		
LAGREPUB						.044	
						(2.9)	
MRTB	.0024						
	(1.4)						
LAGUSUK							.110
							(.8)
Adj. R^2	.35	.67	.67	.11	.16	.65	.62
D.W.	.52	1.56	3.20	1.48	2.04	1.84	1.47
1st-order autocorr.	.41	−.04	−.65	.26	−.04	.05	.13

Note: Variables are defined and sources given in Appendix Table A.13.1.

endowment, increase with the U.S. terms of manufacturing trade and unemployment, and decrease with the higher inflation.

A modeling as well as conceptual issue arises at this point. If one accepts the hypothesis that a country's factor endowment influences very-long-run movements in protection (say, with a lag of several decades), then it might be acceptable to relate levels of tariffs to the level of the U.S. labor–capital ratio. It is possible that the long-run downward trend in tariffs is caused by the endowment effect, so that the trend effect should be allocated to the factor endowment variable. If the endowment effects have very long lags, even our eighty-year time series may be too short. However, if the long-run tariff and the endowment trends are unrelated to each other, then allocating the trend in tariffs to factor endowments is inappropriate. Our next experiment is to first-difference all of the variables (see equation 3). The labor–capital ratio remains insignificant, and is dropped: Apparently there are no short-run (4–8-year) endowment effects. However, all of the remaining variables – the terms of trade, unemployment, and inflation – remain significant and have the right signs. Surprisingly, the real dollar foreign exchange rate between the United States and the United Kingdom was never significant, in either levels or first differences. This was true both with and without the inflation variable present. A dummy variable for the period before the adoption of the income tax in 1917 (NOTAX) is significant and attempted in some equations not shown. The share of tariff revenue in U.S. federal government revenue should not be included on the right-hand side directly because it contains the dependent variable. It has an acceptable R^2 of .67, although it displays negatively correlated errors. Also, the trend effect (which we would have anticipated in a significantly negative constant) is not apparent.

When a party dummy was included in equation 3, it was insignificant. However, this does not mean that the party of the president does not affect the level of protection, because both the unemployment rate and the inflation rate are affected by a president's macro policy. We tested the effect of presidential administrations on macro policy by regressing the unemployment rate as well as the inflation rate on the presidential dummy (REPUB = 1 for Republicans occupying the White House and = 0 for Democrats). Equation 4 indicates that the unemployment rate increases by 3.8 percentage points with Republican presidents, although the relationship is only significant at the .11 level. Since we included the Franklin Roosevelt administrations in these regressions, the party unemployment effect was apparently marginally insignificant because of the Great Depression. Thus, in subsequent data summaries by administrations, we omit the three Franklin Roosevelt administrations. (We also omitted his third term so as not to let World War II bias the unemployment rate in our favor.) With regard to inflation, equation 5 reports that after a transition from a Democratic to a Republican administration, the rate drops by 6.3 percentage points (significant at the .07 level). We also investigated the effect of the party of the president using equations for the level of tariffs and their first differences. The best such equation using levels is reported in equation 6. Notice in this equation that both the lagged labor–capital endowment ratio (LAGLPERK) and a Republican in office in the previous administration (LAGREPUB) are statistically significant and have positive effects on U.S. tariffs. When we break the Republican dummy into two subperiods, we find that its coefficient is stable and significant, both pre- and post-1932. The results for both levels and first differences show that Republican administrations generate significantly more protection than Democratic ones. This reveals Republican protectionism, which will be addressed in detail in section 13.5. Since Republicans have higher unemployment rates and lower inflation rates, equation 2 indicates that the Republican protectionist influence is immediate; the lagged Republican dummy in equation 6 indicates that there may also be lagged effects. Equation 3 predicts heavy pressure for increased protection in the 1920s and early 1930s, in the late 1950s (in 1958 the oil import quota was imposed), and in the 1980s (recall that the first Reagan administration is after the period of estimation for the equation). Note that tariff pressure is low during the Ford administration (1974).

The first Reagan term reveals the highest increase in protariff pressure since Fordney–McCumber in 1922 under Harding and Smoot–Hawley in 1930 under Hoover. Notice in Figures 13.2–13.4 that all three of the indicators of protection increased from the Carter to the first Reagan administration. The unemployment rate rose from 6.4% to 8.5%; the terms of trade for manufactures rose from 87 to 100; and the inflation rate dropped from 10% per year to 4%.

13.5   The isoprotection curve and the macroeconomic by-product theory of Republican protectionism

Republican protectionism is the phenomenon of procapital Republican presidential administrations generating more protection (which helps labor and hurts capital) whereas prolabor Democratic administrations generate freer trade (which hurts labor). One explanation is provided by Ferguson (1984), who argues that Democratic presidents since Franklin Roosevelt favor freer trade because they have obtained substantial campaign financing from U.S. multinationals. According to his argument, the multinationals do not care about the prolabor stance of the Democrats because they have low wage bills, specializing instead in physical- and human-capital-intensive activities that benefit from free world trade. Ferguson's argument is ingenious but incomplete: It does not explain why Democratic presidents would support free trade when this works counter to the interests of blue-collar and much union labor.

Our explanation of the puzzle is the *macroeconomic by-product effect*. It suggests that protection is a by-product of each administration's macro policy. We have noted that two important determinants of protection are unemployment and the inflation rate. The level of protection generated by post–World War II presidents is influenced by each administration's macroeconomic policies as well as the exogenous macroeconomic shocks that it experiences.

The amount of protectionist pressure generated by each administration is derived largely from its macroeconomic policies, and these generate pressures for protection whose redistributive effects are opposite to that of the macro policies. Democratic presidents favor macroeconomic policies that benefit labor: low unemployment and high inflation. The loose monetary policy that generated the higher inflation causes the dollar to weaken. Republicans do the reverse, favoring high unemployment and low inflation, resulting in a strong dollar. These macroeconomic policies benefit the economic clienteles of the parties in the expected way: The Republican macro policies favor capital, creditors, and perhaps financial intermediaries; the Democratic macro policies favor labor, debtors, and so on. The first Reagan administration fits this historical pattern: It experienced the worst minidepression since the Great Depression and favored Volcker's Federal Reserve policy of monetary stringency and a strong dollar. The reduced inflation reduced consumer pressure on Congress against protection, and the stronger dollar increased pressure on Congress from labor and the U.S. importable sector because of cheaper imports. Notice that Republican protectionism will not separate the parties and their lobbies so long as the redistributive effect of the trade policy is smaller than that of the macro policy. For example, labor is still better off economically under the Democratic administrations, because the Democratic prolabor macro policy effects should dominate the Democratic freer trade effects.

To illustrate our solution to the puzzle of Republican protectionism, we estimate *isoprotection curves* based on Magee's (1982) isoprotection curves [for a published discussion of these curves see Frey (1984a, pp. 56–8)]. Figure 13.5 shows that they are drawn in the Phillips curve diagram. Isoprotection curves show combinations of unemployment and inflation that generate equal levels of protection. They are derived by regressing tariffs on unemployment, inflation, and all other determinants of endogenous tariffs. The total derivative of the tariff equation is taken, with only inflation and unemployment changing. Set the total change in the tariff equal to zero and solve for the changes in inflation divided by the changes in unemployment in

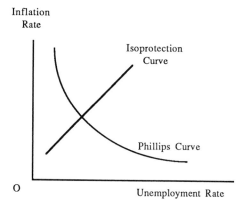

Figure 13.5. Magee's isoprotection curve.

terms of their coefficients in the tariff equation:

$$dI/dU = -(u/i) = 2$$

where u is the coefficient on unemployment and i is the coefficient on inflation in the tariff equation. In equation 2 in Table 13.3, the coefficient $u = .0045$ and $i = -.0024$, yielding a slope of approximately 2. Thus, a one-percentage-point increase in the U.S. unemployment rate requires a two-percentage-point increase in the U.S. inflation rate to keep the equilibrium level of protection constant.

Figure 13.6 shows two isoprotection curves drawn through the means of the Democratic and Republican average inflation and unemployment rates in this century. The data for calculating these means exclude the three terms of Franklin Roosevelt because of the Great Depression effects discussed earlier. The average Democratic president has favored macroeconomic policies on low isoprotection curves (toward the upper left corner of the figure), which generate freer trade, whereas the average Republican president has favored macroeconomic policies on high isoprotection curves (toward the lower right corner). Note that inflation rates are higher under the Democrats while unemployment rates are lower. Isoprotection curves can be drawn through each of these points: The one associated with the Democrats will have lower protection ($t = .071$) while the one through the Republican point will have higher protection ($t = .107$).

The issue of protection and *stagflation* can be illustrated using Figure 13.5. If the Phillips curve shifts out with no change in the party in power, no

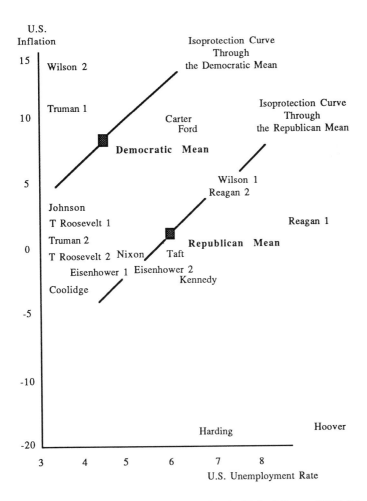

Figure 13.6. Isoprotection curves for the United States, 1900–88.

change in protection will occur if inflation and unemployment are increasing in the ratio of 2 to 1 (i.e., equal to the slope of the curves) and no other determinants of protection are changing. On the issue of worldwide stagflation see Bruno and Sachs (1985). They argue that, since wages are more indexed in Europe than in the United States, the usual Mundellian result is reversed, so that tight monetary and loose fiscal policy in the United States caused stagflation in Europe.

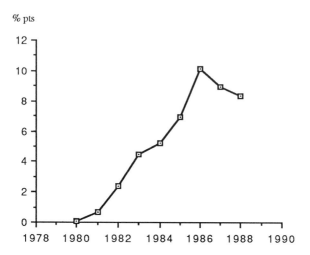

Figure 13.7. Change in the predicted level of U.S. protection above 1980 levels.

13.6   Republican protectionism in the 1980s

The *first Reagan administration is on the third-highest isoprotection curve of the century*. Notice in Figure 13.6 that only Harding and Hoover would lie on isoprotection curves to the right of Reagan's first term. Reagan's first term also has the third-highest predicted increase in protection this century because of (1) an increase in the U.S. terms of trade index from 87 to 100; (2) a rise in the U.S. unemployment rate from 6.4% to 8.5%; and (3) a drop in the U.S. inflation rate for producer prices from 9.7% per annum to 4.2% (all compared to the Carter administration). Macroeconomic considerations contribute to a decline in protectionist pressure for the second Reagan term as unemployment falls, inflation rises, and the dollar falls.

The rise in protectionist pressure has been dramatic. Our equation predicts a fourfold increase in protection in the 1980s, based on the 1900–80 estimation period. Figure 13.7 shows the predicted rise above 1980 levels in the level of U.S. protection (using our tariff equation 7 as a proxy measure for all protection). It starts in 1980 at the actual tariff of 3.1%, increases to over 13% in 1986, and then falls to the 1988 value of 11.5%. The moderately protectionist trade bill of 1988 is a consequence of this pressure.

How much of this predicted increase in protection during the 1980s is attributable to each cause is shown in Table 13.4. Figure 13.8 shows four of these variables by year and their percentage-point contribution to the predicted rise in U.S. protection from 3.1% in 1980 to 11.5% in 1988. Two of the

Table 13.4. *Variables explaining the rise in U.S. protectionism,
1980–8*

	Percentage points	Percent
Decreased prices of U.S. imports (Increase in the U.S. terms of trade)	+4.0	48
Decrease in U.S. inflation	+3.4	42
Strengthening of the dollar	+1.9	22
Decline in the U.S. labor–capital ratio	−.5	−7
Decrease in the unemployment rate	−.4	−5
Total increase	+8.4	100

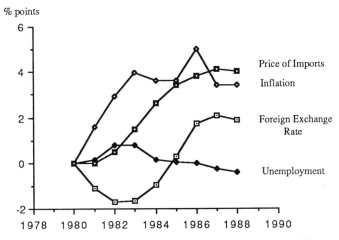

Figure 13.8. Contributions to U.S. protection in the 1980s.

three primary causes are Republican policy oriented and hence transitory:
decreased inflation and the strengthened dollar. The decreased price of U.S.
imports may be a longer-term phenomenon explained by the erosion in the
competitive position of the United States. While the real value of the dollar
has weakened between 1985 and 1988, its 1988 value is still above that of
1980. Both the labor–capital ratio and the unemployment rate declined, causing an implicit decline in protection. The capital–labor ratio, the terms of trade
variable, and the real foreign exchange rate had four-year lags in the estimating equation. For the simulations reported in Figure 13.8, they are represented by a moving average of the previous four years; the rest of the variables
were contemporaneous.

The pattern of Republican presidents being more protectionist than Democratic administrations holds for both Reagan administrations, Harding, Hoover, Eisenhower, and Nixon. Democratic presidents Franklin Roosevelt, Johnson, and Carter are on freer-trade isoprotectionist curves, characterized by lower unemployment and higher inflation.

What are the long-term trends for protection? A factor reducing U.S. protection is the shift in the factor endowment away from blue-collar labor and toward more human and physical capital. All of the other indicators signal increased protection. First is the long-term erosion in the competitive position of many U.S. industries. Next is the decline in union participation, suggesting continued decline for the prolabor Democratic party. Thus, if the recent success rate of Republican presidential candidates continues, this indicates increasing protection. The move toward lower inflation and higher unemployment was dramatic in the first Reagan administration. If continued in future Republican administrations, this phenomenon shifts the American political equilibrium in a southeasterly direction in Figure 13.6. *Increasing protectionism* in the United States is a consequence because of Republican policy preferences for high unemployment, low inflation, and a strong dollar.

Historically, Congress has been more protectionist than the Executive Branch. In the past two decades, however, *the Executive Branch has become increasingly protectionist* in its negotiation of voluntary export restraint agreements with the Far East and in its administrative protection (antidumping, etc.). Congress now appears to be battling the White House to regain control of protectionist policy. In addition to the current high demand for protection, Congress may wish to recapture both protectionist and proexport lobbying resources, which have been concentrated on the White House.

In contrast, *the 1970s was a period of low long-run protection*. We speculate that this is true even if the ad valorem equivalent of all nontariff barriers was measured along with tariff rates. The reason is that three out of four factors pointed to lower protection: the continued decline of labor in the U.S. factor endowment, the low level of the U.S. terms of manufacturing trade, and the high level of U.S. inflation (which mobilized consumers against protection and contributed to the weak dollar). The only protectionist pressure came from the increase in the U.S. unemployment rate.

There are two implications of this work in other policy areas. One implication of increasing Republican electoral success is that fiscal deficits will become an increasingly secular (rather than cyclical) problem. Paul Roberts (1984), among many others, has noted that deficits are large in troughs and small at peaks. Since Democrats overstimulate while Republicans understimulate real economic activity, fiscal deficits may be a growing problem if Republican presidents keep getting elected.

The second implication is that inflation can also be interpreted in a redistributive framework. Since Democrats tend to be debtors and Republicans creditors, Republican electoral success would predict future deflation relative to inflation.

President Bush will be the first third-term Republican president since Herbert Hoover in 1929 and Theodore Roosevelt in 1905. Both of these third termers experienced major stock crashes. If history repeats itself in this way, we shall be in for greater protection in the 1990s.

CHAPTER 14

A Cobb–Douglas model of endogenous protection

This chapter extends the endogenous policy model by using Cobb–Douglas production functions and Cobb–Douglas utility functions for the economic actors. As before, lobbies contribute resources to politics, equating their returns to political and economic activity at the margin, while the parties maximize their probability of election, trading off general voter dissatisfaction with protection against the electioneering resources that favorable policies elicit from the lobbies. Given the Cobb–Douglas case, this chapter covers the following:

14.1. a review of the literature;
14.2. closed-form solutions to the $2 \times 2 \times 2 \times 2$ model;
14.3. political independence [all political variables (probabilities of election of the parties, the fractions of both factors devoted to lobbying and the policies) are independent of world prices, and all except the policies are independent of country capital–labor ratios];
14.4. the endowment effect on protection (protection increases the greater the country's endowment of the scarce factor);
14.5. the policy bifurcation effect (a change in a country's factor endowment always increases one policy and reduces the other);
14.6. increasing returns to politics (the return to a factor increases with the country's endowment of that factor);
14.7. Prisoner's Dilemma tariffs occur with countervailing power (i.e., when the factors are more evenly balanced);

Chapter 14 in Stephen P. Magee, William A. Brock, and Leslie Young, *Black Hole Tariffs and Endogenous Policy Theory*. New York: Cambridge University Press, 1989. Adapted from Leslie Young and Stephen P. Magee, "Endogenous Protection, Factor Returns and Resource Allocation," *Review of Economic Studies* 53 (1986), 407–19.

14.8.   the magnification paradox (decreasing protection is accompanied by increasing lobbying and welfare losses);
14.9.   the party magnification effect (greater factor price sensitivity hurts the factor's party);
14.10. deceptively intuitive general equilibrium effects; and
14.11. generalizations of these results.

In Chapter 10, we obtained solutions for the reaction functions of the four players, but numerical methods were needed to solve for the equilibrium of the game, which was determined by a system of four nonlinear equations in four unknowns. In this chapter, we find closed-form solutions for the equilibrium actions of the four players for the case of Cobb–Douglas utility and production functions and a logit probability of election function. Given these solutions, the general equilibrium effects of comparative static changes are particularly transparent. This is important because the multiplicity of feedbacks among the actions of the four players makes intuitive speculation treacherous. To simplify, we begin by assuming that the elasticities of the electoral odds with respect to the four political variables (the two lobbying levels and the two party policies) are all unity. We relax this assumption in section 14.10.

To review, the structure of the endogenous policy model is the neoclassical $2 \times 2 \times 2 \times 2$ model of Chapter 9 with two goods, two factors, two lobbies, and two political parties. We assume that the production functions exhibit constant returns to scale and no factor intensity reversals. The country is small and faces an exogenous international price P, which is the price of good 2 in terms of good 1. However, domestic special-interest politics generates trade distortions so that the domestic price Q can differ from P. Q will be higher than P because of the tariff but lower than P because of the export subsidy. Given nonspecialized production, the factor price equalization theorem implies that the equilibrium wage and rental rates depend only on Q and are independent of factor endowments. The impact of Q on the returns to capital and labor motivates their owners to form lobbies that contribute resources to politics. For simplicity, we assume that the capital and labor lobbies make direct contributions K and L of the factor that they own to their favored party. We assume that one party is procapital while the other is prolabor, and each uses its policies to bid for votes and for political contributions. The procapital party's policy is to subsidize exports of the capital-intensive good 1, while the prolabor party's policy is to raise the domestic price of the labor-intensive good by a tariff on imports of good 2.

Assume that each lobby chooses its political contributions to maximize the expected utility of a representative owner of the corresponding factor, while each party chooses its policy in order to maximize its probability of election.

Many combinations of Nash and Stackelberg behavior are possible among the four players in this political game. Assuming vigorous party competition, each party leads one lobby in a Stackelberg fashion, but adopts Nash behavior toward the other two players, while each lobby adopts Nash behavior toward the other three players (see section 3.8). All four players internalize voter behavior and the behavior of economic agents. We assume that the procapital party leads the capital lobby and the prolabor party the labor lobby, with the prolabor party always announcing the higher domestic price for the labor-intensive good in order to attract labor contributions. In this chapter, factor owners take account of the impact of the election on their cost of living because the domestic price Q appears independently in their indirect utility functions. We are now ready to examine the results.

14.1   The literature

The entire Keynesian revolution may be less about economic theory and more about a special-interest movement to create a massive middle class with the spending power to support the domestic success of automobiles, chemicals, electricals, and other capital-intensive industries. This approach has the side effect of being Pareto superior to the marketing of steel through armaments. Furthermore, Keynesianism is implicitly protectionist because of its focus on domestic spending. Exports play a role but net exports for the average country equal zero. These ideas and many more are supported by a fascinating study by Kurth (1979).

This chapter builds a formal model of the connections between economic markets, lobbying, and political control by governments. Kurth tells the history of these connections in several countries, but particularly Germany before World War II.

An interesting question is how major powers market their steel. Kurth notes that the German steel industry was at a disadvantage relative to Britain's after World War I because Germany did not have a strong consumer goods sector as did Britain, nor a domestic automobile industry (Britain was rated second in the world), nor an overseas empire that consumed steel in the construction of railroads. The two best outlets for steel in Germany in the 1920s were exports to Eastern Europe and the production of armaments. Thus, the steel industry in Germany in the 1920s supported the National People's Party, which favored rearmament, revision of the Treaty of Versailles, and tariff barriers against steel imports from Western Europe.

Two other sectors emerged in Germany in the 1920s: chemicals and electricity. The chemical industry had a very strong interest in free trade because I. G. Farben was the world's largest chemical corporation and the largest corporation in all of Europe. Both the chemical and electrical industries wished to promote mass consumption; therefore these industries supported parties favoring social welfare, democratic politics, and free trade (these industries joined with labor in opposition to the coalitions of the steel industry and the agriculturalists). A strategic mistake was made by I. G. Farben when it diverted most of its new capital investment in the 1920s into building enormous plants to produce gasoline from coal using a process known as hydrogenation. This was based on widespread forecasts (reminiscent of the 1970s) that world petroleum supplies would soon be exhausted.

The stock market crash in the United States and the beginning of the Great Depression, however, dealt a serious blow to the free trade policy of the German chemical and electrical industries because of the Smoot–Hawley tariff and the rise in world tariff barriers. Suddenly, a coercive trade option (Ostpolitik) of the German steel industry became much more attractive to chemicals and electricity. Furthermore, the depression induced declines in world oil prices during 1930–1, and the opening up of the vast East Texas oil fields in 1931 meant that I. G. Farben would face massive imports of cheap American oil. The only solution for Farben now was a strong protectionist government that would guarantee a market for its coal-based gasoline, or a government that would actually buy the gasoline itself for rearmament and military expansion.

In 1932, these developments caused the German chemical and electrical industries to switch from opposition to cooperation with the nationalistic and protectionist German steel and grain producers. The National People's Party was not popular enough to win the elections of 1932, so that first the steel industry and later the chemical and electrical industries shifted their financial lobbying support to a National Socialist Party under Hitler. In 1933, when the Nazis came to power, the foreign policy goals of the steel industry (rearmament, the revision of the Treaty of Versailles, high protection, and the domination of Eastern Europe) became the foreign policy of Germany under Hitler.

Thus, Kurth documents the fascinating tale of special-interest support for Nazi Germany. The steel industry in the United States in the 1920s took a very different course because 30% of American steel production went into the booming American automobile industry. Thus, the American steel industry did not have the same need for armaments, foreign entanglements, and the military–industrial complex that was necessary for a profitable steel industry in Germany.

Kurth notes that, after World War II, steel did not need the militarization of the 1920s and 1930s. In Britain, West Germany, France, and Italy, the automobile age boomed, and the general economic prosperity legitimized liberal democratic systems and reduced the radical positions of the European and American working classes. With the transformation of blue-collar workers into the middle class, labor shifted its focus from political activities and radical propaganda to individual consumption.

Kurth argues that partial saturation of markets with automobiles led in the 1960s and early 1970s to detente, which would lead to automobile ventures that would allow sales in Eastern Europe and the Soviet Union. This created profits both for the American automobile industry and for American international banks. However, by the mid-1970s the American oil industry discovered that, in communist countries, volume might be high but profits are low. By 1977, he notes, international banks had loaned over $50 billion to communist countries, but these countries were approaching their limits to repay. He shows the close relationship between special interests and political ideology, even on detente.

The last decade has seen conflict in the West between protectionist industries (textiles, steel, and, more recently, chemicals) versus free trade industries (aerospace, computers, and telecommunications) with the automobile industry being in a swing position with ambiguous interests. This concludes the discussion of the Kurth (1979) paper.

The level of protection fell among the advanced countries for about a quarter of a century following World War II. Most economists viewed this as a welfare improvement. There are two serious problems with this view. First, when protection is declining, export subsidies are very likely to be rising. Since the latter are more indirect in the United States (e.g., increased subsidization of education, research and development, military R&D, and research for explorations in space), they are harder to observe. Subsidies to the dominant factor in the United States, the well educated, are implicitly export subsidies. Since the policies are moving in opposite directions and lobby levels are changing, the welfare effects are far from obvious. Second, we show in this chapter that, although both protection and export subsidies may be falling, welfare can also be falling because of increases in lobbying. This result can be the outgrowth of the magnification paradox, to be described in this chapter.

For an example of the magnification paradox see Dougan (1984). He argues, for reasons that differ somewhat from ours, that the level of protection in an industry is not a valid indicator of the industry's political influence. In the language of this chapter, an industry can have high returns from political activity even if the policy favoring it is small. He argues too that an industry's power depends on the domestic demand and supply elasticities it faces.

Frey and Schneider (1982) point out that much of the empirical work on international political economy has been applied to the United States. This makes it difficult to generalize the results to other countries. Frey and Ramser (1986) note that there is substitutability between economic policies. They find that regulation and taxation are substitutes.

What is the relationship between domestic groups and the international power of a country? Although we do not attempt to model that question in this book, it is clear our domestic policy model of protection has certain implications for foreign policy. The declining U.S. tariffs over the past fifty years, coupled with government encouragement of R&D, sophisticated military technologies, and subsidies to American higher education, are the policy reflection of the political power of America's abundant factor. The U.S. multinational corporation is the greatest embodiment of U.S. comparative advantage, namely, skilled labor and capital. Our own view is that U.S. multinationals are the single largest economic force behind the emergence of the United States as a hegemonic power in the twentieth century. It is in their interest to have a stable and well-ordered international economy.

Hegemonic theory provides an ideological justification for the international extension of national self-interest. There were powerful forces in Britain pursuing free trade abroad going back to the East India Company. As we just noted, multinational corporations have been a powerful force favoring open systems overseas. The special-interest behavior of U.S. multinationals acting through Franklin Roosevelt and other Democratic internationalist presidents has been documented by Ferguson (1984). He shows that New York investment bankers and multinationals contributed heavily to Roosevelt in 1932 in exchange for the pursuit of freer world trade.

Kindleberger (1975) examines the rise of free trade in Western Europe. He notes that Bastiat argued that free trade inevitably accompanied the spread of democracy. With respect to special-interest origins, Kindleberger notes that free trade was favored by the bourgeois in England while it was favored by the landed aristocracy on the Continent. Conversely, protection was preferred by the aristocracy in England and by the bourgeois manufacturing class on the Continent.

Kindleberger (1986) provides evidence for the hegemonic theory of tariffs. According to the hegemonic theory, international trade was relatively open in portions of the nineteenth and twentieth centuries because of the existence of a large, stable nation more powerful than its rivals: the United Kingdom in the nineteenth century and the United States in much of the twentieth. Kindleberger notes that both the IMF and the World Bank were the exclusive ideas of the U.S. Treasury and that the power of these institutions grew out of U.S. support.

Our view is that what appears to be hegemonic behavior by the United States really comprises special-interest policies driven by U.S. multinational corporations. McKeown (1983) examines the hegemonic theory of tariffs discussed by Kindleberger, Gilpin, Krasner, Keohane, and Nye. While the theory is appealing, McKeown finds significant empirical departures from it. Its predictive accuracy in explaining nineteenth-century tariff levels is poor:

For example, British efforts were not successful in producing major changes in tariff levels of other countries, and the tariff liberalization that did occur was frequently in the absence of British pressure. In addition, the major motivation for reduction in world tariff laws in both centuries was world prosperity, whereas increases in protection generally occurred during periods of worldwide depression.

14.2   Closed-form solutions and no multiple equilibria

The first result of our mathematical analysis using the Cobb–Douglas model is closed-form solutions for all of the key political variables (see the two-part Appendix to this chapter). This is an important extension of the work in the earlier chapters, since the solutions are difficult. The earlier chapters were able to obtain solutions, but not in closed form: They had the other endogenous variables on the right-hand side of some complex nonlinear equations. Thus, the equilibrium values of tariffs, export subsidies, the proportions of each factor devoted to lobbying, and the probabilities of election of the parties can each be written in terms of the model parameters alone. Extreme values of a country's factor endowment ratio force specialization of the economy in one of the two products: Theorem 5 in the Appendix gives the conditions required for production nonspecialization. However, for intermediate values of the country's endowment ratio, we get a unique interior equilibrium for the five political variables. Another point to stress is that the solutions are unique, so that multiple interior equilibria are not present in the Cobb–Douglas model.

14.3   Political independence

There are two independence results. The first states that the five political variables (the fractions of both factors lobbying, both policies, and the probabilities of election of both parties) are independent of world prices (the country's terms of trade). This is a bit surprising because important redistributions of income occur when the terms of trade change. In earlier chapters we showed that, with Leontief production, an increase in the terms of trade (caused, say, by a decline in import prices) reduces wages, causing an expansion in labor lobbying, an increased tariff, and an increased probability of success for the prolabor party. *In the Cobb–Douglas model, a rise in the terms of trade causes a decline in wages and an increase in the returns to capital, but neither the lobbying ratios, the policies, nor the electoral outcomes are ultimately affected.* Since the Leontief and the Cobb–Douglas models have contrasting implications, there are grounds for empirical tests of the two models in future research.

The second independence result is derived in Theorem 8. It states that *changes in a country's endowment ratio do not affect the proportions of each factor devoted to lobbying and the probabilities of election of the parties.* To illustrate the logic of the first part of this proposition, consider an increase in an economy's capital stock. This increases the equilibrium export subsidy and decreases the equilibrium tariff. The increased export subsidy makes the procapital party's election more important to the capital lobby, which is a reason for it to increase the proportion of capital devoted to lobbying. However, the equilibrium tariff has declined, so victory by the prolabor party is less harmful, which is a reason for the capital lobby to decrease the proportion of capital devoted to politics. It turns out that these two opposing forces exactly cancel in the Cobb–Douglas model, leaving the proportion of each factor devoted to politics unchanged. This result could be tested across countries if national lobbying data were available.

The second part of the proposition in Theorem 8 is that *electoral outcomes are independent of country factor endowments;* i.e., the ability of the procapital party to get elected is unaffected by the level of the country's capital–labor ratio. This surprising result contrasts with the Leontief model result that procapital party electoral success increases with the country's capital–labor endowment. To explain the Cobb–Douglas model effect, let there be an increase in an economy's capital endowment. From the previous paragraph, we know that the fraction of capital stock devoted to politics will be unaffected. Thus, the procapital party will now have more lobbying resources. However, it increases its export subsidy while the labor party decreases it tariff, and these two policy changes hurt the procapital party with the voters. According to the mathematics, the electoral benefits of the increased capital to the procapital party are just offset by the electoral declines caused by the two policy changes.

14.4   The endowment effect on protection

The factor endowment effect suggests that the higher the ratio of the scarce factor to the abundant factor, the higher will be the level of protection of the scarce-factor-intensive good. Theorem 7 implies that when the odds of electoral success have unitary elasticities with respect to lobbying resources and with respect to each party's policy, the equilibrium tariff increases with the square root of the economy's labor–capital endowment. Similarly, the equilibrium subsidy on exports decreases with the square root of the economy's labor–capital endowment. In general, any increase in the endowment of a factor in an economy always leads to an increase in the policy favored by that factor.

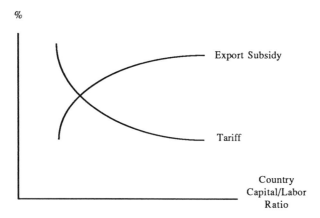

Figure 14.1. The policy bifurcation effect: One policy increases and the other decreases with factor endowment changes.

14.5   The policy bifurcation effect

Changes in endowment ratios lead to bifurcated policy changes: *All country factor endowment changes increase one policy and reduce the other.* This stresses a point often missed in policy discussions of protection. There is a tendency to think that if tariffs are dropping, welfare must be improving. In a special-interest world with pro- and antitariff forces at work, any decline in protection must be examined carefully. If the forces that caused the tariff decline are endowment changes, then we can expect proexport lobby effects to generate higher export subsidies. Any welfare analysis of the tariff decline must include these general equilibrium effects.

The bifurcation effect is illustrated in Figure 14.1. There has been continuous capital deepening since World War II, meaning increases in most advanced country capital–labor ratios. At the same time, from the mid-1940s until the early 1970s, tariffs were falling and export subsidies were rising. Casual empiricism suggests conformity with the endowment effect and the bifurcation effect. Since the early 1970s, nontariff protection has been rising, so that the simple story must be rescued with industry aging effects and other intellectual epicycles.

14.6   Increasing returns to politics

Theorem 9 states that *an increase in the endowment of one factor increases that factor's rate of return in the country and decreases the return of the other factor*. To illustrate, consider an increase in a country's capital endowment. The average owner of capital still devotes the same percentage of its capital to lobbying and the procapital party still has the same long-run electoral chances as before. In addition, the equilibrium export subsidy is higher and the equilibrium tariff is lower. Thus, capital returns are unambiguously higher.

The increasing returns effect illustrates how political effects can reverse economic effects. For a neoclassical closed economy, diminishing returns cause decreased returns in response to an increase in the domestic endowment of capital. However, with endogenous politics, the increased supply of capital increases the demand for redistribution to capital in the political market. In the new political equilibrium, the increased political demands of capital generate a higher export subsidy and a higher probability of election for the procapital party. The two of these more than offset the diminishing returns to capital (see section 12.2).

14.7   Prisoner's Dilemmas and countervailing power

Protection is usually viewed as a mechanism whereby one group gains at the expense of other groups. Theorem 10 highlights an important general equilibrium qualification: The relative strength of the group must be sufficient to ensure that the increase in its factor price more than compensates for the larger fraction of resources it devoted to political activity. If neither lobby in a country is predominant in terms of its factor endowment, then both groups end up worse off than under free trade. Thus, *we can expect Prisoner's Dilemma-type outcomes in redistributive struggles in countries with factor endowment ratios near the world average.* Theorem 10 provides an explicit calculation of the range of factor endowment ratios over which the country will be trapped in a Prisoner's Dilemma equilibrium. For countries with capital–labor endowments above this range, capital is better off with endogenous politics than it would have been under free trade. For countries with capital–labor endowments below this range, labor is better off than it would have been with free trade. (The free trade case is not an equilibrium – merely a benchmark.)

For the next three results, we analyze the effects of factor intensities and consumer preferences. Assume an increase in the responsiveness of capital returns to the product price ratio. Does this make capital more or less powerful politically, and what happens to the political equilibrium? Since capital returns are more sensitive to product price changes, capital will have a greater interest in manipulating prices through the political system and, hence, will increase the amount of capital devoted to lobbying. However, as noted above in the analysis of an increased endowment of capital, the procapital party

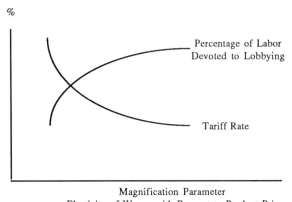

Figure 14.2. The magnification paradox: Protectionist lobbying increases and tariffs decrease with increased magnification.

reasons that it can not only have more lobbying resources but also increase its populist appeal by setting a lower special-interest export subsidy. Since both garner more votes, it is unambiguous that the procapital party's probability of election increases. Since capital lobbies more and gets a less favored policy, its welfare declines. The latter is counterintuitive; however, the result applies only in partial equilibrium. We consider below what happens in general equilibrium.

Consider also a technological change that causes production technologies to become more similar. If this happens, we would observe that the capital–labor ratios for the two products get closer together. When this occurs, magnification is said to increase because both factor prices become more responsive to changes in product prices. What does this do to the domestic political equilibrium? Assume for simplicity that the elasticities of capital returns and wages are initially equal and that both increase by equal amounts.

14.8   The magnification paradox: increasing lobbying and welfare losses but with decreasing distortions

In Theorem 12 we get conditions under which *increasing similarity of production technologies causes redistributive policies to fall but the proportions of both factors devoted to lobbying to increase.* This result is illustrated in Figure 14.2. Increased magnification is associated with movements to the right in the figure.

Theorem 12B´ then shows that there is a critical value for the elasticities of factor returns with respect to product prices such that, at lower values, the increase in magnification lowers the expected utility of both factors of production. Thus, we have developed conditions under which magnification changes cause both policies and welfare to fall. This is a reminder that, in a second-best world, decreases in tariffs do not imply that welfare is increasing. Whether this result is important empirically depends, of course, on the validity of the model and whether the elasticities of factor returns with respect to product prices are greater or less than this critical value. If they are greater, then increases in tariffs and export subsidies will be associated with declines in welfare. We assume that the elasticites of both factor returns are equal.

Thus, *the level of distortions sponsored by the parties can be a poor indicator of the intensity of the political struggle and of the welfare losses from the distortions.* Under the parameter changes described in Theorem 12, the level of distortions can be negatively correlated with the level of resources in political activities because parties need only mild policies to elicit large political contributions.

14.9   The political magnification effect: greater factor price sensitivity hurts the factor's party

Theorem 13 develops results when the elasticities of the two factor returns are unequal. Assume that wages are more responsive to product price changes than are capital returns ($n > m$). In this case, labor will devote a larger fraction to lobbying than will capital. Let the capital–labor endowment of the country equal 1 to abstract from the effects of relative factor endowments on the policies. Does the procapital party offer a larger or smaller export subsidy than the prolabor party's tariff? Partial equilibrium reasoning would lead us to expect a lower tariff, since the prolabor party gets the benefit of relatively more resources and might garner even more votes by cutting its tariff in a populist move. However, this reasoning is incorrect: The equilibrium tariff exceeds the export subsidy when wages are more responsive to product price changes than are capital returns. In short, *the party leading the more price sensitive lobby proposes more extreme distortions.*

What are the effects of increased factor price responsiveness on the electoral success of the parties? Again, let wages become more responsive to product price changes than capital returns. From the proof of Theorem 13 in the second part of the Appendix, observe in equation (A.32) that the procapital party's odds of election a exceed unity. Thus, the prolabor party is worse off, and we get the counterintuitive result that *the party of the factor with more responsive factor prices does worse than the other party.* The explanation is that the prolabor party gains from a more favorable lobbying ratio (a higher ratio of labor to capital is devoted to lobbying) but loses even more votes from the increase in its equilibrium tariff relative to the export subsidy.

14.10 Deceptively intuitive general equilibrium results

The result in Theorem 7 that an increase in the capital stock leads to an increase in the export subsidy is deceptively complicated. An increase in a country's endowment of capital has the following initial partial equilibrium effects: More capital is given to the procapital party. The party reasons that it now has greater advertising capability and could acquire even more voters by cutting its export subsidy, which it does. Ironically, the increased demand for an export subsidy results in a partial equilibrium decrease in the subsidy. It is only after the full general equilibrium effects of the adjustments by the other party and other lobby that the procapital party ultimately increases its export subsidy. We are currently incapable of giving a good intuitive explanation of the complicated feedback effects that lead to the rise in the export subsidy. The irony is that the *general equilibrium effects are intuitive but the partial equilibrium effects are counterintuitive.*

14.11 Generalizing the logit function for voters and the government budget constraint

We now relax the assumption that the behavior of voters is unit elastic with respect to resources and policies, and get this intuitive result: If voters oppose distortions more, the equilibrium distortions become smaller and less sensitive to changes in the country's factor endowment ratio; also, the proportion of the economy's resources devoted to lobbying falls. If voters become sufficiently insensitive to the lobbying funds that a party has at its disposal, then the increasing returns result can be reversed. Theorem 14 treats the implications of the government budget constraint.

CHAPTER 15

Black hole tariffs

How much of an economy's resources can be wasted in special-interest political activity? We find that there are conditions under which *there are no upper limits to redistributive lobbying: Virtually all of the economy can disappear into an economic black hole (in which the economy's output approaches zero).* If the factors have extreme values of relative risk aversion, then there are upper limits on the amount of waste. However, for intermediate values of relative risk aversion, the economy can approach a black hole. One parametric change that pushes the economy toward it is increased magnification effects, by which a change in product prices has a greater effect on both wages and returns to capital. Ironically, as the black hole is approached, the magnification paradox is present: The policies of both parties are moving toward free trade (i.e., zero tariffs and export subsidies), but lobbying is increasing and welfare is declining.

This chapter examines the following:

15.1. the literature;
15.2. the assumptions;
15.3. the 50% limit on rent seeking with risk neutrality;
15.4. the black hole; and
15.5. post–World War II movements toward gray holes.

Consider now the welfare losses from rent seeking.

Early theories of economic doom generated by Malthus, Marx, and Schumpeter each had identifiable culprits: the poor or the capitalists or the

Chapter 15 in Stephen P. Magee, William A. Brock, and Leslie Young, *Black Hole Tariffs and Endogenous Policy Theory*. New York: Cambridge University Press, 1989. Adapted from Leslie Young and Stephen P. Magee, "Risk Aversion and the Black Hole in the Political Economy of Protection," mimeo, University of Texas at Austin, 1984; presented at the American Economic Association Meetings, Chicago 1987.

intellectuals. Who are the culprits here? The answer is "everyone," driven by rational self-interest: We all dig black holes since we all participate in redistributive activity. This chapter illustrates conditions under which the welfare losses from lobbying have no lower limits. Obviously, the conditions required for economic black holes seldom occur, although wars, ghettos, and revolutions may be examples. Can they be avoided? Redistributive competition cannot be legislated away because those who benefit from redistribution stand at the legislative, executive, and judicial gates.

15.1   The literature

The black hole described in this chapter follows a long tradition of fatalism in economics. David Ricardo labeled economics the "dismal science." Malthus believed that the poor would reproduce at such a rate that economic surpluses would be eroded and wages would decline to subsistence levels. Marx argued that redistributive conflict between capital and labor, and ultimately among capitalists themselves, would cause capitalism to destroy itself. Schumpeter (1950) predicted the fall of capitalism because of the ascent of intellectuals, who would fail to share adequately in the wealth and would foment redistributive conflict through organized labor, politics, and the bureaucracy.

What are the political implications of the black hole? Totalitarianism? Schumpeter's (1950) criterion for the success of an economic-political system is that it did not create conditions that lead to an undemocratic régime. Another possibility is Hirschman's (1970) idea that, in deteriorating political and economic situations, the primary options are either "exit" or "voice." Lindbeck (1985a) suggests the underground economy. Due to progressive taxation, the increased income coming from productive activity declines because of higher marginal tax rates. To compensate, individuals substitute toward redistributive activity and underground activities.

What empirical evidence do we have about the proportion of country GNPs that are devoted to redistributive activity? Krueger (1974) found that 7% of Indian GNP was absorbed in rent seeking, whereas 15% of Turkish GNP was lost to rent seeking over import licenses alone. She indicates that, with competitive rent seeking, the entire value of the redistributive effect in tariff analysis can be wasted. Krueger indicates, as do Brock and Magee (1974), that the entire value of a rent-seeking individual's income is wasted if the factor markets equate marginal returns between redistributive and productive activities. That is, in the traditional Corden (1957) diagram that decomposes the effect of a tariff change into the tariff revenue, the producer's surplus, and the deadweight loss, the producer's surplus will be exhausted. Thus, the production cost of rent seeking is equal to the value of the rents.

(In a more complicated model, it would equal the expected value of the rents.) One implication of Krueger's (1974) paper was that welfare in an economy would be higher with a monopolist seeking rents because fewer resources would be wasted in rent seeking. This analysis, however, ignores any political value of the resources in educating voters. See also Takacs (1987).

In a non–black hole context, Hillman and Riley (1987) examine conditions under which all versus part of the rents will be dissipated by rent seeking. They find that asymmetric valuation reduces the cost of political contestability and that the equilibrium number of active contenders for rents can be small – perhaps generally two. This parallels the usual pattern of a political incumbent and a challenger. For the measurement of deadweight loss triangles resulting from trade distortions in general equilibrium see Helpman (1978).

Mohammad and Whalley (1984) indicate that redistributive activity might consume as much as 25–40% of Indian GNP. Hamilton, Mohammad, and Whalley (1984) have worldwide measurements of the rent-seeking costs of trade restrictions across countries. Ross (1984) finds that rent seeking accounts for approximately 38% of the gross domestic product in Kenya. For papers on recent protectionism and potential harm to world welfare see the series edited by Salvatore (1985). On the possibility that lobbying can increase welfare see Bhagwati's (1980, 1982a) work on directly unproductive activities (DUP), as extended by Dinopolous (1982), Mitra (1987), and others. The opportunity costs of lobbying can have a negative shadow price so that, in fact, lobbying for a tariff could improve welfare in a second-best situation. In this same area, Fries (1982) shows that if quotas are allocated to firms in a particular way, governments can eliminate the inefficiency caused by rent seeking by international financial flows. Hamilton, Mohammad, and Whalley (1984) examined the North–South terms of trade in an eight-region numerical general equilibrium model. They find that import restrictions in the developing countries should have improved their terms of trade. However, once the rent-seeking costs are included in the welfare calculations, it is possible for the total terms of trade for all regions to decline.

A basic tenet of both Chapter 3 and this chapter is that increased party competition reduces economic efficiency. Anecdotal evidence for this proposition comes from Switzerland and Sweden. Lindbeck (1985a) notes that Sweden has very strong political competition coupled with a centralized public sector and infrequent referenda, whereas Switzerland has permanent coalition governments but characterized with a federal structure and frequent referenda. Could it be true that vigorous party competition leads to greater redistribution? Lindbeck shows that public spending is 68% of GNP in Sweden but only 30% in Switzerland. Lindbeck (1986a) extends this discussion, noting that while Sweden is high in public spending, the U.K.

devotes 45% of its GNP to public spending and the United States devotes only 33%. He does not perform an analysis of the levels of political competition in these three countries. A parallel to the notion of high political competition is our assumption in this chapter of equal sized parties and equally powerful factors of production. It is reasonable that party competition would be greater in such a case compared to a country with only one strong party.

While the developing countries should be in the midst of a Rostovian takeoff, rent seeking reduces their ability to grow effectively. Lindbeck (1986b) notes that although output in developing countries increased 5.0% per annum during the period 1960–81, the increase in labor inputs was 3.7%, so that labor productivity grew at only 1.3% per year.

A theoretical paper by Blomqvist and Mohammad (1984) indicates that the results of measurements of rent seeking are heavily dependent on the institutional mechanism by which they are collected. For example, if there were perfect competition among bureaucrats for corrupt government jobs, then the rent-seeking costs of obtaining fixed import quotas might be low. As Rose-Ackerman (1984) points out, competition in the market for bureaucrats may simply shift the political rents to owners of inelastically supplied factors in markets without close substitutes. Presumably these would be the most capable rent seekers. Niskanen (1976) proposed a solution to bureaucratic rent seeking: Reduce bureaucratic inefficiency by bureaucratic competition, well-structured reward systems for efficiency, and private bidding to produce government outputs.

Lake (1986) points out that in May 1930 over 1,000 members of the American Economic Association signed a petition to Congress urging them to vote down the tariff bill then pending before them. It had no effect: One month later, Herbert Hoover signed the Smoot–Hawley Tariff into law. The inability of economists to convince the political system to adopt Pareto-optimal outcomes is well known.

The obvious explanation of distortionary policies is that these policies redistribute income. Tullock (1985) has argued that the Industrial Revolution itself may have occurred in England because of rent seeking. He follows up Tollison's (1982) earlier research indicating that the cause of the English Civil War was the desire of the House of Commons to take over the profits from the rent-seeking activities of the king emanating from his royal monopoly.

Historically, the Chicago school has been concerned about the growth of government bureaucracies. Casstevens (1984) applies a birth–death demography model to Kaufman's (1976) data on bureaus of the U.S. government over the period 1923–73, much as one might estimate a rabbit population. There were 175 bureaus in 1923 and 394 in 1973. By extrapolation, there would be 700 bureaus by 2003 and almost 1,600 bureaus by 2054, revealing intellectual limits to exponential extrapolation. His model suggests that the number of bureaus doubles every forty years.

A contrary view is Brittan's (1975) efficiency argument for government bureaucracies. He argues that politicians have a comparative advantage in getting votes but not in administering programs; hence, the virtue of a professional bureaucracy.

Consider now inefficiency related to trade policy. Page (1979, 1981) estimates that approximately 20% of OECD manufactured trade and 44% of OECD total trade is managed by nontariff restrictions. Nogues, Olechowski, and Winters (1986) place the latter number at 27%. This chapter does not provide empirical estimates to parallel these; rather, we use theory to place upper limits on potential losses. The interested reader is encouraged to extend the theoretical work in this chapter empirically.

The results in this chapter are at great variance with the low welfare costs of protection emerging from traditional measures – two examples being Magee (1972) and Tarr and Morkre (1984). Szenberg, Lombardi, and Lee (1977) found that the welfare gain to the United States of abolishing footwear import restrictions was only $79 million. For other studies of the welfare effects of trade restrictions see Easton and Grubel (1982). For a survey of welfare economics generally under democracy see van den Doel (1979). For a survey of techniques used to measure the welfare effects of protection see Jeon and von Furstenberg (1986). For a theoretical paper on exact measurement of welfare losses see Helpman (1978). Harris (1984) finds that, because of economies of scale, 50% tariff cuts in Canada would produce a 5% increase in gross national product. Melvin (1985) notes that one welfare consequence of tariffs is that it stimulates greater interregional trade within countries. For an analysis of the welfare effects of tariff reductions under the Tokyo round see Kreinin and Officer (1979). For an analysis of how to calculate the consumer costs of trade restrictions see the work by Rousslang and Soumela (1985).

The results in this chapter are at variance with the results of Coughlin (1982), who obtains Pareto-optimal outcomes with probabilistic voting. However, his formulation did not have campaign contributions affecting the probabilities of election.

The degree of relative risk aversion plays a role in the economic black hole. For a formal treatment of power and taxation with risk aversion see Aumann and Kurz (1977a). For a formal treatment of the problem of political myopia (the application of higher than market discount rates by politicians) see Cohen and Noll (1984).

For theoretical papers on the relationship between uncertainty and trade policy see Cassing, Hillman, and Long (1986), Helpman and Razin (1980),

Jensen and Thursby (1986), and Young and Anderson (1980, 1982). For the relationship between uncertainty and voter behavior see Aranson (1986), Enelow and Hinich (1981), Ferejohn and Noll (1976), and Palfrey and Rosenthal (1985). For analysis of uncertainty applied in a voter context see Palfrey and Rosenthal (1985). It is well known from Bhagwati's (1971) work that subsidizing the output of the import-competing sector is welfare superior to a tariff. Helpman and Razin examined this contention in the presence of uncertainty and observed that, if short sales on equity securities are prohibited or restricted, then a tariff may be welfare superior to subsidies. In general, however, they find that subsidizing the sales of equity securities in the import-competing sector is superior to a tariff. For a survey of the literature and a theory of rent seeking see Hartle (1983). Ferejohn and Noll (1976) analyze the effects of uncertainty on formal theories of politics. On this same subject see also Enelow and Hinich (1981), who analyze how each voter's idea point shifts in the presence of uncertainty.

Bernholz (1966) argues that the perverse tendencies of economic policies to demonstrate proproducer bias may not simply be a phenomenon plaguing democracies, but rather are dependent on certain economic structures in an economy. On the global question of the Schumpeterian malaise see the discussion by Nelson and Winter (1982). For an interesting international example of Olson's (1965) exploitation of large groups by small groups in an economy see Wellisz and Wilson (1986).

Some political scientists are less pessimistic about the economic effects of political conflict between groups – for example, Brittan (1975). Brittan also notes the following failure of electoral politics. Because of the absence of a budget constraint among voters, the populace expects too much from government and at too low a cost. This is consistent with the observation that government workers in some jurisdictions are overworked and underpaid relative to their private counterparts. A related point is his observation is that public frustration may grow over time: The more equality and efficiency our public institutions inspire, the greater our outrage at the inefficiencies that remain.

The analysis in this chapter is a static version of perverse outcomes possible in a redistributive game. The dynamic parallel might be an arms race between two superpowers such as the United States and the Soviet Union. On this issue see the analysis by Intriligator (1975). For a recent discussion of a similar problem involving the "Dove's Dilemma" see Dunn (1981).

The international economic equivalent of domestic rent seeking is for a nation to levy an optimum tariff (see the works cited on this in Chapter 2). Mann (1985) shows that the optimal tariff rate on imports will be positive and depends on the degree of economies of scope and scale in technology. Thurow and Tyson (1987) discuss economic black holes caused by inconsistent policies.

15.2   The assumptions

The analytical framework of this chapter is the Cobb–Douglas version of the Heckscher–Ohlin–Samuelson trade model developed in Chapter 14. Recall that the two lobbies, representing the interests of factor owners, contribute resources to politics and equate at the margin the returns to political and economic activity. The parties maximize their probabilities of election, trading off voter dissatisfaction with distortionary policies against votes gained from lobbying resources that the policies elicit. As before, rationally ignorant voters select parties based on a logit probability of election function. We now explore conditions sufficient to yield the black hole.

First, we assume *countervailing power* by the two factors, meaning that they have equal political power. Technically, we define countervailing power as equal probabilities of election for the prolabor and procapital parties when the country's entire factor endowment is devoted to politics. We set the problem up symmetrically so that what is true for capital is also true for labor. Thus, if 70% of capital is devoted to lobbying, then the same will be true for labor. While this is a mathematical convenience, there is an economic rationale: The more equally balanced are two protagonists in a domestic battle over redistribution, the more likely they will expend large resources in a close race. In track, two runners will expend more energy if the race is close than if it is not.

Second, we assume that capital and labor have *constant relative risk aversion*. Third, an important parameter in our black hole experiment is the elasticity of factor prices with respect to product prices. This is also called the *magnification elasticity* because it is always greater than one in the general equilibrium Heckscher–Ohlin–Samuelson trade model; that is, any percentage change in product prices leads to a larger percentage change in factor prices. The effect is important here because changes in tariffs and export subsidies change relative product prices, and relative prices change factor prices. The larger the magnification effect, the greater the payoff to the lobbies from getting product prices changed through the political process.

15.3   Limits on rent seeking related to risk aversion

What are the upper limits on the resources that the capital lobby will commit to the battle over relative prices? By our symmetry assumption, all of the analysis for capital applies equally to labor. If the capital lobby devotes another unit of capital to the procapital party, its income is reduced because fewer units are employed in production. This is called the *negative units effect*. However, the additional unit of capital in the hands of the procapital party ultimately results in a higher export subsidy and a higher return to cap-

Percentage of Capital and
Labor Devoted to Lobbying

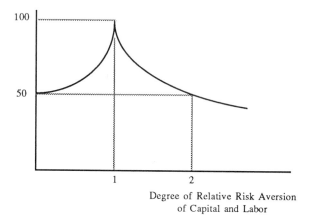

Degree of Relative Risk Aversion
of Capital and Labor

Figure 15.1. Upper limits on GNP loss due to rent seeking related to degree of risk aversion.

ital. This is called the *positive returns effect*. The positive returns effect is not under the conscious control of the capital lobby, by our necessary assumption that the parties are Stackelberg leaders (see Chapter 3). However, the units effects and the returns effects do change with the parameters of the model. In general, the larger the positive returns effect, the larger the fraction of capital that will be devoted to politics.

We consider next two possible ranges for the degree of relative risk aversion ρ by the two lobbies. Consider first values of this parameter for which $\rho < 1$. In this case, the proportion of capital (and, by our symmetry assumption, labor) devoted to politics will be bounded above in the following way:

$$K^*/K_0 < 1/(2 - \rho)$$

Notice that for risk neutrality ($\rho = 0$), no more than 50% of an economy's capital and labor will be devoted to rent seeking. Second, consider degrees of relative risk aversion for which $\rho > 1$. In this range we have the following upper limit on the proportion of rent seeking by capital (and labor):

$$K^*/K_0 < 1/\rho$$

Figure 15.1 shows the upper limits on predatory lobbying related to the degree of relative risk aversion ρ. Risk neutrality or values of the parameter ρ greater than 2 guarantee that, at most, half of an economy would be lost in redistributive activity. Simulations indicate that actual rent seeking may be closer to 33%, well below the 50% upper limit with risk neutrality.

Percentage of Capital and
Labor Devoted to Lobbying

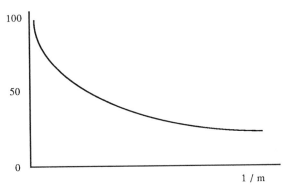

Figure 15.2. Upper limits on GNP loss due to rent seeking related to the magnification parameter *m*.

For degrees of relative risk aversion not equal to 1, there are upper limits on the proportion of an economy that will be devoted to rent seeking. Interestingly, these upper limits are independent of other parameters in the model.

15.4 The black hole

Consider now an economy whose factors are risk averse and have degrees of relative risk aversion equal to 1. Let the factor intensities of production in the two industries move together. This means that the capital–labor ratio in the labor-intensive import sector rises relative to the same ratio in the export sector. When this happens, product price changes have increasingly large effects on both wages and capital returns. The parameter *m* measures the percentage change in factor prices with respect to product price changes. Figure 15.2 shows that as *m* gets arbitrarily large, $(1/m)$ approaches zero and the upper limits on the equilibrium amount of an economy wasted in predatory redistributive activity can approach 100%. *With high magnification, the transfer of capital into lobbying generates an arbitrarily large increase in capital returns.* In this case, it is rational for the capital lobby to throw nearly all its capital into the redistributive battle; by symmetry, so will labor. *This carries us into the economic black hole.*

Figure 15.3 is a three-dimensional illustration of the black hole. The black hole is approached as *m* gets large and ρ approaches 1. The parameter *m* has just been described; the other axis plots the degree of relative risk aversion ρ. In the black hole, the economy loses nearly 100% of its free trade, politics-free income. The black hole suggests that the politically efficient equilibrium

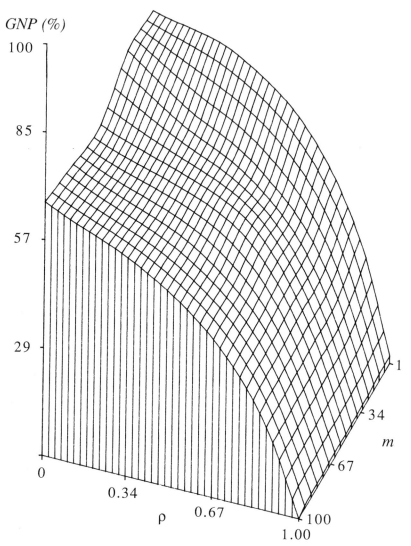

Figure 15.3. The black hole.

P in Figure 3.1 is virtually on the x axis. Political efficiency implies the absence of a functioning economy.

An interesting property is that *the equilibrium tariff and export subsidy approach zero near the black hole*. A moment's reflection will make clear why this is the case: A very small policy change can generate an arbitrarily large change in factor prices. Thus, both equilibrium policies are low with high magnification. This is an example of the magnification paradox of Chapter 14.

Another mathematical property is that, although the economy does get arbitrarily close to zero in the black hole, it does not go entirely to zero. The intuitive explanation is that, in a redistributive battle between capital and labor over the shares of the pie, there must be some pie left to battle over. There is also a mathematical explanation why a small fraction of the economy must remain in operation. In equilibrium, each of the lobbies must be indifferent between transferring another unit out of production and into politics. In effect, the rate of return on the last unit of capital employed in economic production must equal its rate of return in the hands of the procapital party. For this arbitrage condition to hold, a tiny fraction of capital and labor must remain in the economy.

15.5   Empirical implications: postwar movement toward gray holes

Do economic black holes really exist? Obviously not for long periods of time – otherwise the nation-state would collapse. Of course, some countries do collapse, although the reasons are usually not clear. One sees both advanced and developing countries torn by national strikes and internal strife. Two such countries in the recent past have been Poland and Argentina. Beksiak (1987) argues that the roots of Poland's economic problems are political. As an empirical matter, a study of the economic causes of governmental collapse and coups d'état might uncover case studies.

On a more modest level, every economy experiences ebbs and flows in the level of redistributive conflict at work. Although few economies approach the black hole, they are likely to move somewhat toward it in troughs of business cycles. Recall that the compensation principle states that rational lobbies will transfer resources toward politics when economic prospects are bad.

A gray hole describes a situation in which nontrivial levels of resources are wasted in redistributive conflict. The country's productivity and economic well-being are hampered by overregulation, excessive redistributive lawyering, and inefficient economic conflict resolution. In effect, our analysis in Chapter 8 of the invisible foot was about older economies with gray holes. We speculate that 10–20% of most economies is lost in redistributive rent seeking of this sort.

What light does our mathematics throw on the problem of gray holes? Since World War II, the automation boom has made it possible to replace labor in many labor-intensive industries such as textiles, shoes, steel, and now automobiles. If labor-intensive industries become more capital intensive, factor-price magnification increases. Thus, increasing automation may be responsible for the increase in factor-price magnification that led to increasing lobbying, decreasing tariffs, and moves toward a gray hole since World War II.

Since the early 1970s, tariff protection has been replaced with VERs and other nontariff barrier forms of protection. Casual empiricism suggests that both protection and the fraction of the U.S. economy devoted to predatory redistributive activity have been increasing since then.

CHAPTER 16

The endowment effect: cross-national evidence on endogenous tariffs

By regressing tariff rates on country factor endowment ratios, we are able to reveal country comparative advantage in both a political and an economic sense. This chapter explores the following:

16.1. the literature;
16.2. tariff rates and national factor endowment ratios;
16.3. the endowment effect (empirical evidence);
16.4. the inverted U between tariffs and national capital–labor ratios; and
16.5. evidence of nontariff barriers and overprotection.

The endowment effect in our $2 \times 2 \times 2 \times 2$ model of endogenous tariffs suggests that tariffs help labor and harm capital in the advanced countries. Heckscher–Ohlin–Samuelson symmetry dictates that the reverse should be true in the developing countries. Thus, all things considered, there should be an inverted-U shape relating tariffs to country capital–labor ratios. In the developing countries, the tariff rate should rise with capital–labor endowment ratios (since capital-intensive goods are imported), but it should fall with the capital–labor endowment ratios in the advanced countries. We have modest success in confirming this hypothesis.

16.1 The literature

For a comprehensive study of the relationship between trade patterns and comparative advantage see Leamer (1984). He estimates net export pat-

Chapter 16 in Stephen P. Magee, William A. Brock, and Leslie Young, *Black Hole Tariffs and Endogenous Policy Theory*. New York: Cambridge University Press, 1989. Adapted from Stephen P. Magee, "The Endowment Effect," mimeo, University of Texas at Austin, June 1987.

227

terns among sixty countries with ten goods, and eleven factors to explain comparative advantage during 1958 and 1975. He shows how net trade patterns and levels of gross domestic product are linearly related to factor endowments in a Heckscher–Ohlin–Samuelson model of international trade. For a similar study covering the years 1966 and 1980 see Bowen (1984). For a historical study of the factor endowments derivable from national balance sheets for 1688–1978 see Goldsmith (1985). For general background discussions of the Heckscher–Ohlin–Samuelson tests of factor endowments in trade patterns see Baldwin and Hilton (1983) and Hamilton and Svensson (1984).

Conybeare (1983b) examines national tariff levels across thirty-five countries in 1971. He finds that tariff rates were positively correlated across countries with indirect taxes (such as tariffs and excise taxes) as a percentage of government revenue, the size of the central government as a percentage of total government, and the instability of exports. Tariffs were negatively correlated with the commodity diversification of exports (and imports), gross national product, GNP per capita, manufacturing as a percentage of GNP, and government as a percentage of GNP. The following variables were uncorrelated with national tariff levels: the geographical diversification of exports (and imports), military expenditures, the degree of urbanization, and the rate of growth of GNP. He notes that many of his correlations may be explained by the level of economic development of a country. Tariffs are negatively correlated with GNP per capita, and many of the variables above are also associated with GNP per capita. Thus, a major difficulty in explaining cross-national tariff rates is disentangling causal forces from these development effects.

Conybeare (1982) examines the empirical determinants of revenue diversification across countries. He finds that government revenue sources become more diversified the higher the level of GNP per capita for the developing countries, whereas no relationship exists between the two variables for the developed countries. He confirms Wagner's law of expanding activity: Government as a percentage of GNP rises with the level of development. He finds that the more open the economy, the more diversified the sources of taxation. Along with the more obvious explanations, openness generates greater opportunities for taxable assets to escape the tax authorities, so that more sources of taxation are employed. Finally, developing countries with large trade sectors collect more revenue because the cost of collecting import duties is lower.

We present brief evidence in this chapter on inflation across countries. We find that inflation is lower in economies with larger endowments of capital relative to labor, supporting the view that if capitalists tend to be creditors and labor debtors, then unanticipated inflation redistributes wealth from creditors to debtors. Maier (1978) noted that the Bolsheviks performed a similar redistribution in the Soviet Union, using inflation to tax their class enemies.

The view expressed in this book is that aggregate protection has fallen because of factor endowment evolution away from the scarce factor, labor, and has increased in recent years because of specific industry senility and the success of the procapital Republican party in obtaining its redistributive objectives through contractionary macro policy. High unemployment and low inflation (i.e., a strong dollar under floating rates) have the byproduct of increasing the equilibrium level of protection (see Chapter 13). This differs from the theory of hegemonic tariffs offered by Gilpin (1975), Kindleberger (1986), and Krasner (1976). They assert that U.S. protection fell during this century to promote the collective good of a liberal international trading régime and that U.S. protection has been rising since the mid-1960s as U.S. power has waned. See Balassa and Balassa (1984) for a recent discussion of protection in the advanced countries. For a survey of how trade policy affects patterns of world trade and manufactures see Winters (1987).

A number of studies also contain useful data. On elasticities of import and export demand for a number of industrial and developing countries see Gylfason (1987). For parameters from cross-national tests of the permanent income hypothesis see Kormendi and LaHaye (1984). For an analysis of nontariff barriers across countries see Nogues, Olechowski, and Winters (1986). For analyses of the size of the public economy see Cameron (1979). For an analysis of long-term trends in the openness of economies see Grassman (1980). For an analysis of subsidies as a percentage of government revenues across countries see Fig (1987). For estimates of tariff rates both through time and across countries see So (1986). For estimates of cross-national economic inequality see the study by Cowen (1986). Waldrup (1985) analyzes cross-national unemployment rates. Harvey (1985) relates redistributive activities to foreign direct investment across countries. McDaniel (1984) has cross-national data on the degree of unionization. Han (1986) has interpolated capital stock data for countries that did not appear in Leamer's (1984) data. Wang (1985) analyzes the effect of national corporate income tax rates on country debt–equity ratios. Licon and Lockwood (1985) analyze cross-national divorce rates. Vith (1985) has collected data on arms sales to the third world. Molina (1984) attempts to explain cross-national variance in concentration ratios in the commercial banking industry. Nimo (1986) attempts to explain how government as a percentage of GNP varies across countries. For data on protective rates by country in Latin America see Macario (1964). For estimates of price elasticities of demand for fifteen developed and nine developing countries see Gylfason (1987). For data on levels of protection for eight Latin American countries by product see Macario (1964). For calculations of both tariff and

Table 16.1. *Correlations between tariff rates and Leamer's national factor endowment ratios across thirty-two countries (mid-1970s data)*

Country factor endowment	Tariff rate	Log of the tariff rate
1. Skilled labor/labor[a]	$-.52^b$	$-.62^b$
2. Semiskilled labor/labor	$-.73^b$	$-.59^b$
3. Unskilled labor/labor	$.75^b$	$.65^b$
4. Tropical land/labor	.02	.20
5. Dry land/labor	.04	.07
6. Humid aresothermal land/labor	$-.08$	.02
7. Humid microthermal land/labor	$-.18$	$-.16$
8. Coal/labor	$-.14$	$-.15$
9. Minerals/labor	$-.19$	$-.09$
10. Oil/labor	$-.19$	$-.29$
11. Capital/labor	$-.58^b$	$-.65^b$

[a]Labor = skilled + semiskilled + unskilled labor.
[b]Significant at the 1% level.

nontariff barriers in major industrialized countries see Deardorff and Stearn (1983).

We discuss in this chapter the tendency for Japan to underimport. For a background paper on industrial policy in Japan see Uekusa and Ide (1986). For a discussion of Japan's trade structure and problem of trade surpluses see Saxonhouse (1985, 1986). Ray and Marvel (1984) found that most advanced countries have lower tariff rates on their high-technology industries whereas Japan does the reverse: It protects high-tech industries in an infant-industry sense. Ishii, McKibbin, and Sachs (1985) find that tariff retaliation by the United States against Japanese trading practices would be particularly harmful to Japan. Their econometric model predicts a significant contraction in Japan, a sharp end depreciation, and a rise in inflation.

16.2   Tariff rates and national factor endowment ratios

Leamer (1984) provides national factor endowment data on eleven variables for thirty-two countries in the mid-1970s: capital, three kinds of labor, four types of land, and three forms of natural resources (coal, minerals, and oil). Our tariff rates equal each country's tariff duties divided by the value of the country's imports in the mid-1970s (see So 1986). In Table 16.1, we report simple correlations between these endowment ratios and national tariff rates. Based on these simple results, it appears that *tariffs protect unskilled labor while they harm physical capital and human capital* (skilled and semiskilled labor). Aggregate country tariff rates are unrelated to the four types of land and the three forms of natural resources. This is also true at higher levels of aggregation: tariffs are uncorrelated with aggregate land–labor ratios and resource–labor ratios. Leamer's results suggest that there are three important endowment variables at work: skilled labor, unskilled labor, and capital. Use of more than two factors carries us outside the confines of the $2 \times 2 \times 2 \times 2$ framework of our Cobb–Douglas model in Chapter 13, and we leave to other scholars the job of building a three-factor political economy model; however, we proceed with an analysis of the data, applying insights from our model. We interpret these results as preliminary evidence for the endowment thesis: namely, that a factor's political power increases with its importance in a country's factor endowment.

16.3   The endowment effect: empirical evidence

One problem with the analysis in section 16.2 is that the Leamer endowment data plus our tariff data cover only thirty-two countries. In this section we expand the sample to fifty-eight countries and include other variables (see Appendix Table A.16.1 for our basic 58-country sample). Leamer defines unskilled labor as individuals who are "illiterate." His other two groups are basically "literate" labor. We used country literacy rates as a proxy for the proportion of the labor force that is skilled. From the analysis above, tariffs should decrease across advanced countries with the proportion of literate labor in an economy and with the capital–labor ratio. We used Han's (1986) data on 1975 national capital stocks, derived using techniques similar to Leamer's. The country labor data is for 1980 and was obtained from the World Bank annual reports.

Figure 16.1 plots tariff rates on country capital–labor ratios. Figure 16.2 plots tariff rates on the percentage of the population that is literate. Notice the negative relationships in both cases. The axes in Figure 16.1 are in the natural logarithms of the variables.

We obtained other variables suggested by our analysis of the U.S. case, by Conybeare, and others. Unemployment rates could be obtained for only about half of the desired number of countries. For this smaller data set, we found that tariffs were generally uncorrelated with total unemployment and male unemployment rates. However, tariffs were positively correlated with female unemployment rates across countries. This is explained by female unemployment rates being higher in the developing countries, which have higher tariffs.

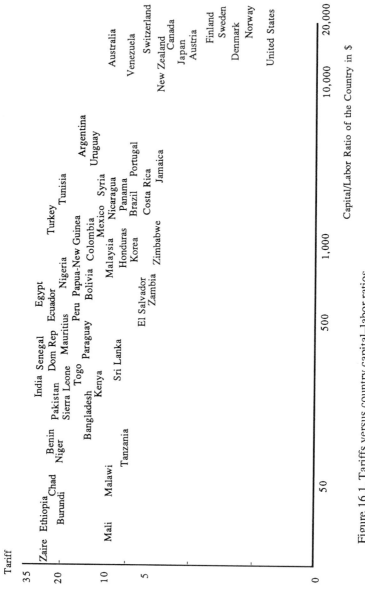

Figure 16.1. Tariffs versus country capital–labor ratios.

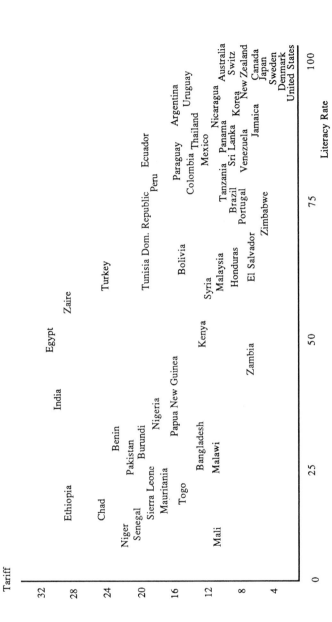

Figure 16.2. Tariffs versus country literacy rates.

Table 16.2. *Equations explaining tariffs, openness, and inflation across countries (t-ratios in parentheses)*

	Tariff rates (mid-1970s)			Openness (imports/GNP)		Inflation (1960–80)	
	1	2	3	4	5	6	7
Constant	23.1	21.7	19.9	29.1	22.5	5.2	9.3
	(9.1)	(7.7)	(9.6)	(5.2)	(4.9)	(2.9)	(6.2)
GNP/capita			−2.3		.12		−.17
			(−3.4)		(.1)		(−.4)
(GNP/capita)^2			0.12		−.007		−.013
			(2.5)		(−.1)		(−.4)
Capital/labor	−.00027					−.00047	
	(−2.1)					(−4.9)	
Labor/capital				−441.2			
				(−2.6)			
Literate labor/	−.09			−.08		.08	
labor	(−3.4)			(−1.5)		(3.2)	
Capital/labor <$750			.0018				
			(.6)				
≥$750			−.0002				
			(−1.6)				
Literate/labor <70%			−.055				
			(−1.2)				
≥70%			−.084				
			(−3.0)				
Tariff rev./	.16	.16	.18				
govt. rev.	(3.8)	(3.9)	(4.6)				
Imports/GNP	−.27	−.27	−.29			−.08	−.07
	(−5.1)	(−5.2)	(−5.4)			(−2.4)	(−1.9)
Country area					−.0026	−.0027	
					(−3.7)	(−3.7)	
Govt./GNP					.64	.59	
					(2.7)	(2.3)	
Subsidies/						47.4	50.6
govt. rev.						(3.5)	(3.2)
R^2	.66	.66	.64	.27	.19	.44	.26
n	58	58	58	71	71	40	40

The tariff regressions are shown in Table 16.2. In tariff equation 1, both the capital–labor ratio and the literate labor ratio are quite significant in explaining tariffs across fifty-eight countries. Two other significant variables are the share of tariff revenue in total government revenue and the degree of openness of the economy (measured by imports/GNP). Developing countries use tariffs to generate much of their government revenue. The negative effect of openness on tariffs is puzzling. One might think that the result is due to the reverse causation: that is, high tariffs reduce openness. However, experimentation with simultaneous equation estimation of both tariff and openness equations revealed that tariff rates do not have negative effects on openness whereas openness does have negative effects on tariffs. For this reason, imports/GNP was left in the tariff equation. We leave to future researchers the explanation of why open economies have lower endogenous tariff levels. We speculate that either tariff and nontariff protection are complements across countries, or that voters in open economies are more sophisticated in ways that are not picked up by our literacy variable.

The effect of the two endowment ratios on national tariff rates is striking. We note a potential identification problem with the literacy variable that may confound an endowment effect and a sophisticated voter effect. The endowment effect suggests that skilled labor is hurt by protection. However, the same effect could have been generated by sophisticated voters having a larger negative voter effect in the probabilistic voting function.

16.4   The inverted U between tariffs and capital–labor endowments

In our Heckscher–Ohlin–Samuelson political economy trade model, the relationship between factor endowments and policies should not be monotonic. If the advanced countries are protecting low-wage labor, the developing countries cannot also be protecting low-wage labor, because some group of countries must export low-wage goods to the advanced countries. Since we know that the tariff rate decreases with country capital–labor endowments in advanced countries, symmetry demands that tariffs rise with capital–labor endowments in developing countries. In short, symmetry suggests an inverted-U shape for tariffs plotted against country capital–labor endowments. We extend the logic of the two-factor model to the three-factor situation, realizing the dangers of doing so.

We test for symmetry by breaking both factor endowment ratios in equation 1 into two groups (at the median value). Tariff equation 2 in Table 16.2 reports these results. The median capital–labor ratio is $750 per laborer while the median literacy ratio for the labor force is 70%. Notice that for advanced coutnries, the negative coefficient on the capital–labor ratio is just barely statistically significant while the negative coefficient on literacy is very significant. Thus, *the political economy model fits the advanced countries.* For the developing countries, neither endowment variable is significant, though the capital–labor coefficient is positive, as suggested by the inverted-U hypothesis. With respect to capital–labor, the data do not refute an inverted U; unfortunately, it also does not reject the null hypothesis. The insignificance of the endowment coefficients for the developing countries is suggestive. In tariff regression 3, we replace the endowment ratios with GNP/capita and (GNP/capita)^2. It is no better or worse than the endowment equations. We leave to future research the global question of whether development effects on tariffs are endowment effects or something else.

Future research on this question could have three possible outcomes. First, if the lowest-income developing countries follow the same pattern as the middle- and upper-income countries, then all countries in the world protect unskilled labor. In this case a new trade theory would be required to explain why *skilled labor and capital gain in all countries from greater exports while unskilled labor gains in all countries from reduced imports.* One bizarre implication of this outcome is that the worldwide academic bias for free trade may be self-serving, since academics gain economically from expanded exports. The second scenario is that the lower-income developing countries follow the inverted-U hypothesis and protect physical capital while harming skilled labor. The third possibility is that political interventions in the lower-income developing countries prevent the Heckscher–Ohlin–Samuelson theorem from predicting patterns of protection and trade. In this case, our model would not apply.

16.5   Nontariff protection and overprotection

We examine next the issue of overprotection by examining the residuals from the tariff equation 1 and from the openness equation 4 of Table 16.2. These results are shown in Tables 16.3 and 16.4. The countries at the top of the list for the tariff equation are less restrictive (and hence more "open") than the equation predicted. Thus, the United States, Brazil, Japan, and Mexico have much lower tariff restrictions than expected, based on peer group performance, whereas Turkey and India have the reverse.

Tariffs are not the only means of protecting an economy from foreign trade. Nontariff barriers abound. One way around the difficulty of nonobservable nontariff barriers is to examine openness. Equations 4 and 5 are openness equations in which we estimate imports as a percentage of GNP for an expanded sample of 71 countries. Labor-abundant countries are less open and capital-abundant economies more open. In contrast to the tariff equation, skilled-labor-abundant economies are less open, though not statistically significantly so. Equation 5 indicates that openness is not a level of development issue.

The residuals from the openness equation provide an indirect measure of nontariff protection. This time, excessively closed economies are at the top of the list. The rent seekers Turkey and India again made the list, having lower import/GNP ratios than peer group behavior predicts. Japan is no surprise,

Table 16.3. *Tariff rates (mid-1970s) by country: actual and predicted[a]*

Code	Country	Actual	Predicted	Act. – pred.
2	Bangladesh	13	21.2	−8.2
3	Mali	9.9	17.8	−7.9
8	Malawi	9.5	17.2	−7.7
117	United States	0.6	8.2	−7.6
77	Brazil	8.1	14.4	−6.3
44	Zambia	5.9	11.7	−5.8
108	Japan	2.7	8.1	−5.4
49	Zimbabwe	5.2	10.3	−5.1
47	El Salvador	6.1	10.8	−4.7
11	Niger	20.7	24.9	−4.2
24	Sierra Leone	18.5	22.7	−4.2
12	Tanzania	8.8	11.8	−3
82	Mexico	11.3	14.2	−2.9
67	Colombia	12.4	15.2	−2.8
18	Benin	21.9	24.4	−2.5
65	Paraguay	14	16.4	−2.4
27	Pakistan	21	23.2	−2.2
53	Nigeria	17.6	19.5	−1.9
40	Bolivia	14.1	15.5	−1.4
87	Venezuela	7.5	8.9	−1.4
113	Denmark	1.2	2.6	−1.4
103	New Zealand	5	6.3	−1.3
25	Sri Lanka	8.4	9.4	−1
78	Republic of Korea	7.4	8.3	−0.9
64	Dominican Republic	19.4	19.4	0
45	Honduras	9.1	9.1	0
26	Kenya	12.7	12.7	0
81	Portugal	7.2	7.2	0
106	Austria	2.8	2.7	0.1
10	Burundi	20.8	20.6	0.2
114	Canada	4.9	4.7	0.2
55	Thailand	12.3	11.9	0.4
57	Costa Rica	6.2	5.7	0.5
74	Syria	11.4	10.8	0.6
115	Sweden	1.9	1.2	0.7
110	Finland	2.3	1.5	0.8
75	Malaysia	9.6	8.7	0.9
116	Norway	1.1	0.04	1.06
80	Panama	8.7	7.6	1.1

Table 16.3 (cont.)

Code	Country	Actual	Predicted	Act. – pred.
85	Uruguay	12.5	11.4	1.1
17	Togo	14.4	13.1	1.3
112	Australia	8.6	7.2	1.4
56	Nicaragua	9.6	8	1.6
51	Papua New Guinea	16.5	14.6	1.9
39	Mauritania	16.2	14.2	2
63	Jamaica	5	2.2	2.8
79	Argentina	14.9	12	2.9
58	Peru	17.5	14.4	3.1
36	Senegal	20.7	16.2	4.5
62	Tunisia	19.2	14.4	4.8
118	Switzerland	6.8	2	4.8
31	Chad	24.1	19	5.1
66	Ecuador	19.3	14.2	5.1
1	Ethiopia	28.5	22	6.5
61	Turkey	24	17.2	6.8
14	India	29.8	21.3	8.5
5	Zaire	28.3	16.8	11.5
46	Egypt	30.8	18.8	12

[a]Predictions use equation 1 from Table 16.2.

given the woeful tales of American and European businesspeople who return as if they had preceded Admiral Perry. The striking feature about Japan is that the equation predicts Japan's import/GNP ratio as being fourteen percentage points too low. This translates into their international trade level being $167 billion too low: Japan should more than double its imports for it to just come up to average peer country behavior. Of course, this calculation says nothing about the appropriate trade balance. Other low-trade economies include Mexico, Sweden, New Zealand, and France, as well as a surprise – West Germany. The last column of the table gives the dollar value of the trade shortage. Figure 16.3 shows those economies that are more open than we expected (had higher import/GNP ratios than predicted) and those that are more closed (had lower ratios).

Finally, as an afterthought, we included in Table 16.2 equations explaining inflation rates over the period 1960–80 for a smaller sample. Although inflation is not a focus of this work, endowment effects on inflation are striking and are not explained by level of development effects: Notice the insig-

Table 16.4. *Openness by country: actual and predicted[a] imports/GNP*

Code	Country	Actual	Predicted	Act. – pred.	GNP ($M)	Import shortfall
61	Turkey	11.6	31.1	−19.5	66,003	−12,871
50	Morocco	23	37.8	−14.8	18,180	−2,691
108	Japan	12.2	26.6	−14.4	1,155,152	−166,342
14	India	7.9	21.9	−14	161,568	−22,620
46	Egypt	21	33.9	−12.9	23,084	−2,978
53	Nigeria	17.5	30.3	−12.8	85,547	−10,950
58	Peru	15.7	27.9	−12.2	16,182	−1,974
44	Zambia	30.8	42.3	−11.5	3,248	−374
65	Paraguay	12.4	23.8	−11.4	4,160	−474
111	West Germany	22.7	33.5	−10.8	827,631	−89,384
67	Colombia	14.3	24.2	−9.9	31,506	−3,119
87	Venezuela	18.6	28.5	−9.9	54,087	−5,355
113	Denmark	29.3	38.7	−9.4	66,045	−6,208
82	Mexico	13.4	22.8	−9.4	145,882	−13,713
85	Uruguay	19.8	29	−9.2	8,149	−750
48	Ivory Coast	27.7	36.6	−8.9	9,545	−850
115	Sweden	29.8	38.6	−8.8	112,216	−9,875
103	New Zealand	23.4	31.7	−8.3	23,397	−1,942
66	Ecuador	22.1	30.3	−8.2	10,160	−833
109	France	21.5	29.5	−8	627,555	−50,204
49	Zimbabwe	27.6	34.9	−7.3	4,662	−340
86	Yugoslavia	24	31.2	−7.2	58,426	−4,207
105	United Kingdom	27.1	34.2	−7.1	442,728	−31,434
79	Argentina	15.9	23	−7.1	66,203	−4,700
51	Papua New Guinea	33.6	40.4	−6.8	2,340	−159
23	Madagascar	25.2	31.2	−6	3,045	−183
1	Ethiopia	12.3	18.1	−5.8	4,354	−253
39	Mauritania	38.6	44.4	−5.8	660	−38
2	Bangladesh	21.2	26.8	−5.6	11,505	−644
27	Pakistan	21.7	26.5	−4.8	24,660	−1,184
64	Dominican Republic	22.9	27.6	−4.7	6,264	−294
28	Sudan	21.1	25.6	−4.5	7,667	−345
102	Italy	27	31	−4	368,712	−14,748
74	Syria	34.2	37.9	−3.7	12,060	−446
5	Zaire	11.6	14	−2.4	6,226	−149
40	Bolivia	26.1	27.5	−1.4	3,192	−45
3	Mali	21.8	22.9	−1.1	1,330	−15
106	Austria	31.9	32.4	−0.5	76,725	−384
10	Burundi	20.5	21	−0.5	820	−4

Table 16.4 (cont.)

Code	Country	Actual	Predicted	Act. – pred.	GNP ($M)	Import shortfall
116	Norway	32.7	32.8	–0.1	51,865	–52
47	El Salvador	32.5	32.5	0	2,970	0
26	Kenya	34.5	34.5	0	6,678	0
31	Chad	29.6	29.2	0.4	540	2
110	Finland	32.7	32.3	0.4	47,628	191
56	Nicaragua	34.3	33.8	0.5	1,924	10
12	Tanzania	24	23.1	0.9	5,236	47
55	Thailand	29.2	28.1	1.1	31,490	346
117	United States	9.8	8.5	1.3	2,586,672	33,627
112	Australia	14.3	12.3	2	142,390	2,848
80	Panama	36.9	34.4	2.5	3,114	78
77	Brazil	10.3	6.8	3.5	243,335	8,517
118	Switzerland	34	29	5	106,860	5,343
36	Senegal	46.7	41.2	5.5	2,565	141
57	Costa Rica	40.1	33.8	6.3	3,806	240
18	Benin	34.1	27	7.1	1,054	75
8	Malawi	31.3	23.8	7.5	1,403	105
81	Portugal	40.5	32.4	8.1	23,226	1,881
62	Tunisia	42.2	32.7	9.5	8,384	796
78	Republic of Korea	38.4	27.8	10.6	58,064	6,155
24	Sierra Leone	42.8	30.5	12.3	980	121
75	Malaysia	47.1	34.5	12.6	22,518	2,837
11	Niger	39.6	25.1	14.5	1,590	231
107	Netherlands	47.5	32.6	14.9	161,727	24,097
63	Jamaica	51.5	36.3	15.2	2,288	348
114	Canada	24.2	8.4	15.8	242,107	38,253
45	Honduras	49.2	32.8	16.4	2,072	340
38	Liberia	63.5	38.3	25.2	1,007	254
17	Togo	61.5	36.3	25.2	1,025	258
25	Sri Lanka	51.1	25.7	25.4	3,969	1,008
104	Belgium	59.6	33	26.6	119,364	31,751
101	Ireland	69.3	34.8	34.5	16,104	5,556

[a]Predictions use equation 4 in Table 16.2.

nificance of the GNP/capita variables in equation 7. Unemployment did not generally work in these inflation equations and was omitted (also for lack of data). Note, however, the surprising significance of factor endowments in explaining national inflation rates. Capital-abundant economies have lower

Relatively Open Economies	Relatively Closed Economies
Tunisia	Turkey
Korea	Morocco
Sierra Leone	Japan
Malaysia	India
Niger	Egypt
Netherlands	Nigeria
Jamaica	Peru
Canada	Zambia
Hondurus	Paraguay
Liberia	W. Germany
Togo	Colombia
Sri Lanka	Venezuela
Belgium	Denmark
Ireland	Mexico

Figure 16.3. Open and closed economies based on import/GNP ratios.

inflation rates, but skilled-labor-endowed economies have higher inflation rates; closed economies are more inflation prone, although the causation is probably two-way, and countries with greater subsidies have higher inflation. We conclude that endowment effects appear to be important in explaining three variables of interest to students of political economy: tariffs, openness, and inflation. Inflation is also a redistributive contest between capital and labor.

CHAPTER 17

The senile-industry argument for protection

Since most economists favor free trade, it must not be the best policy. As America ages, more and more economists are getting on the protectionist bandwagon. The first indicator that free trade is overrated is the absence of any country with free trade. A second is that the advanced countries with the freest trade are moving away from it. In short, all consumers seem to want it but cannot get it, and those countries that do have it are giving it up.

There are three types of industries: young, middle-aged, and old. Young ones should have protection but old ones do have it. This book has already advanced one theory: Age doesn't matter – only political power. We have seen through the compensation effect that when economic capability declines, political influence grows. Senile-industry protection is best explained by this effect. The sclerosis of advancing economic age can only be relieved by the elixir of protection.

This chapter covers the following:

17.1. the literature;
17.2. the product life cycle;
17.3. the industry life cycle and infant- and senile-industry protection;
17.4. the country life cycle and the U-shaped relationship between protection and GNP per capita;
17.5. the dominance of economic over political explanations of protection;
17.6. endogenous industrial policy; and
17.7. our conclusions.

Chapter 17 in Stephen P. Magee, William A. Brock, and Leslie Young, *Black Hole Tariffs and Endogenous Policy Theory*. New York: Cambridge University Press, 1989. Based on remarks made by Stephen P. Magee at the Kiel Conference, Kiel, West Germany, June 1986.

Historically, a widely accepted rationale for protection has been the infant-industry argument. The argument is that young industries cannot grow without temporary protection from foreign competition. The infant-industry argument suggests that industries go through life cycles. If we accept the life-cycle argument, then there is also an argument for senile-industry protection. As a grammar student once quipped, life is separated into three parts: infancy, adultery, and senility. Upon this intellectual foundation we launch a senile-industry argument for protection.

17.1   The literature

Frey, Pommerehne, Schneider, and Gilbert (1984) find that there is little consensus among economists that protection reduces economic welfare. They find that while 79% of American economists believe that protection reduces welfare, the proportion is only 70% in Germany, 47% in Switzerland, 44% in Austria, and 27% in France. It would be interesting to correlate these percentages with pre-EEC levels of protection by these countries.

See Kindleberger (19878) and Norton (1986) on the aging of economies. International product life cycles have been described by Vernon (1966). For a fascinating discussion of the national political consequences of product cycles see Kurth (1979). He argues that in many countries, the textile industry has been powerful since its inception. Textile manufacturers were a major force in the revolutions of the 1830s in France, Belgium, and Switzerland. Thus, the political power of textiles in protectionism is not just a senile-industry phenomenon. Following the textile industry, the second stage of a country's industrialization typically involves the creation of a steel industry and the related emergence of steel users such as railroads, shipbuilding, and, in this century, automobiles. Kurth argues that most of the major industrial countries have gone through this industrial life cycle, starting with textiles, then steel, and then one or more of the associated rail, shipping, or auto industries.

For rent-seeking approaches to declining industry, see the work by Cassing and Hillman (1986) and Hillman (1982). As dying industries become smaller, their political support fades as well, so that the political and economic processes are reinforcing. This contrasts with our compensation result of Chapter 11, in which political activity offset economic declines. One would think that protection would increase both capital and labor returns in senile industries. However, Canto (1986) and Canto, Dietrich, Jain, and Mudaliar (1986) found that protection and the Standard and Poor's 500 stock market returns were negatively correlated. Presumably, this reflects a Smoot–Hawley/Great Depression–type effect. For a study of the infant-industry argument for protection see Mayer (1984a). For discussion of trade policy in multiple-product industries see Mann (1985).

One of the most difficult things in the theory of protection is measuring the tariff equivalent of quantitative restrictions. A comprehensive study of thirty-one different restrictions in the United States is provided by Hufbauer, Berliner, and Elliott (1985). See also the discussion by Deardorff and Stearn (1984a) of various ways to measure nontariff barriers in the major industrialized countries. For both a discussion of theory and measurement see Hamilton (1984a, 1985a, 1986a,b). For a theoretical discussion of old-industry behavior and industrial policy see Flam and Helpman (1987). On the use of coverage ratio to measure nontariff barriers see Nogues, Olechowshi, and Winters (1986). For a time series analysis of dumping in the United States see Takacs (1981) and B. Brown (1985).

Hillman, Katz, and Rosenberg (1987) note that when some industries decline, the government will step in to assist the affected firms. Since many of its programs are designed to protect jobs, these authors find that the prospect of protection makes the firm's choice of labor endogenous to the political equilibrium. That is, firms will hire more labor if there is the prospect that their benefits from protection will be related to the number of jobs affected. Two weak banks in Texas, Republic and Interfirst, merged partially to maximize their size and hence the likelihood of a substantial political bailout by the U.S. government. Subsequently, the merged bank failed.

Protectionists take a cynical view of adjustment assistance in the United States: As Hughes (1979) notes, they view it as "burial assistance." De la Torre et al. (1978) find that some dying industries facing vigorous import competition were able to revitalize by simultaneously becoming more efficient and coping with internal redistributive activity by fighting off unionization. The U.S. apparel industry shifted to low-wage areas in the southeastern United States and adopted a hub-and-wheel locational strategy that placed the headquarters in the center and the production facilities in a circle around it, each about 100 miles apart. Since each production facility was small (less than 250 employees), this reduced the likelihood of successful unionization.

Yoffie (1983) argues that we are now witnessing a new pattern of protectionism; that is, that of voluntary export restraints and orderly marketing agreements. For a discussion of a life cycle for voluntary export trade agreements (VERs) internationally, based on life cycle models, see Aggarwal, Keohane, and Yoffie (1987). They find very different effects of protection in industries with low barriers to entry and high barriers to exit. These are industries with low opportunity costs for the industry's factors. Low barriers to entry mean that protection will encourage large-scale entry of firms into the industry and a dissipation of the politically created rents. High barriers to exit traps factors and generates a higher demand for protection (than without barriers) because the industry is larger in down cycles, returns are low, and so on. This generates a pattern that Aggarwal, Keohane, and Yoffie call increasing "institutional protection" over time, as is the case for textiles and apparel. Because of foreign entry, more countries must be added to VER agreements over time. A pattern of "sporadic" protection exists for industries such as steel because the imposition of protection generates high profits and wage increases that linger because of high barriers to entry. This reduces the demand for protection temporarily.

Hamilton (1985b) finds that voluntary export constraints levied against Japan, for example, will stimulate exports from other countries. In general, it may be true that VERs of this sort actually promote world development because they raise the price of some labor-intensive goods. For a theory of VERs see Hamilton (1985a). For analysis of the allocation of VERs within exporting countries see Hamilton (1986a). Hamilton (1986b) finds that the import tariff equivalents of U.S. voluntary export restraints applied to Hong Kong were well over 100% in 1983. Those applied by Sweden were also particularly high, exceeding 50% in the same period.

Hillman and Ursprung (1988) devise a formal theoretical framework of voluntary export restraints, examining conditions under which VERs will be mutually beneficial to both domestic and foreign producers' interests. In effect, VERs provide compensation to foreigners who have been restricted from a domestic (e.g., U.S.) market. Hamilton (1986b) finds that when tariffs and VERs are combined, the United States had higher levels of protection in the early 1980s than did Europe. For empirical estimates of VERs in both the United States and Europe see Kalantzopoulos (1986). For a discussion of the political economy of VERs see Jones (1984).

Husted (1986) analyzes foreign lobbying in the United States. Obviously, foreign lobbying can be welfare improving if it has the effect of overcoming U.S. trade restrictions. Husted provides the following data on foreign lobbying expenditures in the United States in 1984 (in millions of dollars):

France	$50.1	South Africa	22.4
Australia	31.0	Japan	20.0
Colombia	26.7	West Germany	18.9
Great Britain	24.7		

These expenditures reflect only country expenditures by governments, trade associations, and firms. When a broader view of expenditures is taken, foreign industries spent $108.2 million in 1984. The principal industries are tourism ($56 mil.), coffee ($25.6 mil.), airlines ($13.0 mil.), and oil ($2.8 mil.). The principal expenditures within individual countries were made in the following areas:

Australia, export promotion and the steel industry;
Canada, the government, weapons, oil, and natural gas;
Colombia, coffee;
Federal Republic of Germany, the government and airline firms;
France, tourism;
Great Britain, export promotion and airlines;
Israel, the government;
Jamaica, the government; and
Japan, government export promotion and the auto industry.

For a study of the power of the Japanese lobby in the United States see Lidell (1987). For a discussion of foreign lobbying in the United States on the 1987 trade bill see Mossberg (1987). For a theoretical paper on the effects of foreign lobbying in a political economy model see Das (1986).

One phenomenon associated with senile-industry protection is the evolution of adjustment policies to facilitate the movement of capital and labor into other industries. For papers on this subject see Aho and Bayard (1982), Bhagwati (1982b), Hillman, Katz, and Rosenberg (1987), and the OECD (1983). Aho and Bayard discuss the inevitable trade-offs among equity, efficiency, and political justifications of trade adjustment assistance. For a background paper on the United States in trade and investment generally see Lipsey (1982).

A number of studies deal with industry protection: on U.S. institutional pressures toward greater auto protection see Nelson (1986); on restrictions in high-tech products see Kreinin (1985); and on textiles see Pelzman (1982). For exceptions to the rule that old industries get more protection, consider the electronics industry. Considered a sunrise industry, electronics has recently succeeded in obtaining protection, perhaps because of the political expertise it obtained in getting defense contracts.

For a discussion of how the new protectionism relates to old industries, see Hamilton (1986c) and Yoffie (1983). Microeconomic shocks can accentuate the decline in senile industries: See Genberg, Swoboda, and Salemi (1984), who show that foreign variables have significant effects on Switzerland, even during the floating foreign exchange rate régime since 1973. Insofar as foreign economic variables generally have increased their impact on domestic economies because of increased openness, the demand for endogenous protection might be raised as ex post insurance against foreign shocks. For the observation that older regions of the United States tend to file more antidumping claims, see Cassing, McKeown, and Ochs (1986). For an interesting historical account of tariff policy and the stimulus it provided to the U.S. iron and steel industries see Baack and Ray (1983).

For a model of industrial policy with monopolistic competition see Flam and Helpman (1987). They find that small levels of protection are welfare improving, whereas changes in export subsidies, output subsidies, and R&D subsidies have ambiguous welfare effects.

Mayer (1984b) examines the infant-industry argument, noting that export subsidies are justified if there are externalities present; that the optimal export subsidy may well rise before it falls; and that export subsidies result in significant short-run welfare losses to society as a whole, offset by benefits only in the future. David (1970) examines carefully the infant-industry argument applied to tariff protection of the pre–Civil War U.S. cotton textile industry, and finds that learning by doing was important: Between 1833 and 1839, it accounted for 80% of the growth in total productivity. However, he concludes that the cotton tariff was little more than the means of redistributing income in favor of cotton textile producers.

For a paper on the behavior of bureaucracies in the United States on the issue of administered protection see Finger, Hall, and Nelson (1982). For discussions of voters, legislators, and bureaucrats see Fiorina and Noll (1977a,b). Their model predicts that as the demand for public goods grows exogenously over time, incumbent legislators experience a growing advantage.

17.2   The product life cycle

Vernon (1966, 1979) suggests that products go through life cycles. New (young) products are introduced in high-income countries because of high demand for new products, and in high-technology countries due to the supply of scientific innovators. Assume, for purposes of illustration, that the product in question is a new computer that is first introduced in the United States. After demand for the computer increases in Western Europe and other developed countries, the innovating firm exports the adolescent product from the United States or transfers it abroad through its multinational subsidiaries. As European firms acquire the computer through legitimate or other means, they begin production. In this middle age of the product's life, both the United States and the Europeans start exporting the product to the developing countries. Finally, in the product's old age, the production technology becomes so standardized that it is copied worldwide, and the locus of production shifts to the developing countries or the Far East, which have the lowest production costs in the world. Old products are exported from the developing countries back to the United States and Europe. Examples of new products include Star Wars technologies, medical technologies, and high-tech computers; middle-aged products are automobiles, machine tools, and chemicals; and old products are steel, textiles, and shoes. The Far East is currently in the process of shortening the life cycle of many products, and Japan is transforming middle-aged products such as autos into old ones for the United States.

What are the implications of this product life cycle for the life cycle of protection? New products do not need infant-industry protection in the innovating country because they face no international competition. For example, U.S. high-tech computer technologies do not need protection since they face no import competition. It is only after the product has become middle-aged that protection emerges in Western Europe and Japan to protect their computer firms from U.S. exports. Then, when the product gets old, it will be exported from the developing countries to the United States and Europe. Compensation behavior and increased lobbying by those injured cause the equilibrium level of protection to rise in the United States and Europe.

In short, *infant-industry protection applies only to middle-aged products outside of their country of origin, whereas senile-industry protection applies to old products.*

It appears that tariffs were used early in this century to protect U.S. industry against imports of manufactures from the United Kingdom and Europe. The decline in tariffs and the rise in nontariff barriers in the United States in recent decades are illustrated in the next chapter (see Figure 18.1). The increases have been primarily in America's aging and senile industries: textiles, steel, and autos. For data on these from Hufbauer, Berliner, and Elliott (1986) see Table 18.1. By 1984, these forms of nontariff protection had a tariff equivalent equal to that for all U.S. tariffs.

17.3   The industry life cycle

17.3.1   Infant-industry protection

Let us turn our attention now to the aging process at the industry level. Consider the human parallel: Individuals require protection early and late in their lives. For the first two decades or so of an individual's life, consumption exceeds production. For individuals, this pattern of deficit spending is funded by parental altruism. Parents also protect their offspring against direct competition in the market. The present value of an individual increases if he or she accepts this protection against market competition and accumulates human capital through schooling. The protection itself is of lower value if the child does not invest in learning and does not learn to compete. The ability to compete economically is acquired slowly: It starts at home, is refined at school and in athletics, and is tested in part-time and summer jobs through learning by doing. It would be foolhardy to subject a small child to full-scale economic competition against adults. Protection is rational for the young individual.

The same appears to hold for industries. Young industries need greater protection than older ones. If a government acted like a beneficent parent, it would reduce protection and increase competition until its industries could compete on world markets on their own. Postadolescent industries that do best on world markets are those that use the principles of comparative advantage; that is, they specialize in products in which they have the greatest relative advantage over foreigners. They also accumulate human capital in new product areas that require sophisticated technologies and thereby earn larger profits. Like individuals, industries with entrepreneurs who plan ahead do better than those that do not. Also, industries that invest in research and development do better than those that do not, and those that encourage hard work do better than those with undisciplined labor relations.

The problem, of course, is that in a special-interest world, the industries partially run the government. Thus, the government cannot be viewed as a parent and the industries as children. In a world of special-interest governments, behavior is better described as a fraternity house run by the members. Although there are outside constraints, most of the variance in group behavior is explained by the preferences of the inmates.

It is here that Japan comes to mind. It would appear to an outsider that Japanese economic policy follows a rational model of prudent parental behavior: Industries are protected but not permitted wasteful self-indulgence. They appear to be guided toward careers involving strong competition on world markets. This contrasts with the more self-indulgent government behavior in Europe and the United States, better described by the fraternity house model.

Another parallel between individual and industry aging is late adolescence. In both human and animal cultures, the weaning process is a painful one. Offspring are physically booted out of the nest by some birds. With humans, the process is eased a bit by institutional halfway houses such as universities. Industries, like children, are reluctant to give up the warmth of protected domestic markets and the easy life of protected profits. Industries fight the end of protection, but the maturing process requires the pain of separation from protection.

What happens to the industry that carries heavy protection into middle age? We have all known children who were supported too long by their parents. Such individuals underaccumulate the skills and the drive necessary to compete successfully. The same is true for infant industries too long protected. Westerners complain that Japan still overprotects its domestic industry from outside competition. If this is true, then these industries will eventually suffer from this overprotection.

Underprotection of young industries can be as bad as overprotection. Child labor laws are evidence of society's disapproval of economic underprotection. Although we have not studied the case, the very interesting University of Chicago experiment in Chile may be a case of premature removal of protection for an adolescent economy.

One sad consequence of life is that not everyone grows up. There are immature, disorganized individuals who did not have either the right parents, the right teachers, or the right breaks – or who may have had everything. In any case, they are incapable of personal or economic success. They bounce around in their jobs and in their relationships, and their lives are painful to behold. The same is true of some industries: High levels of protection are required if the industry is to survive. Sadly, these deadbeat industries seem incompetent at all undertakings except manipulating the public purse. The general point is that some industries, like some individuals, cannot succeed without protection.

17.3.2   Senile-industry protection

The question facing every economy with an old industry is whether it should import the good at a lower cost and a higher quality, or pay a higher price for a lower-quality domestic version. The question is one of free trade versus protection.

There are economic parallels between old industries and old people. Middle-aged individuals run trade surpluses (earn more than they spend), whereas the elderly run trade deficits. Old individuals experience a planned reduction in their wealth such that spending can exceed earnings. Similarly, old industries import more than they export. In so doing, they contribute to a reduction in the net foreign assets held by their country. If the industry's decline is as predictable as old age, it may parallel the personal life cycle of the industry's retiring workers.

We observe increasing protection in older industries such as autos, steel, and textiles. Does senile-industry protection of these industries provide public benefits of the infant-industry sort? Perhaps so. The most charitable argument is that *senile-industry protection provides efficiency in the transfer of resources out of old and dying industries, reduces social risks, and improves the welfare of the agents in the dying industry more than it reduces the welfare of others.* Following the compensation effect, lobbies in old industries will also invest more in obtaining protection than lobbies in middle-aged industries will invest in preventing it.

Should there be protection for senile industries? A traditional argument for protection in general is risk. Relying on foreign markets is risky around wartime or during OPEC-type periods. Early in World War II, the Japanese separated the United States from Far Eastern rubber, tin, and diamonds. The reduction in world trade in these items forced the United States and its allies to make difficult economy moves and construct costly alternatives; for example, synthetic substitutes for rubber and diamonds and electrolytic coating for tin cans. Research and development can provide alternatives but require expensive crash programs.

Consider the analogy of an individual with poor eyes choosing whether to wear glasses (e.g., protect a weak bodily industry) or get an eye transplant. Arch free traders should opt for the eye transplant; rational individuals who take the risks into account would prefer the protection of glasses to free trade in the form of imported Japanese eyes. The risks are real.

Does civilized society offer protection to the old? Of course – in the form of senior citizen discounts, institutionalized protection from the marketplace (social security), and mandatory retirement and public pensions. Protection abounds for the elderly, as well it should.

What about senile industries? Should we keep the heat of foreign competition breathing down the necks of the increasingly decrepit steel and textile industries, with autos not far behind? U.S. industry is getting transplants and taking whole blood a pint at a time from the Far East in the form of offshore sourcing of components that are merely assembled in the United States.

Experience with both automobiles and the human body suggests that they collapse one part at a time. The rational approach is to repair for as long as is feasible (i.e., protection) and then run in a new part or get a transplant (import). All of the industries in an economy do not weaken at the same time. Similarly, senile industries apply for protection seriatim: first textiles, then steel, and now autos.

Card-carrying free traders would insist that textiles and steel be entered in 100-yard dashes with the Japanese. It is obvious that the Americans and British would get clobbered in world trade sprints: Their joints would give out long before the finish was in sight. In fact, it is quite ungentlemanly to pit virile 20-year-old Japanese industries against 70-year-old occidentals.

The thing to do is have old-age races in which 70-year-olds race other 70-year-olds. Presumably this is what the Common Market had in mind when it admitted the British to compete with German and French agriculture: a race of the aged with no stopwatch. Given this view, senile-industry protection is respect awarded for one's past efforts, and as such is worked for and looked forward to by every middle-aged industry.

17.4 The country life cycle and the U-shaped relationship between protection and GNP per capita

For an analysis of younger economies see Rostow (1960); for older ones see Kindleberger (1978) and Olson (1982). Older economies are more plagued by redistributive coalitions than are younger economies, according to

Olson. Perform with us, if you will, the following mental exercise: Think of industries as bodily organs and the body itself as a country. (We are aware of the perils of the body analogy.)

When individuals get really old, the body is more prone to systemic failure. Hardening of the arteries and heart and kidney diseases are major threats. Olson talks of economic sclerosis, and one gets a vision of industries so separated by redistributive strife that they can no longer function together. The press would lead Americans to believe that each of the major organs of the British economy take turns at being on strike, with the result being that the economic body can scarcely function.

Although we cannot relate tariffs directly to country age, we can relate them to a proxy – country levels of economic development. Figure 17.1 shows the average tariff rate plotted against national income per capita for a sample of countries. Notice that as GNP per capita increases, national tariff rates fall until GNP per capita reaches $10,000. Thereafter, national levels of protection begin to rise again. A quadratic relationship between tariff rates and GNP per capita was estimated in equation 3 of Table 16.2. It is from that equation that the critical value of GNP per capita was derived by solving for the minimum value of the tariff (the precise value was $9,583). There may be other explanations for these results, including the greater dependence of young countries on tariffs as sources of government revenue (e.g., in 1900, tariff revenue was a major source of revenue for the U.S. government). If these arguments hold, then young and old countries get greater protection than middle-aged countries.

17.5   Economic versus political explanations of protection

Do industry economic factors or country political variables give us a greater understanding of protection? This question may seem impossible, but cheap answers are possible. By now it should be clear that both matter. The French, Germans, British, and Americans have sufficiently different political systems so that these institutional factors across countries might outweigh differences across industries within a given country. However, if industry age matters, then industry factors may have greater weight. A straightforward approach would be to see whether industry (economic) factors were more important in explaining tariffs than country (political) factors.

As a statistical matter, the question boils down to whether cross-sectional variability in tariff rates is better explained by country factors or industry factors. The test uses Deardorff and Stern's (1984b) and Stephen's (1986) data on the tariff rates for nineteen products imported into ten developed countries (see Stephen's paper for the test). The data are shown in Table 17.1. The procedure is to regress the 190 observations on the country means in one

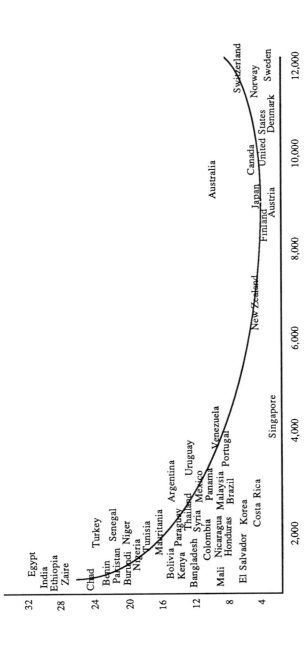

Figure 17.1. The U-shaped relationship between protection and GNP per capita: Tariff protection is minimal at 1980 GNP per capita of $10,000.

regression and the industry means in another. If national political institutions are more important than industry factors, then the regression of the tariff rates on country tariff means should explain more of the tariff variability than the regression on the industry tariff means, and vice versa.

We find that, although both country and industry considerations are important, industry factors are relatively more important, accounting for 53% of the variance in tariffs, compared to 20% explained by country effects. Industry factors explain over 2.5 times the variance in tariffs that country factors explain. The industry regression is significantly better than the country regression.

These results are not surprising in light of the similarity in factor endowments among the advanced countries and the past fifty years of negotiated mutual tariff reductions under GATT, which had their origins early in the Roosevelt administration and the Reciprocal Trade Agreements Act of 1934. Although we have not performed similar analysis for the developing countries, we suspect that the reverse might be true there; that is, that country factors would provide greater explanatory power.

17.6   Endogenous industrial policy

On industrial policy see Lawrence (1984); Norton (1986) provides a good summary of the issues, and Krugman (1983) gives a critical view, noting that the only economic rationale for government intervention in aging industries is to offset other government policies, compensate for external economies or R&D appropriability problems (see Magee, 1977a–c), or offset Japanese intervention in duopolistic industries with steep experience curves.

Pressures for industrial policies illustrate the compensation effect: As the economic success of America's sunset industries declines because of foreign industrialization, they will turn to political activity. The greatest pressure for such policies should be in industries with high power-function indexes (Chapter 6) or those with accumulated lobbying experience. Industrial policies are endogenous, like other redistributive policies. The fancy academic rationales for them are camouflage used to reduce voter opposition to their redistributive intent. The policies are caused by economic shocks and aging but are adopted to enhance political efficiency.

17.7   Conclusions

Senile-industry protection is good just as infant-industry protection is good: It enhances efficiency, albeit political efficiency. It may also be economically efficient. Would you want your hair cut or your throat shaved by a laid-off longshoreman? Following the conservative social welfare function,

Table 17.1. *Nominal tariff rates for the developed countries by industry*

	Austria	Finland	Norway	Sweden	Switz.	Denmark	Canada	Japan	U.S.	EEC	Avg.
Textiles	18.7	24.1	16.2	10.9	8.2	12.1	18.9	3.3	14.4	10.1	12.3
Wear & apparel	36.3	37.2	22.8	14.4	15.5	16.4	25.4	13.8	27.8	16.7	20.4
Leather	9.1	12.6	6.6	4.8	2.8	3.6	8.2	3.0	5.6	3.9	5.2
Footwear	24.1	17.5	24.6	13.8	12.4	11.5	24.5	16.4	8.8	11.6	14.7
Wood products	4.8	0.5	2.0	0.9	5.0	4.4	5.8	0.3	3.6	3.3	3.2
Furniture	23.0	8.7	7.6	5.4	13.2	8.4	19.4	7.8	8.1	8.5	10.1
Paper	15.9	8.0	2.9	3.0	6.6	10.8	11.8	2.1	0.5	8.1	7.4
Printing	2.4	1.8	4.3	0.2	0.9	4.4	5.7	0.2	1.1	3.2	2.7
Chemicals	8.1	3.1	8.1	6.3	1.1	11.9	7.9	6.2	3.8	11.5	8.6
Rubber	14.6	13.9	7.3	6.5	2.0	6.7	12.2	1.5	3.6	5.5	6.7
Nonmetallic	8.9	3.8	2.8	3.1	3.5	6.7	9.5	0.6	9.1	5.2	5.3
Glass	17.5	25.4	10.5	9.3	4.5	9.7	11.3	7.5	10.7	9.8	10.9
Iron & steel	6.2	5.7	2.2	4.7	2.1	7.2	6.7	3.3	4.7	6.5	5.5
Nonferrous metal	4.5	1.2	1.1	0.9	4.3	8.1	2.0	1.1	1.2	4.0	3.3
Metals	19.3	9.6	6.3	5.3	3.8	7.9	14.1	6.9	7.5	7.9	8.5
Nonelec. machines	10.8	8.7	8.8	4.9	1.5	6.4	6.1	9.1	5.0	6.4	6.6
Elec. machines	18.7	11.0	8.6	7.0	2.0	9.3	12.9	7.4	6.6	9.8	9.5
Transport	24.5	6.0	3.5	8.2	6.7	8.5	2.4	6.0	3.3	10.3	8.8
Misc.	13.7	18.1	8.9	6.1	1.5	10.0	8.8	6.0	7.8	8.5	8.8
Country avg.	14.8	11.4	8.2	6.1	5.1	8.6	11.2	5.4	7.0	7.9	8.3

Sources: Deardorff and Stern (1984b) and Stephens (1986).

individuals benefit from stable environments and the remembrance of things past. Because protection increases predictability, it increases welfare. Like the deaths of individuals, industrial deaths that are anticipated are less painful than catastrophic ones. Senile-industry protection is also inevitable because old industries have greater experience than young industries at lobbying. There are also equity arguments. If an industry has paid corporate taxes for decades, it has a social investment in the society, which should yield dividends when the industry becomes old. Should not new industries, which have paid no past taxes, contribute to aging industries that have supported the country in the past?

There are four conclusions: First, perhaps we should not oppose senile-industry protection too strenuously. It is not crutches but broken legs that are bad. Broken legs are exogenous, so it is silly to rail against crutches. The problem is not protection but the inevitable aging of industries and the loss of competitive advantages to countries whose labor forces earn less and who prefer to work harder. Protection just reduces localized pain. An industry-specific nontariff barrier is a local anesthetic whereas countrywide protection is a general anesthetic, which has greater risks and costs.

Second, protection can be postponed by jogging and other economic fitness programs, such as occasional cold showers in the international market, but this only postpones the pain.

Third, diseased organs eventually threaten the health of the entire country. Subsidized shipbuilding carries an enormous cost in several advanced countries. Continuing protection is maladaptive to national economic survival and may threaten the entire *corpus economique*. In this case, gangrenous industries must be removed and replaced with foreign competition. The termination of senile-industry protection is even more painful than the weaning process that terminates infant-industry protection. Industry euthanasia is difficult for the political process to contemplate.

Fourth, on the question of protection, economists play the role of doctors. Doctors usually know before the patient that, say, a diseased tonsil must be removed. So, too, economists know early the costs of continued protection and get impatient with the silly rationalizations by diseased industries against minor surgery in the form of somewhat freer trade. However, like doctors, economists need patience in dealing with older industries. These industries have very real fears about death and dying, and free-trade surgery is not without risk.

It is ironic that so many free traders perch in tenure-protected academic roosts. It is clear why the world pays so little attention to the squawkings of our academic free-trade choir.

CHAPTER 18

Optimal obfuscation and the theory of the second worst: the politically efficient policy

Mayer and Riezman (1987) argue correctly that political economy models cannot explain why tariffs are preferred as redistributive mechanisms over factor or production subsidies. We address their question in this chapter. Specifically, we examine the following:

18.1. the literature;
18.2. the politically efficient policy;
18.3. optimal obfuscation and the theory of the second worst; and
18.4. the voter information paradox.

In an early paper on optimal policy, Bhagwati (1971) showed that economic policies could be ranked in terms of economic efficiency. He argued that direct policies are more efficient than indirect ones. Consider the position of the prolabor party in Part II of this book. According to Bhagwati,

> the most efficient way to help labor would be with a labor subsidy;
> the next best would be a production subsidy for labor-intensive industries;
> the next would be a tariff on imports of labor-intensive goods;
> the next would be a quota on labor-intensive imports; and
> the next a voluntary export restraint agreement by foreign suppliers of labor-intensive goods.

What we observe politically is virtually the reverse of Bhagwati's ordering. The proliferation of nontariff barriers, quotas, and voluntary export restraint

---

Chapter 18 in Stephen P. Magee, William A. Brock, and Leslie Young, *Black Hole Tariffs and Endogenous Policy Theory*. New York: Cambridge University Press, 1989. Adapted from Stephen P. Magee, "The Principle of Political Indirection," mimeo, University of Texas, October 1983.

agreements over the past two decades demonstrate that political institutions may prefer inefficient policies. In this chapter, we outline a structure for the trade-off between economic and political efficiency discussed in Chapter 3. The focus here is on the *politically efficient policy,* namely, which policy will be chosen to redistribute income to a given well-organized group.

Welfare economics invented the *theory of the second best* to explain the optimality of certain policy inefficiencies. For example, if there are high U.S. steel prices because of a producer cartel, then, according to the theory of the second best, the welfare-maximizing price for U.S. autos might be higher than the perfectly competitive price.

We assert that with endogenous politics, the equilibrium policies that emerge can be economically inefficient. Rational calculations of the vote-maximizing policy for each party often leads to one of the worst economic policies being chosen. This we call the *theory of the second worst.* We develop the principle of *optimal obfuscation* in this chapter to explain why such inefficient policies emerge in endogenous political equilibria. From Chapter 3 we know that maximum political efficiency implies minimum economic efficiency.

When voters are rationally uninformed, an important element in political competition is the level of economic resources possessed by each party. Resources allow each party to inform voters of their virtues and their opponents' vices. To collect resources, parties sponsor redistributive policies that yield particularized benefits but generalized costs. For a given redistributive policy, a vote-maximizing party will increase the value of its policy so long as the resource benefits exceed the voter hostility costs. Our focus until now has been to explain the equilibrium level of a given policy – namely, a tariff.

In this chapter, our attention shifts to the choice of the politically efficient policy. Why is a tariff chosen instead of another policy to perform the same redistribution? This decision requires sophistication, since a party must compute optimal levels of each policy before picking which of those policies yields the most votes. We find that imperfectly informed voters can cause the equilibrium values of the politically efficient portfolio of policies to be economically inefficient. Further, the political parties will choose the level of economic inefficiency which is in their interest.

Our thesis is that they will choose indirect policies to obfuscate the redistributive process. By indirect, we mean policies that are roundabout, circuitous, oblique, and labyrinthine.

18.1   The literature

A number of references advocate trade intervention as first-best policies. For example, Deardorff and Stern (1987) note that tariff retaliation may be the best in response to exploitative policies by other governments. Brander and Spencer (1985) give an example in which an export subsidy can move a domestic firm from a Cournot–Nash equilibrium to a position of Stackelberg leadership over a rival foreign firm. For a good critical discussion of this type of work, see, inter alia, Dixit (1987) and Krugman (1987).

A number of popular news sources note that foreign lobbying in Washington has helped to dilute the most restrictive provisions in the 1987 Trade Bill. On the inefficiencies of tariffs relative to other policies see Donges (1984). For an interesting theoretical paper on why one trade policy might be chosen over another see Mayer and Riezman (1985). Deardorff and Stern (1983, 1984a) analyze nontariff barriers.

There is a saying on the boardroom wall of a major corporation in America that "Perception is everything." This statement applies to politics even more than business. In Schattschneider's (1935) analysis of the passage of the Smoot–Hawley tariff bill, he states that "the sentimental basis of the protective system is nationalism. Following the orgy of tariff increases, Congress said to business in effect, as the dodo said to Alice after the caucus race, 'everybody has won and all should have prizes!' "

18.2   The politically efficient policy

As before, assume that a labor lobby channels resources to a prolabor party in exchange for a tariff on imports of labor-intensive goods while a capital party gives resources to a procapital party in exchange for an export subsidy on capital-intensive goods. For the analysis in this chapter, consider only the behavior of the prolabor party; symmetric arguments apply to the procapital party and are developed in the Appendix to this chapter.

Let us now arrange all of the policy choices for a party from the most efficient economically to the least efficient. As noted earlier, the labor subsidy would be the most efficient economically and thus first; a production subsidy for labor-intensive industries second; next would be a tariff on imports of labor-intensive goods; the next would be a quota on labor-intensive imports; the next a voluntary export restraint agreement (VER) by foreign suppliers of labor-intensive goods; and so on. We shall construct an index of "obfuscation" O, for which $O = 0$ is the most direct whereas $O = \infty$ is the most indirect. Assume that the most direct policies are also the most economically efficient (and vice versa). Assume further that the vote-maximizing values of the policy at each level of obfuscation causes more indirect policies to channel fewer resources to the capital party. Thus, the optimal level of procapital lobbying resources channeled to the procapital party R^* declines with the level of obfuscation O.

The problem is more complicated for voters. Greater obfuscation will hurt the party with regard to the voters because it introduces more waste, but will help the party to the extent that the waste is less recognizable to voters. We might expect that the former effect would dominate with more fully informed voters, whereas the latter would be more important with uninformed ones. We continue the assumption of rationally ignorant Downsian (1957) voters. We suspect that the vast majority of the American electorate does not understand the conditions under which quotas are welfare inferior to tariffs. Not even the expert writers of this book know whether U.S. welfare falls if the Democratic party switches from a 12% tariff to a 9% quota. Only a presidential candidate with limited faculties would try to explain to American voters the economic differences between a tariff and a quota. In short, rationally ignorant voters are assumed to perceive decreased economic costs at the optimal values of more indirect policies.

What are the calculations of the parties? A party could obviously choose too indirect a policy. If it attempted to enrich capital in the United States by altering regulations on the thickness of glass-bottom boats, the voters will not penalize the procapital party because the policy is so indirect as to be undetectable by voters as a redistributive plan. However, the capital lobby would get so little benefit that it would contribute nothing to the party. Thus, such a policy is too indirect. Somewhere between no obfuscation and total obfuscation is the politically efficient policy that parties choose.

18.3   Optimal obfuscation and the theory of the second worst

What happens when the protectionist party resorts to a policy that is harder for the voters to figure out? By increasing obfuscation, there is a decline in the votes that the party loses because of the perceived distortion effects of the policy. This is shown by the decline in the L curve in Figure 18.1 (see Figure 2.4 for a discussion). However, with increased obfuscation, votes also decline because of reduced campaign contributions (the protectionist lobby gets less of a benefit). The politically efficient policy chosen by the protectionist party will be that which maximizes the difference between the gain and the loss curves. The optimal level of obfuscation in Figure 18.1 will be at obfuscation level O', which maximizes the votes at EH.

To summarize, *a party will increase the indirectness of its policy if the party's vote gain from greater voter obfuscation exceeds its loss from reduced resources. It will choose a policy that just balances these marginal effects. The one chosen will be the politically efficient policy.*

Over the past two decades U.S. protection has moved away from tariffs and U.S.-administered quantitative restrictions. Antiprotectionist public agitation coupled with sophisticated Japanese political maneuvers have led the administration of U.S. protectionism to shift to voluntary export restraints administered in Tokyo. The economic costs in 1984 for VER-type trade restrictions on U.S. imports of automobiles, steel, and textiles exceed those for all U.S. tariffs. Indirect methods such as voluntary export restraint agreements are now the dominant form of American protection.

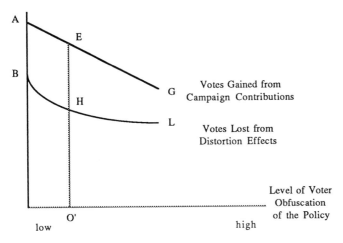

Figure 18.1. The optimal level of obfuscation for the protectionist party.

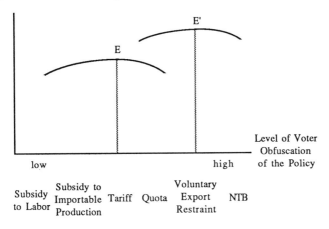

Figure 18.2. Evolution of the politically efficient policy, 1930s–1980s.

The evolution of the vote-maximizing level of obfuscation for protectionist policies is shown in Figure 18.2. In that figure, the vertical axis is the difference between the gain and loss curves in Figure 18.1. In the 1930s, the tariff was a primary redistributive tool. By the 1950s, quotas were in vogue,

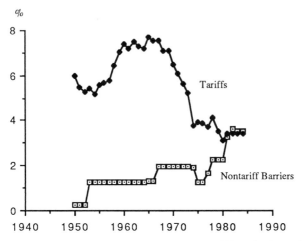

Figure 18.3. U.S. tariff rates and the tariff equivalent of nontariff barriers, 1950–84.

Table 18.1. *Hufbauer, Berliner, and Elliott's (1986) nontariff barrier data*

Product	Period in effect	Import value (millions of $)	Year	Share of imports	Tariff equiv.	Contrib. to U.S. protection
Shoes	1977–81	$2,480	1981	0.009	18.5	0.17
TVs	1977–82	1,543	1982	0.006	15.0	0.09
Sugar	1934–present	1,258	1984	0.004	30.0	0.12
Meat	1965–present	1,363	1983	0.005	14.0	0.07
Chemical	1922–86	2,698	1984	0.008	15.0	0.12
Fish	1977–present	3,627	1983	0.014	10.0	0.14
Autos	1981–84	29,260	1984	0.089	11.0	0.98
Textiles/apparel	1957–73	3,497	1973	0.050	20.0	1.00
	1974–81	9,500	1981	0.036	27.0	0.97
	1982–present	16,498	1984	0.050	30.0	1.50
Carbon steel	1967–74	4,830	1974	0.047	13.3	0.63
	1978–82	8,958	1982	0.036	15.9	0.59
Oil	1959–73	7,858	1973	0.111	96.0	10.66

the most important of which was the oil import quota imposed under Eisenhower. By the 1970s, voters were getting increasingly sophisticated, and the political system hatched the voluntary export restraint movement, which cleverly let foreigners set the level of protection. Thus, the best policy for the protectionists has evolved from the tariff to the quota to the VER.

Figure 18.3 shows how the tariff equivalent of nontariff forms of protection has grown since 1950. The nontariff curve was drawn by adding up the values in the last column of Table 18.1 for the years in which each restriction was in force. For example, the tariff equivalent of all nontariff restrictions in 1965 was 1.31 (= 0.12 for sugar + 0.07 for meat + 0.12 for chemicals + 1.0 for textiles). The data in Table 18.1 are adapted from Hufbauer, Berliner, and Elliott (1986).

With increases in voter sophistication, parties must disguise their redistributive activities more effectively. We have more nontariff barriers now because they are more indirect and increase the votes of protectionist politicians.

18.4   The voter information paradox

With parties playing obfuscation strategies, the following voter information paradox emerges: *Voters can become better informed, but the parties can respond with higher equilibrium levels of distortions.* The change from tariffs to VERs in the past few decades illustrates the point. Voters became increasingly sophisticated in opposing tariffs restrictions, causing tariffs to fall initially. The final result was the adoption of VERs, which are more opaque to voters and have greater economic costs and higher tariff equivalents.

The moral: Political efficiency has an economic cost.

Mathematical appendixes

Appendix to Chapter 2

This appendix derives an alternative diagrammatic approach to endogenous tariff theory. Figure A.2.1 shows how the total benefit curves from lobbying increase as the tariff increases from t_1 to t_3. These cause the endogenous lobbying levels to rise from L_1^e to L_3^e. Figure A.2.2 makes this positive relationship explicit between higher tariffs and higher lobby contributions.

OS is the supply curve of lobby contributions from the protectionist lobby to the protectionist party associated for alternative tariff levels. All values of L not on the curve OS do not satisfy lobby rationality and hence are not endogenous.

It would be nice to add the endogenous tariff level to this diagram. We redraw the curve OS in Figure A.2.3, and to it we add voter and protectionist party behavior. The curve OS ends at the prohibitive tariff level t_p. Any tariff higher than this has no domestic effect because there are no more imports at any tariff level at or above t_p.

Following the probabilistic voting function, voters have a higher probability of voting for parties with more campaign funds, but are less likely to vote for a party the higher the value of its special-interest policy. These contribution and distortion effects we can describe using *isovote curves*, loci of points along which the number of votes for the protectionist party (or, equivalently, the probability of election of the protectionist party) is constant. The curves must be positively sloped because an increase in the tariff alienates voters (due to the distortion costs) and must be offset by more campaign funds. They are also concave from below because the distortion costs (deadweight loss triangles) increase with the square of the tariff, and because there are diminishing returns to campaign advertising past some point (the probability of a party's election has an upper bound of 1.0). In other words, to keep votes constant, lobbying funds must be more than doubled if the tariff rate is dou-

Mathematical Appendixes to Stephen P. Magee, William A. Brock, and Leslie Young, *Black Hole Tariffs and Endogenous Policy Theory*. New York: Cambridge University Press, 1989.

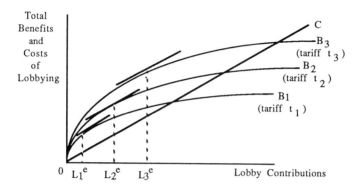

Figure A.2.1. How endogenous lobby contributions (L_e) increase with more favorable policies (tariffs: $t_3 > t_2 > t_1$).

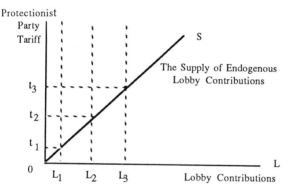

Figure A.2.2. The supply curve of endogenous lobby contributions to the protectionist party.

bled along a given isovote curve. Curves to the right have more votes than those to the left: As we move right along the line t^eE, the tariff is constant and the protectionist party receives more lobbying funds. Thus, curve v_2 yields more votes to the protectionist party than v_1.

Politics resolves conflicts. Here, the role of the parties is to reconcile conflicts between general voter interests and special protectionist interests. The general interest would be maximized at the economically efficient Pareto-optimal point O. Other things being equal, the welfare of the special-interest protectionist lobby would be maximized at point S at the prohibitive tariff level t_p. The protectionist party will not choose either of these points because neither maximizes its probability of election. To achieve its objective, however, the protectionist party must operate under the constraint of the level of funds provided by the protectionist lobby (i.e., along the lobby funds supply curve OS). A self-interested strategy by the protectionist party is to search along the lobby funds supply curve OS for the tariff rate that

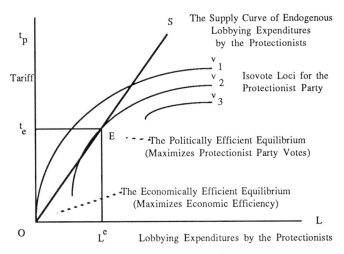

Figure A.2.3. Alternative description of the endogenous policy and lobbying equilibrium: economic efficiency at O and political efficiency at E.

maximizes its votes. This is the Stackelberg-leadership strategy adopted by the parties, and is discussed formally in Chapter 3.

When the protectionist party sets a tariff that maximizes its votes (or, equivalently, probability of election), we obtain the politically efficient equilibrium E. At E, there will be an isovote locus v_2 just tangent to OS. Since the isovote locus v_1 goes through the origin, v_1 is the number of votes the protectionist party would receive if it supported free trade. The difference between v_2 and v_1 is the net vote gain to the protectionist party from choosing its endogenous tariff level t_e and is equal to the net vote gain AB in Figure 2.1 in the text. Will a party ever choose Pareto optimality as its vote-maximizing strategy? As voters increase in sophistication, the isovote loci rotate clockwise, reflecting the voters' decreased dependence on information funded through party advertising. If voters had been fully informed, the slope of isovote locus v_1 would have been flatter than the lobby funds curve OS at the origin, and the party would have chosen the Pareto-optimal zero tariff as its vote-maximizing strategy. Any other tariff level would reduce its votes below v_1. In this case, economic efficiency and political efficiency would be at the same equilibrium (point E would coincide with point O).

Appendix to Chapter 3

The following two equations describe an Arrow–Debreu redistributive political equilibrium with A individuals and P parties, each of whom sets a tariff. Each of the a individuals employs the following strategy:

$$\max_{C^a} U^a(t, C^a, C^o) \tag{3.1}$$

U^a = the indirect utility function for individual a
t = a vector of the tariff levels of the P parties
C^o = the contributions of the other individuals besides a
C^a = the contribution by individual a

Each of the political parties does the following:

$$\max_{t^p} V_p \underset{-}{(t_p}, \underset{+}{t_o}, C_p\underset{+}{(t_p, t_o)}) \qquad p = 1, \dots, P \qquad (3.2)$$

V_p = the indirect utility function for party p (= 1, ... , P)
t_p = the tariff level chosen by party p
t_o = a vector of tariff levels for other parties besides p
$C_p(t_p, t_o)$ = contributions by all individuals to party p
          $\underset{+}{}\;\underset{-}{}$

When we narrow the problem to two lobbies and two political parties, the strategies of the four players can be stated in the following four equations. Primed values of a variable denote the proexport lobby 1.

proexport lobby 1
$$\max_{C^{1\prime}, C^{2\prime}} R = (1-p)\, r^{1\prime} + pr^{2\prime} - C^{1\prime} - C^{2\prime} \qquad (3.3)$$

protectionist lobby 2
$$\max_{C^1, C^2} R = (1-p)\, r^1 + pr^2 - C^1 - C^2 \qquad (3.4)$$

proexport party 1
$$\max_{s} q = q\underset{+}{(C^{1\prime}}, \underset{-}{C^2}, \underset{-}{s}, \underset{+}{t}) \qquad (3.5)$$

protectionist party 2
$$\max_{t} p = p\underset{-}{(C^{1\prime}}, \underset{+}{C^2}, \underset{+}{s}, \underset{-}{t}) \qquad (3.6)$$

where $p + q = 1$ and $t \geq 0$ and $s \geq 0$. Equations (3.5) and (3.6) describe the reaction curves of the voters: They are not explicitly derived because the voters are rationally ignorant, following Downs (1957). If the protectionist party derives no benefit from setting a positive tariff, we would obtain

$$t = 0 \qquad (3.7)$$

The solutions to (3.3) for $C^{1\prime}$ and to (3.4) for C^2 yield the familiar reaction curves for the lobbies:

$$C^{1\prime} = C^{1\prime}(t, s) \qquad (3.8)$$
$$C^2 = C^2(t, s)$$

[i.e., each lobby's optimal contribution with respect to t and s from the solution to Eqs. (3.3) and (3.4)].

The assumption that the lobbies are Stackelberg leaders vis-à-vis the voters allows us to incorporate the reaction function of the voters [Eqs. (3.5) and (3.6)] into the strategy of the lobbies, yielding

the proexport lobby:
$$\max_{C^{1\prime}, C^{2\prime}} R' = [1 - p(C^{1\prime}, C^{2\prime}, s, t)] \, r^{1\prime} + p \, (C^{1\prime}, C^{2\prime}, s, t) \, r^{2\prime} - C^{1\prime} - C^{2\prime} \tag{3.9}$$

the protectionist lobby:
$$\max_{C^{1}, C^{2}} R = [1 - p(C^{1}, C^{2}, s, t)] \, r^{1} + p \, (C^{1}, C^{2}, s, t) \, r^{2} - C^{1} - C^{2} \tag{3.10}$$

Our assumption that the parties are Stackelberg leaders vis-à-vis the lobbies causes each party to incorporate the reaction function of its lobby [Eqs. (3.8)] into its own strategy, yielding

the proexport party:
$$\max_{s} q \, (C^{1\prime}[t, s], C^{2}, s, t) \tag{3.11}$$

the protectionist party:
$$\max_{t} p \, (C^{1\prime}, C^{2}[t, s], s, t) \tag{3.12}$$

We show below that the lobbies do not contribute to their nonfavored party, so that in equilibrium, $C^{1} = C^{2\prime} = 0$.

The solutions to the endogenous policy model are contained in the following four equations: the values of $C^{1\prime}$, C^{2}, s, and t. These are the classic Brock and Magee equations that form the basis of the book.

$C^{1\prime}$ contributions by the proexport lobby to the proexport party

$$dR/dC^{1\prime} = \underset{-}{dp/dC^{1\prime}} \, (\underset{-}{r^{2\prime} - r^{1\prime}}) \quad -1 = 0 \qquad \text{yields } C^{1\prime} > 0 \tag{3.13}$$

C^{2} contributions by the protectionist lobby to the protectionist party

$$dR/dC^{2} = \underset{+}{dp/dC^{2}} \, (\underset{+}{r^{2} - r^{1}}) \quad -1 \quad = 0 \quad \text{yielding } C^{2} > 0 \tag{3.14}$$

[marginal political   [marginal
revenue]   cost]

s the equilibrium export subsidy set by the proexport party

$$\underset{+}{dq/dC^{1\prime}} \, (\underset{+}{dC^{1\prime}/ds}) \quad + \underset{-}{dq/ds} = 0 \tag{3.15}$$

t the equilibrium tariff set by the protectionist party

$$\underset{+}{dp/dC^{2}} \, (\underset{+}{dC^{2}/dt}) \quad + \underset{-}{dp/dt} = 0 \quad \text{yielding } t > 0 \tag{3.16}$$

[positive contribution   [negative
effect]   distortion
effect]

To illustrate the campaign-contribution specialization theorem, consider the decision of whether the protectionist lobby should give to the proexport party in (3.18) below. The first part of the negative first term, dp/dC^{1}, shows that the probability of election for the protectionists' favored party 2 declines when the protectionists contribute to the proexport party 1. When this is multiplied by the economic difference to the lobby in the value of the two political parties ($r^2 - r^1$), there is a negative marginal revenue effect of giving to the lobby's less-favored party. Because this first term is negative, there is no marginal benefit to offset the -1 that reflects the $1 marginal cost of contributing to party 1. Because the entire left-hand side of (3.18) is negative, the inequality holds, causing the optimal contribution by the protectionist party to the proexport party to be zero. Similar reasoning applied to (3.17) explains why the proexport lobby does not contribute to the protectionist party.

$C^{2'} = 0$ proexport contributions to the protectionist party

$$dR'/dC^{2'} = dp/dC^{2'} (r^{2'} - r^{1'}) - 1 < 0 \qquad (3.17)$$
$$\phantom{dR'/dC^{2'} = } \underset{+}{\phantom{dp/dC^{2'}}} \underset{-}{\phantom{(r^{2'} - r^{1'})}}$$

$C^1 = 0$ protectionist contributions to the proexport party

$$dR/dC^1 = dp/dC^1 (r^2 - r^1) - 1 < 0 \qquad (3.18)$$
$$ \underset{-}{} \underset{+}{}$$

Appendix to Chapter 4

In this appendix, we consider only the behavior of the protectionist lobby; parallel arguments apply to the proexport lobby. The protectionist lobby's calculations of the benefits of *access* are the positive effects of the contributions C^i on the expected economic returns r^i when party i is elected:

$$r^1 = r^1 (s, C^1) \qquad r^2 = r^2 (t, C^2) \qquad (4.1)$$
$$\underset{-}{}\ \underset{+}{} \qquad \underset{+}{}\ \underset{+}{}$$

When these access effects are inserted into the maximand of the protectionist lobby, we obtain the following objective function of the lobby:

$$\max_{C^1, C^2} R = [1 - p (C^1, C^2, s, t)] r^1 (s, C^1)$$
$$+ p (C^1, C^2, s, t) r^2 (t, C^2) - C^1 - C^2 \qquad (4.2)$$

The first-order conditions for (4.2) are as follows:

$$dR/dC^1 = dp/dC^1 (r^2 - r^1) + (1 - p) dr^1/dC^1 - 1 = 0 \qquad (4.3)$$
$$ \underset{-}{}\ \underset{+}{}\ \underset{+}{}\ \underset{+}{}$$

$$dR/dC^2 = dp/dC^2 (r^2 - r^1) + p (dr^2/dC^2) - 1 = 0 \qquad (4.4)$$
$$ \underset{+}{}\ \underset{+}{}\ \underset{+}{}\ \underset{+}{}$$
$$ [\ \text{policy effect}\ ]\quad [\ \text{access effect}\ ]$$

Notice that a positive term now appears in the equation for C^1; that is, it is possible that the protectionist lobby may contribute to the proexport party because of the access effect. In addition, the access effect adds a new term C^2 to the equation for the contribution to the protectionist party; this was not present in (3.14) and increases contributions to the preferred party.

The *retribution* effect is the negative effect on returns that spiteful parties inflict on contributors to the opposition. If both parties do it, there is a negative effect of C^2 on r^1 and a negative effect of C^1 on r^2.

$$r^1 = r^1 (s, C^1, C^2) \qquad r^2 = r^2 (t, C^1, C^2) \qquad (4.5)$$
$$\underset{-}{}\ \underset{+}{}\ \underset{-}{} \qquad \underset{+}{}\ \underset{-}{}\ \underset{+}{}$$

When these r^i are inserted into (3.10), the following first-order conditions result:

$$dR/dC^1 = dp/dC^1 \; (r^2 - r^1) \; + (1 - p)(dr^1/dC^1) \; + p(dr^2/dC^1) \qquad - 1 = 0 \qquad (4.6)$$

$$dR/dC^2 = dp/dC^2 \; (r^2 - r^1) \; + p(dr^2/dC^2) \qquad\qquad + (1 - p)(dr^1/dC^2) \; - 1 = 0 \qquad (4.7)$$

[policy effect]   [access effect   ]   [retribution effect]

When there are three parties present, the protectionist lobby has the following objective in the normal endogenous policy case of Chapter 3 (in which there are no access or retribution effects):

$$\max_{C^1,C^2,C^3} R \;=\; p^1 \, r^1 + p^2 \, r^2 + p^3 \, r^3 - C^1 - C^2 - C^3 \qquad (4.8)$$

$$p^i \;=\; \text{probability of election of party } i$$
$$C^i \;=\; \text{contribution by the lobby to party } i$$

Transposing the marginal cost of a \$1 contribution to the right-hand side of the equations, we obtain the following Kuhn–Tucker first-order conditions:

$$\sum_i (dp^i/dC^j)r^i \;\leq 1 \qquad = 1 \Rightarrow C^j > 0 \qquad (4.9)$$
$$< 1 \Rightarrow C^j = 0 \qquad j = 1, \dots , 3$$

Letting $p^i_j = dp^i/dC^j$, (4.9) can be written in matrix form as $[p^i_j][r^i] \leq 1$ or as

$$\begin{bmatrix} p_1{}^1 & p_1{}^2 & p_1{}^3 \\ p_2{}^1 & p_2{}^2 & p_2{}^3 \\ p_3{}^1 & p_3{}^2 & p_3{}^3 \end{bmatrix} \begin{bmatrix} r^1 \\ r^2 \\ r^3 \end{bmatrix} \;\leq\; \begin{bmatrix} 1 \\ 1 \\ 1 \end{bmatrix} \qquad (4.10)$$

The most reasonable assumption is that the diagonal elements of (4.10) are nonnegative and the off-diagonal elements are nonpositive. This is somewhat restrictive because it means that the voters view the parties as substitutes but not as complements. We know that the sum of each row must equal zero because the changes in the probabilities associated with a marginal contribution to any party must sum to zero. Without loss of generality, let us number the parties so that party 3 is the most protectionist; party 2 is less so; and party 1 is the least protectionist. Thus, the pattern of returns to the protectionist lobby is $r^3 > r^2 > r^1$. As the sum of the electoral probabilities equals 1, replace p^1 in (4.8) with $(1 - p^2 - p^3)$. This yields the following objective for the protectionist lobby:

$$\max_{C^1,C^2,C^3} (1 - p^2 - p^3) \, r^1 + p^2 \, r^2 + p^3 \, r^3 - C^1 - C^2 - C^3 \qquad (4.11)$$

When the first-order conditions are rewritten in terms of the differences in the returns, we obtain

$$p_1{}^3 \, (r^3 - r^1) + p_1{}^2 \, (r^2 - r^1) \qquad \leq 1$$

$$p_2{}^3 \, (r^3 - r^1) + p_2{}^2 \, (r^2 - r^1) \qquad \leq 1 \qquad (4.12)$$

$$p_3{}^3 \, (r^3 - r^1) + p_3{}^2 \, (r^2 - r^1) \qquad \leq 1$$

By assumption, all of the differences in returns are nonnegative, which is to say that $(r^3 - r^1) > (r^2 - r^1) > 0$. Clearly, positive contributions to the second and third parties are possible because both the second and the third rows in (4.12) contain a positive term (the "own" probability effect) multiplied by a positive return differential. However, there can be no contributions to the first party from the protectionist lobby because all of the terms in row 1 contain only negative cross-probability effects multiplied by nonnegative return differentials. Our earlier results for the two-politician race are obviously a special case: with three parties, a special-interest lobby will contribute to, at most, two of the three parties. The protectionists do not contribute to the least favored party 1.

The generalization of the pattern of optimal contributions by a lobby to n parties is now evident. With n parties, the objective function of the protectionist lobby is

$$\max R = \sum_i p_{ij}\,(r^{n-i+1} - r^i) - \sum_j C_j \qquad j = 1, \dots , n \qquad (4.13)$$

The first-order conditions associated with (4.13) are as follows:

$$\sum_i^{n-1} p_j^{n-i+1}\,(r^{n-i+1} - r^i) \qquad\qquad j = 1, \dots , n \qquad (4.14)$$

Given our assumptions, the left-hand side of (4.14) is always nonpositive for the first party (i.e., the least favored one). In general, a lobby will contribute to, at most, $n - 1$ out of n parties.

Appendix to Chapter 5

A reduced-form version of party behavior in the endogenous policy model from Chapter 3 can be written as follows:

the proexport party 1 $\qquad \min_s p(s,t)$ $\qquad\qquad\qquad$ (5.1)

the protectionist party 2 $\qquad \max_t p(s,t)$ $\qquad\qquad\qquad$ (5.2)

We have redefined the p function in (3.12) to be the reduced form in (5.1) and (5.2). We assume interior solutions for all of this chapter. The associated first-order conditions are as follows (subscripts denote first derivatives):

$$p_s(s,t) = 0 \qquad\qquad\qquad (5.3)$$
$$p_t(s,t) = 0 \qquad\qquad\qquad (5.4)$$

These yield the following reaction functions:

reaction function of party 1: $\quad s = R^1(t,a)$ $\qquad\qquad$ (5.5)
reaction function of party 2: $\quad t = R^2(s,a)$ $\qquad\qquad$ (5.6)

where a is a shift parameter. Assume that the s in (5.5) and the t in (5.6) are unique.

These reaction functions represent the optimal policy choice of the party, given the policy of the other party. Let p be twice continuously differentiable so that the following second-order conditions hold for a proper minimum for party 1 and a proper maximum for party 2:

$$d^2p/ds^2 = p_{ss} > 0 \qquad \text{for all } t \tag{5.7}$$
$$d^2p/dt^2 = p_{tt} < 0 \qquad \text{for all } s \tag{5.8}$$

A.5.1   The reverse-slope theorem (see §5.2)

If we insert the reaction functions back into (5.3) and (5.4), we obtain

$$p_s(R^1(t,a),t) = 0 \tag{5.9}$$
$$p_t(s,R^2(s,a)) = 0 \tag{5.10}$$

Differentiating these with respect to s and t yields

$$p_{ss}R_t^1 + p_{st} = 0 \tag{5.11}$$
$$p_{ts} + p_{tt}R_s^2 = 0 \tag{5.12}$$

Since p is twice continuously differentiable, $p_{st} = p_{ts}$. Thus

$$R_s^2 = [p_{ss}/p_{tt}] \, R_t^1 \tag{5.13}$$

Because from (5.7) and (5.8) the bracketed term is negative, the slopes of the reaction functions must have opposite signs in the neighborhood of the political equilibrium.

A.5.2   The reverse-shift theorem (see §5.3)

Assume that some shock causes both parties to prefer a higher level of their redistributive policy. We show that in the new equilibrium one of the policies will increase while the other may decrease. Assume that the shift parameter a increases in the reaction functions of the two parties in (5.5) and (5.6). Assume that this reflects an increased desire by both parties for higher redistributive policies; that is, $R_a^1 > 0$ and $R_a^2 > 0$. Differentiate (5.5) and (5.6) totally with respect to a, beginning at equilibrium values for s and t:

$$s_a = R_t^1 t_a + R_a^1 = R_t^1(R_s^2 s_a + R_a^2) + R_a^1 \tag{5.14}$$
$$t_a = R_s^2 s_a + R_a^2 = R_s^2(R_t^1 t_a + R_a^1) + R_a^2 \tag{5.15}$$

The solution to these equations is

$$s_a = (1 - R_t^1 R_s^2)^{-1} \, (R_t^1 R_a^2 + R_a^1) \tag{5.16}$$
$$t_a = (1 - R_t^1 R_s^2)^{-1} \, (R_s^2 R_a^1 + R_a^2) \tag{5.17}$$

We know from the reverse-slope theorem that the sign of $R_t^1 R_s^2$ is negative, so that

$$(1 - R_t^1 R_s^2) > 0 \tag{5.18}$$

All that is required is that if

$$\text{sign } (R_t^1 R_a^2 + R_a^1) = -\text{ sign } (R_s^2 R_a^1 + R_a^2) \tag{5.19}$$

then we get the reverse-shift paradox:

$$\text{sign } s_a = - \text{sign } t_a. \tag{5.20}$$

The reverse-shift result is not inevitable, merely possible. The text indicates graphically that if there is an outward shift in the two reaction curves that result in a reverse shift, *it is always the equilibrium policy of the counteractor that declines.*

A.5.3   *The policy-distance paradox (see §5.4)*

The policy distance H between parties on trade policy can be measured by the sum of the policies (because an export subsidy is a negative tariff):

$$H = s + t \tag{5.21}$$

Let both parties become more special-interest, so that a increases. From (5.16) and (5.17), we have

$$
\begin{aligned}
H_a = s_a + t_a &= (1 - R_t^1 R_s^2)^{-1} [R_t^1 R_a^2 + R_a^1 + R_s^2 R_a^1 + R_a^2] \\
&= (1 - R_t^1 R_s^2)^{-1} [R_a^1 (1 + R_s^2) + R_a^2 (1 + R_t^1)]
\end{aligned} \tag{5.22}
$$

From the reverse-slope theorem, we know that either R_s^2 or R_t^1 must be negative. The negative one identifies the counteractor. Let $R_s^2 < 0$. For $H_a < 0$, it must be true that $|R_s^2| > 1$, and that R_a^1 is sufficiently large. In general, the more negative the counteractor's slope and the larger the shift in the emulator party's reaction function (relative to the other party's shift), the more likely a decline in the policy distance between the parties.

A.5.4   *The distortion paradox (see §5.5)*

This result indicates that the parties could become increasingly special-interest, yet the long-run average level of the two policy distortions could still fall. Let the mean distortion D be denoted by

$$
\begin{aligned}
D &= [1 - p] s + pt \\
&= [1 - p(s,t,a)] s + p(s,t,a) t
\end{aligned}
$$

The change in the mean, following the increase in special-interest activity (denoted by an increase in a), is

$$
\begin{aligned}
D_a &= s_a [1 - p] - s[p_s s_a + p_t t_a + p_a] + t_a p + t[p_s s_a + p_t t_a + p_a] \\
&= s_a [1 - p] + t_a p + (t - s) [p_s s_a + p_t t_a + p_a]
\end{aligned} \tag{i}
$$
$$ \qquad\qquad\qquad\qquad\qquad\qquad + \qquad\; - $$

$$
= s_a [(1 - p) + p_s (t - s)] + t_a [p + (t - s)p_t] + (t - s)p_a \tag{ii}
$$
$$ \qquad\qquad + \qquad\qquad\qquad\qquad - $$

If the reverse-shift paradox did not occur, s_a and t_a would both be positive so that the mean D_a could fall only if $(t - s)$ was positive and the negative term $p_t t_a$ was sufficiently large in (i). If the reverse-shift phenomenon did occur, D_a might be negative if the policy that fell (say, $t_a < 0$) had a sufficiently large and positive bracketed term attached to it in (ii). One factor contributing to this is that the party whose policy fell (say, $t_a < 0$) had a high probability of election (i.e., p is large).

A.5.5   Three generalizations of the reverse-slope theorem (see §5.7)

1. A unity-sum policy game with many political parties. In order to avoid losing the reader in a sea of subscripts, let us develop the many-party, one-issue, nonconstant-sum case first. The situation may be described as follows: Party i solves

$$\max_{t_i \in R^1} p^i (t_1, t_2, \dots , t_{i-1}, t_i, t_{i+1}, \dots , t_n, a) \qquad (5.23)$$

for $i = 1, 2, \dots , n$. We will put $(t_1, t_2, \dots , t_{i-1}, t_i, t_{i+1}, \dots , t_n) = (t^i, t^{io})$ to simplify notation. Think of t_i^o as "all tariffs other than t_i." First- and second-order necessary conditions for a proper noncooperative equilibrium are given by (5.24) below. All subscripts i indicate differentiation of the variable by t_i.

$$p^i_i (R^i(t_i^o, a), t_i^o, a) \quad = 0, \qquad (5.24)$$
$$p^i_{ii} (R^i(t_i^o, a), t_i^o, a) \ < 0, \qquad i = 1, 2, \dots , n$$
$$t_i = R^i(t_i^o, a) \qquad\qquad i = 1, 2, \dots , n \qquad (5.25)$$

Condition (5.25) follows from the assumption that the reaction $R^i(t_i, a)$ of i to the play of the others t_i^o is a proper maximum. Equation (5.25) is the requirement of noncooperative equilibrium. To simplify notation, write

$$\sigma x = \max \left\{ \frac{x}{|x|}, \frac{-x}{|x|} \right\} \ \text{ for } x \neq 0 \quad \sigma x = 0 \quad \text{for } x = 0$$

where σx is the sign of x.

Let us examine the determinants of the sign of change in party i's reaction curve with respect to a change in the tariff position of party j; that is,

$$\sigma R^i_j \quad i, j = 1, 2, \dots , n.$$

Differentiate (5.24) totally with respect to t_j:

$$p^i_{ii} R^i_j + p^i_{ij} = 0 \qquad (5.26)$$

Because $\sigma p^i_{ii} = -1$, it must follow that $\sigma R^i_j = \sigma p^i_{ij}$. This implies

Theorem 1: Assume that p^i is twice continuously differentiable and that the solution function $R^i(t_i^o, a)$ of (5.23) is well defined and is a proper maximum for each t_i^o, a. Then

$$\sigma R^i_j = \sigma p^i_{ij} \qquad (i, j) = 1, 2 \dots , n, \qquad i \neq j \qquad (5.27)$$

where R^i_j, p^i_{ij} are evaluated at $(R^i(t_i, a), t_i, a)$.

Proof: The proof is the application of the implicit function theorem given above. The result states that the slope of party i's reaction curve with respect to a change in the tariff of party j has the same sign as p^i_{ij}. In other words, if party i's reaction function is positively sloped when plotted in $t_i t_j$ space, party j's reaction function must be negatively sloped in the neighborhood of the political equilibrium. See Figures 5.1 and 5.2 for examples of this result when $n = 2$.

2. A constant-sum policy game with two political parties. Here, for all (t_1, t_2, a),

$$p^1(t_1, t_2, a) + p^2(t_1, t_2, a) = k(a) \tag{5.28}$$

where $k(a)$ is a constant that may depend upon a. Obviously from (5.28), since p is twice continuously differentiable,

$$p^2_{21} = -p^1_{21} = -p^1_{12}. \tag{5.29}$$

Therefore, from (5.27), at any noncooperative equilibrium,

$$\begin{aligned} \sigma R^1_2 &= \sigma p^1_{12} \, (R^1(t_2, a), t_2, a) \\ &= -\sigma p^2_{21} \, (t_1, R^2(t_1, a), a) \\ &= -\sigma R^2_1 \end{aligned}$$

Note that we used the equation (5.25) of noncooperative equilibrium in order to guarantee that

$$p^1_{12}(R^1(t_2, a), t_2, a) = p^1_{21} \, (t_1, R^2(t_1, a), a)$$

From (5.27) we see the basic reason for the phenomena of opposite-signed reaction functions at any noncooperative equilibrium:

$$\sigma p^1_{12} = -\sigma p^2_{21} \tag{5.30}$$

Equation (5.30) describes an asymmetric externality. In other words, the marginal payoff p^1 for party 1 is affected by an increase in t_2 in an opposite manner than is the marginal payoff p^2_1 to party 2 affected by increased t_1.

An economic example of this is two firms producing different products with asymmetric externalities: for example, the case of a real estate development polluted by a steel mill. If transactions costs are large enough so that the noncooperative equilibrium concept applies, then it is reasonable to expect reaction functions with opposite slopes. In more detail, suppose t_i is the output level of the ith firm, where "party 1" is the developer. Look now at equation (5.30): p^1_{12}, (p^2_{21}) is the shift in marginal profits to the developer number 1 (steel producer number 2) when steel output (product 2) increases (subscript i denotes differentiation by t^i). It is natural to expect that pollution is proportional to steel output. On the other hand, the developer makes it more attractive to work at the steel plant (thereby lowering labor costs) and makes the plant's land more valuable; thus it is reasonable to expect that an increase in the developer's activity will lead to an increase in marginal profits to the steel plant owner. Thus, $p^2_{21} > 0$. Therefore, $R^1_2 < 0$ and $R^2_1 > 0$. Suppose now that an increase in a represents an increase in the demand for steel. Assume, as is reasonable, $R^2_a > 0$ and $R^1_a = 0$. Then, from the equations, we must have $t^1_a < 0$ and $t^2_a > 0$. That is, development activity falls when steel output goes up.

Consider next a constant-sum multi-issue game with two political parties. Here equilibrium is defined by (5.23) and (5.24) except that $t_i \in R^m$, and we assume that the equilibrium is unique (implying that p is strictly concave in t_1 and strictly convex in t_2). Thus, $R^1(t_2, a)$, $R^2(t_1, a)$ are defined by

$$p^1(R^1(t_2, a), t_2, a) = 0, \qquad t_2 \in R^m \tag{5.31}$$
$$p^2(t_1, R^2(t_1, a), a) = 0, \qquad t_1 \in R^m \tag{5.32}$$

Differentiate (5.31) and (5.32) totally with respect to t_2 and t_1, respectively, to obtain

$$p_{11} R^1_2 + p_{12} = 0 \tag{5.33}$$
$$p_{21} + p_{22} R^2_1 = 0 \tag{5.34}$$

Because at any noncooperative equilibrium (t_1, t_2),

$$t_1 = R^1(t_2, a) \tag{5.35}$$
$$t_2 = R^2(t_1, a) \tag{5.36}$$

it therefore follows that

$$p_{12} = p^T_{21} \tag{5.37}$$
$$p_{11} R^1_2 = (p_{22} R^2_1)^T \tag{5.38}$$

where p^T indicates a transposed matrix. Assume that the noncooperative equilibrium (t_1, t_2), is regular in that p_{11} is negative definite, and p_{22} is positive definite at (t_1, t_2). This requires that the second-order conditions for (t_1, t_2) to be a maximum of p hold with strict inequality in all directions.

Equation (5.38) says roughly that the $n \times n$ matrices, R^1_2, R^2_1 differ by negative definite and positive definite matrices, respectively. In particular, we obtain

$$\sigma \det(R^1_2) = \sigma \det(R^2_1). \tag{5.39}$$

Here $\det A$ denotes the determinant of the matrix A. It appears to be difficult to get any more qualitative information out of (5.38) without making stronger assumptions on the matrices p_{ij}.

The formulas (5.31) and (5.32) for t_{1a}, t_{2a} might generalize to the many-issue two-party constant-sum case. We are unable to say anything qualitatively about t_{1a}, t_{2a} without stronger assumptions on the p_{ij} matrices. The many-issue case is plagued by Arrow cycling and other problems. This is a useful area for future study.

3. A constant-sum policy game with many political parties. In this case, equation (5.28) becomes

$$\sum_j p^j(t_j, t^o_j, a) = k(a) \tag{5.40}$$

Since the proof of Theorem 1 does not depend upon whether or not the game is constant-sum, equation (5.27) still holds. There is an additional requirement that follows directly from (5.40):

$$P^n = k(a) - \sum_{i \neq n} p^i \tag{5.41}$$

Therefore, from (5.27) and (5.41)

$$\sigma R^n_j = \sigma p^n_{nj} = \sigma[-\sum_{i \neq n} p^i_{nj}] \tag{5.42}$$

In order to generate hypotheses about the p^i_{nj} and to get sign restrictions on σR_{nt} out of (5.42), let us rank the parties in terms of some notion of "external distance." That is, the closer are two parties' indices, the larger are their external effects upon each other's marginal revenue. Assume the following:

$$\sigma(\Sigma_{i\neq n} p^i_{nj}) = \sigma p^j_{nj} \qquad j = 1, 2, \ldots, n-1 \qquad (5.43)$$

Equation (5.43) is a type of dominant diagonal assumption; it is implied by

$$|p^j_{nj}| > \Sigma_{i\neq n,\, j} |p^i_{nj}| \qquad (5.44)$$

In more detail, the impact of t_n on j's marginal revenue p^j_{nj} from t_j is greater than the sum over all parties but n, j of the impacts of t_n on marginal revenues from t_j. It may be reasonable to assume that the parties may be indexed in such a way so that (5.43) holds at least for $j = n - 1$. Thus,

Theorem 2: Assume (5.43). Then, from Theorem 1,

$$\sigma R^i_j = \sigma p^i_{ij}, \qquad i = 1, 2, \ldots, n-1, \quad j = 1, 2, \ldots, n, \quad i \neq j \qquad (5.45)$$
$$\sigma R^n_j = -\sigma R^j_n, \qquad j = 1, 2, \ldots, n-1 \qquad (5.46)$$

Because

$$\sigma R^n_j = \sigma p^n_{nj} = -\sigma(\Sigma_{i\neq n} p^i_{nj}) = -\sigma p^j_{nj} = -\sigma R^j_n$$

Appendix to Chapter 6

A.6.1   The industry lobby as a noncooperative n-person game (see §6.2)

Consider n individuals who stand to obtain supplier surplus gains $S_1(t), \ldots$, $S_n(t)$ and m individuals who stand to lose consumer surplus amounts $C_1(t), \ldots , C_m(t)$, if it is proposed that an industry's tariff be changed from 0 to t. Assume the absence of a proexport lobby. Let

$$G_i = G_i(X, Y, x_i, S_i(t)) \qquad (6.1)$$
$$L_j = L_j(X, Y, y_j, C_j(t)) \qquad (6.2)$$
$$X = \sum x_i \qquad (6.3)$$
$$Y = \sum y_j \qquad (6.4)$$

where

G_i = expected net gain by i ($= 1, \ldots , n$)
L_j = expected net loss by j ($= 1, \ldots , m$)
$X(Y)$ = total lobbying resources raised by n gainers (m losers) from the tariff
$x_i(y_j)$ = lobbying contribution by gainer i (loser j)

This is a model of the voluntary provision of a public good whose net benefits are $S_1(t) \ldots S_n(t), -C_1(t) \ldots -C_m(t)$ for individuals $1, 2, \ldots , n$ and $1, 2, \ldots , m$.

Consider $G_i(X, Y, x_i, S_i(t))$. The perceived net gain to i of using his resources to back the tariff is a function of the total perceived backing for protection X, total lobbying against protection Y, his own backing x_i above and beyond his contribution to the perceived total X, and his supplier surplus gain $S_i(t)$ if the tariff passes.

The reader might well ask why t itself is not made a function of X,Y too. The impact of the X, Y, and x_i upon the ultimate outcome as seen by i is assumed to be already reflected in $G_i(X, Y, x_i, S_i(t))$. This follows our Stackelberg formulation in earlier chapters in which the political system chooses the tariff t against which the potential gainers and losers respond.

Definition 1: x_i^e and y_j^e is a noncooperative equilibrium (NCE)
  if for each i, j;   (6.5)

$$G_i(X_i^e + x_i^e, Y^e, x_i^e, S_i(t)) \geqq G_i(X_i^e + x_i, Y^e, x_i, S_i(t)) \qquad (6.6)$$
$$-L_j(X^e, Y_j^e + y_j^e, y_j^e, C_j(t)) \geqq -L_j(X^e, Y_j^e + y_j, y_j, C_j(t)) \qquad (6.7)$$

for all $x_i \geqq 0$ and $y_j \geqq 0$, where $X_i^e = \sum_{s \neq i} x_s$ and $Y_j^e = \sum_{u \neq j} y_u$, where

  X_i = contributions by all gainers except individual i
  Y_j = contributions by all losers except individual j

In words, x_i^e, y_j^e is an NCE if no player can make himself better off by choosing some resource level other than his equilibrium level, given that all others choose their equilibrium levels. An NCE is identical to the concept of current equilibrium in oligopoly theory.

If for each t there is a unique equilibrium, $X^e(t)$, $Y^e(t)$, satisfying (6.5), then:

Definition 2: The functions $X^e(t)$, $Y^e(t)$ are called "lobbying functions"
  of the gainers and losers, respectively.   (6.8)

We do not analyze explicitly how the political process chooses t; this has been addressed in earlier chapters.

We turn now to the properties of the endogenous lobbying functions $X^e(t)$ and $Y^e(t)$. The functions G_i, L_j are subjective, so we must make assumptions about the form of these functions. The problem is similar to that in consumer demand theory, in which very general assumptions are made about the utility functions (e.g., quasi-concavity and monotonicity). Let $S_i(t) = S_i$ and $C_j(t) = C_j$ to simplify the notation.

Consider the gains to protectionist agent i, $G_i(X, Y, x_i, S_i)$. It is reasonable to postulate that G_i is increasing in his supplier surplus S_i and in the contributions by others X_i. It is plausible to suppose that G_i is decreasing in Y. What about x_i? The arguments X and x_i in G_i are an attempt to capture precisely Olson's (1965) notions of perceived effectiveness and noticeability, respectively. Suppose that a compensated change in X takes place such that X is constant but x_i increases. Because G_i measures the net benefit to i ($G_i = B_i - x_i$, where B_i equals the gross benefit and x_i equals the amount contributed to the campaign), it is reasonable to postulate that G_i increases for small values of x_i and then decreases for large values. We would expect B_i to increase for low values of x_i because

1. individual i may feel that he has an impact on the chances of passage of the legislation above and beyond the total X;
2. he derives personal satisfaction from defending his group's interest; and

3. he feels negatively about his noticeability and group sanctions that might be levied against him if he does not contribute.

Also it seems reasonable to postulate diminishing returns to (X,x_i) at least for large values of X, x_i. Second-order necessary conditions imply that NCE values must occur in concave portions of G_i (we do not analyze here increasing returns). In what follows, we make several assumptions.

Assumption 1:

(a) Each function G_i is concave in (X,x_i) for each (Y,S_i).
(b) For each X, Y, S_i, the function G_i is increasing in x_i for small x_i but decreasing for values of x_i beyond a unique maximum value.
(c) G_i is increasing in X, S_i for each Y, x_i.
(d) G_i is nonincreasing in Y for each (X,x_i,S_i).   (6.9)

The same properties are assumed for each function $-L_j$. In addition, twice continuous differentiability is assumed throughout.

We now impose a second assumption on the lobbying functions.

Assumption 2: Each G_i-L_j is additively separable in Y and X, respectively; that is G_{iX}, G_{ix_i}, $-L_{jY}$, $-L_{jy_j}$ are independent of Y, X respectively (subscript symbols denote partial derivatives).   (6.10)

Thus, first- and second-order necessary conditions for an NCE x_i^e, y_j^e are given by:

$$G_{iX} + G_{ix_i} \leq 0 \qquad (= 0 \text{ if } x_i > 0) \tag{6.11}$$

$$G_{iXX} + G_{iXx_i} + G_{ix_iX} + G_{ix_ix_i} = G_{iXX} + 2G_{iXx_i} + G_{ix_ix_i} \leq 0 \tag{6.12}$$

$$-L_{jY} - L_{jy_j} < 0 \qquad (= 0 \text{ if } y_j > 0) \tag{6.13}$$

$$-L_{jYY} - 2L_{jYy_j} - L_{jy_jy_j} < 0 \tag{6.14}$$

A.6.2   Existence and uniqueness (see §6.3)

For given (X,Y,S_i), let $Y_i(X,Y,S_i) \equiv \{x_i \geq 0 \mid (6.11) \text{ holds}\}$. In order to study Y_i in more detail, we define:

$$G_i(X, Y, x_i, S_i) \equiv G_{ix_i}(X, Y, x_i, S_i) + G_{iX}(X, Y, x_i, S_i) \quad x_i \geq 0 \tag{6.15}$$

G_i is the perceived net marginal value product of x_i. By definition of G_i, for $x_i \geq 0$

$$x_i \in Y_i(X, Y, S_i) \Leftrightarrow G_i(X, Y, x_i, S_i) \leq 0 \qquad (= 0 \text{ if } x_i > 0) \tag{6.16}$$

In order for G_i to be well behaved, we shall assume the following.

Assumption 3: G_i is

(a) continuous,   (c) increasing in S_i,
(b) decreasing in x_i,   (d) decreasing in X.   (6.17)

In Figure A.6.1, G_i is plotted as a function of x_i in the case where $X_1 < X_2$. By inspection of Figures A.6.1 and A.6.2, the reader can easily show that Assumption

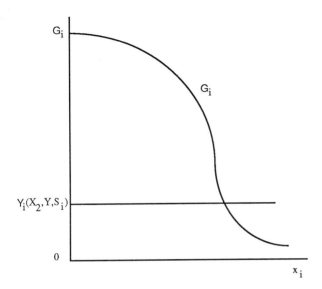

Figure A.6.1. G_i plotted as a function of x_i in the case where $X_1 < X_2$.

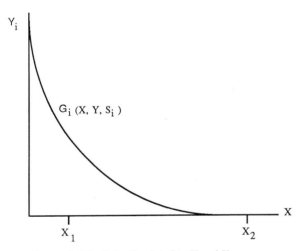

Figure A.6.2. Gain G_i related to X and Y.

3 implies that for each $i, Y, Y_i(X, Y, S_i)$, if it exists, is nonincreasing in X and nondecreasing in S_i. Hence, define:

$$Y(X, Y, S) \equiv \Sigma_j^n Y_j(X, Y, S_i) \qquad (6.18)$$
$$S \equiv (S_1, \dots, S_n)$$

and observe that if X solves (6.19), then (6.20) holds.

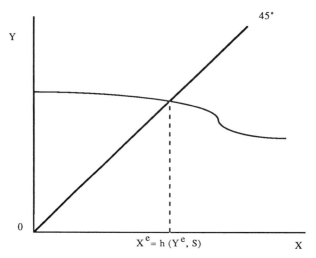

Figure A.6.3. Total protectionist contributions X related to total opposition contributions Y.

$$X^e = Y(X^e, Y, S) \tag{6.19}$$
$$x_i^e = Y_i(X^e, Y, S_i) \tag{6.20}$$

This an NCE for the n gainers given Y. This is so because (6.20) satisfies (6.11) by construction and concavity of G_i in (X, x_i) yields first-order necessary conditions sufficient for G_i to achieve a maximum at $x_i = x_i^e$. Notice that the concavity of G_i is more than is needed for this property: All that is needed is that the first-order condition (6.11) be necessary and sufficient for a maximum of G_i in x_i. This is important for cases where G_i is interpreted as a subjective expected value as in Olson (1965).

Each Y_i is nonincreasing in X; therefore Y is nonincreasing in X (see Figure A.6.3 in which Y is plotted against X). We see immediately that Assumption 3(a,b,d) imply existence and uniqueness of an NCE for the gainers, provided that Y is fixed. So, in particular, for Assumption 2, in which G_i is independent of Y for each i, we have existence and uniqueness of an NCE. Furthermore, if x_i^e is > 0, since assumption 3(c) implies G_i increases in S_i, Y increases in S_i; so by inspection of Figure A.6.3, X^e increases in S_i. For all $j \neq i$ we have $x_j^e = Y_j(X^e, S_j)$, which does not increase and decreases if $x_j^e > 0$ when S_i increases. But $x_i^e = Y_i(X^e, S_i)$ must increase because X^e does when S_i increases.

A.6.3   *Exploitation of the large by the small (see §6.4)*

The previous results ensure that the following holds.

Result 1: In the case that all G_r ($r = 1, 2, \ldots, n$) are independent of Y, Assumption 3 implies that if $x_i^e > 0$ and if S_i increases, ceteris paribus, then X^e increases and x_j^e decreases for j unequal to i provided that $x_j^e > 0$. Furthermore, x_i^e increases when S_i increases. (6.21)

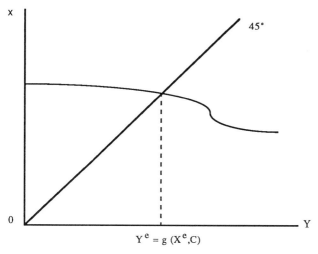

$$Y^e = g (X^e, C)$$

Figure A.6.4. Opposition contributions Y related to protectionist contributions x.

This result is essentially Olson's (1965) effect of the small exploiting the large. For if a stake becomes larger – that is, S_i increases – then, ceteris paribus, the other contributions fall due to free-riding. A similar result holds for the losers.

Define $\Delta_j (X,Y,y_j,C_j)$ by

$$\Delta_j \equiv -L_{jy_j} (X,Y,y_j,C_j) - L_{jY}(X,Y,y_j,C_j) \tag{6.22}$$

Let $x_j (X,Y,C_j)$ be defined by

$$x_j (X,Y,C_j) = \{y_j\} \ge 0, \; \Delta_j (X,Y,y_j,C_j) \le 0 \quad (= 0 \text{ if } y_j > 0) \tag{6.23}$$

Assumption 4: Δ_j is continuous, decreasing in Y, decreasing in y_j, and increasing in C_j. $\tag{6.24}$

The same argument as for the gainers yields:

Result 2: Assume that X is fixed. An NCE Y^e such that $\{y_j^e\}, j = 1, \dots, m$ exists for the losers and is depicted in Figure A.6.4. Furthermore, for a fixed X if $y_j^e > 0$, then an increase in C_j implies that Y^e increases, y_r^e decreases for $r \ne j$, provided that $y_r^e > 0$ and y_j^e increases. $\tag{6.25}$

Here,

$$x(X,Y,C) \equiv \Sigma_{r=1} x_r(X,Y,C_r), \qquad C = (C_1, \dots, C_m) \tag{6.26}$$

The relations $Y^e = x$, $X^e = Y$ (in Figures A.6.3 and A.6.4) define a pair of NCE equilibrium response functions.

$$X^e = h(Y^e,S), \qquad\qquad Y^e = g(X^e,C) \tag{6.27}$$
$$\quad\; ? \;\; + \qquad\qquad\qquad\qquad ? \;\; +$$

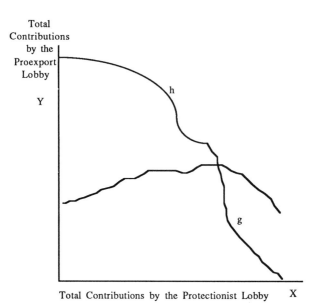

Figure A.6.5. Total contributions by both lobbies.

where h is the solution of (6.19) for X^e as a function of Y^e, S and g is the solution of $Y^e = x$ for Y^e as a function of X^e and C. Obviously, an NCE will exist if the functions h, g are continuous in Y, X, respectively, and the situation is depicted as in Figure A.6.5, which shows equilibrium contributions. The random slopes of the curves h, g indicates that it is difficult to determine a priori the sign of the partial derivatives h_Y and g_X. The most plausible hypothesis is that $G_i(X,Y, x_i,S_i)$ decreases in Y and $\Delta_j(X,Y,y_j,C_j)$ decreases in X, because these are marginal products of own contributions and should fall as perceived opposition increases. If this is the case, the situation is as described in Figure A.6.6. There may be one or more than one intersection, or none at all.

Comparative statics may be performed in Figure A.6.6b. An increase in S_i, for example, will lead to a rightward shift in h, which leads to an increase in X and a decrease in Y. We get the reassuring result that an increase in the stake of an individual protectionist leads the total level of protectionist lobby contributions to rise and the total level of opposing contributions to fall. The same comparative statics result obtains at equilibria that are stable with respect to the following dynamics.

$$X^{t+1} = h(Y^t, S), \qquad Y^{t+1} = g(X^t, S), \qquad t = 1, 2, \ldots \qquad (6.28)$$

Little more can be said at this level of generality.

A.6.4   Perceived effectiveness and noticeability: concentration and homogeneity (see §6.5)

   In order to obtain empirical implications, we shall work with specific lobbying functions $X^e = X^e(S_1, \ldots, S_n)$, $Y^e = Y^e(C_1, \ldots, C_m)$ from this point to illustrate

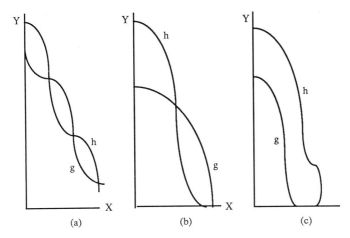

Figure A.6.6. Types of equilibria for protectionist and proexport contributions: (a) multiple equilibria; (b) single equilibrium; (c) no equilibrium.

spillover and free-rider effects. Consider the following lobbying functions for gainer i and loser j from the tariff:

$$S_i[a/X^e + b/x_i^e] \leq 1 \quad (=1 \text{ if } x_i^e > 0) \quad a, b \geq 0 \quad a+b \leq 1 \quad (6.29)$$

$$C_j[A/Y^e + B/y_j^e] \leq 1 \quad (=1 \text{ if } y_j^e > 0) \quad A, B \geq 0 \quad A+B \leq 1 \quad (6.30)$$

Recall that a,b and A,B, are Olson's perceived effectiveness and ("free-riding") noticeability coefficients for gainers and losers, respectively, and are assumed identical for each gainer and each loser. Equations (6.29) and (6.30) are first-order necessary conditions that would emerge from the following objective functions of the two actors:

$$\max G_i \equiv S_i[a \log(\sum_{j \neq i} x_j^e + x_i) + b \log x_i] - x_i \quad (6.31)$$

$$\min L_j \equiv M_j - AC_j \log Y - BC_j \log y_j + y_j \quad (M_j \text{ constant}) \quad (6.32)$$

Here coefficient a provides a measure of spillover effects on the free-rider problem: The larger is a, the greater the benefits accruing to i of contributions by others. Coefficient b captures the effect of individual j's own contribution on his own gain, apart from his contribution to the total. It may be helpful in one context to view a as the perceived effect of one's contribution to the pecuniary returns (via the tariff) and b as nonpecuniary gains, such as political access or future unspecified benefits. Equations (6.29) and (6.30) and $a + b < 1, A + B < 1, a \geq 0, b \geq 0, A \geq 0, B \geq 0$ imply the following:

$$x_i^e (S_1, \dots, S_n) \leq S_i, \quad i = 1, \dots, n \quad (6.33)$$

$$y_j^e (C_1, \dots, C_n) \leq C_i, \quad j = 1, \dots, m \quad (6.34)$$

$$X^e (\lambda S_1, \dots, \lambda S_n) = \lambda X^e(S_1, \dots, S_n) \quad \text{for all } \lambda > 0, \quad S_i \geq 0, \quad i = 1, \dots, n \quad (6.35)$$

$$Y^e\,(\lambda C_1, \ldots, \lambda C_m) = \lambda Y^e(C_1, \ldots, C_m) \quad \text{for all } \lambda > 0, \quad C_j \geq 0, \quad j = 1, \ldots, m$$
$$(6.36)$$

$$X^e\,(S_1, \ldots, S_n) \text{ is maximum subject to } \sum_i S_i = R \quad \text{when } S_k = R \text{ for some } k$$
$$(6.37)$$

$$Y^e\,(C_1, \ldots, C_m) \text{ is maximum subject to } \sum_j C_j = R \quad \text{when } C_f = R \text{ for some } f$$
$$(6.38)$$

if $S_{i_1} = S_{i_2} = S$ for some $i_1 < i_2$,

      then $X^e(\ldots, S_{i1} - d, \ldots, S_{i2} + d, \ldots) > X^e(\ldots, S_{i1}, \ldots, S_{i2},)$

      for $d > 0, \quad d < S$ (6.39)

if $C_{j_1} = C_{j_2} = C$ for some $j_1 < j_2$,

      then $Y^e(\ldots, C_{j_1} - d, \ldots, C_{j_2} + d, \ldots) > Y^e(\ldots, C_{j_1}, \ldots, C_{j_2},)$

      for $d > 0, \quad d < C$ (6.40)

These properties are what one would expect from an Olson (1965) theory of the voluntary provision of public goods. The least surprising result is (6.33) and (6.34), in which no actor contributes more than his stake (i.e., what he will get back from the political system). In (6.35) and (6.36), lobby contributions are homogeneous of degree 1 with respect to the stakes: If each lobby member's stake increases by a factor of λ, the entire lobby's effort rises by λ. The superiority of the monopolist lobby is reflected in (6.37) and (6.38). Total lobby contributions are maximum for a single-member lobby, holding the total stake constant. A related result is Olson's enhancement of concentration result shown in (6.39) and (6.40). Any increase in the inequality of the stakes increases the level of total lobby contributions.

A.6.5   A simplified model: firms of equal size (see §6.6)

We simplify the model by assuming that each of the protectionist firms is the same size and that each of the proexport firms is the same size. Put

$$B_i = [a \log(\textstyle\sum x_i) + b \log x_i]\, S_i(t)$$

and

$$A_j = -[A \log(\textstyle\sum y_j) + B \log y_j]\, C_j(t).$$

The proexport lobby game is

$$\min\{-y_j + C_j[A \log(\textstyle\sum y_j) + B \log y_j]\}.$$

Solving the game B_i ($i = 1, \ldots, n$) and noting that $X = nx$ yields

$$x = S(a/n + b) \qquad\qquad (6.41)$$
$$X = S(a + nb) \qquad\qquad (6.42)$$

where $S = S(t)$ is the gain of each identical protectionist in the tariff change from 0 to t, x is the individual's lobbying expenditure, and X is the total lobby's expenditure. A similar procedure applied to the proexport lobby yields

$$y = C[A/m + B] \qquad\qquad (6.43)$$
$$Y = C[A + mB] \qquad\qquad (6.44)$$

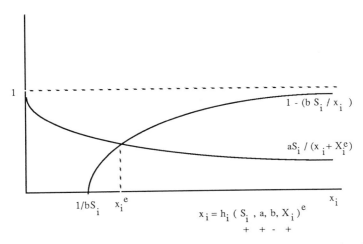

Figure A.6.7. The optimal response of protectionist i from equation (6.47).

Note the following three issues:

1. Addition of another member with an identical stake leads to a fall in x but a rise in X.
2. Increasing the number who share a given gain S has no effect on the total lobbying effort only if $a = 0$. With the parameter $a = 0$, there is no free-rider problem, so each contributor appropriates the entire benefit of his lobbying activity.
3. What happens if the number of protectionists is increased but the total dollar value of the protectionist stake remains unchanged? Mathematically, this is similar to replacing S by S/n in (6.42) and C by C/m in (6.44). The total lobbying of the protectionists and the proexport lobby becomes

$$X' = (S'/n)\,(a + nb) \qquad = S'(a/n + b) \qquad\qquad (6.45)$$
$$Y' = (C'/m)\,(A + mB) \qquad = C'(A/m + B) \qquad\qquad (6.46)$$

respectively, and both of these fall as the numbers of players increase.

To examine the general case in more detail consider the best-response function of protectionist i given his expectation of what the others will contribute (X_i^e) and his stake S_i. Protectionist i chooses x_i to equate expected marginal gain to marginal cost, which is assumed to be unity. If the contributions of others increase (X_i^e), then the expected marginal gain to i falls, provided that $a > 0$. When $a = 0$, increases in X_i^e have no effect on protectionist i because there is no free-riding. When $a = 0$, then $x_i = 1/bS_i$. Notice that when b increases, x_i falls. (See Figure 6.7.) Let S_i be the stake of player i. Then best-response x_i solves

$$S_i[a/(x_i + X_i^e) + b/x_i] = \quad 1 \qquad\qquad (6.47)$$

The parameters a and b are restricted to $(a + b) \le 1$ so that for all values of X_i^e, S_i we have $x_i \le S_i$. If $X_i^e = 0$, then x_i that solves (6.47) is maximum. So $aS_i/x_i = 1 = bS_i/x_i$ implies $x_i = (a + b)S_i < S_i$ if and only if $a + b \le 1$.

A.6.6   The lobbying power function (see §6.7)

The literature on lobbying and regulation has investigated extensively the issue of the concentration of benefits. A frequently used measure of concentration is the Herfindahl index, which equals the sum of the squared market shares. In terms of the lobbying problem here, the Herfindahl index of the stakes H is defined as:

$$H = H (S_1, \ldots , S_n) = \sum_i [S_i/(\sum_k S_k)]^2 \qquad (6.48)$$

Here, H is associated here with the structure of the supplier surplus stakes among the n gainers from the tariff. The Herfindahl can be combined with the total stakes of the gainers to yield our power function P:

$$P = P (S_1, \ldots , S_n) = H(\sum S_i) \qquad (6.49)$$

This index satisfies (6.33), (6.35), (6.37), and (6.39). In particular, the power function increases in the concentration of the stakes and is homogeneous of degree 1 in the level of the stakes.

Because $1/H$ can be interpreted as the number of equal-size gainers from the tariff, we can simplify the problem further. Let us use the power function to solve (6.20) and (6.22) for the case of identically sized actors, $S_i = S$ and $C_j = C$ for all i, j. The results were shown in equations (6.41)–(6.44). As in the discussion there, the following is true for the power function P in (6.49): Addition of another member with an identical stake leads to a fall in x but a rise in X. The empirical implication is that per-member contributions should fall with group membership, whereas total contributions should increase.

A.6.7   Endogenous lobbying and the size of political jurisdictions

How are the levels of lobbying expenditures by well-organized protectionists (relatively less well-organized consumer groups) affected by the size of the political jurisdiction? We examine here the net contributions for protection, which equal the total protectionist contributions minus the proexport lobby contributions. Suppose that all political jurisdictions (districts) are identical and that there are n identical gainers and m identical losers in each of the D districts $(d = 1, \ldots , D)$. We will examine the net protectionist contributions over the union of the d districts. Now suppose the D districts are consolidated into one large district with one representative to represent it. From (6.41)–(6.44), the solution for the gainers and losers with consolidation is

$S(a/n + b)$	$= x$	unconsolidated:	X	$= S(a + nb)$	(6.50)
$S[a/nd + b]$	$= x'$	consolidated:	X'	$= nxd$	$= S[a + nbd]$
$C[A/m + B]$	$= y$	unconsolidated:	Y	$= C[A + mB]$	(6.51)
$C[A/md + B]$	$= y'$	consolidated:	Y'	$= myd$	$= C[A + mBd]$

The equilibrium in the larger geographical district (i.e., after consolidation) is indicated by a prime (´). Figure A.6.8 shows these functions, assuming that both pro- and antiprotectionist lobbying funds are an increasing function of the tariff rate. We

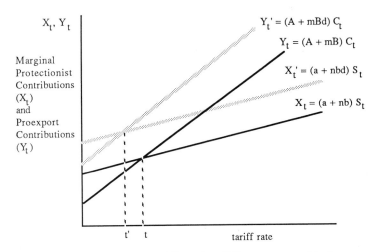

Figure A.6.8. Equilibrium tariffs under different geographical aggregations of voters.

assume for the moment that the equilibrium tariff is determined simply by the intersection of the protectionist and the proexport lobby curves.

Assume that Congress chooses a tariff to maximize $(X - Y)$. If either C_t or m increases, ceteris paribus, then expenditures against the tariff increase and hence net protectionist lobbying expenditures fall. (C_t is the derivative of C with respect to the tariff.) Thus, the tariff would fall. Conversely, if S_t or n increases, protectionist lobbying expenditures rise and the tariff rises. It will be a general result that a rise in the marginal stake S_t will increase lobbying expenditures, whereas a rise in the number of identical players may go either way. That is, adding another identical player along with his additional stake increases the total stake but decreases the lobbying put forth by each individual.

With geographical consolidation, the results can go either way: Figure A.6.8 indicates that if $b = 0$, then net protectionist pressure falls. If $B = 0$, then the pressure rises. What is the meaning of $b = 0$? Because only the total lobbying expenditures matter, another individual contribution has no impact. When $b = 0$ there is complete free-riding: Thus, protectionist i feels that increasing his contribution x_i by \$1 reduces the expected contribution by the rest of the protectionists by \$1. If $b > 0$, there is not complete free-riding, so there is a positive expected gain to i when he contributes. Consolidation will increase net protectionist lobbying and increase the tariff when $B = 0$, assuming that the X curve shifts upward and the Y curve does not move. That is, when consumers – the losers – feel anonymous, then consolidation generates more special-interest behavior and hence a higher tariff. The logic goes like this: Consolidate two equal-sized congressional districts into a state. There are now twice as many gainers and losers. Contribution per person of the losers falls. But if $B = 0$, total contributions of the losers remain the same even though $2mC$ is the financial interest. That is, contribution per person falls so much that even though there is twice as much potential contribution as before, total lobbying in the state is the same as the lobbying directed to each of the two representatives in the congressional districts. Things are different with the firms, however. Because they are larger, they feel less anonymous: that is, $b > 0$. Thus, even though lobbying per person falls due to free-riding ($a > 0$) the total lobbying rises. Thus, general interests can lose their relative clout as we move to larger political jurisdictions.

A.6.8   Estimation of the lobbying power function (see §6.9)

The lobbying power function in equation (6.49) could be estimated for protectionists as follows. First, estimate the value of the protectionist stake for the entire industry V as the product of industry sales and the tariff rate ($t \times$ sales). Then simply estimate the power function directly:

$$\log X = a_0 + a_1 \log H + a_2 \log V \tag{6.52}$$

Unfortunately, the coefficients are not precise estimates of the perceived effectiveness and noticeability coefficients. The coefficients a and b can be estimated from the following regression after calculating the number of "equal-sized" firms in each industry ($=1/H$).

$$r = X/V = a + nb \tag{6.53}$$

where

r = the lobbying ratio (ratio of lobbying expenditures to the value of the stakes)

X = total lobbying expenditures by the industry for protection

V = value of the industry stake (= tariff rate times industry sales)

H = Herfindahl index of concentration for the industry ($0 \le H \le 1$)

n = number of equal-sized firms in each industry($= 1/H$)

There is a problem with this formulation. Many highly competitive industries and consumer groups will have very small Herfindahl ratios. In some cases, it may be impossible to calculate n, which equals the inverse of the Herfindahl. It may be more straightforward to estimate the following equation [derived from (6.41)].

$$r = X/V = aH + b \tag{6.54}$$

This regression provides an explicit test of our assumption that $a \ge 0, b \ge 0, a + b \le 1$, and so on. It would also provide empirical evidence on the relative importance of perceived effectiveness ($a > 0$) relative to noticeability effects ($b > 0$). A diagram of interest would be the plot of r on H or n. Positive residuals (actual values exceeding predicted ones) would indicate above average lobbying success by an industry.

Another issue is the possible dependence of the noticeability coefficient b on the number of equal-sized firms n. The theory predicts that an increase in n with the total stake held constant causes the lobby to decrease its total lobbying effort X. The coefficient a measures an external effect, and b measures an internal effect: If $a = 0$, there are no spillover effects or externalities; if $b = 0$, individual effort has no effect.

Table A.7.1. *Results for test 2: value of z in a normal approximation of the binomial*

	Hypothesis tested			
	Number of industries (1)	Proportion of cases (2)	Stolper– Samuelson (3)	Factor- specific (4)
Capital's position:				
Protectionism	15	$p_1 = 0.63$	4.49	0.50
Free trade	9	$p_2 = 0.37$	$(0.000003)^a$	(0.31)
Labor's position:				
Protectionism	16	$p_1 = 0.76$	2.10	4.01
Free trade	5	$p_2 = 0.24$	$(0.018)^a$	$(0.000003)^a$

[a]The hypothesis is rejected at this level of significance.

A parallel is the case of n farmers spraying their crops with insecticides. If $a = 0$, there are no spillover effects, so that one farmer's spraying benefits no other farmer. The value x corresponds to the cost of insecticide spray for individual farmer i; $nS =$ the total value of the crop; and $t =$ price of the crop. The case $b = 0$ and $a > 0$ captures the case in which spillover effects are so great that as n approaches infinity, X approaches zero. In the opposite case of $a = 0$ and $b > 0$, there are no external effects, implying that $X = bnS > 0$, no matter how large n is. The case of $b > 0$ does not necessarily make a great deal of sense when n is large: This equation implies that, as n gets large, each lobby member still perceives that his individual effort has the same effect on his personal welfare, despite his growing personal anonymity. This problem could be rectified by letting b be a decreasing function of n so that b approaches 0 as n approaches infinity. Estimation of (6.54) could proceed along such lines.

Appendix to Chapter 7

This appendix presents a more detailed analysis of tests 2 and 3 in the text (see §§7.3.2 and 7.3.3). Test 2 tests the degree of unanimity of each factor on one position or the other. Table A.7.1 summarizes the data from Table 7.1 for capital and labor. More observations are possible for capital here because its position does not have to be paired with knowledge of labor's position. We find that only 63% of the industries selected show capital supporting the preferred alternative (protectionism). Stolper–Samuelson predicts that all capital would choose one alternative or the other (100% vs. 0%) and should not split this way (63% vs. 37%).

Because it is impossible to test the sample observations in Table A.7.1 against the hypothesis that $p_1 = 1.0$ and $p_2 = 0$, we must set some arbitrary value of p_1 that is less than 1.0. We arbitrarily set $p_1 = 0.9$ and $p_2 = 0.1$ as the hypothesized Stolper–Samuelson values. Thus, a sample that showed 90% of capital supporting the preferred alternative (say, protection) and only 10% supporting the other (free trade) would be consistent with the factor mobility assumption implicit in Stolper–Samuelson. Similarly, we arbitrarily set $p_1 = p_2 = 0.5$ as the hypothesized population values associated with the factor-specific model. Notice that we bias against acceptance of Stolper–Samuelson if p_1 is set too close to 1, and the test of factor specificity is influenced by the random breakdown of the sample between protectionists and free traders. If there is a tendency for only one group to lobby, there is also a tendency to reject the Ricardo–Viner–Cairnes model of factor specificity.

The test is conducted as follows: What is the probability that the sample proportions in column 2 of Table A.7.1 would have been obtained if the true population proportions were those hypothesized ($p_1 = 0.9$ for Stolper–Samuelson and $p_1 = p_2 = 0.5$ for Ricardo–Viner–Cairnes)? We use the binomial distribution for the test. Because the number of trials is $n = 24$ for capital and $n = 21$ for labor, an approximation must be used. The Poisson distribution could be used but is recommended only when $p_1 = 0.05$; thus, we must use the normal approximation. We transform the number of cases ($x = 15$ for capital and $x = 16$ for labor) apparently satisfying the hypothesis into the standardized normal random variable z (see Freund 1971, pp. 75, 175):

$$z = (x - np_1) / [(np_1(1 - p_1)]^{1/2} \qquad (7.1)$$

The tabulated values of z are shown in columns 3 and 4 of Table A.7.1, along with their significance levels.

Consider capital: If the true population proportion is 0.9 (Stolper–Samuelson), the chances of obtaining a proportion of $p_1 = 0.63$ are only 0.0003%, whereas the chances of getting $p_1 = 0.63$ are 31% when the hypothesized value is 0.5 (Ricardo–Viner–Cairnes). Thus, for capital the results reject the factor mobility hypothesis implicit in Stolper–Samuelson and cannot reject the factor-specific Ricardo–Viner–Cairnes hypothesis. The sample proportion of labor favoring protection is 0.76: Both Stolper–Samuelson and Ricardo–Viner–Cairnes are rejected, with the latter rejected more decisively. The results for labor are thus inconclusive. Notice that we biased the test in favor of Stolper–Samuelson by choosing the larger of the two sample proportions to compare with the hypothesized value of 0.9.

As an aside, the data in Table A.7.1 permit a test of the Burgess (1976) result that American labor would gain at the expense of American capital with greater protection. If this result is correct, we should observe that labor would support protection in a larger proportion of the industries than capital. Using the test described in (7.1), we find that $p_1 = 0.76$ is significantly greater than 0.63 at the 0.11 level ($z = 1.25$), while 0.63 is significantly less than 0.76 at the 0.06 level ($z = 1.58$). Thus, the data here are not inconsistent with the Burgess result; they support him using one test and almost confirm his result when the order of the test is reversed. We view our results as mixed, however, and turn instead to a third and stronger test of the factor mobility assumption than is provided by either test 1 or 2.

Test 2 indicated the degree of unanimity (or lack thereof) that a factor has for a specific trade policy. In test 3 we test whether or not a factor prefers a policy that is beneficial to the industry in which it is currently employed. If it does, factor specificity is implied; if not, factor mobility (among other things) is more likely. Two versions of this test are presented: The first is a proportions test; the second allows continuous variation in the industry's trade balance.

Table A.7.2. *Results for test 3: number of industries with capital's or labor's position on free trade related to the trade sector*

Industry	1. Protectionist	2. Free trade	Odds ratio (s.e.(o))	Signif. (χ^2)
Position of capital ($n = 24$)				
1. Import-competing	n_{11} =10	n_{12} = 3	4.0	4.1
	(p_{11} =0.42)	(p_{12} = 0.12)		
2. Export	n_{21} =5	n_{22} = 6	(3.6)	(0.05)
	(p_{21} =0.21)	(p_{22} = 0.25)		
Position of labor ($n = 21$)				
1. Import-competing	n_{11} =11	n_{12} = 1	8.8	3.3
	(p_{11} =0.53)	(p_{12} = 0.04)		
2. Export	n_{21} =5	n_{22} = 4	(10.9)	(0.10)
	(p_{21} =0.24)	(p_{22} = 0.19)		

Consider the data in Table A.7.2. These are approximately the same industries that were used in test 2. The rows in Table A.7.2 classify the industries according to whether they are export or import competing. A tendency for dominant diagonality indicates Ricardo–Viner–Cairnes factor specificity; independence of the sectors and the trade positions is consistent with Stolper–Samuelson factor mobility. The usual test of association in these tables is a straightforward application of the chi-square test χ^2. Although χ^2 is a good measure of the significance of the association, it is not useful as a measure of the degree of association between sectoral location and the factor's preferred trade policy (Fleiss 1973, p. 41). The odds ratio, however, does provide such a test (Fleiss 1973, pp. 43–6). The sample odds ratio o is defined as

$$o = \frac{(p_{11}/p_{12})}{(p_{21}/p_{22})} \qquad (7.2)$$

Notice that the odds of a factor favoring protection relative to free trade are p_{11}/p_{12} if the factor is in the import-competing sector and p_{21}/p_{22} if it is in the export sector. If these odds are the same, then knowledge of the factor's sectoral location gives us no information about the factor's most likely policy preference. In this case, the numerator and denominator in (7.2) are equal and the odds ratio equals 1. Stolper–Samuelson predicts that the odds ratio $o = 1$ whereas factor specificity implies $o > 1$. Let us test these hypotheses.

The standard error of the odds ratio s.e.(o) is approximately

$$\text{s.e.}(o) = (o/n^{1/2}) \, [(1/p_{11} + 1/p_{12} + 1/p_{21} + 1/p_{22})^{1/2}] \qquad (7.3)$$

[Fleiss 1973, p. 45]. The values of o and s.e.(o) from (7.2) and (7.3) are reported in Table A.7.2. The calculations indicate that the odds of capital in the import-competing sector favoring protection are four times those of capital in the export sector; for labor, the same odds ratio is 8.8. The standard errors are 3.6 and 10.9, respectively. The significance tests should not be performed using just these standard errors.

Rather, calculate the variable Y,

$$Y = [(o - o^h) / (s.e.(o)/n^{1/2})]^2 \qquad (7.4)$$

which has a χ^2 distribution with one degree of freedom (Freund 1971, p. 214). The obtained sample value o is tested against the hypothesized value o^h.

The values of χ^2 computed from (7.4) for Y, as well as their significance levels, are shown in the last column of Table A.7.2. Both capital and labor differ significantly from the hypothesized Stolper–Samuelson independence of lobbying positions and sectoral location: Stolper–Samuelson is refuted for capital at the 5% level and labor at the 10% level.

Appendix to Chapter 8

A.8.1   Model 1: wealth redistribution (see §8.2)

We analyze here two economies: an invisible hand economy without redistribution and an invisible foot economy with part of the labor force devoted to capturing the wealth of others. In the invisible foot economy, the total labor supply T follows one of two activities: L is engaged in productive activity whereas R pursues redistributive activity.

$$T = L + R \qquad (8.1)$$

Productive labor helps produce economic income, whereas redistributive labor re-labels wealth, transferring it from one member of society to another. All redistributed wealth is converted to income. The division of this income into consumption and savings is not important for the points we wish to make here. Total income Y in the invisible foot economy comes from two sources: economic income F and redistributive income Kr.

$$Y = F(K,L) + Kr(R) \qquad (8.2)$$

where

K,L = capital and labor in production;
r = fraction of capital that is redistributed each period and converted to income; and
R = labor engaged in redistributing capital.

In contrast, total income in the invisible hand economy can be written

$$Y = F(K,T) \qquad (8.3)$$

As discussed in §8.2, we assume that the two economies have identical labor forces and identical capital stocks. From Eqs. (8.2) and (8.3) it is clear that the hand economy will have more economic income because $T > L$, but the foot economy will have redistribution income if $r > 0$ because redistribution transforms part of the capital stock back into income during each period. GNP and GNP per capita can be higher in the invisible foot economy because of that transformation (if r is sufficiently high and early in the redistribution phase). This can be seen by transferring one unit of labor from economic activity to redistributive activity in (8.2), starting at a low R.

This labor would not have made the transition voluntarily from productive activity into redistributive activity unless the income it received from redistribution Kr' exceeded the forgone wage F_L. But this is the very condition that guarantees that the transfer to redistribution increases GNP, that is, $(Kr' - F_L) > 0$. Because of the reduction in productive labor in the invisible foot economy, the higher capital–labor ratio causes wages to be higher and returns to capital to be lower (the marginal product of capital is lower, and the marginal product of labor is higher).

To determine the effects of redistribution on growth, differentiate (8.2) totally (all derivatives are with respect to time):

$$dY = F_K dK + F_L(dT - dR) + r dK + Kr_R dR \qquad (8.4)$$
$$= \{F_K dK + F_L dT\} + \{r dK + (Kr_R - F_L) dR\} \qquad (8.5)$$

Consider the growth rates of income in two economies, each starting with identical stocks of K and T and with identical production and redistribution technologies. Let the invisible foot economy be initially at $R = 0$ and not in a redistributive equilibrium. This will be the case if the marginal payoff to increasing redistribution (Kr_R) exceeds the cost of one less laborer in production (F_L), by the earlier discussion. The second expression in braces in equation (8.5) indicates that invisible foot economies will have unambiguously higher growth rates of GNP than invisible hand economies. The reason for this is simple: Collectors of GNP statistics value all services at the amount the wage earner receives, and wealth is being converted into income.

Early in invisible foot economies, GNP growth rates will be higher the more rapid the growth of labor in the redistributive sector; that is, so long as the economy's redistribution equilibrium in labor markets has not yet been reached. Because ($Kr_R - F_L$) is positive, the redistributive growth term in (8.5) increases with dR. In the earliest phases of redistribution, dR will be large simply because R is near zero. Also, note in (8.5) that the marginal payoff to entering redistribution will also increase with the capital stock if ($r_R - F_{LK}) > 0$. If this is the case, capital-abundant economies will initially demonstrate more rapid growth with increasing redistribution than will labor-abundant economies.

A.8.2   Model 2: static income redistribution (see §8.3)

In this model, redistributive activity is directed at income rather than at wealth. Let there be $N(t)$ people at date t who own one unit of labor each. Suppose that one unit of labor produces $w(t)$ units of final goods output using a single-input, constant-returns technology. Then each individual j solves the following problem (we suppress t until it is needed):

$$\max wL_j \phi (R_j, R_{-j}) \qquad (8.6)$$
$$\text{s.t. } L_j + R_j = 1 \qquad (8.7)$$

where L_j denotes productive labor; R_j denotes labor devoted in redistribution; $R_{-j} = (R_1, \dots, R_{j-1}, R_{j+1}, \dots, R_N) = $ the vector of redistributive inputs by everyone but j; and ϕ denotes the impact of redistribution upon j's income as a function of all redistributive activity in society. We shall assume that ϕ increases in R_j, decreases in R_{-j}, and is the same function for everybody. (The assumption of homogeneous individuals will be made throughout.)

The interpretation of ϕ is the following: If j increases R_j enough, he will obtain more than perfectly competitive earnings wL_j from his labor. But large enough input R_{-j} of his $N-1$ rivals will make $\phi < 1$, so that he gets less than his perfectly competitive earnings. We shall assume $\phi\,(R_j, R_{-j}) = 1$, where $R_1 = R_2 = \cdots = R_N$ to dramatize the zero-sum nature of noncooperative equilibrium.

In order to derive some specific illustrative results, consider the following special case for ϕ :

$$\phi(R_j, R_{-j}) \equiv R_j^\alpha \{\Sigma_{k\neq j} R_k^{-\alpha}/(N-1)\}, \alpha > 0 \tag{8.8}$$

The solution of (8.6) must satisfy the first-order necessary conditions

$$\partial\phi_j/\partial R_j = \phi/L_j \tag{8.9}$$

by which we obtain from (8.8)

$$R_j \equiv R = \alpha L_j \equiv \alpha L, \qquad L = 1/(1+\alpha), \quad R = \alpha/(1+\alpha) \tag{8.10}$$

Let Y denote observable GNP. Because all income earned by labor (whether wasteful or not) is recorded in GNP accounts, we put, by definition,

$$Y \equiv wN \tag{8.11}$$

The reader may be uneasy about (8.11) because each j is using his own labor to redistribute. But that labor, through (8.10), is valued at w for each unit. In a model having specialists who were better at redistribution than j, the equilibrium would be for j to sell R_j units at w and purchase R_j units from someone else. In this model all redistributive labor income would show up in GNP accounts. Because analysis of this more elaborate model would be straightforward but more complicated, we stick with (8.11).

Let $Y = $ GNP; $X = $ value of final goods production; and $Z = $ total value of resources in redistribution. From (8.10) we have

$$Y = wN, \qquad X = (1-r)Y, \qquad Z = rY, \qquad r = \alpha/(1+\alpha) \tag{8.12}$$

Using (8.12) to calculate rates of growth, and letting α vary over time:

$$g_Y = g_w + g_N \tag{8.13a}$$
$$g_Z = g_r + g_Y = g_\alpha/(1+\alpha) + g_Y \tag{8.13b}$$
$$g_X = -\alpha g_\alpha/(1+\alpha) + g_Y \tag{8.13c}$$
$$g_Y = \alpha g_Z/(1+\alpha) + g_X/(1+\alpha) \tag{8.14}$$

The quantity $\alpha(t)$ determines the share of resources diverted to redistribution and must be less than unity in order for our model to be sensibly posed. The rate of growth of α can be anything over short periods of time.

We make four points:

1. In the short run just about any patterns of rates of growth of real output are possible. As in the first model, large positive rates of growth of GNP are

compatible with large positive rates of growth of both productive activity and redistributive activity.

2. An important case is where $g_\alpha \to 0$ as $t \to \infty$. In this case, the share of GNP going to redistribution settles down in the long run. Then, under modest regularity of the function $\alpha(t)$ we have

$$\alpha(t) \to \bar\alpha, \qquad t \to \infty \tag{8.15}$$

Hence the growth rates of Y, X, and Z converge.

3. As indicated by (8.13), the negative association, if any, between rates of growth of redistribution and rates of growth of GNP is more likely to show up in young countries. This contrasts with the results in model 1, and thus is the reverse of Olson's view.

4. This model is consistent with the stylized fact that distributive activity is countercyclical. As an economy falls into recession, it is most likely that g_w is negative and g_α is positive. Therefore $g_Z = g_Y + g_\alpha/(1 + \alpha) > g_Y$ when falling into a recession. On the rise out of the recession, it is natural to expect that $g_\alpha < 0$ and $g_w > 0$. Therefore on the upswing we should expect that $g_Z = g_Y + g_\alpha/(1 + \alpha) < g_Y$.

Although these results depend on our specific functional forms, we suspect that similar results will turn up in more general models that capture the decline in the rewards of production relative to redistribution in the business cycle. For theoretical and empirical development of the negative covariation of political and economic returns in a general equilibrium, see the compensation effect in Chapter 11.

A.8.3   Model 3: dynamic income redistribution (see §8.4)

We explore next the economic impact of income redistribution in an intertemporal model. We assume that N homogeneous individual households maximize their life-cycle utility. We will not derive the explicit optimization in what follows. The budget of household h is

$$C_h + dK_h/dt = (rK_h + wL_h + d_h\pi)\, \phi\, (R_h, R_{-h}), \qquad K_h(0) = K_{h0} \tag{8.16}$$

where C_h is consumption by h, K_h is capital owned by h, r is the rental rate on capital, w is the wage rate on labor L_h, π is corporate profits (whose dividends are assumed to be redistributed lump sum in fraction d_h, à la Arrow and Debreu), and ϕ is the impact of redistribution on income, which is increasing in own redistribution labor R_h and decreasing in the redistributive labor of others R_{-h}.

Assume that the households are homogeneous and have time-stationary preferences

$$\int_0^\infty e^{-\rho t}\, U(C_h(t))\, dt. \tag{8.17}$$

where ρ is the subjective rate of time preference. The variables ρ, r, and C_h are related by Irving Fisher's equation,

$$\rho = (dU_h'/dt)/U_h' = r\phi \tag{8.18}$$

where $U_h{'}$ is the marginal utility of consumption. The constant-returns productive sector income is given at date t by

$$Y = F(K,L,t) = rK + wL \tag{8.19}$$
$$\pi \equiv F(K,L,t) - rK - wL = 0$$

Each household has one unit of labor to allocate each period. Therefore (since $\pi = 0$ in equilibrium) the household solves

$$\max_{0 \leq L_h \leq 1} (rK_h + wL_h)\, \phi\, (1 - L_h, R_{-h}) \tag{8.20}$$

Using the function developed in model 2, we find

$$L_h = [1/(1 + \alpha)]\, (1 - \alpha rK_h/w) \tag{8.21}$$
$$R_h = [1/(1 + \alpha)]\, (\alpha + \alpha rK_h/w)$$

Notice that, all other things being equal, the more wealthy an economy, the more resources are used in protecting wealth from redistribution (because R_h increases with K_h). Competitive markets require that

$$r = F_K(K, L, t) = F_K(K/L, 1, t) \tag{8.22}$$
$$w = F_L(K/L, 1, t)$$

where subscripted symbols denote partial derivatives and the equalities follow from constant returns. Since we are not focusing on population growth in this model, we put $N = 1$ for convenience.

Suppose that there is no technical progress so that F is independent of t. Then, in steady state $dU_h{'}/dt = 0$ so that

$$\rho = r = F_K(K/L, 1) \tag{8.23}$$

Let $k(\rho)$ solve (8.23); $k(\rho)$ falls in ρ since F is concave. Notice that $k(\rho)$, the capital–labor ratio, is independent of redistributive activity. This is partially an artifact of the assumed absence of redistributive activity by firms. Substitute $k(\rho) = K/L$ into (8.21) to obtain

$$L_h = 1/(1 + \alpha\tau(\rho))$$
$$R_h = \alpha t(\rho)/(1 + \alpha\tau(\rho)) \tag{8.24}$$
$$\tau(\rho) \equiv 1 + \rho k(\rho)/w(\rho)$$

$$K = k(\rho)L = k(\rho)/(1 + \alpha\tau(\rho)) \tag{8.25}$$
$$X \equiv F(K,L) = LF(k(\rho),1) = F(k(\rho),1)/(1 + \alpha\tau(\rho))$$

We draw three main conclusions from behavior in the steady state:

1. Although the national capital stock and national output are smaller with redistribution ($\alpha > 0$), the fraction of redistributive waste is the same for national output and the national capital stock.
2. Economies with higher ratios of capital incomes ρK to labor income wL in the productive sector have higher propensities to redistribute.
3. All growth rates will be the same. Hence, there need not be an association between growth rates of economic variables and redistributive activity in the long run.

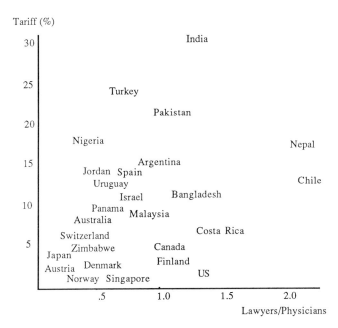

Figure A.8.1. Tariffs versus lawyers/physicians.

Appendix to Chapter 9

A.9.1   The economy (see §9.2)

The standard "two-by-two" pure trade model has a country producing two goods by two factors of production. To simplify, we assume that this economy is small, so that world prices are independent of its behavior. Production of the two goods, X and Y, is linearly homogeneous in the inputs, capital and labor:

$$X = X(K_x, L_x) \tag{9.1}$$
$$Y = Y(K_y, L_y) \tag{9.2}$$

where K_i and L_i are the factors devoted to producing good i ($= X,Y$). Profit maximization and zero economic profits in each industry dictate that the following first-order conditions hold:

$$X_k/Y_k = P^d \tag{9.3}$$
$$X_l/Y_l = P^d \tag{9.4}$$

where X_i and Y_i are partial derivatives with respect to input i and P^d is the domestic price of good Y in terms of good X (i.e., P_y/P_x). We deviate now from the standard general equilibrium trade model by suggesting that factors of production will be devoted both to economic activities (producing goods X and Y) and to political activities:

$$K = K_x + K_y + K_p \tag{9.5}$$
$$L = L_x + L_y + L_p \tag{9.6}$$

where K_p and L_p are the amounts of the economy's capital and labor that engage in the political process. As in the standard models, we take a long-run view so that full employment holds. Real income available to consumers, evaluated at world prices, equals the value of their production plus their receipts of tariff revenue on imports, expressed in terms of good X:

$$I_x = X + P^d Y + tMP^i \tag{9.7}$$

where I_x is income in terms of good X, P^i is the international price of Y in terms of good X, t is the ad valorem tariff rate, and M is imports.

The demand side of the model is standard. Consumption of the two goods (X^c and Y^c) plus resources transferred to the government (lump sum) to fund the export subsidy is assumed to satisfy the budget constraint

$$I_x = X^c + P^i Y^c + sE \tag{9.8}$$

where s is the ad valorem export subsidy on exports E of good X. The utility of identical and homothetic consumers is maximized, yielding

$$U_y/U_x = P^d \tag{9.9}$$

where U_i is the marginal utility of good i ($i = X^c$, Y^c) and P^d is the domestic relative price of Y that consumers face. If the goods markets clear, exports of X (E) and imports of Y (M) equal the difference between domestic demand and supply:

$$E = X - X^c \tag{9.10}$$
$$M = Y^c - Y \tag{9.11}$$

If domestic markets are in full equilibrium, the trade balance will equal the government budget deficit, because from (9.7), (9.8), (9.10), and (9.11),

$$E - P^i M = sE - tMP^i$$

We assume, without loss of generality, that the country is capital-abundant and conforms to the Heckscher–Ohlin theorem. Thus, the country has a comparative advantage in the export of good X, the capital-intensive good. It also conforms to the Stolper–Samuelson theorem in that increases in P^d lead to rises in the price of good Y (i.e., they raise the real wage, because good Y is the labor-intensive good).

Finally, we define the relationships between the domestic relative price of Y and the international price. This relationship is influenced by the equilibrium values of the commercial policy variables (the export subsidy on good X and the import tariff on good Y) and the probabilities of election of the two parties:

$$\begin{aligned} P^d &= (P_y/P_x)^i \, \pi/(1+s) + (P_y/P_x)^i (1+t)(1-\pi) \\ &= P^i \pi S + P^i T(1-\pi) \quad = P^i[\pi(S-T)+T] \end{aligned} \tag{9.12}$$

where

P^d = domestic price of Y in terms of X;

$(P_y/P_x)^i$ = international price of Y in terms of X;

    π = probability of election of the first (procapital) party;

    T = $(1 + t)$ one plus the ad valorem tariff rate on Y;

    S = $1/(1 + s)$ inverse of one plus the ad valorem export subsidy on X.

We have introduced T and S for notational simplicity. Because we are dealing with a small open economy, P^i is exogenous.

An important economic consideration underlies (9.12). If the economy adjusted rapidly relative to the frequency of elections, the economy would face a low relative price of Y when the first party was elected (i.e., relative prices would equal P^iS) and the economy would face a relatively high price of good Y when the second party was elected (i.e., P^iT). By writing equation (9.12) in the form above, we are implicitly assuming that the political market clears more frequently than the economic market so that the economy stays at the long-run "expected value" of the relative goods prices rather than moving to either of the two extreme realizations following each election. This assumption is a reasonable one if the entire political process is captured in this model. If we think of the probability of success of the two parties in the broader context of bureaucratic decisions, court decisions, and legislative outcomes – and if these occur frequently (e.g., monthly) – then the formalization in (9.12) is reasonable.

A.9.2   The voters (see §9.3)

We assume that neither capital nor labor holds a majority of the votes. This is an admittedly artificial assumption in a two-factor model; however, the disadvantage of the additional economic complexity of moving to a three-or-more-factor model is felt to outweigh the advantages of voter realism. We will label the probability of election of the procapital party π and the probability of election of the prolabor party $1 - \pi$. The procapital party will support policies such as export subsidies, which would raise the price of good X, the capital-intensive good. Via the Stolper–Samuelson theorem, this will increase the real income of capital. This leads to the following function defining the probability of election of the procapital party:

$$\pi = \pi(K_p, L_p, s, t) \qquad\qquad (9.13)$$
$${}^+{}^-{}^-{}^+$$

where

    π = probability of election of party 1, the party supporting an export subsidy on good X favoring capital (e.g., Republicans);

$1 - \pi$ = probability of election of party 2, the party supporting an import tariff on good Y favoring labor (e.g., Democrats);

    K_p = capital supplied to party 1 by the capital lobby;

    L_p = labor supplied to party 2 by the labor lobby;

    s = the proportional ad valorem export subsidy on good X supported by party 1;

    t = the proportional ad valorem import tariff on good Y supported by party 2.

Notice that if party 1 supports a higher export subsidy, this hurts it with voters, but if it has more capital resources at its disposal, it has a higher probability of election. Similar arguments hold for contributions of labor to party 2 and higher redistributive policies supported by party 2. To simplify, we assume that the capital lobby contributes only capital to the political process whereas the labor lobby contributes only labor. The value of this simplification is felt to outweigh the cost of more tedious calculations.

A.9.3   The lobbies (see §9.4)

In Part I, the campaign contribution specialization theorem showed that in an n-party race a lobby should give, at most, to $n - 1$ parties. Thus, in a two-party race, each lobby should contribute to one party, if at all. The same proposition holds in general equilibrium. To see this, consider the capital lobby's objective function. It wishes to maximize the expected rental income in the economy less the cost of running the lobby:

$$\max_{K_p^1,\, K_p^2} (\pi r^1 + (1 - \pi)r^2)\, K - (\pi r^1 + (1 - \pi)\, r^2)\, K_p = (\pi r^1 + (1 - \pi)r^2)(K - K_p)$$

The first-order conditions are

$$\partial \pi/\partial K_p^1\, (r^1 - r^2)(K - K_p)\ = \pi r^1 + (1 - \pi)r^2\, \partial K_p^1 \tag{A}$$
$$\partial \pi/\partial K_p^2\, (r^1 - r^2)(K - K_p)\ = \pi r^1 + (1 - \pi)r^2 \tag{B}$$

where

$r^i\ =$ real rentals if party i is elected;
$K^i_p\ =$ contributions by the capital lobby to party i;
$K_p\ = K_p^1 + K_p^2$;
$\pi\ =$ probability of election of party 1.

By the Stolper–Samuelson theorem, r^1 is greater than r^2 because party 1 raises the price of good X, the capital-intensive good, and increases in the price of good X increase the real rentals. Notice that the left-hand side of (B) is negative, because contributions by the capital lobby to party 2 lower the probability of election of party 1 $(\partial \pi/\partial K_p^2 < 0)$.

The economic reasoning underlying the specialization theorem is straightforward. As the lobby cannot influence the position chosen by the parties [i.e., in Eqs. (A) and (B), r^1 and r^2 are fixed by our assumption that the lobbies are Stackelberg followers vis-à-vis the parties], the payoff to the lobby comes only from influencing the outcome of the election. This is reflected in the partial derivatives of the probability of election. However, as the probabilities are constant-sum, anything that benefits one party hurts the other.

An important problem plaguing all lobbies is the free-rider problem, which was studied extensively by Olson (1965). The phenomenon can be modeled, albeit ad hoc, by adding an appropriability parameter α to the gross revenue rK received by the lobby. If $\alpha = 1$ the lobby possesses no free-rider problem, but if $\alpha = 0$, the free-rider problem will so dominate that the lobby will not participate in political activity.

We write the objective functions of the lobbies as follows:

Capital lobby $\max\limits_{K_p} \alpha_k rK - rK_p$ (C)

Labor lobby $\max\limits_{L_p} \alpha_l wL - wL_p$ (D)

These yield the following first-order conditions for the optimal K_p and L_p (assuming interior solutions):

$$(\partial r/\partial P^d)\,(\partial P^d/\partial K_p)(\alpha_k K - K_p) = r \qquad (9.14)$$
$$(\partial w/\partial P^d)\,(\partial P^d/\partial L_p)(\alpha_l L - L_p) = w \qquad (9.15)$$

where

α_i = appropriability of the ith lobby $(0 \le \alpha_i \le 1)$
$\alpha = 0$, lobby ineffective – serious free-rider problem
$\alpha = 1$, lobby completely effective – no free-rider problem;
r,w = real rental or wage in terms of good X (marginal factor productivity);
K_p, L_p = capital and labor contributed by the lobbies to parties 1 and 2, respectively.

Notice that we have decomposed the marginal effect of the contributions on real factor returns into two components [appearing as the first two terms in (9.14) and (9.15)]. The first term is a Stolper–Samuelson effect that captures the behavior resulting from the change in relative prices. Because r is the real return to capital expressed in terms of good X, it equals the marginal physical product of capital X_k in industry X. Similarly, w is the real wage in terms of good X. These two terms can be obtained by implicit differentiation of (9.3) and (9.4), using (9.5) and (9.6). The solutions are as follows:

$$\frac{\partial r}{\partial P^d} = \frac{\partial X_k}{\partial P^d} = Y_k + P^d\left(Y_{kk}\frac{\partial K_y}{\partial P^d} + Y_{kl}\frac{\partial L_y}{\partial P^d}\right) \qquad (E)$$

$$\frac{\partial w}{\partial P^d} = \frac{\partial X_1}{\partial P^d} = Y_1 + P^d\left(Y_{lk}\frac{\partial K_y}{\partial P^d} + Y_{ll}\frac{\partial L_y}{\partial P^d}\right) \qquad (F)$$

where

$$\frac{\partial K_y}{\partial P^d} = \frac{-Y_k(X_{ll} + P^d Y_{ll}) + (X_{kl} + P^d Y_{kl})\,Y_1}{(X_{kk} + P^d Y_{kk})(X_{ll} + P^d Y_{ll}) - (X_{kl} + P^d Y_{kl})} > 0 \qquad (G)$$

$$\frac{\partial L_y}{\partial P^d} = \frac{Y_k\,(X_{kl} + P^d Y_{kl}) - (X_{kk} + P^d Y_{kk})Y_1}{(X_{kk} + P^d Y_{kk})\,(X_{ll} + P^d Y_{ll}) - (X_{kl} + P^d Y_{kl})^2} > 0 \qquad (H)$$

We turn now to the second terms in (9.14) and (9.15). The effects of political activity by the two lobbies influence relative prices through the effects of the resources on the probabilities of election. This reflects our equilibrium concept that the lobbies internalize the behavior of the voters while accepting as given the stated position of the parties on the issues (i.e., S and T). These terms are obtained by differentiation of (9.12) with respect to K_p:

$$\partial P^d/\partial K_p = P^i (S - T) [\partial \pi/\partial K_p] < 0 \tag{I}$$
$$\partial P^d/\partial L_p = P^i (S - T) [\partial \pi/\partial T_p] < 0 \tag{J}$$

Because S is less than T, and additional units of capital raise the probability of election of the first party, the addition of resources by the capital lobby to the political process will lower the relative price of the labor-intensive good.

The economic reasoning underlying the optimal contribution levels by the two lobbies is straightforward. For the moment, abstract from the free-rider problem by assuming it away (set $\alpha_k = 1$). Assume that the rental on an additional machine allocated to the political process came at a real cost of $5. If there were one thousand machines still working in the private economy, the lobby should continue to allocate capital to lobbying so long as the marginal effect of the additional units of capital on the real return to capital exceeds $0.005. Other things being equal, lobbying will have larger marginal benefits for the lobby the larger the proportion of capital in productive activities. If the first two terms on the left-hand side of the first order of conditions are independent of lobby size, it is clear that the third term on the left-hand side decreases linearly in K_p for (9.14) and in L_p for (9.15). Finally, it is clear that lobbies will be more effective the higher the value of their appropriability parameter.

A.9.4   The political parties (see §9.5)

The strategy of the two parties is straightforward: The protectionist (first) party will choose the tariff so as to minimize π. The objectives of the two parties and the consequent first-order conditions follow:

Party 1 $\max_t \pi$ (K)

Party 2 $\min_s \pi$ (L)

$$\underset{A}{(\partial \pi/\partial K_p)}\underset{B}{(\partial K_p/\partial s)} + \underset{C}{(\partial \pi/\partial L_p)}\underset{D}{(\partial L_p/\partial s)} + \underset{E}{(\partial \pi/\partial s)} = 0 \tag{9.16}$$
$$\quad + \quad + \qquad\qquad - \quad + \qquad\qquad -$$

$$(\partial \pi/\partial L_p)(\partial L_p/\partial t) + (\partial \pi/\partial K_p)(\partial K_p/\partial t) + (\partial \pi/\partial t) = 0 \tag{9.17}$$
$$\quad - \quad + \qquad\qquad + \quad + \qquad\qquad +$$

Consider the optimum behavior of party 1 described in (9.16). Terms B and D reflect the Stackelberg-leader role of the parties versus the lobbies. Term B captures the increased resources that would flow from the capital lobby to party 1 if it increases the export subsidy. Term D captures the increased resources that would flow from the labor lobby to party 2 if the first party raised the export subsidy. Let us perform an experiment in which the first party raises its proposed export subsidy from 15% to 20%. Terms A and B capture the favorable effect this move would have on the first party's chances of election because of the increased resources it would obtain from the capital lobby. Terms C and D represent the negative effect this policy change would have, caused by increased labor resources flowing to the other party. Term E reflects the increased hostility voters would have toward party 1, emanating from the distortion that the higher export subsidy causes. We assume that voters do not possess sufficient knowledge to make sophisticated second-best calculations about the distortionary effects of the export subsidy. For example, if the tariff by party 2 were set at 20%, this could lead to the improvement of welfare as relative prices would be closer to international prices. Because second-best calculations more than tax most practicing economists, it is reasonable to expect that voters would not be so sophisticated. Thus, the negative sign of term E for party 1 assumes that any increase in a redistributive policy variable will meet with greater voter hostility. Similar considerations, with the arguments reversed, apply to the optimal decision by party 2 in its choice of the export subsidy.

We can distinguish two levels of Stackelberg leadership by the two parties. The first is a "limited-information Stackelberg equilibrium" in which the political parties have knowledge of and take into account the effect of their policy only on the resources that flow directly to them. In this case, terms C and D would equal zero in both (9.16) and (9.17). If it is difficult for parties to calculate the effect of their own policies on resource flows to the other party, this is a reasonable assumption. The other equilibrium concept is that of a "full-information Stackelberg equilibrium." In this case, terms C and D will be nonzero. Because it is a nontrivial matter to calculate the resource flows that will come directly to each party as a result of its own policy choice, the limited information approach is more reasonable and is used in this work. Even in this case, term B in both equations requires rather tedious implicit differentiation of equation (9.14) for the capital lobby and (9.15) for the labor lobby.

Note that the system is consistent with regard to the number of equations and unknowns. There are twelve endogenous economic variables (Y, X, K_x, K_y, L_x, L_y, X^c, Y^c, E, M, I_x, and P^d) and five endogenous political variables (K_p, L_p, s, t, and π). The seventeen equations determining these variables are numbered above. There are five parameters in the system: (P^i, K, L, α_k, and α_l). The variables r and w are identically equal to the marginal product of capital in the X industry and the marginal product of labor in the X industry and thus have not been counted as unknowns. The equilibrium values of K_p and L_p denote the level of lobbying present in the economy, and π is the equilibrium probability of election of party 1. Political variables s and t denote the country's export subsidy and its import tariff.

Appendix to Chapter 10

Our endogenous policy model explores whether, in equilibrium, lobbies and political parties will wish to redistribute income in exchange for resources to gain votes. If the answer to this question is "yes," then we say that the lobbies and the parties "enter the redistributive political market." The terms "procapital party" and "Republican party" are used interchangeably; the same holds for "prolabor party" and "Democratic party."

Recall that each party leads one lobby in a Stackelberg fashion, but adopts Nash behavior toward the other two major players, and each lobby adopts Nash behavior toward the other three major players. All four players internalize voter behavior and the behavior of economic actors. The procapital party leads only the capital lobby; the prolabor party leads only the labor lobby and always announces a higher domestic price in order to attract labor contributions. Renters own κ_0 units of capital and choose the level of political contributions κ in order to maximize the expected profits on their productive capital. Since they behave in a Nash fashion with respect to the other players, they solve the problem:

$$\max_{0 \leq \kappa \leq \kappa_0} (\kappa_0 - \kappa)\{\pi (\kappa,\lambda,S,T) R(PS) + (1 - \pi (\kappa,\lambda,S,T)) R(PT)\}$$

Workers own λ_0 units of labor and choose political contributions λ to maximize the expected wages earned by their productive labor; that is, they solve:

$$\max_{0 \leq \kappa \leq \kappa_0} (\lambda_0 - \lambda)\{\pi (\kappa,\lambda,S,T) W(PS) + (1 - \pi (\kappa,\lambda,S,T)) W(PT)\}$$

Let $\kappa^*(\lambda,S,T)$ and $\lambda^*(\kappa,S,T)$ be the optimal contributions by the two lobbies. We shall assume that $\kappa_S^* < 0$ and $\lambda_T^* > 0$; that is, if a party proposes a domestic price more favorable to the lobby it leads, then it will attract more resources from that lobby. Since the procapital party is a Stackelberg leader with respect to the capital lobby and adopts Nash behavior toward the other players, it maximizes its probability of victory by solving:

$$\max_{S} \pi (\kappa^*(\lambda,S,T),\lambda,S,T)$$

Similarly, the prolabor party maximizes its probability of victory by solving:

$$\max_{T} \pi (\kappa,\lambda^*(\kappa,S,T),S,T)$$

Let the optimal policies of the two parties be $S^*(\lambda,T)$ and $T^*(\kappa,S)$ respectively. While capital lobby contributions reduce the proportion of productive capital, the rental rate increases by the Stolper–Samuelson effect (because higher capital contributions to the procapital party increase the expected domestic price of good 1).

The actions of each player in the political game depend on the actions of two or three of the other players, as expressed by the reaction functions $\kappa^*(\lambda,S,T)$, $\lambda^*(\kappa,S,T)$, $S^*(\lambda,T)$ and $T^*(\kappa,S)$. An equilibrium of the game is a set of mutually consistent actions κ^e, λ^e, S^e, T^e satisfying:

$$\kappa^e = \kappa^e(\lambda^e, S^e, T^e), \qquad \lambda^e = \lambda^*(\kappa^e, S^e, T^e)$$
$$S^e = S^*(\lambda^e, T^e), \qquad T^e = T^*(\kappa^e, S^e)$$

We shall confine attention to equilibria such that $S^e \leq T^e$, that is, such that the prolabor party's policies are more favorable to labor so that it indeed attracts labor contributions. If $1 < S \leq T$, then the procapital party would gain by reducing S – both from the direct effect of this on voters and from the induced increase in contributions from the capital lobby. Similarly, if $S \leq T < 1$, then the prolabor party would gain by increasing T. Thus, in equilibrium $S^e \leq 1 \leq T^e$.

A.10.1 Leontief production and logit probabilities of election

The model above is difficult to analyze because of the generalized forms of the players' maximization problems and the complexity of the Nash and Stackelberg interactions among the four players. However, in the special case of a Leontief production technology and a logit probability of election function, it is possible to solve explicitly for the reaction functions. This permits us to analyze the conditions under which the parties will and will not sponsor redistributive trade policies.

Henceforth, suppose that production involves fixed input–output coefficients. Measure capital and labor so that one unit of good 1 requires one unit of capital and one unit of labor. Then measure good 2 so that one unit requires one unit of labor. Let A be the units of capital required to produce a unit of good 2. In standard notation, we have chosen units so that:

$$1 = a_{\lambda 1} = a_{\kappa 1} = a_{\lambda 2} \quad \text{and} \quad a_{\kappa 2} = A \tag{10.1}$$

These conventions simplify our formulas and entail no loss of generality within the Leontief model. We assume that $A < 1$ so that good 2 is indeed relatively labor-intensive. We confine our attention to equilibria in which both factors are fully employed and both goods are produced, that is, where

$$A < (\kappa_o - \kappa)/(\lambda_o - \lambda) < 1 \tag{10.2}$$

and

$$A < Q < 1 \tag{10.3}$$

If profit maximization leads to a finite demand for both factors, then, recalling that good 1 is the numeraire,

$$W + R = 1 \qquad W + AR = Q$$

Therefore, the equilibrium rental and wage rates are

$$R = (1 - Q)/(1 - A) \qquad W = (Q - A)/(1 - A) \tag{10.4}$$

Notice that $\partial R/\partial Q < 0$ and $\partial W/\partial Q > 0$, as implied by the Stolper–Samuelson theorem.

Let the odds of victory by the procapital party be

$$\Phi \equiv \pi/(1 - \pi)$$

It is easier to specify functional forms for Φ than for π directly because Φ need only be nonnegative, whereas $0 \leq \pi \leq 1$. For example, if Φ is loglinear in κ, λ, S, and T,

$$\log \Phi = a_0 + a_1 \log \kappa - a_2 \log \lambda + a_3 \log S + a_4 \log T \quad \text{for} \ \ S \leq 1, T \geq 1$$

where the elasticities $a_1, \dots, a_4$ are positive constants, then π would have the logit form, which is widely used to model dichotomous choices. The sign is positive on $\log S$ because $S < 1$.

It might appear that the above functional form would be useful for exploring the conditions under which the lobbies and parties enter the redistributive political market. Intuitively these should be related to the elasticities $a_1, \dots, a_4$ of the electoral odds with respect to political contributions and policies. However, Φ then behaves perversely for small values of κ and λ – and it is precisely the behavior of Φ for such values that is important for determining the entry of the lobbies into politics. For example, if $a_1 < 1$, then $\partial\Phi/\partial K = a_1\kappa^{a_1-1} \to \infty$ as $\kappa \to 0$; whereas if $a_1 > 1$, then $\partial\Phi/\partial\kappa \to 0$ as $\kappa \to 0$. Thus, the marginal impact of κ on Φ becomes large for small κ when $a_1 < 1$, and the reverse is true when $a_1 > 1$. This can be shown to lead to the unacceptable conclusion that if the electoral odds are inelastic (elastic) with respect to κ, then in equilibrium the capital lobby will (will not) enter the redistributive political market.

To avert such perverse results, which arise from the boundary behavior of Φ, while retaining mathematical tractability, we shall assume that all the a_i's are unity but we shift the origin of the independent variables; that is, we assume that

$$\log \Phi = \log(\kappa + K_1) - \log(\lambda + L_1) + \log(S + S_1) + \log(T + T_1) \quad \text{for } S \le 1, T \ge 1$$

where K_1, L_1, S_1, and T_1 are constants. Then the elasticity of the electoral odds with respect to κ, for example, is

$$\partial \log \Phi/\partial \log \kappa = \kappa/(\kappa + K_1).$$

Thus, a higher K_1 implies a lower value of this elasticity for all values of κ. The corresponding probability of election function is

$$\pi(\kappa,\lambda,S,T) = \left[\frac{1 + (\lambda + L_1)}{(\kappa + K_1)\,(S + S_1)\,(T + T_1)} \right]^{-1} \tag{10.5}$$

There is another reason to introduce the parameters K_1 and L_1. If $K_1 = 0$ and $L_1 = 0$, then (10.5) would imply that $\pi(0,0,S,T)$ is undefined, while for any $\kappa > 0$ we would have $\pi(\kappa,0,S,T) = 1$. This would mean that if workers make no political contributions, then an arbitrarily small contribution by the capital lobby makes victory by the prolabor party impossible – whatever the policies adopted by the two parties. The assumption that $L_1 > 0$ precludes this implausible behavior. For similar reasons, we assume that $K_1 > 0$. However, there is no corresponding need to assume that $T_1 > 0$ and $S_1 > 0$ because (10.3) ensures that S and T are always positive. To simplify the algebra, we shall assume that $T_1 = 0$ and $S_1 = 0$. This implies a probability of election function:

$$\pi(\kappa,\lambda,S,T) = 1/\{1 + (\lambda + L_1)/(\kappa + K_1)ST\}, \qquad S \le 1, T \ge 1 \tag{10.6}$$

Note that

$$0 \le \pi \le 1, \qquad \pi_\lambda < 0, \qquad \pi_{\lambda\lambda} > 0, \qquad \pi_\kappa > 0, \qquad \pi_{\kappa\kappa} < 0$$
$$\pi_S > 0, \qquad \pi_{SS} < 0, \qquad \pi_T > 0, \qquad \pi_{TT} < 0$$

(A subscript denotes partial differentiation with respect to the corresponding variable.)

In (10.6), the effect of increases in K_1 (L_1) is similar to the effect of increases in κ (λ). Henceforth, we can simplify our formulas by carrying out the analysis in terms of the "effective" capital and labor political contributions:

$$K \equiv K_1 + \lambda, \qquad L \equiv L_1 + \lambda$$

With these definitions (10.6) becomes

$$\pi = 1/(1 + L/KST) = KST/(KST + L) \quad (10.7)$$

We recast the choices of the two lobbies in terms of K and L. Let the total endowments of effective capital and labor be

$$K_o \equiv \kappa_0 + K_1, \qquad L_o \equiv \lambda_0 + L_1 \quad (10.8)$$

Then the quantities of capital and labor used in production are

$$\kappa_o - \kappa = K_o - K, \qquad \lambda_o - \lambda = L_o - L \quad (10.9)$$

By (10.4), the expected rates of factor reward are

$$R = \{\pi(1 - PS) + (1 - \pi)(1 - PT)\}/(1 - A) \quad (10.10)$$
$$W = \{\pi(PS - A) + (1 - \pi)(PT - A)\}/(1 - A) \quad (10.11)$$

The capital lobby maximizes its expected return on productive capital $(K_o - K)R$. By (10.9), (10.10), and (10.7), it solves

$$\max_{K_1 \leq K \leq K_o} \quad e(K) \equiv (K_o - K)\frac{KST(1 - PS) + L(1 - PT)}{(KST + L)(1 - A)} \quad (10.12)$$

The labor lobby maximizes its expected return on productive labor $(L_o - L)W$. By (10.9), (10.11), and (10.7), it solves:

$$\max_{L_1 \leq L \leq L_o} \quad f(L) \equiv (L_o - L)\frac{KST(PS - A) + L(PT - A)}{(KST + L)(1 - A)} \quad (10.13)$$

Notice that, in the Leontief model, the expected rates of factor reward R and W can also be interpreted as the factor rewards that would result if entrepreneurs in both industries ignored the randomness in domestic price of the importable and made production choices as if Q always assumed its expected value: $Q' = \pi PS + (1 - \pi)PT$. This interpretation is reasonable if we think of politics as a continuous process in which resources are used not simply in elections but also to influence legislative, executive, and judicial decisions. Entrepreneurs might then ignore politically induced price fluctuations and make their production decisions according to the long-run average outcome. Under this interpretation Q' should replace Q in constraint (10.3).

A.10.2 Endogenous tariffs and export subsidies

We now calculate the reaction functions of the four players. As explained above, the expressions for W, R, and π on which they are based are valid over the following subset of R^4:

$$C = \{<K,L,S,T>: K_1 \leq K \leq K_o, L_1 \leq L \leq L_o, A/P \leq S \leq 1, 1 \leq T \leq 1/P\} \quad (10.14)$$

Theorem 1: Let

$$K'(L,S,T) = (L/ST)[\{[P(T - S)(1 + K_oST/L)]/(1 - PS)\}^{1/2} - 1] \quad (10.15)$$

The optimal effective political contribution of the capital lobby is

$$K^*(L,S,T) = \max\{K_1, K'(L,S,T)\}$$

(For the proof of this and other theorems presented here, see §A.10.4.)

Theorem 2: Let

$$L'(K,S,T) = KST[\{[P(T - S)(1 + L_o/KST)]/(PT - A)\}^{1/2} - 1] \qquad (10.16)$$

The optimal effective political contribution of the labor lobby is

$$L^*(K,S,T) = \max\{L_1, L'(K,S,T)\}$$

Theorem 3: Let

$$S'(L,T) = [1 - \{(1 - PT)(1 + LP/K_oT)\}^{1/2}]/P \qquad (10.17)$$

If

$$(P - 2 + T)TK_o/(1 - PT) < L \qquad (10.18)$$

and

$$K_1 < K'(L,S'(L,T),T)S'(L,T) \qquad (10.19)$$

then the optimal policy of the procapital party is

$$S^*(L,T) = S'(L,T) < 1$$

If either (10.18) or (10.19) is violated, then its optimal policy is

$$S^*(L,T) = 1$$

Theorem 4: Define $T'(K,S)$ by

$$A/PT'(K,S) = 1\{(1 - A/PS)(1 + AKS/L_oP)\}^{1/2} \qquad (10.20)$$

If

$$[(P - 2PS + AS)L_o]/[S(PS - A)] < K \qquad (10.21)$$

and

$$L_1 < [L'(K,S,T'(K,S))]/T'(K,S) \qquad (10.22)$$

then the optimal policy of the prolabor party is

$$T^*(K,S) = T'(K,S) > 1$$

If either (10.21) or (10.22) is violated, then its optimal policy is no intervention:

$$T^*(K,S) = 1$$

In Theorems 3 and 4, hypotheses (10.19) and (10.22) are difficult to interpret because K', S', L', and T' are complex functions. We now give a simpler set of conditions determining when the parties enter the redistributive political market.

Theorem 3': (A) If

$$(P - 2 + T)K_oT/(1 - PT) < L < PK_oT^3/4(1 - PT) \qquad (10.23)$$

then, for sufficiently small values of K_1, the procapital party sets

$$S^*(L,T) = S'(L,T) < 1$$

    (B) If L does not satisfy (10.23), then, whatever the value of K_1,

$$S^*(L,T) = 1$$

Theorem 4': (A) If

$$(P - 2PS + AS)L_o/S(PS - A) < K < L_oP/S(PS - A) \qquad (10.24)$$

then for sufficiently small values of L_1, the prolabor party sets

$$T^*(K,S) = T'(K,S) > 1$$

    (B) If L does not satisfy (10.24), then, whatever the value of L_1,

$$T^*(L,T) = 1$$

Theorem 3'B shows that entry by the procapital party into the redistributive game is blocked either if L is large compared to T or if L is small compared to T. In the first case, there is no procapital policy that will attract capital contributions because, given the comparatively moderate policies of the prolabor party, the capital lobby will not attempt to offset the labor lobby's large contribution. In the second case, voters are sufficiently alienated by extreme policies of the prolabor party that the procapital party need not itself incur voter hostility by bidding from the capital lobby contributions. Theorem 4'B has similar implications for entry by the prolabor party. We now give conditions under which free trade will/will not be an equilibrium of the tariff-setting game.

Theorem 5: Free trade. Suppose that

$$K_1 \geq PL_o/(P - A) \qquad (10.25)$$
$$L_1 \leq PK_o/(4(1 - P)) \qquad (10.26)$$

Then the following is an equilibrium of the political game:

$$K = K_1, \quad L = L_1, \quad S = 1, \quad T = 1 \qquad (10.27)$$

that is, neither lobby makes political contributions, and both parties espouse free trade.

    Thus if K_1 and L_1 are sufficiently large – that is, if the elasticity of the electoral odds with respect to political contributions is sufficiently low – then free trade will be an equilibrium of the political game. In this case, the negative voter effect of any intervention outweighs the meager vote benefits of the political contributions that they attract.

Theorem 6: Redistributive intervention. Suppose that

$$K_1 < PL_o/(P - A) \qquad (10.28)$$
$$L_1 < L'(K_1, 1, T'(K_1, 1))/T'(K_1, 1) \qquad (10.29)$$

Then, in any equilibrium of the political game, at least one party espouses a distortion and at least one lobby makes political contributions.

Thus, if K_1 and L_1 are sufficiently small – that is, if the electoral odds are sufficiently elastic with respect to political contributions – then free trade will not be an equilibrium. For example, if the procapital party espouses nonintervention, then the prolabor party can increase its probability of victory by espousing a tariff.

In the more general case, where F has nonunitary elasticity with respect to S and T, Theorems 5 and 6 can be extended to show that free trade would be an equilibrium if the elasticities of F with respect to K and L are low relative to its elasticities with respect to S and T, whereas free trade would never be an equilibrium if the reverse were true.

We next compare the expected income of the two lobbies in a lobbying equilibrium with that under free trade with no lobbying. In the former case, at least one lobby has fewer units in production, but then expected rates of return of the two factors cannot both be higher than under free trade. Hence, at least one lobby will be worse off. The following result characterizes a class of situations where one factor is better off than under free trade whereas the other is worse off.

Theorem 7: In any equilibrium in which one party espouses nonintervention and the other espouses intervention, the lobby associated with the noninterventionist party will be worse off than under free trade whereas the other lobby will be better off.

We shall illustrate these equilibria shortly. A more intriguing possibility is that both factors could be worse off in a lobbying equilibrium than under free trade. We cannot give precise conditions for this paradoxical possibility because of the difficulty of solving explicitly for the equilibrium from Theorems 1–4. Instead, we enumerate the possibilities using simulations.

A.10.3   The Prisoner's Dilemma

This section simulates conditions under which both factors can end up worse off with lobbying and special-interest policies. We do this by varying over wide ranges the exogenous parameters that the economy faces. These parameters are the economy's effective capital endowment (K_o), the relative price of the labor-intensive good on world markets (P), the capital–labor ratio of good 2 relative to good 1 (A), and the parameters determining the effectiveness of capital and labor lobbying resources in influencing voters (K_1 and L_1). We are interested in discovering how many of the distorted economies are characterized by Prisoner's Dilemma outcomes. To fix the scale of the economies under consideration, we arbitrarily set the labor endowment of the economy (L_o) at 101. Theorem 7 tells us that both factors can be worse off only if both parties espouse intervention. Theorem 6 indicated that this would occur if the parameters K_1 and L_1 were small. Therefore, we set $K_1 = 1 = L_1$, that is, about 1% of L_o. (Equal values of K_1 and L_1 ensure that under free trade, each party's probability of election is .5.) We construct a grid covering the entire range of the parameter values of A, P, and K_o. We let A and P

range from 0.1 to 0.9 in steps of 0.1, subject to

$$A < P < 1$$

which is a necessary condition for nonspecialized production under free trade. For each A, we considered values of K_o such that the country's endowment ratio $(K_o - K_1)/(L_o - L_1)$ ranged from A to 1 in steps of 0.1; that is, subject to the condition that, under free trade, both goods were produced and both factors are fully employed:

$$A < (K_o - K_1)/(L_o - L_1) < 1$$

We thus consider all economies that satisfy these conditions – subject to the coarseness of the grid and the assumptions about the sensitivity of the electoral odds to K and L that are implicit in our values for K_1 and L_1. This generates 204 different possibilities, each described as a "different economy" even though two "economies" may differ only in the international price that they face. Of the 204 possibilities, 61 had equilibria in which both parties proposed intervention; that is, had $T_e > 1 > S_e$. We investigate these in some detail.

In twenty-four of the sixty-one economies with both parties sponsoring redistributive policies, both factors had lower expected incomes net of lobbying expenditures than they had under free trade. In twenty-seven economies the capital lobby was better off than under free trade, whereas in ten economies labor was better off. For reasons that will emerge, we refer to these three cases as "Prisoner's Dilemma" (PD), "capital-dominant" (CD), and "labor-dominant" (LD) economies, respectively.

In all these cases, the proposals by political parties to manipulate prices draws resources into the political struggle, but in PD economies (about 40% of the double-distortion equilibria) the opposing resources neutralize each other sufficiently that both factors are worse off: Any gains through improved factor returns are more than offset because fewer units earn this higher return. It turns out that free trade is never an equilibrium in these sixty-one economies – as we would expect from Theorem 6 because of the low values of K_1 and L_1. Thus in PD economies free trade would be Pareto superior to the double-distortion equilibrium for the two lobbies, but free trade cannot be an equilibrium. Of course, if the parties are also considered, then free trade is not Pareto superior – one party has a lower probability of election than under the double-distortion equilibrium.

The situation just described for the two lobbies resembles the famous "Prisoner's Dilemma." To complete the analogy, we considered a "metagame" involving the two lobbies, each of which chooses whether or not to commit resources to politics. The 2×2 payoff matrix is shown in Figure 10.4 in the text and is constructed as follows. If both lobbies commit resources, then their payoffs are the equilibrium incomes in the double-distortion equilibrium of Theorem 6 (denoted by e_{22} and f_{22}, respectively). If both choose to commit no resources, then their payoffs are their free trade incomes (denoted by e_{11} and f_{11}). If the capital lobby voluntarily desisted from lobbying, then the procapital party would set the export subsidy $s = 0$. We assume that the labor lobby and the prolabor party then maximize according to Theorems 2 and 4 with $K = K_1$ and $S = 1$. Let the payoffs to the two lobbies that result be e_{12} for capital and f_{12} for labor. Taking the reverse of the above situation (with only the labor lobby desisting from lobbying) yields the payoffs e_{21} and f_{21}.

An argument similar to that yielding Theorem 7 shows that $e_{21} > e_{11} > e_{12}$ and $f_{12} > f_{11} > f_{21}$; that is, each factor is better off if it is the only factor that is lobbying than it would be under free trade. Moreover, free trade is better for it than if it were the only factor not lobbying. In PD economies we have $e_{11} > e_{22}$ and $f_{11} > f_{22}$; that is, free trade is better for both factors than is both factors lobbying. Moreover, for all our PD economies we found that $e_{22} > e_{12}$ and $f_{22} > f_{21}$. To summarize, in PD economies:

$$e_{21} > e_{11} > e_{22} > e_{12} \quad \text{and} \quad f_{12} > f_{11} > f_{22} > f_{21}$$

Thus, the payoff matrix of the metagame has the form of the Prisoner's Dilemma game. The best possible situation for a factor is to lobby while the other factor does not; the next best is free trade; the third best is when both lobby; the worst is to be the only factor that does not lobby. Therefore, each factor's dominant strategy is to lobby: No matter what capital does, it pays for labor to lobby for a tariff; no matter what labor does, it pays for capital to lobby for an export subsidy. The lobbying equilibrium is a (noncooperative) equilibrium of dominant strategies in the metagame played by the two lobbies -- even though it is Pareto inferior to free trade for the lobbies. Full knowledge by a lobby of what the other lobby plans to do does not avert this outcome. The only way out would be for the lobbies to collude and jointly to refuse to contribute to politics. This possibility is examined more closely in Chapter 11.

Figure 10.4 in the text provides an example of one of the twenty-four economies whose Figure 10.1 payoffs conformed to the Prisoner's Dilemma game (it contains the data for Figure 10.1). We have normalized capital and labor income so that they equal 1 in the free trade case. Notice that in the double-distortion noncooperative equilibrium (outcome 22 in Figure 10.1), the tariff is 11.7%, the export subsidy is 39.2%, and the probability of Republican election is .19. Both capital and labor are worse off compared to free trade; only the procapital party gains. If only capital lobbies (outcome 21), labor income drops 33% below its income with free trade, whereas if only labor lobbies (outcome 12), capital income drops 74% below its free trade level.

Our simulations permit some interesting generalizations about the parameter values yielding a Prisoner's Dilemma outcome. L_o, L_1, and K_1 were the same for all economies. For a fixed value of K_o, the CD economies all had lower values for R^f/W^f, the free trade relative return to capital, than the PD economies; these, in turn, all had lower values of R^f/W^f than the LD economies. The intuition is that if a factor receives relatively low returns under free trade, then it faces relatively low opportunity costs of entering politics. This can be seen in Theorems 1 and 2 where a high P and a low A (which tend to make R^f/W^f small) tend to lead to a high K^* and a low L^*, ceteris paribus. The intrusion of a large amount of capital lobbying versus relatively little labor lobbying raises the return to capital so much that, in equilibrium, it more than compensates for the fewer units of capital in production. This creates a capital-dominant situation. The reverse applies for high values of R^f/W^f. For intermediate values, both factors face similar opportunity costs and end up neutralizing each other's political contributions. Hence, both factors are worse off than under free trade.

Next, for fixed values of P and A, our simulations revealed that all the CD economies had higher values of K_0 than all the LD economies. A higher value of K_0 means that a greater absolute amount of resources can be marshaled for the political struggle while still leaving an increased number of units to enjoy the resulting higher returns. This political mechanism, in effect, creates "increasing returns" to increases in capital endowment. The same applies for increases in L_0. In CD economies, where K_0/L_0 is relatively large, the increasing returns to capital overwhelm those to labor; the reverse holds for LD economies. We explore this case in detail in §14.6. In PD economies, with intermediate values of K_0/L_0, the increasing-returns effects for both factors are offsetting. Because both cannot be better off than under free trade, both end up worse off.

A.10.4   Proofs of the theorems (see §A.10.2)

Theorem 1: Let

$$K'(L,S,T) = (L/ST)[\{[P(T - S)(1 + K_0ST/L)]/(1 - PS)\}^{1/2} - 1] \qquad (10.15)$$

The optimal effective political contribution of the capital lobby is

$$K^*(L,S,T) = \max\{K_1, K'(L,S,T)\}$$

Proof: By (10.12), the capital lobby chooses K to maximize

$$e(K) \equiv (K_0 - K)\frac{KST(1 - PS) + L(1 - PT)}{(KST + L)(1 - A)} \qquad (10.12)$$

subject to $K_1 \leq K \leq K_0$. The turning points of the function $e(K)$ are determined by the first-order condition

$$0 = \partial \log e/\partial K = -(K_0 - K)^{-1} - ST(KST + L)^{-1} + \frac{ST(1 - PS)}{KST(1 - PS) + L(1 - PT)}$$

Elementary algebra reduces this to

$$0 = \frac{K^2 S^2 T^2}{L^2} + \frac{2KST}{L} + 1 - \frac{P(T - S)(1 + K_0 ST/L)}{(1 - PS)} \qquad (A1)$$

The roots of this quadratic equation in K are

$$K = (L/ST)[-1 \pm \{(P(T - S)(1 + K_0 ST/L))/(1 - PS)\}^{1/2}] \qquad (A2)$$

In the set **C** of feasible solutions to the game, $T \geq 1 \geq S$ and $1 \geq PS$, so both roots are real.

We now construct the graph of $e(K)$, which is a twice-differentiable function of K_0 except at the vertical asymptote $K = -L/ST$. By (A2), one turning point of $e(K)$ lies on each side of this asymptote. Moreover, $e(K)$ crosses the K axis at

$$K = K_0 \quad \text{and} \quad K = K_2 \equiv -(L/ST)(1 - PT)/(1 - PS)$$

Because $T \geq S$ and $1 \geq PT$, both these crossings occur to the right of the asymptote $K = -L/ST$. It is readily checked that $e_K(K_2) > 0$ and $e_K(K_o) < 0$. Therefore, the larger turning point K' of $e(K)$ [which is defined by (10.15)] lies between K_2 and K_o and is the maximum of $e(K)$ in this region.

It follows that if $K' > K_1$, then K' maximizes $e(K)$ subject to $K_1 \leq K \leq K_o$. (This situation arises when K_1 has the value K_1' in Figure 10.1.) If $K' \leq K_1$, then $e_K(K) < 0$ in the region $K_1 \leq K \leq K_o$, and $K^* = K_1$ maximizes $e(K)$ in this region. (This situation arises when K_1 has the value K_1'' in Figure 10.1.) ‖

Theorem 2: Let

$$L'(K,S,T) = KST[\{[P(T-S)(1 + L_o/KST)]/(PT - A)\}^{1/2} - 1] \qquad (10.16)$$

The optimal effective political contribution of the labor lobby is

$$L^*(K,S,T) = \max\{L_1, L'(K,S,T)\}$$

Proof: By (10.13), the labor lobby maximizes

$$f(L) \equiv (L_o - L)\frac{KST(PS - A) + L(PT - A)}{(KST + L)(1 - A)}$$

subject to $L_1 \leq L \leq L_o$. The turning points of the function $f(L)$ are determined by the first-order condition

$$0 = \partial \log f / \partial L = -(L_o - L)^{-1} - (KST + L)^{-1} + (PT - A)/[KST(PS - A) + L(PT - A)]$$

Elementary algebra reduces this to

$$0 = \frac{L^2}{K^2S^2T^2} + \frac{2L}{KST} + 1 - \frac{P(T-S)(1 + L_o/KST)}{(PT - A)} \qquad (A3)$$

The roots of this quadratic equation in L are

$$KST[-1 \pm \{(P(T-S)(1 + L_o/KST))/(PT - A)\}^{1/2}]$$

In the set C of feasible solutions to the game, $T \geq S$ and $PT \geq A$, so both roots are real. $L'(K,S,T)$ is the positive root. An argument like that in Theorem 1 shows that $L^*(K,S,T)$ is the maximum of $f(K)$ subject to $L_1 \leq L \leq L_o$. ‖

Theorem 3: Let

$$S'(L,T) = [1 - \{(1 - PT)(1 + LP/K_oT)\}^{1/2}]/P \qquad (10.17)$$

If

$$(P - 2 + T)TK_o/(1 - PT) < L \qquad (10.18)$$

and

$$K_1 < K'(L,S'(L,T),T)S'(L,T) \qquad (10.19)$$

then the optimal policy of the procapital party is

$$S^*(L,T) = S'(L,T) < 1$$

If either (10.18) or (10.19) is violated, then its optimal policy is

$$S^*(L,T) = 1$$

Proof: The argument just before §A.10.1 showed that the procapital party always chooses $S \le 1$ in equilibrium. We impose this as a constraint because the functional form (10.7) for $\pi(K,L,S,T)$ is valid only in this region. Since the procapital party is the Stackelberg leader with respect to the capital lobby and adopts Nash behavior toward the other players, it chooses $S \le 1$ to maximize

$$\pi(K^*(L,S,T),L,S,T) = 1/(1 + L/K^*(L,S,T)ST)$$

For given (L,T), this is equivalent to maximizing $K^*(L,S,T)S$. We first maximize $K'(L,S,T)S$ subject to $S \le 1$.

Lemma 1: If (10.18) holds, then $S'(L,T)$ maximizes $K'(L,S,T)S$ subject to $S \le 1$. If (10.18) does not hold, then the constrained maximum is at $S = 1$.

Proof: By (10.15), the maximization of $K(L,S,T)S$ for given (L,T) is equivalent to the maximization of

$$g(S) \equiv (T - S)(1 + K_o ST/L)/(1 - PS) \tag{A4}$$

The turning points of $g(S)$ are determined by the first-order condition

$$0 = \partial \log g(S)/\partial S = P/(1 - PS) - 1/(T - S) + K_o T/(L + K_o ST)$$

Elementary algebra reduces this to

$$P^2 S^2 - 2PS + PT(1 + L/K_o T) - LP/K_o T = 0$$

The roots of this quadratic equation in S are

$$S = [1 \pm \{(1 - PT)(1 + PL/K_o T)\}^{1/2}]/P \tag{A5}$$

In the set **C** of feasible solutions to the game, $1 \ge PT$, so both roots are real; that is, $g(S)$ has two turning points.

To relate these turning points to the maximum of $g(S)$ in the region of $S \le 1$, consider the graph of $g(S)$. By (A4), $g(S)$ has a vertical asymptote at $S = 1/P > 1$. To show that S' is the maximum of $g(S)$ in the region $S \le 1/P$, we note that $g_S(S) < 0$ for S just less than $1/P$, whereas $g_S(L/KT) > 0$. It follows that $g(S)$ has at least one local maximum for $S \le 1/P$. But S' is the only turning point of $g(S)$ in the region $S \le 1/P$, so S' must be the global maximum of $g(S)$ in this region.

Since $1/P \ge 1$, S' will be the global maximum of $g(S)$ subject to $S \le 1$, provided that $S'(L,T) < 1$; that is, provided that

$$(1 - P)^2 < (1 - PT)(1 + LP/K_o T)$$

Elementary algebra reduces this condition to (10.18).

Conversely, if (10.18) is violated, then $S' \ge 1$. Because $g_S(S) > 0$ for $S \le S'$, it follows that $S = 1$ maximizes $g(S)$ subject to $S \le 1$. ‖

We now return to the proof of Theorem 3. Since the capital lobby's contribution is not $K'(L,S,T)$ but $K^*(L,S,T) \equiv \max\{K_1, K'(L,S,T)\}$, further analysis is required to determine when the procapital party will propose a distortion. We first show that (10.18) and (10.19) imply that $S^*(L,T) = S'(L,T) < 1$.

By Lemma 1, if (10.18) holds, then $S'(L,T) < 1$ and S' maximizes $K'(L,S,T)S$ subject to $S \leq 1$. Therefore, for any $S \leq 1$,

$$K'(L,S',T)S' \geq K'(L,S,T)S \tag{A6}$$

Moreover (10.19) implies that, for any $S \leq 1$,

$$K'(L,S',T)S' > K_1 \geq K_1S \tag{A7}$$

(A6) and (A7) imply that, for any $S \leq 1$,

$$K^*(L,S',T)S' \geq K'(L,S',T)S' \geq \max\{K_1,K'(L,S,T)\}S = K^*(L,S,T)S$$

Therefore S' indeed maximizes $K^*(L,S,T)S$ (and hence $\pi(K^*(L,S,T),L,S,T)$) subject to $S \leq 1$. Therefore $S^* = S' < 1$.

Next, suppose that (10.19) is violated but that (10.18) holds. Then $S'(L,T) < 1$ and S' maximizes $K'(L,S,T)S$ subject to $S \leq 1$. Therefore, for any $S \leq 1$,

$$K'(L,S,T)S \leq K'(L,S',T)S' \tag{A8}$$

Since (10.19) is violated, $K'(L,S',T)S' \leq K_1$, so (A8) implies that

$$K'(L,S,T)S \leq K_1 \tag{A9}$$

Moreover,

$$K_1S \leq K_1 \tag{A10}$$

(A9) and (A10) imply that, for any $S \leq 1$,

$$K^*(L,S,T) = \max\{K_1, K'(L,S,T)\}S \leq K_1 \tag{A11}$$

But

$$K_1 \leq \max\{K_1, K'(L,1,T)\} \equiv K^*(L,1,T)$$

so (A11) implies that, for any $S \leq 1$,

$$K^*(L,S,T)S \leq K^*(L,1,T)1$$

Therefore $S^* = 1$ maximizes $K^*(L,S,T)S$ subject to $S \leq 1$.

Finally, suppose that (10.18) is violated. By Lemma 1, for any $S \leq 1$,

$$K'(L,S,T)S \leq K'(L,1,T)$$

Moreover, for any $S \leq 1$,

$$K_1S \leq K_1$$

Therefore, for any $S \leq 1$,

$$K^*(L,S,T)S = \max\{K_1,K'(L,S,T)\}S \leq \max\{K_1,K'(L,1,T)\} = K^*(L,1,T)$$

Therefore $K^*(L,S,T)S$ is maximized by $S^* = 1$. ‖

Theorem 4: Define $T'(K,S)$ by

$$A/PT'(K,S) = 1\{(1 - A/PS)(1 + AKS/L_oP)\}^{1/2} \tag{10.20}$$

If

$$[(P - 2PS + AS)L_o]/[S(PS - A)] < K \qquad (10.21)$$

and

$$L_1 < [L'(K,S,T'(K,S))]/T'(K,S) \qquad (10.22)$$

then the optimal policy of the prolabor party is

$$T^*(K,S) = T'(K,S) > 1$$

If either (10.21) or (10.22) is violated, then its optimal policy is no intervention:

$$T^*(K,S) = 1$$

Proof: Arguing as in the proof of Theorem 3, we suppose that the prolabor party chooses $T \geq 1$ to minimize

$$\pi(K,L^*(K,S,T),S,T) = 1/\{1 + L^*(K,S,T)/KS\}$$

For given K,S, this is equivalent to maximizing $L^*(K,S,T)/T$. We first determine the maximum of $L'(K,S,T)/T$ subject to $T \geq 1$.

Lemma 2: If (10.21) holds, then $T'(K,S)$ maximizes $L'(K,S,T)/T$ subject to $T \geq 1$. If (10.21) does not hold, then the constrained maximum is at $T = 1$.

Proof: By (10.16), the maximization of $L'(K,S,T)/T$ for given K,S subject to $T \geq 1$ is equivalent to the maximization of

$$(T - S)(1 + L_o/KST)/(PT - A)$$

subject to $T \geq 1$. This, in turn, is equivalent to the choice of $t \equiv 1/T \leq 1$ to maximize

$$h(t) \equiv ((1 - ST)(1 - L_o t/KS))/(P - At)$$

The turning points of $h(t)$ satisfy the first-order condition

$$0 = d \log h(t)/dt = A/(P - At) - S/(1 - St) + L_o/(KS + L_o)$$

Elementary algebra reduces this to

$$A^2 t^2/P^2 - 2tA/P + A(1 + AKS/L_o P)/PS - AKS / L_o P = 0$$

The roots of this quadratic equation in t satisfy

$$At/P = 1 \pm \{(1 - A/PS)(1 + AKS/L_o P)\}^{1/2} \qquad (A12)$$

An argument like that for Lemma 1 shows that the smaller root t' in (A12) is the maximum of $h(t)$ subject to $t \leq P/A$. Since $P/A \geq 1$, t' will be the maximum $h(t)$ subject to $t \leq 1$, provided that $t' < 1$, that is, provided that $At'/P < A/P$, or

$$At/P = 1 \pm \{(1 - A/PS)(1 + AKS/L_o P)\}^{1/2} \qquad (A12)$$

Elementary algebra reduces this to (10.21).

Conversely, if (10.21) is violated, then $t' \geq 1$. Because $h_t(t) > 0$ for $t \leq t'$, it follows that $t = 1$ maximizes $h(t)$ subject to $t \leq 1$. The conclusion of Lemma 2 now follows because $T = 1/t$ and $T' = 1/t'$. ‖

The rest of the proof of Theorem 4 is similar to that of Theorem 3. ‖

Theorem 3': (A) If

$$(P - 2 + T)K_oT/(1 - PT) < L < PK_oT^3/4(1 - PT) \qquad (10.23)$$

then, for sufficiently small values of K_1, the procapital party sets

$$S^*(L,T) = S'(L,T) < 1$$

  (B) If L does not satisfy (10.23), then, whatever the value of K_1,

$$S^*(L,T) = 1$$

Proof: (A) If the second inequality in (10.23) holds, then for $S = T/2$,

$$L < K_oPTS(T - S)/(1 - PT)$$

or

$$1 \leq P(T - S)(1 + K_oST/L)/(1 - PS)$$

By (10.15), for $S = T/2$,

$$K'(L,S,T)S > 0$$

Because $T/2 < T \leq 1/P$ and S' maximizes $K'(L,S,T)S$ subject to $S \leq 1/P$, it follows that

$$K'(L,S',T)S' > 0$$

Therefore, for sufficiently small K_1,

$$K'(L,S',T)S' > 0$$

The conclusion then follows from Theorem 3.

  (B) Suppose that the second inequality in (10.23) is violated; that is,

$$L \geq PK_oT^3/4(1 - PT) \qquad (A13)$$

Elementary calculus shows that, given any T, $T^2/4 \geq S(T - S)$ for all S. Therefore (A13) implies that

$$L \geq K_oPTS'(T - S')/(1 - PT)$$

Therefore, the argument of part A can be reversed to show that

$$K'(L,S',T) < 0$$

so for any $K_1 \geq 0$,

$$K'(L,S',T)S' < K_1$$

Therefore, by Theorem 3, $S^* = 1$.

  On the other hand, if

$$L > (P - 2 + T)K_oT/(1 - PT)$$

then Theorem 3 again implies that $S^* = 1$. ‖

Theorem 4': (A) If

$$(P - 2PS + AS)L_o/S(PS - A) < K < L_oP/S(PS - A) \qquad (10.24)$$

then for sufficiently small values of L_1, the prolabor party sets

$$T^*(K,S) = T'(K,S) > 1$$

(B) If L does not satisfy (10.24), then, whatever the value of L_1,

$$T^*(L,T) = 1$$

Proof: (A) If the second inequality in (10.24) holds, then for sufficiently large T,

$$K < L_oP(1 - S/T)/S(PS - A)$$

or:

$$KTS(PS - A) < L_oP(T - S)$$

By (10.16),

$$0 < L'(K,S,T)/T$$

Because T' maximizes $L'(K,S,T)/T$, we conclude that

$$0 < L'(K,S,T)/T'$$

By Theorem 4, if

$$L_1 < L'(K,S,T')/T'$$

and the first inequality in (10.24) holds, then the prolabor party sets

$$T^*(K,S) = T'(K,S)$$

(B) If the first inequality in (10.24) holds but the second is violated, then $T' > 1$ and

$$K \geq L_oP(1 - S/T')/S(PS - A) \qquad \text{or} \qquad KT'S(PS - A) \geq L_oP(T' - S)$$

By (10.16),

$$L'(K,S,T') \leq 0$$

Hence for any L_1,

$$L'(K,S,T') \leq 0$$

Therefore, by Theorem 4, $T^* = 1$.

On the other hand, if the first inequality in (10.24) is violated, then by Theorem 4, $T^* = 1$. ‖

Theorem 5: Free trade. Suppose that

$$K_1 \geq PL_o/(P - A) \qquad (10.25)$$
$$L_1 \leq PK_o/(4(1 - P)) \qquad (10.26)$$

Then the following is an equilibrium of the political game:

$$K = K_1, \quad L = L_1, \quad S = 1, \quad T = 1 \qquad (10.27)$$

Proof: By (10.15),

$$K'(L_1,1,1) < 0$$

so by Theorem 1,

$$K^*(L_1,1,1) = K_1 \tag{A15}$$

By (10.16),

$$L'(K_1,1,1) < 0$$

so by Theorem 2,

$$L^*(K_1,1,1) = L_1 \tag{A16}$$

If $T = 1$ and (10.26) holds, then clearly

$$L_1 \geq PT^3/4(1 - PT)$$

so by Theorem 3´,

$$S^*(L_1,1) = 1 \tag{A17}$$

If $S = 1$ and (10.27) holds, then clearly

$$K_1 \geq PL_o/S(PS - A)$$

so by Theorem 4´,

$$T^*(K_1,1) = 1 \tag{A18}$$

Equations (A15)–(A18) establish that (10.27) indeed defines an equilibrium. ‖

Theorem 6: Redistributive intervention. Suppose that

$$K_1 < PL_o/(P - A) \tag{10.28}$$
$$L_1 < L'(K_1,1,T'(K_1,1))/T'(K_1,1) \tag{10.29}$$

Then, in any equilibrium of the political game, at least one party espouses a distortion and at least one lobby makes political contributions.

Proof: Suppose that $K = K_1$ and $S = 1$; that is, the capital lobby makes no political contributions and the procapital party espouses free trade. The proof of Theorem 4´ shows that if (10.28) holds, then $L'(K_1,1,T'(K_1))/T'(K_1,1)$ is positive. Therefore, we can indeed choose L_1 satisfying (10.29). Moreover, when $K = K_1$ and $S = 1$,

$$L_1 < L'(K_1,1,T'(K_1,1))/T'(K_1,1) \tag{10.29}$$

Equations (A14) and (10.25) and Theorem 4 then imply that $T^*(K_1,1) > 1$. ‖

Theorem 7: In any equilibrium in which one party espouses nonintervention and the other espouses intervention, the lobby associated with the noninterventionist party will be worse off than under free trade whereas the other lobby will be better off.

Proof: Suppose that the procapital party espouses free trade while the prolabor party espouses a tariff. Then the expected price of good 2 exceeds the free trade price. By (10.4), the expected rate of return for labor will be higher than that under free trade, whereas the reverse will be true for capital. Hence, the capital lobby will be worse off than under free trade, whatever its level of political contributions. On the other hand, the labor lobby can exceed its free trade expected income even if it made no political contributions. Hence, if it made the optimal level of political contributions, it would certainly do better than under free trade. A similar argument applies when the prolabor party espouses free trade and the procapital party espouses a tariff. ‖

Appendix to Chapter 11

Recall that in our model of the tariff-setting game, four types of equilibria are possible:

A. positive tariff and positive export subsidy;
B. positive tariff, zero export subsidy;
C. zero tariff, positive export subsidy; and
D. zero tariff, zero export subsidy (free trade).

Table 11.1 in the text reports the incidence of equilibria in the sixty-one economies that had at least one equilibrium of type A. As expected from Theorem 6 of Chapter 10, the low values of K_1 and L_1 ensure that no economy had a type D (free trade) equilibrium. Recall that low values of K_1 and L_1 are associated with high values of the elasticity of electoral outcomes with respect to lobbying resources. Let π continue to denote the probability of procapital party victory and let e and f continue to denote the expected net income of renters and workers. We attach subscripts to indicate the type of equilibrium at which these quantities are evaluated. For all twenty-five economies with three equilibria we have the following:

$$\pi_B > \pi_A > \pi_C \tag{11.1}$$
$$e_B < e_A < e_C \tag{11.2}$$
$$f_B > f_A > e_C \tag{11.3}$$

For the economies with only two equilibria, the above inequalities held whenever they were applicable. Thus, compared to a type A (double-distortion) equilibrium, a type B (zero-subsidy) equilibrium always involved a higher probability of victory by the procapital party, a lower expected income for the capital lobby, and a higher expected income for the labor lobby. The reverse held for a type C (zero-tariff) equilibrium. The same remarks held when type B and C outcomes were compared with those under free trade with no lobbying. Using a subscript F to indicate quantities associated with the latter, we obtained the following:

$$\pi_B > \pi_F > \pi_C \tag{11.4}$$
$$e_B < e_F < e_C \tag{11.5}$$
$$f_B > f_F > e_C \tag{11.6}$$

The last two equations follow from Theorem 7 of Chapter 10.

The multiplicity of equilibria has an interesting implication for our Prisoner's Dilemma theory of tariffs. Our discussion of this was based on a metagame in which the noncooperative (outcome 22) entries of the payoff matrix were calculated from the type A equilibrium. In a Prisoner's Dilemma economy, both lobbies are worse off under this equilibrium than the cooperative (free trade) outcome with no lobbying. However, according to (11.5) and (11.6), this statement would no longer be true if the noncooperative payoffs were calculated according to a type B or a type C equilibrium.

Appendix to Chapter 12

We warn the reader that the variables are reversed in this chapter because we are considering a labor-abundant developing country. We consider the effects of technology and terms of trade changes on movements of capital between free trade (non–rent-seeking) economies and politically distorted economies (hereafter referred to as "nondistorted" vs. "distorted" economies). Consider first technology in Table A.12.1. Generally, technical changes increasing the capital output ratio for good Y (this is parameter $A < 1$) cause the factor intensities of the two goods to converge (the capital output ratio = 1.0 for good X). Low (high) values of A are associated with high (low) domestic capital returns relative to international returns. Low values of A generate higher returns to capital in distorted economies than returns in nondistorted economies. If technology moves factor intensities for goods further apart (A decreases), capital will move from nondistorted to distorted economies. Notice that if $P = 0.8$, a distorted economy would have net capital returns everywhere higher than a nondistorted economy if the capital output ratio for good Y were 0.4 (this parameter is identical worldwide); it would have mixed returns (some above, some below, depending on factor endowments) if $A = 0.5$; and its net returns would be lower than foreign (nondistorted) returns if $A = 0.6$ or higher. The simulations reported in Chapter 12 apply to the "mixed" economy cases in Table A.12.1 (wherein countries with low capital endowments lose capital whereas those with large endowments acquire more).

Now hold technology and endowments constant and increase P, the price in nondistorted (world) markets of the exportable (labor-intensive) good. It is reasonable to assume that developing countries are probably more politically distorted than advanced ones. If this is the case, *major improvements in the terms of trade of developing countries can move them from a situation with total capital flight to unending capital inflows.* This is a movement to the right in Table A.12.1 (i.e., from L's to H's). This is true despite the rent-seeking and politically created distortions. For example, at $P = 0.8$ and $A = 0.3$, the returns to capital net of lobbying costs are higher in politically distorted economies than in nondistorted ones. Conversely, *low prices for LDC exports generate a political as well as an economic curse:* Returns are lower than in nondistorted regions, and the capital stock implodes (the only exception would be LDCs so capitalized that they produced only the capital-intensive good; but this is outside the scope of the present analysis).

The analysis in the table must be read with care because the result is a subtle one. An increase in P raises the price of the labor-intensive good, and this lowers rentals in our model (the usual result). But increases in P raise the return to capital in politically distorted areas *relative* to nondistorted areas.

Table A.12.1. *Equilibrium net domestic capital returns in politically distorted economies relative to nondistorted international returns as functions of world prices P and the relative factor intensities of production A*

Value of A	0.3	0.4	0.5	0.6	0.7	0.8
0.7						L
0.6					L	L
0.5				L	L	M
0.4			L	L	L	H
0.3		L	L	L	M	H
0.2	L	L	L	M	M	H
0.1	L	L	M	L	H	H
Value of P	0.3	0.4	0.5	0.6	0.7	0.8

Note: L = domestic (distorted) returns less than international ones for wide ranges of domestic K/L endowments;

M = domestic returns mixed (lower at low K/L and higher at high K/L) relative to international returns;

H = domestic returns higher than international ones for wide ranges of domestic K/L endowments.

We use the same Leontief model as in Chapter 10, but reverse some of the variables because the economy is a developing rather than a developed economy. The probability of election of the procapital party is still p, but the capital-intensive good X is now imported while the labor-intensive good Y is exported. The procapital party sponsors a tariff t on imports of X; the prolabor party sponsors an export subsidy s on exports of good Y. As before, P^d is the domestic price of good Y in terms of good X (i.e., P_y/P_x). The domestic price is determined as follows:

$$P^d = [(P_y/P_x)^t [p/(1+t)] + (P_y/P_x)^t (1+s)(1-p)] \qquad (12.1)$$
$$\equiv P^t [p/(1+t) + (1+s)(1-p)]$$

where

P^d = domestic price of Y in terms of X

P^t = $(P_y/P_x)^t$ = international price of Y in terms of X (the terms of trade)

p = probability of election of the first (procapital) party

t = tariff rate on imports of X

s = export subsidy on Y

Because we are dealing with a small economy, the international price P^t is exogenous. We assume that the economy is labor-abundant and exports good Y and imports good X with free trade. Thus, increases in t and p both raise, ceteris paribus, the domestic price of X, the capital-intensive good, and hence raise the return to capital. By assuming that the political market clears more frequently than the economic market, the economy stays at the "expected value" of the relative goods prices.

Consider next the political outcomes. The higher a distortionary policy supported by either party, the less success it will have politically. However, the greater the level of economic resources possessed by a party, the greater will be its success. The capitalist lobby gives all of its K_p to the procapital party; and the labor lobby gives all of its L_p to the prolabor party. Hence,

$$p = p(K_p, L_p, s, t) \qquad\qquad (12.2)$$
$$ + \quad - \quad + \; -$$

where

$\quad p \;=\;$ probability of election of the procapital party 1 (the party supporting a tariff on imports of good X)

$1 - p \;=\;$ probability of election of the prolabor party 2 (the party supporting an export subsidy on good Y)

$\quad K_p \;=\;$ capital supplied to party 1 by the capital lobby

$\quad L_p \;=\;$ labor supplied to party 2 by the labor lobby

$\quad s \;=\;$ the proportional ad valorem export subsidy on labor-intensive good Y supported by party 2

$\quad t \;=\;$ the proportional ad valorem import tariff on capital-intensive good X supported by party 1

Appendix to Chapter 13

Table A.13.1 shows the data from Table 13.2 by year rather than by administration. Table A.13.2 defines the variables in our model and shows the sources for our data. Table A.13.3 reports changes in actual tariffs (DTARTOT) and the predicted change in tariffs (PDTAR) using equation 3 in Table 13.3 in the text. It also reports the percentage of the predicted change accounted for by the macro variables, inflation, and unemployment (ACTMACRO). The midyear of the administration is in the last column. Notice that the first Reagan administration had the third-highest increase in protection, based on equation 3 in Table 13.3.

Table A.13.1. *The data by year*

Year	Tariff (%)	Un-emp.	Infla-tion	Terms of trade	K/L	Real FX rate	WPI U.K.	$/U.K. £	PPI U.S.
1901	29	2.4	−1.5	114.9	4,768	93.5	19.7	4.87	26.9
1902	27.9	2.7	6.3	118.6	4,916	100.9	19.4	4.87	28.6
1903	27.9	2.6	4.9	122.5	4,886	105.8	19.4	4.87	30
1904	26.3	4.8	−3.3	122.5	4,930	100.8	19.7	4.87	29
1905	23.7	3.1	0.7	113.8	5,047	98.5	20.3	4.87	29.2
1906	24.2	0.8	3.1	113.3	5,119	94.9	21.7	4.87	30.1
1907	23.3	1.8	5.3	114.2	5,207	96.4	22.5	4.87	31.7
1908	23.9	8.5	−3.5	120.7	5,327	101.7	20.6	4.87	30.6
1909	24.8	5.2	7.5	122.6	5,431	108.3	20.8	4.87	32.9
1910	21.1	5.9	4	123.8	5,503	106.9	21.9	4.87	34.2
1911	20.3	6.2	−7.6	114.7	5,577	96.1	22.5	4.87	31.6
1912	18.6	5.2	6.3	110.5	5,734	96.2	23.9	4.87	33.6

Table A.13.1 (*cont.*)

Year	Tariff (%)	Un- emp.	Infla- tion	Terms of trade	K/L	Real FX rate	WPI U.K.	$/U.K. £	PPI U.S.
1913	17.7	4.4	0.9	108.4	5,766	97.1	23.9	4.87	33.9
1914	14.9	8	-2.4	112.5	5,787	93.6	23.9	4.93	33.1
1915	12.5	9.7	2.1	120.9	5,884	77.9	30.4	4.76	33.8
1916	9.1	4.8	23.1	126.3	5,942	75.9	38.3	4.77	41.6
1917	7	4.8	37.5	119.6	6,072	81.3	49.3	4.76	57.2
1918	5.8	1.4	11.7	102.1	6,347	82.7	54	4.77	63.9
1919	6.2	2.3	5.5	111.2	6,373	87.4	58	4.43	67.4
1920	6.4	4	11.4	110.9	6,241	96.7	70.7	3.66	75.1
1921	11.4	11.9	-36.8	114.7	6,265	94.3	43.6	3.85	47.5
1922	14.7	7.6	-1.1	104.5	6,309	95.8	36.9	4.43	47
1923	15.2	3.2	4	96	6,399	98.3	36.3	4.57	48.9
1924	14.9	5.5	-2.5	98.2	6,511	92	39.1	4.42	47.7
1925	13.2	4	5.5	91.2	6,613	93.1	37.3	4.83	50.3
1926	13.4	1.9	-3.4	96.3	6,768	97.5	34.2	4.86	48.6
1927	13.8	4.1	-4.5	90.9	6,836	97	32.8	4.86	46.4
1928	13.3	4.4	1.3	86.2	6,895	99.3	32.4	4.87	47
1929	13.5	3.2	-1.3	92.8	6,814	100.4	31.7	4.86	46.4
1930	14.8	8.7	-9.5	99.4	6,796	104	27.7	4.86	42
1931	17.8	15.9	-15.5	94	6,577	108.4	24.1	4.53	35.5
1932	19.6	23.4	-11.3	104.9	6,212	126.8	23.6	3.51	31.5
1933	19.8	24.6	1.9	107.5	5,848	107.8	23.4	4.24	32.1
1934	18.4	21.7	13.4	108.6	5,545	99.5	24.2	5.04	36.4
1935	17.5	20.1	6.9	112.5	5,315	108	24.5	4.9	38.9
1936	16.8	16.9	1	116	5,210	101.4	26	4.97	39.3
1937	15.6	14.3	6.9	117.3	5,185	95.7	29.6	4.94	42
1938	15.4	19	-9	107.8	5,030	94	27.7	4.89	38.2
1939	14.4	17.2	-1.8	107.6	4,914	99.5	28.3	4.44	37.5
1940	12.5	14.6	1.9	105.8	4,898	88.4	37.6	3.83	38.2
1941	13.6	9.9	11.3	103.8	4,963	84.1	41.8	4.03	42.5
1942	11.5	4.7	13.2	115.7	4,795	90.6	43.9	4.03	48.1
1943	11.6	1.9	4.4	116.9	4,689	92.7	44.7	4.04	50.2
1944	9.4	1.2	0.8	123.2	4,679	91.6	45.6	4.04	50.6
1945	9.3	1.6	1.8	118.9	4,824	92.2	46.2	4.03	51.5
1946	9.9	3.9	14.6	89.9	4,863	101.7	48	4.03	59
1947	7.6	3.6	25.4	84	5,203	116.6	52.5	4.03	74
1948	5.7	3.4	8	81.6	5,513	109.8	60.2	4.03	79.9
1949	5.5	5.5	-2.9	80.3	5,711	110.9	63.2	3.69	77.6
1950	6	5	1.8	80.3	5,908	130.3	72.2	2.8	79
1951	5.5	3	9.5	76.1	6,222	117.6	87.6	2.8	86.5
1952	5.3	2.7	-0.6	77.3	6,455	113.9	90.2	2.79	86

Table A.13.1 (*cont.*)

Year	Tariff (%)	Un- emp.	Infla- tion	Terms of trade	K/L	Real FX rate	WPI U.K.	$/U.K. £	PPI U.S.
1953	5.4	2.5	-1	79.5	6,638	111.9	90.2	2.81	85.1
1954	5.2	5	0.2	78.5	6,797	111.1	91.1	2.81	85.3
1955	5.6	4	0.2	81	6,941	108.9	93.8	2.79	85.5
1956	5.7	3.8	2.8	82.7	7,095	109	96	2.8	87.9
1957	5.8	4.3	3.6	86.3	7,356	109.9	99	2.79	91.1
1958	6.4	6.6	2.3	89.2	7,657	110.6	100	2.81	93.2
1959	7	5.3	-0.2	91.1	7,562	110.3	100	2.81	93
1960	7.4	5.4	0.8	90.9	7,655	109	102	2.81	93.7
1961	7.2	6.5	0	92.3	7,765	107.3	104	2.8	93.7
1962	7.5	5.4	0.3	94.1	8,006	104.2	107	2.81	94
1963	7.3	5.5	-0.3	93.8	8,137	103.3	108	2.8	93.7
1964	7.2	5	0.4	94.9	8,339	101.3	111	2.79	94.1
1965	7.7	4.4	3.3	98.1	8,675	99.1	115	2.8	95.7
1966	7.6	3.7	2.2	98.5	9,096	100	118	2.79	98.8
1967	7.5	3.7	1.6	100	9,381	101	120	2.75	100
1968	7.1	3.5	3.1	104	9,693	115.6	124	2.39	103
1969	7.1	3.4	4.8	105.3	9,940	115.3	129	2.39	107
1970	6.5	4.8	2.2	103	10,072	111	138	2.4	110
1971	6.1	5.8	3.2	98.5	10,185	104.2	149	2.44	114
1972	5.7	5.5	3.8	93.1	10,223	98.9	158	2.5	117
1973	5.2	4.8	11.8	86.2	10,393	102.5	170	2.45	128
1974	3.8	5.5	18.3	80.2	10,496	101	208	2.34	148
1975	3.9	8.3	6.6	83.4	10,460	96.4	254	2.22	163
1976	3.9	7.6	3.7	89	10,389	105.3	298	1.81	171
1977	3.7	6.9	6.9	88.6	11,004	96.8	357	1.75	182
1978	4.1	6	9.2	85.1	11,103	87.2	390	1.92	196
1979	3.5	5.8	12.8	86	11,286	78.2	438	2.12	218
1980	3.1	7	11.8	88.5	11,467	69.4	509	2.33	247
1981	3.4	7.5	7.1	96.1	11,673	79.8	558	2.02	270
1982	3.6	9.5	3.7	99.6	11,799	89	600	1.75	281
1983	3.7	9.5	0.6	102.5	11,917	98.7	634	1.52	285
1984	3.7	7.4	1.7	99.9	12,067	109.5	662	1.34	291
1985	3.8	7.1	1.8	103	12,217	132			294
1986	3.6	6.9	-2.3	104.7	12,367	103.3			290
1987	3.5	6.1	2.2	100	12,517	90.6			296
1988	3.4	5.6	4.0	100	12,667	87			308

Table A.13.2. *The variables and data sources (each observation is one four-year presidential administration)*

Variable	Definition
LTAR	the dependent variable = *t* (approximately equal to log of 1 plus the average ad valorem tariff rate = tariffs duties collected/the value of total U.S. imports)
LAGTAR	the dependent variable lagged one period
LAGLPERK	the lagged number of U.S. employees per $100,000 of real capital (in 1972 dollars) = $100,000/(K/L)
LAGTMT	lagged value of the U.S. terms of manufacturing trade = the price of U.S. manuf. exports/price of U.S. manuf. imports
INFLATE	the average inflation rate in the current administration (PPI)
UNEMP	the average unemployment rate for the current administration
LAGUNEMP	the U.S. unemployment rate lagged one period
REPUB	Republican dummy = 1 if the administration contained a Republican president
LAGREPUB	the Republican dummy lagged one administration
DREPUB	the change to a Republican administration from a Democratic administration (=1); otherwise, DREPUB = 0
LR1	= 1 if the previous obs. was a Repub. president 1900–32
LR2	= 1 if the previous obs. was a Repub. president 1933–84
MRTB	the real U.S. trade balance
NOTAX	= 1 in the period 1900–20 (no income tax period)
LAGUSUK	Lagged value of U.S. prices over U.K. prices (=U.S. PPI/(FX rate • U.K. wholesale prices); after 1973 = trade weighted dollar (real FX rate)

Variable	Years	Source (page/table number)		
U.S. export and import unit value indexes for finished manufactures (terms of trade)	1900 – 70	4, 892, 893	U226	
	1971 – 82	3		
	1983 – 4	2		
U.S. wholesale price indexes/ producer price indexes (inflation)	1900 – 47	4, 116	E13	(WPI)
	1948 – 84	1, 297		(PPI)
U.S. unemployment	1900 – 57	4, 73	D47	
	1958 – 83	1, 259		
	1984	5		
Compensation of employees as percent of national income (capital share)	1905 – 30	4, F55 141	(every 5 yrs +	
	1929 – 65	6, 14–15	interpolated)	
	1966 – 84	1, 256		
Federal government receipts	1900 – 28	4, 712	Y259	
	1929 – 84	1, 318		
Exports, Imports (free and dutiable) for trade balance and tariff revenue	1900 – 57	4, 539	U16–18	
	1958 – 70	4, 888	U208–210	
	1971 – 81	3		
U.S. civilian labor force	1900 – 46	4, 126–7		
	1947 – 84	1, 266		
Net stock of fixed nonresidential private capital (total equipment and structures)	1900 – 29	4, 256	F450 (structures) & F455 (equip) + interpolation	
	1925 – 75	7, 49	1976	
	1976 – 83	7, 54	1984	

Table A.13.2. (cont.)

Variables	Years	Source (page/table number)
U.K. wholesale prices and U.K.	1900 – 70	8
foreign exchange rate	1971 – 84	9
Antidumping cases	10	

1. Economic Report of the President, February 1985
2. Highlights of U.S. Export and Import Trade
3. Statistical Abstracts of the U.S., 1975, 1979, 1984
4. Historical Statistics of the U.S., 1976 and 1957
5. Economic Indicators, 1985
6. National Income and Product Accounts of the U.S., 1929–65
7. "Survey of Current Business" articles by John Musgrave 8/84 and 4/76
8. Lee, *Purchasing Power Parity* (NY: Marcel Dekker)
9. IMF, *International Financial Statistics*
10. B. Brown (1985)

Table A.13.3. *Actual and predicted change in tariffs, 1905–84 and rank starting with the largest increase in protection*

Rank	President	DTARTOT	PDTAR	ACTMACRO	Year
1	Harding	0.069829	0.038796	72.11	1922
2	Hoover	0.026069	0.041224	140.46	1930
3	Reagan 1		0.025886	52.90	1982
4	F. Roosevelt 1	0.014641	0.006383	–34.29	1934
5	Eisenhower 2	0.011299	0.10834	18.39	1958
6	Kennedy	0.006044	0.005007	48.02	1962
7	Johnson	0.001611	–0.003512	–476.11	1966
8	Eisenhower 1	–0.001031	0.001–94	–165.34	1954
9	Coolidge	–0.005405	–0.040125	412.59	1926
10	Carter	–0.005481	–0.000313	0.13	1978
11	Nixon	–0.010686	–0.002819	–7.21	1970
12	Ford	–0.020320	–0.028938	32.01	1974
13	Taft	–0.021114	–0.038920	–14.91	1910
14	Truman 2	–0.023847	–0.004645	–79.59	1950
15	F. Roosevelt 3	–0.026274	–0.039165	156.57	1942
16	Truman 1	–0.031113	–0.038158	35.92	1946
17	F. Roosevelt 2	–0.031269	–0.005790	2.51	1938
18	T. Roosevelt 2	–0.031556	–0.047106	–4.24	1906
19	Wilson 1	–0.065208	–0.048013	4.25	1914

DTARTOT   actual change in the tariff
PDTAR   predicted change in the tariff using equation 3 in Table 13.3
ACTMACRO   percentage of the actual change explained by macro variables (inflation and unemployment)

Appendix 1 to Chapter 14

The economic sector of the model is the neoclassical $2 \times 2 \times 2 \times 2$ model developed above. There are two goods, each produced using two factors, capital and labor. We assume that the production functions exhibit constant returns to scale and no factor intensity reversals. The numeraire is good 1, the more capital-intensive good. The country is small and faces an international price P for good 2, which is exported. However, politically motivated trade distortions can lead to a domestic price Q, which differs from P. Let W and R be the wage and rental rates. If Q does not induce specialization in production, then, by the factor price equalization theorem, the equilibrium wage and rental rates depend only on Q and are independent of factor endowments:

$$W = W(Q), \qquad R = R(Q)$$

Because good 2 is relatively labor-intensive, the Stolper–Samuelson theorem implies that $\partial W/\partial Q > 0$ and $\partial R/\partial Q < 0$.

The impact of Q on the returns to capital and labor motivates their owners to form lobbies that contribute resources to politics. For simplicity, we assume that the capital and labor lobbies make direct contributions K and L of the factor that they own to the party proposing the policy more favorable to themselves. The alternative assumption, that the lobbies contribute funds that are used by the parties to purchase resources, would complicate the model but yield similar results. We assume that there are procapital and prolabor parties, each using its policies to bid for votes and for political contributions. The procapital party's policy is to set a domestic price of P/S – for example, by a subsidy on exports of good 1, which is more capital-intensive – whereas the prolabor party's policy is to set a domestic price of PT – for example, by a tariff on imports of good 2.

We assume that the probability of victory by the procapital party is

$$\pi = \pi(K,L,S,T)$$

where

$$
\begin{aligned}
&\partial\pi/\partial K > 0 &&\partial\pi/\partial L < 0 \\
&\partial\pi/\partial S <(>) 0 &&\text{for } S >(<) 1 \\
&\partial\pi/\partial T >(<) 0 &&\text{for } T >(<) 1
\end{aligned}
$$

We shall suppose that each lobby chooses its political contributions in order to maximize the expected utility of a representative owner of the corresponding factor, while each party chooses its policy in order to maximize its probability of election. We assume that the capital lobby's choices are as if made by a representative individual who owns K_o units of capital and has an indirect utility function:

$$V_R = V_R(Q, I_R)$$

where I_R is his income. Contribution K is chosen to maximize expected utility; that is, the lobby solves

$$
\begin{aligned}
\max_{0 \leq K \leq K_o} \ &\pi(K,L,S,T)V_R\,(P/S,(K_o - K)R(P/S)) \\
&+ \{1 - \pi(K,L,S,T)\}V_R\,(PT,(K_o - K)R(PT))
\end{aligned}
$$

Note that the capital owner takes account of the impact of the election on his cost of living because Q appears independently in his indirect utility function. The representative labor owner owns L units of labor and has an indirect utility function:

$$V_W = V_W(Q, I_W)$$

where I_W is his income. Contribution L is chosen to maximize his expected utility:

$$\max_{0 \leq L \leq L_o} \pi(K,L,S,T)V_W(P/S,(L_o - L)W(P/S))$$
$$+ \{1 - \pi(K,L,S,T)\}V_W(PT,(L_o - L)W(PT))$$

Let $K^*(L,S,T)$ and $L^*(K,S,T)$ be the optimal policies of the two lobbies. We shall assume that $K_S^* > 0$ and $L_T^* > 0$; that is, if a party proposes a domestic price more favorable to the lobby that it leads, then it attracts more resources from that lobby. Because the procapital party is a Stackelberg leader with respect to the capital lobby and adopts Nash behavior toward the other players, it maximizes its probability of victory by solving

$$\max_{S \geq 1} \pi(K^*(L,S,T),L,S,T)$$

Similarly, the prolabor party maximizes its probability of victory by solving

$$\min_{T \geq 1} \pi(K,L^*(K,S,T),S,T)$$

Let the optimal policies of the two parties be $S^*(L,T)$ and $T^*(K,S)$, respectively. The action of each player in the political game depends on the actions of two or three of the other players, as expressed by the reaction functions $K^*(L,S,T)$, $L^*(K,S,T)$, $S^*(L,T)$, and $T^*(K,S)$. An equilibrium of the game is a set of mutually consistent actions (K_e,L_e,S_e,T_e) satisfying

$$\begin{aligned} K_e &= K^*(L_e,S_e,T_e), & L_e &= L^*(K_e,S_e,T_e) \\ S_e &= S^*(L_e,T_e), & T_e &= T^*(K_e,S_e) \end{aligned} \qquad (14.1)$$

A.14.1   The Cobb–Douglas model

We wish to calculate the effects of comparative static changes on the actions of the individual players and on the equilibrium of the game. In principle, this can be done by implicit differentiation of the first-order conditions determining the actions of the players. However, the first-order condition determining the Stackelberg choices of the parties (each internalizing the optimal choice of one lobby) will involve second derivatives of π, R, W, V_R, and V_W. Therefore, comparative static results would involve third derivatives. Because general equilibrium results would require inverting a 4×4 matrix involving such derivatives, there is little prospect of obtaining useful general conclusions. Even with restrictions on the forms of the utility and production functions and of the probability of election function, equilibrium would be determined by a system of four nonlinear equations in four unknowns. However, for the special case of Cobb–Douglas utility and production functions and a logit probability of election function, we have found closed-form solutions for the equilibrium actions of the four players. Because these solutions are expressed in terms of the model parameters alone, the general equilibrium effects of comparative static changes are particularly transparent. This is important for confirming the results outlined in the introduction, as the multiplicity of feedbacks among the actions of the four players makes intuitive speculation particularly treacherous.

Henceforth, we shall suppose that the production functions for goods 1 and 2 are Cobb–Douglas. With a suitable choice of units, the unit cost functions of the two industries can then also be written in the Cobb–Douglas form:

$$C_1(R,W) = R^\alpha W^{1-\alpha}, \qquad C_2(R,W) = R^\beta W^{1-\beta}$$

where α,β are constants such that $0 < \beta < \alpha < 1$. The *numeraire* is the more capital-intensive good 1. If the domestic price of good 2 is Q, then, in a nonspecialized equilibrium, the wage and rental rates are determined by the conditions for equilibrium in the two industries:

$$1 = R^\alpha W^{1-\alpha} \qquad \text{and} \qquad Q = R^\beta W^{1-\beta}$$

A routine calculation shows that the equilibrium factor prices are

$$W = Q^N \qquad \text{and} \qquad R = Q^{-M} \qquad (14.2)$$

where $N \equiv \alpha/(\alpha - \beta)$ and $M \equiv (1 - \alpha)/(\alpha - \beta)$. We shall suppose that the representative owners of capital and labor are risk neutral and have Cobb–Douglas utility functions. Hence, their indirect utility functions have the form

$$V_R(I_R,Q) = I_R Q^{-\gamma}, \qquad V_W(I_W,Q) = I_W Q^{-\delta} \qquad (14.3)$$

where V_R, I_R are the incomes of the respective factor owners and $0 \le \gamma, \delta \le 1$. By (14.2):

$$I_R = (K_o - K)Q^{-M}$$

Therefore, the utility of the capital lobby when the domestic price is Q is

$$V_R = (K_o - K)Q^{-m}$$

where $m \equiv M + \gamma$. Similarly the utility of the labor lobby is

$$V_W = (L_o - L)Q^n$$

where $n \equiv N - \delta$. Since $1 > \alpha > \beta > 0$, we have $m > 0$. Moreover, $N \equiv \alpha/(\alpha - \beta) > 1 \ge \delta$ so $n > 0$. Thus, an increase in Q harms the capital lobby and benefits the labor lobby, as implied by the Stolper–Samuelson theorem.

By (14.3), combinations of income I_R and commodity price Q such that $I_R Q^{-\gamma}$ is fixed will yield the same utility for the capital owner. Hence, Q^γ is an index of his cost of living. We can interpret $Q^{-m} = Q^{-M}/Q^\gamma$ as the "real" return to capital: the return Q^{-M} in terms of the numeraire, deflated by the cost of living index Q^γ. Similarly, Q^n is the real return to labor. Respectively, m and n are the elasticities of the real returns to capital and labor with respect to the commodity price Q. They measure the sensitivity of the lobbies to the political outcome.

In the political sector, we shall suppose that the function $\pi(K,L,S,T)$ giving the procapital party's probability of election has the logit form, which is widely used to model dichotomous choices (see, e.g., Theil 1971, pp. 628–33). Under the most general logit model, the procapital party's odds of victory would be a loglinear function of the explanatory variables:

$$\log[\pi/(1-\pi)] = e + k \log K - l \log L - s \log S + t \log T$$

where e, k, l, s, t are positive constants. To simplify the exposition, we begin by assuming that the elasticities k, l, s, t of the electoral odds with respect to K, L, S, T are all unity. (The consequences of nonunitary elasticities are examined in §A.14.4.) We also assume that $e = 0$. This ensures that $\pi = 1/2$ when $K = L$ and $S = T$, and yields the probability of election function

$$\pi(K,L,S,T) = \frac{1}{1 + LS/K} = \frac{KT}{KT + LS}$$

Thus, the capital lobby solves

$$\max_{0 \le K \le K_0} e(K) = (K_0 - K) \frac{KT(P/S)^{-m} + LS(PT)^{-m}}{KT + LS} \tag{14.4}$$

whereas the labor lobby solves

$$\max_{0 \le L \le L_0} f(L) = (L_0 - L) \frac{KT(P/S)^n + LS(PT)^n}{KT + LS} \tag{14.5}$$

The reaction functions of the four players are given by the following results.

Theorem 1: Let

$$K(L,S,T) = (LS/T)[\{(1 - (ST)^{-m})(1 + K_0T/LS)\}^{1/2} - 1] \tag{14.6}$$

The optimal policy of the capital lobby is

$$K^*(L,S,T) = \max \{0, K(L,S,T)\}$$

(Proofs for this theorem and the other theorems that follow appear in §A.14.6.)

Theorem 2: Let

$$L(K,S,T) = (KT/S)[\{(1 - (ST)^{-n})(1 + L_0S/KT)\}^{1/2} - 1] \tag{14.7}$$

The optimal policy of the labor lobby is $L^*(K,S,T) = \max \{0, L(K,S,T)\}$

Theorem 3: (A) The first-order condition determining the optimal procapital policy S^* is

$$1 + m + mSL/K_0T - (ST)^m = 0 \tag{14.8}$$

(B) If

$$m > 1 \tag{14.9}$$

or

$$m = 1 \quad \text{and} \quad L < K_0T^2 \tag{14.10}$$

then (14.8) is satisfied by a unique positive value of S that also satisfies the second-order condition. If

$$m < 1 \quad \text{and} \quad L < K_0T^2m(1-m)^{(1-m)/m} \tag{14.11}$$

then (14.8) can have two solutions, but only the one in the interval $0 < S < (K_oT^{1+m}/L)^{1/(1-m)}$ satisfies the second-order condition.

  (C) If, in addition

$$(T^m - 1 - m)TK_o/m < L \tag{14.12}$$

then the solution S to (14.8) defined in (B) is greater than 1 and is the optimal procapital policy S^*. However, if neither (14.9), (14.10), nor (14.11) holds or if (14.12) is violated, then the optimal procapital policy is free trade, that is, $S^* = 1$.

Theorem 4: The optimal prolabor policy T^* can be obtained from Theorem 3 by replacing m with n, interchanging K and L, and interchanging S and T.

For completeness, Theorems 1–4 included an analysis of the boundary conditions and the second-order conditions on the players' choices. It turns out that the latter are always satisfied in an interior solution of the game as defined below.

Definition: An interior solution to the game is an equilibrium set of policies (K_e, L_e, S_e, T_e) [as defined in (14.1)] such that $K_e > 0$, $L_e > 0$, $S_e > 1$, $T_e > 1$; that is, both lobbies allocate resources to politics and both parties espouse intervention. The set of interior solutions in our model can be characterized in terms of the solution to equation (14.13), which follows.

Lemma 1: For $m > 0$, $n > 0$ the following equation in r,

$$1 = \frac{\{1 - (1 + m)r^{-m}\}^{1/2}}{1 - r^{-m}} + \frac{\{1 - (1 + n)r^{-n}\}^{1/2}}{1 - r^{-n}} \tag{14.13}$$

has a unique solution $r_e(m,n) > 1$.
  Let

$$a(m,n) \equiv -1 + (1 - r_e^{-m}) \{1 - (1 + m)r_e^{-m}\}^{1/2} \tag{14.14}$$
$$b(m,n) \equiv -1 + (1 - r_e^{-n}) \{1 - (1 + n)r_e^{-n}\}^{1/2} \tag{14.15}$$
$$c(m,n) \equiv m/(r_e^m - m - 1) \tag{14.16}$$
$$d(m,n) \equiv n/(r_e^n - n - 1) \tag{14.17}$$

Theorem 5: Suppose that

$$1/r_e < (d/bc)K_o/L_o < r_e \tag{14.18}$$

Then the game has a unique interior equilibrium (K_e, L_e, S_e, T_e) given by

$$K_e = K_o a/c \tag{14.19}$$
$$L_e = L_o b/d \tag{14.20}$$
$$S_e = \{K_o r_e d/L_o bc\}^{1/2} \tag{14.21}$$
$$T_e = \{L_o r_e c/K_o ad\}^{1/2} \tag{14.22}$$

If (14.18) is violated, then the game has no interior equilibrium.

  Notice that

$$a = K_e T_e/L_e S_e = 1/b \tag{14.23}$$
$$r_e = S_e T_e \tag{14.24}$$

Thus, a and b are respectively the odds of victory for the procapital and the prolabor parties, while r_e is the product of the distortions that they propose. Because $r_e > 1$, condition (14.18) for an interior equilibrium will certainly be satisfied for a range of values of K_o/L_o.

The parameters of the model are the world price P, the endowments K_o, L_o, and the elasticities m and n. World price P does not influence the equilibrium political choices of the players, a result special to the Cobb–Douglas model. If production functions are Leontief, then P does affect these choices. In both cases, P affects the expected utility of the factors.

A.14.2 The effects of factor endowments

We first consider the "partial equilibrium" effects of an increase in factor endowment on the actions of each player when the actions of the other players are given.

Theorem 6: Partial equilibrium. At an interior equilibrium, an increase in K_o:

    (A) increases $K^*(L,S,T)$ and $K^*_S(L,S,T)$;
    (B) decreases $S^*(L,T)$;
    (C) does not affect $L^*(K,S,T)$ or $T^*(L,T)$ (for fixed values of the arguments of the respective functions).

Thus, an increase in K_o increases the political demand for export subsidies because more units of capital stand to benefit from them. This is manifested in the increased contributions of the capital lobby and in their increased responsiveness to a rise in the export subsidy (Theorem 6A). Surprisingly, Theorem 6B shows that the partial equilibrium response of the procapital party to this increased demand is to reduce the export subsidies supplied. The reason is that, because the increase in K_o increases not only K^*_S but also K^*, it increases not only the electoral benefits to the procapital party of raising S but also the electoral costs. In effect, the party now has more to lose from antagonizing the larger constituency that has been created by the increased capital contributions. In our model, this second effect dominates, reducing the export subsidies offered by the procapital party.

Although the increase in K has no direct effect on the actions of the remaining two players, they will respond to the new actions taken by the capital lobby and the procapital party, generating "general equilibrium" effects. The outcome is as follows:

Theorem 7: General equilibrium. The equilibrium ratio S_e/T_e of the distortions proposed by the procapital and the prolabor parties increases in proportion to the ratio K_o/L_o of the endowments of the capital and labor lobbies. $S_e(T_e)$ increases (decreases) with the square root of K_o/L_o.

Theorem 7 has the intuitively appealing interpretation that an increase in K_o, which increases the political demand for protection, will result in a greater amount being supplied. However, Theorem 6B makes it clear that this response of the political system arises only because the general equilibrium interactions among the four players reverses the partial equilibrium response of the procapital party, which, left to itself, would have reduced the supply of protection. We thus have two contrasts with the usual operation of economic markets:

1. an increased demand for protection can reduce the amount supplied for given actions by the other players, and
2. the general equilibrium response of a player to a parameter change can be the reverse of his partial equilibrium response.

The more favorable policies brought about by a relatively larger endowment need not improve the welfare of the capital lobby: This also depends on how the endowment ratio affects the proportion of resources diverted from production and the equilibrium electoral odds.

Theorem 8: In general equilibrium, changes in the endowment ratio do not affect:

(A) the proportion of resources entering politics from each lobby;
(B) the equilibrium electoral odds.

Theorem 8A arises because an increase in K_o/L_o increases the export subsidy proposed by the procapital party but reduces the tariff proposed by the prolabor party. This makes a procapital victory more beneficial to the capital lobby but a victory by the prolabor party less harmful. These effects cancel, leaving unchanged the proportion of resources devoted to politics by the capital lobby. Similar remarks apply to the labor lobby. Moreover, an increase in K_o/L_o increases the relative contributions K_e/L_e of the capital lobby, which improves the electoral odds of their party, but also makes their party's policies relatively more extreme, which reduces these odds. The upshot is that the equilibrium electoral odds are independent of endowments. Since an increase in the endowment ratio K_o/L_o induces a set of policies more favorable to capital without affecting the electoral odds or the proportion of resources entering politics, we have the following:

Theorem 9: An increase in the endowment of one factor increases that factor's expected rate of return and decreases the expected return to the other factor. This holds for returns in terms of the numeraire and for the real returns, whether calculated on the basis of the entire endowment or of only those units productively engaged.

We next compare the welfare of the two lobbies under a political equilibrium and under free trade. We have the following:

Theorem 10: Prisoner's Dilemma. If

$$\frac{K_o}{L_o} > (<) \frac{bc}{r_e d} \left(\frac{c(a + 1)}{(c - a)(a + r_e^{-m})} \right)^{2/m} \equiv F_K$$

then the capital lobby has a higher (lower) expected utility in an interior equilibrium than under free trade. If

$$\frac{K_o}{L_o} > (<) \frac{ad}{r_e c} \left(\frac{d(b+1)}{(d-b)(b+r_e^{-n})} \right)^{2/n} \equiv F_L$$

then the labor lobby has a higher (lower) expected utility in an interior equilibrium than under free trade. Moreover,

$$\frac{bc}{r_e d} < F_K, \qquad\qquad \frac{1}{F_L} < \frac{r_e bc}{d} \qquad\qquad (14.25)$$

that is, the critical values K_o, L_o defined above lie within the interval over which there is an interior equilibrium.

Protection is usually viewed as a mechanism whereby one group gains at the expense of other groups. Theorem 10 highlights an important general equilibrium qualification: The relative strength of the group must be sufficient to ensure that the improvement in its economic return more than compensates for the loss of resources in political activity. If neither lobby is overwhelmingly strong, then both groups end up worse off than under free trade. This can be seen from Theorem 10, which shows that this will be true provided that: $F_K > K_o/L_o > 1/F_L$. Such values of K_o/L_o can certainly be found if the elasticities m and n are sufficiently similar in value, because if $m = n$, then $a = b = 1$ and $c = d$, so

$$F_K = F_L = \{ \{2c/(c-1)(r_e^{m/2} + r_e^{-m/2})\}^{2/m} > 1 > 1/F_L$$

In these cases, intermediate values of the endowment ratio make both factors worse off than under free trade. This situation has the flavor of a Prisoner's Dilemma: The lobbies are drawn into politics by their maximizing choices, but the departure from free trade makes both lobbies worse off. This issue is explored more fully in §A.10.3 in the context of a metagame in which the lobbies decide whether or not to enter the political market.

A.14.3 Elasticities of factor returns with respect to commodity prices

This section considers how political outcomes are influenced by the price elasticities of the real returns to capital and labor, that is, by $m \equiv (1-\alpha)/(\alpha-\beta) + \gamma$ and $n \equiv \alpha/(\alpha-\beta) - \delta$. An increase in m and n would occur, for example, if factor intensities in the two industries drew closer together (i.e., $\alpha - \beta$ becomes smaller) so that the "magnification effect" of commodity prices on factor prices becomes larger. The "partial equilibrium" effects of an increase in m on the capital lobby and on the procapital party are given by

Theorem 11: At an interior equilibrium, an increase in m:

(A) increases $K^*(L,S,T)$ for fixed values of L,S,T; and
(B) decreases $S^*(L,T)$ for fixed S,T.

The effects of n on L^* and T^* are similar.

An increase in m constitutes an increase in the "demand for protection" because the capital lobby's returns now become more sensitive to the commodity price:

For given actions of the other players, the capital lobby will increase its political contributions. However, this increased demand for protection also increases the marginal electoral cost of supplying protection (by raising K^*). The upshot of all this analysis is that less protection will be supplied for given actions by the other players.

We consider next the general equilibrium effects of changes in the elasticities. We focus on the case described above when a and b move closer together. This increases m and n simultaneously. A simple result is available for the case where $m = n$ and both elasticities increase together. Since

$$m \equiv (1 - \alpha)/(\alpha - \beta) + \gamma \qquad \text{and} \qquad n \equiv \alpha/(\alpha - \beta) - \delta$$

this occurs, for example, when $\gamma = \delta = 0$, $\alpha = 1/2$, and β approaches α.

Theorem 12: Suppose that $m = n$.

(A) Equal increases in m and n decrease the distortions proposed by each party but increase the proportion of resources devoted to politics by each lobby.

(B) If $K_o = L_o$, then within the interval $0 < m < 2.14$ equal increases in m and n decrease each lobby's expected utility, expressed as a ratio of free trade utility. For higher values of m, this ratio is increased by equal increases in m and n.

Thus, the level of distortions sponsored by the parties can be a poor indicator of the intensity of the political struggle and of the welfare losses from the distortion. Under the parameter changes described in Theorem 12, the level of distortions can be negatively correlated with the level of resources in political activities. This is because when the lobbies are highly sensitive to commodity prices, parties need only mild policies to elicit large political contributions. Although the low distortions lead to a relatively efficient use of the resources that are productively engaged, there is simultaneously a heavy diversion of resources into unproductive activities. As Theorem 12B shows, the upshot can be that low distortions are accompanied by welfare levels that are low compared to the free trade level. Again, we need to be cautious in interpreting changes in the ratio of expected utilities. Because the free trade utility levels of the capital and labor lobbies are $K_o P^{-m}$ and $L_o P^n$, we can avoid this problem in the following special case:

Theorem 12B´: If $P = 1$, then an increase in $m = n$ does not affect the free trade utility level of either lobby. Over the interval $0 < m < 2.14$ it decreases the distortions proposed by each party but also decreases the expected utility of both lobbies.

Similar results hold when there are increases in m and n for $m \neq n$, but the results are more complicated to state and prove. We next contrast the choices of the capital lobby and their party with the choices of their opponents in terms of which lobby's real return is more sensitive to the commodity price.

Theorem 13: If $m < n$, then

(A) $K_e/K_o < L_e/L_o$
(B) $S_e/K_o < T_e/L_o$
(C) $K_e T_e/L_e S_e > 1$

As one would expect, the factor whose real return is more sensitive to the commodity price devotes proportionately more resources to political manipulation of this price in equilibrium. One might infer that its party would then need to adopt less extreme policies because it can attract more contributions for the same degree of distortion; however, general equilibrium considerations in fact dictate the reverse conclusion. In Theorem 13B, if we assume that $K_o = L_o$ (to abstract from the effect of relative factor endowments on party policies), then we see that the party leading the more price-sensitive lobby proposes the more extreme distortion. The last two considerations have opposite effects on the electoral odds: The greater resources contributed to politics by labor increase their odds of victory; however, this is countered by the negative voter effect of the more extreme policy proposed by its party. Theorem 13C shows that the latter effect dominates: In equilibrium, the odds of victory are lower for the party leading the more price-sensitive lobby.

A.14.4 Impact of the elasticities of the electoral odds with respect to policies and electoral resources

So far, our analysis has assumed that the electoral odds $\Phi = \pi/(1 - \pi)$ have unit elasticity with respect to K,L,S,T. If the elasticities of Φ with respect to T and S have constant values $s,t \neq 1$, then our results are modified as follows. In (14.13) determining r, and in the definitions (14.14)–(14.17) of a,b,c,d, replace m by m/s and n by n/s everywhere except in the exponents of r. The equilibrium solutions (14.19) and (14.20) remain valid; that is, $K_e/K_o = a/c$ and $L_e/L_o = b/d$. However, (14.21) and (14.22) become

$$S_e = \{(K_o/L_o)r_e^s \, d/bc\}^{1/(s+t)} \tag{14.26}$$
$$T_e = \{(L_o/K_o)r_e^t c/ad\}^{1/(s+t)} \tag{14.27}$$

It follows that the elasticity of S_e/T_e with respect to K_o/L_o is $2/(s+t)$. Thus, if the voters become more sensitive to the distortions proposed by either party (i.e., $s+t$ becomes higher), then the equilibrium ratio of distortions becomes less sensitive to the endowment ratio. This change has no qualitative effect on the analysis in §A.14.2 of the impact of factor endowments, or on the analysis of §A.14.3 on the impact of m and n. Moreover, an analysis like that in §A.14.3 shows that an increase in s and t will decrease the equilibrium levels of distortions and the equilibrium proportion of resources devoted to politics.

If the elasticities of Φ with respect to K and L also have constant values not equal to 1, then it becomes impossible to obtain a closed form for the reaction functions of the players, let alone for the general equilibrium solution. To obtain an idea of the consequences of nonunitary elasticities here, we suppose that the electoral odds have the form:

$$\Phi = \frac{(uK + v)T}{(wL + x)S}$$

where u,w are positive constants and v,x are constants that can have either sign. Different elasticities of Φ with respect to K and L can be modeled by different choices of u,v,w, and x. It is readily checked that the general equilibrium solutions (14.19)–

(14.23) remain valid when K_e, K_o, L_e, L_o are replaced by $uK_e + v$, $uK_o + v$, $wL_e + x$, $wL_o + x$, respectively.

The results of §A.14.3 would be modified as follows. Because S_e is now proportional to $\{(K_o + v)/(wL_o + x)\}^{1/2}$, if the electoral odds have a low (high) elasticity with respect to K, then the equilibrium export subsidy will have a low (high) elasticity with respect to the capital endowment. Next, note that the elasticity of Φ with respect to K is $1/(1 + vK/u)$. This is greater (less) than 1 if v is less (greater) than 0. Because $K_e/K_o = a/c - (1 - a/c)v/uK_o$, it follows that an increase in K_o then decreases (increases) the proportion of capital entering politics. However, the equilibrium electoral odds are not affected.

Because the expected nominal returns to productive capital are proportional to $S_e M$, the above results imply that these returns still increase with increases in the capital endowment. However, if v is positive (i.e., $K\Phi_K/\Phi < 1$) and M is sufficiently small, then this effect could be reversed by the increasing proportion of capital absorbed into politics. In these circumstances, an increase in K_o could decrease the expected return to capital, when account is taken of the units absorbed into politics. In effect, the diminishing returns to capital in political activity induce diminishing returns overall. Similar remarks apply for the expected real returns.

A.14.5   The government's budget constraint

In the above model of political activity, the lobbies do not take account of the revenue that is generated or absorbed by government intervention. If allocated to factors in proportion to their income, the revenue generated by a tariff would benefit both lobbies, whereas the revenue requirements of an export subsidy would harm both lobbies. We shall not attempt to calculate how these considerations would affect the behavior of the players: They would merely add another layer of complexity to the mathematics without affecting our conclusions qualitatively. A more important issue is whether changes in the government's revenue are the driving force behind the changes in factor returns and welfare in our comparative static results. The following result shows that this is not the case for the results in §A.14.2 on factor endowments.

Theorem 14: For any values of α, β, γ, δ such that

$$\frac{r_e^{(1-\beta)/(\alpha-\beta)} - r_e^{-\beta/(\alpha-\beta)}}{r_e - 1} < \frac{2 + 1/(\alpha - \beta)}{\alpha} \tag{14.28}$$

there is a range of world prices P such that the government's budget deficit, averaged over electoral outcomes, is zero for two different values of the endowment ratio K_o/L_o, both of which are consistent with interior equilibria. This condition will always be satisfied for β sufficiently close to 0 and α sufficiently close to 1.

No changes in government revenue, averaged over electoral outcomes, would be required as a result of changes in the endowment ratio between the two values identified in Theorem 14 or in a move to free trade when the endowment ratio is one of those identified in the theorem. Thus, our results in §A.14.2 on the welfare effects of such comparative static changes are indeed generated by the changes themselves and not by variations in the revenue that the government is obtaining from unspecified third parties. A similar analysis is possible for the results in §A.14.3 on the elasticities of factor returns on commodity prices.

A.14.6   Proofs to the theorems

This appendix contains the proofs of the theorems in §§A.14.1–A.14.5.

Theorem 1: Let

$$K(L,S,T) = (LS/T)[\{(1 - (ST)^{-m})(1 + K_oT/LS)\}^{1/2} - 1] \tag{14.6}$$

The optimal policy of the capital lobby is

$$K^*(L,S,T) = \max\{0,K(L,S,T)\}$$

Proof: Differentiating (14.4), the turning points of $e(K)$ satisfy

$$0 = -\frac{\partial \log e}{\partial K} = \frac{1}{K_o - K} + \frac{T}{KT + LS} - \frac{T(P/S)^{-m}}{KT(P/S)^{-m} + LS(PT)^{-m}}$$

Elementary algebra deduces this to

$$0 = (KT/LS)^2 + 2KT/LS + 1 - (1 - (ST)^{-m})(1 + K_oT/LS)$$

The roots of this quadratic equation in K are

$$(LS/T)[-1 + \{(1 - (ST)^{-m})(1 + K_oT/LS)\}^{1/2}]$$

Because $e(K) \to -\infty$ as $K \to \infty$, the larger root is the maximum of $e(K)$. ‖

The proof of Theorem 2 is similar to that of Theorem 1.

Theorem 3: (A) The first-order condition determining the optimal procapital policy S^* is

$$1 + m + mSL/K_oT - (ST)^m = 0 \tag{14.8}$$

(B) If

$$m > 1 \tag{14.9}$$

or

$$m = 1 \quad \text{and} \quad L < K_oT^2 \tag{14.10}$$

then (14.8) is satisfied by a unique positive value of S that also satisfies the second-order condition. If

$$m < 1 \quad \text{and} \quad L < K_oT^2m(1 - m)^{(1-m)/m} \tag{14.11}$$

then (14.8) can have two solutions, but only the one in the interval $0 < S < (K_oT^{1+m}/L)^{1/(1-m)}$ satisfies the second-order condition.

(C) If, in addition

$$(T^m - 1 - m)TK_o/m < L \qquad\qquad (14.12)$$

then the solution S to (14.8) defined in (B) is greater than 1 and is the optimal procapital policy S^*. However, if neither (14.9), (14.10), nor (14.11) holds or if (14.12) is violated, then the optimal procapital policy is free trade, that is, $S^* = 1$.

Proof: The procapital party chooses S so as to maximize its electoral odds $K^*(L,S,T)T/LS$. We first consider the maximization of $K(L,S,T)/S$. By Theorem 1, this is equivalent to maximizing

$$g(S) = (1 - (ST)^{-m})(1 + K_oT/LS)$$

Differentiating

$$\begin{aligned}dg/dS \ &= mS^{-m-1}T^{-m}(1 + K_oT/LS) - (K_oT/LS^2)(1 - (ST)^{-m}) \qquad (A1)\\ &= yf\end{aligned}$$

where

$$\begin{aligned}y(S) &\equiv 1 + m + mLS/KT - (ST)^m \qquad\qquad (A2)\\ f &\equiv (K_oT/LS^2)(ST)^{-m}\end{aligned}$$

Thus, the first-order condition for the maximization of $K(L,S,T)/S$ is $y = 0$, that is, (14.8).

We next check when $y(S) = 0$ has a positive solution. Note that $y(0) = 1 + m > 0$. If $m > 1$, then as $S \to \infty$, $y \to -\infty$ so $y(S) = 0$ certainly has a solution. For the other cases note that

$$dy/dS = mL/K_oT - mS^{m-1}T^m \qquad\qquad (A3)$$

If $m = 1$ and (14.10) holds (i.e., $L < K_oT^2$), then y has a constant negative slope, so $y(S) = 0$ again has a solution. If $m < 1$, then

$$dy/dS = (1 - m)mS^{m-1}T^m > 0$$

so the (positive) solution to (A3) is the unique minimum of y. This solution is

$$S' \equiv (K_oT^{1+m}/L)^{1/1-m} \qquad\qquad (A4)$$

so the minimum value of y is

$$\begin{aligned}y_{min} = \ &1 + m + m(L/K_o)^{1+1/(m-1)}T^{(1+m)/(1-m)-1} - (L/K_o)^{m/(m-1)}T^{m\{(1+m)/(1-m)+1\}}\\ = \ &1 + m + (m-1)(K_oT^2/L)^{m/(1-m)}\end{aligned}$$

Thus, $y_{min} < 0$ provided that

$$(1 + m)/(1 - m) < (K_oT^2/L)^{m/(1-m)}$$

or

$$L < K_oT^2\{(1 - m)/(1 + m)\}^{1/m-1}$$

But for all positive m

$$m < (1 + 1/m)^{1/m-1}$$

so if $m < 1$ and (14.11) holds, then $y_{min} < 0$ and $y(S) = 0$ has at least one solution.

Next, we consider the second-order condition for the choice of S. By (A1),

$$d^2g/dS^2 = y \, df/dS + f \, dy/dS$$

At a turning point of g (where $y = 0$), this has the same sign as dy/dS or as

$$S \, dy/dS - y = (ST)^m(1 - m) - (1 + m)$$

by (A3) and (A2). If $m \geq 1$, then this is negative, so any turning point of g is a maximum. For the case $m < 1$, recall that S' is the unique turning point of y and yields a negative minimum value of y. Hence, to the left of S' there is a unique solution S to $y(S) = 0$ and $dy(S)/dS < 0$, so that the second-order condition is satisfied at S. Moreover, for any $S > S'$, $dy/dS > 0$, so any solution to $y(S) = 0$ in this region would violate the second-order condition.

The S defined above will be a maximum of $K^*(L,S,T)/S$ provided that $K(L,S,T) > 0$. Because S maximizes $K(L,S,T)/S$, this will be true provided that $K(L,S,T) > 0$ for some S. By (14.6) $K(L,S,T) > 0$ provided that

$$(1 - (ST)^{-m})(1 + K_oT/LS) > 1$$

or

$$L < K_oT(S^{m-1}T^m - S^{-1}) \tag{A5}$$

If $m > 1$, then (A5) will hold for sufficiently large S. If $m = 1$ and (14.10) holds, then again (A5) will hold for sufficiently large S. If $m < 1$, then elementary calculus shows that the maximum value of $S^{m-1}T^m - S^{-1}$ is $Tm(1 - m)^{1/m-1}$, so (A5) will be satisfied for some S provided that (14.11) holds. Thus, we have confirmed that S maximizes $K^*(L,S,T)/S$.

The above reasoning also shows that if neither (14.9), (14.10), nor (14.11) holds, then $K(L,S,T) < 0$ for all S, so the optimal policy is to set $S^* = 1$. This will also be true if $S < 1$, that is, if $dy(1)/dS < 0$ [i.e., if (14.12) is violated]. However, if (14.12) holds, then $dy(1)/dS > 1$, so $S > 1$ and the optimal policy is to set $S^* = S$. ‖

The proof of Theorem 4 is similar to that of Theorem 3.

Lemma 1: For $m > 0$ and $n > 0$, the following equation in r

$$1 = \frac{\{1 - (1 + m)r^{-m}\}^{1/2}}{1 - r^{-m}} + \frac{\{1 - (1 + n)r^{-n}\}^{1/2}}{1 - r^{-n}} = G(r) \tag{14.13}$$

has a unique solution $r_e(m,n) > 1$.

Proof: If $m = n$, then the above lemma follows immediately if we regard (14.13) as a quadratic equation in r^{-m}. Next we suppose, without loss of generality, that $n > m$. We show that

$$1 > G((1 + m)^{1/m}) = \frac{\{1 - (n + 1)(1 + m)^{-n/m}\}^{1/2}}{1 - (1 + m)^{-n/m}} \tag{A6}$$

The expression inside the square root is well defined because $n > m$ implies that

$$(1 + n)^{1/n} < (1 + m)^{1/m}$$

(A6) is equivalent to

$$1 - (n + 1)(1 + m)^{-n/m} < 1 - 2(1 + m)^{-n/m} + (1 + m)^{-2n/m}$$

or

$$1 - n < (1 + m)^{-n/m} \tag{A7}$$

This certainly holds if $n \geq 1$. If $n < 1$, then (A7) is equivalent to

$$(1 - n)^{-1/n} > (1 + m)^{1/m}$$

This is always true for $n > m$, as can be seen from the binomial series expansions of the two sides of the inequality.

We have shown that $G(r) < 1$ when $r = (1 + m)^{1/m}$. Moreover, as $r \to \infty$, $G(r) \to 2$. Therefore Rolle's theorem implies that equation (14.13) has a solution in the interval $(1 + m)^{1/m} < r < \infty$. To establish the uniqueness of the solution note that

$$\frac{d}{dr}\left[\log \frac{\{1 - (m + 1)r^{-m}\}^{1/2}}{1 - r^{-m}}\right] = \frac{m(m + 1)r^{-m-1}}{2\{1 - (m + 1)r^{-m}\}} - \frac{mr^{-m-1}}{1 - r^{-m}}$$

This expression has the same sign as

$$(m + 1)r^{-m} + m - 1 \tag{A8}$$

Any solution r_e to (14.13) must satisfy

$$\frac{1 - (m + 1)r^{-m}}{(1 - r^{-m})^2} \leq 1$$

or

$$1 - (m + 1)r^{-m} \leq 1 - 2r^{-m} + r^{-2m}$$

or

$$0 < r^{-m} + m - 1$$

Thus at any solution to (14.13), (A8) must be positive; that is, at any solution

$$\frac{d}{dr}\left[\frac{\{1 - (m + 1)r^{-m}\}^{1/2}}{1 - r^{-m}}\right] > 0$$

Hence the solution is unique.

The above argument remains valid when m is replaced by n. It follows that at any solution to (14.13) $dG/dr > 0$. Hence the solution is unique.

Theorem 5: Suppose that

$$1/r_e < (d/bc)K_0/L_0 < r_e \tag{14.18}$$

Then the game has a unique interior equilibrium (K_e, L_e, S_e, T_e) given by

$$K_e = K_0 a/c \tag{14.19}$$
$$L_e = L_0 b/d \tag{14.20}$$
$$S_e = \{K_0 r_e d/L_0 bc\}^{1/2} \tag{14.21}$$
$$T_e = \{L_0 r_e c/K_0 ad\}^{1/2} \tag{14.22}$$

If (14.18) is violated, then the game has no interior equilibrium.

Proof: By Theorems 1–4 any interior solution (K,L,S,T) to the game satisfies the first-order conditions:

$$KT/LS = -1 + \{(1 - (ST)^{-m})(1 + K_oT/LS)\}^{1/2} \tag{A10}$$
$$LS/KT = -1 + \{(1 - (ST)^{-n})(1 + L_oS/KT)\}^{1/2} \tag{A11}$$
$$0 = 1 + m - (ST)^m + mLS/K_oT \tag{A12}$$
$$0 = 1 + n - (ST)^n + nKT/L_oS \tag{A13}$$

By (A12),

$$K_oT/LS = m/\{(ST)^m - m - 1\} \tag{A14}$$

By (A13),

$$L_oS/KT = n/\{(ST)^n - n - 1\} \tag{A15}$$

Substituting (A14) into (A10), we have

$$KT/LS = -1 + \{(1 - r^{-m})(1 + m/(r^m - m - 1))\}^{1/2}$$

where $r = ST$. This simplifies to

$$KT/LS = -1 + (1 - r^{-m})/\{1 - (m + 1)r^{-m}\}^{1/2} \tag{A16}$$

Similarly, substituting (A15) into (A11), we have

$$LS/KT = -1 + (1 - r^{-n})/\{1 - (n + 1)r^{-n}\}^{1/2} \tag{A17}$$

Multiplying (A16) and (A17) yields

$$1 = 1 - \frac{1 - r^{-m}}{\{1 - (m + 1)r^{-m}\}^{1/2}} - \frac{(1 - r^{-n})}{\{1 - (n + 1)r^{-n}\}^{1/2}}$$

$$+ \frac{(1 - r^{-m})(1 - r^{-n})}{\{1 - (n + 1)r^{-n}\}^{1/2}\{1 - (m + 1)r^{-m}\}^{1/2}}$$

This simplifies to

$$1 = \frac{\{1 - (m + 1)r^{-m}\}^{1/2}}{1 - r^{-m}} + \frac{\{1 - (n + 1)r^{-n}\}^{1/2}}{1 - r^{-n}}$$

that is, to (14.13). Lemma 1 established that this has a unique solution $r_e(m,n) > 1$.

Substituting this value of r_e into (A10), (A11), (A14), and (A15) and recalling definitions (14.14)–(14.17):

$$K_eT_e/L_eS = a(m,n) \tag{A18}$$
$$L_eS_e/K_eT = b(m,n) \tag{A19}$$
$$K_oT_e/L_eS = c(m,n) \tag{A20}$$
$$L_oS_e/K_eT = d(m,n) \tag{A21}$$

By (A18) and (A20),

$$K_e/K_o = a/c, \quad \text{that is, (14.19) holds}$$

By (A19) and (A21),

$$L_e/L_o = b/d, \quad \text{that is, (14.20) holds}$$

By (A20),

$$T_e/S_e = cL_e/K_o = c(L_e/L_o)(L_o/K_o) \tag{A22}$$

But

$$S_e T_e = r_e \tag{A23}$$

(A23), (A22), and (14.20) imply that $T_e{}^2 = (L_o/K_o)r_e cb/d$.
    By (14.23),

$$T_e = \{L_o/K_o r_e c/ad\}^{1/2}$$

Thus, (14.22) holds. Similarly, (14.21) holds.
    If (14.18) holds, then by (14.21) and (14.22),

$$T_e > 1 \quad \text{and} \quad S_e > 1$$

Moreover, $K_e > 0$ and $L_e > 0$, so we indeed have defined an interior equilibrium. ‖

Theorem 6: Partial equilibrium. At an interior equilibrium, an increase in K_o:

    (A) increases $K^*(L,S,T)$ and $K^*_S(L,S,T)$;
    (B) decreases $S^*(L,T)$;
    (C) does not affect $L^*(K,S,T)$ or $T^*(L,T)$ (for fixed values of the arguments of
the respective functions).

Proof: (A) Differentiating (14.6),

$$dK/dK_o = (1 - (ST)^{-m})^{1/2}/2(1 + K_o T/LS)^{1/2}$$

At an interior equilibrium, this is positive and increases as S increases. This proves
(A).
    (B) The procapital party maximizes KT/LS. By (14.16) this is equivalent to
maximizing

$$g(S) \equiv (1 - (ST)^{-m})(1 + K_o T/LS).$$

But

$$d\{dg/dS\}/dK_o = \{(1 + m)(ST)^{-m} - 1\}T/LS^2$$

At an interior equilibrium, $ST = r$ satisfies (14.13), so this is negative. Because S is
determined by the first-order condition $dg/dS = 0$, it follows that S is decreased by
an increase in K_o. This proves (B).
    (C) Because K does not appear in the first-order conditions determining L and
T, (C) follows immediately. ‖

Theorems 7 and 8 follow immediately from (14.21) and (14.22).

Theorem 9: An increase in the endowment of one factor increases that factor's
expected rate of return and decreases the expected return to the other factor. This
holds for returns in terms of the numeraire and for the real returns, whether cal-

culated on the basis of the entire endowment or of only those units productively engaged.

Proof: The expected return on each unit of capital in production in terms of the numeraire is

$$\frac{K_eS_e(P/S_e)^{-M}+L_eT_e(PT_e)^{-M}}{K_eS_e + L_eT_e} = P^{-M}S_e^M \frac{K_eS_e/L_eT_e + (S_eT_e)^{-M}}{K_eS_e/L_eT_e + 1}$$

$$= P^{-M}S_e^M \frac{a + r_e^{-M}}{a + 1}$$

Recall that a and r_e are independent of K_o/L_o. By Theorem 5, an increase in K_o/L_o increases S_e so it increases the expected return on each unit of capital in production in terms of the numeraire. In this argument, if M is replaced by m, then we would reach the same conclusion regarding the expected real return on capital.

The equilibrium ratio of productive to total capital is

$$(K_o - K_e)/K_o = 1 - K_e/K_o \tag{A25}$$

By Theorem 5, this is independent of K_o/L_o. The expected return on total endowment in terms of the numeraire is the product of (A24) and (A25). Clearly this also increases with K_o/L_o. A similar argument holds for the real return on total endowment. The analysis of the rate of return on labor is similar. ‖

Theorem 10: Prisoner's Dilemma. If

$$\frac{K_o}{L_o} > (<) \frac{bc}{r_ed} \left(\frac{c(a + 1)}{(c - a)(a + r_e^{-m})}\right)^{2/m} \equiv F_K$$

then the capital lobby has a higher (lower) expected utility in an interior equilibrium than under free trade. If

$$\frac{K_o}{L_o} > (<) \frac{ad}{r_ec} \left(\frac{d(b + 1)}{(d - b)(b + r_e^{-n})}\right)^{2/n} \equiv F_L$$

then the labor lobby has a higher (lower) expected utility in an interior equilibrium than under free trade. Moreover,

$$\frac{bc}{r_ed} < F_K, \qquad \frac{1}{F_L} < \frac{r_ebc}{d} \tag{14.25}$$

that is, the critical values K_o, L_o defined above lie within the interval over which there is an interior equilibrium.

Proof: The expected utility of the capital lobby in equilibrium is

$$(K_o - K_e)\frac{K_eT_e(P/S_e)^{-m} + L_eT_e(PT_e)^{-m}}{K_eT_e + L_eS_e}$$

whereas its utility under free trade is

$$K_oP^{-m}$$

Thus, the ratio of these utility levels is

$$S_e^m \left(1 - \frac{K_e}{K_o}\right) \frac{(K_e T_e/L_e S_e) + (S_e T_e)^{-m}}{K_e T_e/L_e S_e + 1}$$

An argument like that in Theorem 9 shows that this equals

$$\left(\frac{K_o}{L_o}\right)^{m/2} \left(\frac{r_e d}{bc}\right)^{m/2} \left(1 - \frac{a}{c}\right) \left\{\frac{a + r_e^{-m}}{a + 1}\right\}$$

Our conclusion for the capital lobby follows immediately. A similar argument holds for the labor lobby.

To prove (14.25), note that the following propositions are equivalent:

$$bc/r_e d < F_K < r_e bc/d$$

$$1 < \left\{\frac{c(a + 1)}{(c - a)(a + r_e^{-m})}\right\}^{2/m} < r_e^2$$

Because $r_e > 1$, the left-hand inequality clearly holds. The right-hand inequality is equivalent to the following:

$$c(a + 1)/(c - a)(a + r_e^{-m}) \; < r_e^m$$
$$c(a + 1)/(c - a) \; < a r_e^m + 1$$
$$\{c(a + 1) - (c - a)\}/(c - a) \; < a r_e^m$$
$$a(1 + c)/(c - a) \; < a r_e^m$$
$$a \; < c - (1 + c) r_e^{-m}$$
$$1 + a \; < (1 + c)(1 - r_e^{-m})$$

Substituting from (14.14) and (14.16), this is equivalent to

$$\frac{1 - r_e^{-m}}{1 - (m + 1) r_e^{-m}} < \frac{(1 - r_e^{-m})^2}{1 - (m + 1) r_e^{-m}}$$

Because r_e is the solution to (14.13), the last inequality always holds. The proof for F_L is similar. ‖

Theorem 11: At an interior equilibrium, an increase in m:

    (A) increases $K^*(L,S,T)$ for fixed values of L,S,T; and
    (B) decreases $S^*(L,T)$ for fixed S,T.
The effects of n on L^* and T^* are similar.

Proof: (A) follows immediately from Theorem 1. By (14.6), the procapital party seeks to maximize KT/LS or:

$$g(S) \equiv (1 - (ST)^{-m})(1 + K_o T/LS)$$

Conclusion (B) will hold provided that an increase in m decreases dg/dS. A direct calculation shows that this will be true provided that

$$1/\log ST < m + 1/\{1 + K_o T/LS\}$$

At an interior equilibrium, (A14) holds, so this condition is equivalent to each of the following:

$$1/\log r < m + m/(r^m - 1)$$
$$\log r^m < r^m - 1$$
$$r^m < \exp(r^m - 1)$$

But this last inequality always holds, as can be seen by expanding the Taylor series for the right-hand side.

Theorem 12: Suppose that $m = n$.

(A) Equal increases in m and n decrease the distortions proposed by each party but increase the proportion of resources devoted to politics by each lobby.

(B) If $K_o = L_o$, then within the interval $0 < m < 2.14$ equal increases in m and n decrease each lobby's expected utility, expressed as a ratio of free trade utility. For higher values of m, this ratio is increased by equal increases in m and n.

Proof: By (14.14)–(14.17), if $m = n$, then

$$a = b = 1, \qquad c = d$$

so by (14.19) and (14.20),

$$K_e/K_o = L_e/L_o \tag{A26}$$

By (14.21) and (14.22), equal increases in m and n will decrease the distortions provided that $dr_e(m,m)/dm < 0$. Moreover, (14.6) can be written as

$$(1 + KT/LS)^2 = (1 - r_e^{-m})(1 + K_o/K)KT/LS \tag{A27}$$

Since $1 = a = KT/LS$ this reduces to

$$4 = (1 - r_e^{-m})(1 + K_o/K)$$

By (A26), equal increases in m and n will increase K_e/K_o and L_e/L_o provided that $dr_e^m(m,m)/dm > 0$.

When $m = n$, equation (14.13) defining r_e reduces to

$$1 - r_e^{-m}/\{1 - (m + 1)r_e^{-m}\}^{1/2} = 2$$

This simplifies to

$$3r_e^{2m} - 2(1 + m)r_e^m - 1 = 0 \tag{A28}$$

The variable r_e is given by the positive solution to this quadratic equation; that is,

$$r_e^m = \{1 + 2m + 2\{m^2 + m + 1\}^{1/2}\}/3 \tag{A29}$$

Applying the implicit function theorem to (A28) and using (A29),

$$\frac{dr^m}{dm} = \frac{2r^m}{3r^m - 1 - 2m} = \frac{r^m}{\{m^2 + m + 1\}^{1/2}} \tag{A30}$$

Because $dr^m(m,m)/dm > 0$, equal increases in m and n will increase the proportion of resources devoted to politics.

The expression $dr_e(m,n)/dm$ has the same sign as

$$\frac{d \log r_e}{dm} = \frac{d\{\log r^m/m\}}{dm} = -\frac{\log r^m}{m^2} + \frac{1}{mr^m}\frac{dr^m}{dm}$$

Thus $dr_e/dm < 0$ provided that

$$\log r^m > \frac{m}{r^m}\frac{dr^m}{dm} = \frac{m}{\{m^2 + m + 1\}^{1/2}}$$

by (A30). By (A29) this will be true provided that

$$G(m) \equiv m\{m^2 + m + 1\}^{-1/2} - \log\{1 + 2m + 2\{m^2 + m + 1\}^{1/2}/3\} < 0$$

But $G(0) = 0$, so the above inequality certainly holds if for $m > 0$ we have

$$0 > \frac{dG}{dm} = \frac{1}{Z^{1/2}} - \frac{m(1 + 2m)}{Z^{1/2}} - \frac{2 + (1 + 2m)Z^{-1/2}}{1 + 2m + 2Z^{1/2}}$$

where $Z \equiv m^2 + m + 1$. This will be true provided that

$$0 > \frac{1 + m + m^2 - m^2 - m/2}{Z} - \frac{2Z^{1/2} + 1 + 2m}{1 + 2m + 2Z^{1/2}}$$

that is,

$$0 > \frac{1 + m/2}{1 + m + m^2} - 1$$

But the last inequality always holds for $m > 0$, so we indeed have

$$dr_e(m,n)/dm < 0 \tag{A31}$$

that is, equal increases in m and n decrease the distortions proposed by each party. This proves (A).

To prove (B), note that when $K_o = L_o$ and $m = n$, (A25) and (A26) imply that the ratio of equilibrium expected utility to free trade utility is

$$r_e^{m/2}(1 - 1/c)(1 + r_e^{-m})/2$$

By (14.16),

$$1 - 1/c = 2 + 1 - r_e^{-m}/m$$

so the ratio of expected utilities is

$$r_e^{m/2}(1 - r_e^{-m})\{2 + (1 - r_e^{-m})/m\}/2$$

Writing $y(m) \equiv r_e(m,m)^{m/2}$ this equals

$$H(y) \equiv (y + 1/y) + (y^{-1} - y^3)/2m$$

$$2\frac{dH}{dm} = \frac{y^3 - y^{-1}}{m^2} + \frac{dy}{dm}\left[2 - \frac{2}{y^2} - \frac{1}{my^2} - \frac{3y^2}{m}\right]$$

Because $dy/dm = (dr^m/dm)/2y$,

$$2m^2y^2\,dH/dm = y^5 - y + (m/2y)(dr^m/dm)[2my^2 - 2m - 1 - 3y^4]$$

Substituting from (A30),

$$2m^2y^2\, dH/dy = y^5 - y + (m/2y)\, 2y^2\, \frac{2my^2 - 2m - 1 - 3y^4 - 1}{3y^2 - 1 - 2m}$$

$$2m^2y\, dH/dy = y^4 - 1 + m\, \frac{2my^2 - 2m - 3y^4 - 1}{3y^2 - 1 - 2m}$$

$$= y^4 - 1 - my^2 - m\, \frac{y^2 + 2m + 1}{3y^2 - 1 - 2m}$$

$$= r_e^{2m} - 1 - mr_e^m - m\, \frac{r_e^m + 2m + 1}{3r_e^m - 1 - 2m}$$

Substituting from (A29),

$$2m^2y^2\, dH/dy = r_e^m(r_e^m - m) - 1 - m\, \frac{(1 + 2m)\frac{4}{3} + (1 + m + m^2)^{1/2}\frac{2}{3}}{2\{1 + m + m^2\}^{1/2}}$$

$$= r_e^m(r_e^m - m) - 1 - \frac{m}{3} - \frac{2m(1 + 2m)}{3\{1 + m + m^2\}^{1/2}}$$

$$18m^2y\, dH/dy = 3r_e^m(3r_e^m - 3m) - 9 - 3m - 6m(1 + 2m)/3Z^{1/2}$$

where $Z \equiv 1 + m + m^2$. Substituting from (A29),

$$3r_e^m(3r_e^m - 3m) = (1 + 2m + 2Z^{1/2})(2Z^{1/2} + 1 - m)$$
$$= (1 + 2Z^{1/2})^2 - 2m^2 + mZ^{1/2}$$
$$= 1 + (4 + m)Z^{1/2} + 2m^2 + 4m + 4$$

Therefore

$$18m^2y\, dH/dm = 2m^2 + m - 4 + \{(4 + m)Z - 6m(1 + 2m)\}/Z^{1/2}$$
$$= 2m^2 + m - 4 + \{m^3 - 7m^2 - m + 4\}/\{m^2 + m + 1\}^{1/2}$$

A direct calculation shows that this has only one positive zero at $m = 2.14$. Differential dH/dm (and hence dr_e/dm) is negative (positive) when m is less (greater) than this zero. This completes the proof of (B).

Theorem 13: If $m < n$, then

    (A) $K_e/K_o < L_e/L_o$
    (B) $S_e/K_o < T_e/L_o$
    (C) $K_eT_e/L_eS_e > 1$

Proof: By (A31), $dr_e(m,m)/dm < 0$. As $r(m,n)$ lies between $r_e(m,m)$ and $r_e(n,n)$, $m < n$ implies that $r_e(m,n) < r_e(m,m)$. Because $r_e(m,m)$ is the solution to (14.13), it follows that

$$3r_e^2(m,n) - 2(2m + 1)r_e(m,n) - 1 < 0$$

This can be rearranged as

$$\frac{1 - 2r_e(m,n)^{-m} + r_e(m,n)^{-2m}}{1 - (m + 1)r_e^{-m}(m,n)} > 4$$

$$\frac{1 - r_e^{-m}(m,n)}{\{1 - (m + 1)r_e^{-m}\}^{1/2}} > 2$$

or

$$a = K_e T_e / L_e S_e > 1 \qquad (A32)$$

by (14.14) and (14.23). This proves (C).

To prove (A), note that by (14.23) and (14.6),

$$(1 + a) = (1 - r_e^2)(1 + aK_o/K)$$

or

$$K_o/K_e = [(1 + a)^2/(1 - r_e^{-m}) - 1]/a = (a + 2 + r_e^{-m/a})/(1 - r_e^{-m}) \qquad (A33)$$

Similarly

$$L_o/L_e = (b + 2 + r_e^{-n/b})/(1 - r_e^{-n}) \qquad (A34)$$

Because $m < n$, (A33) implies that

$$K_o/K_e > (a + r_e^{-n/a} + 2)/(1 - r_e^{-n}) \qquad (A35)$$

Because $r_e^{-n} < 1$ and $a > 1 > 1/a = b$,

$$a + r_e^{-n/a} > b + r_e^{-n/b}$$

so

$$K_o/K_e > b + r_e^{-n/b} + 2/1 - r_e^{-n} = L_o/L_e$$

by (A34). This proves (A). Part (B) follows immediately from (A) and (C). ‖

A.14.7 Derivation of results in §A.14.4

Suppose that the electoral odds are

$$f = KT^\tau/LS^\sigma$$

Let $t \equiv T^\tau$, $s \equiv S^\sigma$ so that $T = t^{1/\tau}$, $S = s^{1/\sigma}$. The capital lobby maximizes

$$e(K) \equiv (K_o - K)\{(Kt\,(P/s^{1/\sigma})^{-m} + Ls(Pt^{1/\tau})^{-m}\}/\{Kt + Ls\}$$

It is readily checked that the first-order conditions for the capital lobby and procapital party are

$$Kt/Ls = -1 + \{(1 - (s^{1/\sigma}t^{1/\tau})^{-m})(1 + K_o t/Ls)\}^{1/2}$$
$$0 = 1 + (m/s)(1 + Ls/K_o t) - (s^{1/\sigma}t^{1/\tau})^m$$

Similarly, the first-order conditions for the labor lobby and the prolabor party are

$$Ls/Kt = -1 + \{(1 - (s^{1/\sigma}t^{1/\tau})^{-n})(1 + L_o s/Kt)\}^{1/2}$$
$$0 = 1 + (n/\tau)(1 + Kt/L_o s) - (s^{1/\sigma}t^{1/\tau})^n$$

With these modifications to (A10)–(A13) we can now duplicate the steps (A14)–(A21) to obtain (14.19) and (14.20) using the new definitions of a,b,c,d given in §A.14.4. Moreover, the analogue of (A22) implies that

$$T_e^\tau S_e^\sigma = t_e/s_e = (L_o/K_o)cb/d \qquad (A36)$$

while $S_e T_e = r_e$, so

$$S_e^\sigma T_e^\sigma = r_e^\sigma \qquad (A37)$$

(A36) and (A37) imply that

$$T^{\tau+\sigma} = (L_o/K_o)cbr_e{}^s/d$$

This implies (14.26). The derivation of (14.27) is similar.

Next, suppose that the electoral odds are

$$\Phi = (uK + v)T/(wL + x)S$$

Let $k \equiv uK + v$, $l \equiv wL + x$, $k_o \equiv uK_o + v$, and $l_o \equiv wL_o + x$. The capital lobby maximizes

$$e(K) \equiv \frac{(K_o - K)kT \ (P/S)^{-m} + lS(PT)^{-m}}{kT + lS}$$

that is, it maximizes

$$ue(K) = \frac{(k_o - k)kT \ (P/S)^{-m} + lS(PT)^{-m}}{kT + lS}$$

This can be obtained from the objective function for the case $u = 1$, $v = 0$ by replacing K and K_o by k and k_o. Similarly, the objective function of the labor lobby can be obtained from that for the case $w = 1$, $x = 0$ by replacing L and L_o by l and l_o. The conclusions claimed are obtained by applying these transformations to the equations defining an interior equilibrium.

Theorem 14: For any values of α, β, γ, δ such that

$$\frac{r_e{}^{(1-\beta)/(\alpha-\beta)} - r_e{}^{-\beta/(\alpha-\beta)}}{r_e - 1} < \frac{2 + 1/(\alpha - \beta)}{\alpha} \tag{14.28}$$

there is a range of world prices P such that the government's budget deficit, averaged over electoral outcomes, is zero for two different values of the endowment ratio K_o/L_o, both of which are consistent with interior equilibria. This condition will always be satisfied for β sufficiently close to 0 and α sufficiently close to 1.

Proof: A routine calculation shows that, in the Cobb–Douglas economy with domestic price Q, $K_o - K_e$ units of productive capital, and $L_o - L_e$ units of productive labor, the domestic output of the importable is

$$Y_2(Q) = (L_o - L_e)NQ^{N-1} - (K_o - K_e)MQ^{-M-1}$$

[Recall that $N \equiv \alpha/(\alpha - \beta)$, $M \equiv (1 - \alpha)(\alpha - \beta)$.] Hence, the domestic value of domestic production is

$$QY_2 = NI_W - MI_R$$

where

$$I_W \equiv (L_o - L_e)Q^N, \qquad I_R \equiv (K_o - K_e)Q^{-M}$$

are the labor and capital incomes. Because the lobbies have Cobb–Douglas preferences and spend, respectively, d and g of each dollar on the importable, the domestic value of imports is

$$\delta I_R + \gamma I_W - QY_2 = mI_R(Q) - nI_W(Q) \tag{A38}$$

where $m \equiv M + \gamma$, $n \equiv N - \delta$. Under the tariff regime, $Q = PT$ and tariff revenue is

$$G^T \equiv \{mI_R(PT) - nI_W(PT)\}(1 - 1/T) \tag{A39}$$

units of the exportable.

At domestic price Q, the lobbies spend all of their production income, so the domestic value of exports equals that of imports. Because exports are the numeraire, (A38) also gives the quantity of exports. Under the subsidy regime, the domestic price of the export is S times the world price. Hence the government pays out a subsidy equivalent to

$$G^S \equiv \{mI_R(P/S) - nI_W(P/S)\}(S - 1) \tag{A40}$$

units of exportable.

The government's budget constraint is

$$\pi G^S = (1 - p)G^T$$

Substituting from (A39) and (A40) this becomes:

$$\pi(S - 1)\{m(K_o - K_e)(P/S)^{-M} - n(L_o - L_e)(P/S)\}$$
$$= (1 - \pi)(1 - 1/T)\{m(K_o - K_e)(PT)^{-M} - n(L_o - L_e)(PT)^N\}$$

Substituting from (14.19)–(14.22), we can write this as the following equation in $x \equiv (K_o/L_o)^{1/2}$:

$$g(x) = h(x,P) \tag{A41}$$

where

$$g(x) \equiv x^{M+N+2}f^{M+N}\{xf(a + r^{-M-1}) - (a + r^{-M})\}$$
$$h(x,P) \equiv \{xf(a + r^{-N-1}) - (a + r^N)\}kP^{M+N}$$

where a is defined in (14.14), $f \equiv (rd/bc)^{1/2}$, $k \equiv n(1 - b/d)/m(1 - a/c)$. The condition (14.18) for K_o/L_o to lead to an interior equilibrium can be written as

$$r/f > x > 1/f \tag{A42}$$

We have to show that it is possible to choose P so that the graph H of $y = h(x,P)$ cuts the graph G of $y = g(x)$ twice in the region (A42). Their horizontal intercepts A,B have x coordinates

$$x^A \equiv (a + r^{-M})/(a + r^{-M-1})f$$
$$x^B \equiv (a + r^N)/(a + r^{N-1})f$$

Note that

$$r/f > x^B > x^A > 1/f$$

Changes in P would swivel the straight line graph H around B.

Let C be the point $(1/f, g(1/f))$ on G. A routine calculation shows that if hypothesis (14.28) holds, then BC is steeper than G at $x = 1/f$, so that BC will cut G again for $x < x^A < r/f$. For values of P such that H has slope just less than BC, H will cut G twice in the region (A42).

Appendix to Chapter 15

The economic sector of the model is the Heckscher–Ohlin–Samuelson trade model using two factors, capital and labor. We suppose that the production functions in the two industries are Cobb–Douglas and exhibit constant returns to scale. The unit cost functions are then also Cobb–Douglas. With a suitable choice of units they can be written as

$$C_1(R,W) = R^\alpha W^{1-\alpha}, \qquad C_2(R,W) = R^\beta W^{1-\beta}$$

where α and β are constants such that $0 < \beta < \alpha < 1$. The numeraire is the more capital-intensive good 1. The country is small and faces an international price P for good 2, which is imported. Politically motivated trade distortions can lead to a domestic price Q for good 2 that differs from P. In a nonspecialized equilibrium, the wage and rental rates are determined by the zero-profit conditions in the two industries:

$$1 = R^\alpha W^{1-\alpha} \qquad \text{and} \qquad Q = R^\beta W^{1-\beta}$$

A routine calculation shows that the equilibrium factor prices are

$$W = Q^N \qquad \text{and} \qquad R = Q^{-M} \tag{15.1}$$

where $N \equiv \alpha/(\alpha - \beta)$ and $M \equiv (1 - \alpha)/(\alpha - \beta)$. Note that $W_Q > 0$ and $R_Q < 0$ as implied by the Stolper–Samuelson theorem.

The impact of Q on the returns to capital and labor motivates their owners to form lobbies that contribute resources to politics. For simplicity, we assume that the capital and labor lobbies make direct contributions K and L of the factor that they own to the party proposing the policy more favorable to themselves. As before, the alternative assumption that the lobbies contribute funds that are used by the parties to purchase resources would complicate the model but would yield similar results. We assume that there is a procapital party and a prolabor party, each using its policies to bid for votes and for political contributions. The procapital party's policy is to set a domestic price of P/S ($S \geq 1$) – for example, by a subsidy on exports of good 1 – whereas the the prolabor party's policy is to set a domestic price of PT ($T \geq 1$) – for example, by a tariff on imports of good 2.

We assume that the probability of victory by the procapital party $\pi(K,L,S,T)$ increases with the political contributions K of the capital lobby and the tariff T proposed by the prolabor party, and decreases with the political contributions L of the labor lobby and the export subsidy S proposed by the procapital party. The rationale of this probability of election function is that voters own various combinations of goods and factors such that increased departures from free trade inflict increasing losses on increasing numbers of voters. Because voters are imperfectly informed and find voting costly, electioneering resources can be used by parties to influence both voters' perceptions of these losses and voter turnout – and hence electoral probabilities. The resources are supplied by the lobbies: well-informed groups with a clear preference for one party because their members own predominantly one factor. We assume that π has the logit form, which is often used to model dichotomous choices. In addition, we assume that the electoral odds are unit elastic with respect to each of its arguments; that is,

$$\log(\pi/(1 - \pi)) = \log K + \log T - \log L - \log S$$

or

$$\pi(K,L,S,T) = KT/(KT + LS) \qquad \text{for } K \geq 0, L \geq 0, T \geq 1, S \geq 1 \qquad (15.2)$$

In our model, each lobby chooses its political contributions in order to maximize the expected utility of the factor that it represents, equating the marginal returns to politics and to productive activity. It behaves in a Cournot fashion with respect to the other players. Each party maximizes its probability of election, calculating in a Stackelberg fashion that more extreme policies will attract more political contributions from its lobby but will antagonize voters. It is assumed to behave in a Cournot fashion with respect to the other lobby and the other party.

We assume that the capital lobby's choices are as if made by a representative individual who owns K_0 units of capital and has an indirect utility function $V_R(I_R,Q)$ where I_R is his income. By (15.1), we get

$$I_R = (K_0 - K)Q^{-M}$$

The domestic price will be P/S or PT according to whether the procapital or the prolabor party wins. Because these events have probabilities $KT/(LS + KT)$ and $LS/(KT + LS)$, respectively, the capital lobby's expected utility is

$$e(K) = \frac{KTV_R((K_0 - K)(P/S)^{-M},P/S)+ LSV_R((K_0 - K)(PT)^{-M},PT)}{(KT + LS)} \qquad (15.3)$$

An increase in K decreases expected utility by decreasing the number of units of capital employed in production but increases it by increasing the probability of a low price for the labor-intensive good 2 and hence of a high return to capital. We shall refer to these as the "units effect" and the "returns effect," respectively. The level of political contributions balancing these two effects optimally is the solution $K^*(L,S,T)$ to

$$\max e(K) \qquad \text{subject to} \quad 0 \leq K \leq K_0 \qquad (15.4)$$

Similarly, the labor lobby is assumed to own L_0 units of capital and chooses $L^*(K,S,T)$ to maximize its expected utility.

The procapital party calculates in a Stackelberg fashion that increases in the export $K^*(L,S,T)$ from the capital lobby but will reduce its electoral odds because the distortion alienates more voters. The policy balancing these two effects optimally is the solution $S^*(L,T)$ to

$$\max K^*(L,S,T)T/LS \qquad \text{subject to} \quad S \geq 1 \qquad (15.5)$$

Similarly, the optimal policy of the prolabor party is the solution $T^*(K,S)$ to

$$\max L^*(K,S,T)S/KT \qquad \text{subject to} \quad T \leq 1 \qquad (15.6)$$

An equilibrium of the political game is a set of actions (K_e, L_e, S_e, T_e) by the four players that are mutually consistent; that is, such that

$$K_e = K^*(L_e,S_e,T_e), \qquad L_e = L^*(K_e,S_e,T_e)$$
$$S_e = S^*(L_e,T_e), \qquad T_e = T^*(K_e,S_e)$$

We now relate the risk aversion of the lobbies to the proportion of resources K_e/K_o, L_e/L_o that they devote to politics in equilibrium. Suppose that both lobbies have Cobb–Douglas direct utility functions. If ρ is the capital lobby's coefficient of relative risk aversion and γ is its (constant) expenditure share on good 2, then its indirect utility function is

$$V_R(I_R,Q) = \frac{Q^{-\gamma(1-\rho)} I_R^{1-\rho}}{1 - \rho} \qquad \rho \neq 1 \qquad (15.7)$$

$$V_R(I_R,Q) = \log I_R - \gamma \log Q \qquad \rho = 1 \qquad (15.8)$$

Substituting these expressions for V_R into (15.3) gives the expected utility of the capital lobby:

$$e(K) = \frac{(K_o - K)^{1-\rho}\{KT(P/S)^{-m(1-\rho)} + LS(PT)^{-m(1-\rho)}\}}{(1 - \rho)(KT + LS)} \qquad \rho \neq 1 \qquad (15.9)$$

$$e(K) = \log(K_o - K) - m\frac{KT\log(P/S) + LS\log(PT)}{KT + LS} \qquad \rho = 1 \qquad (15.10)$$

where $m \equiv \gamma + (1 - \alpha)/(\alpha - \beta)$ measures the sensitivity of the capital lobby to the commodity price Q and hence to the political outcome. If $\rho = 0$ and the commodity price is Q, then the lobby has real income $(K_o - K)Q^{-m}$, so m is the elasticity of real income with respect to Q. The corresponding expressions for the labor lobby with relative risk aversion σ and a constant expenditure share δ on good 2 can be obtained by replacing K_o, K, L,S, T, ρ, and m in (15.9) and (15.10) by L_o, L, K, T, S, σ, and $-n$, where $n \equiv \alpha/(\alpha - \beta) - \delta$ measures the sensitivity of the labor lobby to the political outcome.

The first and second terms in the product in (15.9) and in the sum in (15.10) give the "units effect" and the "returns effect" of K on the capital lobby's expected utility e, as discussed below in the proof of Theorem 1. For $\rho \neq 1$, the proportional impact of K on e operating via these two effects corresponds to the two terms in

$$\frac{\partial \log e}{\partial \log K} = \frac{1 - \rho}{K_o/K - 1} + \frac{1}{1 + KT/LS} \cdot \frac{(ST)^{m(1-\rho)} - 1}{(ST)^{m(1-\rho)} + LS/KT} \qquad (15.11)$$

Consider first the case $1 > \rho$. The second term in (15.11) is always less than 1, whatever the values of K,L,S,T, and m; that is, however extreme the policies of the two parties and however high the sensitivity of the lobby to the political outcome, there is a limit to the benefits of allocating resources to politics via the returns effect. This is because K affects not the returns themselves, but only the odds of achieving high returns. By contrast, as K approaches K_o, the first term becomes arbitrarily large and negative: As increasing resources are devoted to politics, the proportional losses via the units effect become arbitrarily large and negative, reflecting the fact that, as increasing resources are devoted to politics, the proportional losses via the units effect become arbitrarily large. Because the optimal K^* equates at the margin the proportional gains from the returns effect and the proportional losses from the units effect, K^* will always be chosen so that the latter is less than 1, that is, $(1 - \rho)/(K_o/K - 1) < 1$. It follows that for $\rho < 1$,

$$\frac{K^*}{K_o} < \frac{1}{2 - \rho}$$

For the case $\rho > 1$, e is negative so, at the margin, the proportional gain in expected utility via the returns effect is

$$\frac{1 - (ST)^{m(1-\rho)}}{(1 + KT/LS)\{(ST)^{m(1-\rho)} + LS/KT\}} < \frac{1}{(1 + KT/LS)LS/KT} < 1 \tag{15.12}$$

whereas the proportional loss via the units effect is $(\rho - 1)/(K_o/K - 1)$. By (15.12), at the optimum K^*, the latter term is always less than 1, so for $\rho > 1$,

$$\frac{K^*}{K_o} < \frac{1}{\rho}$$

We have thus proved the following theorem:

Theorem 1: In the Cobb–Douglas model with $\rho \neq 1$, K^*/K_o is bounded above by a number less than 1 that depends only on ρ and is independent of the parameters of the model and of the policies of the other players.

A similar result holds for the labor lobby. Now suppose that the capital lobby's relative risk aversion ρ approaches 1 from below. For fixed K,L,S,T, and m in (15.11) the first term decreases in absolute magnitude: The increase in ρ reduces the proportional losses from the units effect. The second term in (15.11) also decreases; but if it does so at a sufficiently slower rate, then the optimal K^*, which equates the two terms, could approach K_o for suitable choices of parameters. A similar possibility arises when ρ approaches 1 from above. We now confirm these possibilities in the limiting case where $\rho = 1$.

Differentiating (15.10), we have

$$\frac{\partial e}{\partial K} = \frac{-1}{K_o - K} + \frac{m(\log ST)T/LS}{(1 + KT/LS)^2} \tag{15.13}$$

The two terms in (15.13) give the impact of K on expected utility e via the units effect and the returns effect. In contrast to the case $\rho \neq 1$, the returns effect is not bounded above by 1 but can be made arbitrarily large if $m\log ST$ is sufficiently large. Thus, the lobby could devote an arbitrarily large proportion of its resources to politics if it were highly sensitive to the political outcome, or if the parties' policies were extreme. To confirm that this can occur in an equilibrium of the game, we must consider the simultaneous optimization of both lobbies and both parties. Define

$$\rho(m) \equiv \exp(2\{(1+m)^{1/2} - 1\}/m) \tag{15.14}$$

Theorem 2: Suppose that both lobbies have Cobb–Douglas utility functions with unit relative risk aversion. There will be an equilibrium with both parties advocating intervention if and only if

$$m = n \quad \text{and} \quad \rho(m) > K_o/L_o > 1/\rho(m) \tag{15.15}$$

In this case,

$$K_e/K_o = 1 - \log\rho(m) = L_e/L_o \tag{15.16}$$

$$S_e = \left(\frac{\rho(m)K_o}{L_o}\right)^{1/2} \quad \text{and} \quad T_e = \left(\frac{\rho(m)L_o}{K_o}\right)^{1/2} \tag{15.17}$$

As $m = n$ becomes large, K_e/K_o and L_e/L_o approach 1 from below, and S_e and T_e approach 1 from above.

Proof: By (15.13), the first-order condition defining the choice of K^* reduces to the quadratic equation

$$(KT/LS + 1)^2 - (KT/LS)(K_o/K - 1)m\log ST = 0 \qquad (15.18)$$

It is readily checked that the second-order condition is satisfied by the larger root $K^*(L,S,T)$, which is given by

$$K^*T/LS = -1 - (m/2)\log ST + B^{1/2} \qquad (15.19)$$

where

$$B \equiv (1 + K_o/LS)m\log ST + (m^2/4)(\log ST)^2$$

The procapital party maximizes $K^*(L,S,T)T/LS$, that is, the right-hand side of (15.19). The first-order condition for this is

$$0 = -\frac{m}{2S} + \frac{B^{-1/2}}{2}\left(\left(1 + \frac{K_oT}{LS}\right)\frac{m}{s} - \frac{K_oTm\log ST}{LS^2} + \frac{m^2\log ST}{2S}\right) \qquad (15.20)$$

This simplifies to

$$(1 - \log ST)K_oT/LS = -1 - (m/2)\log ST + B^{1/2} \qquad (15.21)$$

Comparing (15.19) and (15.21), we see that when both lobby and party are optimizing,

$$K/K_o = 1 - \log ST \qquad (15.22)$$

Substituting (15.22) into (15.18) yields

$$KT/LS + 2 + LS/KT = m(\log ST)^2/(1 - \log ST) \qquad (15.23)$$

A similar argument shows that when both the labor lobby and the prolabor party are optimizing

$$L/L_o = 1 - \log ST \qquad (15.24)$$

and

$$LS/KT + 2 + KT/LS = n(\log TS)^2/(1 - \log TS) \qquad (15.25)$$

Comparing (15.23) and (15.25) we see that if $m \neq n$, then there is no set of values of (K,L,S,T) at which all players are maximizing unless $S = 1 = T$. Hence, there will be an equilibrium with both parties advocating intervention only if $m = n$.

The quadratic equation (15.23) determines KT/LS as a function of m and ST, and (15.25) determines LS/KT as a function of n and TS. Because of the symmetry between the two lobbies and between the two parties, if $m = n$ and the larger (smaller) root of (15.23) leads to a K satisfying the second-order condition for K^*, then the larger (smaller) root of (15.25) leads to an L satisfying the second-order condition for L^*. However, if $m = n$, then the two equations are identical and have identical larger roots and identical smaller roots. Hence, if $m = n$ and all players are maximizing, then

$$KT/LS = LS/KT$$

It follows that $KT/LS = 1$, so (15.23) implies that, in equilibrium,

$$4 = m(\log ST)^2 / (1 - \log ST)$$

If $S_e, T_e > 1$, then $\log S_e T_e$ is the positive root of this quadratic equation in $\log ST$. Recalling (15.14), this implies that

$$S_e T_e = r(m) \tag{15.26}$$

Equations (15.22) and (15.13) then imply (15.16). Moreover, because $K_e T_e/L_e S_e = 1$, (15.22) and (15.24) also imply that

$$S_e/T_e = K_e/L_e = K_o/L_o \tag{15.27}$$

(15.26) and (15.27) imply (15.17).

As $0 < \log r(m) < 1$, we have $0 < K_e < K_o$ and $0 < L_e < L_o$. Moreover, (15.15) and (15.17) imply that $S_e > 1$ and $T_e > 1$. Because all the feasibility constraints in K,L,S,T are slack at the equilibrium given by (15.16) and (15.17), we are justified in determining the equilibrium via first-order conditions like (15.18) and (15.20), which ignore these constraints. The last conclusions of Theorem 2 hold because as m becomes large, $\log r(m)$ approaches 0 and $r(m)$ approaches 1. If these hypotheses are violated, then there can be equilibria in which one party advocates free trade and the other advocates intervention. Indeed, such equilibria can occur even under parameter values satisfying (15.15); that is, both types of equilibria are possible for given parameter values. Section 11.4 discusses the implications of such multiple equilibria. In any equilibrium of the present model, at least one party advocates intervention. ‖

As an example of the application of Theorem 2, suppose that $\gamma = \delta = 0$ (neither lobby consumes good 2), and $\alpha = 1/2$. Then $m = n = 1/(1 - 2\beta)$ becomes arbitrarily large as β approaches 1/2 from below. In this case, the capital intensities of the two sectors draw closer together, increasing the "magnification effect" of commodity prices on factor returns. With unit relative risk aversion, the impact of political contributions via the returns effect becomes large, drawing an arbitrarily high proportion of each lobby's resources into politics. Interestingly, this occurs despite the fact that as m and n increase, the equilibrium policies of the two parties become less extreme and approach free trade. Because $r(m) > 1$, hypothesis (15.15) will be satisfied, for example, if $K_o/L_o = 1$.

Appendix to Chapter 16

Table A.16.1 shows the expanded country data used in our work on the endowment effect.

Table A.16.1. *The country data*

Country	Tariff	Liter. (%)	Capital/ labor	Imports/ GNP	Duties/ govt. rev	GNP per capita	Popul. (mil.)
Argentina	14.9	93	3,986	16.32	18.0	2,390	27.7
Australia	8.6	100	14,886	8.89	4.4	9,820	14.5
Austria	2.8	99	13,498	5.55	0.8	10,230	7.5
Bangladesh	13.0	26	104	8.75	16.3	130	88.5
Benin	21.9	28	83	17.93	43.7	310	3.4
Bolivia	14.1	63	765	21.34	28.0	570	5.6
Brazil	8.1	76	1,709	9.37	8.2	2,050	118.7
Burundi	20.8	25	31	24.09	39.5	200	4.1
Canada	4.9	99	14,208	5.98	1.4	10,130	23.9
Chad	24.1	15	48	27.13	30.0	120	4.5
Colombia	12.4	81	890	15.72	25.1	1,180	26.7
Costa Rica	6.2	90	1,807	8.67	2.8	1,730	2.2
Denmark	1.2	99	14,053	2.77	0.1	12,950	5.1
Dominican Republic	19.4	67	370	30.56	73.4	1,160	5.4
Ecuador	19.3	81	438	29.18	38.1	1,270	8.0
Egypt	30.8	44	479	32.63	54.0	580	39.8
El Salvador	6.1	62	429	11.04	4.5	660	4.5
Ethiopia	28.5	15	27	28.65	53.3	140	31.1
Finland	2.3	100	16,202	3.64	0.4	9,720	4.9
Honduras	9.1	60	747	13.41	8.3	560	3.7
India	29.8	36	191	29.86	88.1	240	673.2
Jamaica	5.0	90	2,834	3.50	0.7	1,040	2.2
Japan	2.7	99	11,720	5.08	1.3	9,890	116.8
Kenya	12.7	47	165	15.92	9.7	420	15.9
Malawi	9.5	25	48	10.04	9.7	230	6.1
Malaysia	9.6	60	1,313	12.52	6.7	1,620	13.9
Mali	9.9	10	25	10.23	4.3	190	7.0
Mauritania	16.2	17	356	15.05	7.5	440	1.5
Mexico	11.3	83	1,229	19.63	24.3	2,090	69.8
New Zealand	5.0	99	9,429	5.76	1.6	7,090	3.3
Nicaragua	9.6	90	1,561	11.57	5.7	740	2.6
Niger	20.7	10	72	13.40	28.7	300	5.3
Nigeria	17.6	34	559	18.45	29.2	1,010	84.7
Norway	1.1	99	20,702	1.90	0.1	12,650	4.1
Papua New Guinea	16.5	32	462	6.87	4.5	780	3.0
Pakistan	21.0	24	106	16.02	38.4	300	82.2
Panama	8.7	85	1,620	9.56	4.2	1,730	1.8
Paraguay	14.0	84	285	15.60	35.0	1,300	3.2
Peru	17.5	80	552	15.70	18.8	930	17.4
Portugal	7.2	78	2,623	10.12	4.6	2,370	9.8
Republic of Korea	7.4	93	970	6.26	4.3	1,520	38.2
Senegal	20.7	10	331	27.68	24.8	450	5.7
Sierra Leone	18.5	15	124	42.86	79.3	280	3.5

Table A.16.1 (*cont.*)

Country	Tariff	Liter. (%)	Capital/ labor	Imports/ GNP	Duties/ govt. rev	GNP per capita	Popul. (mil.)
Sri Lanka	8.4	85	233	13.43	13.1	270	14.7
Sweden	1.9	99	19,239	2.87	0.2	13,520	8.3
Switzerland	6.8	99	21,865	8.62	4.7	16,440	6.5
Syria	11.4	58	2,294	14.94	7.7	1,340	9.0
Tanzania	8.8	79	72	11.71	7.4	280	18.7
Thailand	12.3	86	730	18.30	18.4	670	47.0
Togo	14.4	18	203	61.46	51.6	410	2.5
Tunisia	19.2	62	2,071	23.31	31.0	1,310	6.4
Turkey	24.0	60	1,422	22.67	38.2	1,470	44.9
United States	0.6	99	12,177	5.73	0.2	11,360	227.7
Uruguay	12.5	94	3,345	4.25	4.2	2,810	2.9
Venezuela	7.5	82	12,437	7.12	4.0	3,630	14.9
Zaire	28.3	55	20	25.98	26.6	220	28.3
Zambia	5.9	44	600	8.77	1.7	560	5.8
Zimbabwe	5.2	69	991	27.61	7.2	630	7.4

Appendix to Chapter 18

The probability of election π of the procapital party increases with the economic resources R it holds but decreases with the distortions D it introduces. We focus on the behavior of the capital party only; symmetric arguments apply to the other party.

$$\pi = \pi\,(R,D) \qquad \pi_r > 0, \quad \pi_d < 0, \quad \pi_{rr} < 0, \quad \pi_{dd} < 0 \qquad (18.1)$$

Assume that this general relationship from the vote-maximizing model of Chapter 3 holds for any policy that the party introduces. As policies get more indirect, they are less effective in eliciting funds from their clientele lobbies. This makes lobbying resources decrease with more obfuscation (with higher values of O):

$$R = R(O) \qquad R' < 0 \qquad (18.2)$$

Let D represent the economic distortions that voters perceive. We assume that

$$D = D(O) \qquad (18.3)$$

$D' > 0$ with fully informed voters and $D' < 0$ with rationally uninformed voters. With $D' > 0$, fully informed voters correctly perceive that the party is harming them by moving to more indirect policies. With $D' < 0$, rationally uninformed voters do not recognize that the more indirect policy is harming them more: They incorrectly perceive that distortions have fallen when a more indirect policy is employed. Although the text might seem to suggest that O is discrete, we assume that it is continuous for mathematical convenience. In short, we assume that fully informed voters can detect that quotas are worse than tariffs, whereas rationally uninformed voters do the reverse. Before pursuing the implications of (18.2) and (18.3) we must discuss the voters.

The political party is assumed to pick the policy that is best for it by its choice of the level of obfuscation O. For every value of O there will be an associated policy p. Let p be a variable ranging from factor subsidies at one extreme to complicated voluntary export restraint agreements on the other. The rational party will choose an election-maximizing value of p, call it p^*. Associated with this policy will be an equilibrium level of the perceived economic distortion D^*. Because the party is a Stackelberg leader vis-à-vis the lobby, it anticipates the vote-maximizing value of policy p on the level of resources R^* that it will receive from its lobby.

To summarize, for every level of the obfuscation variable there will a policy level optimal from the party's point of view; the attendant distortion level D^* that the policy causes; the resource flow R^* optimal from the point of view of the lobby; and the resulting probability of election π^* of the procapital party. To simplify, we do not consider each optimal policy explicitly because there is a single policy associated with each level of obfuscation. The party's strategy is to maximize its probability of election by its choice of the level of obfuscation:

$$\max \pi^*(R^*(O), D^*(O)) \tag{18.4}$$

The first-order conditions associated with (18.4) are

$$
\begin{array}{cccc}
\text{(a)} & \text{(b)} & \text{(c)} & \text{(d)} \\
(d\pi^*/dR^*)(dR^*/dO) & + & (d\pi^*/dD^*)(dD^*/dO) & = 0 \\
+ & - & - & ?
\end{array}
\tag{18.5}
$$

(d) > 0 for fully informed voters
(d) < 0 for rationally uninformed voters

The question mark under term (d) indicates that the sign depends on whether voters are fully informed or not. The second-order conditions are left to interested readers. We stated earlier that an increase in obfuscation could cause the perceived level of distortions by voters to go either way. Consider now each of the two groups of voters: fully informed and rationally uninformed.

With fully informed voters, marginal waste effects are assumed to exceed marginal detection effects so that more obfuscation will increase perceived distortions, making $(dD^*/dO) > 0$. That is, a fully informed voter is able to detect both the redistributive policy and the economic costs it imposes. When $(dD^*/dO) > 0$, both of the terms on the left-hand side of (18.5) are negative. With fully informed voters, a political party would always choose the most direct policies ($O = 0$). Since we see an abundance of inefficient and indirect redistributive policies worldwide, apparently the assumption of a fully informed electorate is of limited empirical relevance.

Consider now less sophisticated, rationally ignorant Downsian (1957) voters, so that $(dD^*/dO) < 0$. Thus, the positive second term [(c) × (d) in equation (18.5)] means that movement by the party to a more indirect policy makes voters think that the party is less perverse than before. If the positive term in (18.5) exceeds the negative one at $O = 0$, then we know that the procapital party will choose an indirect policy. Given certain second-order conditions, (18.5) identifies the level of obfuscation that generates the most votes and hence the policy chosen by the party.

References

Ackerman, Bruce, 1975, *Economic Foundations of Property Law*. Boston: Little Brown.

Adamany, David, 1977, "Money, Politics and Democracy: A Review Essay," *American Political Science Review*, 71, 289–304.

Aggarwal, Vinod K., 1985, *Liberal Protectionism*. Berkeley: University of California Press.

Aggarwal, Vinod K., Robert O. Keohane, and David B. Yoffie, 1987, "The Dynamics of Negotiated Protectionism," *American Political Science Review*, 81, 345–66.

Agmon, Tamir, 1985, *Political Economy and Risk in World Financial Markets*. Lexington: D.C. Heath and Co.

Ahmad, J., 1978, "Tokyo Round of Trade Negotiations and the Generalized System of Preferences," *Economic Journal*, 88, 285–95.

Ahmad, Kabir V., 1983, "An Empirical Study of Politico-Economic Interaction in the United States," *Review of Economics and Statistics*, 65, 170–7.

Aho, C. M., and J. D. Aronson, 1985, *Trade Talks*. Council on Foreign Relations.

Aho, C. M., and T. O. Bayard, 1982, "Cost and Benefits of Trade Adjustment Assistance," paper presented at National Bureau of Economic Research Conference on the Structure and Evolution of Recent U.S. Trade Policy, Cambridge.

Aitken, N. D., and R. S. Obutelewicz, 1976, "A Cross-Section Study of EEC Trade with the Association of African Countries," *Review of Economics and Statistics*, 58, 425–33.

Alexander, Herbert E., 1971, *Financing the 1964 Election*. Princeton: Citizen's Research Foundation.

1976, *Financing Politics*. New York: Congressional Quarterly Press.

Anderson, Kym, 1980, "The Political Market for Government Assistance to Australian Manufacturing Industries," *Economic Record*, 56, 132–45.

Anderson, Kym, and Robert E. Baldwin, 1981, "The Political Market for Protection in Industrial Countries: Empirical Evidence, 1981," World Bank Staff Working Paper No. 492.

Andrain, Charles R., 1980, *Politics and Economic Policy in Western Democracies*. North Scituate, Mass.: Duxbury Press.

Aranson, Peter H., 1986, "Risk, Uncertainty and Retrospective Voting," Conference on Political Information and Political Theory, Austin, Texas, February 13–15.

Aranson, Peter H., and Melvin J. Hinich, 1979, "Some Aspects of the Political Economy of Election Campaign Contribution Laws," *Public Choice*, 34, 435–61.

Aranson, Peter H., and Peter C. Ordeshook, 1981, "Regulation, Redistribution and Public Choice," *Public Choice*, 37, 69–100.

Arndt, H. W., 1984, "Political Economy," *Economic Record*, 60, 266–73.

Atkinson, Anthony B., and Joseph E. Stiglitz, 1980, *Lectures on Public Economics*. London: McGraw-Hill.

Aumann, R. J., and Mordecai Kurz, 1977a, "Power and Taxes," *Econometrica*, 45, 1137–61.

1977b, "Power and Taxes in a Multi-Commodity Economy," *Weizmann Science Press of Israel*, 27, 185–234.

Aumann, R. J., Mordecai Kurz, and A. Neyman, 1980, "Power and Public Goods," Technical Report No. 273, Economics Series, Stanford, California.

Austen-Smith, D., 1981, "Voluntary Pressure Groups," *Economica*, 48, 143–53.

1984, "Interest Groups, Campaign Contributions and Spatial Voting," presented to the Allied Social Science Association Annual Meeting, Dallas, Texas.

Austin, Erik W., 1986, *Political Facts of the United States since 1789*. New York: Columbia University Press.

Axelrod, Robert, 1980a, "Effective Choice in the Prisoner's Dilemma," *Journal of Conflict Resolution*, 24, 3–25.

"More Effective Choice in the Prisoner's Dilemma," *Journal of Conflict Resolution*, 24, 379–403.

1981, "The Emergence of Cooperation," *American Political Science Review*, 75, 306–18.

1984, *The Evolution of Cooperation*. New York: Basic Books.

Baack, Bennett D., and Edward J. Ray, 1973, "Tariff Policy Comparative Advantage in the Iron and Steel Industry: 1870–1929," *Explorations in Economic History*, 10, 3–23.

1983, "The Political Economy of Tariff Policy: A Case Study of the United States," *Explorations in Economic History*, 20, 73–93.

1985a, "The Political Economy of the Origin and Development of the Federal Income Tax," *Research in Economic History, Supplement*, JAI Press.

1985b. "The Political Economy of the Origins of the Military–Industrial Complex in the United States," *Journal of Economic History*, 45, 369–75.

Badgett, L. D., 1978, "Preferential Tariff Reductions: The Philippine Response, 1900–1940," *Journal of International Economics*, 8, 79–92.

Balassa, Bela, 1965, "Tariff Protection in Industrial Countries: An Evaluation," *Journal of Political Economy*, 73, 573–94.

1967, *Trade Liberalization among Industrial Countries*. New York: McGraw-Hill.

1974, "Trade Creation and Trade Diversion in the European Common Market: An Appraisal of the Evidence," *The Manchester School*, 42, 93–135.

Balassa, Bela, and C. Balassa, 1984, "Industrial Protection in the Developed Countries," *The World Economy*, 7, 179–96.

Baldwin, David A., 1985, *Economic Statecraft*. Princeton: Princeton University Press.

Baldwin, Robert E., 1970, *Nontariff Distortions of International Trade*. Washington, D.C.: Brookings Institution, chap. 3.

1976a, "The Political Economy of U.S. Postwar Trade Policy," Bulletin No. 4, Center for the Study of Financial Institutions, Graduate School of Business Administration, New York University.

1976b, "Trade Employment Effects in the United States of Multilateral Tariff Reduction," *American Economic Review*, 66, 142–8.

1976c, "U.S. Tariff Policy: Formation and Effects," Discussion Papers on International Trade, Foreign Investment Employment, U.S. Dept. of Labor, Office of Foreign Economic Research.

1978, "The Economics of the GATT," in Peter Oppenheimer (ed.), *Issues in International Economics*. Stocksfield, England: Oriel Press, pp. 82–93.

1982a, "The Inefficacy of Trade Policy," *Essays in International Finance*, 150, 1–26.

1982b, "The Political Economy of Protectionism," in Jagdish N. Bhagwati (ed.), *Import Competition and Response*. Chicago: University of Chicago Press, pp. 263–86.

1983, "Trade Policies Under the Reagan Administration," paper presented at Pre-Conference Working Meeting, Washington.

1984a, "The Changing Nature of U.S. Trade Policy Since World War II," in Robert E. Baldwin and Anne O. Krueger (eds.), *The Structure and Evolution of Recent U.S. Trade Policy*. Cambridge: National Bureau of Economic Research.

1984b, "Rent-seeking and Trade Policy: An Industry Approach," National Bureau of Economic Research Working Paper No. 1499.

1984c, "Trade Policies in Developed Countries," in Ronald W. Jones and Peter B. Kenen (eds.), *Handbook of International Economics*. Amsterdam: North Holland, pp. 571–619.

1985a, *Economic Statecraft*. Princeton, New Jersey: Princeton University Press.

1985b, "Trade Policies Under the Reagan Administration," in Robert E. Baldwin (ed.), *Recent Issues and Initiatives in U.S. Trade Policy*. Cambridge, Mass.: National Bureau of Economic Research, pp. 10–33.

1986a, "Alternative Liberalization Strategies," National Bureau of Economic Research Working Paper No. 2045.

1986b, "Lobbying for Public Goods: The Case of Import Protection," Cambridge: National Bureau of Economic Research.

1986c, *The Political Economy of U.S. Import Policy*. Cambridge: MIT Press.

1987, "The New Protectionism: A Response to Shifts in National Economic Power," in Dominick Salvatore (ed.), *The New Protectionist Threat to World Welfare*. Amsterdam: Elsevier Science Publishing Co., pp. 95–112.

Baldwin, Robert E., and R. Spence Hilton, 1983, "A Technique for Indicating Comparative Costs and Predicting Changes in Trade Ratios," *Review of Economics and Statistics*, 65, 105–10.

Baldwin, Robert E., and W. Lewis, 1978, "U.S. Tariff Effects on Trade and Employment in Detailed SIC Industries," in W. G. Dewald (ed.), *The Impact of International Trade and Investment on Employment*. Washington, D.C.: U.S. Dept. of Labor, pp. 241–59.

Baldwin, Robert E., and T. Murray, 1977, "MFN Tariff Reductions and Developing Country Trade Benefits Under the GSP," *Economic Journal*, 87, 30–46.

Baldwin, Robert E., and J. David Richardson, 1973, "Government Purchasing Policies, Other NTBs and the International Monetary Crisis," Fourth Pacific Trade and Development Conference, Ottawa.

Baldwin, Robert E., and T. S. Thompson, 1984, "The Appropriate Response to Trade Barriers and 'Unfair' Trade Practices in Other Countries," *American Economic Review*, 74, 271–6.

Baldwin, Robert E., J. Mutti, and J. David Richardson, 1980, "Welfare Effects on the United States of a Significant Multilateral Tariff Reduction," *Journal of International Economics*, 10, 405–23.

Bale, M. D., 1973, "Adjustment to Free Trade: An Analysis of the Adjustment Assistance Provisions of the Trade Expansion Act of 1962," Ph.D. thesis, University of Wisconsin and Report No. DLMA 91-55-73-05-1 of the National Technical Information Service, Springfield, Virginia.

1977, United States Concessions in the Kennedy Round and Short-Run Labour Adjustment Costs, *Journal of International Economics*, 7, 145–8.

Bale, M. D. and J. Mutti, 1980, "Output and Employment Changes in a 'Trade Sensitive' Sector: Adjustment in the U.S. Footwear Industry," World Bank Staff Working Paper No. 430, Washington, D.C.

Ball, D. S., 1967, "United States Effective Tariffs and Labor's Share," *Journal of Political Economy*, 75, 183–7.

Banzhaf, John F., III, 1965, "Weighted Voting Doesn't Work: A Mathematical Analysis," *Rutgers Law Review*, 19, 317–43.

Barnet, R. J., and Mueller, R. E., 1974, *Global Reach*. New York: Simon and Schuster.

Baron, David P., 1983, *The Export–Import Bank*. New York: Academic Press.

1986, "Service-Induced Campaign Contributions and the Electoral Equilibrium," Conference on Political Information and Political Theory, University of Texas, February.

Baron, David P., and John Ferejohn, 1987, "Bargaining and Agenda Formation in Legislatures," *American Economic Review*, 77, 303–9.

Barro, Robert, 1973, "The Control of Politicians: An Economic Model," *Public Choice*, 14, 19–42.

Barry, Brian, 1978, *Sociologists, Economists and Democracy*. Chicago: University of Chicago Press.

Barry, Frank G., 1986, "Profitability, Investment and Employment: A Survey of Recent Developments in Medium-Term Growth Theory," *Economic and Social Review*, 17, 159–73.

1987, "Fiscal Policy in a Small Open Economy," *Journal of International Economics*, 22, 103–21.

Bartlett, Randall, 1978, "Economics, Power and the Myth of the Public Interest," Research Paper Series, Dept. of Economics, Williams College, Williamstown, Mass., June.

Basevi, G., 1966, "The United States Tariff Structure: Estimates of Effective Protection of United States Industries and Industrial Labor," *Review of Economics and Statistics*, 48, 147–60.

1968, "The Restrictive Effect of the U.S. Tariff and Its Welfare Value," *American Economic Review*, 58, 840–52.

Basevi, Giorgio, Flavio Delbono, and Vincenzo Denicolo, 1988, "International Monetary Cooperation Under Tariff Threats," Centre for Economic Policy Research, London, Paper No. 235, May.

Bauer, R. A., Ithiel de Sola Pool, and Lewis A. Dexter, 1963, *American Business and Public Policy: The Politics of Foreign Trade*. New York: Atherton Press.

Becker, Gary S., 1968, "Crime and Punishment: An Economic Approach," *Journal of Political Economy*, 76, 169–217.

1983, "A Theory of Competition among Pressure Groups for Political Influence," *Quarterly Journal of Economics*, 98, 371–400.

Becker, Gary S., and William Landes, 1974, *Essays in the Economics of Crime and Punishment*. Cambridge: National Bureau of Economic Research.

Becker, Gary S., and George J. Stigler, 1974, "Law Enforcement, Malfeasance and Compensation of Enforcers," *Journal of Legal Studies*, 3, 1–8.

Becker, William H., and Samuel F. Wells, Jr. (eds.), 1984, *Economics and World Power*. New York: Columbia University Press.

Beksiak, Janusz, 1987, "Economic Crises in Poland," Seminar Paper No. 396, Institute for International Economic Studies, Stockholm, December.

Bell, Daniel, 1976, *The Cultural Contradictions of Capitalism*. New York: Basic Books.

Ben-Dor, Y., and Y. Shilony, 1982, "Power and Importance in a Theory of Lobbying," *Behavioral Science*, 27, 69–76.

Ben-Zion, U., and Z. Eytan, 1974, "On Money, Votes and Policy in a Democratic Society," *Public Choice*, 17, 1–10.

Berg, Larry L., Larry L. Eastland, and Sherry Bebitch Jeffe, 1981, "Characteristics of Large Campaign Contributions, *Social Science Quarterly*, 62, 409–23.

Berglas, Eitan, 1976, "On The Theory of Clubs," *American Economic Review*, 66, 116–21.

Bergsten, C. Fred, 1972, *The Cost of Import Restrictions to American Consumers*. New York: American Importers Association, pp. 2–16.

Bergsten, C. Fred, and William R. Cline, 1982, *Trade Policy in the 1980s*. Washington, D.C.: Institute for International Economics.

Bergsten, C. Fred, and Lawrence B. Krause (eds.), 1975, *World Politics and International Economics*. Washington, D.C.: Brookings Institution.

Bergsten, C. Fred, and John Williamson, 1982, "Exchange Rates and Trade Policy," paper presented at a conference on Trade Policy in the Eighties, June 23–25, Institute for International Economics, Washington, D.C.

Bernholz, Peter, 1966, "Economic Policies in a Democracy," *Kyklos,* 29, 48–79.
1974, "Logrolling, Arrow-Paradox and Decision Rules – A Generalization," *Kyklos*, 27, 49–61.
1977, "Dominant Interest Groups and Powerless Parties," *Kyklos,* 30, 411–20.
1982, "Externalities as a Necessary Condition for Cyclical Social Preferences,"*Quarterly Journal of Economics*, 97, 699–705.
1984, "The Political Economy of Growth," *Kyklos,* 37, 291–94.
1987, "A General Constitutional Possibility Theorem," mimeo.
Bhagwati, Jagdish N., 1969, *Trade, Tariffs and Growth: Essays in International Economics.* London: Weidenfeld and Nicholson.
1971, "The Generalized Theory of Distortions and Welfare," in Jagdish N. Bhagwati et al. (eds.), *Trade, Balance of Payments and Growth: Papers in International Economics in Honour of Charles P. Kindleberger.* Amsterdam: North Holland, pp. 69–90.
1980, "Lobbying and Welfare," *Journal of Public Economics*, 14, 355–63.
1982a, "Directly Unproductive, Profit-Seeking DUP Activities," *Journal of Political Economy*, 90, 988–1002.
1982b, "Structural Adjustment and International Factor Mobility: Some Issues," International Economics Research Center Paper No. 6, Discussion Paper Series No. 163, Columbia University, New York.
1987, "VERs, Quid Pro Quo DFI and VIEs: Political-Economy-Theoretic Analysis," *International Economic Journal*, 1, 1–14.
Bhagwati, Jagdish N., and T. N. Srinivasan, 1980, "Revenue Seeking: A Generalization of the Theory of Tariffs," *Journal of Political Economy*, 88, 1069–87.
Bhandari, Jagdeep S., and Bluford H. Putnam (eds.), 1984, *Economic Interdependence and Flexible Exchange Rates.* Cambridge: MIT Press.
Bird, Peter J. W. N., 1984, "The Costs and Benefits of Protection: A Comment," *Kyklos,* 37, 102–3.
Blackhurst, R., 1981, "The Twilight of Domestic Economic Policies," *World Economy*, 4, 357–73.
Blake, David H., and Robert S. Walters, 1976, *The Politics of Global Economic Relations.* Englewood Cliffs, New Jersey: Prentice-Hall.
Bliss, Christopher, and Barry Nalebuff, 1984, "Dragon-Slaying and Ballroom Dancing: The Private Supply of a Public Good," *Journal of Public Economics*, 25, 2–12.
Bloom, R., and H. J. Price, 1975, "Voter Response to Short-Run Economic Conditions," *American Political Science Review*, 69, 1240–54.
Blomqvist, Ake, and Sharif Mohammad, 1984, "Controls, Corruption and Competitive Rent-Seeking in LDCs," Working Paper No. 8418C, Centre for the Study of International Economic Relations, Dept. of Economics, University of Western Ontario.
Bluestone, Barry, and Bennett Harrison, 1982, *The Deindustrialization of America.* New York: Basic Books.
Boadway, Robin, and J. M. Treddenick, 1978, "A General Equilibrium Computation of the Effects of the Canadian Tariff Structure," *Canadian Journal of Economics*, 11, 424–46.

Boller, Paul F., 1981, *Presidential Anecdotes*. New York: Penguin.

Borcherding, John D., 1979, "Toward a Positive Theory of Public Sector Supply Arrangement," mimeo, Dept. of Economics, Simon Fraser University.

Bornschier, Volker, 1980, "Multinational Corporations and Economic Growth," *Journal of Development Economics*, 7, 91–210.

Borooah V. K., and F. van der Ploeg, 1983, *Political Aspects of the Economy*. Cambridge: Cambridge University Press.

Bowen, Harry P., 1984, "The Resource Determinants of Developing Country Comparative Advantage in Manufactured Goods, 1966 and 1980," prepared for the Office of International Economic Affairs, U.S. Dept. of Labor, Contract No. B9K36138.

Bowen, Howard, 1943, "The Interpretation of Voting in the Allocation of Economic Resources," *Quarterly Journal of Economics*, 58, 38.

Bowles, Samuel, and Richard Edwards, 1985, *Understanding Capitalism: Competition, Command and Change in the U.S. Economy*. New York: Harper and Row.

Bowls, Roger, and David K. Whynes, 1981, *The Economic Theory of the State*. Oxford: Martin Robertson.

Brams, Steven J., 1975, *Game Theory and Politics*. New York: Free Press.

Brander, James A., 1981, "Intra-Industry Trade in Identical Commodities," *Journal of International Economics*, 1, 1–14.

Brander, James A., and Paul R. Krugman, 1980, "A 'Reciprocal Dumping' Model of International Trade," Dept. of Economics, MIT.

Brander, James A., and Barbara J. Spencer, 1984, "Tariff Protection and Imperfect Competition," in H. Kierzkowski (ed.), *Monopolistic Competition in International Trade*. Oxford: Oxford University Press, pp. 194–206.

1985, "Export Subsidies and International Market Share Rivalry," *Journal of International Economics*, 18, 83–100.

Brennan, Geoffrey, and James M. Buchanan, 1980, *The Power to Tax: Analytical Foundations of a Fiscal Constitution*. Cambridge: Cambridge University Press, chaps. 1, 3, 4, 7, 9.

1984, "The Logic of the Levers: The Pure Theory of Electoral Preference," Conference on the Political Economy of Public Policy, Stanford University.

1985, *The Reason of Rules*. Cambridge: Cambridge University Press.

Breton, A., 1974, *The Economic Theory of Representative Government*. Chicago: Aldine-Atheron.

Brito, Dagobert L., and J. David Richardson, 1984, "Power and Trade," University of Wisconsin and Rice University, mimeo.

Brittan, Samuel, 1975, "The Economic Contradictions of Democracy," *British Journal of Political Science*, 5, 129–59.

Brock, William. A., 1972, "On Models of Expectations that Arise from Maximizing Behavior of Economic Agents Over Time," *Journal of Economic Theory*, 5, 348–76.

1980, "The Design of Mechanisms for Efficient Allocation of Public Goods," in Lawrence Klein, Marc Nerlove, and S. C. Tsiang (eds.), *Quantitative Economics and Development*. New York: Academic Press, pp. 45–80.

Brock, William A., and Stephen P. Magee, 1974, "The Economics of Politics," paper presented at the Workshop on Industrialization Organization, University of Chicago, January; also "An Economic Theory of Politics: The Case of the Tariff," mimeo, University of Chicago, May.

1975, "The Economics of Pork-Barrel Politics," Report 7511, Center for Mathematical Studies in Business and Economics, University of Chicago.

1977, "Understanding Collective: A Formal Analysis of the Voluntary Provision of Public Goods," mimeo, University of Chicago, December.

1978, "The Economics of Special-Interest Politics: The Case of the Tariff," *American Economic Review*, 68, 246–50.

1980, "Tariff Formation in a Democracy," in John Black and Brian Hindley (eds.), *Current Issues in Commercial Policy and Diplomacy*. New York: St. Martin's Press, pp. 1–9.

1984, "The Invisible Foot and the Waste of Nations: Redistribution and Economic Growth," in D. C. Colander (ed.), *Neoclassical Political Economy*. Cambridge: Ballinger Press, pp. 177–85.

Bronfenbrenner, Martin, 1971, *Income Distribution Theory*. Chicago: Aldine-Atheron.

Brown, B., 1985, "Protectionist Pressure in the Eighties," professional report, University of Texas at Austin.

Brown, Cloufifird W., Jr., Roman B. Hedges, and Lynda W. Powell, 1980, "Modes of Elite Political Participation: Contributors to the 1972 Presidential Candidates," *American Journal of Political Science,* 24, 259–90.

Brown, Drusilla, 1985a, "A Computational Analysis of Japan's Generalized System of Preferences," Seminar Discussion Paper No. 162, Research Seminar in International Economics, Dept. of Economics, University of Michigan.

1985b, "General Equilibrium Effects of the U.S. Generalized System of Preferences," Seminar Discussion Paper No. 160, Research Seminar in International Economics, Dept. of Economics, University of Michigan.

Brown, F., and John Whalley, 1980, "General Equilibrium Evaluations of Tariff-Cutting Proposals in the Tokyo Round and Comparisons with More Extensive Liberalization of World Trade," *Economic Journal*, 90, 838–66.

Brunner, Karl (ed.), 1979, *Economics and Social Institutions*. Rochester, New York: Rochester Studies in Economics and Policy Issues.

Bruno, Michael, and Jeffrey Sachs, 1985, *Economics of Worldwide Stagflation*. Cambridge: Harvard University Press.

Buchanan, James M., 1975, *The Limits of Liberty: Between Anarchy and Leviathan*. Chicago: University of Chicago Press.

Buchanan, James M., and Gordon Tullock, 1962, *The Calculus of Consent*. Ann Arbor: University of Michigan Press.

1968, *The Demand and Supply of Public Goods*. Chicago: Rand-McNally.

Buchanan, James M., Robert D. Tollison, and Gordon Tullock, 1980, *Toward a Theory of the Rent-Seeking Society*. College Station, Texas: A&M University Press.

Buckley, P. J., and M. Casson, 1976, *The Future of the Multinational Enterprise*. London: Macmillan.

Burgess, David F., 1976, "Tariffs and Income Distribution: Some Empirical Evidence for the United States," *Journal of Political Economy*, 84, 17–46.

Cabeza, Carlos, 1987, "Protectionism in Developing Countries," term paper, Finance 396, University of Texas at Austin.

Cable, C., 1977, "British Protectionism and LDC Imports," *ODI Review*, 2, 29–48.

Cable, Vincent, and Ivonia Rebelo, 1980, "Britain's Pattern of Specialization in Manufactured Goods with Developing Countries and Trade Protection," World Bank Staff Working Paper No. 425, Washington, D.C.

Cahoon, L. S., Melvin J. Hinich, and Peter C. Ordeshook, 1978, "A Statistical Multidimensional Scaling Method Based on the Spatial Theory of Voting," in Peter Wang (ed.),*Graphical Representation of Multivariate Data*. New York: Academic Press, pp. 243–78.

Cairnes, John E., 1884, *Some Leading Principles of Political Economy*. London: Macmillan.

Calvert, Randall L., 1986, "Reputation and Political Leadership: A Game-Theoretic Approach," Conference on Political Information and Political Theory, University of Texas at Austin.

Calvert, Randall L., and Wilson, R., 1984, "Comment" [on Van de Kragt et al. (1983)], *American Political Science Review*, 78, 456–97.

Cameron, David R., 1979, "The Expansion of the Public Economy: A Comparative Analysis," *American Political Science Review*, 72, 4.

Canto, Victor A., 1983–4, "U.S. Trade Policy: History and Evidence," *Cato Journal*, 3, 679–96.

1986, *The Determinants and Consequences of Trade Restrictions in the U.S. Economy*. New York: Praeger.

Canto, Victor A., J. Kimball Dietrich, Adish Jain, and Vishwa Mudaliar, 1986, "Protectionism and the Stock Market: The Determinants and Consequences of Trade Restrictions," *Financial Analysts Journal*, 42, 32–42.

Cassing, James H., 1981, "On the Relationship Between Commodity Price Changes and Factor Owners' Real Positions, *Journal of Political Economy*, 89, 593–5.

Cassing, James H., and Arye L. Hillman, 1981, "A Social Safety Net for the Impact of Technical Change," *Economic Record*, 57, 232–7.

1985, "Political Influence Motives and the Choice Between Tariffs and Quotas," *Journal of International Economics*, 19, 279–90.

1986, "Shifting Comparative Advantage and Senescent Industry Collapse," *American Economic Review*, 76, 516–23.

Cassing, James H., Arye L. Hillman, and Ngo V. Long, 1986, "Risk Aversion, Terms of Trade Uncertainty and Social-Consensus Trade Policy," *Oxford Economic Papers*, 38, 234–42.

Cassing, James H., Timothy McKeown, and John Ochs, 1986, "Regional Demands for Protection: An Empirical Analysis of the Tariff Cycle," paper presented at Conference on the Political Economy of Trade Policy, National Bureau of Economic Research.

Casstevens, Thomas W., 1984, "Population Dynamics of Governmental Bureaus," *Undergraduate Mathematics and Its Applications Project Journal*, 5, 178–99.

Caves, Richard E., 1971, "International Corporations: The Industrial Economics of Foreign Investment," *Economica*, 38, 1–27.

1976, "Economic Models of Political Choice: Canada's Tariff Structure," *Canadian Journal of Economics*, 9, 278–300.

Chamberlin, John R., 1978, "The Logic of Collective Action: Some Experimental Results," *Behavioral Science*, 23, 441–5.

Cheh, J. H., 1974, "United States Concessions in the Kennedy Round and Short-Run Labor Adjustment Costs," *Journal of International Economics*, 4, 323–40.

Cheung, Stephen N. S., 1973, "The Fable of the Bees: An Economic Investigation," *Journal of Law and Economics*, 16, 11–33.

Chipman, John S., 1966, "A Survey of the Theory of International Trade: Part 3, The Modern Theory," *Econometrica*, 34, 18–76.

Chow, Gregory C., 1976, "Control Methods for Macroeconomic Policy Analysis," *American Economic Review*, 66, 340–5.

Chubb, John E., 1984, "The Political Economy of Federalism," Conference on the Political Economy of Public Policy, Stanford University.

Clegg, Patrick, and Karen Forsythe, 1984, "International Stock Market Returns," term paper, Finance 396, University of Texas at Austin.

Clements, Kenneth W., and Larry A. Sjaastad, 1984, "How Protection Taxes Exporters," London: Trade Policy Research Centre, Thames Essay No. 39.

Cline, William R., 1982, "Reciprocity: A New Approach to World Trade Policy?," *Policy Analyses in International Economics*, No. 2, Washington, D.C.: Institute for International Economics.

(ed.), 1983, *Trade Policy in the 1980s*. Cambridge: MIT Press.

1984, *Exports of Manufactures from Developing Countries*. Washington, D.C.: Brookings Institution.

Cline, William R., N. Kawanabe, T. O. M. Kronsjo, and T. Williams, 1978a, "Multilateral Effects of Tariff Negotiations in the Tokyo Round," in W. G. Dewald (ed.), *The Impact of International Trade and Investment on Employment*. Washington, D.C.: U.S. Dept. of Labor, pp. 265–85.

1978b, *Trade Negotiations in the Tokyo Round: A Quantitative Assessment*. Washington, D.C.: Brookings Institution.

Coase, Ronald, 1937, "The Nature of the Firm," *Economica*, 4, 386–405.

1960, "The Problem of Social Costs," *Journal of Law and Economics*, 3, 1–44.

Cohen, Benjamin, 1973, *The Question of Imperialism: The Political Economy of Dominance and Dependence*. New York: Basic Books, chaps. 5–7.

1983, "Trade and Unemployment: Global Bread-and-Butter Issues," *Worldview*, 26, 9–11.

Cohen, Linda, and Roger Noll, 1984, "Electoral Influences on Congressional Policy Preferences," Conference on the Political Economy of Public Policy, Stanford University.

Cohen, R. B., 1982, "The Prospects for Trade and Protection in the Auto Industry," paper presented at a conference on Trade Policy in the Eighties, Institute for International Economics, Washington, D.C.

Collier, P., 1979, "The Welfare Effects of Customs Union: An Anatomy," *Economic Journal*, 89, 84–95.

Condorcet, Marquis de, 1785, "Essai sur l'application de l'analyse a la probabilité des décisions rendues à la pluralité des voix," Paris.

Conlon, Richard P., 1987, "The Declining Role of Individual Contributions in Financing Congressional Campaigns," *Journal of Law and Politics,* 3, 467–507.

Connolly, Michael, 1970, "Public Goods, Externalities and International Relations," *Journal of Political Economy,* 78, 279–90.

Constantopoulos, M., 1974, "Labour Protection in Western Europe," *European Economic Review,* 5, 313–28.

Conybeare, John A. C., 1978, "Public Policy and the Australian Tariff Structure," *Australian Journal of Management,* 3, 49–63.

1982, "The Rent-Seeking State and Revenue Diversification," *World Politics,* 35, 25–42.

1983a, "Politicians and Protection: Tariffs and Elections in Australia," *Public Choice,* 41, 113.1–7.

1983b, "Tariff Protection in Developed and Developing Countries: A Cross-Sectional and Longitudinal Analysis," *International Organization,* 37, 441–67.

1984a, "A Comparative Study of Selected Trade Wars: Anglo-Hanse, Late 19th Century European, Hawley Smoot, Chickens and Steel," Columbia University, American Political Science Association.

1984b, "Politicians and Protection: Tariffs and Elections in Australia," *Public Choice,* 43, 203–9.

1984c, "Public Goods, Prisoners' Dilemmas and the International Political Economy," *International Studies Quarterly* 2, 5–22.

Cook, J. H., 1981, "The Effects of U.S. Tariffs on Production, Prices, Employment and Trade: Numerical Results Under Alternative Model Structures," School of Economics, LaTrobe University, Melbourne, Australia.

Cook, W. D., M. J. L. Kirby, and S. L. Mehndiratta, 1974, "Models for the Optimal Allocation of Funds Over *N* Constituencies During an Election Campaign," *Public Choice,* 20, 1–16.

Cooper, Richard N., 1972, "The European Community System of Generalized Preferences: A Critique," *Journal of Development Studies,* 8, 379–94.

1987, "Trade Policy as Foreign Policy," in Robert M. Stern (ed.), *U.S. Trade Policies in a Changing World Economy.* Cambridge: MIT Press, pp. 291–322.

Cooter, R., 1982, "The Cost of Coase," *Journal of Legal Studies,* 11, 1–33.

Corden, W. Max, 1957, "The Calculation of the Cost of Protection," *Economic Record,* 33, 29–51.

1966, "The Structure of a Tariff System and the Effective Rate of Protection," *Journal of Political Economy,* 74, 221–37.

1971, *The Theory of Protection.* London: Oxford University Press, esp. pp. 45–50.

1974, *Trade Policy and Economic Welfare.* Oxford: Oxford University Press.

1975, "The Costs and Consequences of Protection: A Survey of Empirical Work," in P. B. Kenen (ed.), *International Trade and Finance: Frontiers for Research.* Cambridge: Cambridge University Press, pp. 51–91.

1981, "Exchange Rate Protection" in R. N. Cooper et al. (eds.), *The International*

Monetary System Under Flexible Exchange Rates. Cambridge, Mass: Ballinger Publishing, pp. 17–34.

1984a, Booming Sector and Dutch Disease Economics: Survey and Consolidation, *Oxford Economic Papers*, 36, 359–88.

1984b, "Market Disturbances and Protection: Efficiency Versus the Conservative Social Welfare Function," Conference on Trade Problems and Policies, Monash University.

1985, *Protection, Growth and Trade: Essays in International Economics*. New York: Basil Blackwell.

1987, *Protection and Liberalization: A Review of Analytical Issues*. Occasional Paper No. 54, International Monetary Fund, Washington, D.C., August.

Cornell, Nina W., Roger G. Noll, and Barry Weingast, 1976, "Safety Regulation," in Henry Owen and Charles L. Schultze (eds.), *Setting National Priorities: The Next Ten Years*. Washington, D. C.: Brookings Institution, pp. 464–7, 470–7.

Corson, W., W. Nicholson, and J. David Richardson, 1979, "Final Report: Survey of Trade Adjustment Assistance Recipients," report by Mathematica Policy Research. to U.S. Dept. of Labor, Bureau of International Labor Affairs, Office of Foreign Economic Research, Princeton.

Coughlin, Peter J., 1982, "Pareto Optimality of Policy Proposals with Probabilistic Voting," *Public Choice,* 39, 427–33.

1983, "Davis–Hinich Conditions and Median Outcomes in Probabilistic Voting Models," *Journal of Economic Theory*, 34, 1–12.

Coughlin, Peter J., and S. Nitzan, 1981, "Directional and Local Electoral Equilibria with Probabilistic Voting," *Journal of Economic Theory*, 24, 226–39.

Coughlin, Peter J., and Thomas R. Palfrey, 1984, "Pareto Optimality in Spatial Voting Models," *Social Choice and Welfare*, 1, 307–19.

Courant, P., et al., 1979, "Why Voters Support Tax Limitation Amendments: The Michigan Case," *Tax and Expenditure Limitations, National Tax Journal,* Supplement.

Cowen, David G., 1986, "Cross-National Economic Inequality," term paper, Finance 396, University of Texas at Austin.

Cox, J., B. Robertson, and Vernon L. Smith, 1982, "Theory and Behavior of Single Object Auctions," in Vernon Smith (ed.), *Research in Experimental Economics*. JAI Press, pp. 1–43.

Craig, Steven G., and Joel W. Sailors, 1985, "Interstate Barriers to Trade in a Federalist Economy," mimeo, Dept. of Economics, University of Houston.

Crain, W. Mark, 1977, "On the Structure and Stability of Political Markets," *Journal of Political Economy,* 85, 829–42.

Crandall, R. W., 1981, *The U.S. Steel Industry in Recurrent Crisis*. Washington, D.C.: Brookings Institution.

Crossman, Richard, 1973, "European Economic Community: Labour Party Attitude," *Times* (London), April 11, p. 16A.

Curzon, Gerard, and Victoria Price, 1984, "Is Protection Inevitable?" Discussion Paper No. 8401, Graduate Institute of International Studies, Geneva.

Dantzig, George B., 1975, "An Institutionalized Divvy Economy," *Journal of Economic Theory*, 11, 372–84.

Darley, John M., and Bibb Latane, 1968, "Bystander Intervention in Emergencies: Diffusion of Responsibility," *Journal of Personality and Social Psychology*, 8, 377–83.

Das, Satya, 1986, "Foreign Lobbying and the Political Economy of Protection," Dept. of Economics, University of Milwaukee, mimeo.

David, Martin, and Timothy Smeeding (eds.), 1985, *Horizontal Equity, Uncertainty and Economic Well-Being*. Chicago: University of Chicago Press.

David, Paul A., 1970, "Learning by Doing and Tariff Protection," *Journal of Economic History*, 30, 521–601.

Davies, O. A., and Melvin J. Hinich, 1966, "A Mathematical Model of Policy Formation in a Democratic Society," in Joseph L. Bernd (ed.), *Mathematical Applications in Political Science, II*. Dallas: SMU Press, pp. 175–208.

1967, "Some Results Related to a Mathematical Model of Policy Formation in a Democratic Society," in Joseph L. Bernd (ed.), *Mathematical Applications in Political Science, II*. Dallas: SMU Press, pp. 14–38.

Davies, S.W., and A. J. McGuinness, 1982, "Dumping at Less than Marginal Cost," *Journal of International Economics*, 12, 169–82.

Davis, John, and Patrick Minford, 1986, "Germany and the European Disease," International Finance Discussion Paper No. 296, Federal Reserve Board, Washington, D.C., December.

Davis, Lance E., 1980, "It's a Long, Long Road to Tipperary, or Reflections on Organized Violence, Protection Rates and Related Topics: The New Political History," *Journal of Economic History*, 40, 1–16.

Davis, Lance E., and Douglass North, 1970, "Institutional Change and American Economic Growth," *Journal of Economic History*, 30, 131–49.

Dawes, Robyn M., 1980, "Social Dilemmas," *Annual Review of Psychology*, 31, 169–93.

Dawes, Robyn M., John M. Orbell, and Alphons J. C. van de Kragt, 1985, "A 'Great Society' or a 'Small Society'?: The Threshold-of-the-Room Effect in Social Dilemmas," paper presented at the annual meeting of the Western Psychological Association, San Jose, April.

with Sanford R. Braver and L. A. Wilson, II, 1986, "Doing Well and Doing Good as Ways of Resolving Social Dilemmas," in H. Wilkes and D. Messick (eds.), *Social Dilemmas*, Frankfurt am Main: Lang GambH.

De Alessi, L., 1980, "The Economics of Property Rights: A Review of the Evidence," *Research in Law and Economics*, 2, 1–47.

Deardorff, Alan V., 1986, "Safeguards Policy and the Conservative Social Welfare Function," Seminar Discussion Paper No. 173, Research Seminar in International Economics, University of Michigan.

Deardorff, Alan V., and Robert M. Stern, 1978, "The Effects of Domestic Tax/Subsidies and Import Tariffs on the Structure of Protection in the United States, United Kingdom and Japan," paper presented to International Economic Study Group, Sixth Annual Conference, Sussex, U.K., pp. 18–20.

1979, "An Economic Analysis of the Effects of the Tokyo Round of Multilateral Trade Negotiations on the United States and Other Major Industrial Countries," MTN Studies 5, Committee on Finance, U.S. Senate. Washington, D.C.: U.S. Government Printing Office.

1980, "Changes in Trade and Employment in Industrialized Countries, 1970–76," Sixth World Congress of the International Economic Association, Mexico City.

1981, "A Disaggregated Model of World Production and Trade: An Estimate of the Impact of the Tokyo Round," *Journal of Policy Modeling*, 3, 127–52.

1983, "The Effects of Foreign Tariffs and Existing Nontariff Barriers on the Sectoral Structure of Protection in the Major Industrialized Countries," Seminar Discussion Paper No. 126, Reserarch Seminar in International Economics, University of Michigan.

1984a, "Methods of Measurement of Nontariff Barriers," Seminar Discussion Paper No. 136, Research Seminar in International Economics, Dept. of Economics, University of Michigan.

1984b, "Tariff and Exchange Rate Protection under Fixed and Flexible Exchange Rates in the Major Industrialized Countries," in J. S. Bhandari and B. H. Putnam (eds.) *Economic Interdependence and Flexible Exchange Rates*. Cambridge: MIT Press, pp. 472–99.

1987, "Current Issues in Trade Policy: An Overview," in Robert M. Stern (ed.), *U.S. Trade Policies in a Changing World Economy*. Cambridge: MIT Press, pp. 15–68.

de la Torre, Jose, Michael Jay Jedel, Jeffrey S. Arpan, E. William Ogram, and Brian Toyne, 1978, *Corporate Responses to Import Competition in the U.S. Apparel Industry*, Atlanta: College of Business Administration Publishing Services Division, Georgia State University.

de Melo, J. A. P., and K. Dervis, 1977, "Modelling the Effects of Protection in a Dynamic Framework," *Journal of International Economics*, 4, 149–12.

Demsetz, Harold, 1970, "The Private Production of Public Goods," *Journal of Law and Economics*, 13, 293–306.

Denzau, Arthur T., and Michael C. Munger, 1984, "Legislators and Interest Groups: How Unorganized Interests Get Represented," paper prepared for presentation at the Public Choice Society Meetings, March 30.

Dewees, Donald N. (ed.), 1983, *The Regulation of Quality*. Toronto: Butterworths.

Diebold, W., Jr., and H. Stalson, 1982, "Negotiating Issues in International Services Transactions," paper presented at conference on Trade Policy in the Eighties, Institute for International Economics, Washington, D.C.

Dinopoulos, Elias, 1982, "Optimum Tariff With Revenue-Seeking: A Contribution to the Theory of DUP Activities," working paper, Columbia University.

1987, "Quid Pro Quo Foreign Investment," Conference on Political Economy, World Bank, Washington, D.C.

Dixit, Avinash K., 1980, *Theory of International Trade*. New York: Cambridge University Press.

1987, "How Should the United States Respond to Other Countries' Trade Policies?," in Robert M. Stern (ed.), *U.S. Trade Policies in A Changing World Economy*. Cambridge: MIT Press, pp. 245–82.

Dixon, Peter B., B. R. Parmenter, J. Sutton, and D. P. Vincent, 1982, *ORANI: A Multi-Sectoral Model of the Australian Economy.* Amsterdam: North-Holland.

Donges, Juergen B., 1984, "The International Trading Order at the Crossroads," Working Paper No. 199, Kiel Institute of World Economics.

Dornbusch, Rudiger, 1987, "External Balance Correction: Depreciation or Protection?," *Brookings Papers on Economic Activity*, 249–69.

Dornbusch, Rudiger, and Jeffrey A. Frankel, 1987, "Macroeconomics and Protection," in Robert M. Stern (ed.), *U.S. Trade Policies in a Changing World Economy.* Cambridge: MIT Press, pp. 77–130.

Dougan, William R., 1981, "The Political Economy of Protection," dissertation, Dept. of Economics, University of Chicago.

    1984, "Tariffs and the Economic Theory of Regulation," *Research in Law and Economics,* 6, 87–210.

Downs, Anthony, 1957, *An Economic Theory of Democracy.* New York: Harper and Row.

Dunn, Lewis A., 1981, "Some Reflections on the 'Dove's Dilemma,'" *International Organization*, 35, 181–92.

Dunn, Ray, 1983, "Lawyers Per Capita and National Growth," term paper, Finance 396, University of Texas at Austin.

Dunn, Robert M., Jr., 1980, "Economic Growth Among Industrialized Countries," NPA Committee on Changing International Realities, Report No. 179, National Planning Association.

Dunning, J. H. (ed.), 1971, *The Multinational Corporation.* London: George Allen and Unwin.

    1973, "The Determinants of International Production," *Oxford Economic Papers*, 25, 289–336.

Easton, Stephen T., and H. Grubel, 1982, "The Costs and Benefits of Protection in a Growing World," *Kyklos*, 36, 213–30.

Eaton, Jonathan, and Gene Grossman, 1985, "Tariffs as Insurance: Optimal Commercial Policy When Domestic Markets Are Incomplete," *Canadian Journal of Economics*, 18, 258–72.

Edwards, Richard C., 1970, "Economic Sophistication in Nineteenth Century Congressional Tariff Debates," *Journal of Economic History*, 30, 802–37.

Ehrlich, I., 1975, "The Deterrent Effect of Capital Punishment: A Question of Life and Death," *American Economic Review*, 65, 397–417.

Eichengreen, Barry J., 1982, "U.S. Antidumping Policies: The Case of Steel," paper presented at National Bureau of Economic Research Conference on the Structure and Evolution of Recent U.S. Trade Policy, Cambridge, Mass., December 3–4.

Eiteman, Wilford J., 1930, "The Rise and Decline of Orthodox Tariff Propaganda," *Quarterly Journal of Economics*, 45, 22–39.

Eliasson G., 1984, Micro Heterogeneity of Firms and the Stability of Industrial Growth, *Journal of Economic Behavior and Organization*, 5, 249–74.

Enelow, James, and Melvin J. Hinich, 1981, "A New Approach to Voter Uncertainty in the Downsian Spatial Model," *American Journal of Political Science,* 25, 483–93.

1982a, "Ideology, Issues and the Spatial Theory of Elections," *American Political Science Review*, 76, 493–501.

1982b, "Nonspatial Candidate Characteristics and Electoral Competition," *Journal of Politics*, 44, 115–30.

1984, *The Spatial Theory of Voting: An Introduction*. Cambridge: Cambridge University Press.

Erzan, Refik, and Guy Karsenty, 1987, "Products Facing High Tariffs in Major Developed Market Economy Countries: An Area of Priority for Developing Countries in the Uruguay Round?," Seminar Paper No. 401, University of Stockholm, Institute for International Economic Studies, December.

Ethier, Wifred J., 1971, "General Equilibrium Theory and the Concept of Effective Protection," in H. G. Grubel and Harry G. Johnson (eds.), *Effective Tariff Protection*, Geneva: GATT and Graduate Institute of International Studies, pp. 17–43.

1979, "Internationally Decreasing Costs and World Trade," *Journal of International Economics*, 9, 1–24.

1982, "Dumping," *Journal of Political Economy*, 90, 487–506.

1986, "The Multinational Firm," *Quarterly Journal of Economics*, 101, 805–33.

Evans, H. D., 1971, "Effects of Protection in a General Equilibrium Framework," *Review of Economics and Statistics*, 53, 147–56.

Fair, Ray, 1978, "The Effects of Economic Events on the Vote for President," *Review of Economics and Statistics*, 60, 159–73.

Falvey, Rodney E., 1979, "The Composition of Trade within Import-Restricted Product Categories," *Journal of Political Economy*, 87, 1105–14.

Feenstra, Robert C., 1982, "Voluntary Export Restraints in U.S. Autos, 1980–81: Quality, Employment, Welfare Effects," paper presented at National Bureau of Economic Research Conference on the Structure and Evolution of Recent U.S. Trade Policy, Cambridge, Mass., December 3–4.

Feenstra, Robert C., and Jagdish N. Bhagwati, 1982, "Tariff Seeking and the Efficient Tariff," in Jagdish N. Bhagwati (ed.), *Import Competition and Response*. Chicago: University of Chicago Press, pp. 245–58.

Ferejohn, John A., 1983, "Congress and Redistribution," in A. Schick (ed.), *Making Economic Policy in Congress*. American Enterprise for Public Policy Research, Washington, D.C., pp. 131–57.

Ferejohn, John A., Morris P. Fiorina, and Herbert F. Weisberg, 1978, "Toward a Theory of Legislative Decision," *Game Theory and Political Science*. New York: New York University Press, pp. 165–90.

Ferejohn, John A., and Roger G. Noll, 1976, "Uncertainty and Formal Theory of Political Campaigns," Social Science Working Paper No. 75, California Institute of Technology.

Ferguson, Thomas, 1983a, "Elites and Elections or What Have They Done to You Lately? Toward an Investment Theory of Political Parties and Critical Realignment," Political Science, MIT.

1983b, "Party Realignment and American Industrial Structure," *Research in Political Economy*, 6, 1–82.

1984, "From Normalcy to New Deal: Industrial Structure, Party Competition and American Public Policy in the Great Depression," *International Organization,* 38, 41–94.

Ferguson, Thomas, and Joel Rogers, 1986, *Right Turn.* New York: Hill and Wang.

Fieleke, Norman S., 1976, "The Tariff Structure for Manufacturing Industries in the United States: A Test of Some Traditional Explanations," *Columbia Journal of World Business,* 11, 98–104.

Fig, John Francis, 1987, "Rent Seeking Theory and Testing," M.A. thesis, University of Texas at Austin.

Findlay, Ronald J., and Stanislaw Wellisz, 1982, "Endogenous Tariffs, the Political Economy of Trade Restrictions and Welfare," in Jagdish N. Bhagwati (ed.), *Import Competition and Response.* Chicago: University of Chicago Press, pp. 223–38.

1983, "Some Aspects of the Political Economy of Trade Restrictions," *Kyklos,* 36, 469–81.

Findlay, Ronald J., and John D. Wilson, 1984, "The Political Economy of Leviathan," Seminar Paper No. 285, Institute for International Economic Studies, University of Stockholm; published in A Razin and E. Sadka (eds.), 1987, *Economic Policy in Theory and Practice.* London: Macmillan, pp. 289–304.

Finger, J. Michael, 1976, "Trade and Domestic Effects of Offshore Assembly Provision in the U.S. Tariff Code," *American Economic Review,* 66, 598–611.

1980, "The Industry–Country Incidence of 'Less Than Fair Value' Cases in United States Import Trade," presented at NBER–FIPE Conference on Trade Prospects Among the Americas: Latin American Export Diversification and the New Protectionism, Saõ Paulo, Brazil, March 23–26.

1983–4, "The Political Economy of Trade Policy," *Cato Journal,* 3, 743–50.

Finger, J. Michael, H. K. Hall, and D. R. Nelson, 1982, "The Political Economy of Administered Protection," *American Economic Review,* 72, 452–66.

Fiorina, Morris P., and Roger G. Noll, 1977a, "Voters, Bureaucrats and Legislators: A Rational Choice Perspective on the Growth of Bureaucracy," Social Science Working Paper No. 159, California Institute of Technology, Division of the Humanities and Social Sciences.

1977b, "Voters, Legislators and Bureaucracy: Institutional Design in the Public Sector," Social Science Working Paper No. 194, California Institute of Technology, Division of the Humanities and Social Sciences.

Fisher, Eric, and Charles A. Wilson, 1987, "International Duopoly with Tariffs," International Finance Discussion Paper No. 308. Washington, D.C.: Federal Reserve Board.

Flam, Harry, and Elhanan Helpman, 1987, "Industrial Policy under Monopolistic Competition," *Journal of International Economics,* 22, 79–102.

Fleisig, H., and C. Hill, 1982, "The Benefit and Cost of Official Export Credit Programs," paper presented at National Bureau of Economic Research Conference on the Structure and Evolution of Recent U.S. Trade Policy, Cambridge, Mass., December 3–4.

Fleiss, J. L., 1973, *Statistical Methods for Rates and Proportions*. New York: John Wiley.

Floyd, R. H., 1977, "Some Long-Run Implications of Border Taxes for Factor Taxes," *Quarterly Journal of Economics*, 91, 555–78.

Foley, Duncan, 1975, "Problems Versus Conflicts: Economic Theory and Ideology," *American Economic Review*, 65, 231–6.

1978, "State Expenditures from a Marxist Perspective," *Journal of Public Economics*, 9, 221–38.

Frank, C., Jr., 1977, *Foreign Trade and Domestic Aid*. Washington, D.C.: Brookings Institution, chap. 3.

Frank, I., 1979, "The 'Graduation' Issue in Trade Policy toward LDCs," World Bank Staff Working Paper No. 334, World Bank, Washington, D.C.

Frank, Robert H., and David A. Freeman, 1978, *Distributional Consequences of Direct Foreign Investment*. New York: Academic Press.

Fraser, Niall M., and Keith W. Hipel, 1984, *Conflict Analysis, Models and Resolutions*. Amsterdam: North-Holland Publishing.

Fratianni, Michele, and John Pattison, 1982, "The Economics of International Organizations," *Kyklos*, 3, 244–62.

Freund, J. E., 1971, *Mathematical Statistics*. Englewood Cliffs: Prentice-Hall, 2nd ed.

Frey, Bruno S., 1978, *Modern Political Economy*. Oxford: Martin Robertson.

1979, "Politometrics of Government Behavior in a Democracy," *Scandinavian Journal of Economics*, 8, 308–22.

1984a, *International Political Economics*. Oxford: Basil Blackwell.

1984b, "The Public Choice View of International Political Economy," *International Organization*, 38, 199–223.

Frey, Bruno S., and Lawrence J. Lau, 1968, "Towards a Mathematical Model of Government Behaviour," *Zeitschrift für Nationalokonomie*, 28, 355–80.

Frey, Bruno S., Werner W. Pommerehne, Friedrich Schneider, and Guy Gilbert, 1984, "Consensus and Dissension among Economists: An Empirical Inquiry," *American Economic Review*, 74, 986–94.

Frey, Bruno S., and Jans Jurgen Ramser, 1976, "The Political Business Cycle: A Comment," *Review of Economic Studies*, 43, 553–55.

1986, "Where Are the Limits of Regulation," *Journal of Institutional and Theoretical Economics*, 142, 571–80.

Frey, Bruno S., and Friedrich Schneider, 1978, "An Empirical Study of Politico-Economic Interaction in the United States," *Review of Economics and Statistics*, 60, 174–83.

1981, "A Politico-Economic Model of the U.K.: New Estimates and Predictions," *Economic Journal*, 9, 737–40.

1982, "International Political Economy: An Emerging Field," Seminar Paper No. 227, Institute for International Economic Studies, University of Stockholm.

Frieden Jeffrey A., and David A. Lake, 1987, *International Political Economy: Perspectives on Global Power and Wealth*. New York: St. Martin's Press.

Friedman, James W., 1974, "Non-Cooperative Equilibria in Time-Dependent Supergames," *Econometrica*, 42, 221–37.

Friedman, Milton, 1962, *Capitalism and Freedom*. Chicago: University of Chicago Press.

Fries, Timothy, 1982, "Protection and Rent-Seeking in a Stock Market Model of Trade under Uncertainty," Economics Dept., Williams College, Williamstown, Mass., December.

Frohlich, Norman, and Joe A. Oppenheimer, 1974, "The Carrot and the Stick: Optimal Program Mixes for Entrepreneurial Political Leaders," *Public Choice*, 19, 43–61.

1984, "Democracy and Distributive Justice: A First Cut," Conference on the Political Economy of Public Policy, Stanford University, March.

Frohlich, Norman, Joe A. Oppenheimer, and O. R. Young, 1971, *Political Leadership and Collective Goods*. Princeton: Princeton University Press.

Froman, L. A., 1963, "A Review of Bauer, Pool and Dexter, American Business and Public Policy: The Politics of Foreign Trade," *American Political Science Review*, 5, 671–2.

Gallarotti, G. M., 1985, "Toward a Business-Cycle Model of Tariffs," *International Organization*, 39, 155.

Gant, M. M., and L. Sigelman, 1985, "Anticandidate Voting in Presidential Elections," *Polity*, 18, 329–39.

Gardner, Ray, 1981, "Wealth and Power in a Collegial Policy," *Journal of Economic Theory*, 25, 353–66.

Gates, Paul W., 1981, "Pressure Groups and Recent American Land Policies," *Agricultural History*, 55, 103–27.

Genberg, Hans, Alexander K. Swoboda, and Michael Salemi, 1984, "The Relative Importance of Foreign and Domestic Disturbances for Aggregate Fluctuations in the Open Economy: Switzerland 1964–1981," Discussion Papers in International Economics, No. 8407, November.

General Agreement on Tariffs and Trade, 1984, *International Trade 1983/84*, Geneva.

Gerschenkron, Alexander, 1962, *Economic Backwardness in Historical Perspective*. Cambridge: Harvard University Press.

Giersch H., and Wolter F., 1983, "Towards an Explanation of the Productivity Slowdown : An Acceleration–Deceleration Hypothesis," *Economic Journal*, 93, 35–55.

Gilpin, Robert, 1975, *U.S. Power and the Multinational Corporation*. New York: Basic Books.

Glazer, Amihai, Henry McMillan, and Marc Robbins, 1985, "Politics and Corporate Profits," Irvine Economics Paper No. 85-22, University of California.

Glismann H. H., and A. Neu, 1971, "Towards New Agreements on International Trade Liberalization," *Weltwirtschaftliches Archiv*, 2, 235–70.

Glismann, H. H., and F. D. Weiss, 1980, "On the Political Economy of Protection in Germany," World Bank Staff Working Paper No. 427, Washington, D.C.

Goehring, D. J., and J. P. Kahan, 1976, "The Uniform N-Person Prisoner's Dilemma Game," *Journal of Conflict Resolution*, 20, 111–28.

Goldberg, Victor P., 1977, "On Positive Theories of Redistribution," *Journal of Economic Issues*, 11, 119–32.

Goldsmith, Raymond W., 1985, *Comparative National Balance Sheets*. Chicago: University of Chicago Press.

Goldstein, Judith, 1986, "Ideas, Institutions and American Trade Policy," Cambridge: National Bureau of Economic Research.

Goodin, Robert E., 1982, *Political Theory and Public Policy*. Chicago: University of Chicago Press.

Goodman, John C., 1976, "A Theory of Competitive Regulatory Equilibrium," Dept. of Economics, Dartmouth College.

Goodwin, C., 1972, "Economic Theory and Society: A Plea for Process Analysis," *American Economic Review*, 62, 409–15.

Gordon, Roger H., 1985, "Taxation of Investment and Savings in a World Economy: The Certainty Case," Seminar Discussion Paper No. 157, Research Seminar in International Economics, Dept. of Economics, University of Michigan.

Gould, J. P., 1973, "The Economics of Legal Conflicts," *Journal of Legal Studies*, 2, 279–300.

Gourevitch, Peter Alexis, 1977, "International Trade, Domestic Coalitions and Liberty: Comparative Responses to the Crisis of 1873–1896," *Journal of Interdisciplinary History*, 8, 281–313.

Gowa, Joanne, 1986, "Comment" on Robert E. Baldwin, "Lobbying for Public Goods," a paper presented at the Conference on the Political Economy of Trade Policy, Cambridge: MIT.

Grassman, Sven, 1980, "Long-Term Trends in Openness of National Economies," *Oxford Economic Papers*, 32, 123–33.

Graves, Quart, "Religious Diversity as Related to Per Capita GNP Growth Rates," term paper, Finance 396, University of Texas at Austin.

Green, Robert T., 1972, *Political Instability as a Determinant of U.S. Foreign Investment*. Austin, Texas: Bureau of Business Research, University of Texas.

Greenaway, David, 1984, "Multilateral Trade Policy in the 1980s," *Lloyds Bank Review*, 151, 30–44.

Grilli, Enzo, 1980, "Italian Commercial Policies in the 1970s," World Bank Staff Working Paper No. 428, Washington, D.C.

Grossman, Gene M., 1980, "Border Tax Adjustments: Do They Distort Trade?" *Journal of International Economics*, 10, 117–28.

1981, "The Theory of Domestic Content Protection," *Quarterly Journal of Economics*, 96, 583–603.

1982a, "Offshore Assembly Provisions and the Structure of Trade," *Journal of International Economics*, 12, 301–12.

1982b, "On Measuring the Employment Effects of Import Competition," in Jagdish N. Bhagwati (ed.), *Import Competition and Response*. Chicago: University of Chicago Press, for the National Bureau of Economic Research, pp. 396–9.

1982c, "The Employment and Wage Effects of Import Competition in the United States," Discussion Paper in Economics No. 35, Woodrow Wilson School, Princeton University, Princeton, N.J.

1984, "International Trade, Foreign Investment, and the Formation of the Entrepreneurial Class," *American Economic Review*, 74, 605–14.

Grossman, Gene M., and J. David Richardson, 1985, "Strategic Trade Policy: A Survey of Issues and Early Analysis," Princeton University, *Special Papers in International Economics*, 15, 1–38.

Grossman, Sanford J., and Oliver D. Hart, 1980, "Takeover Bids, the Free-Rider Problem and the Theory of the Corporation," *Bell Journal of Economics,* 11, 42–64.

Groves, T., and Ledyard, J., 1977, "Optimal Allocation of Public Goods: A Solution to the 'Free Rider' Problem," *Econometrica,* 45, 783–809.

Gupta, Dipak K., and Yiannis Venieris, 1981, "Introducing New Dimensions in Macro Models: The Sociopolitical and Institutional Environments," *Economic Development and Cultural Change,* 30, 31–58.

Guttman, Joel M., 1977, "Understanding Collective Action: Matching Behavior," Rand Corporation, Santa Monica, California.

Gylfason, Thorvaldur, 1987, "Does Exchange Rate Policy Matter?," *European Economic Review,* 31, 375–81.

Haefele, Edwin T., 1971, "A Utility Theory of Representative Government," *American Economic Review,* 61, 350–67.

Hall, Robert E., 1980, "Stabilization Policy and Capital Formation," *American Economic Association,* 70, 157–63.

Hamburger, Henry, 1979, *Games as Models of Social Phenomena.* San Francisco: W. H. Freeman and Co.

Hamilton, Bob, Sharif Mohammad, and John Whalley, 1984, "Rent Seeking and the North–South Terms of Trade," Centre for the Study of International Economic Relations, Working Paper No. 8426C, Dept. of Economics, University of Western Ontario.

Hamilton, Carl, 1981a, "A New Approach to Estimation of the Effects of Non-Tariff Barriers to Trade: An Application to the Swedish Textile and Clothing Industry," *Weltwirtschaftliches Archiv,* 117, 298–325.

1981b, "Public Subsidies to Industry: The Case of Sweden and Its Shipbuilding Industry," Institute for International Economic Studies, University of Stockholm, Seminar Paper No. 174.

1984a, "Voluntary Export Restraints: ASEAN Systems for Allocation of Export Licences," Seminar Paper No. 275, Institute for International Economic Studies, University of Stockholm.

1984b, "Voluntary Export Restraints on Asia: Tariff Equivalents, Rents and Trade Barrier Formation," Seminar Paper No. 276, Institute for International Economic Studies, University of Stockholm.

1985a, "Economic Aspects of Voluntary Export Restraints in D. Greenaway," *Current Issues in International Trade.* London: Macmillan, 99–117.

1985b, "Voluntary Export Restraints and Trade Diversion", *Journal of Common Market Studies,* 23, 345–355.

1986a, "ASEAN Systems for Allocation of Export Licences under VERs and Import Quotas and Voluntary Export Restraints: Focusing on Exporting Countries, reprint from *The Political Economy of Manufacturing Protection: Experiences of ASEAN and Australia,* Reprint Series No. 324, Institute of International Economic Studies, University of Stockholm.

1986b, "An Assessment of Voluntary Restraints on Hong Kong Exports to Europe and the USA," *Economica,* 53, 339–50.

1986c, "Restrictiveness and International Transmission of the 'New' Protectionism," Seminar Paper No. 367, Institute for International Economic Studies, University of Stockholm.

1986d, "The Upgrading Effect of Voluntary Export Restraints," *Weltwirtschaftliches Archiv*, 122, 358–64.

Hamilton, Carl, and Lars E. O. Svensson, 1984, "Do Countries' Factor Endowments Correspond to the Factor Contents in Their Bilateral Trade Flows?," *Scandinavian Journal of Economics*, 86, 84–97.

Hammack, David C., 1981, "Economic Interest Groups and Path Analysis: Two Approaches to the History of Power," *Journal of Interdisciplinary History*, 11, 694–704.

Han, Xiaoyue, 1986, "The Relationship of Capital Stock and GNP: A Cross Country Analysis and Estimation," term paper, Finance 396, University of Texas at Austin.

Hanke, Steve H., 1983–4, "U.S.–Japanese Trade: Myths and Realities," *Cato Journal,* 3, 757–70.

Hansen, Stephen, Thomas R. Palfrey, and Howard Rosenthal, 1987, "The Downsian Model of Participation: Formal Theory and Empirical Analysis of the Constituency Size Effect." *Public Choice.*, 52, 15–33.

Harberger, Arnold C., 1962, "The Incidence of the Corporation Income Tax," *Journal of Political Economy*, 70, 215–40.

Hardin, G., 1975, "The Tragedy of the Commons," in Bruce Ackerman (ed.), *Economic Foundations of Property Law.* Boston: Little Brown, pp. 2–11.

Hardin, Russell, 1971, "Collective Action as an Agreeable *n*–Prisoners' Dilemma," *Behaviorial Science*, 16(5), 472–81.

1979, "Comment," on paper by Mancur Olson, in Clifford S. Russell (ed.), 1979, *Collective Decision Making.* Baltimore: Johns Hopkins Press, pp. 122–9.

Harris, Richard G., 1984, "Market Structure and Trade Liberalization: A General Equilibrium Assessment," paper for presentation at the Workshop on Applied General Equilibrium Models in International Trade, Columbia University, April.

Harrison, Glenn W., and E. E. Rutstrom, 1986, "Trade Wars: Computing Nash Equilibria in General Equilibrium Trade Models," University of Western Ontario.

Harsanyi, John, 1967–8, "Games with Incomplete Information Played by Bayesian Players, I–III." *Management Science,* 14, 149–82, 320–34, 486–502.

Hartle, D. G., 1983, "The Theory of 'Rent Seeking': Some Reflections," *Canadian Journal of Economics*, 16, November 4, 539–54.

Harvey, Alan, 1985, "Redistributive Activities and Its Relationship to Foreign Direct Investment," term paper, Finance 396, University of Texas at Austin.

Haveman, R., 1976, "Policy Analysis and the Congress: An Economist's View," *Policy Analysis*, 2, 235–50.

Hays, W. L., and Winkler, R. L., 1971, *Statistics.* New York: Holt, Rinehart and Winston.

Hayek, Friedrich A., 1979, *The Political Order of a Free People*, Vol. 3 of *Law, Liberty and Legislation*. London: Routledge and Kegan Paul.

Helleiner, Gerald K., 1977, "The Political Economy of Canada's Tariff Structure: An Alternative Model," *Canadian Journal of Economics*, 10, 318–36.

Helpman, Elhanan, 1978, "The Exact Measure of Welfare Losses Which Result from Trade Taxes," *International Economic Review*, 19, 157–63.

1984, "A Simple Theory of International Trade with Multinational Corporations," *Journal of Political Economy*, 92, 451–71.

Helpman, Elhanan, and Paul R. Krugman, 1985, *Market Structure and Foreign Trade*. Cambridge: MIT Press.

Helpman, Elhanan, and Assaf Razin, 1980, "Efficient Protection under Uncertainty," *American Economic Review*, 70, 716–31.

Henderson, Dale W., 1979, "Financial Policies in Open Economies," *American Economic Review Papers and Proceedings*, 69, 232–8.

Heyne, Paul, 1983–4, "Do Trade Deficits Really Matter?," *Cato Journal*, 3, 705–16.

Hibbs, Douglas A., Jr., 1977, "Political Parties and Macroeconomic Policy," *American Political Science Review*, 71, 1467–87.

1987, *The American Political Economy: Macroeconomics and Electoral Politics*. Cambridge: Harvard University Press.

Hibbs, Douglas A., Jr., and H. Fassbender (eds.), 1981, *Contemporary Political Economy*. Amsterdam: North-Holland Publishing.

Hicks, John, 1983, "Structural Unemployment and Economic Growth: A Labor Theory of Value Model," in Dennis C. Mueller (ed.), *The Political Economy of Growth*. New Haven: Yale University Press, pp. 53–6.

Hildebrand, David K., James D. Laing, and Howard Rosenthal, 1977, *Prediction Analysis of Cross Classifications*. New York: Wiley.

Hillman, Arye L., 1977a, "The Brigden Theorem," *Economic Record*, 53, 434–46.

1977b, "The Case for Terminal Protection for Declining Industries," *Southern Economic Journal*, 44, 155–60.

1982, "Declining Industries and Political-Support Protectionist Motives," *American Economic Review*, 72, 1180–7.

1988a, "Policy Motives and International Trade Restrictions," in Hans-Jurgen Vosgerou (ed.), *New Institutional Arrangements for the World Economy*. New York: Springer-Verlag.

1988b, *The Political Economy of Protection*. Fundamentals of Pure and Applied Economics. New York: Harwood Academic Publishers.

1988c, "Tariff-Revenue Transfers to Protectionist Interests: Compensation for Reduced Protection or Supplementary Reward for Successful Lobbying?" *Public Choice*, 58, 169–85.

Hillman, Arye L., and Eliakim Katz, 1987, "Hierarchical Structure and the Social Cost of Bribes and Transfers," *Journal of Public Economics*, 34, 129–42.

Hillman, Arye L., Eliakim Katz, and Jacob Rosenberg, 1987, "Workers as Insurance: Anticipated Government Assistance and Factor Demand," *Oxford Economic Papers*, 3, 1–8.

Hillman, Arye, and John G. Riley, 1987, "Politically Contestable Rents and Transfers," Conference on Political Economy, World Bank, Washington, D.C.

Hillman, Arye L., and Doy Samet, 1987, "Dissipation of Contestable Rents by Small Numbers of Contenders," *Public Choice*, 54, 63–82.

Hillman, Arye L., and Heinrich W. Ursprung, 1988, "Domestic Politics, Foreign Interests and International Trade Policy, *American Economic Review*, 78, 729–45.

Hillman, J. S., 1978, *Non-Tariff Agricultural Barriers*. Lincoln: University of Nebraska Press.

Hilton, R. S. "An Estimable Model of the Commodity Version of Trade," Ph.D. thesis, University of Wisconsin–Madison, 1981.

Hinckley, Barbara, 1981, *Coalitions and Politics*. New York: Harcourt Brace Jovanovich.

Hindley, B., 1984, "Empty Economics in the Case for Industrial Policy," *World Economy*, 7, 277–94.

Hinich, Melvin J., 1978, "Spatial Voting Theory When Voter Perceptions of Candidates Differ," Virginia Tech, CE 78-11-4.

1981, "Voting as an Act of Contribution," *Public Choice*, 36, 135–40.

Hinich, Melvin J., John Ledyard, and Peter C. Ordeshook, 1972, "Nonvoting and the Existence of Equilibrium Under Majority Rule, *Journal of Economic Theory*, 4, 144–53.

1973, "A Theory of Electoral Equilibrium: A Spatial Analysis Based on the Theory of Games," *Journal of Politics*, 35, 154–93.

Hinich, Melvin J., and Peter C. Ordeshook, 1970, "Plurality Maximization vs. Vote Maximization: A Spatial Analysis with Variable Participation," *American Political Science Review*, 64, 772–91.

Hinich, Melvin J., and W. Pollard, 1981, "A New Approach to the Spatial Theory of Electoral Competition," *American Journal of Political Science*, 25, 323–41.

Hirschman, Albert O., 1945, *National Power and the Structure of Foreign Trade*. Berkeley: University of California Press, reprinted 1969.

1970, *Exit, Voice and Loyalty*. Cambridge: Harvard University Press.

Hirshleifer, Jack, 1980, *Price Theory and Application*. Englewood Cliffs, N.J.: Prentice-Hall, 3rd ed.

Hochman, H., and J. D. Rodgers, 1969, "Pareto Optimal Redistributions, *American Economic Review*, 59, 542–5.

Holsen, John, 1987, "Tax Evasion, Corruption and Administration: Monitoring Agents under Symmetric Dishonesty," Conference on Political Economy, World Bank, Washington, D.C.

Hotelling, Harold, 1929, "Stability in Competition," *Economic Journal*, 39, 41–57.

Hudec, R. 1980, "GATT Dispute Settlement After the Tokyo Round: An Unfinished Business," *Cornell International Law Journal*, 13, 221–37.

Hufbauer, Gary C., D. T. Berliner, and K. A. Elliott, 1986, *Trade Protection in the US: 31 Case Studies*. Washington, D.C.: Institute for International Economics.

Hufbauer, Gary C., and Joanna S. Erb, 1984, *Subsidies in International Trade*. Washington, D.C.: Institute for International Economics.

Hughes, Gordon A., and David M. G. Newbery, 1986, "Protection and Developing Countries' Exports of Manufactures," *Economic Policy*, 2, 410–53.

Hughes, H., and Anne O. Krueger, 1982, "Effects of Protection in Developed Countries on Developing Countries' Exports of Manufactures," paper presented at National Bureau of Economic Research Conference on the Structure and Evolution of Recent U.S. Trade Policy, Cambridge, Mass., December.

Hughes, K. H., 1979, *Trade, Taxes and Transnationals: International Economic Decision Making in Congress*. New York: Praeger.

Husted, Steven, 1986, "Foreign Lobbying and the Formation of Domestic Trade Policy," paper presented at 61st Annual Western Economic Association Meetings, San Francisco.

Hymer, Stephen, 1970, "The Efficiency (Contradictions) of Multinational Corporations," *American Economic Review*, 60, 441–8.

Ingberman, Daniel, 1985, "Spatial Competitions with Imperfectly Informed Voters," mimeo, University of Pennsylvania.

Inman, R. P., 1978, "Testing Political Economy's 'As If' Proposition: Is the Median Income Voter Really Decisive?" *Public Choice*, 33, 44–65.

1981, "On Setting the Agenda for Pennsylvania School Finance Reform: An Exercise in Giving Policy Advice," *Public Choice*, 36, 449–74.

1982, "The Economic Case for Limits to Government," *American Economic Review*, 72, 176–83.

1985, "Markets, Government and the New Political Economy," in Alan Auerbach and Martin Feldstein (eds.), *Handbook of Public Economics*. Amsterdam: North-Holland, Sections I and II.

International Bar Directory, 1985. Chicago: American Bar Foundation, 4th ed.

Intriligator, Michael D., 1971, *Mathematical Optimization and Economic Theory*. Englewood Cliffs, N.J.: Prentice-Hall.

1975, "Strategic Considerations in the Richardson Model of Arms Races," *Journal of Political Economy*, 83, 339–53.

Isaac, R. Mark, Ken F. McCue, and Charles R. Plott, 1985, "Public Goods Provision in an Experimental Environment," *Journal of Public Economics*, 26, 51–74.

Isaac, R. Mark, James W. Walker, and Susan H. Thomas, 1984, "Divergent Evidence on Free Riding: An Experimental Examination of Possible Explanations," *Public Choice*, 42, 113–49.

Ishii, Naoko, Warwick McKibbin, and Jeffrey Sachs, 1985, "The Economic Policy Mix, Policy Cooperation and Protectionism: Some Aspects of Macroeconomic Interdependence Among the United States, Japan and Other OECD Countries," *Journal of Policy Modeling*, 74, 533–72.

Jackson, J. H., 1982, "GATT Machinery and the Tokyo Round Agreements," paper presented at a Conference on Trade Policy in the Eighties, June, Institute for International Economics, Washington, D.C.

Jackson, John E., 1974, *Constituencies and Leaders in Congress: Their Effects on Senate Voting Behavior*. Cambridge: Harvard University Press, chaps. 1, 2, 4, 7.

Jacobson, Gary C., 1978, "The Effects of Campaign Spending in Congressional Elections," *American Political Science Review*, 72, 469–91.

Jacobson, O. L. S., 1978, "Earnings Losses of Workers Displaced from Manufacturing Industries" in W. Dewald (ed.), *The Impact of International Trade and Investment on Employment.* U.S. Dept. of Labor, Washington, D.C.: U.S. Government Printing Office, pp. 87–98.

Jenkins, G. P., 1981, "Costs and Consequences of the New Protectionism: The Case of Canada's Clothing Sector," mimeo, North–South Institute, Ottawa.

Jenkins, G. P., G. Glenday, J. C. Evans, and C. Montmarquette, 1978, "Trade Adjustment Assistance: The Costs of Adjustment and Policy Proposals," report by Econanalysis Incorporated to the Dept. of Industry, Trade and Employment, Canada.

Jenkins, G. P., and C. Montmarquette, 1979, "Estimating the Private and Social Opportunity Cost of Displaced Workers," *Review of Economics and Statistics,* 61, 342–53.

Jensen, Richard, and Marie Thursby, 1981, "A Conjectural Variation Approach to Strategic Tariff Equilibria," Dept. of Economics, Ohio State University.

1986, "Endogenous Tariff Policy under Uncertainty," research report, Dept. of Economics, Ohio State University.

Jeon, Bang Nam, and George M. von Furstenberg, 1986, "Survey: Techniques for Measuring the Welfare Effects of Protection: Appraising the Choices," *Journal of Political Modeling,* 82, 273–303.

Johansen, Leif 1960, *A Multi-Sectional Study of Economic Growth.* Amsterdam: North-Holland.

1965, *Public Economics.* Amsterdam: North-Holland.

Johns, R. A., 1985, *International Trade Theories and the Evolving Internatonal Economy.* New York: St. Martin's Press.

Johnson, A. S., 1908, "Protection in the Formation of Capital," *Political Science Quarterly,* 23, 220–41.

Johnson, Harry G., 1960, "The Cost of Protection and the Scientific Tariff," *Journal of Political Economy,* 68, 327–45.

1965, "The Theory of Tariff Structure with Special Reference to World Trade and Development," in Harry G. Johnson and Peter Kenen (eds.), *Trade and Development.* Geneva: Librairia Droz, pp.9–29.

1971, *Aspects of the Theory of Tariffs.* London: George Allen and Unwin, chap. 11.

Jones, Kent, 1984, "The Political Economy of Voluntary Export Restraint Agreements," *Kyklos,* 37, 82–101.

Jones, Ronald W., 1971, "A Three-Factor Model in Theory, Trade and History," in Jagdish N. Bhagwati et al. (eds.), *Trade, Balance of Payments and Growth: Papers in International Economics in Honor of Charles P. Kindleberger.* Amsterdam: North-Holland, pp. 3–21.

1979, *International Trade: Essay in Theory.* Amsterdam: North-Holland.

Jones, Ronald W., and Jose Scheinkman, 1977, "The Relevance of the Two-Sector Production Model in Trade Theory," *Journal of Political Economy,* 85, 909–35.

Jungenfelt, Karl, and Douglas Hague (eds.), 1985, *Structural Adjustment in Developed Open Economies.* New York: St. Martin's Press.

Kalantzopoulos, Orsalia, 1986, "The Cost of Vountary Export Restraints for Selected Industries in the U.S. and E.E.C," mimeo.

Kalt, Joseph P., and Mark A. Zupan, 1983, "Further Evidence on Capture and Ideology in the Economic Theory of Politics," Discussion Paper No. 979, Harvard Institute of Economic Research, Cambridge, Mass.

   1984, "The Ideological Behavior of Legislators: Rational On-the-Job Consumption or Just a Residual," Conference on the Political Economy of Public Policy, Stanford University, March.

Katzenstein, Peter J. (ed.), 1978, *Between Power and Plenty: Foreign Economic Policies of Advanced Industrial States*. Madison: University of Wisconsin Press.

Kau, James B., and Paul H. Rubin, 1979, "Self-Interest, Ideology and Logrolling in Congressional Voting," *Journal of Law and Economics*, 22, 365–84.

   1982, *Congressmen, Constituents and Contributors*. Boston: Martinus Nijhoff.

Kaufman, Herbert, 1976, *Are Government Organizations Immortal?* Washington, D.C.: Brookings Institution.

Keesing, D. G., and Wolf, M., 1980, *Textile Quotas Against Developing Countries*. London: Trade Policy Research Centre, Thames Essay No. 3.

Kegley, Charles W., and Patrick McGowan (eds.), 1981, *The Political Economy of Foreign Policy Behavior*. Beverly Hills: Sage Publishers.

Kemp, Murray C., and Henry Y. Wan, 1976, "An Elementary Proposition Concerning the Formation of Customs Unions," *Journal of International Economics*, 6, 95–7.

Keohane, Robert O., 1984, *After Hegemony*. Princeton: Princeton University Press.

Keohane, Robert O., and Joseph Nye, 1977, *Power and Interdependencee*. Boston: Little Brown Publishing.

Kim, Olive, and Mark Walker, 1984, "The Free Rider Problem: Experimental Evidence," *Public Choice,* 43, 3–24.

Kinder, D. R., 1981, "Presidents, Prosperity and Public Opinion," *Public Opinion Quarterly,* 45, 1–21.

Kinder, D.R., and D. R. Kiewiet, 1981, "Sociotropic Politics – The American Case," *British Journal of Political Science*, 11, 129–61.

Kindleberger, Charles P., 1951, "Group Behavior and International Trade," *Journal of Political Economy*, 59, 30–46.

   1963, *International Economics*. Homewood, Illinois: Irwin, 3rd ed.

   1969, *American Business Abroad: Six Lectures on Direct Investment*. New Haven: Yale University Press.

   (ed.), 1970a, *The International Corporation*. Cambridge: MIT Press.

   1970b, *Power and Money. The Economics of International Politics and the Politics of International Economics*. New York: Basic Books.

   1975, "The Rise of Free Trade in Western Europe, 1820–1875," *Journal of Economic History,* 35, 20–55.

   1978, "The Aging Economy," *Weltwirtschaftliches Archiv*, 114, 407–21.

   1980, "Economic Laws and Economic History," Massachusetts Institute of Economics, lecture at Luigi Bocconi University, Milan, Italy.

   1983–4, "International Trade and National Prosperity," *Cato Journal,* 3, 623–38.

1986, "International Public Goods Without International Government," *American Economic Review,* 76, 1–13.

Kindleberger, Charles P., and David B. Audretsch (eds.), 1983, *The Multinational Corporation in the 1980s.* Cambridge: MIT Press.

Klapp, Merrie G., 1982, "The State – Landlord or Entrepreneur?," *International Organization,* 36, 575–607.

Klein, Lawrence R., 1985, "Empirical Aspects of Protectionism: LINK Results," *Journal of Policy Modeling,* 7, 35–47.

Knetsch, J., and Thomas Borcherding, 1979, "Expropriations of Private Property and the Basis for Compensation," *(University of) Toronto Law Journal,* 29, 237–52.

Knorr, Klaus, 1973, *Power and Wealth: The Political Economy of International Power.* London: Macmillan.

Kohler, Wilhelm K., 1987, "Modeling Heckscher–Ohlin Comparative Advantage in Regression Equations: A Critical Survey," Seminar Discussion Paper No. 211, Research Seminar in International Economics, Dept. of Economics, University of Michigan, December.

Komorita, S. S., and C. W. Lapworth, 1982, "Alternative Choices in Social Dilemmas," *Journal of Conflict Resolution,* 26, 692–708.

Kormendi, Roger C., 1983, "Government Debt, Government Spending and Private Sector Behavior," *American Economic Review,* 73, 994–1010.

Kormendi, Roger C., and Laura LaHaye, 1984, "Cross-Regime Tests of the Permanent Income Hypothesis," mimeo.

Kormendi, Roger C., and Philip G. Meguire, 1984a, "Cross Country Evidence on Some Macroeconomic Hypotheses Relating to Economic Growth," mimeo.

1984b, "Cross Regime Evidence of Macoeconomic Rationality," *Journal of Political Economy,* 92, 875–908.

Korstecki, M. M. (ed.), 1982, *State Trading in International Markets.* London: MacMillan.

Kotlikoff, Laurence J., and Torsten Persson, and Lars E. O. Svensson, 1987, "Social Contracts as Assets: A Possible Solution to the Time-Consistency Problem," Seminar Paper No. 397, University of Stockholm, Institute for International Economic Studies, December.

Kramer, Gerald H., 1966, "A Decision-Theoretic Analysis of a Problem in Political Campaigning," in Joseph L. Bernd (ed.), *Mathematical Applications in Political Science, II.* Dallas: SMU Press.

1971, "Short-Term Fluctuations in U.S. Voting Behavior, 1896–1964," *American Political Science Review,* 65, 131–43.

1977, "A Dynamical Model of Political Equilibrium," *Journal of Economic Theory,* 16, 310–35.

1983, "Electoral Politics in the Zero-Sum Society," Social Science Working Paper 472, California Institute of Technology, Pasadena.

Kramer, Gerald H., and James M. Snyder, 1984, "Linearity of the Optimal Income Tax: A Generalization," Conference on the Political Economy of Public Policy, Stanford University, March.

Krasner, Stephen D., 1976, "State Power and the Structure of International Trade," *World Politics,* 283, 317–47.

1977, "U.S. Commercial and Monetary Policy: Unravelling the Paradox of External Strength and Internal Weakness," *International Organization,* 314, 635–71.

1978, *Defending the National Interests.* Princeton: Princeton University Press.

1985, *Structural Conflict.* Berkeley: University of California Press.

Krauss, Melvyn, 1983–4, "Protectionism, the Welfare State and the Third World," *Cato Journal,* 3, 673–8.

Kreinin, Mordechai E., 1981, "Static Effect of E.E.C. Enlargement on Trade Flows in Manufactured Products," *Kyklos,* 34, 60–71.

1985, "United States Trade and Possible Restrictions in High Technology Products," *Journal of Policy Modeling* 71, 69–105.

Kreinin, Mordechai E., and Lawrence H. Officer, 1979, "Tariff Reductions Under the Tokyo Round," *Weltwirtschaftliches Archiv,* 3, 543–72.

Krueger, Anne O., 1974, "The Political Economy of the Rent-Seeking Society," *American Economic Review,* 64, 291–303.

1978, *Foreign Trade Regimes and Economic Development: Liberalization Attempts and Consequences.* Cambridge: Ballinger Publishing, for the National Bureau of Economic Research, Vol. X.

1980, "Impact of Foreign Trade on Employment in United States Indusry," in John Black and Brian Hindley (eds.), *Current Issues in Commercial Policy and Diplomacy.* London: MacMillan, pp. 73–98.

Krugman, Paul R., 1979, "Increasing Returns, Monopolistic Competition and International Trade," *Journal of International Economics,* 9, 469–80.

1981, "Intra-Industry Specialization and the Gains from Trade," *Journal of Political Economy,* 86, 959–73.

1983, "Targeted Industrial Policies: Theory and Evidence," *Federal Reserve Bank of Kansas City,* 123–55.

(ed.), 1986, *Strategic Trade Policy and the New International Economics.* Cambridge: MIT Press.

1987, "Strategic Sectors and International Competition," in Robert M. Stern (ed.), *U.S. Trade Policies in a Changing World Economy.* Cambridge: MIT Press, pp. 207–32.

Kurth, James R. 1979, "The Political Consequences of the Product Cycle: Industrial History and Political Outcomes," *International Organization,* 33, 1–34.

Lage, G. M., 1970, "A Linear Programming Analysis of Tariff Protection," *Western Economic Journal,* 53, 147–56.

Lake, David A., 1986, *Political and Cosmopolitical Economy Revisited: Japan and Theories of Trade Policy.* Cambridge: National Bureau of Economic Research.

Landes, William, and Richard Posner, 1975, "The Private Enforcement of Law," *Journal of Legal Studies,* 4, 1–46.

Lasswell, Harold D., 1974, "Some Perplexities of Policy Theory," *Social Reseerach,* 41, 176–89.

Lavergne, Real P., 1983, *The Political Economy of U.S. Tariffs: An Empirical Analysis.* Toronto: Academic Press.

Lawrence, Robert Z., 1984, *Can America Compete?* Washington: Brookings Institution.

Lawrence, Robert Z., and Litan, Robert E., 1986, *Saving Free Trade.* Washington: Brookings Institution.

Leamer, Edward E., 1984, *Sources of International Comparative Advantage.* Cambridge: MIT Press.

Leamer, Edward E., and Robert M. Stern, 1970, *Quantitative International Economics.* Boston: Allyn and Bacon.

Ledyard, John O., 1983, "The Pure Theory of Large Two Candidate Elections," mimeo, Northwestern University, Evanston, Illinois.

Leff, Nathaniel H., 1979, "Monopoly Capitalism and Public Policy in Developing Countries," *Kyklos*, 32, 718–38.

Leibenstein, Harvey, 1976, *Beyond Economic Man.* Cambridge: Harvard University Press.

Lenway, Stefanie Ann, 1985, *The Politics of U.S. International Trade: Protection, Expansion and Escape.* Boston: Pitman.

Leone, R., and Jackson, J., 1981, "The Political Economy of Federal Regulator Activity: Water Pollution Controls in the Pulp and Paper Industry," in G. Fromm (ed.), *Studies in Public Regulation.* Cambridge: MIT Press, pp. 231–71.

Lerner, Abba P., 1936, "The Symmetry between Import and Export Taxes," *Economica (n.s.)*, 3, 306–13.

Levinsohn, James, 1987, "Strategic Trade Policy and Direct Foreign Investment: Tariffs Versus Quotas," Seminar Discussion Paper No. 210, Research Seminar in International Economics, Dept. of Economics, University of Michigan, September.

Licon, David, and Lockwood, Mike, 1985, "Cross-National Divorce Rates," term paper, University of Texas at Austin.

Liddell, Lise Marie, 1987, "The Power of the Japanese Lobby in Washington, D.C.," professional report, Graduate School of Business, University of Texas at Austin.

Lindbeck, Assar, 1975a, "Business Cycles, Politics and International Economic Dependence," *Skandinaviska Enskilda Banken Quarterly Review*, 53–68.

　1975b, "Inequality and Redistribution Policy Issues: Principles and Swedish Experience," Seminar Paper No. 44, Institute for International Economic Studies, University of Stockholm.

　1976, "Stabilization Policy in Open Economies with Endogenous Politicians," Seminar Paper No. 54, Institute for International Economic Studies, University of Stockholm.

　1977, *The Political Economy of the New Left: An Outsider's View.* New York: Harper and Row.

　1983, "Budget Expansion and Cost Inflation," *American Economic Review*, 73, 285–90.

　1985a, "Redistribution Policy and Expansion of the Public Sector,"*Journal of Public Economics*, 28, 309–28.

　1985b, "What Is Wrong with the Western European Economies?," *World Economy*, 8, 153–70.

1986a, "Limits to the Welfare State," *Challenge*, 28, 31–45.

1986b, "Public Finance for Market-Oriented Developing Countries," Seminar Paper No. 348, Institute for International Economic Studies, University of Stockholm.

1987, "Individual Freedom and Welfare State Policy," Seminar Paper No. 389, Institute for International Economic Studies, University of Stockholm, September.

1988a, "Consequences of the Advanced Welfare State," *World Economy*, 11, 19–38.

1988b, "Individual Freedom and Welfare State Policy," *European Economic Review*, 32, 295–318.

Lindbeck, Assar, and Dennis J. Snower, 1987a, "Efficiency Wages Versus Insiders and Outsiders," *European Economic Review*, 31, 407–16.

1987b, "Union Activity, Unemployment Persistence and Wage-Employment Ratchets," *European Economic Review*, 31, 157–67.

Lindbeck, Assar, and Jorgen W. Weibull, 1987a, "Balanced-Budget Redistribution as the Outcome of Political Competition," *Public Choice*, 52, 273–97.

1987b, "Strategic Interaction with Altruism – The Economics of Fait Accompli," Seminar Paper No. 376, Institute for International Economic Studies, University of Stockholm.

1988, "Welfare Effects of Alternative Forms of Public Spending," *European Economic Review*, 32, 101–27.

Lindberg, Leon N., and Charles S. Maier (eds.), 1985, *The Politics of Inflation and Economic Stagnation*. Washington, D.C.: Brookings Institution.

Lindblom, Charles E., 1977, *Politics and Markets*. New York: Basic Books.

Lipsey, Richard E., 1982, "Recent Trends in U.S. Trade and Investment," Reprint No. 565, National Bureau of Economic Research. Reprinted from *Problems of Advanced Economies*, Proceedings of the Third Conference on New Problems of Advanced Societies, Tokyo, Japan, November.

Lipson, Charles, 1985, *Standing Guard*. Berkeley: University of California Press.

Lloyd, Peter J., 1977, *Antidumping Actions and the GATT System*. London: Trade Policy Research Centre, Thames Essays No. 9.

Lowi, T. J., 1964, "American Business, Public Policy, Case-Studies and Political Theory," *World Politics*, 16, 677–715.

Lowinger, T., 1976, "Discrimination in Government Procurement of Foreign Goods in the U.S. and Western Europe," *Southern Economic Journal*, 42, 451–60.

Lucas, Robert E., Jr., and Prescott, Edward C., 1971, "Investment under Uncertainty," *Econometrica*, 39, 659–81.

Luce, R. D., and Raiffa, H., 1957, *Games and Decisions*. New York: John Wiley, pp. 94–102.

Lundberg, L., 1981, "Patterns of Barriers to Trade in Sweden: A Study in the Theory of Protection," World Bank Staff Working Paper No. 494, Washington, D.C.

Macario, Santiago, 1964, "Protectionism and Industrialization in Latin America," *Economic Bulletin for Latin America*, 9, 61–101.

McCarthy, J. E., 1975, *Trade Adjustment Assistance: A Case Study of the Shoe Indusry in Massachusetts*. Research Report No. 58, Federal Reserve Bank of Boston.

McCormick, Robert E., and Robert D. Tollison, 1979, "Rent-Seeking Competition in Political Parties," *Public Choice*, 34, 5–14.

1981, *Politicians, Legislation and the Economy*. Boston: Martinus Nijhoff.

McCubbins, Mathew D., and Thomas Schwartz, 1984, "The Politics of Derustication," Conference on the Political Economy of Public Policy, Stanford University, March.

McCulloch, Rachel, 1978, *Research and Development as a Determinant of International Competitiveness*. Washington, D. C.: National Planning Association.

1979, "Trade and Direct Investment: Recent Policy Trends," in Rudiger Dornbusch and Jacob Frenkel (eds.), *International Economic Policy: Theory and Evidence*. Baltimore: Johns Hopkins University Press, pp. 76–104.

1985, "U.S. Direct Foreign Investment and Trade: Theories, Trends and Public Policy Issues," in A. Erdilek (ed.), *Multinationals as Mutual Invaders: Intraindustry Direct Foreign Investment*. Beckenham, England: Croom Helm, pp. 129–59.

McCulloch, Rachel, and R. Owen, 1984, "Linking Negotiations on Trade and Foreign Investment," in C. P. Kindleberger and D. B. Audretsch (eds.), *The Multinational Corporation in the 1980s*. Boston: MIT Press, pp. 334–58.

McDaniel, Kenneth A., 1984, "Unions and a Nation's Economic Performance," term paper, Finance 396, University of Texas at Austin.

McGuire, Martin, 1983, "The Anatomy of Income Distribution," mimeo, University of Maryland.

McKelvey, Richard D., and Peter C. Ordeshook, 1986, "Information and Elections: Retrospective Voting and Rational Expectations," Conference on Political Information and Political Theory, University of Texas at Austin.

McKenzie, Richard B., 1979, *The Political Economy of the Educational Process*. Boston: Martinus Nijhoff.

McKeown, Timothy J., 1983, "Hegemonic Stability Theory and 19th Century Tariff Levels in Europe," *International Organization*, 37, 73–91.

McKinnon, Ronald I., 1973, *Money and Capital in Economic Development*. Washington: Brookings Institution.

MacKuen, M., 1984, " Exposure to Information, Belief Integration, and Individual Responsiveness to Agenda Change," *American Political Science Review*, 78, 372–91.

McPherson, C. P. 1972, "Tariff Structures and Political Exchange," Ph.D. thesis, University of Chicago.

MacRae, C. D., 1977, "A Political Model of the Business Cycle," *Journal of Political Economy*, 85 239–63.

Magee, Stephen P., 1972, "The Welfare Effects of Restrictions on U.S. Trade," *Brookings Papers on Economic Activity*, 3, 645–701.

1976, *International Trade and Distortions in Factor Markets*. New York: Marcel Dekker.

1977a, "Application of the Dynamic Limit Pricing Model to the Price of Technology and International Technology Transfer," in Karl Brunner and Allan H. Meltzer (eds.), *Optimal Policies, Control Theory and Technology Exports.* Amsterdam: North-Holland, pp. 203–24.

1977b, "Information and the Multinational Corporation: An Appropriability Theory of Direct Foreign Investment," in Jagdish N. Bhagwati (ed.), *The New International Economic Order: The North–South Debate.* Cambridge: MIT Press, pp. 317–40.

1977c, "Multinational Corporations, the Industry Technology Cycle and Development," *Journal of World Trade Law,* 9, 297–321.

1980, "Three Simple Tests of the Stolper–Samuelson Theorem," in Peter Oppenheimer (ed.), *Issues in International Economics.* London: Oriel Press, pp. 138–53.

1982, "The Isoprotection Curve: Protection in the United States," mimeo, University of Texas at Austin. [For a published discussion, see Frey (1984b, pp. 56–88).]

1984, "Endogenous Tariff Theory: A Survey," in David C. Colander (ed.), *Neoclassical Political Economy.* Cambridge: Ballinger Press, pp. 41–54.

1987, "The Political Economy of U.S. Protection," in Herbert Giersch (ed.), *Free Trade in the World Economy: Towards an Opening of Markets.* Tubingen: J. C. B. Mohr, pp. 368–402.

Magee, Stephen P., and William A. Brock, 1976, "The Campaign Contribution Specialization Theorem," mimeo, University of Chicago, February.

1983, "A Model of Politics, Tariffs and Rent Seeking in General Equilibrium," in Burton Weisbrod and Helen Hughes (eds.), *Human Resources, Employment and Development: Vol 3, Problems of Developed Countries and the International Economy* (Proceedings of the Sixth World Congress of the International Economic Association held in Mexico City, 1980). London: Macmillan, pp. 497–523.

1986, "Third World Debt and International Capital Market Failure as a Consequence of Redistributive Political Risk Sharing," in Michael P. Claudon (ed.), *World Debt Crisis: International Lending on Trial.* Cambridge: Ballinger, pp. 173–98.

Magee, Stephen P., and Thomas Noe, 1989, "Economic Policy Failure with Endogenous Voting," *Hong Kong Economic Papers* , forthcoming.

Magee, Stephen P., and Ramesh K. S. Rao, 1980, "Vehicle and Nonvehicle Currencies in International Trade," *American Economic Review,* 70, 368–73.

Magee, Stephen P., and Leslie Young, 1983, "Multinationals, Tariffs and Capital Flows with Endogenous Politicians," in C. P. Kindleberger and D. Audretsch (eds.), *The Multinational Corporation in the 1980s.* Cambridge: MIT Press, pp. 21–37.

1987, "Endogenous Protection in the United States, 1900–1984," in Robert M. Stern (ed.), *U.S. Trade Policies in a Changing World Economy.* Cambridge: MIT Press, pp. 145–195.

Magee, Stephen P., Leslie Young, and William A. Brock, 1984, "The Compensation Effect of Endogenous Tariffs in General Equilibrium," paper presented at the Conference on International Political Economy, Dept. of Finance, University of Southern California, March.

Maier, Charles S., 1978, "The Politics of Inflation in the Twentieth Century," in Fred Hirsch and John H. Goldthorpe (eds.), *The Political Economy of Inflation.* Cambridge: Harvard University Press, pp. 37–72.

Malbin, Michael J., 1979, "Campaign Financing and the 'Special Interests,'" *Public Interest,* 56, 21–42.

Mandel, Ernest, 1978, *Late Capitalism.* New York: Shocken.

Mann, Catherine L., 1985, "Trade Policy for the Multiple Product Declining Industry," International Finance Discussion Paper No. 259, Federal Reserve Board, Washington, D.C.

1987, "Protection and Retaliation: Changing the Rules of the Game," International Finance Discussion Paper No. 309, Federal Reserve Board, Washington, D.C., May.

Manne, Henry G. (ed.), 1975, *The Economics of Legal Relationships.* St. Paul: West.

Marguez–Ruarte, J., 1973, "An Elementary Framework of Inter-run Analysis," mimeo, University of Chicago.

Markusen, James R., 1986, "Explaining the Volume of Trade," *American Economic Review,* 76, 1002–11.

Markusen, James R., and Anthony J. Venables, 1986, "Trade Policy with Increasing Returns and Imperfect Competition: Contradictory Results from Competing Assumptions," Centre for Economic Policy Research, London, Paper No. 120, July.

Martin, J. P., and J. M. Evans, 1981, "Notes on Measuring the Employment Displacement Effects of Trade by the Accounting Procedure," *Oxford Economic Papers,* 33, 154 –64.

Marvel, Howard P., and Edward J. Ray, 1985, "The Kennedy Round: Evidence of the Regulation of International Trade in the United States,"*American Economic Review,* 75, 190–7.

1987, "Intraindustry Trade: Sources and Effects on Protection," *Journal of Political Economy,* 95, 1278–91.

Marwell, Gerald, 1980, "Experiments on the Provision of Public Goods II: Provision Points, Stakes, Experience and the Free Rider Problem," *American Journal of Sociology,* 85, 926–37.

"Economists Free Ride, Does Any One Else: Experiments on the Provision of Public Goods," *Journal of Public Economics,* 15, 295–310.

Marwell, Gerald, and R. Ames, 1979, "Experiments on the Provision of Public Goods I: Resources, Interest, Group Size and the Free Rider Problem," *American Journal of Sociology,* 84, 1335–60.

Mayer, Wolfgang, 1974, "Short-run and Long-run Equilibrium for a Small Open Economy," *Journal of Political Economy,* 82, 955–67.

1981, "Theoretical Considerations on Negotiated Tariff Adjustments," *Oxford Economic Papers,* 33, 135–53.

1984a, "Endogenous Tariff Formation," *American Economic Review*, 74, 970–85.

1984b, "The Infant-Export Industry Argument," *Canadian Journal of Economics*, 17, 249–69.

Mayer, Wolfgang, and Ray Riezman, 1985, "Endogenous Choice of Trade Policy Instruments," Working Paper Series No. 85-8, College of Business Administration, University of Iowa.

1987, "Tariff Formation in Political Economy Models," Conference on Political Economy, World Bank, Washington, D.C.

Melman, S., 1983, *Profits without Production*. New York: Alfred A. Knopf.

Meltzer, Allan H., and Scott F. Richard, 1981, "A Rational Theory of the Size of Government," *Journal of Political Economy*, 89, 914–27.

Melvin, James R., 1975, *The Tax Structure and Canadian Trade*. Economic Council of Canada, Ottawa.

1985, "The Regional Economic Consequences of Tariffs and Domestic Transportation Costs," *Canadian Journal of Economics*, 18, 237–57.

Mendeloff, John, 1984, "Theories of Regulation and the Politics of OSHA," Conference on the Political Economy of Public Policy, Stanford University.

Mercenier, J., and Jean Waelbroeck, 1984a, "Effect of a 50% Tariff Cut in the 'VARUNA' Model," Conference on General Equilibrium Trade Policy Modeling, Columbia University, New York.

1984b, "The Sensitivity of Developing Countries to External Shocks in an Interdependent World," *Journal of Policy Modeling*, 6, 209–35.

Messerlin, Patrick A., 1981, "The Political Economy of Protectionism: The Bureaucratic Case," *Weltwirtschaftliches Archiv*, 117, 469–95.

Michaely, Michael, 1977, *Theory of Commercial Policy: Trade and Protection*. Chicago: University of Chicago Press.

1984, *Trade, Income Levels and Dependence*. Amsterdam: North-Holland.

1985, "The Demand for Protection against Exports of Newly Industrializing Countries," *Journal of Policy Modeling*, 7, 123–32.

Miller, M. H., and J. E. Spencer, 1977, "The Static Effects of the U.K. Joining the Common Market: A General Equilibrium Approach," *Review of Economic Studies*, 41, 71–94.

Mintz, S., 1974, *U.S. Import Quotas: Costs and Consequences*. Washington, D.C.: American Enterprise Institute.

Mitra, Pradeep, 1987, "Tax Reform in the Presence of DUP Activities," Conference on Political Economy, World Bank, Washington, D.C.

Miyagiwa, Kaz F., and Leslie Young, 1986, "International Capital Mobility and Commercial Policy in An Economic Region," *Journal of International Economics*, 20, 329–41.

Moe, Terry M., 1980, *The Organization of Interests*. Chicago: University of Chicago Press.

1981, "Toward a Broader View of Interest Groups," *Journal of Politics*, 43, 531–43.

Mohammad, Sharif, and John Whalley, 1984, "Rent Seeking in India: Its Costs and Policy Significance," *Kyklos*, 37, 387–413.

Molina, Carlos, 1984, "Cross-National Concentration in the Commercial Banking Industry," term paper, Finance 396, University of Texas at Austin.

Morkre, M. E., and D. G. Tarr, 1980, *Staff Report on Effects of Restrictions on United States Imports: Five Case Studies and Theory*. Federal Trade Commission, Washington, D.C.: U.S. Government Printing Office.

Mossberg, Walter S., 1987, "Foreign Diplomats Adopt Lobbying U.S.-Style to Dilute Trade Bill Provisions on Capitol Hill," *Wall Street Journal*, July 8, 46.

Moulin, H., 1983, *The Strategy of Social Choice*. New York: North-Holland.

Mueller, Dennis C., 1979, *Public Choice*. Cambridge: Cambridge University Press.

(ed.), 1983, *The Political Economy of Growth*. New Haven: Yale University Press.

Mundell, Robert A., 1957, "International Trade and Factor Mobility," *American Economic Review*, 47, 321–35.

Musgrave, Richard A., 1981, "Leviathan Cometh – or Does He?" *Tax and Expenditure Limitations*. Washington D.C.: Urban Institute Press, pp. 77–120.

Musgrave, Richard A., and Peggy B. Musgrave, 1984, *Public Finance in Theory and Practice*. New York: McGraw-Hill.

Mussa, Michael, 1974, "Tariffs and the Distribution of Income: The Importance of Factor Specificity, Substitutibility, and Intensity in the Short and Long Run," *Journal of Political Economy*, 82, 1191–1203.

Mutti, J., 1977, "Aspects of Unilateral Trade Policy and Factor Adjustment Costs," *Review of Economics and Statistics*, 60, 102–10.

1982, *Taxes, Subsidies and Competitiveness Internationally*. Washington, D.C.: National Planning Association.

Mutti, J., and H. Grubert, 1982, "D.I.S.C. and Its Effects," paper presented for a National Bureau of Economic Research Conference on the Structure and Evolution of Recent U.S. Trade Policy, Cambridge, Mass., December.

Neary, J. Peter, 1978, "Short-Run Capital Specificity and the Pure Theory of International Trade," *Economic Journal*, 88, 488–510.

1985, "International Factor Mobility, Minimum Wage Rates and Factor-Price Equalization: A Synthesis," *Quarterly Journal of Economics*, 100, 551–70.

Neary, J. Peter, and Cormac O'Grada, 1986, "Protection, Economic War and Structural Change: The 1930s in Ireland," Discussion Paper Series, No. 117, Centre for Economic Policy Research, London.

Nelson, Douglas, 1986, "The Public Politics of Protection: Automobiles," mimeo.

1987, "U.S. Trade Policy: Liberal Structure and Protectionist Dynamics," Conference on Political Economy, World Bank, Washington, D.C.

Nelson, Richard R., and Sidney G. Winter, 1982, "The Schumpeterian Tradeoff Revisited," *American Economic Review*, 72, 114–31.

Neumann, G., 1978, "The Direct Labor Market Effects of the Trade Adjustment Assistance Program: The Evidence from the TAA Survey," in W. Dewald (ed.), *The Impact of International Trade and Investment on Employment*. U.S. Dept. of Labor, Washington, D.C.: U.S. Government Printing Office, pp. 107–26.

1979, "Adjustment Assistance for Trade-Displaced Workers," in D. B. H. Denoon (ed.), *The New International Economic Order: A U.S. Response.* New York: New York University Press, pp. 109–40.

Neville, Cliff, 1986, "Effect of Lawyers on National Economic Performance," term paper, Finance 396, University of Texas at Austin.

Niemi, Richard G., and Herbert F. Weisberg, 1972, *Probability Models of Collective Decision Making.* Columbus, Ohio: Charles E. Merrill.

Nimo, Richard B., 1986, "General Government Consumption as a Factor Affecting Economic Growth: An International Comparison," term paper, Finance 396, University of Texas at Austin.

Niskanen, W., 1976, "Bureaucrats and Politicians," *Journal of Law and Economics,* 19, 617–43.

Nogues, Julio J., Andrzej Olechowski, and L. Alan Winters, 1986, "The Extent of Nontariff Barriers to Industrial Countries' Imports," *World Bank Economic Review,* 1, 181–99.

Nordhaus, William D., 1975, "The Political Business Cycle," *Review of Economic Studies,* 42, 169–90.

Nordinger, E., 1981, *On the Autonomy of the Democratic State.* Cambridge: Harvard University Press.

North, Douglass C., 1981, *Structure and Change in Economic History.* New York: W. W. Norton.

Norton, R. D., 1986, "Industrial Policy and American Renewal," *Journal of Economic Literature,* 24, 1–40.

Nozick, Robert, 1974, *Anarchy, State and Utopia.* New York: Basic Books.

Oakland, William H., 1974, "Public Goods, Perfect Competition, and Underproduction," *Journal of Political Economy,* 82, 927–39.

Olson, Mancur, 1965, *The Logic of Collective Action: Public Goods and the Theory of Groups.* Cambridge: Harvard University Press.

 1982, *The Rise and Decline of Nations: Economic Growth Stagflation and Social Rigidities.* New Haven: Yale University Press.

Olson, Mancur, and Hans H. Landsberg (eds.), 1973, *The No-Growth Society.* New York: W. W. Norton.

Ordeshook, Peter C., and Kenneth A. Shepsle (eds.), 1982, *Political Equilibrium.* Boston: Kluwer-Nijhoff.

Organisation for Economic Co-Operation and Development, 1983, *Positive Adjustment Policies.* Paris, France: OECD.

 1985, *Costs and Benefits of Protection.* Paris, France: OECD.

Otani, Yoshihiko, 1980, "Strategic Equilibrium of Tariffs in General Equilibrium," *Econometrica,* 48, 643–62.

Page, S. B., 1979, "The Management of International Trade," in Robin Major (ed.), *Britain's Trade and Exchange Rate Policy.* London: Heinemann Educational Books.

 1981, "The Revival of Protectionism and Its Consequences for Europe," *Journal of Common Market Studies,* 20, 17–40.

Paldam, Martin, 1981, "A Preliminary Survey of the Theories and Findings on Vote and Popularity Functions," *European Journal of Political Research,* 9, 181–99.

Palfrey, Thomas R., and Howard Rosenthal, 1984, "Participation and Provision of Discrete Public Goods: A Strategic Analysis." *Journal of Public Economics,* 79, 171–93.

1985, "Voter Participation and Strategic Uncertainty," *American Political Science Review,* 79, 62–78.

1986, "Private Incentives in Social Dilemmas," Conference on Political Information and Political Theory, University of Texas at Austin, February.

Pashigian, Peter B., 1975, "On the Control of Crime and Bribery," *Journal of Legal Studies;* 4, 311–26.

Pearson, C., 1981, "Discriminatory Trade Restraints: OMAs on Rubber Footwear," School of Advanced International Studies, Johns Hopkins University, Washington, D. C.

Peltzman, Sam, 1976, "Toward a More General Theory of Regulation," *Journal of Law and Economics,* 19, 211–40.

1980, "The Growth of Government," *Journal of Law and Economics,* 23, 209–87.

1987, "Economic Conditions and Gubernatorial Elections," *American Economic Review,* 77, 293–7.

Pelzman, Joseph, 1981, "Economic Costs of Tariffs and Quotas on Textile and Apparel Products Imported in to the United States," paper presented for a Conference on Crisis Industries and the Safeguards Provisions of the GATT, sponsored by the Trade Policy Centre, London.

1982, "The Impact of the Multifiber Arrangement on the U.S. Textile Industry," paper presented at Conference on the Structure and Evolution of Recent U.S. Trade Policy, National Bureau of Economic Research, December.

Pelzman, Joseph, and D. Rousslang, 1982, *Effects on U.S. Trade and Employment of Tariff Elimination Among the Countries of North America and the Caribbean Basin.* Office of Foreign Economic Research, U.S. Dept. of Labor, Washington, D.C.: U.S. Government Printing Office.

Persson, Mats, and Lars E. O. Svensson, 1985, "Time Consistency of Fiscal and Monetary Policy," Seminar Paper No. 331, Institute for International Economic Studies, University of Stockholm.

1987, "Checks and Balances on the Government Budget," Seminar Paper No. 380, Institute for International Economic Studies, University of Stockholm.

Persson, Mats, and Pehr Wissen, 1984, "Redistributional Aspects of Tax Evasion," *Scandinavian Journal of Economics,* 86, 131–49.

Petith, H., 1977, "European Integration and the Terms of Trade," *Economic Journal,* 87, 262–72.

Pincus, J. J., 1975, "Pressure Groups and the Pattern of Tariffs," *Journal of Political Economy,* 83, 757–78.

1984, "Tariff Policies," *Encyclopedia of American Political History,* 3, 1259–70.

Plott, C., and Levine, H., 1978, "A Model of Agenda Influences on Committee Decisions," *American Economic Review,* 68, 146–60.

Polanyi, Karl, 1944, *The Great Transformation.* Boston: Beacon Press.

Polinsky, A. Mitchell, 1980, "Private Versus Public Enforcement of Fines," *Journal of Legal Studies*, 9, 105–8.

  1983, *An Introduction to Law and Economics*. Boston: Little Brown.

Pommerehne, Werner W., and Bruno S. Frey, 1978, "Bureaucratic Behavior in Democracy: A Case Study," *Public Finance/Finances Publiques*, 33, 1–2.

Poole, Keith T., 1986, "The Dynamics of Interest Group Evaluations of Congress," Conference on Political Information and Political Theory, University of Texas, February.

Poole, Keith T., and Thomas Romer, 1985, "Patterns of Political Action Committee Contributions to the 1980 Campaigns for the United States House of Representatives," *Public Choice*, 47, 63–111.

Poole, Keith T., Thomas Romer, and Howard Rosenthal, 1987, "The Revealed Preferences of Political Action Committees," *American Economic Review*, 77, 298–302.

Pope, Clayne, 1964, "The Impact of the Ante-Bellum Tariff on Income Distribution," in *Explorations in Economic History*, 9, 375–422.

Porter, Robert H., 1984, "Tariff Policies in a Small Open Spatial Economy," *Canadian Journal of Economics*, 17, 270–82.

Posner, Richard A., 1977, *Economic Analysis of Law*. Boston: Little Brown, 2nd ed.

  1983, *The Economics of Justice*. Cambridge: Harvard University Press.

Pruitt, D. G., and Kimmel, M. J., 1977, "Twenty Years of Experimental Gaming: Critique, Synthesis and Suggestions for the Future," *Annual Reviews in Psychology*, 28, 363–92.

Pryor, Frederick L., 1983, "A Quasi-Test of Mancur Olson's Theory," in Dennis C. Mueller (ed.), *The Political Economy of Growth*. New Haven: Yale University Press, pp. 90–105.

  1984, "Rent Seeking and the Growth and Fluctuations of Nations: Empirical Tests of Some Recent Hypotheses," in David C. Colander (ed.), *Neoclassical Political Economy*. Cambridge, Mass.: Ballinger, pp. 155–76.

Pugel, Thomas A., and Ingo Walter, 1985, "U.S. Corporate Interests and the Political Economy of Trade Policy," *Review of Economics and Statistics*, 67, 465–73.

Rabinowitz, G., 1978, "On the Nature of Political Issues: Insights from a Spatial Analysis," *American Journal of Political Science*, 22, 793–817.

Rae, Douglas, 1980, "An Altimeter for Mr. Escher's Stairway: A Comment on William H. Riker," *American Political Science Review*, 74, 451–5.

Rapoport, Anatol, 1966, *Two-Person Game Theory*. Ann Arbor: University of Michigan Press.

Rappaport, Ammon, 1985, "Public Goods and the MCS Experimental Paradigm," *American Political Science Review*, 79, 148–55.

Rappaport, Ammon, and Albert M. Chammah, 1965, *Prisoner's Dilemma*. Ann Arbor: University of Michigan Press.

Ratner, S., 1972, *The Tariff in American History*. New York: Van Nostrand.

Rawls, John, 1971, *A Theory of Justice*. Cambridge: Harvard University Press.

Ray, Edward J., 1981a, "The Determinants of Tariff and Nontariff Trade Restrictions in the United States," *Journal of Political Economy*, 89, 105–21.

198lb, "Tariff and Non-Tariff Barriers to Trade in the United States and Abroad," *Review of Economics and Statistics*, 63, 161–8.

1985, "Trade Liberalization, Preferential Agreements and Their Impact on U.S. Imports from Latin America," in Connally and Gonzalez-Vega (eds.), *Economic Reform and Stabilization in Latin America*. New York: Praeger, pp. 253–79.

1987, "The Impact of Special Interests on Preferential Tariff Concessions by the United States," *Review of Economics and Statistics*, 69, 187–93.

Ray, Edward J., and Howard P. Marvel, 1984, "The Pattern of Protection in the Industrialized World," *Review of Economics and Statistics*, 66, 452–8.

Rees, Albert, 1980, "Improving Productivity Measurement," *American Economic Review*, 70, 340–2.

Richardson, J. David, 1971, "Some Sensitivity Tests for a 'Contant-Market-Shares' Analysis of Export Growth," *Review of Economics and Statistics*, 53, 300–4.

1982a, "New Nexes Among Trade, Industrial and Balance-of-Payments Policies," paper presented at a Conference on the Future of the International Monetary System, New York University, October.

1982b, "Trade Adjustment Assistance Under the United States Trade Act of 1974: An Analytical Examination and Worker Survey," in Jagdish N. Bhagwati (ed.), *Import Competition and Response*. Chicago: University of Chicago Press, for the National Bureau of Economic Research, pp. 321–63.

Riedel, J., 1977, "Tariff Concessions in the Kennedy Round and the Structure of Protection in West Germany: An Econometric Assessment," *Journal of Political Economy*, 84(7), 133–43.

Riker, William H., 1980, "Implications from the Disequilibrium of Majority Rule for the Study of Institutions," *American Political Science Review*, 74, 432–46.

Riker, William H., and Peter C. Ordeshook, 1973, *An Introduction to Positive Political Theory*. Englewood Cliffs, N.J.: Prentice-Hall.

Roberts, Brian E., 1985, "Assets Values and the Political Process: The Integration of Political Information in Political and Economic Markets," mimeo.

1986, "Voters, Investors and the Consumption of Political Information," Conference on Political Information and Political Theory, University of Texas at Austin, February.

Roberts, Paul Craig, 1984, *The Supply-Side Revolution: An Insider's Account of Policymaking in Washington*. Cambridge: Harvard University Press.

Roberts, Russell D., 1984, "A Positive Model of Private Charity and Public Transfers," *Journal of Political Economy*, 92, 136–53.

Rogoff, Kenneth, and Anne Sibert, 1985, "Elections and Macroeconomic Policy Cycles," Federal Reserve Board, International Finance Discussion Papers No. 271, pp. 1–27.

Romer, T., 1975, "Individual Welfare, Majority Voting and the Properties of a Linear Income Tax," *Journal of Public Economics.*, 4, 163–85.

Romer, T., and Howard Rosenthal, 1979, "The Elusive Median Voter," *Journal of Public Economics*, 12, 143–70.

Rose-Ackerman, Susan, 1980, "Inefficiency and Re-Election," *Kyklos*, 33, 287–307.

1982, "A New Political Economy?" *Michigan Law Review,* 80, 872–84.

1984, "Bureaucracy and Competition," Conference on the Political Economy of Public Policy, Stanford University, March.

Rosecrance, Richard, 1981, "International Theory Revisited," *International Organization,* 35, 691–713.

Rosen, Benson, and Hillel J. Einhorn, 1972, "Attractiveness of the 'Middle of the Road' Political Candidate," *Journal of Applied Social Psychology,* 2, 157–65.

Rosen, Harvey S., 1980, "What Is Labor Supply and Do Taxes Affect It?," *American Economic Review Papers and Proceedings,* 70, 171–5.

Ross, Victoria B., 1984, "Rent-Seeking in LDC Import Regimes: The Case of Kenya," Discussion Papers in International Economics, No. 8408, Graduate Institute of International Studies, Geneva.

Rostow, Walt W., 1960, *The Stages of Economic Growth..* Cambridge: Cambridge University Press.

1962, *The Process of Economic Growth.* Oxford: Clarendon.

1970, "The Past Quarter-Century as Economic History and the Tasks of International Economic Organization," *Journal of Economic History,* 30, 150–87.

1971, *Politics and the Stages of Growth.* Cambridge: Cambridge University Press.

1975, *How It All Began; The Origins of the Modern Economy.* New York: McGraw-Hill.

1978, *Getting From Here to There.* New York: McGraw-Hill.

1980, *Why the Poor Get Richer and the Rich Slow Down.* Austin: University of Texas Press.

1982, *Economics in the Long View: Essays in Honor of W. W. Rostow.* Austin: University of Texas Press.

Rothbard, Murray, 1977, *Power and Market.* Kansas City: Sheed Andrews and McMeel.

Rousslang, Donald J., and John W. Suomela, 1985, "Calculating the Consumer and Net Welfare Costs of Import Relief," Staff Research Study No. 15, Office of Economics, United States International Trade Commission, Washington, D.C.

Rubinstein, Ariel, 1986, "Finite Automata Play the Repeated Prisoner's Dilemma," *Journal of Economic Theory,* 39, 83–96.

Ruffin, Roy, 1979, "Border Tax Adjustments and Countervailing Duties," *Weltwirtschaftliches Archiv,* 115, 351–5.

Rugman, A. M., 1980, "Internalization as a General Theory of Foreign Direct Investment: A Re-Appraisal of the Literature," *Weltwirtschaftliches Archiv,* 116, 365–79.

Russell, Clifford S. (ed.), 1979, *Collective Decision Making.* Baltimore: Johns Hopkins University Press.

Sabato, Larry J., 1987, "The Political Parties and PACs: Novel Relationships in the New System of Campaign Finance," *Journal of Law and Politics,* 3, 423–48.

Sachs, Jeffrey, and Alberto Alesina, 1986, "Political Parties and the Business Cycle in the United States, 1948–1984," National Bureau of Economic Research Working Paper No. 1940.

Safarian, A. E., 1982, "Trade-Related Investment Issues," paper presented at the

Conference on Trade Policy in the Eighties, Institute for International Economics, Washington, D.C., June.

Sah, Raaj, 1987, "Persistence and Pervasiveness of Corruption: New Perspectives," Conference on Political Economy, World Bank, Washington, D.C., June.

Salvatore, D., 1985, "The New Protectionism and the Threat to World Welfare: Editor's Introduction," *Journal of Policy Modeling*, 7, 1–22.

Samuelson, Paul A., 1954, "The Pure Theory of Public Expenditure," *Review of Economics and Statistics*, 36, 387–9.

1955, "The Diagrammatic Exposition of the Theory of Public Expenditures," *Review of Economics and Statistics*, 37, 350–6.

Sandler, Todd (ed.), 1981, *The Theory and Structures of International Political Economy*. Boulder, Colo.: Westview Press.

Sapir, A., 1981, "Trade Benefits Under the EEC Generalized System of Preferences," *European Economic Review*, 15, 339–55.

Sapir, A., and L. Lundberg, 1982, "The U.S. Generalized System of Preferences and Its Impact," paper presented for a National Bureau of Economic Research Conference on the Structure and Evolution of Recent U.S. Trade Policy, Cambridge, Mass.

Sapir, A., and E. Lutz, 1981, "Trade in Services: Economic Determinants and Development-Related Issues," World Bank Staff Working Paper No. 480, Washington, D.C.

Saunders, Ronald S., 1980, "The Political Economy of Effective Tariff Protection in Canada's Manufacturing Sector," *Canadian Journal of Economics*, 13, 340–8.

Saxonhouse, Gary R., 1985, "What's Wrong with Japanese Trade Structure," Seminar Discussion Paper No. 166, Research Seminar in International Economics, Dept. of Economics, University of Michigan.

1986, "Japan's Intractable Trade Surpluses in a New Era," Seminar Discussion Paper No. 178, Research Seminar in International Economics, Dept. of Economics, University of Michigan.

Schattschneider, E. E., 1935, *Politics, Pressures and the Tariff*. New York: Prentice-Hall.

Schneider, Friedrich, and Bruno S. Frey, 1983, "An Empirical Study of Politico-Economic Interaction in the United States: A Reply," *Review of Economics and Statistics*, 65, 178–81.

1988, "Politico-Economic Models of Macroeconomic Policy: A Review of the Empirical Evidence," in Thomas D. Willett (ed.), *Political Business Cycles*. Durham: Duke University Press, pp. 240–75.

Schotter, Andrew, 1981, *The Economic Theory of Social Institutions*. Cambridge: Cambridge University Press.

Schuknecht, Ludger Wilhelm, 1987, "The Constitutional Economics of International Trade," masters thesis, George Mason University, Fairfax, Virginia.

Schumpeter, Joseph A., 1950, *Capitalism, Socialism, and Democracy*. New York: Harper and Brothers.

Sen, Amartya K., 1970, "The Impossibility of a Paretian Liberal," *Journal of Political Economy*, 78, 152–7.

1973, *On Economic Inequality*. New York: W. W. Norton and Co.

1981, "Ethical Issues in Income Distribution: National and International," in Sven Grassman and Erik Lundberg (eds.), *The World Economic Order*. London: Macmillan, pp. 464–94.

1985, "Well-Being, Agency and Freedom, The Dewey Lecture, 1984," *Journal of Philosophy*, 82, 169–221.

Shelp, R. K., 1981, *Beyond Industrialization*. New York: Praeger.

Sherman, Howard, 1979a, "Inflation, Unemployment and the Contemporary Business Cycle," *Socialist Review*, 9, 75–102.

1979b, "Technology vis-à-vis Institutions," *Journal of Economic Issues*, 13, 175–91.

1981, "Marx and Determinism," *Journal of Economic Issues*, 15, 61–71.

Shouda, Y., 1980, "A Quantitative Analysis of Protection in Japan," Japan Economic Research Center, mimeo.

Shubik, Martin, 1984, *A Game-Theoretic Approach to Political Economy*. Cambridge: MIT Press.

Shubik, Martin, and L. Van der Heyden, 1978, "Logrolling and Budget Allocation Games," *International Journal of Game Theory*, 7, 151–62.

Shubik, Martin, and H. P. Young, 1978, "The Nucleolus as a Noncooperative Game Solution," in Peter C. Ordeshook (ed.), *Game Theory and Political Science*. New York: New York University Press, pp. 511–27.

Simmons, Randy T., Robyn M. Dawes, and John M. Orbell, 1983, "An Experimental Comparison of the Two Motives for Not Contributing to a Public Good: Desire to Free Ride and Fear of Being Gypped," mimeo.

Smart, Bruce, 1986, "Administration Trade Initiatives," *Business America*, 9, 2–4.

Smith, A. D., D. M. W. N. Hitchens, and S. W. Davies, 1985, *International Industrial Productivity*. Cambridge: Cambridge University Press.

Snidal, Duncan, 1979, "Public Goods, Property Rights and Political Organizations," *International Studies Quarterly*, 23, 532–66.

So, Daphne, 1986, "Cross-Country Tariffs," masters report, University of Texas at Austin.

Spann, Robert M., 1977, "The Macroeconomics of Unbalanced Growth and the Expanding Public Sector: Some Simple Tests of a Model of Government Growth," *Journal of Public Economics*, 8, 397–404.

Spinelli, Franco, 1985, "Protectionism and Real Wage Rigidity: A Discussion of the Macroeconomic Literature," *Journal of Policy Modeling*, 7, 157–80.

Staelin, C. P., 1976, "A General Equilibrium Model of Tariffs in a Non-Competitive Economy," *Journal of International Economics*, 6, 39–63.

Staiger, Robert W., 1985, "Heckscher–Ohlin Theory in the Presence of Market Power," Seminar Discussion Paper No. 154, Research Seminar in International Economics, Dept. of Economics, University of Michigan.

Staiger, Robert W., Alan V. Deardorff, and Robert M. Stern, 1985a, "An Evaluation of Factor Endowments and Protection as Determinants of Japanese and American Foreign Trade," Seminar Discussion Paper No. 158, Research Seminar in International Economics, Dept. of Economics, University of Michigan.

1985b, "The Effects of Protection on the Factor Content of Japanese and American Foreign Trade," Seminar Discussion Paper No. 159, Research Seminar in International Economics, Dept. of Economics, University of Michigan.

1985c, "The Employment Effects of Japanese and American Protection," Seminar Discussion Paper No. 165, Research Seminar in International Economics, Department of Economics, University of Michigan.

Staniland, Martin, 1985, *What Is Political Economy?* New Haven: Yale University Press.

Stephens, Craig, 1986, "Tariffs: Country vs. Industry Effects," professional report, Graduate School of Business, University of Texas at Austin.

Stern, Nicholas H., 1987, "Uniformity Versus Selectivity in Tax Structures," Conference on Political Economy, World Bank, Washington, D.C., June.

Stern, Robert M. (ed.), 1987, *U.S. Trade Policies in a Changing World Economy.* Cambridge: MIT Press.

Stern, Robert M., and K. Maskus, 1981, "Determinants of the Structure of U.S. Foreign Trade, 1958–1975," *Journal of International Economics*, 11, 207–24.

Stigler, George J., 1970a, "Director's Law of Public Income Redistribution," *Journal of Law and Economics*, 13, 1–10.

1970b, "The Optimum Enforcement of Laws," *Journal of Political Economy*, 78, 526.

1971, "The Theory of Economic Regulation,"*Bell Journal of Economics and Management Science*, 2, 3–21.

1972, "Economic Competition and Political Competition," *Public Choice*, 13, 91–106.

1974, "Free Riders and Collective Action: An Appendix to Theories of Economic Regulation," *Bell Journal of Economics and Management Science,* 5, 359–65.

1983, "Nobel Lecture: The Process and Progress of Economics," *Journal of Political Economy*, 91, 529–45.

1984, "Laissez-Faire: Policy or Circumstance," Conference on the Political Economy of Public Policy, Stanford University, March.

Stockman, Alan C., and Harris Dellas, 1984, "Asset Markets, Tariffs and Political Risk," Discussion Papers in International Economics, No. 8404, Graduate Institute of International Studies, Geneva.

Stolper, Wolfgang, and Paul A. Samuelson, 1941, "Protection and Real Wages," *Review of Economic Studies,* 9, 58–73.

Strange, Susan, 1979, "The Management of Surplus Capacity," *International Organization*, 3, 303–35.

1985, "Protectionism and World Politics," *International Organization,* 39, 233–59.

Stulz, Rene M., 1984, "The Current Account, Optimal Consumption Choices and Unanticipated Changes in the Terms of Trade," Working Paper Series, No. 84-81, Ohio State University.

Sugden, Robert, 1981, *The Political Economy of Public Choice.* New York: John Wiley and Sons.

Szenberg, M., J. W. Lombardi, and E. Y. Lee, 1977, *Welfare Effects of Trade Restrictions.* New York: Academic Press.

Takacs, Wendy E., 1981, "Pressures for Protectionism: An Empirical Analysis," *Economic Inquiry,* 19, 687–93.

    1987, "Auctioning Import Licenses: An Economic Analysis," Seminar Paper No. 390, Institute for International Economic Studies, University of Stockholm, September.

Tarr, David G., 1979, "Cyclical Dumping: The Case of Steel Products," *Journal of International Economics,* 9, 57–63.

Tarr, David G., and Morris E. Morkre, 1984, *Aggregate Costs to the United States of Tariffs and Quotas on Imports.* Washington, D.C.: Federal Trade Commission.

Taussig, Frank W., 1931, *The Tariff History of the United States.* New York: G. P. Putnam & Sons.

Taylor, Lance, and S. L. Black, 1974, "Practical General Equilibrium Estimation of Resource Pulls under Trade Liberalization," *Journal of International Economics,* 4, 37–58.

Telser, Lester G., 1972, *Competition, Collusion and Game Theory.* New York: Aldine-Atherton.

Tharakan, P. X. M., 1980, "Political Economy of Protection in Belgium," World Bank Staff Working Paper No. 431, Washington, D.C.

Theil, Henri, 1971, *Principles of Econometrics.* New York: John Wiley.

Thurow, Lester C., 1980, *The Zero-Sum Society.* New York: Penguin Books.

    1985, *The Zero-Sum Solution.* New York: Simon and Schuster.

Thurow, Lester C., and Laura D'Andrea Tyson, 1987, "The Economic Black Hole," *Foreign Policy,* 67, 3–21.

Tichy, Gunther, 1985, "Is the Product Cycle Obsolete?," Research Memorandum 8502, University of Graz, Dept. of Economics, June.

Tiebout, Charles, 1956, "A Pure Theory of Local Expenditures," *Journal of Political Economy,* 64, 416–24.

Tollison, Robert D., 1982, "Rent Seeking: A Survey," *Kyklos,* 35, 28–47.

Tosini, Suzanne C., and E. Tower, 1987, "The Textile Bill of 1985: The Determinants of Congressional Voting Patterns," *Public Choice,* 54, 19–25.

Tower, Edward, 1975, "The Optimum Quota and Retaliation," *Review of Economic Studies,* 42, 623–30.

Tufte, Edward R., 1974, *Data Analysis for Politics and Policy.* Englewood Cliffs, N.J.: Prentice-Hall.

    1976, *Political Control of the Economy.* Princeton, N.J.: Princeton University Press.

Tullock, Gordon, 1965, *The Politics of Bureaucracy.* Washington, D.C.: Public Affairs Press.

    1967a, *Toward a Mathematics of Politics.* Ann Arbor: University of Michigan Press.

    1967b, "The Welfare Cost of Tariffs, Monopolies and Theft," *Western Economic Journal,* 5, 224–32.

    1971a, "The Cost of Transfers," *Kyklos,* 24, 629–43.

    1971b, *The Logic of the Law.* New York: Basic Books.

    1979, "Public Choice in Practice," in Clifford S. Russell (ed.), *Collective Deci-*

sion Making: Applications from Public Choice Theory. Baltimore: Johns Hopkins Press, pp. 27–45.

1983, *Economics of Income Redistribution.* Boston: Kluwer-Nijhoff.

1985, "Why Did the Industrial Revolution Occur in England?," mimeo.

1986, *The Economics of Wealth and Poverty.* New York: New York University Press.

Tullock, Gordon, and James M. Buchanan, 1962, *The Calculus of Consent.* Ann Arbor: University of Michigan Press.

Uekusa, Masu, and Hideki Ide, 1986, "Industrial Policy in Japan," Pacific Economic Paper No. 135, Australia–Japan Research Centre, May.

United Nations Conference on Trade and Development, 1983, *Handbook of International Trade and Development Statistics.* New York: United Nations.

United States Congress, 1973, Committee on Ways and Means, Hearings on HR:6767, The Trade Reform Act of 1973, 15 Parts, May 9–June 15, 1973. Washington, D.C.: U.S. Government Printing Office.

United States Dept. of Treasury, *International Sales Corporation Legislation: 1979 Annual Report.* Washington, D.C.: U.S. Government Printing Office.

Utgoff, K. D., 1982, *Reduction of Adjustment Costs Associated with Trade.* Public Research Institute of the Center for Naval Analyses, Washington, D.C.

Van de Kragt, Alphons, John M. Orbell, and Robyn Dawes, 1983, "The Minimal Contributing Set as a Solution to Public Goods Problems," *American Political Science Review,* 77, 112–21.

van den Doel, Hans, 1979, *Democracy and Welfare Economics.* New York: Cambridge University Press.

Varian, Hal R. 1975, "Distributive Justice, Welfare Economics and the Theory of Fairness," *Philosophy and Public Affairs,* 4, 223–47.

1987, "Measuring the Deadweight Costs of DUP and Rent Seeking Activities," Conference on Political Economy, World Bank, Washington, D.C., June.

Vernon, Raymond, 1966, "International Investment and International Trade in the Product Cycle," *Quarterly Journal of Economics,* 80, 190–207.

1979, "The Product Cycle Hypothesis in a New International Environment," *Oxford Bulletin of Economics and Statistics,* 41, 255–67.

Viner, Jacob, 1948, "Power Versus Plenty as Objectives of Foreign Policy in the Seventeenth and Eighteenth Centuries," *World Politics,* 1, 1–29.

Vith, Susanne, 1985, "U.S. Arms Sales to the Third World," term paper, Finance 396, University of Texas at Austin.

von der Schulenberg, J. M. Graff, and G. Skogh (eds.), 1986, *Law and Economics and the Economics of Legal Regulation,* Vol. 13 in International Studies in Economics and Econometrics. Boston: Kluwer Academic Publishers.

Wade, Larry L. (ed.), 1983, *Political Economy.* Boston: Kluwer-Nijhoff.

Waldrup, James L., 1985, "Cross-National Unemployment Rates," term paper, Finance 396, University of Texas at Austin.

Walker, Jack L., 1983, "The Origins and Maintenance of Interest Groups in America," *American Political Science Review,* 77, 390–406.

Wallace, M., 1983, "Managing Resources That Are Common Property: From Kathmandu to Capitol Hill," *Journal of Policy Analysis and Management*, 2, 220–37.

Wallerstein, Immanuel, 1984, *The Politics of the World-Economy*. Cambridge: Cambridge University Press.

Wallerstein, Michael, 1986, "The Micro-Foundations of Solidarity: Protectionist Policies, Welfare Policies and Union Centralization," Working Paper No. 109, Dept. of Political Science, UCLA, April.

Walter, Ingo, 1982, "Structural Adjustment and Trade Policy in the Eighties," paper presented at a Conference on Trade Policy in the Eighties, Institute for International Economics, Washington, D.C.

Walter, Ingo, and Kaj Areskoug, 1981, *International Economics*. New York: John Wiley, 3rd ed.

Walter, Ingo, and H. P. Gray, 1983, "Protectionism and International Banking," *Journal of Banking and Finance*, 7, 445–648.

Wang, Ko, 1985, "Cross-National Corporate Income Tax Rates and Debt/Equity Ratios," term paper, Finance 396, University of Texas at Austin.

Warr, P. G., and Peter J. Lloyd, 1982, "Do Australian Trade Policies Discriminate Against Less Developed Countries?," Centre for Economic Policy Research Discussion Paper No. 50, Australian National University, Canberra.

Weidenbaum, Murray L., 1983–4, "The High Cost of Protectionism," *Cato Journal*, 3, 777–92.

Weingast, Barry R., 1981, "Regulation, Re-regulation and De-regulation: The Political Foundations of Agency–Clientele Relationships," *Law and Contemporary Problems*, 44, 147–76.

Weisberg, H., and J. Rusk, 1970, "Dimensions of Candidate Evaluation," *American Political Science Review*, 64, 1167–85.

Weiss, Frank D., 1986, "A Political Economy of European Community Trade Policy against the Less Developed Countries?," revised version of paper presented at First European Economic Association Congress in Vienna, Austria.

Weisskopf, T., 1979, "Marxian Crisis Theory and the Rate of Profit," *Cambridge Journal of Economics*, 3, 342–53, 471–5.

1981, "The Current Economic Crisis in Historical Perspective," *Socialist Review*, 57, 9–35.

Weitzman, Martin L., 1984, *The Share Economy*. Cambridge: Harvard University Press.

Welch, W. P., 1974, "The Economics of Campaign Funds, " *Public Choice*, 2, 83–97.

Wellisz, Stanislaw, and Ronald Findlay, 1988, "The State and the Invisible Hand," *Research Observer* 3, 59–80.

Wellisz, Stanislaw, and John D. Wilson, 1986, "Lobbying and Tariff Formation: A Deadweight Loss Consideration," *Journal of International Economics*, 20, 367–75.

Weston, A., V. Cable, and A. Hewitt, 1980, *The EEC's Generalized System of Preferences*. London: Overseas Development Institute.

Weymark, John A., 1980, "Welfare Optimal Tariff Revenues and Maximum Tariff Revenues," *Canadian Journal of Economics*, 13, 615–31.

Whalley, John, 1980a, "Discriminatory Features of Domestic Factor Tax Systems in a Good Mobile–Factors Immobile Trade Model: An Empirical General Equilibrium Approach," *Journal of Political Economy*, 88, 1177–1202.

1980b, "An Evaluation of the Recent Tokyo Round Trade Agreement Through a General Equilibrium Model of World Trade Involving Major Trading Areas," Working Paper No. 8009, Centre for the Study of International Economic Relations, Dept. of Economics, University of Western Ontario, London, Canada.

1984, "Impacts of a 50% Tariff Reduction in an Eight-Region Global Trade Model," Conference on General Equilibrium Trade Policy Modelling, Columbia University, New York, April.

1985, *Trade Liberalization Among Major World Trading Areas*. Cambridge: MIT Press.

Whalley, John, and R. Wigle, 1982, "Price and Quantity Rigidities in Adjustment to Trade Policy Changes: Alternative Formulation and Initial Calculations," paper presented at International Economics Association Conference on Structural Adjustment in Trade Dependent Advanced Economics, Stockholm, August.

Wijkman, Per Magnus, 1982, "Managing the Global Commons," *International Organizations*, 36, 511–36.

Wildavsky, 1966, "The Political Economy of Efficiency: Benefit Analysis Systems, Analysis and Program Budgeting," *Public Administration Review*, 26, 292–310.

Willett, Thomas D. (ed.), 1988, *Political Business Cycles: The Political Economy of Money, Inflation and Unemployment*. Durham: Duke University Press.

Willett, Thomas D., and Mehrdad Jalalighajar, 1983–4, "U.S. Trade Policy and National Security," *Cato Journal*, 3, 717–28.

Williamson, O. E., 1975, *Markets and Hierarchies: Analysis and Antitrust Implications: A Study in the Economics of Internal Organization*. New York: Free Press.

Wilson, John Oliver, 1985, *The Power Economy*. Boston: Little Brown.

1987, "An Optimal Tax Treatment of Leviathan," Conference on Political Economy, World Bank, Washington, D.C., June.

Wilson, W., 1971, "Reciprocation and Other Techniques for Inducing Cooperation in the Prisoner's Dilemma Game," *Journal of Conflict Resolution*, 15, 167–95.

Winters, L. Alan, 1987, "Pattern of World Trade in Manufactures: Does Trade Policy Matter?" Discussion Paper Series, No. 160, Centre for Economic Policy Research, London.

Wolff, A., 1982, "The Need for New GATT Rules for Safeguard Actions," paper presented at a Conference on Trade Policy in the Eighties, Institute for International Economics, Washington, D.C., June.

Wolter, Frank, 1977, "Adjusting to Imports from Developing Countries," in H. Giersch (ed.), *Reshaping the World Economic Order*. Tubingen: Mohr.

Wong, Kar-yiu, 1987, "Optimal Threat of Trade Restriction and Quid Pro Quo Foreign Investment," Conference on Political Economy, World Bank, Washington, D.C., June.

Wooton, Ian, 1986, "Preferential Trading Agreements: An Investigation," *Journal of International Economics*, 21, 80–97.

World Bank, 1982, *World Development Report*. Washington, D.C.: World Bank.

Worth, D., 1984,"The Growth of Government in the United States," mimeo.

Yaari, Menahem E., 1981, "Rawls, Edgeworth, Shapley, Nash: Theories of Distributive Justice Re-examined," *Journal of Economic Theory*, 24, 1–39.

Yarbrough, Beth V., and Robert M. Yarbrough, 1986, *Opportunism and Governance in International Trade: After Hegemony, What?* Cambridge: National Bureau of Economic Research.

Yeager, Leland B., and David G. Tuerck, 1983–4, "Realism and Free-Trade Policy," *Cato Journal*, 3, 645–66.

Yeats, Alexander J., 1984, "On the Analysis of Tariff Escalation: Is There a Methodological Bias against the Interest of Developing Countries?," *Journal of Development Economics*, 15, 77–88.

Yoffie, David B., 1983, "The Structure of Modern Protectionism: Past Patterns and Future Prospects," Working Paper 9-783-50, Harvard Business School.

Young, H. P., 1977a, "Extending Condorcet's Rule," *Journal of Economic Theory*, 16, 335–53.

1977b, "Power, Prices and Incomes in Voting Systems," *Mathematical Programming*, 14, 129–48.

1978a, "The Allocation of Funds in Lobbying and Campaigning," *Behavioral Science*, 23, 21–31.

1978b, "A Tactical Lobbying Game," *Game Theory and Political Science*. New York: New York University Press, pp. 391–405.

Young, Leslie, 1982, "Comment on Findlay and Wellisz," in Jagdish N. Bhagwati (ed.), *Import Competition and Response*. Chicago: University of Chicago Press, pp. 238–43.

1985, "A Generalization of the Optimal Tariff Argument," Dept. of Finance Working Paper 85/86-2-10, University of Texas, Graduate School of Business.

Young, Leslie, and James E. Anderson, 1980, "The Optimal Policies for Restricting Trade under Uncertainty," *Review of Economic Studies*, 46, 927–32.

1982, "Risk Aversion and Optimal Trade Restrictions," *Review of Economic Studies*, 49, 291–305.

Young, Leslie, and Stephen P. Magee, 1982, "A Prisoners' Dilemma Theory of Tariffs," paper presented at Econometric Society Meetings, New York, December; also presented at the Conference on Rational Actor Models in Political Economy, Stanford University, April 1984.

1984, "A Black Hole in the Political Economy of Protection," mimeo, Dept. of Finance, University of Texas at Austin; presented at the American Economic Association Meetings, 1987.

1986, "Endogenous Protection, Factor Returns and Resource Allocation" *Review of Economic Studies*, 53, 407–19.

Author index

415

Subject index

access effects, 6, 270, 271
adding machine model, 45, 75
adjustment assistance, 244, 246
administered protection, 247
agricultural protection, 44, 88, 154
airlines, 245–6
Algeria, 119–20
altruism, 87, 248
aluminum, 95
America, *see* United States
American Economic Association, 218
American Medical Association (AMA), 92
Annecy, trade negotiations, 182
antidumping claims, 246
apparel, 106, 108, 244
appropriability, 88
    effects, 92
    parameter, 132, 302, 303
    theory, 170
appropriation mechanisms, 167
arbitrage, 1, 46
Argentina, 119–20, 225, 232–3, 238–9,
    253, 299, 362
Arrow–Debreu model, 4, 52, 267, 297
asymmetric externality, 8, 84
Australia, 88, 120, 127, 128, 232, 233,
    240, 245, 246, 253, 299, 362
Austria, 119, 120, 232, 237, 239, 243,
    253, 255, 299, 362
automobiles, 155, 170, 206, 246, 262
aviation, 107, 108

Bangladesh, 119, 120, 232, 233, 237, 239,
    253, 299, 362
banking, 206, 207
bearings, 107, 108
beggar-thy-neighbor, 187

Belgium, 120, 240, 241, 243
Benin, 232, 233, 237, 240, 253, 362
Bhagwati's rankings, 257
black hole, 28, 215–16, 223–5, 356–61
Bolivia, 51, 232, 233, 237, 239, 253, 362
Brazil, 232, 233, 236, 237, 240, 253, 362
Brazilian vitality, 21, 166–76
Britain, 204, 205, 207, 252
British disease, 171
Brock–Magee political apparatus, 13
bureaucracy, 75, 218–19, 247
    model, 141
    tariffs, 42
Burke–Hartke Bill, 178, 182, 187
Burundi, 232, 233, 237, 239, 253, 362
business cycles
    political, 35, 179, 180
    troughs, 117, 153, 225
by-product argument, 92

campaign contributions, 34, 62–71, 81,
    270–2
    large contributors, 6, 63
    see also contributions
Canada, 90, 119, 120, 127, 232, 233, 237,
    240, 241, 246, 253, 255, 299,
    362
capital, 127, 231, 309, 315
    accumulation, 166, 184
    abundance, 26, 116, 147, 168, 173,
      295
    benefits from inflows of, 175
    cross flows, 21, 168, 175
    deepening, 184, 210
    dominance, 148–50, 313–15
    fixed nonresidential private capital,
      U.S., 329